A HANDBOOK OF
LITERARY CRITICISM

*A comprehensive analysis of all the literary forms,
including the letter, the essay, the oration,
history, fiction, biography, the
lyric poem, drama,
and the epic.*

WILLIAM HENRY SHERAN

NOBLE AND NOBLE, *Publishers*
76 FIFTH AVENUE   NEW YORK

4318

TO THE MEMORY OF

THE LATE

PROFESSOR FREDERICK MAX MÜLLER

With whom the Author spent many delightful days

as a pupil in the

UNIVERSITY OF OXFORD

PREFACE

The purpose of the writer is to supply teachers and students of literature with a suitable manual of literary criticism. As Sidney Lanier pointedly remarked, there is no book extant in any language which gives an analytical and comprehensive survey of all the well-marked, widely varying, literary forms which have differentiated themselves in the course of time — the letter, the essay, the oration, history, fiction, biography, the lyric, the drama, the epic. I have attempted to furnish such a survey as the vast range of subjects and the limitations of a handbook allow. The student thus enjoys the advantage of viewing critically the whole field of letters — an advantage which no other manual offers.

As a preliminary study, this handbook treats literature from the viewpoint of a fine art. In common with all the fine arts literature has its own province, its own form and content. And the art-form and art-content of literature should be ascertained before the student makes any detailed study of the various departments in which literary art finds expression. The introductory chapters of this manual are devoted to such an analysis.

A special claim in favor of this handbook is conciseness as well as comprehensiveness. While dealing in a practical way with all the departments of literature, I have endeavored to give the briefest possible compendium of the best criticism. The " first principles " of literary art are tersely set forth and their application to the various prose-forms and verse-forms is equally terse. In thus economizing the student's time and attention, I have abbreviated the history of literary forms and neglected to estimate their more minute differentiations — work which, after all, can only be suggested within the limits of a manual covering such a large field. In drawing upon the various sources of literary criticism, I have adopted the same method of condensation; often compressing into a single paragraph the ideas of a critic, which have been elaborated through several pages. The condensed account often takes the place of, and is preferable to, the verbatim quotation.

In making selections from German and French sources for this volume, I have availed myself of the criticism of Professor Francis J. Schaefer, Ph. D., who has personally supervised much of the work. The thanks of the author are also due to the late Prof. Max Müller, of Oxford, who suggested the plan of this handbook, and made some valuable suggestions as to the selection of the subject-matter.

A full list of the writers, ancient and modern, to whom this handbook is in any way indebted, will be found at the close of the volume. References are also made in the text, and those which usually occupy the place of foot-notes are incorporated in the work itself, as I believe such an arrangement is more satisfactory to the student.

If this handbook shall prove helpful to teachers and students, the object for which it was written will be attained.

WILLIAM HENRY SHERAN.

CONTENTS

PART I

INTRODUCTION

CHAPTER		PAGE
I.	Literature as a Fine Art	1
II.	Art-Form in Literature	7
III.	The Word	15
IV.	The Sentence	24
V.	The Paragraph	33
VI.	The Complete Composition	40
VII.	Art-Content in Literature: Sublimity	52
VIII.	Beauty	61
IX.	Feeling	69
X.	Wit and Humor	75
XI.	Melody	80
XII.	Personality in Literary Art	84
XIII.	Personality in Literary Art (continued)	93

PART II

ANALYSIS OF PROSE-FORMS

CHAPTER		PAGE
XIV.	The Letter	108
XV.	The Letter (continued)	113
XVI.	The Letter (continued)	118
XVII.	The Letter (continued)	121
XVIII.	The Letter (continued)	128
XIX.	The Letter (continued)	137
XX.	The Letter (concluded)	142
XXI.	The Essay	150
XXII.	The Essay (continued)	153
XXIII.	The Essay (continued)	160
XXIV.	The Essay (continued)	165

CHAPTER		PAGE
XXV.	The Essay (continued)	175
XXVI.	The Essay (continued)	178
XXVII.	The Essay (concluded)	185
XXVIII.	Biography	193
XXIX.	Biography (continued)	201
XXX.	Biography (concluded)	213
XXXI.	History	225
XXXII.	History (continued)	235
XXXIII.	History (concluded)	248
XXXIV.	The Oration	263
XXXV.	The Oration (continued)	274
XXXVI.	The Oration (continued)	282
XXXVII.	The Oration (continued)	295
XXXVIII.	The Oration (concluded)	306
XXXIX.	Fiction	327
XL.	Fiction (continued)	340
XLI.	The Novel	348
XLII.	Representative Authors of Fiction	356

PART III

ANALYSIS OF POETIC FORMS

CHAPTER		PAGE
XLIII.	Poetry	388
XLIV.	Poetry (continued)	394
XLV.	The Drama	404
XLVI.	Characters of the Drama	419
XLVII.	Ethics of the Drama	432
XLVIII.	Representative Authors	439
XLIX.	The Epic	466
L.	The Epic (continued)	487
LI.	The Lyric	514
LII.	The Lyric (continued)	534
LIII.	Conclusion	548

APPENDIX

I. Special Bibliographies of the Letter, Essay, Biography, History, Oration, Fiction, Poetry.

II. General Index.

AN ACKNOWLEDGMENT TO PUBLISHERS AND AUTHORS

NOTE.— The student, teacher, and general reader are invited to read the literary critics mentioned below, from whose works selections have been made in the compilation of this handbook; they are also requested to remember the courtesy of the publishers who granted permission to the author to use these selections.

G. P. PUTNAM'S SONS, New York.
Raymond, George Lansing......Poetry as a Representative Art.
Bain, Alexander...............English Composition and Rhetoric.
Hardwicke, Henry.............Oratory and Orators.
Sears, Lorenzo................Occasional Addresses.

A. C. McCLURG & COMPANY, Chicago.
Rabb, Kate Milner............National Epics.
Spalding, John Lancaster.......Collected Works.
Chesterfield, Lord.............Letters.

LONGMANS, GREEN & COMPANY, New York.
Newman, John Henry..........Collected Works.
Thomson, Daniel Greenleaf.....The Philosophy of Fiction.

HOUGHTON, MIFFLIN & COMPANY, Boston.
Bates, Arlo....................Talks on Literature.
Browning, Robert..............Collected Works.
Stedman, Edmund Clarence.....Poets of America.
Stedman, Edmund Clarence.....Nature and Elements of Poetry.

DODD, MEAD & COMPANY, New York.
Mabie, H. W...................Collected Works.

THE CLARENDON PRESS, Oxford.
Moulton, Richard Green........Shakespeare as a Dramatic Artist.

ix

SCOTT, FORESMAN & COMPANY, Chicago.
Mathews, William............Oratory and Orators.
Welsh, Alfred H.............English Literature and Language.

A. C. ARMSTRONG & SON, New York.
Hunt, Theodore W...........Literature and Style.

D. C. HEATH & COMPANY, Boston.
Moulton, Richard Green......Literary Study of the Bible.
O'Connor, J. F. X............Rhetoric and Oratory.

THE AMERICAN BOOK COMPANY, New York.
Shaw, Thomas B.............Manual of English Literature.

HENRY HOLT & COMPANY, Boston.
Perry, Thomas Sergeant......History of Greek Literature.

HARPER & BROTHERS, New York.
English Men of Letters.......Series.

BENJAMIN H. SANBORN & COMPANY, Boston.
Mead, William Edward........Composition and Rhetoric.

THE WERNER COMPANY, Akron, Ohio.
The New Werner Twentieth Century Encyclopedia (Britannica).

CHARLES SCRIBNER'S SONS, New York.
Forsyth, William............Life of Cicero.
Marsh, George P.............Origin and History of the English
                                                    Language.

GEORGE BELL & SONS, London.
Bohn's Classical Libraries......

THE MACMILLAN COMPANY, New York.
Arnold, Matthew............Essays in Criticism.
Pater, Walter................Appreciations.

GINN & COMPANY, Boston.
Caley & Scott................Literary Criticism.
Mace, William H.............Method in History.
Hudson, Rev. H. N...........Shakespeare, Life and Art.

JOHN J. McVEY & COMPANY, Philadelphia.
    Fénelon, Archbishop...........Three Dialogues on Eloquence.

J. H. COATES & COMPANY, Philadelphia.
    Hutton, Richard Holt..........Essays in Criticism.

PENN PUBLISHING COMPANY, Philadelphia.
    Beecher, Henry Ward..........Oratory.

W. J. WIDDLETON & COMPANY, New York City.
    Trench, Richard Chenevix......Study of Words.

THE CENTURY COMPANY, New York City.
    The Century Dictionary.........

A full list of the Authors quoted in this Handbook will be found among the Bibliographies at the close of the volume. See Appendices.

PART I

CHAPTER I

LITERATURE AS A FINE ART

Literature as a Fine Art.—In the treatment of literature the proposition which seems to stand most in need of assertion at the present moment is, that literature is a *fine art,* and should be studied in connection with the other fine arts. For the same "first principles" which apply to painting, music, sculpture, architecture, apply with equal force to literature. Likewise, literature has its own form and content, and a medium far more subtle and complex than sound or color or stone.

The Affinity of Literature to Other Fine Arts.—The relation that literary art sustains toward the other arts is aptly expressed by Cicero: *Omnes artes quasi uno vinculo conjunguntur* — all the arts are bound together as by a common bond. Hence, literary art must have some affinity with sculpture, painting, architecture; and this affinity is found in the underlying principles of all art. These principles, as expressed by the Greeks, are unity, harmony, balance, proportion. They form the common bond which binds all the arts together.

The Source of These Principles.—They are all found in nature, and they were appropriated by the human artist. "Art," says Aristotle, "is *mimesis* or imitation of nature." The things of nature are individualized, marked off as separate units; and, thus separated, they exhibit unity, harmony,

1

balance, proportion. The more common illustrations are a tree or a flower. Even a superficial examination of these objects reveals the "first principles" of art. Wherever one of these principles is wanting, we call a thing *deformed:* where all are absent we apply the term chaotic — we call it chaos. Man imitated the divine Artist; and in building, carving, painting, writing, he applied the selfsame principles. His art increased or decreased in merit according to the manner in which these principles were applied. A Gothic cathedral, a poem, a painting, will illustrate the manner of application: each work of art is one, embodying the principle of unity; the parts of each work harmonize, one with the other; balance and proportion strike the eye at a glance, as in the leaves of a flower or the branches of a tree.

The Relation of Literary Art to Science.— Both unite in expressing the true; but the former adds beauty to the truth of the assertion. Some illustrations:

Science: "The sun has spots upon its surface."
  Art: "The orb of day is dashed with wandering isles of night."
Science: "Autumn changes the leaves from green to red or yellow."
  Art: "Autumn lays a fiery finger on the leaves."
Science: "The rock-walls of my castle are impregnable."
  Art: "My castle's strength will laugh a siege to scorn."
Science: "The rays of the sun grow in intensity as the sun mounts toward the zenith."
  Art: "The sun tricks his beams and with new spangled ore flames in the forehead of the morning sky."

The primary object of all art is to express beauty, and it is clear from these examples that literary art adds beauty to the bare scientific assertion of a truth.

Other Relationships of Science and Literary Art.— Science is limited to the true: literary art covers a much larger field; as a basis it may have the wholly true, the partially true or the wholly false. As illustrations of the first class we may take Biblical literature or popularized science; of the second class there is the historical drama or novel, the great epics; of the third class there is the realm of pure fiction.

Again, literary art is concrete, synthetical, creative; science is abstract, analytical, impersonal. While the latter appeals to the intellect, the former makes its primary appeal to the æsthetic sense and to the emotions. It is art that addresses itself to the *human* in man; hence, in the older universities the classics are called " the humanities." Literary art may truthfully employ the language of Terence — *Homo sum: humani nihil a me alienum puto.*

Once more, science deals with parts; literary art with wholes. Plato has this to say of the literary structure: " Every literary work ought to be put together like a living creature, with due proportion of head, hands or feet and body." As the parts in the animal organism are determined by the vital principle animating them in such a manner that all unconsciously develop into fitness and harmony, so is it with a literary production — a central thought or idea acts in it like the animating principle in the living organism, making a complete creation to which it gives unity and harmony.

Literary Art and the Æsthetic Sense.—Inasmuch as literature is a fine art, its primary object is beauty, and its primary appeal is to the æsthetic sense. This sense is described as our faculty, or power, of appreciating the beautiful, whether in the physical, moral or intellectual order. Lessing describes it as our faculty of appreciating those ideals which art externalizes and renders concrete. The old rhetoricians described it under the heading of good taste or the capability of perceiving and estimating the beauties of nature and of art. It is, therefore, a certain natural and instinctive sensibility to beauty. As a fine taste judges food; so, metaphorically, a fine taste, or the æsthetic sense, judges beauty.

A Universal Endowment.—The æsthetic sense is as innate to man as his physical sense of taste or touch, and it is quite as universal. For the most ignorant savages have some discernment of beauty. They possess an art, although it be primitive and exceedingly crude. Witness their dress, war ornaments, the painting of their bodies, their ballads, tales and death-songs. The æsthetic sense varies in degree according to the peculiar gifts, the location, the advantages of culture, refinement, civilization, enjoyed by nations. Thus, for example, the ancient Greeks possessed the keenest appreciation of beauty; nature provided them with this special gift, and also a most beautiful natural environment upon which this talent could be exercised. They also enjoyed the advantages of the rarest culture and the highest degree of civilization. Add to all this their wonderful creative faculty, and it is not surprising that they left the best models in every department of the fine arts.

Improvement of the Æsthetic Sense.—It is improved by locality. Witness the effect of the skies and landscape of Italy or Greece upon the artists who have flourished in those places. It is improved by discipline. In the same nation note the difference between those who study the fine arts and the untaught multitude. It is improved by intelligence. The extraordinary mental power of the Greeks was a strong factor in the development of their æsthetic sense. It enabled them to judge a work of art, compare it with nature's original, show the connection of parts and their relation to the whole.

Thus, in analyzing an intricate masterpiece, reason told them why and upon what grounds their artistic work was beautiful. Finally, the æsthetic sense is developed by a good heart — by strong and virtuous affection. As Edmund Burke writes: " He whose heart is indelicate or hard, he who has no admiration of what is truly noble or praiseworthy, nor the proper sympathetic sense of what is soft and tender, must have a very imperfect appreciation of the highest beauties of art."

Lines of Development. —They are two: delicacy and correctness. As our appreciation of beauty grows it becomes delicate; we see hidden beauties that escape the vulgar eye; we become sensible to the smallest blemishes. As our power of appreciation develops it becomes more correct; we are able to distinguish genuine from counterfeit beauties; our judgment improves so that we can classify and estimate works of genius. The value of delicacy lies chiefly in discerning the true merit of a work; the value of correctness, in rejecting false pretensions to merit.

The Ultimate Judge of Merit.—Our æsthetic sense is just and true when it agrees with the general judgment of men. The supreme court in this matter is not a school, nor a faction, nor the popular fancy, but mankind in general. *What all men agree in admiring must be beautiful.* The concurring judgment or feeling of the race is the last court of appeal. And the sound and natural state of our æsthetic sense is ultimately determined by the general taste of mankind. As illustrations of this irreversible and infallible judgment there are the epics of Homer, Virgil, Milton; the dramas of Æschylus, Sophocles, Shakespeare; the sculpture of Phidias; the architecture of the Gothic cathedral; the painting of the Italian masters, the music of Wagner; and so on through the long list of the artists of every age, who, in spite of years, are immortally young.

Practical Value.—The literary artist should develop his faculty for appreciating the beautiful, for he thus becomes his own critic in choosing words and sentences, in writing graceful and harmonious composition, and, above all, in selecting high and worthy ideals for his art.

CHAPTER II

ART-FORM IN LITERATURE. WORDS

Elements of Art-Form.— These elements are the word, sentence, paragraph, complete composition. Each element claims its own definition, analysis and place in relation to the art-form of literature. In the case of poetry, the paragraph yields its name to the stanza, section, or to some other title, but the idea of subordinate topics and divisions for which the paragraph stands, is quite the same whether in verse or prose. It remains to view each of the elements in detail.

Words in Relation to Literary Art.— Words are the material which the literary artist uses, as the painter uses colors, as the musician uses the keys of a piano, as the sculptor uses marble. They are the simplest element of composition; yet upon their mastery the excellence of literary art depends in a large measure. The right word, like the right key of the piano, or the right color in painting, always gives the proper tone to the composition; any other word would mar the harmony — lessen or destroy the effect. The skill of the artist is shown in the selection of words as it is shown in the harmony of keys or colors.

Various Definitions of Words.— Words, says Plato, form the body of composition, and thought forms its soul. Marsh also describes words as the living vesture which thoughts find for themselves. Schlegel likens words to amber in which thousands of precious thoughts are preserved. Emerson goes to geology for a suitable illustration: " Just as in some fossil, curious and beautiful shapes, the graceful fern or the finely vertebrated lizard are preserved; so in words are beautiful thoughts and images — the imagination and feeling of past ages." "Words," says Trench, "are not merely arbitrary signs denoting ideas, but living powers; they are not like the sands of the sea, innumerable, disconnected atoms, but growing out of roots clustering in families, they connect and intertwine themselves with all that men have been doing and thinking and feeling from the beginning of the world till now. They are a glorious inheritance which other generations by their truth and toil have made ready for us."

The Origin of Words.— As Trench remarks, there are two theories concerning the origin of language. "One theory would put language on the same level with the various arts and inventions with which man has gradually adorned and enriched his life. It would make him by degrees to have invented it just as he might have invented any of those, for himself; and from rude, imperfect beginnings, the inarticulate cries by which he expressed his natural wants, the sounds by which he sought to imitate the impression of the natural objects upon him, little by little to have arrived at that wondrous organ of thought and feeling, which his language is often to him now." This theory makes of language a gradual and complete evolution from the broken cries of the Baboon to the glorious periods of a Cicero or a Webster. The second theory is thus set forth by Trench: " God gave man language just as He gave him reason, and just because He gave him reason; for what is man's *word* but his *reason,* coming forth that it may behold itself? They are indeed so essentially one and the same that the Greek language has one word for them both. God gave it to man because he could not be a man, that is, a social being without it. Yet this must not be taken to affirm that man started at the first furnished with a full-formed vocabulary of words. He did not thus begin the world *with names,* but *with the power of naming.* God did not teach man words as one of us teaches a parrot, but gave him a capacity and then evoked the capacity which He gave. This point is clear from Genesis: He brought the animals to Adam to see what he would *call* them, and whatsoever Adam called every living creature, that was the *name* thereof. Here we have the clearest intimation of the origin, at once divine and human, of words."

Partial Agreement of Both Theories.— They agree in admitting an evolutionary process. They disagree in this: the initial power of naming or coining words. One theory maintains that man had from the very beginning the full power and capacity for naming things; the other theory maintains that man gained this power and capacity *gradually,* as his vocal organs were gradually trained to the pronunciation of words. Renan in his history of language says that all languages, like all organisms, are subject to the law of gradual development. Yet the primitive language possessed those elements necessary to its integrity; all were there, but confusedly and without distinction; all were in the germ which slowly expanded into regular form and proportion. This law of language is the law of all life as exhibited in organisms. We may liken it to the growth of a tree springing out of, and unfolding itself from a root, that root being the divine capacity for language with which man was created. In this explanation of Renan we have all that appears to be sound in both theories respecting the origin of language.

How Words have Multiplied.— Words multiplied as man extended his rule over nature. New facts, new discoveries, new inventions, new arts, new philosophies, new religions — all clamored for the new word and the new phrase. In this connection words are called the record of discoveries, the mile-stones of human progress. For example, words like *trinity, christian, pagan, monarchy, patriarch, democracy, theocracy, tyranny, impressionist, realist, nominalist, reformation, revolution, crusade, abolition,* and a host of others, mark whole epochs in human history. With a boundless world lying around him and demanding to be catalogued and named, man was compelled to add to his vocabulary; and as he advanced in civilization and multiplied the arts and sciences, as well as civil and religious institutions, this verbal addition was bound to be enlarged. On this point John Stuart Mill observes: "Hardly any original thoughts on mental or social subjects ever make their way among mankind or assume their proper importance in the minds even of their inventors until aptly selected words or phrases have, as it were, nailed them down and held them fast." Some recent illustrations: the philosophy of evolution represented by the " survival of the fittest "; " the struggle for existence "; " the process of natural selection." The late political movement in Ireland is immortalized by the word "boycott." Similarly, such phrases and words as ' sphere of influence,' ' the cross of gold,' ' abolition,' ' total abstinence,' ' imperialism,' ' state rights,' ' reconstruction,' and hundreds of other terms represent large movements in human history, crystallized fragments of which are thus imbedded in a nation's vocabulary.

And so, as Trench observes, words are the embodiment of the feelings, thoughts and experiences of many nations. They mark how far the moral and intellectual conquests of mankind have advanced. They convey the mental treasures of one period to the generations that follow. They sail safely across gulfs of time in which empires have suffered shipwreck. We speak of " Punic faith " to-day, although Carthage has been in ruins over 2,000 years.

The Two-Fold Function of Words.— A word when used by the literary artist has two functions to perform. First, it calls up an image of the thing it stands for. Secondly, it calls up a set of ideas associated therewith. In the first case, it *denotes* one thing; in the second case it *connotes* many things. The artist must consider this power of denotation and connotation. For example, take the expressions, ' bad faith ' and ' Punic faith.' They denote the same idea. But the second expression connotes much more than the first. A legion of ideas are associated with the word, Punic, which make a vivid and lasting impression, driving home the abstract idea contained in the word, ' bad.' Or, again, take the verb ' to boycott '; it denotes ' to ostracize ' or ' to let severely alone.' But, on the other hand, it connotes a legion of vivid ideas, as the image of Captain Boycott, hated and shunned by the Irish peasantry, comes before the mind. " Mr. Jones, the Alderman, *roots* for popularity in the ninth ward." " Our esteemed contemporary, the democratic Free Press, is braying for a change in the administration." Examples may be multiplied indefinitely. A clever literary artist, like a judge of rare spices, detects at once the flavor of words possessing any power of connotation; and the selection of a word often depends upon this varying and subtle power. As Mr. Bates observes, " To suggest by the choice of words those delicate and subtle ideas which are like a fragrance or like the iridescent sheen of nacre is one of the highest triumphs of literary art; and the nice artist in words is certainly not less careful in regard to the connotation of words than he is of their denotation."

Selection of Nouns.— These are the most ancient part of speech. In the art of writing they first claim our attention. Before man could speak or write about any subject, he had to name it. As the number of subjects is so great and so varied, he soon possessed an unlimited number of substantives, that are commonly called nouns. The selection of the noun is perhaps the easiest task for the literary artist. It is suggested by the subject in hand. The power of connotation common to all words is shared by the noun, especially when the connotation is supported by the rest of the phrase or sentence. For this purpose our language is rich in synonyms. The metaphorical use of gender is also a consideration for the literary artist. The genius of our language permits us, whenever it will add beauty to our composition, to make the names of inanimate objects either masculine or feminine, in a metaphorical sense. For example, " Justice is the law of nature; SHE alone confers honor upon man." No other language offers this advantage, for in other languages every word has a fixed gender which can on no occasion be changed. Finally, the declension of the noun claims attention. By abolishing cases we have made the structure of English most simple. Simplicity and ease are the chief benefits we derive from the use of prepositions instead of case endings. Any foreigner realizes how simple the English is because of this change. But it is a benefit often gained at the expense of harmony : certain words must be placed close by one another in a period to show that they are connected in meaning, and frequently the words so placed do not harmonize, thereby marring the beauty and rhythm of the sentence.

Selection of Verbs.— The verb is the most complex part of speech, and therefore makes the heaviest demand upon the reason of the writer. The choice of the verb depends upon the writer's perception of truth. It contains a predicate or statement and thereby involves an exercise of reason. It carries with it several subtle divisions of time. The exact expression of time usually accompanies the affirmation made by the verb. Reason must weigh the affirmation from the viewpoint of time as well as significance. As Dr. Blair writes, " On account of its importance this part of speech receives its name, verb, from the Latin verbum — *the word*. They (the verbs) must have been coeval with men's first attempts toward the formation of language, although it must have been the work of a long time to rear them up to that accurate and complex structure which they now possess. Owing to their subtle nature, they possess a greater power of connotation than the noun. Like all modern European tongues, the English makes use of the auxiliary verb. It renders language more simple and easy in structure, having the same effect as the change from the case-ending to the preposition. On the whole, it improves the English as an art-medium."

Selection of Adjectives.— The adjective makes a primary appeal to the aesthetic sense. It is the flesh dressing out the skeleton. It is called the cloth of gold on the field of literature. The adjective more than any other part of speech justifies the term art, as applied to writing. The selection of the adjective requires both judgment and taste. The same is true of the adverb, for both are the finishing touches given to the literary canvas. The right adjective is determined partly by the qualities or attributes of the substantives to which it belongs, and partly by the general effect of the whole composition. Often an adjective which of right belongs to a certain substantive, must be modified in the interest of the general effect, just as lively colors must often be " toned down " on the canvas. Perhaps no part of speech requires as much care as the adjective. As Professor Mead observes : " Young writers are tempted to make too free use of adjectives because they furnish superlative forms of expression. They heap epithets upon every substantive till it is smothered under qualifying words. It is the mistake of the young painter with a pot of bright colors."

Use of Particles.— For final consideration there are the connective particles; they mark the movement from one idea to another, and thus form the connection of thoughts. These particles increased as man advanced in civilization. The more perfect language becomes, the more numerous are these particles. No language has such a plentiful supply of them as the Greek — the clearest proof of an unrivalled refinement and civilization. In English a great deal depends upon the proper management of these particles. They make a composition appear firm and compact or disjointed and loose; they cause it to march with a smooth and easy pace, or render its progress rough and irregular. Particles are in constant demand; our words have been brought to us from so many diverse sources that, as it were, they straggle asunder; they do not coalesce so naturally in the structure of a sentence as the words of a language built on one foundation. Hence, the need of particles.

CHAPTER III

THE WORD

SOURCES OF ENGLISH WORDS

Universal Indebtedness.—" The sources of our English vocabulary are extremely various. No other tongue, ancient or modern, has appeared in so many and so different phases; and no other people of high civilization has so completely disregarded the barriers of race and circumstance and adopted into its speech so great a number of un-native words. The making of the English language began, it may be said, with the introduction of Roman rule and Roman speech among the barbarous Celts of Britain. The Latin language, as the vehicle of civilization, affected strongly the Celtic, and also the speech of the Teutonic peoples, Saxons, Angles, and Jutes, who in the fifth century obtained a footing on the island. This Teutonic tongue, while assimilating something both of the native Celtic idiom, and of the Latin in a Celtic guise, in time became the dominant language. The speech thus formed (called *Anglo-Saxon* or, as some prefer, *Old English*) was raised almost to classic rank by the labors of Alfred and of the numerous priests and scholars who sought to convey to their countrymen in their native language the treasures of Latin learning and the precepts of the Roman Catholic church. Though uniting in the ninth century with an influx of Scandinavian speech, and in the eleventh century, through the Norman conquest, with the stream which flowed through France from Rome, it remained the chief fountain of English. From these two elements, the Teutonic and the Latin (the latter both in its original form and as modified in the Romance tongues), our language has been constructed; although materials more or less important have been borrowed from almost every known speech." (See Century Dictionary, Preface, VII.)

The Native English.— It is sometimes called Old English or Anglo-Saxon. This Saxon source first claims our attention. As Herbert Spencer indicates, (Philosophy of Style) there are special reasons for so doing, the most important being early association. A child's vocabulary is almost wholly Saxon: he says, " I have," not " I possess "; " I wish," not " I desire "; he does not *reflect,* he *thinks;* he does not beg for *amusement,* but for *play;* he calls things *nice* or *nasty,* not *pleasant* or *disagreeable.*

The Special Value of Saxon to the Literary Artist.— First of all, our native vocabulary economizes attention because of the brevity of the words; secondly, it makes the widest appeal because most generally understood; thirdly, it is valuable because of the imitative character of the words (*e. g.* splash, bang, roar, etc.); fourthly, it is valuable because the words are concrete and specific, not generic and abstract; fifthly, it is valuable because of its tendency to compounds; sixthly, it is valuable because it furnishes the proper basis and main structure of our present English; lastly, it is valuable on account of being so largely the language of emotion, wit and pleasantry. A word about each of these separate merits.

Brevity.— Saxon words are, for the most part, words of one syllable. On this point Herbert Spencer observes (Philosophy of Style) : " The superiority possessed by Saxon English is its comparative brevity. If it be an advantage to express an idea in the smallest number of words, then will it be an advantage to express it in the smallest number of syllables. If circuitous phrases and needless expletives distract the attention and diminish the strength of the impression produced, then do surplus articulations also. A certain effort must be required to recognize every vowel and consonant; some attention is absorbed by each syllable. Hence, the shortness of Saxon words becomes a reason for their greater force."

Appeal.— The best art makes the widest appeal. Literary art makes the widest appeal when it employs the words most easily understood. Owing to long familiarity and early association, the Saxon element enjoys the distinction of being most easily understood. From childhood we learn the significance of Saxon words. If we remember how slowly and with what labor the appropriate ideas follow unfamiliar words in another language, and how increasing familiarity with such words brings greater rapidity and ease of comprehension; and if we consider that the same process must have gone on with the words of our mother tongue from childhood upwards, we shall clearly see that these words call up images with less loss of time and energy than their later learnt synonyms. Hence, on account of the readiness with which the general reader recognizes their power of denotation and of connotation, the great artists in English literature have given them the preference. Chaucer, Spenser, Shakespeare, Milton, Bryant, Longfellow, Tennyson, not to mention others, have used in certain pieces as high as eighty per cent of Saxon words.

Sound and Sense.— The imitative character of Saxon words is abundantly obvious. Perhaps no other language offers so many illustrations: The *whistling* wind, *roaring* waves, *hissing* serpents, *buzzing* flies, *crashing* timbers, *rattling* hail. The advantage of such a vocabulary to the literary artist who wishes to describe a scene, is equally obvious.

Concreteness.— The work of the artist, no matter what be the medium, is to concrete some ideal. Now Saxon words are concrete and specific; they stand for *things;* the literary artist, therefore, selects such words in order to give his composition definiteness and vividness. The Saxon mind was not philosophical, or speculatively disposed; it demanded not abstractions or generalizations. What it did demand was the image, the reality and the definite attributes of reality. As a consequence only a very small percentage of Saxon words are abstract or vague in meaning.

Tendency to Compounds.—The Saxon element of our speech is of the highest importance, because, like the Teutonic parent tree, it permits compounds. These compounds give scope to men of literary genius who thereby create new and most important epithets. New compounds flash out daily from the English literary mint, and they are soon accepted as current coin. The Saxon element deserves all the credit, for with other languages tributary to ours such compounding is not possible. Our strongest epithets such as ' death-dealing,' ' soul-shrinking,' ' blood-curdling,' come from this source.

Syntactic Structure.—Saxon words are not only the prevailing element in our literary art; they form the proper basis and main structure of the English language. They supply the essential parts of speech: the article, pronoun, preposition, numeral, auxiliary verb, conjunction and all the little particles that bind words into sentences and thus form the joints, sinews and ligaments of the language. Saxon controls the grammatical inflections, the terminations of noun, of verb, and of the comparative and superlative, and the entire syntactic structure. It makes all foreign words bend to its laws of declension and conjugation; so that these foreign words are often abridged and simplified. It is called the mortar of the English building.

French and Latin Elements.— Next to the Saxon these elements are the largest and of most importance. In reality there are two classes of Latin words, one class coming directly from the old Roman; the other class coming indirectly from the same source through the French or Norman. The first class has three subdivisions corresponding to the same number of periods in the history of the language. Concerning the oldest Latin acquisition Marsh observes, they were introduced into England at the time of the Roman conquest. For example, such words as street, cheese; and *cester,* the ending of the names of English towns. Christian missionaries brought the next acquisition when England was brought under the dominion of the cross. Latin was the official language of the Roman Catholic Church, and it became the medium of general religious, moral, and intellectual instruction. But the largest acquisition direct from Roman sources was made during the Humanist and Scholastic periods and in the golden age of English literature when classic scholarship in Western Europe unlocked the literary treasures of Greece and Rome. Since then the flood-gates have been opened by such lexicographers as Johnson, who have practically anglicised the whole Latin dictionary. So that at the present time the percentage of Latin is far in excess of any other element.

Value of this Element.— The largest demand for Latin words comes from science, philosophy and theology. Scientific names are almost invariably either Latin or Greek. The enormous growth of the sciences has had a corresponding effect upon Latin terminology. In like manner, philosophy has made heavy demands upon the Latin element. Philosophical writing, on account of its abstract character, has little use for a Saxon vocabulary. Not more than twenty per cent of the words employed in a modern philosophical treatise are Saxon. The definition of evolution given by Herbert Spencer and the amusing translation of it into Saxon may be taken as a fair example of the preference which must be had for Latin in the department of philosophy.

The Latin Element in Literary Art.— The literary artist employs Latin words in the department of oratory. The *os magna sonans* requires the large polysyllabic words such as are supplied only by the Latin. A word which in itself embodies the most important part of the idea to be conveyed, especially when that idea is an emotional one, may often with advantage be a polysyllabic word. Thus it seems more forcible to say, " it is *magnificent,*" than " it is *grand.*" The word *vast* is not so powerful a one as *stupendous.* Calling a thing *nasty* is not so effective as calling it *disgusting.* There seem to be several causes for this exceptional superiority of certain long words. We may ascribe it partly to the fact that a voluminous, mouth-filling epithet is, by its very size, suggestive of largeness or strength. Witness the immense pomposity of sesquipedalian verbiage; and when great power or intensity has to be suggested, this association of ideas aids the effect. A further cause may be that a word of several syllables admits of more emphatic articulation; and, as emphatic articulation is a sign of emotion, the unusual impressiveness of the thing named is implied in it. A third cause is that a long word (of which the latter syllables are generally inferred as soon as the first are spoken) allows the hearers' consciousness a longer time to dwell upon the quality predicated — an advantage results from keeping it before the mind for an appreciable time. (Spencer, Philosophy of Style.) Not only in oratory, but often in history, the literary artist will employ the long word for the reasons indicated by Spencer. For example, the far-resounding periods of Macaulay or the pompous style of Gibbon — a style, however, more or less in keeping with his grand theme — make frequent demands upon the polysyllabic word and sesquipedalian phrases. *Power* and *euphony* are gained, especially the latter, owing to the large number of vowel sounds in Latin words. Sentence rhythm, which is emphasized in the higher kinds of prose, may be more easily maintained when Latin words are freely interspersed with the Saxon; for the consonants of the latter can easily cause a harsh, grating effect upon the ear, if too many Saxon words are put in juxtaposition.

The French Element.— What has been said concerning words which are derived directly from the Latin, applies in almost equal measure to words of French, Norman or Romance origin. The indirect reception of these words into English, while it has occasioned some changes in orthography and pronunciation, made no essential change in their nature. On account of long domestication, these French and Romance derivatives are more closely identified with our language than the words of direct adoption from the Latin. Immediately after the Norman conquest, French was used in the Court and in English schools. It was the language of the bar. All educated Englishmen used it. French literature came with the conquest, and the translation of this literature into the native speech of England, its naturalization as an English possession, was the first movement in the manifestation of a new literary life.

Domestication of French Words.—How this took place is explained by Marsh : " the want of a sufficient nomenclature and the convenience of rhythm and metre, as is very clearly seen in all the older English writings, led to the employment of many French words; and in an age when French was quite as familiar to an educated man as English, a considerable portion of French words would be introduced almost unconsciously and with no objection on the part of the reader. About the middle of the fourteenth century, schools were established in which English was both taught as itself an object of study, and employed as a vehicle of instruction in other languages and disciplines. Native poets, composing original works in their own tongues, would naturally use the poetic diction in which the productions of French literature had been clothed. French literature had already attained a culture which eminently fitted it for literary purposes, and made it a storehouse of poetic wealth in words as well as in thought. This was a convenient resource to writers struggling in vain to find adequate expression in the vocabulary of Saxon-English. Thus in the course of a single generation a greater number of French words were introduced into English than in the three previous centuries which had elapsed since the Norman Conquest. The newly adopted words were not indigenous, yet they were acknowledged and felt to be as genuinely English as those whose descent from the Gothic stock was most unequivocal."

Other Factors at Work.—It would be a mistake to suppose that the influx of French words was due to literature alone. All the arts and sciences contributed their share. The blending of both races brought to England the French lawyer, architect, painter, glass-maker, brass-founder and the other handicraftsmen; they brought with them the vocabularies of their respective arts. The sciences, too, medicine, physics, geography, alchemy, astrology, all of which became known to England chiefly through French channels, added numerous specific terms to the existing vocabulary; and these words soon passed into the domain of common life and were incorporated into the general tongue.

Present Percentages.— It is difficult to get a correct estimate of the foreign elements in English. In literary art about 40,000 words are employed, of which at least sixty per cent are Saxon. According to the latest computation there are over two hundred thousand words in the English language.

As the Saxon element is almost stationary (only a few old coins are recovered by such artists as Tennyson and Browning) there must be a vast expansion of the Latin element. Other languages, with the possible exception of the Greek, have not appreciably increased their contributions. Of our spoken vocabulary as distinguished from the dictionary vocabulary, it is estimated that eighty per cent is of Saxon origin.

Other Languages.— The Greek element, strange to say, has always been small — possibly five per cent. Most of the Greek words are found in the terminology of science and philosophy. Other languages, Celtic, Italian, Arabic, etc., all combined, yield scarcely five per cent. Here is another strange fact: the process of anglicising the Celtic vocabulary never took on definite shape; scarcely one hundred English words now in use can be traced to the ancient British. The Saxon and the Celt, so it seems, could never unite or amalgamate even on linguistic lines, although bound together for centuries in the closest association.

The Supreme Law of Selection.— In selecting words from the various sources, native and foreign, the literary artist must keep in mind the effect aimed at, and choose the word best fitted to that end, no matter what its origin may be. While as a rule the native element has the preference in all our literary masterpieces, such preference is always subordinate to the demands of the art itself.

CHAPTER IV

THE SENTENCE

WORD COMBINATIONS.

The Sentence.— The smallest combination of words making complete sense is called the sentence. After selecting the right word, the artist must find for it the right place in the sentence.

Places of Emphasis.— In every sentence there are two such places — the beginning, and the end. Important words should occupy both positions. The end of the sentence is the place of greatest emphasis. One illustration: "The red artillery flashed far." How much better the arrangement of the poet: "Far flashed the red artillery."

Purpose of Artistic Arrangement.— Three results are always secured by the best artists in the marshalling of words — variation, coherence, and rhythm or harmony of the sentence. Variation is secured by mixing long and short sentences, periodic and loose. The following rules of choice are laid down: for vigor and emphasis use the short sentence; for detail and rhythm use long sentences; to hold attention and interest use the periodic sentence; for ease and naturalness use loose sentences; for point and antithesis use the balanced sentence.

The Short Sentence.— A sentence of two words is undoubtedly short. A sentence of two or three lines is classified in the same manner; whereas a larger number of lines would pass over into the category of a long sentence. However, a sentence of three lines is too long if one line will answer the purpose. Short sentences are usually clear, and they add vivacity by presenting a complete thought that can be taken in at a glance. When too frequent, they break the main thought of the paragraph into fragments so small that the style becomes jerky, incoherent, and undignified. Yet in certain kinds of composition like the compendium, chronicle, text-book, letter, diary, short sentences are preferred. Wit and epigram likewise demand them.

The Long Sentence.— Long sentences permit the expansion of a thought, and give room for indispensable qualifying circumstances. They also serve to group related facts, and thus establish a medium between the paragraph and the individual statement. Certain kinds of work may, therefore, be best done by long sentences. They best group together the elements of a complex thought; they afford opportunity for climax, and give weight and dignity. On the other hand, long sentences are often difficult to handle, often unduly heavy and confused; dependent clauses are frequently tangled with one another, so that the reader can scarcely follow the thought. Moreover, lightness and grace are not easily united in sentences that require a large space wherein to turn themselves (see Mead, Rhetoric). On this point Minto observes: " No small element in the mechanical art of sentence building is the adjustment of the length of the sentence. The capacity of the reader should first be taken into account; a sentence intelligible to one reader might not be easily grasped by another. A number of long and complex sentences weary and confuse the modern reader. It is true, the great artists of Greece and Rome elaborated their periods, but the average power of attention is not so high as in those ages, and hence many a modern artist fails by imitating classic models too closely. This is seen partic-

ularly in the case of the modern orator who uses long periods
— he is almost always a failure, though he may possess every
other requirement. A cursory glance at our modern magazines will show that the long sentence is no longer a favorite
in English prose."

Periodic Sentences.— A periodic sentence is one in which the
sense is suspended until the end is reached. Since the periodic
structure makes possible a suspension of the most important
elements of the sentence, this form is peculiarly adapted to
forcible writing. One can thus stimulate the reader's attention throughout the sentence, and present the weightiest
thought at the moment when he is best prepared to receive it.
According to Blair " This is the most pompous, musical and
oratorical manner of composing: Cicero abounds with such
sentences." Leading English orators like Burke or Webster,
have imitated Cicero. The periodic sentence is secured " by
bringing on predicates before what they are predicated of;
qualifications before what they qualify; by disposing of descriptive adjuncts, results, conditions and alternatives, at the
outset." In this manner the sentence is raised to the highest
degree of unity; and suspense, provided thought be not unduly
retarded, contributes to force. Moreover, an air of gravity
and dignity is given to the composition. On the other hand,
the disadvantages of the periodic sentence are obvious: they
are apt to be too long, and, if frequently used, they cause im-
patience and weariness, and are difficult to follow. The reader
or hearer is apt to lose the beginning before he arrives at the
end. No critic has expressed more clearly the defects of a
periodic or long sentence than De Quincey: " Such a sentence,
for example, begins with a series of *ifs;* perhaps a dozen lines
are occupied with expanding the conditions under which something is affirmed or denied; here you cannot dismiss and have
done with the ideas as you go along; all is hypothetic; all is

suspended in the air.   The conditions are not fully to be understood until you are acquainted with the dependency; you must
give separate attention to each clause of this complex hypothesis, and yet, having done *that* by a painful effort, you have done
nothing at all; for you must exercise a reacting attention
through the corresponding latter section, in order to follow
out its relations to all parts of the hypothesis which sustained
it.   In fact, under the rude, yet also artificial character of this
style, each separate monster period is a vast arch, which, not
receiving its keystone, not being locked into self-supporting
cohesion until you reach its close, imposes of necessity upon
the unhappy reader all the superincumbent mass of its powerful weight through the main process of its construction."
The labyrinthian complexities of which De Quincey complains,
are fast dying out of modern prose.   While the periodic sentence is still used, it now rarely includes more than four or
five lines.

The Loose Sentence.— The genius of the English language
calls for the loose sentence.   And this kind must be of frequent occurrence since our language does not permit the inversions requisite for the constant practice of suspending the
sense.   The loose sentence is one which may be complete in
meaning at one or several points before the end.   The element
of suspense is wanting; the meaning is gathered piece by
piece.   Loose sentences, says Quackenbos, fulfil their function
as the instruments of familiar expression, and are free from
the stiffness that characterizes uniform periods.   They are
not necessarily languid or unmusical; many of the best sentences in English literature are loose.   The reason why loose
sentences are suited to the genius of the English language is
pointed out by Greenough: " An inflected language generally
has a tendency to arrange ideas in such a manner that the
main predicate is withheld until all the modifications have been

given, and the whole thought, with all its details is thus presented at once in an organized body." Hence, the predominance of the periodic style in such languages; but not so in English, where prepositions take the place of inflections. Prepositions imply the loose construction and the loose sentence. If this grammatical reason did not exist, the literary artist would still need the loose sentence in order to vary his expression as well as for ease and naturalness.

The Balanced Sentence.— The balanced sentence is one in which the words and phrases of one part correspond in form and in position with those of another part. On this point of balance, Hill observes, " The balance is greater or less, according as the correspondence is more or less exact, and according as it extends to a larger or smaller part of the sentence." Balanced sentences often contain antithetical words or clauses; but even when they do not, their advantages and disadvantages are similar to those of antithesis. Balance gives pleasure because it is an expression of symmetry — one of the fundamental principles of art. It captivates the ear and helps to impress the memory and fix the attention. Moreover, it adds clearness and simplicity to the style by facilitating the comparison of things that are to be compared. Likewise, it makes the style impressive. According to Bain, the superior impressiveness of the balanced form can be explained in this fashion: when a second statement runs in the same form as one immediately preceding, the mind is partly relieved from the effort needed to follow the new statement, and thus is better prepared to feel the power of the thought itself. However, excessive use of the balanced sentence imparts to composition an affected and artificial character; for example, the style of Johnson or Macaulay. These styles are often stilted, stiff and unnatural because of the balanced sentence. Two rules govern its use. In the first place, it should be used only when there is a call for it in the nature of the thought — that is, when there is a real correspondence between the meanings of the clauses. In the second place, it must always be moderately employed, even when the sense or meaning calls for it, because it is a general law that all strong effects, of which balance is one, should be used with moderation.

A General Rule.— The literary artist has all the foregoing kinds of sentence from which to choose. Assuming that he is a master in the art, he will not pick any one kind of sentence to the exclusion of the other kinds — he will be governed by the law of variation. Herbert Spencer thus describes the perfect artist: " Now he will be rhythmical and now irregular; here his language will be plain and there ornate; sometimes his sentence will be balanced and at other times unsymmetrical; for a while there will be considerable sameness, and then again great variety. His mode of expression naturally responding to his state of feeling, there will flow from his pen a composition changing to the same degree that the aspects of his subject change; and his work will present to the reader that variety needful to prevent continuous exertion of the same faculties."

Coherence of the Sentence.— Coherence is the law of internal arrangement. The relation of each part of the sentence to other parts is thereby made clear and unmistakable. This law implies that a sentence should be a unit both in thought and in expression. There may be several ideas expressed, but they should be homogeneous and form a whole or a unit. Blair gives the following rules to secure coherence: (1) In the course of the same sentence do not shift the scene. (2) Avoid crowding the sentence with heterogeneous subjects. (3) Avoid excess of parenthetical clauses. (4) Do not add members after a full and perfect close. In all styles of composition it is often requisite to give in the same sentence several distinct facts; in which case, the only guiding consideration is comparative closeness of relationship. Coherence is of three kinds. First, in the order of words: the rule is, all words closely related in thought, should be placed together. Secondly, in the order of phrases: phrases similar in significance should be similar in form and length. Thirdly, in relation to connectives: connectives should denote with precision the relation of words and phrases to the context. The literary artist needs a most precise knowledge of connectives; much of the loose, vague and unsatisfactory writing of the present time is due to ignorance regarding connectives.

Harmony of the Sentence.— Two things are aimed at — agreeable modulation, and the sound so ordered as to become expressive of the sense. Harmony depends upon the selection and collocation of words. The grating consonant must be mixed with the smooth liquid. On this point Blair observes: " It is evident that words are most agreeable to the ear which are composed of smooth and liquid sounds, where there is a proper intermixture of vowels and consonants; without too many harsh consonants rubbing against each other; or too many open vowels in succession, to cause a hiatus or disagreeable opening of the mouth. It may always be assumed as a principle, that whatever sounds are difficult in pronunciation, are, in the same proportion, harsh and painful to the ear. Vowels give softness, consonants strengthen the sound of words. The music of language requires a just proportion of both. As to words, long words are commonly more agreeable to the ear than monosyllables — they please it by the succession of sounds which they present to it. Among words of any length those are the most musical which present an intermixture of long and short syllables. A third consideration is the disposition of words in a sentence; for, let the words themselves be ever so well chosen and well sounding, yet if they be ill-disposed, the music of the sentence is utterly lost."

Harmony in Sentence-Structure.— First of all, the distribution of the several members is to be carefully attended to. It is of importance to observe that whatever is easy and agreeable to the organs of speech, always sounds grateful to the ear. While a period is going on, the termination of each of its members forms a pause or rest for pronunciation; and these rests should be so distributed as to make easy the course of the breathing, and, at the same time, should fall at such distances as to bear a certain musical proportion to each other. The next thing which deserves attention is the close or cadence of the whole sentence, which, as it is always the part most sensible to the ear, demands the greatest care. Quintilian writes: "Let there be nothing harsh or abrupt in the conclusion of the sentence, for on that conclusion the mind pauses and rests. This is the most material part in the structure of discourse. Here everyone expects to be gratified." Though attention to the music of sentences must not be neglected, yet it must be kept within proper bounds, for all appearances of affectation are disagreeable. It may degenerate into childish and puerile ornament, especially when there is no equation between sound and sense. The current of sound ought to be adapted to the tenor of the composition. Sentences constructed with a fulness and swell are fitted to clothe ideas important, magnificently sedate. But manifestly, it would be absurd to use such a swell and cadence in any ordinary description or exposition of a theme. Themes that evoke intense passion or emotion require a corresponding sound of words. But ordinary artistic delicacy will see that there must always be an affinity between the sound and the sense.

How the Artist is Trained.— The best rule to follow in order to master the music and harmony of the sentence is to *read aloud* the best models of prose.   The custom of reading aloud will train the ear to sentence-rhythm; *it imprints upon the mind the correct forms of the sentence;* so that when one comes to write, one will instinctively fill out these forms.   The ear is attuned to sentence rhythm as it is attuned to the airs of music.   The practice of reading aloud is quite common in England — not so common in America.   It is said of Newman, our greatest master of prose, that he read aloud, every day, a chapter of Cicero in order to train his ear to sentence-rhythm. And the literary artist who would produce an English prose masterpiece, cannot do better than train with such models as Cicero, Newman, Arnold, Ruskin, Macaulay, reading aloud their matchless prose music and becoming familiar not only with sentence rhythm and harmony, but with their matchless art in constructing and employing the various kinds of sentence.   These immortal writers training the ear to music, the eye to symmetry and proportion, the mind to logical sequence, and the æsthetic sense to a keen appreciation of beauty are infallible guides to the " promised land."

CHAPTER V

THE PARAGRAPH

Definition.— After mastering the various kinds of sentence, the literary artist proceeds to consider their smallest combination known as the paragraph. Like the sentence, it is a unit, but a larger unit, in the composition. As a unit it is marked off by indentation; and, as a component part of the composition — a link in the chain —,it hints in some way at what has preceded it and foreshadows what is to come. It is defined as a group of sentences clustering around a central idea or topic which is subordinate to the main theme of the composition. The paragraph rests the eye by breaking the text; but its main function is to mark and elaborate the progressive changes in the thought. It helps the reader to follow a writer step by step.

Rules of Construction.— First, let the opening sentence indicate the subject of the paragraph. As a rule, each new paragraph introduces and finishes a definite topic; and this topic ought to be indicated at the outset. Secondly, make the opening sentence short. This is done to secure the attention and interest of the reader. In the beginning the reader is not willing to wind through the mazes of the long sentence. Thirdly, let the bearing of each sentence on what precedes be clear and positive. This rule simply insists upon logical and careful development. Fourthly, give smooth connection to the various sentences comprised in the paragraph. Smooth connection is one of the graces of artistic writing.

Principles Applied.— The principles applied in the paragraph are precisely the same as those applied in the sentence. The same unity, coherence and harmony are demanded. There is precisely the same organization. Unity in a paragraph implies a sustained purpose and forbids digression and irrelevant matter. The most common mistake with reference to unity is to run into one paragraph what should be divided into two or more. Even the best writers at times violate this rule; they introduce unnecessary digressions quite distinct from any legitimate development of the specific topic. Coherence of the paragraph implies consecutive arrangement, so that related ideas are kept as close together as possible: in other words, proximity is governed by affinity of ideas. When an idea is put forward in the paragraph, the way to stamp it on the mind is to give everything connected with it — iterations, examples, illustrations and proofs — before passing to another topic. The nature of the subject and the style of the composition usually dictate a plan in the bringing forward of successive particles. It constantly happens that a topic is related to several others, and as composition can move in only one line it may be impossible to bring a paragraph into entire accordance with the law. In such cases we must be content to study the greatest proximity of related topics on the whole (see Bain, Rhetoric Part I). The harmony of a paragraph applies both to thought-development and to sentence-collocation. The harmonious development of thought excludes all breaks or jarring transitions: it is secured by a rigorous application of logic. Like the collocation of words in a sentence, the collocation of sentences in a paragraph should be made with a view to harmony. It depends on a happy admixture of the various kinds of sentence; it depends on such a gradation of sentence as will bring the climax at the close of the paragraph. Inasmuch as harmony is a constant quality of good style, its application to the paragraph becomes obvious.

Method.— Paragraphs, says Barrett Wendell, are prevised, that is, we arrange beforehand the qualities of a paragraph — its length, the idea it will contain, the prominence it will have in the composition; whereas, in the case of sentences we revise them after they are written, and apply then the principles of criticism. Sentences are seldom deliberately planned; they are written first and then revised. Inasmuch as paragraphs are considerable portions of the complete composition, their prevision becomes a part of the general outline.

The Number of Sentences.— A paragraph may consist of a single sentence only, but commonly contains several. Says Mead: " A single paragraph is often a complete article in miniature, since the paragraph may treat a topic so narrow that the entire discussion will comprise but a few sentences." In a long article a group of paragraphs sometimes discusses with considerable fulness a single topic subordinate to the main theme; and this group can be regarded as an article within an article. Extremes of length or brevity are in any case to be avoided. Paragraphs that are too long require too much attention from the reader; paragraphs that are too short subdivide the thought unduly and make obscure the relations of the larger parts of the discourse. For indicating the topic and giving it some application, there should be at least a half dozen sentences in each paragraph.

The Divisions of the Paragraph.— Paragraphs admit of several divisions. First, the long and short; these are interchanged so as to avoid monotony. The length of the paragraph is largely determined by the subject matter of the composition. As Professor Genung writes: " There is no fixed measurement, but roughly speaking, less than a hundred words make a short paragraph; more than three hundred words, a long one." The use of short or long paragraphs is determined by the effect we wish to have. A solid, heavy and serious subject is best treated in the long paragraph. A light, racy topic demands the short paragraph. A second division is the isolated and linked paragraph. The isolated form is comparatively modern, but its use is growing rapidly in the daily and weekly newspapers and in the magazines. The isolated paragraph is short, varying in length from two or three lines to a dozen — rarely more. It deals with every conceivable subject. It is a whole composition in miniature. The reading public take very kindly to this paragraph. Usually a column or two on the editorial page of our daily and weekly newspapers will contain no other kind of writing. Telegraphic reports are now finding the same channel, while book-reviews in the very best magazines employ it. On the other hand, the linked paragraph is found in more elaborate compositions. As parts of a complete composition they require somewhat different construction from independent or isolated paragraphs. Each paragraph in the series should indicate some relationship with its neighbors — there should be an unbroken thread binding all together.

Paragraph Linking.— This is accomplished in various ways: first, by carrying on an important word or phrase from one paragraph to the following — a favorite method with Matthew Arnold. Second, by carrying on a very brief summary of the thought developed in the preceding paragraph — a favorite method of Newman. It gives to the thought-sequence peculiar power and dignity as well as clearness. Third, by letting the last sentence of the paragraph suggest the topic of the following paragraph; this is the ordinary method of linking paragraphs.

Sentence Linking in the Paragraph.— There are several rules which apply to sentence-linking : first, the use of sentence-echo ; the opening clause of one sentence echoes the thought and wording of the last clause of the preceding sentence. Second, by repeating the subject of the first sentence in the succeeding sentences. This method is very effective in oratory ; it is very emphatic if the same word is employed in the repetition. But in all kinds of literary art the subject is repeated by means of the pronoun or synonyms or paraphrase of meaning. A third method, by repeating the subject and predicate, which is still more emphatic and often employed in such parts of the oration as the exhortation. However, one must guard against the stilted style which results from too much repetition of this kind. Finally, sentences are linked by means of connectives. Concerning their right use, Coleridge observes : " A close reasoner and a good writer is generally known by his pertinent use of connectives. Read a page of Johnson ; you cannot alter one conjunction without spoiling the sense. It is a linked strain throughout." Among connectives, the most important are the cumulative conjunctions.

The Cumulative Conjunction.— It is defined as one which adds a new statement to preceding statements of the same class, and having the same bearing upon the topic of the paragraph. There are more than thirty of these in our language. Those of the first rank are, *and, but, for, yet, so, moreover;* they are the most beautiful connectives in English. *And* is the favorite Biblical connective ; the best prose writers often use it at the beginning of a sentence. *Yet* and *for* as initial particles for the paragraph often appear in the best prose. *Moreover* is the favorite connective of Newman ; and in its usage he is now widely copied. Besides these cumulatives of the first rank, we employ such single words as *also, yea, likewise, similarly, first, secondly, further, further-*

more, etc.; and such combinations as *once more, in like man- ner, yet another, then too, add to this.* Ruskin seems to pre- fer *in like manner;* while Herbert Spencer gives preference to *once more.* *So also* makes a happy paragraph transition. Fa- miliarity with prose masterpieces is the best teacher regarding the right use of connectives. The literary artist needs to be familiar with these words above all others in the language. They are essential to consecutive writing, for they are the hinges and joints of paragraph building. They are subdi- vided into *Adversative,* such as *but, notwithstanding; Illative,* indicating effect or consequence, the use of reasoning or argu- ment, such as *therefore, hence, thus, accordingly; Subordinate,* tying a subordinate clause or sentence to its principal, such as *if, provided that, when.* There are other subdivisions of minor importance. " On the right use of connectives," says Bain, " the coherence of paragraphs depends." As in the con- struction of sentences, so in the construction of paragraphs, they are essential in dove-tailing one's work. Much art is shown in their use. Their number is so large as to give all the necessary connection to English composition. On the abuse of particles, Hill observes: " The judicious use of connective particles promotes clearness." But useful as is a connective particle that expresses a real connection of thought, one that serves no purpose is worse than useless, and one used for an unsuitable purpose leads astray. *But* and *and* are frequent of- fenders in both ways. They are properly used to connect words or clauses closely related in meaning and similar in con- struction.

A composition should never begin with *but* or with *and;* for if nothing precedes the conjunction, there is nothing for it to connect with what follows. A paragraph may so begin when there is real opposition or real connection between two para- graphs as wholes; but usually a new paragraph indicates a break in the sense too important to be bridged by a conjunction.

Method of Study.— The artist learns by having the best models before him in his studio. The paragraph should be studied in the best prose authors — Arnold, Newman, Ruskin, Macaulay, George Eliot, Herbert Spencer. Analyze their work; lay bare the mechanism of their paragraph — its skeleton. This may be done mentally while reading, for one rule of right reading is to make mentally a synthesis of the plot or plan as you read. Again, before writing a paragraph, prepare a skeleton in like manner; that is, arrange the leading topic and the connected items of thought. " All orderly and artistic work," says Pater, " presupposes a careful outline beforehand, not only of the whole composition, but of each paragraph." The writer who does not follow such an outline, will be a loose and slovenly workman. No man builds without a plan for each room; no man should write without a similar guide.

CHAPTER VI

THE COMPLETE COMPOSITION

The Ideal Realized.— The maxim of the ancients applies here — *finis coronat opus:* the end crowns the work. The word, the sentence, the paragraph, are but steps toward this goal. The composition as a whole is the grand aim of the writer, for in it his ideal is concreted, realized. The general effect of the whole composition ought to be like the general effect of a complete building or painting or piece of statuary. The quality and merit of the art are thereby determined. As a work of art, a composition when complete possesses unity, harmony, balance, proportion. These principles are the very alphabet of art; they make an important demand upon the artist.

A Well Defined Plan.— The first demand in all kinds of literary art is a well defined plan for the composition. The writer who works without a plan, cannot escape chaos and confusion; whereas clearness is the first requisite of all good writing. It is called the intellectual quality of style because the intellect elaborates the plan of the composition; the intellect discovers at once the presence or absence of a plan in writing.

Evolution of a Plan.— To work out a plan for a composition one must carefully survey the subject and reduce one's ideas to order. There are various methods employed. Some prefer to write headings, giving form to ideas already clear, afterwards combining and correcting them. This is called the suggestive method, or, "thinking with the pen." One idea set down will suggest another until the paragraph is complete. Some writers cannot think without the aid of the pen. Other writers prefer to revolve the subject in their minds until the plan is fully matured. They wait for the thought to " work itself out," before penning a line. But whatever be the method, a plan must precede clearness of expression. Artists of the first rank, such as Newman, Arnold, Ruskin, always outline their work. The same rule applies to verse as well as to prose. Perhaps the most practical method to follow is to start with the outline that first suggests itself. As the theme is developed, both plan and composition may be altered or corrected. The best writers are hardly ever satisfied with the first draught. For example, Daniel Webster outlined several times his oration on the Pilgrim Fathers; Newman planned his Apologia four times and then was not satisfied with the final draught. Carlyle's " Life of Frederick the Great " underwent several revisions. A plan like a composition improves by careful review; but the first rough sketch, though it should lack completeness, ought to have coherence and unity — there should be some central idea round which all that is written clusters.

Qualities of a Complete Composition.— As a work of art, a complete composition is characterized by three qualities, an intellectual quality, an emotional quality, an æsthetic quality. The first quality is represented by the word *clearness;* the second, by *force;* the third, by *elegance.* Each one of these qualities deserves special notice.

Clearness.— This quality is predicated of a composition when its plan is well defined and when the writing itself appeals to the average intellect. The best art always makes the widest appeal. This is true of sculpture, painting, architecture and music as well as the art of letters. In order to make the widest appeal the literary artist must come down to the level of the average intellect to be intelligible to the average reader. The maxim of Aristotle applies here: "Think the thoughts of the wise, but use the language of the simple." Plainness and simplicity of language are gained only by long practice in picking and choosing words. Once more we may emphasize the native element of our speech: the Saxon word is always understood; it makes the widest appeal. In his lectures on writing English, Arlo Bates has this to say of clearness, and the means of attaining it:

"Clearness is most obviously associated with the word and the structure. If an author has carefully considered his work and the unity of his composition; if he has massed it properly in parts and as a whole, if he has looked well to its coherence — it is hardly possible that he should fail of being readily understood. Close attention to the mechanics of style will generally make a writer intelligible, provided always, that he wishes his meaning to be apprehended easily, and that he himself knows what he is attempting to say. It is no less needful to appeal to the average emotional experiences of mankind in order to be clear to the general reader. It must be remembered that all art is based on the assumption of a community of human feelings; in other words, upon the theory that the fundamental emotions are shared by all mankind. The more closely a writer holds to common humanity, to common human experience, the more wide will be the range of his work, and the more clear will he be in those very matters where clearness is most difficult of attainment. To gain clearness it is necessary first to avoid all vagueness of thought and all vagueness of expression. It is needful to shun ambiguity of word or of phrase, and that more subtle ambiguity which may arise from ill-considered paragraphing, from misproportion, or from bad arrangement of the parts of a composition. Finally, it is no less important to write with a constant remembrance of the audience addressed; to use their language and to appeal to the experiences which are likely to be common to the average individual. These are the principles upon which have been written the masterpieces of the world."

Errors Regarding Clearness.— The inexperienced writer sins against clearness in two ways. First, by so expressing himself that what he writes may mean more than one thing. It is the sin of vagueness and ambiguity. It is often the sin of such writers as Emerson, Carlyle, Browning. Emerson said of his own sentences: "They are infinitely repellant particles." Browning is purposely obscure, and, on that account, the despair of modern criticism. A second error is the introduction of a pedantic terminology. Some compositions, like the garb of the primitive man, are fantastic with feathers — from science, philosophy, theology. The most obscure references flatter the childish vanity of the pedant and the young artist. Among great modern writers James Russell Lowell is a shining example of the pedantic workman. His page is full of literary allusions which appeal only to the select and learned few. On the reception of his book, "My Study Windows," Matthew Arnold wrote him as follows: "My Dear Mr. Lowell: Your latest volume gives me great pleasure, indeed. But your manifold references and allusions often weigh down and crush your subject like the shields of the Romans on the breast of Tarpeia."

Force.— The second quality desirable in a composition is force. As clearness represents the intellectual quality, so force stands for the emotional quality of a composition. It appeals to the emotions; its purpose is to arouse feeling. A composition interests and stirs us because of it. Various names are applied to this quality which awakens sympathy, arouses passion and sets the imagination of the reader or hearer at work. Whately calls it *energy;* Campbell, *vivacity;* Bain, *strength.* Aristotle uses the Greek equivalent for energy. But science supplies the best term — *force.* This quality must be understood to cover more than transient outbreaks of emotion, or feeling at high tide; it is used in the sense of lasting vigor and power.

The Basis of Force in Art-Form.— First of all, there is the specific term which gives force to composition. This term is demanded on account of its vividness and its suggestiveness. It gives concrete form to the work of the artist. For example, compare *sound* with the definiteness and force of *cry, roar, yell, howl.* In the specific term we have the power of connotation or suggestiveness. For example, compare *This man is deficient in common sense,* with, *This man is a donkey.* On this point Baldwin observes: " The connotation or suggestiveness of words and phrases, which is their meaning for style, as distinguished from their denotation, which is their meaning for business and logic, as it measures elegance, measures also strength. The pursuit of force, then, is the pursuit of emotional connotations, and emotional connotations attach especially to words familiar and specifically concrete. The habit of the concrete and specific is the force of Homer, the force of Dante and of Chaucer, the force of Newman and Tennyson, the force of all great writers that choose to move our imaginations directly. It is the strong way of narration and description because it is the way of emotional suggestion. Even the most diverse styles, in so far as they have force, will be found to have it by these means." (Baldwin, Rhetoric.) The value of Saxon as supplying our concrete terms, once more becomes obvious.

Figures of Speech as a Source.— Figures of speech are emphatically the language of power. As soon as a writer wishes to impress his earnestness upon you, he invariably breaks out in figurative language. Even the untutored swain finds a figure quite as handy as a club whenever he wishes to express the vehemence of his emotion. Divine wisdom always employed figurative language to impress the truths of the Gospel upon the mind. For example, " The Devil goeth about like a roaring lion." " Work not for the meat that perisheth, but for the meat of eternal life." "Ye Scribes and Pharisees, ye are whitened sepulchres." Figurative language gives force to composition in proportion to the universality of its appeal. Hence, figures should be drawn from familiar sources. The best models in this regard are the figures and parables in Holy Scripture. We cannot improve upon the choice made by Divine Wisdom. No writing possesses more force than Holy Scripture, because of this wise selection of figurative language. On the value of figures to give strength to style and to heighten emotion Dr. Blair writes as follows: "We can always heighten the emotion by the figures which we introduce, leading the imagination to a train of agreeable or disagreeable, of exalting or debasing ideas which correspond to the impressions that we choose to make. When we want to render an object beautiful or magnificent, we borrow images from the most beautiful or splendid scenes of nature; we thereby throw a lustre over our object; we enliven the reader's mind and dispose him to go along with us in the various impressions which we give him of the subject. All this leads us to reflect on the wonderful power of language. What a fine vehicle it has now become for all the conceptions of the human mind. Not content with a simple communication of ideas, it paints these ideas to the eye in the most forcible and beautiful manner through the medium of figurative language. So that language, from being a rude and imperfect interpreter of men's wants and necessities, has now passed into an instrument of the most delicate and refined luxury."

A Subjective Source.—The great secret of force lies not only in the marvellous power of language, but also in the marvellous power of the human will and character. It lies in the earnestness, sincerity and sympathy of the writer. A reader of Carlyle is impressed at once with the intense earnestness of the man, which gives to his words the force and weight of a sledge hammer. A reader of Newman, whatever be his religious convictions, cannot help seeing that the secret of his powerful style, so forcible, yet so captivating, lies in the sincerity and sympathy of the writer. The great orators of the world — a Demosthenes, or Bossuet, or Burke, or Webster, or Patrick Henry — are perhaps the best examples of this peculiar quality in composition; and no class of men are more earnest, sincere and sympathetic than they.

Elegance.— Elegance is the third and last quality required in a complete composition. It is the quality that appeals to the æsthetic sense or to our appreciation of beauty. For it is the beautiful as expressed in art-form — the select word-combination, variety in the sentence and paragraph, a happy choice of figures and illustration, a harmonious development of the complete composition. It, therefore, pertains to structural beauty; and in the complete structure it reveals the personal taste and culture of the artist. He reveals a quick appreciation of beauty, a keen perception of the fitness of things, a power to convey both in the choicest words; he reveals politeness, a well-bred restraint, a complete freedom from any manner of excess, a perfect adaptation of style to thought. And for these various reasons he is called an elegant writer.

Etymological Meaning.— The word, elegance, implies to select — to pick and choose. When applied to composition, it means to pick and choose from the vast mass of words, phrases, sentences, paragraphs, thoughts, that which best suits our literary purpose and the requirements of art.

Scope of Elegance.—As elegance is an appeal to the æsthetic sense, it has to do with the complete structure of the composition, how it will affect the mind of the reader. The reader must be pleased not only with the various parts, but with the general effect of the whole composition. Hence, elegance is the result of the last touches of the great artist upon the literary canvas. Newman wrote thus concerning Cicero: " Cicero wrote elegantly because he had a keen appreciation of what is fine in literary art. In his writings there is an exquisite adaptation of style to thought. He was acquainted with the best models of Grecian literature — he read them for happy turns of phrase — he read them for the emotion wedded to the thoughts, which makes all thinking *human*. He wrote elegantly because out of those models he would pick and choose whatever made thought pleasing and expression beautiful."

Kinds of Composition.— The complete composition admits of four classifications, according to the subject matter and the manner of writing. Of these four kinds of composition, the first deals with persons or things — it is called *Descriptive;* the second deals with acts or events — it is called *Narrative;* the third deals with whatever admits of analysis or requires explanation — it is called *Exposition;* the fourth deals with any material that may be used to convince the understanding or to affect the will — it is called *Argument.* As a rule, these four kinds of composition are not distinct and separate in literary art. The artist at times necessarily allows one kind to run into another; thus, for example, a narrative work will often be descriptive, an argumentative work will often include exposition. It is possible, however, to have purely argumentative, expository, descriptive or narrative writing. Certain rules guide the artist in each class of work.

Exposition.— When the artist adopts this style, he poses as a teacher; he aims at lucid explanation; his object is to appeal to the minds of his readers; he presents facts, analyses, collates and combines them; he unfolds hidden meanings, the significance of things complex and subtle. Although it appears in artistic synthesis, exposition is only another name for analysis;

and because it is so, the guiding principle for the artist is clearness — clearness in statement of facts, clearness in thought-division, clearness in analytical development of the topic.   So that the artist must give strict attention to his definitions, divisions, generalizations.   A second principle subordinate to this is the principle of selection; that is of taking from the varied details those particulars which, when massed together, make the most vivid impression.   This principle also applies to description where a picture of the object described ought to be presented to the mind.   The necessity of some method is likewise obvious; no one method can be mentioned as best in all cases, but in every expository composition, some method of arrangement should be followed.   This principle applies to all kinds of writing, but in a special manner to exposition, the object of which is to analyze and instruct rather than to please the æsthetic sense.   Along with these principles must go the fundamental principles of all art — unity, harmony, balance, proportion.

Description.— Description may be scientific or literary. *Scientific description* is an exact statement of the truth respecting the qualities, characteristics, details, of an object.   It aims at the truth alone.   *Literary description* mentions likewise the qualities and characteristics of an object, but so arranges and classifies them as to bring before the mind an image or a picture of the object described.   The image of the object in the mind of the writer is transferred by written symbols to the mind of the reader.   This transfer is one of the triumphs of literary art.   There are various rules which assist the writer in making this transfer.   First, a cultivation of the habit of visualizing things; that is. seeing them as clearly in your own imagination as you see them in reality and in fact. The imagination should be trained to hold a photograph of the object before the mind, as a painter keeps your photograph before him when enlarging your picture. The merit of literary description depends largely upon this power. Wordsworth calls it the training of the inward eye. A second rule is to find and express the central idea of the picture thus mentally photographed. Two or three characteristic touches are sufficient to suggest the whole. A third rule is to proceed from the near to the remote; from the physical to the mental; from the obvious to the obscure. This is but the natural process of setting forth the characteristics of anything — to pass from the known to the unknown. A fourth rule is to make the details of the description submit to the central thought. These details are not suppressed; they are incidentally mentioned or suggested, but they are always kept subordinate. A final rule is to open the composition with a general view, a broad idea, of the thing, the person or the scene to be pictured. This rule holds whether the description be long or short. The reader should have a general view at once; hence, the opening paragraph of an essay, the introduction of a speech, the preface of a book, the prologue of a play, the beginning of any work of literary art, will be written for this purpose.

Narration.— Like description, this species of writing has for its subject-matter either persons or things. Its purpose is to tell of acts and events. Unlike description, it is not concerned with pictorial work: what the person does or suffers, not how he appears, is the main concern of the writer. As to its artistic value, in telling the story of some human experience or in supplying a record of events, the highest art is employed. As movement is the law of life, it is the first principle applied to narrative, which aims at telling the story of life. *Action, action, action,* the classic definition of oratory, is the advice given by the trained artist to the novice: keep the story *moving:* cut out all particulars which unnecessarily impede its progress,

Omit every detail which can possibly be spared. A second rule is that of method. As in description, so in narrative: method is demanded for an intelligent presentation of the story. It is looked for, and it constitutes much of the charm in biography, history and fiction where narrative writing predominates. Many biographers and historians fail, because at the outset they adopted no method in their work. As examples of methodical work read the biographical essays of Johnson, Macaulay, the historical essays of Newman, the Biography of Johnson by Boswell, the "Decline and Fall" by Gibbon. On the importance of narrative Bates writes: "It is the form of literature which most invariably appeals to men, and it is no less that form which most affects human conduct. Men who could not be brought to give ear to a sermon may be taught by a parable or moved by a tale. It is in narrative that prose rises most surely and indisputably to the rank of a fine art."

Argument.— It is that kind of composition which appeals rather to the understanding than to the æsthetic sense; for it supplies reasons in support of a proposition. In its literary connection, the word is used collectively, as indicating a body of reasons which, for example, would take the form of an essay. More frequently, however, argument and persuasion are allied, the one appealing to the reason, the other, to the feelings. Taken together they form one department of literature — oratory. Inasmuch as argument addresses the understanding, it presupposes a knowledge of logic. For argument deals with propositions, and propositions are things to be proved or disproved; and proof consists of all that is brought forward to sustain or refute the proposition, and it contains facts and inferences so arranged as to be effective for the purpose. As to the number and kind of arguments which may be employed, it is the province of logic to supply such information, and a detailed account of them cannot be given here. But in the arrangement of them in a composition, the artist is guided by two rules. The first of these rules calls for the strongest arguments at the beginning and the end of the composition, just as the most emphatic words are placed at the beginning and the end of a sentence. The remaining arguments are massed between these two points — they form the body of the composition. The second rule is not to employ too many arguments, for where too many are employed, the weak ones are apt to have the very opposite effect from the one intended; and where very many are employed, some are bound to be weak and ineffective. In the case of those selected, the artist should present them in detail and in the strongest possible manner. Such presentation requires the utmost clearness in style. The short sentence, easily grasped and going directly to the point, is preferable in the argumentative style. All the wealth of language is employed to present the argument in a variety of lights, and hold it before the mind until it is fully grasped. Imagery and illustration also abound in this style. All the wealth of rhetoric is employed to this end — to make the argument so effective that it must prevail. Hence, the appeal to the imagination and to the emotions, which usually accompanies argument. Feeling is the powerful ally of reason in bending and subduing the will. As models of argument, read the speeches of Cicero, Burke, Webster. On the practical application of argument to literary work Bates observes that the most obvious use of it is in the plea of the lawyer, the editorials of the newspaper, the essays or speeches establishing scientific, literary, political and religious opinions. Whoever writes at all is sure to employ argument sooner or later, and to a greater or less degree. Civilization differs from barbarism chiefly in that the strife has become intellectual instead of physical; and intellectual conflict is but another name for argument.

CHAPTER VII

ART-CONTENT IN LITERATURE

SUBLIMITY.

Meaning of the Term.— The elements of art-form so far reviewed — the word, the sentence, the paragraph, the complete composition — have to do with the framework and form of composition. The elements of art-content have to do with the ideas expressed; they are sublimity, beauty, feeling, humor, wit, melody. These elements are called emotional, because they appeal in a special manner to the emotions; and as the primary purpose of all art is to arouse emotion, these elements are of vital importance. For when ideas are expressed without this emotional appeal we have, for example, a mathematical or scientific treatise, but not literature properly so called. These elements humanize writing and make it literature

Sublimity Defined.— Sublimity is defined as that quality of literary art which arouses our emotion by expressing boundless extent or superior might. Longinus describes it as that quality of composition which elevates the mind above itself, and fills it with higher conceptions and noble pride. " The true sense," says Blair, " of sublime writing undoubtedly is such a description of objects or exhibition of sentiments, which are of themselves of a sublime nature, as shall give us strong impressions of them." Bascom describes this element as follows: " Sublimity and beauty are but two extremes, the higher and the lower manifestations of the same quality." When the mind

52

is more than pleased, says Quackenbos, when it is elevated and transported by the grandeur of the perceived idea, the æsthetic emotion induced is commonly described as sublime. Sublimity lies in the concord between majestic means and the highest conceivable end, the noblest and most sacred purpose. It is therefore the element of art-content, which yields the most intense delight, the highest degree of which is united with awe and solemnity. It is the element which makes the strongest emotional appeal.

Sources of Sublimity.— Sublimity in literary art is due to sublimity in nature, for the obvious reason that art is an imitation of nature. There are two chief sources — the physical sublime and the moral sublime. Both are found in nature. The simplest form of the physical sublime is the vast, boundless, prospects of nature — the limitless plain, the expanse of ocean, the firmament of heaven. "All vastness," says Blair, "produces the impression of sublimity. Remove all bounds from any object and you presently render it sublime. And you add to the sublimity by extending the object in depth and height; as, for example, the fathomless gulf, the heaven-ascending mountain, the starry heights above all." Such examples are more impressive than a plain of boundless extent. Sources of the sublime, such as infinite space, endless numbers, eternal duration, evoke the strongest emotion. "The emotion caused by the great and sublime in nature," says Burke, "when those causes operate most powerfully, is astonishment; and astonishment is that state of the soul in which all its motions are suspended with some degree of horror. In this case the mind is so entirely filled with its object, that it cannot entertain any other, nor by consequence reason on that object which employs it. Hence, arises the great power of the sublime, that, far from being produced by them, it anticipates our reasonings and hurries us on by an irresistible force. As the great extreme of dimension is sublime, so the last extreme of littleness is likewise in the same measure sublime. When we attend to the infinite divisibility of matter, when we pursue animal life into those excessively small and yet organized beings, that are known only through the microscope, we become amazed and confounded as at the vast itself." Nature— boundless inward in the atom, boundless outward in the whole — is sublime under both aspects.

Infinity as a Source.— Infinity has a tendency to fill the mind with that source of delightful terror which is the most genuine effect of the sublime. There are two infinites to feed the imagination and inspire sublimity. First, the real Infinite which is God Himself. No literature is so sublime as the Hebrew; and this sublimity is due to the fact that the Hebrew mind struggled to give adequate expression to the qualities and attributes of God — He Who existed before the foundations of the world were laid — Who holdeth all nations and all worlds in the hollow of His hand. The real Infinite has inspired not only the most sublime passages of the Bible, but of all other literature also. Besides the real Infinite, there is what critics call the artificial infinite — a counterfeit presentment, examples of which are supplied by nature and by art. This infinite in order to produce its effect, must have succession and uniformity; succession is required in order that the parts may be continued so long and in such a direction as to impress the imagination with the idea that they are unending. For example, the steppes of a desert, the waves of the ocean, the trees of a forest. Uniformity of parts is necessary to artificial infinity; otherwise the imagination would find a check at every change— variety in parts would break that changeless, smooth progression which alone can stamp on bounded objects the character of infinity. Every artist, no matter what may be his medium, employs the artificial infinite. For example, the aisle or dome in architecture; the background and perspective in painting. In literary art it is extensively employed. First of all, in words which employ a negation of limitations — such words as boundless, limitless, never, forever, immortal, endless. Secondly, in figures of speech which reproduce the artificial infinite of nature. For example, the "all-beholding sun," "plains where winds are weary of travel," "never-dying light of the stars." Thirdly, in oratorical or poetic license, where limitations are removed by the sweeping, unmodified statements of emotion. Finally, in all kinds of literary work where the imagination demands fullest freedom. The highest art in one way or another must give the imagination scope by using this kind of infinity.

Power as a Source.— Like vastness or infinity, power produces sublimity. In general, great exhibitions of power always raise sublime ideas. For example, the earthquake, volcano, thunder and lightning, great conflagrations, tornadoes, the storm-tossed ocean. "I know of nothing sublime," says Burke, "which is not some modification of power." And this is found to be true on final analysis, for power is displayed by the elements in the storm and conflagration; it is displayed by the waves of the ocean engulfing the huge ship as if it were an eggshell; it is displayed by the earth and the planets rolling so swiftly in vast orbits; and finally, by God Himself of Whom the psalmist wrote: "Tremble, thou earth! at the presence of the Lord." The power of God, and the wonderful ways in which that power is exerted, produce as many sublime ideas as do His majesty and His infinity.

Obscurity, Silence, Solitude.— These qualities of nature produce the sublime. For example, the obscurity surrounding ghosts and supernatural beings as typified in Hamlet's ghost and Job's vision in the night. Of silence and solitude nature supplies many examples such as great deserts like the Sahara; gloomy, pathless forests like the Black Forest of Germany; the recesses of large mountain chains like the Andes or Alps; the lonesome ice fields of either pole. Perhaps the most sublime spectacle in nature is the starry heavens, for in those starry expanses all the physical sources of sublimity are present — vastness, power, silence, obscurity. Sublimity arising from these sources depends in a large measure upon an accompanying terror. And the qualities just mentioned add a note of terror. For example, how much the night adds to the terror of the pathless wood or the raging tornado. The value of obscurity is known to all artists. The architect made the heathen temples dark, also the Gothic cathedral, the impressiveness of which depends largely on the dimly lighted aisles, and the gloomy vault soaring away, as it were, into infinity. Painting, like architecture, makes use of obscurity; the dark or obscure background covers details which otherwise would mar the general effect. And that effect is generally best seen by a dim or subdued light. When painters attempt to give clear representations of sublime ideas, says Burke, they always fail. Similarly, the literary artist employs obscurity. The sublime parts of a drama are acted in shadow; imagery in literary art is always most sublime when obscure. For example, take the gloomy pomp and obscure coloring in the sublime passages of Homer or Milton. Burke offers this explanation: "It is our ignorance of things, that causes most of our admiration and chiefly excites our emotion. Knowledge and acquaintance make the most striking causes affect us but little. It is thus with the vulgar, and all men are as the vulgar in what they do not understand. As an example, the ideas of eternity and infinity are among the most sublime and affecting we have, yet there is nothing of which we really understand so little, as of infinity and eternity. The imagination distorts and magnifies whatever is not clearly known." In like manner, solitude, silence and vacuity are sources of the sublime; they excite fear and terror. The solitude of a Siberian prison with its barren wastes of snow on every side stretching far away; the silence and barrenness of the great deserts like those of Africa where the caravan crawls over lone and level sands — treeless, manless, forlorn; the awful silence of the vast ice fields of either pole or of the starry heavens — all stir the deepest emotion. Solitary confinement is a dreadful punishment; hence, the sublimity of Prometheus who endured three thousand years of it. Some of the finest passages of literature draw their sublimity from these sources. As examples, read Milton's description of Hell or Chaos; the "Prometheus Unbound" of Shelley; Byron's "Address to the Ocean"; Dante's "Purgatory"; Goethe's "Faust"; Humboldt's "Description of South American Plains and Mountains"; "The Death of Arthur" by Tennyson; Virgil's "Entrance to Tartarus."

Sound as a Source.— The eye is not the only organ of sensation by which a sublime emotion may be produced. Sound has an equally great power, although it is more limited in range. Excessive loudness alone is sufficient to overpower the soul, to suspend its action and to fill it with terror. The noise of vast cataracts, raging storms, of thunder or artillery, awakens a great and awful sensation. The shouting of multitudes has a similar effect; so also the cries of wild beasts. As literary examples of sublimity in sound, read Poe's "The Bells"; the "Knocking at the Gate" in "Macbeth"; the hovel scene in "King Lear"; the "Debate in Pandemonium" by Milton.

Animated Nature.— Animated nature furnishes two sources — the moral sublime and the intellectual sublime. The moral sublime is shown in two ways: first, in the moral strength of superiority to passing impulse in the pursuit of great objects. For example, the toil and persistence of an Alexander,

Cæsar, Columbus. Hence, heroic examples of this kind always leave an indelible impress on the mind. A second source is self-sacrifice, which is the highest moral heroism. The most sublime moral example in this regard is the Redeemer of mankind. Likewise, the man who sacrifices himself for his friends, family, or country is an example of the moral sublime. Instances in point are daring feats in war — the themes of epic and tragedy. The moral sublime exemplified in human beings makes a far stronger appeal than any other; hence, Divine Wisdom became incarnate and lived the life of man in order to win humanity.

The Intellectual Sublime.— Intellectual power, like moral power, is a source of sublimity. Literature is full of sublime passages dealing with intellectual greatness, as exhibited in men like Solomon, Plato, Aristotle, Aquinas, Newton, Bacon. For a conspectus of these read Pope's " Temple of Fame." Usually, intellectual and moral greatness combine to give us the sublime human specimen. For example, Aquinas, Bossuet, Galileo. The great heroes like Alexander or Cæsar are sublime examples of intellectual greatness and moral endurance.

Maleficent Power in the Moral Order.— Power as exerted by the higher orders of creation is often sublime. This power is of two kinds, maleficent and beneficent. Maleficent power is the infliction of suffering. Human suffering may proceed from physical causes—pestilence, famine, storms, floods, earthquakes, conflagrations; it may proceed from human agencies such as the invasions of the Tartars, the Turks, the Goths, the destruction of great cities, such as the sack of Troy, of Carthage, of Rome; it may proceed from supernatural agencies such as the spiritual ruin of man by malignant spirits. But whatever be the source, it has inspired the largest part of that literature in which sublimity predominates. Some illustrations: Thucydides took for his subject the great plague of Athens; Ovid sang about a pestilence; Virgil and Homer dealt with the ruin of Troy; Milton and Dante sang about the Fall of Man; orators like Webster, Burke, Cicero, Mirabeau, Demosthenes, flourished in times of great national peril and disaster. Tragedy has found its most sublime ideas in connection with the sufferings and ruin of heroes, whether of the natural or supernatural order.

Beneficent Power.— The sublime of beneficent energy may be traced in the great agents of the world working for the good of mankind — the sun, the elements, the forces of nature. Likewise, beneficent power of men, angels, and of God Himself. Eulogistic literature is filled with sublime passages extolling the goodness of God. The great storehouse of such literature is the Bible. Hebrew writers have exhausted the language of sublimity in praise of Divine goodness. For example, read the " Book of Psalms " or the letters in the New Testament. The redemptive work of God who took the chosen people out of the house of Egypt, and Who afterward brought salvation to all mankind, is a most frequent inspiration to sublime literature. It is a cherished department of literary effort to grow sublime over great humanitarians like Solon, King Alfred, Florence Nightingale and Francis Xavier. For example, read the eulogistic literature in the department of the essay and the oration.

Vocabulary of the Sublime.— The sublime in English literature has its own symbols, and these symbols have a two-fold office; first, an adequate representation of an object, situation, or event possessing sublimity. Bain observes: " The goodness of our vocabulary on this head depends upon the abundance and expressiveness of its words and phrases." Whether

for description of still life, or for narrating actions and events
we have an abundant supply.

Literature of the Sublime.— Every nation has made some
contribution to the literature of the sublime. The Bible takes
first rank in this department, inasmuch as the Hebrew writers
and the Hebrew people were constantly occupied with thoughts
concerning the supernatural world; they strove to find adequate
expression for the grandeur and magnificence of deity. Hence,
the constant recurrence of sublime passages in the Bible. Next
to the Bible, Milton may be mentioned for the element of sublimity; it is a distinctive feature of his great epic in which he
has reproduced much of the sublimity of Homer, of Virgil,
and the Bible. The great epics of the world are remarkable
examples in point, and may be fairly classified with the literature of the sublime. Oratory is a department of literature
which deserves special mention on account of the number and
variety of its sublime passages; it may be ranked next to the
epic. The speeches of Burke, Webster, Patrick Henry, O'Connell, Channing, Grattan, Wendell Phillips, Erskine, Everett
and many others, are noteworthy examples. And in this connection Tragedy must not be forgotten. As illustrations of
sublimity the dramas of Shakespeare deserve special mention,
especially his great tragedies, Hamlet, Lear, Othello, Macbeth.
But sublimity does not belong to any single literary department; it is not the exclusive possession of the epic or the
drama or the oration. As an element of art-content it appears in all departments, and whenever the thought justifies
its appearance. Sublime passages may be found in the lyric,
in history, in fiction. Occasionally, the essays of Macaulay,
of Ruskin, and of Newman are as sublime as the best orations
and the best epic poetry. Emotion, obeying the law of climax,
will rise and fall like the ocean wave, and according to the
idea with which it is associated, will reveal more or less sublimity.

CHAPTER VIII

ART-CONTENT IN LITERATURE (CONTINUED)

BEAUTY

Definition.— Beauty is the second emotional element of art-content. Next to sublimity it affords the highest pleasure to the imagination. But the emotion it arouses is not so violent as that of sublimity; it is of a calmer kind, more gentle and soothing. It does not elevate the mind so much, but produces an agreeable serenity. Sublimity arouses an emotion too violent to be lasting; the pleasure arising from beauty admits of longer continuance. Beauty differs from sublimity not only in arousing a gentler and more lasting emotion, but also in the greater variety of objects in which it is found. This variety of objects is so great that no word in the language has a wider application. For example, in the present instance it is applied to art-content: it may also be applied to art-form. It is defined by Aristotle as that quality of an object which excites gentle and pleasurable emotion. This definition would ascribe beauty to almost every external object that pleases the eye or the ear, to a great number of the graces of art and to many dispositions of the heart and the mind. Hence, the expressions — a beautiful flower, a beautiful building, a beautiful character.

Chief Divisions.— The chief divisions are: beauty in nature, beauty in art. There are three sub-divisions of beauty in nature, or, rather, a three-fold natural basis for beauty — color, form or figure, movement.

Color as a Source.— In color we have the simplest example of beauty.   Colors considered beautiful are of two kinds.   The first class are those with which there is a pleasing association of ideas.   For example: *white,* suggestive of innocence; *green,* suggestive of spring and rural scenes.   The second class are those that appear delicate rather than gloomy.   Nature ornaments her work with those delicate colors which are the despair of the artist.   For example: the fine coloring of the morning or evening sky.   As to the reason why color is thus so beautiful, Blair observes: " Here neither variety nor uniformity nor any other principle that I know, can be assigned as the foundation of beauty.   We can refer it to no other cause but the structure of the eye, which determines us to receive certain modifications of the rays of light with more pleasure than others."

Figure or Form as a Source.— Figure, like color, opens to us forms of beauty more complex and diversified.   In figure, regularity is the first source of beauty.   By a regular figure is meant one formed according to some certain rule, and not left arbitrary or loose in the construction of its parts.   For example, a circle, a square or a hexagon pleases the eye by its regularity as a beautiful figure.   The second source of beauty in figure is a graceful variety.   It is a more fruitful source than regularity, requiring more attention in all works designed merely to please the eye.   Plants, flowers and leaves are full of variety and diversity.   A straight canal cannot compare with a meandering river.   Cones and pyramids are beautiful, but trees growing in their natural wildness are infinitely more beautiful than when trimmed into cones and pyramids.   A garden is most beautiful when variety prevails.

Lines of Beauty.— According to Hogarth, there are two lines upon which the beauty of a figure principally depends. One is the waving line or a curve bending backwards and forwards, somewhat in the form of the letter S. This he calls the line of beauty, and shows how often it is found in shells and flowers and other ornamental works of nature. It is also found in the figures designed by painters and sculptors for the purposes of decoration. The second line, which Hogarth calls the line of grace, is the same waving curve, but in spiral form around a solid body. For example, in nature, the vine curving around the tree; in art, the marble thread running around the pillar. Twisted pillars are also examples of it. Variety thus plainly appears as a very important source of beauty. Hogarth defines the art of drawing pleasing forms to be the art of varying well. For the curved line, on account of its perpetual blending and variation, breaks up the stiff regularity of the straight line.

Movement as a Source of Beauty.— Motion of itself is always pleasing, and bodies in motion are preferred to those at rest. Movement is of two kinds — gentle and rapid. Only gentle movement belongs to the beautiful; when it is swift or very forcible, such as that of a torrent, it partakes of the sublime. For example, the movement of a bird gliding through the air is extremely beautiful; the swiftness of lightning darting across the heavens is sublime. Motion in a straight line is not so beautiful as in an undulating, waving, direction. And motion upwards is more agreeable than downwards. For example, the easy, curling motion of smoke and flame. Hogarth observes that in our daily movements the business of life is transacted in straight or plain lines, but all the graceful and ornamental movements are made in waving lines. For example, take the movement of persons behind a counter and compare it with the movement of the same persons in a ball room or a parlor. The truth of Hogarth's observation will appear at once.

A Combination of these Sources.— Although color, form and movement are separate sources of beauty and may be treated, each in a distinct manner, yet in many beautiful objects they all meet, rendering beauty greater and more complex. For example, in the morning or evening sky, the movement of the fleecy clouds, the tints of sunlight, the ethereal forms of " the cloud-capped towers," the convex lines of the sky. Again, in a natural landscape where there are flowers, trees and animals, we have delicacy of color, gracefulness of figure, and movement of bird and beast, all producing a pleasant emotion. Perhaps the most complete assemblage of beautiful objects that can anywhere be found, is presented by a rich, natural landscape where there is a sufficient variety of objects and a wealth of color, form and movement. The beauty of the human countenance is of this complex kind: it arises from color, the delicate shades of complexion, the play or movement of feature, and the various lines that form the contour of the face. Burke gives the following summary of physical beauty: " On the whole, the qualities of beauty, in so far as they are merely sensible qualities, are the following: first, to be comparatively small; secondly, to be smooth; thirdly, to have a variety in the direction of the parts; fourthly, to have those parts not angular, but melted, as it were, into each other; fifthly, to be of a delicate frame, without any remarkable appearance of strength; sixthly, to have its colors clear and bright, but not very strong and glaring, or, if it should have any glaring color, to have it diversified with others." These are the properties on which beauty depends; properties that operate in nature, and are less liable to be altered by caprice, or confounded by diversity of tastes, than any other.

Design as a Source of Beauty.— The more obvious sources of beauty in nature are color, form and movement. But underneath these causes there is another which operates powerfully in the same direction. It is the beauty of design. It arises from the perception of means adapted to some end or of parts adapted to the plan of the whole. For example, in considering the structure of a tree or a plant, we observe how all the parts, the roots, the stem, the bark, the branches and leaves, are suited to the growth and nutriment of the whole. Similarly, when we examine the parts and members of a living organism, the happy adjustment of means to the end is at once pronounced beautiful. The beauty of design is present everywhere in nature, from the tiniest blade or most delicate crystal to the grandest creations of the planetary world. The presence of design seems to be a reflection of the beauty of the Eternal Mind reaching from end to end mightily and ordering all things sweetly.

Design in Art.— As art is an imitation of nature, we may expect to find the same sources of beauty in the one as in the other. To begin with design: if we examine any of the works of art, a clock, a ship, a machine, a painting, a building, a poem, the pleasure we have in the examination is enhanced by a discovery of the beauty of design, the adaptation of parts to the whole. This idea of fitness or design has an extensive influence over all the arts. It is the foundation of the beauty which we discover in the proportions of doors, windows, arches, pillars, in all the orders of architecture. Similarly, in a masterpiece of painting, sculpture, poetry, the beauty of design is always apparent. We cannot look upon any work of art whatsoever, without being led by a natural association of ideas to think of its end and design, and to examine the relation of its parts to that design. And because design is fundamentally only another name for the total effect produced by the primary laws of art, an object without design is an object deformed, according to our ideas of beauty.

Design in Literary Art.— It is of the utmost importance in all kinds of literary art. In the essay, sermon, epic, drama, lyric, we require a fitness, an adjustment of means to the end which the author is supposed to have in view. For let a description be ever so rich, or the figures ever so elegant, yet if they are out of place, if they are not proper parts of the whole, and clash with the main purpose of the composition, they destroy the beauty of the work — nay, they are converted into very deformities.

Beauty in Literary Art.— Beauty is a term applied to all that pleases, either in the style, or sentiment, or from whatever principle pleasure flows. This is the general meaning applied to the term. But there is a specific meaning whereby beauty is used to signify a certain grace and amenity in the turn of style and sentiment for which some authors have been particularly distinguished. In this sense it denotes a style neither sublime nor vehemently passionate nor uncommonly sparkling, but such as raises in the reader an emotion of the gentler kind, similar to what is raised by the contemplation of beautiful objects in nature; which neither lifts the mind very high, nor agitates it very much, but stirs feeling and imagination in an agreeable, while quiet, way. It is the poetry of Virgil as contrasted with that of Homer, the prose of Cicero as compared with Demosthenes, the writings of a Fenelon, an Addison or an Irving as compared with Bossuet, Swift, a Burke or a Webster. Not that Virgil and the authors named are incapable of sublimity, but their general manner is distinguished by the character of beauty and grace, and a quiet charm which differentiates them from such rugged, vehement and sublime writers as Victor Hugo and Carlyle.

Beauty of Form and Content.— Every literary artist expresses the beautiful either in art-form or in art-content — either in the ideas set forth, or in the form of expression; for beauty is the primary object of all artistic work. Regarding art-form, Burke writes as follows: " Words have a considerable share in exciting ideas of beauty — they affect the mind by raising in it ideas of those things for which custom has appointed them to stand. Words, by their original and pictorial power have great influence over the passions; if we combine them properly, we may give new life and beauty to the simplest object. In painting, we may represent any fine figure we please, but we never can give it those enlivening touches which it may receive from words. For example, we can represent an angel in a picture by drawing a young man wingéd : but what painting can furnish out anything so grand as the addition of one word —' the angel of the Lord ' ? Is there any painting more grand or beautiful ? "

Color Applying to Words.— Beauty in literary art, like beauty in nature, depends on color, form and movement. Color applies to words. The English language possesses a large vocabulary of color. First, a class of words used in the literal sense : the names of the various colors themselves, white, green, red, etc. ; the names of objects suggestive of color, snow, water, flowers, etc. Secondly, color in a metaphorical sense : the personal element in composition, the author's personality, style, sympathies, training. In this sense color applies to art-content, for the thought of the composition is invariably colored by the personality of the author ; it is also colored by the environment of the author, and hence the phrase, *local color,* which is frequently employed in literary criticism.

Form a Source of Literary Beauty.— Form in literature, as in all the arts, is a source of beauty. The same rules regarding form in nature apply to art-form in literature.   For example, art-form in literature is as beautiful as form in a tree or flower.   The same fundamental laws of art are applied — unity, harmony, balance, proportion.   Besides these, the many species of prose and verse present almost as great variety of form as nature herself.   The human artist approaches the Divine Artist in the beauty which arises from a happy diversity in his miniature creations.

Movement a Source of Literary Beauty.— Movement applies to thought, to art-content.   All kinds of literary art contain some movement.   The most striking example is the action in the development of the novel or the drama.   Next to these rank oratory and the epic.   Movement when slow in literature, is called beautiful; when rapid, it produces the sublime, like the stream that feeds Niagara.   The succession of our ideas, whether rapid or slow, is similar to movements in nature, and produces similar effects.

CHAPTER IX

ART-CONTENT IN LITERATURE (CONTINUED)

FEELING

Definition.— The third element of art-content is called feeling. Some critics prefer the term *pathos*. This element is associated with the thought and humanizes literature as no other element can do, because it is an expression of the human in man. Feeling originates in the heart as thought originates in the mind. In its actual exercise it makes up a large amount of life-interest; hence, its intimate connection with literature, which is the mirror and reflection of life. As an element of art-content, it is that quality of the thought which produces emotion in the reader; although in a wider sense it belongs to both art-form and art-content. In this general sense the whole composition is intended to arouse some emotion; for an appeal to the aesthetic sense cannot be made successfully without this corresponding result.

The Basis of Feeling.— There are three important relationships of life which furnish the basis of feeling. This threefold basis represents man in relation to the family, in relation to society, and in relation to God.

Family Relationship.— This relationship gives rise to parental, filial and fraternal feeling, while the family itself is a consequence of sexual feeling and regard. Parental feeling holds an important place both in literature and in life; so, also, the reciprocal attachment of brothers and sisters. For example, the grandest creations of the Greek drama depend on filial and parental feeling. King Lear and Hamlet are admirable illustrations in our literature. The typical embodiment of the parental relation is the regard of the mother for her own child. The mother and child, as exemplified in the blessed Virgin and her divine Son, have entered into art as a standing type and conception, and they are clothed with all the tenderness and beauty that the painter can express on canvas or the sacred poet introduce into the hymnal of the church. Literary art has exhausted its power of expression upon the parental relation which God holds toward the human race and which a father and mother hold toward the family. The " fatherhood of God and the brotherhood of man " is the ideal that evokes today the strongest emotion in the human breast. Examples of this kind of feeling are almost coextensive with literature itself; for hardly any class of artistic work is attempted without this feeling entering into a part of it or pervading the whole.

Man in Relation to Society.— Man in this relation excites feeling according to the amount and character of his social attachments. Friendship is the first relation; it is the attachment of persons not of the same family, as determined by community of likings. For example, members of the same club, the same profession, the same country. In the ancient, as in the modern world, this attachment figures — it is found in life and in literature. It was sometimes called " Platonic love." For example, Horace refers to Virgil as *dimidium vitae meae*. " David and Jonathan " is an example from Holy Writ. Cicero's attachment to Atticus has added to the wealth of classic literature. In the modern world we have Moore and Byron; Newman and Faber; Goethe and Schiller. Perhaps the most striking example of modern times is the friendship of Tennyson for Arthur Hallam, a classmate at Cambridge. This friendship enriched our literature with the *In Memoriam* — a poem unique in subject matter, but unrivaled as a work of literary art. Friendship, as a rule, does not evoke the strong emotion which pervades the *In Memoriam*. Cicero's *De Amicitia* is, on the whole, a more just expression of it.

Attachment to Country.— Patriotism is stronger than friendship; the emotion which it evokes is deeper and more abiding, for all nations agree with the orator : *Dulce et decorum est pro patria mori* — it is a sweet and a beautiful thing to die for one's country. Literary art owes a large debt to patriotic feeling, especially the department of the lyric and of oratory. Many of the masterpieces of prose and verse are inspired by this feeling; and all writers of note have given some expression to it. After one's home, one's country stirs the deepest emotion. The Teutonic and Celtic races are remarkable for their love of country. All forms of literary art are used as the vehicle of this universal feeling.

Religious Feeling.— This feeling, like patriotism, is universal. In its ideal form it consists of love of God and love of man for His sake. It is the substance of the answer to the question, "What is the great commandment of the law?" This feeling resembles that of a child toward its parent; it is based on a recognition of divine goodness and protection. From this point of view, God is a benign parent. He is treated as an object to inspire love and affection; His gifts and goodness evoke the strongest feeling of which the human heart is capable. The form of literary art best adapted to religious feeling is the lyric. For example, the Book of Psalms, the various hymnals used by Christian denominations; such works as Keble's Christian Year. Similarly, this feeling has an outlet in oratory, as the large amount of sermon literature bears

witness; the Christian pulpit is aglow with the emotion inspired by Christ, the Savior, Who, because He was human as
well as divine, makes the strongest appeal to human love and
affection; His sufferings and death manifest God's goodness
in a special manner. Milton's Paradise Regained deals adequately with this theme; Tasso and Dante, likewise, have
treated it. The great religious writers of every age and nation never weary of it, for to the believer it is an inexhaustible
fountain of the keenest emotion.

Love as a Source.— Love, as between man and woman, is
called the master passion of the heart. It is the " cords of
Adam " binding the sexes together and insuring the futurity
of the race. It has found the most varied expression in art;
it is called the " everlasting theme " in literature. Browning
calls it " the greatest thing in the world," and devotes most
of his poetry to proofs of the assertion. This tender feeling
has inspired what is known as erotic literature. Literary art
puts in the foreground a description of the object; this includes, first of all, the personal charms of each lover, their
mental, moral and physical excellence, their reciprocal liking;
secondly, the beauty and charm of their surroundings — all that
department of nature akin to affection, such as birds, flowers,
streams, trees, the scenery of repose and quiescence, which reflects the feelings of the entranced lovers; thirdly, the utter-
ances of the lovers themselves, ideas and words athrill with
emotion. As love is the master passion, it is more strongly
expressed than any other feeling. The passionate intensity
of love has taxed the capacity of language. It requires imagery both intense and original. As this passion often rises
to the heroic and sinks to the tragic, it is frequently the inspiration of the drama. For example, Antony and Cleopatra,
Romeo and Juliet, Heloise and Abelard. In this connection
the greatest interest lies in the plot. No other variety of ten-

der feeling is so well suited to give fascination to plot. Hence, love is the main theme of the dramatist and novelist. Parental feeling is strong, but the possibilities of plot are not so numerous as in courtship.

Ancient and Modern Treatment.— Tender feeling and sentiment between the sexes did not reach its highest development in ancient literature. Love was second to war in interest, although it claims some attention. For example, Helen in Homer; Dido in Virgil. But war, nevertheless,— " arms and the man "—, was the main theme. The great tragedians of Greece made their plots turn on the element of strife and hatred rather than love; they introduced female characters like Antigone, but these did not appear in love-relationships. The beginning of erotic art in Greece was in the lyric field; and the first great example was the renowned Sappho. Then followed Theocritus, and Bion. The Greek anthology forms quite a volume of erotic literature. Among the Latins, Catullus, Ovid, Horace, and Propertius make love their main theme. Like the Greek writers, the Latins were all licentious. Hence, the necessity for expurgated editions of the classics. Virgil is perhaps the cleanest of the classic writers. The most remarkable love-poem of antiquity is " Hero and Leander "; it was written during the decadence of Greek literature. It has much of the merit of the Biblical love-story — the story of Ruth. But the licentious Pagan who deified lust, failed to treat love in a manner which would reflect credit on human nature. It remained for Christian influence to redeem Pagan morality and sanctify love in the marriage bond. As we approach modern times love becomes a more important element in literary art. The literary treatment of it was purified by chivalry and christianity. The Troubadours in France; Dante, Petrarch, Boccaccio; Ariosto and Tasso, are evidences of its growing importance. In England, Chaucer was the earliest erotic poet. Spenser worked at the same theme. It remained for Shakespeare to eclipse all his predecessors in writing of love. It inspires the largest part of modern English fiction, and with religious feeling divides the honors of the lyric field.

Summary.— The realm of feeling is as large as life itself, the main channels of which — the family, society, country and creed — have been indicated. In relation to art-content, it is the element sought whenever literature is read. *Cor ad cor loquitur.* The heart of the reader seeks the heart of the writer in the thoughts touched with emotion. It is the presence of this element in oratory, which moves an audience to the acceptance of truth. "There can be no eloquence," says Matthews, "without deep feeling. Thoughts must come red-hot from the heart. It is not enough for the orator to have the ordinary passions of our nature; he must be a magazine of sensibility, an electric battery, a Leyden jar, charged to a plenum; he must have an abnormal emotional system united with the mental — a rare depth and fire of nature." Emotion is the life the very soul of the lyric. Take, for example, "Lead Kindly Light," or "The Holy City," and note the contagious feeling which exhales from each line and thought. Some patriotic lyrics have all the power of a charm or incantation, owing to this element of art-content. The novel and the drama are filled with it; and although history aims at an unemotional style, the thoughts themselves dealing with one's own country, its sorrows and joys, must excite the deepest emotion.

Literary Examples.— Œnone, Antigone, Job, Menelaus, Dido, Hero, Romeo, Jeptha, King John, The Virgin Mary, Desdemona, Cordelia, King Arthur, Hallam, Prometheus, the Redeemer of Mankind. (For a full list of classic themes involving deep feeling, see Bain, Rhetoric, Part II.)

CHAPTER X

ART-CONTENT IN LITERATURE (CONTINUED)

WIT AND HUMOR

Wit and Humor.— These elements of art-content are so nearly allied in meaning, they must be treated together. They are in reality two species of the same element, and they have this characteristic in common, they arise out of some kind of incongruity, some form of contrast. Wit is more purely intellectual than humor. The word, wit, is derived from the Saxon, *witan,* and primarily it meant intellect. In the time of Shakespeare and Pope it was a synonym for mental power. Dryden defined wit as thoughts and words elegantly adapted to the subject. Wit has a narrower meaning now. In its modern sense, as defined by Locke, it is the faculty of associating ideas in a new and unexpected manner, the power of invention, continuance, and ingenuity. Humor, on the other hand, is more elemental, more persuasive, more a matter of character and temperament. While wit is allied to talent, humor partakes of the wider reach, the ampler flow, the deep unconsciousness of genius. Wit is the swift play and flash of mind; humor flows from character, it is an expression of character, and, next to feeling, the most thoroughly humanizing element in literary art. As Pater describes it, humor is the expression of the whole nature of man, it is full of heart, it has tenderness, sympathy, piety, sadness; and the laughter it evokes is without malice or bitterness.

Examples.— Cervantes and Shakespeare may be taken as models in the use of both wit and humor. The wit of Dean Swift and Daniel O'Connell is almost proverbial; although in the former it was associated with a keen and biting sarcasm, and, at times, with a most repulsive vulgarity. Some authors temper this element of art-content with a kindly feeling — as Chaucer, Shakespeare, Addison, Burns, Scott. Other writers, like Swift, Pope and Voltaire, mix with it a fund of bitterness and malignity.

The Basis of Wit.— In its most distinctive feature, wit is a play upon words, owing to the many meanings attached to the same word. The ingenuity which some writers display in this work is remarkable. Often, too, it degenerates into unpardonable silliness, especially in conversation. The punster becomes an inveterate bore. The paradox like the pun lies at the foundation of wit; it is a proposition which contains some apparent and startling contradiction — what oft was thought but ne'er so well expressed. A brilliant simile or metaphor is most frequently the basis of wit, for there is no better way afforded to express incongruities. For example, " Bright like the sun her eyes the gazers strike, and like the sun they shine on all alike."

Mistakes Regarding Its Use.— Bain points out three vices in this connection. First, coarseness. The search for witticism has to be controlled by refinement or delicacy Some of the greatest wits have over-stepped this boundary, such as Aristophanes among the ancients; Rabelais, Swift and Pope among moderns. Secondly, obscurity. Like every other effect of style, wit must be intelligible to those addressed. Far-fetched allusions are condemned, whatever be their purpose. Thirdly, excess. In constantly aiming at wit, the greatest risk is, the tendency toward overdoing it. Like all striking effects, it palls by too much repetition, and the torturing of language may be carried to a point where meaning is wholly sacrificed.

Wit of Different Peoples.— All nations possess wit in some measure, for it is a part of the endowment of our common human nature. But races of a cold, sluggish temperament, like the Germans or Russians, are not remarkable for the gift. It rather belongs to the southern races where the soul sparkles in epigram and paradox and figures of speech. For the sprightliness of intellect displayed in wit, no race equals the Celt. Take away from English literature the Irish and Scotch contributions, and very little wit would be left. Shakespeare, of course, would remain, but the exception only proves the rule.

Value of Wit.— In literary art wit is valuable in the same way that spice is valuable in food — it gives a certain flavor and piquancy not otherwise obtainable. It creates laughter, and this has a wholesome emotional effect. It brightens many a literary page just as it brightens many a life. From some kinds of literary art it is rigidly excluded, owing to the seriousness of the subject-matter. It is a powerful weapon in debate, often winning where heavy argument fails, like the pebble in David's sling. In common with humor, it claims comedy as its special literary channel.

The Basis of Humor.— Like wit, humor rests upon incongruities, and like wit it excites mirth or laughter. It depends upon the follies and foibles of mankind — an unfailing fountain of inspiration. It differs from wit, in that its usual accompaniment is sympathy and tender feeling — an innocent raillery, a good-natured smile. By this mixture of tender and kindly feeling with the ludicrous effect, it offends no one and pleases everybody. Of the basis of humor, Sydney Smith

— himself one of the best humorists in our literature — observes: " As you increase incongruity you increase humor; as you diminish it, you diminish humor. If a tradesman of a corpulent and respectable appearance, with habiliments somewhat ostentatious, were to slide down gently into the mud, and decorate a pea-green coat, I am afraid we would all have the barbarity to laugh. If his hat and wig, like treacherous servants, were to desert their falling master, it would certainly not diminish our propensity to laugh. But if he would sit in the mud and threaten the passers-by with his wrath, he would certainly heighten still more the humor of the situation."

Humor in Fiction.— Humor plays an important part in fiction. Sometimes it pervades a whole work, as, for example, Pickwick Papers. The humor of Dickens has for its background the sorrow and suffering of the poorer classes; and because of its pathetic associations, is always tender and goodnatured. According to some critics, its presence in such abundance is the main reason why Dickens retains his hold upon popular favor. In like manner, George Eliot, Thackeray and Hawthorne have used humor to advantage. In fact, all our novelists have had occasion to employ it, for it is hardly possible to construct a plot or describe human life without introducing situations which are humorous in the extreme.

Value of Humor.— Humor is a fountain of joy in life, the great redeemer of the pessimist. It saves the grave character from absurdity. It is a refuge from crushing care and calamity. It is the most useful resource of men in whose temperament the tragic note is dominant. Similarly, it exercises a redeeming influence upon literature, relieving the tediousness of lengthy narrative, breaking like sunshine through the rifted clouds of tragic drama, and diffusing over the whole field of

pure letters a peculiar warmth and tenderness, as if it bid us
remember the human heart whereby we live.

Comedy in Relation to Wit and Humor.— Comedy will be
treated elsewhere in detail, but it remains to note here that this
species of literature is the store-house of wit and humor.   For
comedy is professedly witty and humorous.   The history of
comedy from the days of Aristophanes is one long effort to
place upon the stage the follies, foibles and idiosyncrasies of
mankind.   The ways in which a man may make a fool of himself are countless, and comic characters have represented this
type in every age.   Perhaps our best illustrations are Pickwick,
Falstaff, Don Quixote.   But comic writers have not confined
themselves to the drama or the novel.   Verse is often employed
as in the case of Moore, Saxe and Holmes.   The short essay
is now the most popular vehicle.   Witness the efforts of " Mr.
Dooley," Mark Twain and William Nye in this prose-form.
The brief paragraph is the favorite form in journalism.   Some
papers, like Punch, Puck, Judge, and Life, are made up of such
paragraphs, and are devoted exclusively to wit and humor.
These paragraphs deal with the oddities, incongruities, irrel-
evances of men, and indulge in all manner of caricature.   The
cosmopolitan character of our American population offers a
tempting field for this kind of journalism.

CHAPTER XI

ART-CONTENT IN LITERATURE (CONTINUED)

MELODY

Definition.— The sixth and last element of art-content is melody. It is defined as a succession of musical or agreeable sounds. It depends essentially upon tones of relative pitch, successively arranged. It is established by any particular rhythmic arrangement, as in some popular dance-times; by the intervals of a single chord, as in arpeggio phrases; by a diatonicorder, as in scale passages; by the harmonic connections between successive chords, as in simple choral writing. In relation to composition it implies rhythm and harmony — such a succession of words as will yield agreeable and musical sounds. It is present both in prose and in verse; although poetry, on account of its more intimate connection with music, possesses a larger amount of melody than prose.

Emotional Value.— The emotional value of music is so pronounced and so obvious that no discussion of it is needed here; and melody is simply an identification, more or less limited, of music with written language. All good prose and verse contain melody, without which their appeal to the emotions would be very much impaired, if not entirely lost.

Basis of Melody.— In securing melody, or a succession of musical sounds, a writer must take into account, first of all, the letters of the alphabet. Some letters are friends of melody;

other letters are enemies. The vowel and the liquid are the chief sources of melody; while the consonant with no music in its soul, is a deadly enemy. Yet language could not maintain its timbre or fibre without the consonant; so that the artist must be careful to keep the consonant while *smothering* it in liquid and vowel sounds. There are twenty-three consonants, fourteen vowels in accent, with the same out of accent, in our language. Our wealth of vowel sounds is uncommon. The harmonious blending of these letters and sounds is in a large measure the basis of melody.

Words the Basis of Melody.— Words are, in respect to melody, a combination of letters; and the same rule applies to the word-variation. Words must be so arranged in the sentence, as to produce a succession of agreeable and musical sounds. For this purpose long words are alternated with short words, and harsh-sounding words are so blended with smooth, liquid ones, as to be agreeable in the combined effect. Undeniably, the harsh-sounding and abrupt words are monosyllabic ones of Saxon origin — not altogether, but in large part. On the other hand, the smooth, liquid words are pollysyllabic and of Latin origin. Besides the due alternation of long and short, there should also be the due alternation of emphatic and unemphatic words. A proper distribution of emphasis is essential to melody. As Blair remarks, the location of the accent must be so varied as not to offend the ear by monotone.

Sentences in Connection with Melody.— Harmony and rhythm of sentence have been considered already. The literary artist both in prose and verse must be very careful about the selection of words that will have a fitness, not only from the view-point of thought, but also from the view-point of sound. For example, a word may exactly express the thought-connection, but fail completely to carry the sentence-rhythm — the sound-connection. To borrow a figure from electricity, a word may easily break the circuit. Alliteration is another source of melody in the sentence. It is used extensively in prose and verse. Similarity in sound arising from alliteration, makes it easier to sustain the melody of the sentence. But alliteration is often carried to excess as in the prose and verse of Swinburne. It was carried to excess by the Anglo-Saxons; for example, see Beowulf. The danger from excessive alliteration is monotone.

Melody in the Paragraph.— Throughout the paragraph there is a larger rhythm than in the sentence. As the voice rises and falls in the sentence, so feeling rises and falls in the paragraph. Its highest point is called the climax. It is a common method of the literary artist so to construct the paragraph that the volume of sound will increase to the very end. For example, paragraphs at the close of orations or at the close of sections in any department of prose. Of course, the rhythm and melody of the paragraph will depend upon the construction of the sentences and the way that they are linked and coördinated. Similarly, the melody of the whole composition will depend upon paragraph-linking as well as upon the construction of the sentence.

Melody in Thought.— Melody is an emotional element belonging to art-content, and as such depends upon the smooth and musical succession of ideas as well as of words. This succession must, first of all, be logical; thoughts must be sequent and coherent, in order to furnish a proper basis for melody. The vigorous march of elocution must be accompanied by the vigorous march of ideas. The two-fold *Logos* — the word and the idea — must be melodious. Otherwise the composition is *vox, et praeterea nihil.* Stedman writes that the very *look* of certain words conveys certain ideas to the mind; they seem as entities to display the absolute color, form, expression, associated with their meanings, just as their *seen* rhythm and melody sound themselves to the ear (Stedman, Elements of Poetry, Page 174). Of ideas he might have written in the same vein, for what is meant by a poetic idea if not one that is musical, melodious at bottom — their *seen* rhythm and melody sound themselves to the ear. Inseparable in all high grades of literary art, the musical word and the musical idea blend in a beautiful whole. It is akin to the rhythm of nature —" not a planet, but in her motion like an angel sings." It is akin to the melody of life —" not sweet bells jangled, out of tune and harsh, but sweet bells of one accord, imitating the music of the spheres."

General Remarks.—All grand speech, whether in prose or verse, is rhythmic. There is a melody in the majestic periods of a Webster, a Cicero, a Gibbon or a Macaulay, just as in the grand organ-voice of a Milton or a Homer. This universal and mysterious potency is felt in all prose worthy of the name, and in all verse which deserves the name of poetry. The ancients studied the melody and musical effects of prose with the same ardor that they displayed in mastering the musical effects of poetry. If Cicero be, as Newman asserts, the greatest master of prose composition that the world has seen, he is so in a large measure because he is the greatest master of prose melody. And if Newman be without a peer in English prose, it is because he imitated Cicero so closely. But when the last word is uttered concerning the mere technique of melody, the conditions under which it is present in prose and verse, it remains to observe that melody is inborn and has its dwelling place in the soul of the artist. Rules may guide, they cannot create it; for it comes forth with the ideas of the true artist, as light comes with the sun. The supreme artist has music in his soul — an incommunicable gift of melodious expression.

CHAPTER XII

PERSONALITY IN LITERARY ART

Definition.— It is a truism that the personality of the artist is reflected in his art. As a matter of fact, all art is personal, in that it is some personal ideal externalized and rendered concrete. It is the thought, the idea, the concept, of some individual made known in color or word or stone. No matter what may be the medium, the informing idea, the creative act, is a personal contribution to art. Personality in literary art is quite as obvious as in painting, sculpture or music. In literature it receives the name of style, although the term is equally applicable to all the arts. For example, we have styles of painting, styles of architecture. The term simply indicates the presence of personality in the manner of artistic expression. Personality is incapable of a scientific definition: it is that peculiar combination of intellect and imagination plus other gifts and soul qualities, which differentiates one human being from another, and which in its totality often gives us the artistic temperament and the artistic genius. A writer speaks about the "abysmal depths of personality:" he might also speak about the abysmal mysteries of personality. For, in the Hebrew turn of phrase, we are fearfully and wonderfully made. But although personality in itself cannot be fathomed or defined, nevertheless, like electricity, it may be known through its manifestations; and its manifestation in literary art is called style

Style in Literature.— Style is defined as the peculiar manner in which a writer expresses his thoughts through the medium of words. It applies to both art-form and art-content, for it is an external picture of the ideas in the mind of the artist, and of the order in which they exist there. The definition of Buffon that the style is the man is but another way of stating that a creative personality is at work upon ideas and words, shaping both according to some preconceived plan. Let two individuals write on the same subject; we see in their productions their peculiar modes of thinking, the extent of their knowledge, their taste and feeling. The portrait executed by the most skilful painter does not more fully represent the countenance than the productions of the pen exhibit the characteristics of the mind.

Four Qualities of Style.— These qualities are common in some degree to all good writing: *correctness, clearness, vividness, naturalness.*

Correctness.— It is a quality of style which implies the use of words that are purely English. It implies that these words be used in their true and proper sense, and that the construction of phrases and sentences follow the rules of grammar. Hence, barbarisms, solecisms, and improprieties of all kinds are opposed to correctness. Correctness is necessary in all kinds of writing and, although it is not regarded as a high excellence, the absence of it is ever thought disgraceful. Incorrectness in the use of words and in the construction of sentences is evidence of careless intellectual habits and unfinished education. Occasional errors are pardoned in conversation, owing to hurry of thought and rapidity of expression; but no excuse can be offered for errors in writing, because there is sufficient time for reflection, for the due arrangement of thought and the right modelling of expression. Correctness may be obtained, first of all, by writing. "Writing maketh an exact man." Such practice makes us familiar with the right use of words and the correct development of thought. A second method is extensive reading — familiarity with the best that has been thought and written. The value of good models is the same in the studio of the literary artist as in the studio of the painter. Our greatest prose writers — Newman, Ruskin, Arnold, Macaulay, Lowell, Burke, Eliot, Scott, Addison, De Quincey — ought to be familiar to all who aim at correctness of style.

Clearness.— It implies that the expressions used are such as convey the true meaning of the writer. Thus defined, it is opposed to ambiguity, and obscurities of every kind, from whatever source they may arise. The value of clearness is obvious: we write in order to communicate our thoughts to others. If we do not make ourselves understood, we fail of our object in writing. The meaning of a written passage should be so clear as to become evident at the first glance. On this point Quintilian observes that the meaning of a written composition should strike the mind as the light of the sun strikes the eyes. Hence, clearness in style is a word similar in meaning to transparency as applied to air, to glass, or to water. Sometimes an exception to this rule is allowed. For example, a regard for delicacy or decency precludes the too distinct expression of a thought. Again, certain artists, like Browning, are purposely vague, defending the use of obscurity on artistic grounds. Occasionally, too, lawyers and debaters are compelled to be obscure, owing to the weakness of their side of the case. But in spite of these exceptions, the general rule obtains to speak and to write our thoughts in the clearest manner possible.

Vividness.— This quality of good style requires that the thoughts be expressed in such a manner as to arrest and fix the attention of the reader. Vividness springs from a desire to awaken interest. Viewed in this light, it is an effort on the part of the writer to supply in a written composition what is effected in conversation by the tones of the voice and the expression of the countenance. It is a quality of the highest excellence and contributes largely to the success of the writer. There are five ways of rendering a style vivid. First, by the use of specific as opposed to general terms. Here we come upon the necessity of using the Saxon word and the well-chosen adjective. Second, by an extraordinary arrangement of words in a sentence. Every language has some manner of arranging the words of a sentence, which, from the frequency of its occurrence, may be called its common or ordinary mode of arrangement. This is especially true of the English language in which the grammatical construction is often made to depend on the juxtaposition of words. Vividness is the result of departing from this common arrangement. It is called the inverted style, more in vogue in poetry than in prose, owing to a greater need for vividness. A third way of securing vividness is by omitting unnecessary words and phrases, by cutting out conjunctions like " and "; by multiplying periods instead. Hence, the use of the short clean-cut sentence in the prose of modern times. A fourth way of securing vividness is by climax and antithesis. Climax is considered a great beauty in composition. It is prominent both in prose and in verse. It consists in making the members of a sentence rise and grow in importance, or in so arranging the sentences of a paragraph that there will be a gradually ascending scale of effects to the very close. Like climax, antithesis renders a style vivid. It is founded on the contrast or opposition of two objects. It has this effect — to make each of the contrasted objects appear in a stronger light. It is employed to advantage by the artist in colors and in words. In order to render an antithesis more complete, the sentences or clauses expressing the contrasted ideas should be similarly constructed. Besides these ways, it remains to notice interrogation and repetition.

The former often arouses interest by challenging denial. Both are favorite methods of the orator to drive a truth home. Certain kinds of prose rarely use the question mark; the sober essay and critical review have scarcely any use for it. A final device to secure vividness is the treatment of past events as if they belonged to the present time, by changing the tense of the verb. Historians often use this device to enliven their pages. It may be used in many kinds of descriptive work.

Naturalness.— The fourth quality of good writing is naturalness. It requires that a writer, in the choice of his words, in the form of his sentences, in the ornaments he uses, in his terms of thought and expression, should commend himself to every man of good sense and good taste as having pursued the course best suited to the subject and to the occasion. Naturalness is opposed to all kinds of affectation. There is hardly any defect of style so painful and offensive as affectation. It is offensive in life and conduct, doubly so in composition. It is a defect peculiar to many young writers. The spell of old classic writers consists largely in this quality of naturalness and simplicity. Naturalness is sacrificed whenever there is an employment of unusual words or idioms, a desire for excessive ornament or an attempt to be forcible through extravagance of expression.

Various Kinds of Style.— Thus far we have seen only those qualities which belong of necessity to any and every class of good composition. It remains to view a number of styles which may be regarded as types. While each individual writer has a manner all his own in expressing thought, still there are forms of expression which in the process of time have become fixed or crystallized. Broadly speaking, there are a number of styles which the artist will instinctively employ in dealing with certain subjects or elaborating certain kinds of thought. Narrative, description, exposition, argument, analytic and synthetic work, will demand a corresponding variation of style, regardless of the manner best suited to the genius of the writer. In other words, there is an objective as well as a subjective quality of style in all art of the highest order. The following types or kinds of style are found in general use.

The Diffuse Style.— One of the first and most obvious distinctions in style is that feature which arises from the spreading out of thoughts. This distinction constitutes the diffuse style. A diffuse writer unfolds his thought fully; he places it in a variety of lights, he gives the reader every possible assistance for understanding it completely. He is not careful to express it at first in its full strength, because he intends to repeat the impression, and what he lacked in strength he proposes to supply by copiousness. Writers of this kind generally love magnificence and amplification. Their periods run out into some length and give room for ornament of every kind, which they admit freely. This style has its faults and advantages. The extreme of diffuseness makes a composition weak and languid. It tires the reader by endless paraphrase and repetition. Besides thus weakening the composition, diffuseness is apt to lead to a confused and chaotic development of the theme; because a writer, especially an inexperienced one, is likely to be led away from the point at issue by a tangled web of sentences. On the other hand, a reasonable degree of diffuseness is sometimes required by the theme. For example, in the works that appeal particularly to the intellect and the understanding there is an advantage in using this style. Some matters must be treated in the fullest detail. Hence, in pleading at the bar diffuseness is permissible; also to the clergyman in the pulpit, for ordinary minds are slow to grasp ideas unless they are iterated and reiterated. Exposition of truth in any department requires the diffuse style.

Concise Style.— This style, as the name indicates, is just the opposite of diffuseness. For it compresses thought, while the diffuse style expands thought. A concise writer uses the fewest possible words. He employs none save those that are most expressive; he lops off every redundancy. Ornament is not rejected, but he uses it for the sake of force rather than grace; he never presents the same thought twice. His sentences are arranged with compactness and strength rather than with cadence and harmony. The utmost precision is studied in theme. The faults and advantages of this style are obvious. Too much conciseness ends in abruptness and obscurity — it leads to a manner too pointed and epigrammatical. Any writer who goes to the extreme of conciseness offends good taste quite as much as the man who would wear his business suit or " talk shop " in the drawing room. But obscurity is the great fault of too great conciseness, as it thereby defeats the purpose of all writing — namely, the communication of ideas. Horace, the great literary critic, points this out: *" Brevis esse laboro, obscurus fio "*— I try to be concise, and in so doing I become obscure. On the other hand, there are certain advantages from its use, if conciseness be not pushed too far. First, economy of attention. The mind is always delighted whenever the attention is economized — that is, whenever ideas can be grasped with little or no strain upon the attention. In this connection Herbert Spencer observes that all writers should have this point — economy of attention — in view. (Spencer, *Philosophy of Style.*) A second advantage of conciseness is to secure the direct treatment of a theme. A writer cannot ramble in his thought if he must weigh and economize his words. Just as in writing a telegraphic message, the cost of each word keeps one from rambling, so a concise style, if adhered to, will save the composition from wearisome paraphrase. The concise style is sometimes employed in descriptive writing, because it is brisk and lively. The strength and vividness of a description often depend on one or two happy strokes rather than in much amplification of details. This style is likewise used in addresses to the passions. In these addresses it is dangerous to be diffuse, because it is difficult to support the proper warmth and emotion for any length of time. Writers who incline toward this style as a general feature of their work, are Prescott, Emerson, Arnold, Addison, Steele. De Quincey, on the other hand, inclines toward the diffuse style, as do also Macaulay, Ruskin and Newman.

The Idiomatic Style.— It is sometimes said of a style that it is easy or idiomatic. These epithets are generally found together, and where one is justly applied, the other follows as a natural consequence. A style which is idiomatic will appear to have been easily practiced and will be easily understood. By an idiomatic style is meant a manner of writing in which the phrases, forms of sentences, and arrangement of the words and clauses are such as belong to the English language. Every language has peculiarities of this kind by which it is characterized; and the style in which these peculiarities abound is called idiomatic. In the employment of the idiomatic style there is some danger lest a writer become loose and slovenly; although such a style is most strictly correct in construction and clear in meaning. It is employed, first of all, in conversation; for then our minds are fixed on the matter rather than on the form, and we employ the natural, idiomatic turns of phrase. Secondly, it is used in letter-writing, which in form approaches conversation; for then the natural, not the artificial, man is at work. There is a tendency to employ this style in all modern prose. Our classic writers are beginning to appreciate the native idiom more and more; and as the influence of Latin and Greek over our speech is apt still further to decline, we may expect this tendency to become more and more pronounced. The idiomatic style is always pleasing to the reader; the expression is free, familiar; and the meaning is gathered at a glance.

Among living writers who are inclined to use the idiomatic style, we may mention Wilfred Ward, William Mallock, Mark Twain, Louise Imogen Guiney, Alice Meynell, Thomas Wentworth Higginson, and a number of others; as time goes on, this style is apt to grow more and more in popular favor.

CHAPTER XIII

PERSONALITY (CONTINUED)

The Labored Style.— Opposed to the easy and idiomatic manner of writing, is what we call the labored style. This style gives evidence of great pains on the part of the writer — the burning of midnight oil; and it requires the closest attention and effort in order that it may be understood. The arrangement of the words and clauses is often inverted; the sentences are long and involved; the whole composition is highly and painfully artificial. This style usually lacks clearness, smoothness and naturalness. Three methods are recommended for overcoming this tendency to over-elaboration. First, compose with greater rapidity; ordinarily, the form of expression that first presents itself is easy and idiomatic. Second, the writing of letters, journals, diaries, where less care is demanded. Third, familiarity with writers whose style is easy and idiomatic — such authors as Goldsmith and Irving.

The Barren Style.— The epithet, barren, applies to style when there is a nakedness and want of connection in the thoughts and expressions, when trains of thought are started but only partially followed out, giving the composition a half-finished character. This is especially true of the paragraph when dismissed with one or two sentences. In this style repetitions of the same words and phrases are frequent, and all that pertains to the use of words and the form of expressions is commonplace. Barrenness of style may owe its origin either to lack of invention, or to lack of ideas and words.

Whenever it arises from the former, the writer is unable to trace the relations between his thoughts; he is unable to make inferences and draw conclusions. This defect is remedied by maturity and by discipline of the mental powers; also by practice in amplification. *Fabricando fit faber.* When barrenness of style results from lack of ideas and words, there is no better remedy than the reading of classic English writers — acquaintance with the best that has been thought and said, not only in English literature, but in all literature.

The Luxuriant Style.— This style is just the opposite of the barren style, in every respect. It is characterized by redundancy of words and phrases, especially by a profusion of imagery, and an exuberance of figurative language. Instead of selecting what is choice and best fitted to the subject, the writer pours out all his wealth of ornament and expression. He attempts to write in a commanding, imposing manner, which takes the form of extravagant epithets and figures of speech. This style belongs to youth; Cicero calls it the overflow of youthful feeling. In luxuriance of style, not only youth, but racial temperament must be taken into account. For example, the races of southern Europe as compared with those of the north. The style of Italian or Spanish prose resembles the gardens of the tropics, so luxuriant is the growth; whereas a more becoming severity prevails in northern climes. Three remedies are suggested for this luxuriance: First, the pruning-knife — the removal of all unnecessary words and phrases. Often whole sentences must be recast with a view to greater simplicity. Secondly, careful attention should be paid to metaphor and simile. A luxuriant style usually offends against good taste in these particulars. Hence, the necessity of watching figures in order that they may not accumulate too rapidly; also, that they may not be mixed. The mixed figure is always a sign of this style. Finally, the choice of a topic which will not be beyond the ability of the writer. Youth is always prone to this error.

The Forcible Style.— The epithet, forcible, is applied to a style which in a plain, distinct and irresistible manner urges upon us the opinions and views of the writer. The forcible style is an evidence of excitement. The writer is interested in his subject, and is desirous that others share the same feelings with himself. It implies a full persuasion of the truth, the importance of what is said, and such an exhibition of reasons as cannot fail to produce conviction. Hence, the forcible style is dependent in a great degree upon intellectual habits, and implies a well-disciplined mind. It requires some skill in the use of language, but derives little benefit from what may be termed mere ornaments of style. The forcible style is well suited to the discussion of political subjects; and in the history of our country, especially in times of great popular excitement, many eminent examples are found. For example, in the Revolution, Patrick Henry, James Otis, President Adams; in the late Civil War and the Abolition Movement that preceded it, Wendell Phillips, Webster, Clay, Calhoun; in the temperance movement, John B. Gough, George Prentiss and others. In our late financial excitement, William Jennings Bryan and Bourke Cochran. All these men are shining examples of the forcible style. This style must often be employed, not only before popular audiences, but at the bar and in the pulpit, whenever an argument needs to be driven home, or a heated controversy is carried on.

The Feeble or Languid Style.—Opposed to the forcible style, is what rhetoricians call the feeble or languid style. The feeble style is indicative of the whole character of the writer. The man whose style is feeble is usually slothful in his habits and inefficient in his plans and conduct. His view of his subject is cold and indifferent; his words are general terms, destitute of vividness; his sentences are long and loose, most likely to resemble his trousers, and fitting the thought quite as poorly. Literary art has no place for this style, although it occasionally creeps in, despite the efforts of watchful criticism.   There is a class of writers who attempt to employ force and vehemence when their style is not supported by strength of thought or real feeling.   Their work is worse than exhibitions of the feeble style; it becomes rant and mere declamation.   In such instances we have confident assertion instead of strong reasoning, and all the artificial helps of exclamation, climax, interrogation, antithesis.   But while force and vehemence of style, like a deep and powerful current, sweep every obstacle before them, rant and declamation are fitly represented by the broad and shallow stream, noisy, but powerless.

The Dignified Style.— The foundations of an elevated or dignified style are laid in the thoughts.   These thoughts have more of originality and sublimity than those which come from ordinary minds.   These thoughts are accompanied by an appropriate and sustained emotion, which elevates the mind of the reader.   In reading a production in an elevated style, our attention is so taken up by the thought that we seldom have any regard for the language; and if at any time we stop with this object in view, it is but to express our admiration. The words used are admirably suited to the feelings and thoughts they clothe.   The selection of these words seems not to be the result of effort and care, and we regard them as the language in which the author ordinarily thinks and converses. The sentences are full and flowing, but at the same time, unlabored and simple in their composition.   There is a uniform dignity about them which is characteristic of an elevated style. There is a majesty and grandeur in the quiet but resistless power with which the language carries one along; as if we were moving down some majestic river. Like the forcible style, this style of writing has little need of ornament; for ornament is required to sustain the common styles — to beautify and refresh the deserts of commonplace thought and expression. But in the elevated style there is sufficient exaltation of thought and feeling without the aid of ornament. Examples of this style: Irving, Prescott, Robertson, Newman. History and biography employ it, as a rule.

The Pedantic or Pompous Style.— Unsuccessful attempts after the elevated or dignified manner of writing, result in what is called the pedantic or pompous style. The pedant is fond of showing book-knowledge; and a pedantic style is characterized by the use of such terms and phrases as are obsolete, uncommon, or derived from dead languages. And the style is made pompous by the use of long, high-sounding words and phrases. The young lawyer, preacher or essayist is often guilty of adopting this style; and he always offends good taste by his efforts to appear learned and weighty. Some literary men of high standing, like James Russell Lowell, Emerson, and Macaulay, often err on the side of pedantry. Many a writer errs in the adoption of a pompous style which neither the subject nor the writer can properly sustain. It is the case of the small boy walking around in a man's clothes.

The Neat or Elegant Style.— These terms are applied to style with particular reference to what is called the turn of expression. They denote, also, especially the latter, the nature of the ornament used. Their force is understood when they are applied to any production in the arts. When so applied, we declare that the work of art is not only free from faults, but that it is executed in such a way as exhibits the skill of the artist and gives us pleasure. So in the case of style. We say that a style is neat and elegant, when the turns of expression are such as happily convey the thoughts and are well suited to the subject and occasion. The turns of expression must necessarily depend both on the choice of words and the composition of the sentence. The neat style is also closely connected with the thought that is conveyed. Thus, for example, in the forcible or vehement style, we have bold turns of expression; in the elevated and dignified style, we have sublime and grand turns of expression. In the *neat* style there is simply a justness in the thoughts and a finish in the mode of expressing them. At the same time, the writer is careful to avoid every fault. The neat style, as thus explained, is ever pleasing; and to some classes of writing, peculiarly well suited. This style differs essentially from the easy idiomatic style, because it gives evidence of labor in the composition. It seems the result to which mediocrity of talent has attained by patient and praiseworthy exertion. Neatness and elegance in style demand that all coarse and homely words be avoided, even though their use may give more vividness to the expression. In the selection of imagery the characteristics of this style are found. The imagery selected is both beautiful and expressive, calculated to excite a pleasurable feeling. It is the imagery chosen by an Irving or an Addison. Of all English writers, Addison is perhaps the finest example; his essays are models of neatness and elegance. Hence, Johnson advises the English student to give his days and nights to the study of Addison. Besides these various styles of writing which come from the various uses of words, phrases, sentences, metaphors, similes, there are four kinds dependent partly on the thought to be expressed, and partly on the readers to whom such writing is addressed. These styles are called the Intellectual, the Literary, the Impassioned and the Popular.

The Intellectual Style.— It is defined as that style wherein the thought or subject-matter is emphasized more than the form. The great question with a writer who employs this style is : How can I make the truth intelligible? How can the minds of my readers be most effectually reached? Hence, the writer emphasizes the intrinsic merit of his composition, not this or that manner. The writer who employs the intellectual style feels, first of all, that he must have a clear and full perception of the truth to be communicated. He must be profoundly convinced that it is the truth; and be filled with the desire to communicate it. Hence, the intellectual style is based on the essential value of the truth as independent of any worth that may lie in the special exposition of it. This style is sometimes called the *philosophical,* because it is used mainly in philosophical treatises; it is the style of Bacon, Spencer, Darwin, Locke. But it is used in all writings marked by a persistent prominence of the subject-matter over the form. The intellectual style is characterized, not only by emphasis of subject-matter over form, but also by breadth of view. The writer who employs this style successfully, is a man with depth of insight and a wide range of information. He is gifted with mental many-sidedness; and his readers are impressed with the vast range of his knowledge. For example, Spencer, Emerson. The intellectual style is characterized, not only by the predominance of subject-matter over form, and comprehensiveness of view on the part of the writer, but also by sobriety of spirit. This is one of the manifest marks of any writer of sterling merit, or any style of permanent influence. It is to this type of authorship that Mr. Arnold refers in his suggestive phrase: " Intellectual seriousness." By this he means a sense of responsibility becoming any one whose mission in the world is the discovery and circulation of the truth. It is what Cicero calls that elevation of spirit and sentiment dealing with high themes in an exalted manner, immeasurably above all that is trivial and common. This feature of style, sobriety of spirit or intellectual seriousness, is ethical as well as intellectual. The writer shows this ethical or moral value in various ways: First, by an impartial accuracy of statement. Secondly, by a judicial gravity of mind that will insure honest results in the face of temptation to the contrary. Thirdly, by the supremacy of judgment over passion, and by the supremacy of conscience over personal preference. Fourthly, by a loyal devotion to the interests of the truth. For example, Edmund Burke; Carlyle.

The Literary Style.— This style lies midway between the intellectual and the popular; it borders more closely upon the former than the latter. It is called literary because it is the style in which literature, strictly so-called, is expressed; it is the style of the library and the man of letters. On the one side, it is far removed from the scientific, technical and speculative manner of expression. On the other side, it carefully excludes the ordinary and the commonplace. For in this style is reflected the best literary art and taste. This style is most strongly emphasized in the golden ages of letters. For example, the Age of Pericles in Greece; the Augustan Age; the Age of Louis XIV; the Age of Elizabeth.

Some Features of this Style.— First, ease and flexibility. There is at all times the evidence of fluency and facility of touch. The impression is that the writer has a vocabulary more than sufficient for all demands. There is also a freedom of mental movement; the thought easily adapting itself to the ever changing temperament of the author. There is nothing rigid, conventional or academic. It is the special charm of the essays of Lamb and of Addison. In addition to ease and flexibility we may note a further and most significant element of the literary style — its artistic finish. Form and thought are quite distinct in literary art, and it is true to say that there is such a feature of style as grace and beauty of form — an outward attractiveness differing in character and independent of the subject-matter itself. And this outward attractiveness is especially emphasized in what is called the literary style. In a word, the element of correct and disciplined taste enters as an integral factor; and where it is especially prominent, makes the style literary rather than intellectual. For example, in the writings of Ruskin or of Hawthorne, where the subject-matter is set forth in a way satisfactory to the demands of the most sensitive taste.

The Impassioned Style.— By the impassioned style is meant a manner of writing which is emotional, persuasive, fervid; appealing not so strongly to the intellect and æsthetic sense as to the passions. Hence, the impassioned style differs materially from the intellectual and the literary style. This is the favorite style among forensic writers; it is the style of the orator: for example, in history, Carlyle's " French Revolution "; in fiction, Walter Scott's " Heart of Midlothian." It has no place in scientific or philosophical works. Three elements are found in this style of writing: First, the element of passion. It is from this element that the name of the style is derived. This element indicates that the heart is engaged as well as the head; that emotion is allied to thought; that there is something more in view than mere instruction or entertainment. This element is called the lyric element of prose expression, because, like the lyric in verse, it is an appeal to the emotions — it stirs our feeling. For example, Speeches of Webster, Burke, Cicero. The second element of the impassioned style is personality. Personality, while it is exhibited in all styles, is more pronounced in this style than in any other. The individual aims at leaving an impression. Hence, the great orators of the world have been invariably men of great personality. The third and final element of the impassioned style is power. By this element, the emotion felt by the writer is transferred to the reader. De Quincey calls the class of literature capable of so arousing the reader the literature of power. Power is allied to personality. It is personality acting, or in a transitive state. But it is larger in scope, for it implies, not only personality, but also a mastery of the cogent elements of expression. In other words, the medium of the thought — the language — must be so handled as to permit the burning thoughts of the writer to set the reader or hearer afire. For example: Webster's Reply to Hayne; Patrick Henry's Speech; Burke on Warren Hastings.

The Popular Style.— By the popular style is meant one that is not altogether unintellectual or unliterary or unemotional; but one that is not distinctly marked by any of these characteristics. For some degree of mental excellence as of literary and persuasive excellence it must possess in order to be assigned a place among the prominent classes of English style. But it reaches the level of the common people by presenting these qualities in a modified degree. It is called popular for three reasons: First, because it is so easily understood; it appeals to the average intellect and the common people. Hence, in the popular style both words and thoughts are plain, simple, easily grasped. Secondly, it is called popular because it is practical. The term practical is opposed to theory, speculation, mere scholarship as such. Hence, the themes treated in this style are those having a practical bearing, those in which the general mass of mankind feel the keenest interest. And in the manner of treatment the author is careful to use only those expressions and illustrations which appeal to the multitude. For example, William Jennings Bryan, in his treatment of the money question. The various sciences are thus popularized. Thirdly, the popular style is unmethodical and rambling. There is no close consecutive reasoning, no attempt at artistic development in sentence or paragraph. The writer is governed by the impulse of the moment rather than by law or logic or careful preparation. Hence, it is sometimes called the capricious or extemporaneous style of writing. Reminiscences, memoirs, speeches to the multitudes, popularized science, all kinds of letters and miscellaneous writing. Irving's "Sketch-Book"; Bunyan's "Pilgrim's Progress"; Holmes' "Autocrat of the Breakfast Table."

Concluding Remarks.— The different styles of writing thus far reviewed indicate the presence of personality in literary art; they reflect the scholarship, the imagination, the intellect, and the peculiar temperament of the artist. But aside from the phenomena which may be classified, and which give to us the barren, concise, luxuriant and other styles of writing, there remains an indefinable element, felt rather than understood or named, which makes a certain piece of literary art the author's own; and we have no other way to designate it except by naming it after the person of the artist. Thus, for example, we call a piece of work Tennysonian, Shakespearian, Baconian, because the personality of the author is indelibly stamped upon it. It is the incommunicable power supplied by every artist that enters into every masterpiece. It is the most elusive and intangible element in art; yet upon its presence and discovery much of our pleasure depends. After art-form and art-content are analyzed and the results tabulated, this elusive element remains — the personal impress which an artist inevitably sets upon his production — an impress which yields as many styles as there are individual artists, for the hackneyed saying of Buffon is true: "The style is the man." In describing how this individuality affects writing, Pater observes: "The ways in which individuality shows itself are numerous. Each writer, for instance, may be said to make his own vocabulary; he consciously increases his knowledge of words, deliberately chooses certain terms for particular uses, and carefully decides upon the special term which in each case seems to him best adapted to convey his meaning. Besides this, he unconsciously has a preference toward this word or that; he is influenced by association, by the suggestions which are aroused in his mind by this synonym or that, and is in every decision swayed in one direction or another by the fineness of his perceptions, the nature of his temperament, and by all those minute and mingled elements which make up what we know as character. All these conscious and all these unconscious causes help to bring it about, that every writer shall make for himself what Walter Pater calls a vocabulary faithful to the coloring of his own spirit; and the same principle may be traced through all the divisions of literary art, whether they be of structure or of quality." Walter Pater in his "Essays on Style" lays stress upon the presence of *mind* in literary art: it is the individual characteristic according to which art must be judged. " I call the necessity of *mind* in style, that *architectural conception* of work, which foresees the end in the beginning and never loses sight of it, and in every part is conscious of all the rest, till the last sentence does but, with undiminished vigor, unfold and justify the first. This is the more intimate quality of good style, to which the aptitudes of the medium and the ornaments of scholarship are both subservient. For all art requires always its logic, its comprehensive reason — insight, foresight, retrospect, in simultaneous action." According to Pater, individuality is expressed, not only by the presence of mind, but by the presence of soul also. He ascribes to mind the plan, the architecture of literary art; to soul he ascribes an immediate sympathetic contact; by soul the artist reaches us through sympathy and a kind of immediate contact. It is the emotional element united to the logical or architectural element; through this quality of soul you recognize *the person* in the book — you feel the personality of the artist. The following descriptions of the perfect artist may fittingly close this discussion: one is from the pen of Herbert Spencer; the other from Cardinal Newman. Spencer writes: " When the powers of speech are fully developed, and the ability of the intellect to utter the emotions is complete, then fixity of style will disappear; the perfect writer will express himself as Junius, when in the Junius frame of mind; when he feels as Lamb felt, will use a like familiar speech; and will fall into the ruggedness of Carlyle when in a Carlylean mood. His mode of expression will naturally respond to his state of feeling, and there will flow from his pen a composition changing to the same degree that the various aspects of his subject change." Cardinal Newman writes:

Criticism by Cardinal Newman.—" The art of letters is the method by which a speaker or writer brings out in words worthy of his subject and sufficient for his audience or readers the thoughts which impress him. Literature is therefore of a *personal* character; it consists in the enunciations and teachings of those who have a right to speak as representatives of their kind, and in whose words their brethren find an interpretation of their own sentiments, a record of their own experiences, and a suggestion for their own judgments. A great author is not one who merely has a *copia verborum,* whether in prose or in verse, and can, as it were, turn out at his will any number of splendid phrases and swelling sentences; but he is one who has something to say, and knows how to say it. I do not claim for him, as such, any great depth of thought, or breadth of view, or philosophy, or sagacity, or knowledge of human nature, or experience of human life, though these additional gifts he may have, and the more he has of them, the greater he is; but I ascribe to him, as his characteristic gift, in a large sense the faculty of expression. He is master of the twofold Logos, the thought and the word, distinct, but inseparable from each other. He may, if so be, elaborate his compositions, or he may pour out his improvisations; but in either case he has but one aim which he keeps steadily before him and is conscientious and single-minded in fulfilling. That aim is to give forth what he has within him; and from his very earnestness it comes to pass that, whatever be the splendor of his diction or the harmony of his periods, he has within him the charm of an incommunicable simplicity. Whatever be his subject, high or low, he treats it suitably and for its own sake. If he is a poet, *nil moliter inepte.* If he is an orator, then, too, he speaks not only *distincte* and *splendide,* but also, *apte.* His page is the lucid mirror of his mind and life. . . . He writes passionately because he feels keenly; forcibly, because he conceives vividly, he sees too clearly to be vague; he is too serious to be otiose; he can analyze his subject, and therefore he is rich; he embraces it as a whole and in its parts, and therefore he is consistent; he has a firm hold of it and therefore he is luminous. When his imagination wells up, it overflows in ornament; when his heart is touched, it thrills along his verse. He always has the right word for the right idea, and never a word too much. If he is brief, it is because few words suffice; when he is lavish of them, still each word has its mark, and aids, not embarrasses, the vigorous march of his elocution. He expresses what all feel, but all cannot say; and his sayings pass into proverbs among his people, and his phrases become household words and idioms of their daily speech, which is tessellated with the rich fragments of his language, as we see in foreign lands the marbles of Roman grandeur worked into the walls and pavements of modern palaces. Such preëminently is Shakespeare among ourselves; such preëminently Virgil among the Latins; such in their degree are all those writers who in every nation go by the name of classics. To particular nations they are necessarily attached from the circumstance of the variety of tongues, and the peculiarities of each; but so far they have a catholic and ecumenical character that what they express is common to the whole race of man, and they alone are able to express it. If then the power of speech is a gift as great as any that can be named; if the origin of language is by many philosophers even considered to be nothing short of divine; if by means of words the secrets of the heart are brought to light, pain of soul is relieved, hidden grief is carried off, sympathy conveyed, counsel imparted, experience recorded, and wisdom perpetuated; if by great authors the many are drawn up into unity, national character is fixed, a people speaks, the past and the future, the East and the West, are brought into communication with each other; if such men are, in a word, the spokesmen and prophets of the human family, then it will not answer to make light of literature or to neglect its study; rather we may be sure that, in proportion as we master it in whatever language, and imbibe its spirit, we shall ourselves become in our own measure the ministers of like benefits to others, be they many or few, be they in the obscurer or the more distinguished walks of life, who are united to us by social ties and are within the sphere of our personal influence."

PART II.

CHAPTER XIV

ANALYSIS OF PROSE-FORMS

THE LETTER

Divisions of Literary Art.— Literary art occupies two dis·tinct fields — the field of verse and the field of prose. In the field of verse there are three principal subdivisions — the drama, the epic, the lyric. In the field of prose there are more subdivisions, six of which deserve attention: the *letter,* the *essay,* the *sermon* or *oration, history, biography, fiction.* These are called prose-forms; taken together they divide and cover the prose department of literary art.

The Letter.— The first standard prose-form is called the letter. A letter is defined as a written message or communication from one person to another. Hence, the use of the word " correspondence " to indicate this branch of composition. Besides this specific meaning, a general meaning attaches to the word. When the plural form of the word is used it is a synonym for all literature, and embraces in its meaning all the departments of literary art. Hence, our expression, " The Republic of Letters," signifying the whole field of literature. Examples of such usage: First, Dean Swift: " Pericles was an able minister, an excellent orator and a man of letters." Second, Matthew Arnold: " The valuable thing in letters is the judgment which forms itself insensibly along with fresh knowledge." Third, James Russell Lowell: " Pupils should be given a tincture of letters as distinguished from mere scholarship."

Importance.— The letter, as a standard prose-form, is one of the most important branches of composition, as it enters so largely into the daily business of life. In our age almost everyone is under the necessity of conveying his opinions or his feelings through the medium of the letter.

Rank Among Prose-Forms.— From a literary point of view the letter ranks next to the essay; it is lowest in the scale of prose-forms, because it approaches the nearest to ordinary conversation, has the least trace of art in its construction and permits the largest freedom. It occupies a middle place between the serious and amusing species of composition. It discloses more of the individual character and personality of the writer than any other prose-form; hence, the expression, " the life and letters " in books of biography. As a matter of fact, we cannot draw near to the personality of a great writer without reading his letters; and no department of literary art affords more pleasure than such reading. An attractive feature of current magazines is the publication of letters. For example, the letters of literary men published in the Century, Scribner's, and Harper's magazine.

Historical Value.— The letter is a vehicle not only for the feelings, opinions and reflections of the writer; it often affords a picture of the times in which it was written, and hence contains valuable material for literary and political history. For example, the best history of our late Civil War, written by the secretaries of President Lincoln, contains several hundred letters from generals and soldiers who were in the struggle. Janssen's " History of the German People " publishes letters of Luther and correspondence of the German princes.   Hence, letters explain and illuminate incidentally much of the national, religious, domestic and social conditions and the course of public events.   Other examples: the War of the Roses in England, explained by the correspondence of the Paston family; the Oxford Movement, illuminated by the letters of Pusey, Ward, Froude, Keble, and Newman.

In Relation to Other Literary Forms.— The letter may be called the literary atom because it is found in so many other literary forms.   Besides the department of history, where the letter is beginning to figure so prominently, it is found in all kinds of biography.   For example, read the letters in Boswell's " Life of Johnson," or Morley's " Life of Gladstone." In the drama it helps to interpret character and complicate the plot.   For example, the letters in " Macbeth," " Hamlet," " King Lear," and " Othello."   In fiction the love-letter is frequently met with.   Sometimes a long correspondence is given, as in the case of Glory Quayle in " The Christian." In journalism letters appear from the regular and casual correspondent.   Perhaps the best known collection of letters is found in the New Testament.   Thus, the letter justifies its claim to be regarded as the literary atom.

Various Kinds of Letter.— There are five kinds of letter which occupy a place in literature: the letter of friendship, the news-letter, the official letter, the open letter, the love-letter. These letters form a part of literature because they are filled with sentiment, emotion, feeling, wit, humor and other qualities that humanize them.   The business letter is excluded from this category, for, although some art is required in its construction, yet it has no claim to be regarded as literature: it appeals to the commercial rather than to the æsthetic sense.   It carefully excludes sentiment, emotion or anything that might suggest imagination. It is in the main impersonal, cold, colorless. If it possesses any persuasive power, this merit is not ordinarily the result of literary excellence.

The Letter of Friendship.— As the name indicates, this letter represents correspondence between friends. Many celebrated examples are found in the history of literature, such as the letters of Cicero, Newman, Moore, Byron, Pope, Goethe, Carlyle, Browning. The literary value of such correspondence is enhanced in three ways: by the importance of the subject treated; by wit, humor, feeling and other humanizing qualities; by the rank and merit of those who write such letters. Hence, the curiosity which the public has ever shown concerning the letters of eminent men; the public expects some revelation of character, and as a rule is not disappointed. As letters from one friend to another make the nearest approach to conversation, there is more character displayed in them than in other productions prepared for public view. The writer is informal, at ease; and heart and fancy wield the pen. Hence, the first requisite for such letters is to be natural and simple. A stiff, formal manner is as bad in a letter as it is in conversation or in company. The style must not be too highly polished — neat and correct, but no more. All nicety about words betrays study; care in the selection of sentences or in the arrangement of thoughts should not appear. For the best letters are such as the authors have written with most facility.

Subject-Matter.— The subject-matter of such letters is as wide in range as the scope of human affection. All things in the heavens above and in the earth beneath and in the waters under the earth have found their way into letters of friendship. But perhaps the most frequent topics are personal welfare, affairs of the heart, business. For example, in the letters of Cicero, what concerned him most was his political success, and he received from Atticus much sound advice in reference to his public conduct — what should, or what should not, be done under certain circumstances.   The character and calling of the correspondents will have a determining influence upon the subject-matter selected; as, for example, the letters of Thomas Carlyle and Matthew Arnold are full of literary topics — a panorama of literary allusions.   On the other hand, the letters of Keble and Newman breathe the spirit of religion.   The environment of the correspondents often furnishes the chief topics; as, for example, in the letters of Walpole and Montague the presence of local color is everywhere discoverable.

Utility of these Letters.— The historical value of letters has been noted; the value of letters of friendship to the department of biography cannot be over-estimated.   For, as Newman writes, " It has ever been a truism with me that the real life of a man is in his letters; not only for biography, but for arriving at the inside of things, the publication of letters is the true method."   " The friendly letter availeth much for the understanding of men," as a wise Elizabethan once wrote.

Amount of Such Literature.— Nearly all literary men of any note have kept letters of friendship; some prominent men like Walpole have left several volumes.   A rather strange exception to this rule is William Shakespeare — no authenticated letter from him has ever been found.   Next to literary men, statesmen and clergymen of high rank or prominence in the church have contributed to this department; also scientists, like Huxley; lawyers, physicians, teachers.   In all, twenty-five thousand volumes would not be an unfair estimate.

CHAPTER XV

THE LETTER (CONTINUED)

THE NEWS-LETTER

Definition.— The title indicates the purpose of this letter which, since the rise of journalism, has become a household word in every land. Like the letter of friendship, it contributes directly to the great body of literature; for, frequently, the newspaper correspondent is a literary artist of high rank. In the early history of journalism it was not uncommon to give a journal the title of *news-letter*. For example, the *News-letter* once published in London, and in Philadelphia. At that time news was supplied by correspondents who would canvass a locality and present their material in the form of a letter. So that the newspaper then was little more than a collection of letters.

Style of the News-Letter.— As a rule it has the same easy style, the same freedom of treatment as the letter of friendship. In the matter of gathering news, no fixed method can be applied, nor can any fixed style be predicated of such correspondence. Much depends upon the temperament and gifts of the writer; much upon the character of the journal for which the news-letter is written. For example, the news-letters appearing in our best journals and periodicals exhibit the graces of style and the methodical treatment which one finds in the essay. They are intended for the public eye — a critical public — and hence the writer pays as much attention to literary form as to subject-matter. For example, compare the style of a news-letter appearing in Harper's or the Century magazine with the news-letter style in the ordinary journal. As a matter of fact, news-letters appearing in our art-journals and magazines are as finished in form and as literary in character as any other department of prose.

Subject-Matter.—With regard to subject-matter, the news-letter enjoys the largest range. War, politics, religion, science, art, fashion, are treated with the fullest freedom — a freedom which justifies Matthew Arnold in the remark that the news-letter is a miniature of all passing events. A large number of news-letters are as ephemeral as the subjects treated. The most permanent news-letter deals with *foreign travel*, with *eminent personages*, with the *latest* and *best books* or *publications*. From these three sources, history, biography, and literary criticism receive valuable and permanent additions. The first source: foreign travel was never so large as at present; never before was there such a study of the institutions, customs and manners of strange peoples; hence, the large and growing volume of news-letters. Again, there is a watchful jealousy among all civilized nations, and accordingly an eager demand for news from the special correspondent; for example, the news-letters of Mr. Russel, in the London Times; Richard Harding Davis, in Harper's Weekly. Among foreign travelers there are bands of scholars representing the large universities and working in the interests of various sciences, such as geology, archæology; their letters and correspondence found in university journals are a valuable addition to literature: for example, correspondence of Russell Harris in the Cambridge University Record. Finally, the news-letter from missionaries in foreign lands is of permanent value to the church historian. Both Catholic and Protestant journals give prominence to these letters. Besides these letters there is the news-letter occupying a permanent place in literature, supplying material not only for history, but for biography as well. Such letters describe eminent men in the various walks of life. The permanence of these letters depends upon the subjects treated rather than upon any graces of literary form. The abiding greatness of the human hero often immortalizes such literary work when the art of the workman has no other claim to immortality. For example, in the late Napoleon revival, news-letters, worthless as examples of literary art, were dug up and published as biography. They will survive because of the subject treated. A whole library of this character has grown up around such men as Bismarck, Leo XIII, Gladstone, Newman; and it will survive because of the permanent interest the world will take in these men.

In Relation to Literary Criticism.— A large body of literary criticism comes from news-letters; they announce the latest books and publications, analyzing and passing judgment upon the contents. Literary criticism in England and in America flows through the news-letter as a favorite channel; and on both sides of the water the best journals and magazines regularly devote some space to this correspondence. The finest literary talent is employed. For example, Lang, Zangwill, in England; Curtis, Howells, in America. Besides their permanent value as criticism, these letters are an invaluable guide to the reading public. As Frederick Harrison observes: " Owing to the enormous activity of the modern press and the modern pen, good books are buried in voluminous seas — *rari nantes in gurgite vasto;* and the critic who discovers those books worth reading conveys an inestimable favor upon the public."

The Official Letter.— The official letter, as the title implies, is the document and product of authority. In the administration of government this prose-form has always been employed. Hence, the archives of church and state possess a large mass of literature from this source. In every capital city of the world the archives are filled with official correspondence. Owing to the increasingly complex relations which governments now sustain toward their subjects and toward each other, the volume of official correspondence is constantly growing.

The Literary Value of these Letters.—As a rule, the official letter, like the business letter, makes no direct contribution to literature in the strict sense of that word. For ordinarily it is a plain formal statement of duty or command, giving no room to fancy or emotion. But indirectly, all official correspondence possesses some literary value, because it furnishes material for history. All historians rely upon official archives. The latest examples: Janssen working in the Berlin archives; Ludwig Pastor in the archives of the Vatican; Bancroft and Freeman in the archives of Washington and London. The historical novel, treating past events with fanciful freedom, likewise employs official correspondence as the basis of imaginary plots. Imaginary letters are introduced as written by prominent officials of church and state. For example, Walter Scott's treatment of medieval history.

Species of this Letter.— Two kinds of official correspondence form an exception to the general laws: encyclical letters and those that come under the head of diplomatic correspondence. These letters, when written by gifted men, are among the finest expressions of literary art. For example: the letters of Cicero when Roman consul; the diplomatic correspondence of Talleyrand; the encyclical letters of Leo XIII. Read the letter of Daniel Webster on the impressment of American seamen, written to Lord Ashburton when Webster was Secretary of State. The official letter, says Arnold, when it takes the form of diplomatic correspondence, gives free rein to certain humanizing qualities that characterize the best literature. Emotion, persuasiveness, beauty of form and of thought, are very often, though not always, the characteristics of such writing. Certain it is, however, that in spite of official chilliness and self-suppression there is a large play of personality. Moreover, the arts of diplomacy require at times all the subtlety and wealth of language, justifying Talleyrand's dictum that language was made to conceal thought. John Morley, writing about the biography of Talleyrand, makes this observation: " I find in his diplomatic correspondence a complete revelation of the man who exhausted all the arts of the primitive serpent in dealing with contemporary rulers." The encyclical letter, like diplomatic correspondence, is often a revelation of personality. If the author happens to be a literary artist, as in the case of Sixtus IV., Leo X., or Leo XIII., the encyclical letter will exhibit all the charm and merit of the best literature. Richard Clarke, speaking about the letters of Leo XIII., observes that they rank among the best specimens of epistolary correspondence. A refinement of taste, a deep and varied scholarship, and above all, the impress of an extraordinary personality give to these letters a permanent place in literature.

Style.— The official letter in form and in style: In form it is suggestive of the essay, giving no place to rambling thought or looseness of expression; it is characterized by precision of statement, method and regularity. In style it aims at preserving official dignity; all the formalities of social, political and religious life are strictly observed.

CHAPTER XVI

THE LETTER (CONTINUED)

The Open Letter.— The open letter may be called the literary paradox, for the term, letter, connotes privacy, whereas the open letter courts publicity. Although addressed to some prominent member of society, nevertheless, it is intended for the public. It is more carefully written than the letter of friendship, because it is meant for publication. In style and finish it approaches the essay or treatise — in fact it may be called an essay plus the formalities of epistolary correspondence.

Occasion for this Letter.— The occasion is usually a grave one — some great political or religious upheaval. For example, the late Armenian massacres which were the occasion of an open letter addressed by Mr. Gladstone to the Duke of Westminster. The war between Spain and America occasioned the writing of an open letter by Minister De Lome to the American people. The first open letter written by an Englishman was that of St. Gildas to the ancient Britons, pleading for certain church reforms. Since that time the open letter has often appeared as an index of vicissitudes in political and religious life. The most elaborate open letter in English literature is that of Cardinal Newman to the Duke of Norfolk, wherein the author attempts to allay public feeling in the matter of Vaticanism.

Publicity of Such Letters.— They attain a wide publicity, owing to the excitement which prevails at the time they are written. As soon as the open letter is received, it is given to the public press by the person to whom it is addressed — this with the full consent and understanding of the author. Sometimes the open letter is made a feature of the weekly periodical or the magazine. For example, the letters that appear in the New York Sun or the Century Magazine — letters addressed to the editor, but intended for the public.

Style.— The style of the open letter is dignified and formal, calm, dispassionate. It is written, as a rule, by some prominent citizen — an official of the church, it may be, or of the state; and it treats of subjects which appeal to the whole community. As it is intended to be a calm, critical survey of some warmly debated problem, the open letter appeals to the understanding, rather than to the imagination. The personality of the writer, which shines through the ordinary letter, is kept out of this work. It is occupied with argument, exposition, a plain statement of facts.

The Love-Letter.— The love-letter, as the name implies, is a branch of erotic literature. It deals with the tender passion which has inspired so much that is pure and vile in the world's classics. Like the letter of friendship, the love-letter possesses the charm of incommunicable individualistic traits; for here, if anywhere, personality appears and appeals. This letter is sometimes defined as a lyric in prose. Heart and fancy wield the pen.

Universality of Appeal— "All the world loves a lover"; and, as a consequence, the whole world reads the love-letter. No man or woman is so poorly educated as to feel incompetent to write a love-letter. Hence, if all the love-letters written could be collected, the world would not contain the books. In every home, under lock and key, there is a small packet of them, too sacred for the public eye, yet withal, the purest kind of literature.

Style.— The style of the love-letter is highly emotional, varying with every mood and fancy, extravagant to a degree almost incredible, but well understood by those who have experienced the spell of this tender passion. The style may be compared to a tropic flower garden, it is so luxuriant, so brimful of beauty; metaphor, simile, all kinds of figure and all kinds of illustration, abound. Perhaps the best examples of its luxuriance are found in the *Epithalamium of* Spenser and the sonnets of Petrarch and Shakespeare. Like the letter of friendship, it is free, easy, familiar — no method but " the heart's way."

Literary Use.— The love-letter is prominent in works of fiction. Sometimes it is introduced to elaborate the plot, frequently adding thereto the element of complexity; sometimes it serves as a summary of the action — a delightful bit of retrospect or a breathing space like the lyric pause in dramatic action. Such modern writers as Hall Caine, Henry James, William Dean Howells, Marion Crawford, and others employ the letter quite extensively. For example, the letters of Glory Quayle in " The Christian "; although hers are not all love-letters.

Publication of these Letters.— The modern tendency to unlock all secrets and reveal all affairs of personal and private character has seriously interfered with the privacy of the love-letter. It is often published now in order to satisfy the somewhat morbid craving of the modern public. Several volumes, like the " Love-Letters of an Englishwoman," have been enjoying an extensive circulation. It is only another example of the popularity of erotic literature. There may be a difference of opinion as to the propriety of publishing such letters, but there is no question as to their literary value.

CHAPTER XVII

THE LETTER (CONTINUED)

History of the Letter.— The letter is one of the oldest prose-forms in literature. It constitutes a part, sometimes a very considerable part, of the literary life of historic peoples. From time immemorial kings and princes sent words of greeting to contemporary rulers, using the letter as their literary vehicle. For example, the letter of Arius, King of the Spartans, to Onias, high priest of Israel. Ambassadors and missionaries through it made known their messages to the nations of the earth. The use of the letter gradually crept into commercial life, and after a time the lower as well as the higher ranks of society began to employ it.

The Letter in Hebrew Literature.— The epistolary literature of the Bible constitutes a department of the highest importance. According to Dr. Moulton, three classes of composition come under the head of letter or epistle. The first and largest class is made up of letters in the strictest sense, the *Epistles of Pastoral Intercourse.* These have the full form of epistolary correspondence, commencing with a salutation from the Apostle, with whom other names are joined in some cases, to a distinct church or fellow worker, and ending with further salutations and sometimes an autograph message, and with greetings general or by name. All pastoral affairs are discussed with freedom. For example, the first letter to the Corinthians, where St. Paul talks about church factions, moral laxity, and other matters which come under pastoral supervision. A second class Moulton calls the *Epistolary Treatise,* wherein the customary form of the letter is preserved while the author enters upon a long dissertation concerning religious doctrine. For example, in the letter to the Romans, the doctrine of Faith. A third class is called the *Epistolary Manifesto;* it is a circular letter addressed to the various churches. For example, the general epistle of Saint Peter. Concluding his analysis, Moulton remarks: " The epistles occupy in the New Testament the place occupied by prophecy in the Old Testament. The prophets could move amongst their fellow countrymen and bring to bear upon them the power of vocal address. On the other hand, the apostles addressed those who were scattered through distant cities, and could communicate with the church as a whole only by letter. The analogous Old Testament form — the gnomic epistle — is to be found in wisdom literature. Like the Old Testament essay, it is crude, poorly organized, yet sufficiently definite to be traceable. For example, the third Book of Wisdom is a gnomic epistle; its introduction makes clear that it is delivered in writing, and on the application of a delegate who represents others besides himself; the suggestion is of the intercourse that prevailed between wise men at a distance, such as Solomon and Hiram of Tyre."

Saint Paul the Representative Hebrew Author of Letters.— Of the large number of letter writers, Saint Paul ought to be given first place, for among men of world-wide reputation there is no author quite so prominent as the Apostle of the Gentiles. Next to the Divine Founder of Christianity, there is no personality so great in the New Testament, and a charming revelation of this personality is given in the letters. These letters are translated into every known language; they are read in the churches of all Christian denominations; they are universally admired on account of the nobility of character which they reveal. These letters are valuable in the highest degree as an exposition of Christian doctrine; but aside from their theological value, they possess a permanent literary value. They are filled with emotion, beauty, sublimity, pathos — those qualities that humanize writing and make it literature. They are fourteen in number, and together form about one-fourth of the New Testament.

How Classified.—The letters of St. Paul are classed as open letters because, although directed to separate churches and communities, they were providentially intended to teach the Church universal. With the exception of the letter to Philemon they are open letters from one of the highest officials of the Church — written for the edification and instruction of all the faithful. The letter to Philemon is private in character and must be classified among letters of friendship.

Special Literary Merit.—The letters of Saint Paul reveal the chief personality of primitive Christian times, excepting, of course, the Divine Founder of Christianity. And the first claim to consideration, from a literary point of view, rests upon this fact — the revelation of Saint Paul's character and personality — his passion for righteousness, his burning zeal and enthusiasm — his intense love of humanity — his courage, charity, learning, eloquence — all those traits that glorify human nature and exalt human character are revealed in his letters. The letters of Saint Paul are not only a revelation of his own personality; they reveal the normal working of the oriental imagination; they reveal its normal development, as the later writings of Saint John and the Book of Job reveal its abnormal flights. The oriental imagination is the chief glory of Hebrew literature. In Saint Paul it finds expression in all kinds of metaphor, simile, personification. The letters are full of such figures as " The Word of God is a two-edged sword; " " The wages of sin is death; " " A door was opened unto me in the Lord;" "We are temples of the Holy Spirit." All his imaginative work is normal, practical, severely simple; like the parables of our Lord, in no way suggestive of the grandeur or weirdness of the Apocalypse. Yet this imaginative work is distinctly oriental. It is nature and life as both appear beneath the Syrian skies. A third characteristic of his letters is the frequent literary allusion. Like all great writers, Saint Paul made many literary allusions. They are drawn chiefly from early Hebrew books; only three or four references are made to profane writers. Quotations from the Old Testament are found in profusion throughout his letters; for example, about one-fifth of the letter to the Hebrews is in the form of quotation. Saint Paul's range of reading beyond Hebrew literature was evidently narrow; although complete as regards his own people. When Saint Paul addressed letters to the Greeks and the Romans an opportunity was afforded to him to display a knowledge of classic literature. Only one or two classic quotations occur; among them one from Aratus of Cilicia, a Greek lyric poet. But Saint Paul did not have classic lore for an object — he sought rather the souls of men, and knew little else save the things of heaven. A fifth characteristic of the letters of Saint Paul is their wealth of feeling and emotion—a characteristic of the best literature. The fulness of a passionate and zealous heart finds expression in his literary work as it found expression in missionary labors. His boundless enthusiasm for religion and his intense, passionate, love of humanity fill his letters with emotion; making him the idolized apostle of the Protestant and the Roman Catholic world. In comparison with him the other apostles are frozen spirits, attractive in the order of grace, but without those splendid passions and affections which immortalize the life and letters of Saint Paul. The only apostle who approaches him in largeness of heart and mind is Saint John. As a consequence of this emotion, Saint Paul in his letters adheres closely to the oriental style of writing, the distinguishing features of which are first the frequent use of exclamations. His letters abound in exclamations. For example, " O the depth of the riches, both of the wisdom and knowledge of God!" "O man, who art thou that repliest against God!" Secondly, the frequent use of the question mark. For example, in the letter to the Romans over two hundred sentences are found in the form of questions. Thirdly, the frequent use of exhortation and the employment of the imperative rather than the subjunctive mood for that purpose. Very frequently the argument is interrupted by exhortations, as if heart and brain were in constant rivalry—emotion continually arresting the processes of thought. All these features render his style vivid and impressive. Judged by our severe northern standards of criticism, this style is ill-suited to letters and much better adapted to purposes of oratory. Saint Paul is accused of emphasizing to excess these features of the oriental style, but the critic must take into account the character of the writer, and the peculiar temperament of southern nations. It is a strange fact that his style was not modified by contact with the Romans, and especially with the Greeks. The supreme test of a great genius is to break the shackles of early environment. Saint Paul bore the test in his religious work, earning the title of Apostle of the Gentiles. But in his literary work he never rose above his early Hebrew environment. In the matter and form of his writings he remained to the very end a Hebrew of the Hebrews.

The Letter Among the Greeks and Latins.— There are very few examples of the letter in ancient classic literature; although many writers of a later period have left letters both in Latin and in Greek. No authentic letter written by Plato or Aristotle or the great dramatists or historians of Greece has come down to us. And, if we except Cicero and Pliny, the same statement applies to classic Roman authors. There are allusions in Thucydides, Herodotus, Plutarch, Livy and other classic historians, going to show that the letter was a familiar prose-form both in Greece and in Rome. But very little care seems to have been exercised in preserving such literary remains until we come to the Christian era. In the case of Greece, the absence of the letter may be explained by the destruction of the national archives — the inevitable result of conquest after conquest. In Christian times, besides the letters of Basil, Chrysostom, Ignatius and other Greek fathers, we have the collection of Alciphron, who lived in the latter half of the second century, A. D. He collected three books of letters, one hundred in all; they are written in the best Attic, and describe rather minutely the social life of Greece; perhaps the best part of the collection are those letters that passed between Glycera and Menander. The letters of Phalaris which, if genuine, would be the oldest in Greek literature, are proven to be spurious by Bentley, the English critic. However, they are written in excellent Greek, and belong most probably to the second century of the Christian era.

Letters of the Church Fathers.— Concerning these letters, Newman in his historical sketches offers the following criticism:

Criticism by Cardinal Newman.—" These ancient Fathers (Greek and Latin) have left behind them just that kind of literature which more than any other represents the abundance of the heart, which more than any other approaches to conversation: I mean correspondence. Why is it that we feel an interest in Cicero which we cannot feel in Demosthenes or Plato? Plato is the very type of soaring philosophy, and Demosthenes, of forcible eloquence; Cicero is something more than orator and sage; he is not a mere ideality, he is a man and a brother; he is one of ourselves. We do not merely believe it or infer it, but we have the enduring and living evidence of it — how? *In* *his letters.* Now the case of the Church Fathers is parallel to that of Cicero. We have their letters in a marvelous profusion. We have above 400 letters of Saint Basil; above 200 of Saint Augustine. Saint Chrysostom has left us about 240; Saint Gregory, the same number; Saint Nilus close on to 1,400; Saint Isidore, 1,440. The Blessed Theodoret, 146; Saint Leo, 140; Saint Cyprian, 80 or 90; Saint Jerome, 100; Saint Ambrose, 90; Saint Bernard, the last of the Fathers, supplies 444 * * * These letters are of very various characters, compared one with another; a large portion of them were intended simply for the parties to whom they are addressed; a large portion of them consist of brief answers to questions asked of the writer, or a few words of good counsel or spiritual exhortation, disclosing his character either by the topic selected, or his mode of dealing with it. Many are doctrinal; great numbers again are strictly ecclesiastical. Many are historical and biographical; some might be called state papers; some narrate public translations, and how the writer felt towards them, or why he took part in them. For example, Pope Gregory's epistles give us the same sort of insight into the holy solicitude for the universal Christian people which possessed him, that minute vigilance, yet comprehensive superintendence of the chief pastor, which in a very different field of labor is seen in the Duke of Wellington's dispatches on the campaign, which tells us so much more about him than any panegyrical sketch. On the other hand, the letters of Saint Isidore and Saint Nilus consist of little more than one or two terse, pithy, pregnant sentences, which may be called sermonets, and are often as vivid as if we heard them. Saint Chrysostom's are for the most part crowded into the three memorable years in which the sufferings of exile gradually ripened into a virtual martyrdom. Others, as some of those of Saint Jerome and Saint Ambrose, are meditations on mystical subjects. Those of Saint Dionysius of Alexandria, which are but fragments, recount the various trials of the time, and are marked with a vigorous individuality which invests the narrative with an interest far higher than historical " (Newman, Historical Sketches).

CHAPTER XVIII

THE LETTER (CONTINUED)

CICERO'S LETTERS

Cicero, the Classic Representative of Ancient Epistolary Writing.— Among ancient classic authors, Cicero holds first place as a writer of letters. In tracing the history of this prose-form, he, like Saint Paul, deserves special notice. A word about his life: on the steep side of one of the Volscian hills, below which the river Liris, now the Garigliano, flowed in a winding channel to the sea, not far distant from the kingdom of Naples, lay the ancient town of Arpinum. In the neighborhood of this town, where the Fibreno joins its small tributary stream to the waters of the Liris, amidst rocks and hills and the loveliest of Italian landscapes, Cicero was born on the third of January, B. C. 106. He was slain in 43 B. C.

His Career in Brief.— He served in the Social War in 89; traveled in Greece and Asia 79-77; Quæstor in Sicily in 75; accused Verres in 70; Edile in 69; Pretor in 66; Consul suppressing Catiline in 63; Proconsul in Sicily, 51-50; joined Pompey 49-48; Philippics against Antony 44; proscribed and slain by the second Triumvirate in 43.

General Estimate.— Cicero is an example of the highest type of pagan culture. Few men have been more praised, and few more vilified than Cicero. Two reasons may be assigned — the distinguished place he holds in history — the weakness and strength of character which he alternately displayed in public office and in private life. The chief fault in Cicero's moral character was a want of sincerity. In a different sense of the word from that expressed by Saint Paul, he wished to become all things to all men. His private correspondence and his public speeches were often in direct contradiction with each other as to the opinions he expressed of his contemporaries; and he lavished compliments in the Senate and the Forum upon men whose conduct he disliked, and whose characters he abhorred. One recognizes in him the arts and the vanity of the politician. But, on the other hand, there were many sterling qualities far outweighing this weakness — qualities which will forever entitle Cicero to the respect and homage of mankind.

As a Writer.— His literary work is divided into three classes: orations, philosophical treatises, letters. His orations are fifty-six in number. They have been the models of oratory in all countries ever since his time. To the second division belong treatises on Philosophy, from which we derive all our knowledge of the Greek systems which succeeded the schools of Plato and Aristotle. The third division embraces Cicero's letters. Cicero found the Latin language barren, crude, dissonant; he found it brick and left it marble. On his merit as a writer, Cardinal Newman observes: " Cicero's art lies in converting the very disadvantages of the Latin language into beauties, in enriching it with metaphors and circumlocutions, in pruning it of harsh and uncouth expressions, in systematizing its structure; and herein we find that *copia dicendi* which gained Cicero the high testimony of Caesar to his inventive powers, and which we may add, constitutes him the greatest master of composition that the world has seen."

His Letters.— The letters of Cicero, next to his orations, are the most valuable part of his literary work. They are valuable, first of all, as a history of his domestic life from his fortieth year almost to the day of his death. Like the letters of Saint Paul in this regard, they reveal a charming personality — a character incapable of the apostle's zeal or aggressiveness, but yet, so upright, pure and noble as to win universal admiration even in Christian times when the standard of moral excellence is so high. "These letters," writes De Quincey, "open a door to his domestic life; to say nothing of their exquisite Latinity they are full of playful wit; they have a freshness and reality which no narrative of by-gone events can ever hope to attain; they show that Cicero was a man of genial soul, of a most kind and amiable disposition; they show that he is always the scholar and the gentleman; no one having more of that refined polish which the Romans described by the expressive word, *Urbanitas.*" For, in the whole of his correspondence, not a single coarse word or vulgar idea occurs.

A Revelation of Private Life.— The letters of Cicero as a revelation of his private life, emphasize some traits of his character, notably his passionate fondness for books and for friends. Regarding books he writes to Atticus: "When my librarian brought in and arranged my books, it seemed as if my house had suddenly gotten a soul." Again he writes: "I would sooner sit in my library with a bust of Aristotle above my head than in a consul's chair. I envy not Croesus with all his wealth and broad acres: give me only the power to purchase books." Cicero was a constant book-buyer, gathering parchments, rolls and manuscripts from all parts of the empire. The letters of Cicero reveal his passionate love, not only for books, but for friends as well. Hence his letters are to some extent a history of many important personages of his time. He corresponded with a number of public men;

for example, Antony, Croesus, Caesar, Brutus. Fully fifty men of note in Roman History are mentioned in his letters.

Friendship for Atticus.— The friendship between Cicero and Atticus occupies the largest space in his letters. It was a friendship cordial, sincere, begun in youth and never varying during all the vicissitudes of their lives. On this point Niebuhr remarks that there is no parallel case of such friendship in early Roman history; as the citizen lived simply for his country, having no regard for private or social affections. Cicero possessed these affections, and cultivated friendship to a degree which few Romans could comprehend.

An Autobiography.— The letters of Cicero have all the merits of autobiography. Cicero and Atticus lived on terms of absolute confidence; and their long unbroken friendship made it possible for Cicero to entrust Atticus with all kinds of secrets respecting himself and his family. Hence, the letters are a complete revelation of his private and domestic life; in them are told his most secret plans and purposes; his cares and troubles, whether at home or before the public. As he writes to Terentia: "I consult Atticus about everything." Accordingly, these letters appeal to our age, so curious to know all the secrets about great lives.

The Character of Cicero as Revealed in His Letters.— Insincerity has already been noted as revealed in his political speeches. Aside from this, two glaring defects appear in his character, otherwise so pure and noble. First, a lack of self-reliance: he seldom trusted his own judgment; he feared too much the hiss of the multitude. If he had not received the counsel and support of Atticus, his public life doubtless would have been a failure. The second defect in the character of Cicero was an excitable, impulsive, disposition. It is surprising to note in his letters how rapidly he sinks from exalted moods to the depths of despair. He writes to Atticus: "I am so disheartened and discouraged at times that, were it not for your friendly counsel, I should commit suicide." And in his last reverses, when the Roman Republic fell, Cicero would certainly have committed suicide if Atticus had not exerted his powerful influence, restraining this mercurial friend.

The Literary Value of His Correspondence.— The letters of Cicero satisfy all critical demands as a revelation of character. They are likewise valuable on account of their literary form and content. The style is that easy, flowing, familiar one, characteristic of letters of friendship. His style is a model for all writings of that class. It is the style of Saint Paul, minus the oriental features; for in it there are few question marks or exclamations, and very little imagery. In this literary work, Cicero impresses the reader not only as artless and unstudied, but as a man with unlimited resources in thought, in language, and in the amplification of his theme; and this impression, doubtless, led Newman to rank him as the greatest master of composition that the world has seen.

Characteristics of His Epistolary Style.— There are three characteristics that lend value to the letters of Cicero: first, a methodical development of thought — a characteristic of all his literary work and one rather too strongly emphasized in these letters of friendship. Cicero was a profound student of philosophy as well as of literature; believing that a thorough study of the former is essential for successful interpretation of and work in the latter; and in his letters he applied too rigorously that method of thought-development, so highly valued in his orations and philosophical works. A second characteristic: a wealth of literary allusions and references; he was familiar with all the departments of classic verse and prose. His favorite authors: in poetry, Homer and Æschylus; in philosophy, Plato, Aristotle and Zeno; in history, Xenophon and Polybius. He writes to Atticus: "The orator, the dramatist and the historian are the great educators of mankind." A final characteristic is the introduction of wit, humor, pleasantry of all kinds. Unlike Saint Paul, Cicero often forgets his seriousness and severity, and his page is brightened with the playful and humorous side of life; hence, humanizing elements find a large expression in his letters. Like Saint Paul, Cicero was capable of most intense feeling, but then he employs the language of despair, not of hope. In the art of writing letters and orations, Cicero, since his time, has been the world's model; his influence upon these departments of prose, always pronounced, has never waned. The following criticism from the pen of an English biographer, Mr. Forsyth, may fittingly close this examination of the letters of Cicero:

Criticism by Forsyth.—"I propose to notice a few of these early letters to Atticus somewhat in detail, for they will give us a good idea of Cicero's style and habits of thought, and also show the cordial friendship that existed between these two eminent men — a friendship as frank as it was sincere, which never varied during all the vicissitudes of their lives, and was terminated only by death. In the first letter written in the latter part of the year to Atticus in Epirus on the Western coast of the Adriatic, where, in the neighborhood of Buthrotus, he had recently purchased an estate, Cicero begins by alluding in feeling language of affectionate sorrow to the death of his cousin, or, as he calls him, *brother* Lucius — the only son of his uncle Lucius — who had, as we have seen, been associated with him in the prosecution of Verres. Cicero greatly deplored his loss, and speaks of him as a man endowed with every excellence, and distinguished by great sweetness of disposition. He next refers to a subject which was a fertile source of domestic annoyance for many years,— the unhappy disagreement between Quintus and his wife Pomponia, who was a sister of Atticus. Quintus was a man of hasty temper, easily vexed, but soon appeased, and Pomponia seems to have been a lady rather apt to take offence, and jealous of her imagined rights, — what we may call *touchy,* and inclined to stand on her dignity. A little anecdote which Cicero relates of her in one of his letters, and which will be afterwards mentioned, exhibits her in a sulky and unamiable mood. Terentia also and Pomponia did not get on very well together. The frequent quarrels of the ill-matched pair, Quintus and Pomponia, caused great distress both to Cicero and Atticus; Atticus naturally took his sister's part, and his displeasure at his brother-in-law's conduct was most probably the reason why, at a later period he abandoned the idea he once entertained of accompanying Quintus, in the capacity of quæstor, to his prætorian government in Asia Minor. Cicero was not at all blind to his brother's faults, but he also knew the many good points of his character; and it is pleasant to read the kind and affectionate terms in which he always speaks of him, until unhappily they quarrelled many years after, as I shall have occasion to relate in a subsequent part of this work. In the letter to which I am now alluding, he tells Atticus that he might appeal to Pomponia herself to say how earnestly he had endeavored to induce her husband to treat her with proper affection. Quintus was displeased at this interference, and Cicero says that he had written to him to appease him as a brother, to admonish him as a junior, and to reprove him as an offender. Other topics in the same letter are two matters of business in which Atticus was interested, but about which nothing certain is now known. Cicero takes occasion also to correct his friend in a point of law, and tells him that the doctrine of adverse possession has no application in a case of trust or question of guardianship; which is very much what an English lawyer would say at the present day. Atticus had asked him to employ his good offices in reconciling Lucius to him, for they had had a quarrel; and Cicero assures him that he had done so, but to little purpose. He next congratulates Atticus on his recent purchase in Epirus, and begs him to remember to get anything which may be suitable for his own Tusculan villa; 'for there,' he says, 'in that place alone do I find rest and repose from all my troubles and toil.' This is the first mention that occurs in Cicero's writings of his favorite villa at Tusculum, which he seems to have bought only a short time before. He concludes the letter by telling Atticus that Terentia is suffering a good deal from rheumatism in the limbs; and that she and his darling Tulliola send their best compliments to him, and his sister and mother. The last words are: ' Be assured that I love you like a brother.' In the next letter, which is short, Cicero promises that Atticus shall not again have to complain of him as a negligent correspondent, and begs his friend, who has plenty of leisure, to copy a good example. He mentions that Fonteius has purchased the home of Rabirius at Naples, which Atticus had had some thoughts of buying; and says that his brother Quintus now seemed to be on good terms with Pomponia, and that they were both staying at his country residence near Arpinum. The manner in which he communicates the next piece of intelligence is disappointing, if we accept the usual reading. It is the death of his own father, and all he says on the subject is this: ' My father died on the 25th of November.' He then turns off to ask Atticus to look out for appropriate ornaments for his Tusculan villa. This looks, to say the least, cold and unfeeling; and yet Cicero was the very reverse of being either cold or unfeeling. We have seen that he deplored in the language of genuine sorrow the loss of his cousin Lucius, and we learn that his grief for the death of his daughter Tullia was so excessive that he was derided for it by his enemies. We are therefore surprised to find him noticing so shortly and dismissing so summarily the death of his excellent father. But the truth is that what we call *sentiment* was almost wholly unknown to the ancient Romans, in whose writings it would be as vain to look for it as to look for traces of Gothic architecture amongst classic ruins. And this is something more than a mere illustration. It suggests a reason for the absence. Romance and sentiment came from the dark forests of the North, when Scandinavia and Germany poured forth their hordes to subdue and people the Roman Empire. The life of a citizen of the Republic of Rome was essentially a public life. The love of country was there carried to an extravagant length, and was paramount to and almost swallowed up the private and social affections. The State was everything; the individual comparatively nothing. In one of the letters of the Emperor Marcus Aurelius to Fronto, there is a passage in which he says that the Roman language had no word corresponding with the Greek φυλοστοργια, the affectionate love for parents and children. Upon this Niebuhr remarks that the feeling was 'not a Roman one; but Cicero possessed it in a degree which few Romans could comprehend, and hence he was laughed at for the grief which he felt at the death of his daughter Tullia.' His divorce from Terentia appears to be a violent exception to the general rule of his character; and we shall have to consider hereafter whether he can or cannot be justified for his conduct on that occasion. In these first letters we get a few glimpses of his domestic life. He tells Atticus that his daughter Tulliola, his darling (*delicæ nostræ*), is betrothed to Calpurnius Piso Frugi. This event, which we should have thought full of interest to him, he mentions in the most laconic manner — *Tulliolam C. Pisoni L. F. Frugi despondimus.* The young lady was then only nine, or at the most eleven years old. Atticus had promised her a present, and Cicero tells him that she looked upon her father as bail for the performance, but he intended rather to forswear the obligation than make it good. In another letter he says that Tulliola has brought her action (*diem dat*), and summoned bail."

Thus we learn the kindly disposition, the playful moods of the real Cicero, about whose letters there is a charm to which we have nothing comparable in all antiquity.

CHAPTER XIX

THE LETTER (CONTINUED)

CHESTERFIELD

Lord Chesterfield.— In English literature we count a number of distinguished authors who have left permanent contributions in the shape of letters; among these, none more distinguished than the " first gentleman of Europe," the glory of the reign of Queen Anne — Lord Chesterfield. Like Saint Paul and Cicero, Lord Chesterfield enjoys a world-wide reputation; and any summary of the history of letter-writing howsoever meagre, could not exclude him from special notice.

Biographical Data.— The fourth Earl of Chesterfield, Philip Dormer Stanhope, was born in London on September 22, 1694; in his early training he had all the advantages that wealth and nobility afforded. His education, begun under private tutors, was completed at Cambridge. He traveled much on the continent, admired the French above all other continental races and resolved on his return to teach his boorish countrymen, their art of deportment and good manners. He observed the sharp contrast between the polite, polished Frenchman and the rough, ill-mannered Saxon. He entered the House of Commons, but his oratory was ineffective; he lacked force and power; he drifted into the House of Lords; was several times a British Ambassador on the continent and once Lord Lieutenant of Ireland. On the whole, his political life was not brilliant, but it brought him into contact with the eminent men

of his time.   Chesterfield is described as a man of splendid
intellect, extraordinary fervor and energy, a close observer
of life and conduct.   He had lived in courts and grew accustomed to all kinds of diplomatic warfare; he knew all the
literary and political lights of his day.   Like Matthew Arnold,
he was an apostle of sweetness and light to the British Philis-
tine.   To him Dr. Johnson was a typical Briton, and as Chesterfield termed him, ' a respectable Hottentot.'   He continually complains about our Teutonic love of the vast, the
vulgar and the horrible.

The Charm of His Manners.— The name of Chesterfield has
become a synonym for good breeding and politeness.   It is
associated in our minds with all that is graceful in manner,
attractive in appearance and polite in speech.   He was the most
popular man of his age.   His manners were so fascinating
and his personal appearance so attractive that he was styled
the first gentleman of Europe.   'He forced life, writes Saintsbury, to yield him all the happiness that it is capable of afford-
ing; socially, his career was like a triumphal procession, not
the dull round of cares allotted to most men.   He may be
considered as a splendid type of the successful man of the
world.

Literary Work.— The literary work of Chesterfield is extensive.   His long life was largely one of leisure; and he
devoted much of it to various kinds of writing.   He wished
to become known as a patron of letters and of literary men.
But his fame as a writer rests exclusively upon a volume of
letters written to his son and grandson, and first published
in 1744.

Subject-Matter of the Letters.— The letters, taken collectively, are a system of precepts intended to train a man for

worldly success. According to Chesterfield, there are three chief sources of success in this world : first, knowledge ; second, energy ; third, manners. The letters of Chesterfield lay almost equal stress upon knowledge, energy and good manners. On the value of knowledge he writes thus : " You cannot expect to succeed in this world without knowledge, for an ignorant man is contemptible and insignificant ; he may be said to exist — he does not live. However industrious or however polite you may be, you will never gain the highest respect of people unless you possess a cultivated intelligence." Lord Chesterfield emphasizes two kinds of knowledge : first, the knowledge of books. " I would have you," he writes to his son, " acquainted with the best that has been thought and written ; for acquaintance with the best thought will bring you into the company of the ablest minds ; it will stimulate high and right thinking in yourself ; and such company will be a refuge from the cares of active life. Those men are unfortunate who have not in youth acquired a taste for such study. They are, so to speak, exiles from the best society." The second kind of knowledge which Chesterfield recommends, is that of men. He writes : " In the word, knowledge, I comprehend not only a knowledge of books, but also a knowledge of the world — that knowledge which is gained from actual contact with living men ; and which for practical purposes is more valuable even than that of books. It is true that a knowledge of the world can be acquired only in the world ; but I would have you begin this study now, in the miniature world around you ; make a careful study of your school companions ; observe their conduct — the chief traits of each character, and compare one character with another These studies will serve as a basis for the knowledge of mankind. Remember that your success in after life depends largely upon your ability to deal with our fellow men ; and you cannot deal with them successfully unless you study and know them. They must be studied as you study books."

Energy and Application.— After knowledge, Chesterfield urges energy as the second source of worldly success. He constantly repeats this advice to his son, to be energetic, active, industrious. And in one of his letters he employs that frequently quoted maxim: Whatever is worth doing at all, is worth doing well. Writing about energy as a factor in worldly success, Chesterfield insists upon the necessity of forming in youth a just estimate of the value of time. " Whoever values time aright will form habits of industry. He will be energetic and active. What I do, and ever shall regret, is the time which while young I lost in mere idleness and in doing nothing. This is a common defect of youth against which I beg you will be most carefully upon your guard. Every moment may be of some use, even moments devoted to pleasure and recreation, for the mind may be always alert; and society will yield knowledge as well as pleasure." Again he writes: " Whatever you do, do it with all your power, with all your energies centered therein for the time being. Success depends upon the concentration and the awakening of all one's energies; while failure is too frequently the result of a slovenly and partial application of these energies. I beg of you to pardon my repetition of this advice, but I would have you energetic in youth, especially in the mastery of knowledge; for remember that whatever knowledge you do not solidly lay the foundation of in youth, you will never be master of while you breathe."

Good Manners.— Finally, the letters of Chesterfield emphasize the necessity of good manners as a condition and source of success in the world. His letters have become famous on account of their extensive and careful treatment of this subject. Fourteen letters are devoted exclusively to a discussion of the rules of right conduct; and —,throughout the remaining letters this subject is repeatedly introduced. He writes: " You must always expect to hear more or less from me upon the subject of good manners. Great talent and industry will gain the esteem of mankind; but politeness and good manners are equally necessary to success. Intrinsic merit will win the admiration of all: it will not win the affections of any. All people are not judges of great learning and talent; but all men understand civility; they understand when conduct is obliging and agreeable; they easily and quickly determine good-breeding." Chesterfield is accused of over-estimating the value of politeness. But the world agrees with him in three particulars: first, that any man who respects himself should on all occasions and under all circumstances act the gentleman; second, that good breeding is to all worldly qualifications what charity is to all Christian virtues; third, that for success in public life, politeness and good manners are absolutely necessary.

Literary Merit of His Letters.—The style, as well as the subject-matter, makes these letters immortal. For the man who advocated the utmost gracefulness in conduct, and who exhibited it in his life, was no less graceful in the manner of his writing. "The letters," says Hutton, "are models of neatness, elegance, purity of diction; they are ideal in the graceful adjustment of form to subject-matter." Chesterfield in this species of composition gives the following advice to his correspondent: "The art of letter-writing is by no means an easy one to master. The familiar letters which you write should be patterned after conversation, where the highest art is to conceal art; a letter of that kind should seem easy, natural and not smell of the lamp; the smallest traces of artifice are offensive. Above all, let your letters speak what I trust in God you will always feel — the utmost gentleness and humanity."

CHAPTER XX

THE LETTER (CONTINUED)

MISCELLANEOUS EXAMPLES

Pliny.— Pliny, surnamed " The Younger," in order to distinguish him from the elder Pliny, his uncle, was born at Como, Italy, 62 A. D.; died 113 A. D.   He took the name of *Caecilius* from his father, who had married Plinia, the elder Pliny's sister.   Pliny is described as a man of refined taste, highly accomplished, devoted to literature, kind and indulgent to his freedmen and his slaves, gentle and considerate in all his family relations, just in his dealings, munificent in the use of his wealth, humane and forgiving to all who had offended him.   He was a lawyer by profession, a pupil of the famous Quintilian.   His letters were directed for the most part, to the Emperor Trajan who had the sincerest regard and affection for their author.

Value of these Letters.—There are few remains of Latin prose literature so elegant, interesting and varied as Pliny's letters.   They were written and published on the model of Cicero's letters, and they cannot fairly be called inferior to those of Cicero himself.   They are all carefully composed and couched in the most graceful and polished Latinity.   Blair writes the following criticism :   " Pliny's letters are one of the most celebrated collections which the ancients have given us, in the epistolary way.   They are elegant and polite, and exhibit a very pleasing and amiable view of the author.   Indeed, they are too elegant and fine; and it is not easy to avoid thinking that the author is casting an eye towards the public, when he is appearing to write only for his friends. Nothing, indeed, is more difficult than for an author, who publishes his own letters to divest himself altogether of attention to the opinion of the world in what he says; by which means he becomes much less agreeable than a man of parts would be, if without any constraint of this sort he were writing to his intimate friend."

Pascal.— He was born at Clermont-Ferrand on June 19, 1623; died at Paris, August 19, 1662. He was a distinguished French philosopher, geometrician, writer. His literary activity was due to his connection with the celebrated monastery of Port-Royal. He rose to the highest literary excellence in setting forth and defending the doctrines of Port-Royal against the Jesuits. As a result we have a collection of letters that enjoy a world-wide reputation.

Value of His Letters.— The following criticism is offered by Professor Saintsbury:

Criticism by Saintsbury.—" These letters of Pascal are the first example of French prose which is at once considerable in bulk, varied and important in matter, perfectly finished in form. They owe not a little to Descartes, for Pascal's indebtedness to his predecessor is unquestionably from the literary side. The unanimity of eulogy as to the style of these wonderful letters has sometimes tempted foreigners who feel or affect to feel an inability to judge for themselves, into a kind of scepticism for which there is absolutely no ground. The first example of polite controversial irony since Lucian, these letters have continued to be the best example of it during more than two centuries, in which the style has been sedulously practiced, and in which they have furnished a model to generation after generation without being surpassed by any of the works to which they have shown the way. The unfailing freshness and charm of the contrast between the importance, the gravity, in some cases

the dry and abstruse nature of their subjects and the lightness, sometimes almost approaching levity in its special sense,
of the manner in which these subjects are attacked, is a triumph
of literary art of which no familiarity dims the splendor, and
which no lapse of time can ever impair. The vividness and
distinction of Pascal's phrase, his singular faculty of inserting
in the gravest and most impassioned meditation, what may
almost be called quips of thought and diction without any loss
of dignity, the intense earnestness of meaning, weighting but
not confusing the style, all appear in his ' Thoughts ' and
' Letters.' "

"**Junius.**"— An unknown writer employing this signature,
wrote a volume of world-famous letters, the authorship of
which has baffled the critics of two centuries. These letters
were written between January 21, 1769, and January 21, 1772.
They were published in the *Public Advertiser,* a popular newspaper of the period. They attacked the King and the officials
of government. Edmund Burke remarked in the House of
Commons, " For my part, when I read this attack upon the
King, I own my blood ran cold; Kings, Lords and Commons
are the sport of his fury." The authorship of these letters
has been attributed to no less than thirty-five persons — probably to none with a better show of reason than to Sir Philip
Francis. But although the authorship is unknown, these letters, next to those of Chesterfield, are the most famous in our
literature.

Value of the Letters.— Mr. Wade, in his preface to *The Letters* offers the following criticism: " As there is little in the
subject-matter of these famous epistles that could confer upon
them such enduring celebrity, they must be mainly indebted
for it to the writer's extraordinary powers, the varied resources
of which have enabled him, with the peculiar characteristic of
genius, to dignify and immortalize that which in its own nature, is secondary and perishable. In this respect Junius

stands alone — he is the Napoleon of public writers; and, like the author of the first and noblest epic, though he has a host of imitators, he is still without an equal." Mr. John M. Good, a contemporary critic, writes: " The classic purity of their language, the exquisite force and perspicuity of their argument, the keen severity of their reproach, the extensive information they evince, their fearless and decisive tone, and, above all, their stern and steady attachment to the purest principles of the constitution, acquired for them, with almost electric speed, a popularity which no series of letters have since possessed, nor perhaps ever will; and, what is of far greater consequence, diffused among the body of the people a clearer knowledge of their constitutional rights than they had ever before attained. Enveloped in the cloud of a fictitious name, the writer of these letters, unseen himself, beheld with secret satisfaction the vast influence of his labors, and enjoyed the universal hunt that was made to detect him in his disguise — he beheld the people extolling him, the court execrating him, the ministers, and more than ministers, trembling beneath the lash of his invisible hand."

Newman.— Cardinal Newman, " the English Cicero," was born in London, Feb. 21, 1801; died at Edgboston, August 11, 1890. An unrivalled master of English prose, Newman has left several volumes of letters, two of which were published recently. The following criticism of his style is offered by the Editor of this Manual: There is a peculiar charm about the prose writings of Newman, particularly so after his literary powers had fully matured. This charm is emphasized in his letters, where the restraints of publicity are thrown off, and a revelation of his winning personality is made. If the letter be a revelation of character, then the letters of Newman are a literary prize, for they reveal those traits and gifts of mind and heart. which endear him to the English world. There is the full play of humor, the vivacity of spirit, which resembles a youth on holiday, the warmth and color of personal experience, the frequent allusion drawn from his stores of classic learning, and above all, a fund of good nature.   In his letters, the asperities of polemic writing give place to ' humanism ' in the strict sense of that word.   As Tennyson says : " A warmth within the breast, melts the freezing reason's colder part."   There is, in the style of Newman, a twofold quality — the intellectual quality resulting from the careful discipline of an extraordinary mind — the freedom from artifice, the colloquial manner; the grace, ease, and charm which result from this happy union, are perceived at a cursory glance.   Perhaps Newman is equaled by no other writer in combining a hap-hazard manner with a very definite purpose.

It is necessary to notice here, in connection with his letters, only that happy colloquial manner, that urbanity and half-careless desultoriness which characterize so much of his epistolary correspondence; for if we accept the open letter addressed to the Duke of Norfolk, a letter which approaches the essay or treatise in style, we must see how closely he modelled his epistolary style upon Cicero, whose urbanity, ease and freedom suggest the polite familiarity of conversation without any accompanying tendency to be either commonplace or vulgar.   But after the last word of criticism is uttered, the charm of Newman's letters is the charm of a unique and delightful personality.

Pope and Swift.— A choice collection of letters comes from the pens of Pope and Swift and their contemporary friends, a collection which Blair calls the most celebrated in our literature.   He writes : " This collection is, on the whole, an entertaining and agreeable one; it contains very much wit and ingenuity.   It is not, however, altogether free from the fault imputed to Pliny's epistles, of too much study and refinement.

In the variety of letters from Pope and his friends, we find many that are written with ease and a beautiful simplicity. The letters of Dean Swift exhibit his character fully, with all its defects; hence they are not open to the charge of artificiality. But such is not the case with Mr. Pope — the censure of writing letters in too artificial a manner falls heaviest upon him; he is too fond of writing like a wit, and his letters to ladies are full of affectation."

Walpole.— Horace Walpole, the fourth Earl of Oxford, was born at London, October 5, 1717; died there March 2, 1797. His literary activity lay chiefly in the department of Memoirs and Letters; of the former the most remarkable are the Memoirs of George II. and George III. Of the latter, many volumes were written, some fourteen in all. The following criticism is offered by William P. Courtney: " The pen was ever in Walpole's hand and his entire compositions would fill many volumes. But his delightful *Letters* are the crowning glory of his life. His correspondents were numerous and widespread." The *Letters* were published at different dates, but the standard collection is that by Peter Cunningham (9 vols., 1857). Walpole has been styled the best letter-writer in the English language; and few, indeed, are the names which can compare with his. In these letters his very foibles are penned for our amusement, and his love of trifles — for, in the words of another Horace, he was ever " *nescis quid meditans nugarum et totus in illis* "— minister to our instruction. Through the medium of the letter he communicated to his friends every fashionable scandal, every social event, and the details of every political struggle in English life. Perhaps the best critical estimate of the author may be found in Macaulay's sketch of his life and character.

Montagu and Sevigné.— Lady Mary Montagu and Madame de Sevigné are perhaps the most distinguished women-writers in this department of literature. The former was a contemporary of Pope, born in London in 1690; died in 1762; the latter was born at Paris, 1626; died, 1696. The letters of both women are classics.

Criticism by Thomas B. Shaw.—"Lady Mary Montagu described her travels over Europe and the East in those delightful *letters* which have given her in English literature a place resembling that of Madame de Sevigné in the literature of France. Lady Mary was the first traveler who gave a familiar, picturesque and animated account of Oriental society, particularly of the internal life and manners of the Seraglio, to which her sex and her high position gave her unusual facilities of access. Admirable common sense, observation, vivacity, extensive reading without a trace of pedantry, and a pleasant tinge of half-playful sarcasm, are the qualities which distinguish her correspondence. The style is perfection; the simplicity and natural elegance of the high-born and high-bred lady combined with the ease of the thorough woman of the world. The moral tone, indeed, is far from being high, for neither the character nor the career of Lady Mary had been such as to cherish a very scrupulous delicacy. I have compared her to Madame de Sevigné, but the differences between the two charming writers are no less striking than the resemblances. In Lady Mary there is no trace of that intense and even morbid maternal affection which breathes through every line of the letters addressed to Madame de Grignan; nor is there any of that fetish-like worship of the court which seems to pervade everything written in the chilling and tinsel atmosphere that surrounded Louis XIV. In wit, animation, and the power of hitting off, by a few felicitous touches, a character or a scene, it is difficult to assign the palm of superiority. Lady Mary was unquestionably a woman of far higher intellectual calibre, and of a much wider literary development. She can reason and draw inferences where Madame de Sevigné can only gossip, though it must be allowed that her gossip is the most delicious in the world." . . .

Owing to her intimacy with the French Court, her letters are valuable from an historical point of view as well as for charm of expression.

Modern Examples.— The singular charm and grace of style found in the following collections is admitted by all critics: The *Letters* of Matthew Arnold, Coleridge, Carlyle, the Brownings, Shelley, Moore, Byron, Johnson, Goldsmith, Cowper, Goethe, Schiller, Voltaire, Balzac, Renan, Gladstone, Emerson, Hawthorne, Lincoln, and the encyclical *Letters* of Leo XIII. Some of these collections are combined with the biographies of the authors, which must tend to make them all the more entertaining and instructive. Almost every literary man of note in modern times has made some contribution to this department of literature. (For choice specimens of the *Letter,* see Appendix I.)

Works of Criticism.— No attempt has been made, as yet, to deal adequately with the criticism of the *Letter*. Criticism exists, but only in a fragmentary form, and in connection with other and more important works. Perhaps the largest amount of it is to be found in prefaces to volumes of Letters; in Biographies and Memoirs, and in the larger Encyclopædias.

CHAPTER XXI

THE ESSAY

A Standard Prose-Form.— The essay is a term applied to a species of prose-writing which ranks just above the letter on the scale of prose-forms. It is recognized as a standard prose-form; and in English literature has held a place since the days of Queen Elizabeth. At the present time it is the most popular form in the prose department, owing to the universal popularity of magazines and other periodical literature.

The Meaning of the Word.— The word, essay, comes directly from the French; indirectly, from the Latin. Originally it denoted a certain weight equivalent to 1½ drachmae. In French it had the meaning of trial, contest, or attempt. In English the word essay, retained this meaning; it signified a trial of strength, and applied equally to physical and mental acts. For example, a boat-race in the English Channel was called a "brilliant essay" by a sixteenth century writer. Outside of literature, the word still retains the meaning of trial or attempt. For example, Irving's *Sketch-Book:* "Our first essay in travel to catch fish was along a mountain brook." Tennyson's *Ode to Memory:* "Thou needs must love thy first essay." The accent is thrown on the last syllable wherever the word is used in its literal meaning.

The Word, Essay, in Literature.— The word essay meant originally a rough draft or first effort in practice. It implied a want of finish, an irregular, crude piece of work. Thus defined, the essay embraced all kinds of miscellaneous writing. For example, Cowley speaks thus of his translations: "This essay is but to show you how the classics look in English habit." Dryden writes: "I have made an essay of a letter to your Highness — one which must needs be corrected." The word essay applied equally to verse. For example, Addison referred to his tragedy of Cato as a "modest essay." The best poetical work of Pope received the title of essay: "The Essay on Man." "The Essay on Criticism." The title of essay is no longer applied to poetry.

Modern Use.— In modern times the word essay is restricted to prose. It is applied by some writers to a whole volume in prose. For example, Cardinal Newman's "Essay in Aid of a Grammar of Assent" or his "Essay on the Development of Christian Doctrine;" both of these are large and complete volumes. Locke's "Essay on the Human Understanding;" Burke's "Essay on the Sublime and Beautiful;" Freeman's "Essay on the Norman Conquest;" Butler's "Essay on Natural and Revealed Religion" are all examples in point. It is so used whenever a writer feels that his effort lacks comprehensiveness or whenever the subject of the prose volume is partially or inadequately treated. This application of the term to a whole volume is gradually dying out. The essay, as now understood, properly applies to a single, distinct, department of prose.

A Definition of the Essay as a Standard Prose-Form.— Lord Bacon, who first employed this prose-form in English, defines his essays as a series of notes set down significantly. He writes in the preface: "I have called these brief notes essays; the word is late, but the thing is ancient; for Seneca's Epistles, if you mark them well, are naught but essays." Bacon adopted this prose-form from the French, using Montaigne as a model; and he evidently employed the term in its primitive meaning as a crude literary attempt, fragmentary rather than complete. In modern times the essay represents something quite different from a rough draft or first sketch. During the past three centuries it has been improved and polished by such writers as Addison, Dryden, Lamb, Macaulay, Arnold, and at present it represents the very best literary work of which a prose writer is capable. It is defined as a brief prose composition, highly finished, with unity of theme and methodical development of thought.

A Work of Art.— Because the essay possesses unity of theme and methodical development, it ranks higher than the letter on the scale of prose-forms. In fact, it is distinguished from all miscellaneous writing by these characteristics. On the other hand, it is distinguished from higher prose-forms by its briefness. This characteristic has always marked the essay. The treatment given to any theme in an essay is necessarily incomplete and inadequate, owing to limitations. In this respect the essay bears the same relation to higher prose-forms that the Lyric bears to higher forms in poetry. Like the Lyric, the essay is brief; and, like the Lyric, it demands the highest literary finish and perfection. Addison, who has done some of the best work in this department, gives the following descriptive definition of the essay: "The essay is neither a dissertation nor a thesis; properly speaking, it is a work of art, and must conform to artistic rules. Hence, it requires unity; it must hang together, and round itself off into a separate literary entity. When written, the essay should be able to remain a lasting contribution to literature." De Quincey writes: "An essayist should make every sentence sparkle; he is never permitted to be a dull or slovenly workman. He should be always at his best; for the narrow limit within which the essayist works demands superior merit in the performance."

CHAPTER XXII

THE ESSAY (CONTINUED)

Origin and Development.— The essay is found in the oldest literature. As Bacon remarks, the name is new, but the thing itself is ancient. In the Bible and in the oldest Greek and Latin literature, the essay holds a place.

The Biblical Essay.— The Hebrews did not give to the essay that isolated character which it now possesses. We have no evidence that it was ranked by them as an independent prose-form; they invariably made it a part of a chapter or a book. And it resembles in the Bible the linked essay of modern times where several essays deal with a single theme, and afterward become chapters in a large volume. The literary study of the Bible demands the separation of verse from prose and their subdivision into the various literary forms. Among these forms, the essay in prose and the lyric in verse are found scattered throughout the mass of Hebrew literature. The essay prevails in those parts occupied with story, history and moral philosophy. For example, Exodus, Judges, Ecclesiasticus and Ecclesiastes and throughout the Wisdom literature.

Definition.— The Biblical essay is defined by Moulton as " a number of miscellaneous thoughts collected around a common theme." It lacks the coherence and literary finish of the modern essay. The Biblical essay is much shorter than the modern essay. It resembles the essays of Lord Bacon. The Biblical essay developed from two sources : In Wisdom literature it came from the proverbs, the order being: first, the proverb; second, the proverb-cluster; finally, the essay. In the historical Books, the essay was the first crude attempt of Hebrew writers to give unity and coherence to incidents of their narrative. Incidents in the life of these wandering nomads became themes or titles for their Historical essays. Hebrew writers, in sharp contrast with the Greeks, cared very little for art-form. Hence, the prose forms of the Bible, including the essay, are not only the oldest but perhaps the poorest models from an artistic point of view. However, there is no doubt that Montaigne, Bacon and Feltham imitated the Biblical essay in some particulars, especially in their synthesis of thought and brevity of sentence. Their talent for packing thought in the smallest compass was evidently stimulated by Biblical example. Montaigne admitted that the Bible taught him how to express his thoughts in the briefest and simplest way. And this is the chief reason why the Bible remains a prose model for writers of every age.

The Essay Among the Greeks.— In Greek literature the essay is found as a distinct prose-form. The Greeks who have furnished all models in verse and prose, have left a body of literature in the form of the essay. Considered as a literary form, the essay among the Greeks was of late growth. The first literary effort of the Greeks consisted in song and narrative, culminating in the epic. After the singer came the historian, when the Greeks were willing to exchange myths and legends for the facts of history. The lyric, the drama, the epic in verse, and history, biography and fiction in prose, preceded the essay in Greek literature.

A Period of Criticism.— When Xenophon, the first Greek essayist appeared, 430 B. C., Greek literature had passed through its greatest creative period; just as English literature had done when Addison and Steele began to write. When Xenophon appeared, an age of criticism had succeeded ages of literary creation, and Greek society had grown complex, self-conscious and introspective. Materials for criticism, both in life and literature, had accumulated before the essays of Xenophon appeared. Xenophon was an Athenian by birth. Like London in the English world, Athens was then the center of literary activity in Greece; and Xenophon found abundant material for criticism in the Athenian life and literature, just as Addison found it in the England of the eighteenth century. Like Addison, Xenophon preferred to treat of social, domestic and political matters in his essays. The literary reputation of Xenophon rests upon three kinds of work: history in the Anabasis; the historical novel in the Cyropædia or boyhood of Cyrus; and finally, the essay. Of his voluminous essays ten are still preserved; by far the larger number are lost. Among those preserved, we find such titles as Domestic Economy, Horsemanship, the Duties of a Cavalry Officer, the Revenues of Athens, Praise of a Spartan King. The essays preserved are, with two exceptions, essays in criticism. They are brief compositions in prose, highly finished, with unity of theme. In these essays Xenophon supplied the literary world with a new prose-form which has been in vogue ever since his time, 430 B. C.

Classifications of Greek Essay.— The Greeks divided the essay into five classes, the *monograph, dialogue, symposium, eulogy* and *memoir.*

Monograph.— The monograph, as the name indicates, is an essay dealing with a single theme and representing the original discoveries or investigations of a single writer. It was supplied by Xenophon in his essay on horsemanship; because the writer believed that his essay contained an original investigation into the methods for raising and training horses. In modern times the monograph is exactly synonymous with the scientific essay. It is applied to all brief prose compositions embodying original research. As science deals with parts and details of a class or species, this prose-form is admirably suited to scientific investigation.

Modern Use.—All scientists of modern times have made use of the monograph. Some celebrated examples of the monograph in modern scientific literature: Pasteur's Monograph on the Silk Worm; Huxley's Monograph on a Piece of Chalk; Mivart's Monograph on the Skeleton; Darwin's Monograph on Coral Reefs; Virchow's Monograph on the formation of Cells; Tyndall's Monograph on Heat as a Mode of Motion. Original investigation in any department of science is now published, as a rule, in the form of the monograph. This use is as old as science itself; for there is in ancient Greek literature a monograph by Euclid on Optics; and another on Harmony of Sounds by the same writer. The monographs of Archimedes on Spirals and on the Measurement of the Circle, are examples in point.

The Dialogue.— In the department of science the Greek essay was called a monograph to indicate its chief characteristics as a work of individual research. In philosophy the essay received two names, it was called either a dialogue or a symposium. It received the title of dialogue when two persons were introduced; when more than two were represented, it was named a symposium.

Definition of Dialogue.— The dialogue is defined as a brief prose composition with unity of theme, wherein the thought-development is carried on by the conversation of two persons. This method of thought-development satisfied the requirements of philosophical discussion; allowing scope for debate and introducing the disputants personally to the reader. Hence, in Greek essays upon philosophy we are introduced to the famous teachers of the Academy and the Lyceum, Socrates, Plato, Aristotle, Xenocrates, Polemo. The dialogue is sometimes called the Socratic method; as it was his favorite method of imparting knowledge. Cicero, who was a member of the Greek Academy, writes: " The Academy employs the dialogue merely to compare together different opinions, to see what may be advanced on either side, and to leave one's listeners free in forming their judgments." This was precisely its purpose in the philosophical essay of the Greeks. It was not introduced for the purpose of character study, as we find it in the drama. The revelation of character was never the primary purpose of the essayist. The subject treated, not the persons treating it, absorbed his attention. If the names of the debaters were introduced, it was done simply to engage the attention of the readers and satisfy the demands of discussion. On this point Aristotle observes: " Whosoever aims at instructing men, should engage their attention in his subject by his manner of treatment." Hence, the Greek use of the dialogue in the unattractive prose of philosophy. It enlivened the work, redeeming to some extent the barrenness of speculation.

Kinds of Dialogue.—In the form of dialogue the ancient philosophers wrote most of the essays handed down to us. The dialogue as found in these essays, is conducted in two ways: first, as direct conversation, where none but the speakers appear; the author himself remaining in the background. This is the method of Plato. Secondly, the dialogue reported with such modifications and comments as will give the author a prominent place in the essay. This is the method of Aristotle which Cicero learned in the Academy, adopted in his work, and which he praises as the most satisfactory way of treating philosophy. Plato intended the dialogue for entertainment and instruction. While he made no attempt to depict characters as they were drawn by Aeschylus or Sophocles there was a studied attempt in all his essays to make the speakers consistent and in a measure true to life. Hence, they were exhibited as polite in conversation, graceful in manner and passionate in debate.

The Greek Essay.— Among the philosophical essays of Greece the dialogues of Plato and Aristotle hold first rank; they were models for Greek and Latin writers; and in English literature they have many imitators. Dr. Blair writes of Plato: "In his dialogues the scenery and circumstances are beautifully painted; the conversation is supported with much dramatic coloring, for Plato was an idealist; he possessed the poetic as well as the philosophic temper; his imagination was quite as active as his intellect; as we may see in Phaedo and the Republic. Philosophy did not furnish the desired scope for his luxuriant imagination; hence, Plato had recourse to allegory and fiction."

The Dialogue-Essay in English Literature.— In English literature Bishop Berkeley imitated Plato. The philosophical essays of Berkeley written in the form of dialogue are unrivalled imitations of the Greek master. One point of difference: Berkeley cares less for the pictorial setting and environment of his characters; whereas, Plato cared as much for scenery as a dramatist. David Hume, like Bishop Berkeley, made use of Plato as a model. A collection of essays called "Dialogues on Natural Religion," were written by Hume in imitation of Plato. Hume is unquestionably one of the finest writers of English prose; but in the management of the dialogue he lacks the imaginative power of Plato. However, his style, less florid and figurative, seems to be better adapted to the requirements of philosophical discussion. Mallock, Lilly, Mivart and Ward are modern writers who occasionally use the form of dialogue in essays on philosophical subjects. But this method is no longer popular; the dialogue and the philosophical theme so treated are rapidly passing from the realm of the essay to the novel with a purpose. Aristotle's method of putting the author in the foreground together with the leaders of the dialogue, was imitated by Lucian and Cicero, but he has no imitators in English literature. The dialogues of Lucian are not philosophy; they are rather satirical essays on the pedantry of philosophy; they also ridicule the Pagan gods; they are gay and humorous; full of pleasantry — after the fashion of Voltaire. They add the comments of the author to the dialogue and manage to keep Lucian in the foreground, just as Aristotle had previously done. Cicero is the only distinguished writer in philosophy, who adopted the method of Aristotle. Of his method Cardinal Newman writes as follows: "A peculiarity of Cicero's philosophical discussions is the form of dialogue in which most of them are conveyed — the method followed by Aristotle. Cicero gained great advantages by adopting this method; in controverted questions he was not obliged to discover his own views; he could detail opposing arguments clearly; he could add his own views and comments throughout the essay; he carried the reader on by short stages and easy journeys. The dignity of his speakers, their mutual courtesy; the eloquence displayed on both sides, the clearness and terseness of the style throw a peculiar charm around his philosophical essays."

CHAPTER XXIII

THE ESSAY (CONTINUED)

The Symposium.— The symposium was a Greek essay in which three or more persons carried on a spirited conversation. It contained more life and movement than the dialogue, owing to the number of speakers engaged. All kinds of themes were discussed, as they are now discussed in the popular magazine.

Origin.— Xenophon wrote the first symposium in Greek. This essay has come down to us: it is called " The Banquet." In it we are introduced to Socrates and a party of disputants around a banquet table. The Greek symposium, unlike the Greek dialogue, offered several topics for discussion, thereby adding variety of theme to variety of speakers. Plato employed the symposium in philosophy, but his favorite form of the essay was the dialogue. In one example he introduces the pupils and the work of the Academy. The symposium was a popular form of Greek and Latin literature during the long struggle between rival schools of philosophy and between Christanity and Paganism. Apologists and sophists employed it. It was intended to appeal to the people, like a certain class of novels written for purposes of controversy. Cardinal Newman introduced the symposium into the Oxford controversy. A collection of essays written by him is called " The Story of a Convert." This work is a story only in name; it contains neither plot nor character-drawing. It is the Greek symposium copied from Xenophon and Plato, and found to be a successful method of defending his position. In the department of fiction

George Eliot's " Scenes from a Clerical Life " is a collection of essays in which clerical characters are grouped after the fashion of the Greek symposium; there is no plot or character-drawing, but the grouping is so arranged as to throw considerable light upon clerical life in the Church of England. The symposium in fiction was the forerunner of the short story which has now attained such great popularity.

Use in Criticism.— In English criticism there is one notable example of the symposium — the first one appearing in English literature; it was written by John Dryden and published in 1668. It is called an essay on dramatic poesy, and deals at considerable length with the principles of dramatic art. This symposium is remembered rather on account of the novel form than the thought; although his justification of rhyme in preference to blank verse in the drama was a new departure. Dryden contended that rhyme was quite as natural in the drama as blank verse and that it gave a necessary check to the imagination. Dryden introduces five speakers and varies the themes as the essay develops, in imitation of the Greeks.

The Modern Symposium.— The modern symposium differs from the Greek model in three ways: first, it deals with a single theme; secondly, it offers a fuller treatment of the subject and usually engages more persons in the discussion; thirdly, instead of being published as a single essay wherein the thought-development is carried on by conversation, the modern symposium is a small collection of essays printed together, linked to a single theme, and presenting that theme from various points of view. The symposium is a leading feature of all high-class periodicals, whether newspapers or magazines. The quarterly magazines alone are excepted from the general rule. All the great problems of modern life are discussed in this manner, and the advantage is obvious. Two magazines make a specialty of the symposium: the Nineteenth Century (British) and the North American Review. Almost every issue contains a symposium on some public question.

The Eulogium.— The fourth class of Greek essays received the name of eulogium. Eulogistic literature in prose took first the form of the essay; afterwards it was about equally divided between the essay and the department of oratory. The eulogy was an essay written in praise of some important personage. It applied equally to the living and the dead. It was an outgrowth of hero-worship which found expression in Homer, Hesiod, and the epic-cycle long before the advent of prose composition. Because of the human theme, the eulogy made a wider and stronger appeal than any other class of essay. It had a place in the miscellaneous writings of all Greek authors of note, and it is found today in every class of periodical literature. Its existence is a proof that the world honors the illustrious living and dead in all countries and in every age.

Origin.— The earliest eulogy found in Greek literature was written by Xenophon in praise of a Spartan king. Xenophon summarizes the virtues of his royal hero, emphasizing two in particular — his piety and strict discipline. Xenophon wrote another eulogy called " The Recollections of Socrates. It is the work of an admiring and affectionate disciple. In both essays the Greek writer idealized his subject; praise is bestowed without discrimination. Among ancient writers the most distinguished author of eulogies, outside the field of oratory, was Plutarch. One hundred and ten essays written by Plutarch are preserved; of these forty-six are eulogies. These eulogies deal with celebrated characters in Greek and Roman history; they are brief biographies such as are now printed in Quarterly Reviews. Quintilian constantly refers to Plutarch as " *Laudator temporis acti.*" The aim of Plutarch was to glorify and popularize the heroes of the past. Hence he dwells continually upon the wonderful deeds and virtues of historic idols. His page glorifies both Greek and Roman. His essays are compared with those of Macaulay: in both there is the sweeping assertion; the startling paradox; the long pompous sentence. Like Macaulay, though often inaccurate, he had a vast range of information. These eulogies were collected and published as " Plutarch's Lives." Besides the eulogies, there are nine examples of the symposium and seventeen dialogues among the essays of Plutarch.

In English.— In English literature, Dr. Johnson imitated Plutarch. He wrote a large number of essays which were used as prefaces in an edition of the English Poets. These essays eulogized the poets of England, each according to his merit; they were biographical and critical. Unlike Plutarch, Johnson mingled praise and blame, as the subject required; and Johnson's fame rests upon this essay work in biographical criticism, not upon his dramas or his ditcionary. The essays were afterward collected and published as " Lives of the Poets." The method of Johnson was adopted by contemporary essayists; he divided the essay into two parts giving about equal space to biographical data and to criticism. Macaulay imitated him in the essay on Milton — the first that he published and the one that made his reputation. Reviewers of any note since the time of Johnson follow his method in their magazine articles. Johnson gave the largest space to the merits and virtues of a writer; he placed the defects and faults in the background; and because the note of praise was the predominant note, his essays on English authors must be classified as eulogies. Eulogistic literature finds a place in all English magazines — the great channels of essay-publication.

Modern Use.—Some reasons are obvious for the surprising growth of eulogistic literature in the form of the essay. This growth is due in a measure to the growth of periodicals and magazines. It follows the law of supply and demand. Topics that appeal to the people are essential to the success of any publication. Hence, the mass of eulogies on persons who are, or who have been popular idols; they satisfy the demands of the multitude. A second reason — the multiplication of themes. The educational and moral advantages of democracy, developing individual life, character and personality, multiply themes suitable to the eulogy. A third reason: the prevailing modern tendency to know the secrets of extraordinary success in every department of human endeavor; hence, the general desire to draw near to great lives and pluck out the heart of their mystery. " It is," says Emerson, " the old story of the moth and the flame — the riddle of the human sphinx."

CHAPTER XXIV

THE ESSAY (CONTINUED)

The Memoir.— Besides the monograph, the dialogue, the symposium and the eulogy, there is a class of essays in ancient and modern literature called memoirs.

Meaning of the Word.— The term memoir in literature has various meanings and is applied to different kinds of literary work. There are two distinct meanings attached to the word. First, it is used as a synonym for memoranda or notes taken by a writer in study, travel, observation; miscellaneous items on any subject, without unity or order. For example, the note-book or scrap-book of an author. Secondly, it is defined as an essay relating to some subject within the writer's memory — some subject personally known to the author.

As an Essay.—As an essay, the memoir embraces three kinds of subjects. First, it deals with events in the life of some person intimately known to the author; in which case, it is classified as biography. For example, the Memorabilia of Xenophon dealing with events in the life of Socrates, with whom Xenophon as a pupil was intimately acquainted. An example in modern literature: Talleyrand's memoirs dealing with the life of Napoleon. Secondly, the memoir as an essay treating events in the author's own life. The memoir is then classified as autobiography. For example, the Apology of Socrates is an essay in defence of his conduct; the Apologia of Newman reviewing religious changes in his own life, is a collection of essays autobiographical in character. The memoirs of Gibbon the historian, Hume the philosopher, and Dryden the critic, belong to the same class. Thirdly, the memoir is an essay in natural history, dealing with the life of some plant or animal. It does not reveal the profound research or enlarged information expected in the monograph. It is rather material for scientific investigation than the result of careful scholarship. For example, the essays of Audubon on the birds of America, collected in five volumes and published as memoirs in ornithology. Darwin's Memoirs on Orchids and Climbing Plants. Memoirs of John Burroughs on the characteristics of American animals. This use of the memoir was adopted from the French, who apply it to any essay or collection of essays on animal or plant life. When animal or plant life was treated in a fictitious manner by ancient writers, or events narrated as if occurring among human beings, and intended to enforce some lesson, then the memoir was called an apologue. An apologue among the Greeks took the form of prose. For example, the essays of Æsop commonly known as fables. In English literature it is found in verse and prose: for example, the Hind and Panther; the story of Gulliver.

Basis of the Memoir.— Throughout its various applications, the memoir is based upon some reminiscences or recollections of the author. It is always written from the point of view of personal contact or experience.

As Biography.— The difference between memoirs and regular biography: Regular biography deals with an individual life in a systematic, consecutive and complete manner; whereas memoirs are at best but fragments, glimpses or partial views of the individual life. Hence memoirs bear the same relation to biography proper as a kaleidoscope does to a picture. Because the themes are fragmentary and disconnected, memoirs always take the form of essays. The plural, memoirs, is used in preference to the singular, because these essays are collected and found in volume form.

Literary Value.— Memoirs are a species of prose. In composition they admit of the same freedom of treatment as a letter. The author has the fullest liberty in the matter of selecting topics, and he may ramble at will; he usually casts aside the dignity of serious prose, and fills his page with anecdote, story, sketch, entertaining trifles of all kinds. But one quality is demanded — the composition should be written in a lively style and convey some knowledge worth acquiring. French writers excel in this class of work. Memoirs are more popular in France than in any other country. The English people, owing to national temperament, demand a more serious kind of prose. One class of memoir, called the apologue, has been popular in England, owing to the national love for moral allegory. The apologue is fictitious biography in essay-form, enforcing some moral lesson.

Tracts and Pamphlets.— English writers employ all the classes of essay found in Greek literature, using the same titles and copying closely the Greek models. They have added certain kinds of essay-writing which came into existence with the art of printing. Of these the pamphlet is first in the order of time. The pamphlet has always been a popular essay in England. Disraeli wrote: " Wherever pamphlets abound, there is freedom; " and therefore the English have been a nation of pamphleteers. The pamphlet is defined as a brief, controversial essay —a treatise in miniature. It deals with problems of current interest, usually with political and religious matters.

A Special Pleader.— The pamphlet is a special pleader, always partisan in tone. In supporting a creed or party, it may be descriptive, satirical, didactic; but it is always controversial. It is a record of popular feeling and its history represents the changeful currents of public opinion, from the time that printing began in England.

Synonyms.— Sometimes the pamphlet was called a tract; the terms are synonymous now and apply to the same kind of essay. For example, the Tracts of Newman and Pusey have the same significance as pamphlets. Originally, however, the pamphlet was more elaborate and had a wider circulation.

History of Tracts and Pamphlets.— The history of tracts and pamphlets is the most interesting chapter in the literary history of England. It is the record of great national debates carried on by the most gifted literary men, with all the bitterness and hostility the Saxon can command. The first national debate in England arose over the subject of religion. In the fourteenth century the Lollard doctrines and those of Wickliffe were warmly debated. Wickliffe and the Lollards sharpened the British appetite for pamphlets. Next came the Humanist movement, multiplying this class of essay in England. Humanism dated from Petrarch who dug up the ancient Latin and Greek classics and started a revival of learning. Humanism reversed the medieval ideals, making the most of this world by centering thought upon man and nature and thus placing the arts and sciences first in the curriculum of study. A craze for the new gospel swept over Europe, England included; the evangelists of resurgent paganism were the tract and pamphlet. Universities poured forth an endless stream of these essays. In the publications of Caxton for 1490, tracts and pamphlets have a large place; they were the source of popular instruction before magazines and newspapers came into existence. Among the Humanists of England, Sir Thomas More was the most illustrious pioneer. The period of his life extending from 1478 to 1535, witnessed the hardest struggles of the New Learning in England. More's first pamphlet, shortly after leaving Oxford, was an attempt to reconcile the New Learning with the Old. This pamphlet called *"Ad Dorpium"* was widely circulated and helped to break down monastic prejudice against the revivalists of the ancient classics, and especially against the sciences. More lamented the treatment of Roger Bacon and pleaded for a liberal attitude toward the sciences. More did not antagonize the ancient religion, but he did believe that the time spent by the Schoolmen in barren speculation could be more profitably employed in studying the arts and sciences. English reformers made use of tracts and pamphlets. In their attacks upon the English Church they invariably employed this kind of essay. Erasmus, the best literary critic of the time, regretted these theological quarrels on account of their evil effects upon literature. The best talent of England was wasted, so he thought, upon vile, unworthy productions. The tract and pamphlet of the Reformation were too hastily prepared to have literary merit. In form and in subject-matter they were cheap, vulgar, degrading — a filthy channel of abuse and calumniation, exhausting the vocabulary of hate and scurrility. Men who might have made lasting contributions to literature spent their days on this ephemeral work of religious controversy.

The Puritan Tract.— The Reformation reached a climax in Puritanism. The best specimens of puritan literature are the " Mar-Prelate Tracts " published in 1589; and the " Root and Branch Pamphlets " published in 1640. These puritan tracts and pamphlets were directed against the Church of England; and their aim was to uproot the idea of a religious hierarchy. Hence, the title " Root and Branch Pamphlets." The Mar-Prelate tracts originated in a religious persecution of the Puritans by Whitgift, archbishop of Canterbury, who acted under orders from Queen Elizabeth. The Puritans refused to subscribe to those doctrines of the English Church maintaining a

hierarchy. In the Mar-Prelate tracts the bishops and clergy
were bitterly attacked. Martin Mar-Prelate contributed forty
numbers to these tracts. Other writers like Penry, Throgmartin, Udal, swelled the list, all of which were named after Martin
Mar-Prelate. The Mar-Prelate Tracts provoked replies, the
most brilliant of which were written by Thomas Nash — a
pamphleteer whose chief weapon was satire. Nash wrote five
pamphlets in reply, after the style of Dean Swift. "A Month's
Mind for Pious Martin," was the most popular of these. The
Church of England employed the pamphlet as effectively as the
Puritans. But notwithstanding an increase in volume, tracts
and pamphlets at the close of the 16th and during the 17th century were a worthless addition to literature.

Essays of Milton.— The Mar-Prelate Tracts were followed
by the " Root and Branch Pamphlets." John Milton was the
chief contributor; he headed the list with a dozen essays
against Prelacy. These essays are unworthy of the author of
Paradise Lost. Outside of religious controversy, Milton wrote
prose with some sanity and merit; his essays on Education and
the Liberty of the Press are preserved from a mass of mediocre
prose. The great author passes this criticism on his own efforts: " I reluctantly left the calm and pleasing fields of literature, fed with cheerful and confident thoughts, in order to em-
bark in a troubled sea of noises and hoarse disputes." During
Milton's lifetime the publication of tracts and pamphlets was
the chief literary industry. Religious and political quarrels
brought on the Revolution. From 1640 to 1662, while the
Revolution was in progress, more than twenty thousand tracts
and pamphlets were circulated; they are preserved, many of
them, in the British Museum — a literary monument to the
fiercest struggle on English soil. Two names deserve mention,
besides that of Milton: Lord Halifax, a political pamphleteer,
three volumes of whose essays are preserved; and Daniel

Defoe, the author of Robinson Crusoe, who was sent to the pillory in 1704 for publishing religious tracts.

Pamphlets of the 18th Century.— In the 18th century the pamphlet underwent a wholesome change. While still controversial in character, it was written with more skill and taste. In the hands of Addison, Steele, Burke and Atterbury, this kind of essay became as polished and refined as any other class of literature. Addison expended as much time and care upon his political pamphlets written in defense of the Government, as he did upon essays for the Spectator. The most valued writings of Edmund Burke are found in pamphlet form. Two political events in the 18th century multiplied the pamphlet. The War of the Spanish Succession and the French Revolution. In the former case Addison, Steele and Dean Swift were the distinguished pamphleteers; in the latter, Edmund Burke. Dean Swift as a pamphleteer had no equal among contemporary writers. His qualifications for controversy included a fund of wit and humor, unrivalled satire, a strong party bias, an unlimited vocabulary of abuse. The political pamphlets which made his reputation are four in number: "The Conduct of the Allies"— a pamphlet dealing with the War of the Spanish Succession. Bolingbroke admitted that the circulation of this pamphlet kept the Whig party in power. The other three are: "The Barrier Treaty;" "Thoughts on Public Affairs;" "The Public Spirit of the Whigs." Dean Swift spent eleven years (1710–1721) writing political tracts and pamphlets, and contributing political essays to the Whig Examiner, the organ of his favorite party. He also contributed several essays to the Tatler and the Spectator. A contemporary of Addison and Steele, Dean Swift lacked their grace and finish; his style was that of the Puritan. According to Addison, he wielded his pen as he would a club. Outside the domain of politics, Dean Swift left some fine specimens of

the pamphlet.   Two essays, humorous and satirical, are worthy
of mention :   " A modest proposal for preventing the children
of poor people in Ireland from being a burden to their parents."
In this essay the proposal was to fatten and eat the surplus
children.   Swift's masterpiece of satire, outside of politics, is
the essay called " An Argument Against Abolishing Christianity."

Essays of Atterbury.— While Dean Swift defended the
Whig party, Atterbury wrote against the Whigs, and, like
Swift, employed the essay in pamphlet form.   Atterbury was
a bishop, the leader of the High Church party, and next to
Swift the ablest pamphleteer of the time.   According to Swift,
Atterbury by his writings, set everything on fire.   These
essayists crossed swords; and in a work called " The Battle
of the Books," Swift administered a crushing blow to his
rival.   Years afterward, he exclaimed :   " Great God ! what a
genius I had when I wrote that book."

Essays of Burke.— The French Revolution, like the Spanish
Succession, engaged the best writers and increased the volumes
of tracts and pamphlets.   The Satanic School of which Byron
and Shelley were the leaders, sang the praises of the Revolution in English verse; Shelley, had he the power, would
have reproduced in England the anarchy that disgraced
France in 1793.   In prose as well as verse, the merits of the
Revolution were discussed by Englishmen.   It was found
necessary to stem the tide of infidelity and anarchy setting
toward England; and Edmund Burke, like Dean Swift, was
the man for the hour.   He wrote two pamphlets : the first
one published in 1756 was called a " Vindication of Natural
Society."   It was a clever satire aimed at Bolingbroke and the
deistic School.   In this pamphlet Burke argued that civilized
society ought to be abolished in favor of savagery or the

purely natural state, because civilization is attended by so many abuses, miseries, crimes. These same reasons were urged against Christianity by the Deistic School of France and England. Burke saw that the rationalism which would overthrow revealed religion, was equally calculated to undermine political government. He foretold the political revolution of '93 fully twenty years before it occurred. The same reasons which justified anarchy in religious society, justified anarchy in political and civilized society. The pamphlet was meant to be a reduction to an absurdity of atheistic principles. In 1790 Burke wrote a second pamphlet called "Reflections on the Revolution in France." Like the first one, it attacked atheism; and added a condemnation of the French Revolution. It established the fame of Burke in England and on the Continent. Diderot, replying, said: "In spite of Edmund Burke, belief in God and submission to Kings will be at an end in a few years." Eleven editions of this pamphlet were sold during the first year of its publication. It was followed by another pamphlet called, "An Appeal from the New to the Old Whigs." This was a vindication of his criticism on the French Revolution. He replied to Diderot and Tom Paine. Paine had written the "Rights of Man"— a pamphlet justifying the French Revolution and attacking Edmund Burke. A War of Pamphlets followed, with the result that anarchy and infidelity, while possessing many friends among Englishmen, gained no considerable power in England.

Tracts and Pamphlets of the 19th Century.— The Tractarian Movement, sometimes called the Oxford Movement, derives its name from the circulation of tracts and pamphlets. The Tractarians, like the Puritans aimed at a religious reformation and employed this kind of essay as the Puritans had done in the days of Milton. Three literary men of note were connected with the movement: Keble, Pusey and Newman.

Their essays were called "Tracts for the Times." Of these Keble wrote four; the remaining eighty-six were written by Pusey and Newman. The most famous essay of the collection was Tract 90, written by Newman. Pusey wrote one remarkable pamphlet, the "Eirenicon." In this essay he tried to establish a basis of unity between the Church of England and the Church of Rome. Tract 90 had a similar purpose — to harmonize the 39 Articles with the Catholic Belief. In the political as well as the religous world tracts continue to play an important part. They are circulated publicly and privately in the interests of every kind of reform. America imitates England in the production of these essays. Men prominent in Church and State have occasion at one time or another to write pamphlets which circulate by thousands and enlighten the public on the problems and issues of the day. Much of the work formerly done by tracts and pamphlets printed in isolated form, is now accomplished by the Leader in our magazines and chief periodicals.

CHAPTER XXV

THE ESSAY (CONTINUED)

The Leader.— Along with the tract and pamphlet, the age of printing added the Leader to the various species of the essay. The leader, as the name indicates, is the most prominent essay in a magazine or periodical. In newspapers it is called the chief editorial; in magazines, the leading article. The Leader in magazines is the best written essay; it is supposed to make the widest appeal to the public; it is written by men of the finest literary culture. It is usually the opening essay, though not always so; and at the present time the title of the Leader and the name of the author are printed in heavy type on the cover of the magazine.

Literary Merit.— The magazine Leader in most cases is a permanent contribution to literature. The essays of Steele, Addison, Coleridge, Carlyle, Macaulay, were first published as Leaders in magazines, and afterward collected in their present form.

Publication of Leaders.— The printing of Leaders is as old as periodical literature itself. When Steele published the first English magazine during the War of the Spanish Succession, 1799, the very first issue contained a Leader from the pen of the editor; and Addison or Steele contributed Leaders as long as the " Tatler " and " Spectator " were published by them. The same method was employed by Jeffrey when the Edinburgh Review was started. For years he contributed the

Leaders, assisted occasionally by Sydney Smith; these men were succeeded by Carlyle, Christopher North and others who followed the same plan. Today the Quarterly Reviews and all magazines of any note publish Leaders.

The Chief Editorial.— The Leader in the newspaper, like the Leader in the magazine, is expected to make a special appeal. But the Editorial work in newspapers cannot compare with literary work in magazines. There are two exceptions: First, the Leader written in the London Times which is the official organ of the government. The chief editorial of the London Times is written by a specialist; it occupies two or three columns daily; it is understood to express in a semi-official way the policy of the British Government. It is an essay as carefully and ably written as any appearing in magazines. In America, the Leader published in the New York Sun is an essay of exceptional merit. So, also, are the Leaders of the New York Tribune, The Pioneer Press and a few other newspapers. But as a rule, this essay is ephemeral, too hastily written for permanence.

Subjects Treated.— In magazines, the Leader may deal with almost any theme. As a rule, however, these themes come under six heads: criticism, biography, history, science, philosophy, religion. Such subjects are of permanent interest and give permanence to literature. The first Leader in magazine literature was an essay in criticism. The author was a self-constituted judge of British society — its weaknesses and short-comings; these themes were the subject-matter of the essays of Steele and Addison. Gradually, the field of criticism widened, taking in history with Macaulay, biography with Carlyle, politics with Burke and Jeffrey. Religion, philosophy, science were added by such writers as Huxley, Arnold, George Eliot, Mivart, Spencer, Lilly, Mallock. The field of Addison and Steele was narrow in comparison with the vast range of subject-matter treated in the modern essay.

Popularity.— The Leader often sells a magazine and creates a demand for several editions. It is the first essay to be read on the editorial page of a newspaper. As might be expected, it has considerable influence in moulding public opinion. Unfortunately, the personal element is dying out of modern journalism — that element which the public sought and respected in former years — the element of which Horace Greeley and James Gordon Bennett and Charles A. Dana were such shining examples. Instead of this, we have the " inspired " articles, the impersonal voices of wealth and creed and party. Concerning Horace Greeley, it was written : " The name of the editor was a household word in thousands of homes, and it was with a feeling very closely akin to that of personal affection that Mr. Greeley was regarded by the readers of the " Tribune." Modern conditions seems to make such a thing an impossibility now ; hence, the waning influence of modern journalism upon the masses.

CHAPTER XXVI

THE ESSAY (CONTINUED)

REPRESENTATIVE ESSAYISTS

Their Number.— Any nation possessing an extensive literature may claim several essayists among its gifted literary
men. Thus Xenophon, Plutarch and Æsop among the
Greeks; Cicero and Nepos among the Latins; Montaigne in
France; Bacon, Addison, Macaulay, Arnold, in England. A
dozen or more names might be added to these, from each
civilized nation, ancient and modern, and the list would not
be complete.

Plutarch as an Essayist.— Plutarch was born at Chæronea,
Bœotia, Greece, about 46 A. D. His famous essays are part
biographical and part moral. The first class consists of forty-
six "parallel lives;" in these essays he devotes equal space
to Greek and Roman heroes. The second class consists of
essays moral and philosophical, known as "Opera Moralia."
The following criticism is offered by Muller: "In spite of all
exceptions on the score of inaccuracy, want of information, or
prejudice, Plutarch's essays must remain one of the most
valuable relics of Greek literature, not only because they stand
in the place of many volumes of lost history, but also because
they are written with a graphic and dramatic vivacity, such as
we find in few biographies, ancient or modern; because they are
replete with reflections which, if not profound, are always
moderate and sensible; and because the author's aim through-

out is to enforce the highest standard of morality of which a heathen was capable. He stands before us as the legate, the ambassador, and the orator, on behalf of those institutions whereby the old-time men were rendered wise and virtuous." Concerning the biographical essays, Mr. Paley writes as follows: "These essays are works of great learning and research, and they must have taken years in their compilation. Plutarch must have had access to a great store of books, and his diligence as an historian cannot be questioned, if his accuracy is in some points impeached." Concerning the Opera Moralia, he writes: "These consist of above sixty essays, some of them long, and many of them rather difficult; their literary value is greatly enhanced by the large number of citations from lost Greek poems, especially verses of the dramatists, among whom Euripides holds first place. They evince a mind of vast and varied resources, historical as well as philosophical — the mind of an inquirer and a seeker after knowledge, rather than that of an exponent or an opponent of any particular philosophical system. Plutarch's Greek is not fluent, easy or even clear. He uses many words not in the ordinary Greek vocabulary, and he too often constructs long sentences, the thread of which separately, as well as the connection, cannot be traced without close attention. Hence, he is not attractive as a writer, so far as style is concerned, and he is often diffuse and carries his discussions to an unnecessary length."

Xenophon, Cicero, Nepos.— Xenophon and Cicero have already been reviewed; their essays are among the best which have come down to us from antiquity. The dialogue-essays of Cicero have never been surpassed in purity and charm of style. The biographical essays attributed to Cornelius Nepos cannot be overlooked in any account of the ancient classic essayists. As a writer of this type, his style is so excellent, pure and attractive that he is used in almost every school and college by the students of Latin literature. As to the biographer of Nepos, nothing definite has been ascertained. He was probably a native of Verona, Italy, and lived in the first century, B. C. From the essays it may be inferred that he was a friend of Cicero. In imitation of Plutarch he wrote essays on the lives of illustrious men. Schwabe in his history of Roman literature offers this criticism: "Nepos has left us specimens of the oldest Latinity; his essays are valuable for their lucidity of arrangement, unpretentious tone, and fair and sympathetic judgments; but they hardly attain even a moderate level of accuracy and trust-worthiness as historical essays; at times, also, the style is inferior owing to the frequency of popular and colloquial idioms."

Montaigne.— The most famous of French essayists, was born in Dordogne, Feb. 28, 1533; died, Sept. 13, 1592. He was educated at home under a private tutor, and at Bordeaux College where he studied law. For a time he was attached to the Court of Francis II. He traveled extensively in Germany, Italy and Switzerland. At the French Court and during these travels, he had an opportunity to study the men and the society of his time. As a close observer of social affairs and of the actions of men, he resembles Bacon and Lord Chesterfield. The benefit of these observations is given to us in his essays, which are, according to some critics, the most valuable collection in this department of French literature. Concerning the style of his essays Montaigne himself offers this criticism: "It is a natural, simple and unaffected speech that I love, so written as it is spoken, and such upon the paper as it is in the mouth, a pithy, sinewy, full, strong, compendious and material speech, not so delicate and affected as vehement and piercing — rather difficult than tedious, void of affectation, free, loose, and bold, so that every member of it seems to make a body; not pedantical, nor friar-like, nor lawyer-like, but rather downright soldier-like. I decided to walk with my pen as I go with my feet, and let my mind move with its own natural step, not the steps of the dancing school or as those who leap on horseback because they are not strong enough in their legs to march on foot. The titles of my chapters embrace not always the matter, they often but glance at it by some mark." "There is," says Morley, "a grace in Montaigne's simplicity, a mixture of the Latin training with the homely vigor of his country's speech, that no translation fairly reproduces. The full enjoyment of Montaigne is reserved for those who read his essays through attentively. One may live long in the world and never come to know even a near friend as completely as one may know Montaigne by an attentive reading of his essays."

Criticism by George Saintsbury.—"The book of Montaigne's essays has hardly been second in influence to any of the modern world. This influence is almost equally remarkable in point of matter and in point of form, as regards the subsequent history of thought and as regards the subsequent history of literature. The latter aspect may be taken first. Montaigne is one of the few great writers who have not only perfected but have also invented a literary form. The essay as he gave it had no forerunner in modern literature, and no direct ancestor in the literature of classical times. It is indeed not improbable that it owes something to the body of tractates by different authors and of different dates, which goes under the name of Plutarch's *Morals,* and it also bears some resemblance to the miscellaneous work of Lucian. But the resemblance is in both cases at most that of suggestion. It has been suggested that the form which the essays assumed was in a way accidental, and this of itself precludes the idea of a definite model even if such a model could be found. Beginning with the throwing together of a few stray thoughts and quotations linked by a community of subject, the author by degrees acquires more and more certainty of hand, until he produces such masterpieces as the essay on the poetry of Virgil." "In the arrangement, as in the selection of his language, he is equally original, mixing Latin archaic and provincial words with a good deal of freedom, but by no means to excess. There is little or no trace in him of the interminable sentence which is the drawback of early prose in all languages when it has to deal with anything more difficult to manage than mere narrative. As a rule, he is careless of definitely rhythmical cadence, though his sentences are always pleasant to the ear. But the principal characteristic of his prose style is its remarkable ease and flexibility. These peculiarities, calculated in themselves to exercise a salutary influence on a language as yet somewhat undisciplined, acquired by accident an importance of an extraordinary kind. For, in the subsequent reformation of the French language only two writers of the older date held their ground, and these two were Rabelais and Montaigne. The essays of Montaigne, the popularity of which no academic censorship could touch, thus kept on through the succeeding centuries, and perpetuated a treasury of French in which every generation could behold the riches of their ancestors. The study of these essays influenced all the great prose-writers of France, and they could not fail to be influenced in the direction which it was most important that they should take by the racy phrase, the quaint and picturesque vocabulary, and unconstrained constructions of Montaigne."

Lord Bacon.— Francis Bacon, the English contemporary of Montaigne, was born in 1561 and died in 1626. A student at Cambridge, an English Ambassador, a member of Parliament, Lord Chancellor, a jurist, statesman, historian, philosopher, Lord Bacon has an additional title to fame for having left among his literary bequests to posterity a small volume of essays which now serve more perhaps than any other achievement to render his name immortal. A volume of criticism has been written on this small volume of essays. For, in every age since their production, and among all peoples critics have arisen who passed judgment upon them.

Criticism by Thomas B. Shaw.—"Among the English writings of Bacon the most important is the little volume entitled *Essays,* the first edition of which he published in 1597, and which was several times reprinted, with additions, the last, in 1625. These are short essays on an immense variety of subjects, from grave questions of morals and policy down to the arts of amusement and the most trifling accomplishments; and in them appears, in a manner more appreciable to ordinary intellects than in his elaborate philosophical works, the wonderful union of depth and variety which characterize Bacon. The intellectual activity they display is literally pretentious; the immense multiplicity and aptness of unexpected illustration is only equalled by the originality with which Bacon manages to treat the most worn-out and commonplace subject, such, for instance, as friendship or gardening. No one was ever so concise as Bacon; and in his mode of writing there is that remarkable quality which gives to the style of Shakespeare such a strongly marked individuality; that is, a combination of the intellectual and imaginative, the closest reasoning in the coldest metaphor, the condensed brilliancy of an illustration identified with the development of thought. Many of the essays are absolutely oppressive from the power of thought compressed into the smallest possible compass."

"Of Bacon's moral works the most valuable are the essays. It is impossible to praise too highly writings which have been so widely read and so universally admired. The matter is of the familiar, practical kind that 'comes home to men's bosoms.' The thoughts are weighty, and even when not original have acquired a peculiar and unique tone by passing through the crucible of Bacon's mind. A sentence from the essays can rarely be mistaken for the production of any other writer. His short, pithy sayings have become popular mottoes and household words. The style is quaint, original, abounding in allusions and witticisms, and rich even to gorgeousness with piled up analogies and metaphors."

Criticism by Dugald Stewart.—"In Bacon's essays the superiority of his genius appears to the greatest advantage; the novelty and depth of his reflections often receiving a strong relief from the triteness of his subject. The volume may be read from beginning to end in a few hours, and yet after the twentieth perusal, one seldom fails to remark in it something overlooked before. This is a characteristic of all Bacon's writings, and is only to be accounted for by the inexhaustible aliment they furnish to our thoughts."

CHAPTER XXVII

THE ESSAY (CONCLUDED)

Representative English Essayists.— Besides Lord Bacon, the representative English essayists are Addison, Carlyle, De Quincey, Jeffrey, Lamb, Macaulay, Smith, Steele, Swift, Mivart, Mallock, Huxley, Lilly, Harrison, Arnold. A large number of others, like Hume and Milton have written essays, but their larger works lie in other departments of literature. Only a few of the many who deserve honorable mention can be dealt with here.

Joseph Addison.— He claims our attention as one of the greatest of the English essayists. His father was an eminent clergyman of the Church of England, at Milston in Wiltshire, where the son was born in 1672; he died in 1719. Originally intended for the Church he drifted into literature and politics, principally through Dryden's influence over him, and the patronage of Lord Somers. Like Bacon, he became celebrated through his essays which are far more voluminous than those of his illustrious predecessor and which have evoked a large amount of criticism.

Criticism by Blair.—" Mr. Addison is, beyond doubt, in the English language, one of the most perfect examples of the writer; and, on the whole, the safest model for imitation. He is freest from considerable defects which the language affords. Perspicuous and pure he is in the highest degree; his precision, indeed, not very great; yet nearly as great as his subjects require; the construction of his sentences is easy, agreeable, and commonly very musical, carrying a character of smoothness more than of strength. In figurative language he is rich, particularly in similes and metaphors which are so employed as to render his style splendid, without being gaudy. There is not the least affectation in his manner. We see no marks of labor — nothing forced or constrained: on the contrary, we discover great elegance joined with great ease and simplicity. He is, in particular, distinguished by a character of modesty and of politeness, which appears in all his writings. No author has a more popular and insinuating manner, and the great regard which he everywhere shows for virtue and religion, recommends him highly. His style, perfectly suited to essays, lacks sufficient strength for the higher and more elaborate species of composition."

Criticism by Allibone.—" Perhaps no English writer has been so fortunate as Addison in uniting so many discordant tastes in a unanimous verdict of approbation. Brown has been thought pedantic, Johnson inflated, Taylor conceited, and Burke exuberant; but the graceful simplicity of Addison delights alike the rude taste of the uneducated and the classic judgment of the learned. All critics must agree with Dr. Johnson, who says — ' whoever wishes to attain an English style, familiar but not coarse, elegant but not ostentatious, must give his days and nights to the volumes of Addison.' The immense fertility of invention displayed in these charming essays, the variety of their subjects, and the singular felicity of their treatment will ever place them among the masterpieces of criticism. Nothing is too lofty or too lowly for his pen — the principles of morality and religion — the colored ribbons of the ladies — the grandeur of Milton — the gossip of the tea-party. This essayist was long esteemed the finest model of elegant yet idiomatic English prose; and even now the student finds qualities that never can become obsolete — a never-failing cleverness and limpidity of expression, and a singular appropriateness between the language and the thought."

Macaulay.— He was born at Rothley Temple, Leicestershire, October 25, 1800; died at Holly Lodge, December 28, 1859. He graduated at Cambridge, giving while there most attention to the classics. He held several official positions, but devoted most of his life to literature. His fame rests upon a " History of England," a volume of ballads, and several volumes of essays.

Criticism by Mark Pattison.—" The literary outfit of Macaulay was as complete as has ever been possessed by any English writer; and if it wants the illumination of philosophy, it has an equivalent resource in a practical acquaintance with affairs, with administration, with the interior of cabinets and the humor of popular assemblies. Nor was this knowledge merely stored in his memory — it was always at his command. Whatever his subject, he pours over it his stream of illustration, drawn from the records of all ages and countries. Figures from history ancient and modern, sacred and secular; characters from plays and novels, from Plautus down to Walter Scott and Jane Austen; images and similes from poets of every age and every nation; shrewd thrusts from satirists, wise saws from sages, pleasantries caustic or pathetic from humorists,— all these fill Macaulay's essays with the bustle and variety of some glittering masque and cosmoramic revel of great books and heroical men. His style is, before all else, the style of great literary knowledge. His essays are not merely instructive as history; they are, like Milton's blank verse, freighted with the spoils of all the ages. They are literature as well as history. In their diversified contents the *Essays* are a library by themselves; for those who, having little time for study, want one book which may be a substitute for many, we would recommend the *Essays* in preference to anything else."

Criticism by Alfred Welch.—" What impresses the reader of Macaulay is his skill in the delineation of character — his energetic, impassioned tone. From his vast and well-digested reading proceed the abounding mass and weight of his style,— a river of ideas and facts urged forward by an internal heat. He is so opulent that he makes criticism almost a creative art, and the author or work reviewed becomes a hint for the construction of picturesque dissertations, magnificent comparisons, and a glowing dialectic. His style is characterized by a wealth of illustration and adornment, antithesis of ideas, regular sequence of thought, harmonious construction and incomparable lucidity."

Criticism by Dean Milman.—" Macaulay's essays, for the most part, relate to English history. In virtue of their inimitable style, these essays will always give Macaulay a high place among English classics. His style was eminently his own, but his own not by strange words, or strange collocation of words, by phrases of perpetual occurrence, or the straining after original and striking terms of expression. Its characteristics were vigor and animation, copiousness, clearness, above all, sound English, now a rare excellence. The vigor and life were unabating; perhaps in that conscious strength which cost no exertion he did not always gauge and measure the force of his own words. Those who studied the progress of his writing might perhaps see that the full stream, though it never stagnated, might at first overflow its banks; in later days it ran with a more direct, undivided torrent. His copiousness had nothing timid, diffuse, Asiatic — no ornament for the sake of ornament. As to its clearness, one may read a sentence of Macaulay twice to judge of its full force, never to comprehend. His English was pure, both in idiom and in words, pure to fastidiousness, not that he discarded, or did not make free use of the plainest and most homely terms, but every word must be genuine English, nothing that approached real vulgarity, nothing that had not the stamp of popular use, or the authority of sound English writers, nothing unfamiliar to the common ear."

Thomas Carlyle.— He was born at Ecclefechan in Dumfrieshire on December 4, 1795; his life and work belong to the nineteenth century. He is one of the most original of all English essayists. Perhaps it would be true to say that his influence has been greater than that of any other English essayist, not excepting Macaulay himself. His voluminous writings belong, for the most part, to the departments of History, Biography and the Essay. The amount of criticism is large and varied, corresponding with the influence of the man, who, in spite of his many defects, is one of the largest and richest personalities in literature.

Criticism by William H. Sheran.— The style of Carlyle was quite normal until he began the study of German literature. Any reader of his early essays would be satisfied with the respect shown toward the English idiom by the young Scotch critic. But as his idiosyncracies developed with years, as he became immersed more and more in German literature — the study of Richter, Goethe, and others — his style lost its normal natural character; foreign idioms and turns of phrase began to appear; the extraordinary passion and intensity of the man broke all the prescribed bonds of speech, and, as a consequence, we have in his later writings a violation of about all the rules of grammar and rhetoric, and all the accepted canons of good taste, as if a cyclone in the literary order, had swept through his pages, tossing fragments of sentences about, wrenching and twisting idioms and phrases into an almost unrecognizable mass of verbal ruin, upheaving and uprooting the very foundations and the finer growth of our speech. Carlyle rides the whirlwind and directs the storm, enjoying, apparently, the havoc he makes with verbs and pronouns, cases and conjunctions. He gives his fiery indignation and enthusiasm full play, regardless of the laws of English speech. He strikes with sledge-hammer force, like Thor with his glittering hammer, dashing mountains to the earth; only, instead of a hammer, he used fragments of sentences. Hence, Carlyle is sometimes called a literary savage. Yet, after making the necessary deductions for his brutal use of rhetoric, one must admit that no English writer is more forcible, more noble in the pursuit of high ideals, than Carlyle. He was dissatisfied with the existing order of society, as he found it in his day, and, accordingly, he became an iconoclast like Shelley. He attacked social institutions with the same vehemence and bitter sarcasm; but, unlike Shelley, he spared religion and morality — he could never be an advocate of free love or pen the blasphemy of the author of "Queen Mab." His early Calvinistic training made him as severe in morals as a prophet of the Old Testament; and although, he lost all faith in Christianity, he never openly attacked the faith of his countrymen. In religion, he was, toward the end of his life, an avowed Agnostic. He frankly admits this in a letter to Emerson. Carlyle is a great name in English Criticism, deserving to rank with Dryden, Johnson, and Arnold. In range of information and devotion to his work, he was greater perhaps than any other English critic. He will be always remembered for his two famous sayings, " Genius is an infinite capacity for taking pains;" " whatever you do, do it with all your might." Carlyle should be remembered, not only for his moral maxims, but also for his interest in German literature, and in Northern Mythology. He was the first Englishman of Letters to devote himself to German studies, and to such an extent that Goethe admitted, Carlyle knew German literature and History better than the Germans themselves. He was also a pioneer in unfolding the literary riches of Northern Mythology; he lamented the fact that while Southern Mythology found adequate treatment at the hands of a Homer or a Virgil, there had been no Homer to sing of the heroes of the North. His own studies, though meagre and superficial, were nevertheless sufficient to show the immense literary possibilities of Northern Mythology.

Criticism by James Russell Lowell.—" Carlyle is the first in insight of English critics and the most vivid of English writers. The remarkable feature of Mr. Carlyle's criticism is the sleuth-hound instinct with which he presses on to the *matter* of his theme — never turned aside by a false scent, regardless of the outward beauty of form, sometimes almost contemptuous of it, in his hunger after the intellectual nourishment which it may hide. The delicate skeleton of admirably articulated and related parts, which underlies and sustains every true work of art, and keeps it from sinking on itself a shapeless heap, he would crush remorselessly, to come at the marrow of meaning. In his critical essays he had the advantage of a well-defined theme, and of limits which kept his natural extravagance within bounds and compelled some sort of discretion and compactness. The great merit of his essays lies in a criticism based on wide and various study, which, careless of tradition, applied its standard to the real and not the contemporary worth of the literary performance to be judged. But in proportion as his humor gradually over-balanced the other qualities of his mind, his taste for the eccentric, amorphous, and violent in men became excessive, disturbing more and more his perception of the more commonplace attributes which give consistency to portraiture. No other writer compares with him for vividness. He is himself a witness, and makes us witnesses of whatever he describes. This is genius beyond question; and of a very rare quality. If not a profound thinker, he had what was next best — he felt profoundly, and his cry came out of the depth. With the gift of song Carlyle would have been the greatest of epic poets since Homer. Without it, to modulate and harmonize and bring parts into their proper relation, he is the most amorphous of humorists, the most shining avator of whim the world has ever seen. Beginning with a hearty contempt for shams, he came at length to believe in brute force as the only reality, and has as little sense of justice as Thackeray allowed to women. Still, with all deductions, he remains the profoundest critic and the most dramatic imagination of modern times — such vivid pictures of events, such living conceptions of character, we find nowhere else in prose. As an inspirer and awakener his value cannot be overestimated."

Matthew Arnold.— A representative English essayist of modern times, Matthew Arnold was born in 1822; died in 1888. He was a son of the famous Dr. Arnold of Rugby, and a member of a family distinguished in English literature. Like Carlyle and Macaulay, he devoted his life to letters, excelling both in verse and prose. His favorite prose-form was the essay, and the bulk of his prose writing lies in this department. His essays, like those of Addison, are most highly finished productions. Like Johnson, he was a critic, but on a larger scale; he resembles Carlyle in the range and freedom of his criticism. To his countrymen he professed to be an apostle of culture in the highest and best sense of that word. The many volumes of his prose deal with the various aspects of culture.

Criticism by William H. Sheran.— The essays of Arnold are among the best in English literature — the result of a splendid literary gift, and the highest classical culture.

The purpose throughout all his criticism is to make known the best that has been thought and said in the world. As a critic of life, he aimed at the highest ideals, sought to make culture, sweetness, and light prevail among his countrymen. He imitated the example set by Lord Chesterfield, in the matter of improving the conduct and manners of his fellows, just as in literature he was a constant student and imitator of Newman. The least valuable part of his criticism deals with the Bible and theological subjects. Arnold had not the mental and scholarly equipment necessary for producing any work of permanent value in those departments. The poetry of Arnold should be noted on account of its quality. Nowhere is his literary gift shown to better advantage. "Dover Beach," "Obermann," "The Future," are lyrics of the best class; as a dramatist, he was a failure, having no talent for character creation.

Criticism by Richard Hutton.—"There is in the style of Arnold much sweetness, beauty and light, calm contemplation and exquisite polish. The essays are a collection of some of our best prose. His style is often plain and business-like, sometimes colloquial, never highly ornamental, occasionally marred by ' damnable iteration.' A vein of sarcasm and of rich humor may be found in it at times, but never the biting cynicism of Carlyle. A finished expression was at most times his studious care. Traces of the French idiom may be found, but for the most part, he exhibits classic purity in idiom and in diction."

CHAPTER XXVIII

BIOGRAPHY

Meaning of the Term.— The word, biography, signifies writing which deals with life. It is life-history; and wherever individual life is manifested, the material for biography is supplied. The word is used in a double sense. In its widest meaning it includes the life-history of plant, animal, man and the orders of life above man so far as they are revealed to us. Thus, for example, we have the Biography of the Climbing Plant; the Biography of Napoleon; the Biography of Christ. Biography in its widest meaning deals with the same subjects as biology, but in a different manner. Biology is a science treating of all the phenomena of life; it aims at discovering and classifying all the data concerning life; whereas biography selects only such data as will make the strongest appeal and awaken the liveliest interest. It selects those facts of life which individualize the subject and mark it off from the species. For example, peculiar traits of character or lines of conduct in the human hero. And these selected facts of life are given not in the form of a scientific treatise, as is the case with the various departments of biology. They are presented in the form of a story which gives scope to the imagination and the personal bias and the creative genius of the author. Biography in the strictest sense is a department of literature dealing with human life. When individual human life is treated we have Biography proper; whereas collective human life, for example, the life of a nation, a race or a period, when so treated, is called History.

The Relation of Biography to History.— The provinces of the historian and biographer are distinct, although closely related. On this point, Leslie Stephen, the author of the Dictionary of National Biography, observes: " Biography is closely related to history because most events are connected with some particular person. For example, it would be impossible to describe the Norman Conquest without some reference to Harold or William the Conqueror. And so with every other period. Hence, history depends upon biography for its material; it selects that part of every man's life which belongs to the public, and leaves the details of his private life to the biographer." It follows that the study of biography is supplementary to that of history; it furnishes those portions of the individual story which the historian passes over. It also gives a better chance to study human character, because the individual life is presented in its completeness.

The Relation of Biography to Other Departments of Literature.— Biography furnishes subject matter for all departments of literature. It supplies those humanizing elements which distinguish literature as such from other kinds of writing, especially from science and philosophy. The amount of biography employed in the different departments of literature varies, but it is present in all, and is of vital interest in all.

Some Illustrations.— The letter tells either of the author's own life and experience, or that some other person. Two departments of the essay are strictly biographical — the memoir and the eulogy. Besides these, the essay in criticism is in a large measure biographical; for example, the critical essays of Macaulay and Johnson divide their space about equally between biography and criticism. One division of oratory is wholly biographical, namely, the panegyric. And when not exclusively such, the oration either employs biographical data or makes some individual life the central topic. For example, the orations of Cicero and Demosthenes hinge upon such characters as Catiline or Philip. Webster and Burke make an equally profitable use of biography. Another department of oratory, the Christian sermon, deals for the most part with important personages of the Church; the bulk of this literature is an exhortation to imitate the individual life of Christ, and biographical data of this life are continually employed. The largest use of biography outside of history, is found in the drama and in fiction, which is a part of dramatic literature. The individual is reproduced in his habit as he lived, and facts of biography are needed for the purpose. The best examples in English are the historical dramas of Shakespeare; and the historical novel as written by Lytton or Walter Scott. A novel or drama which attempts to reproduce any historical personage must do so through the medium of biography. The epic, in like manner owes much to biography, although the bulk of the long narrative poems which receive this title present heroes about whom few details are known; yet the facts, though scant, belong to biography. And, last of all, the lyric tells the brief story of a passing mood or feeling, and thus gives a glimpse of individual life. Although brief, the lyric is intensely human and personal, and a record of the facts of life. Thus, all departments of literature employ biographical matter. As Walter Pater writes: " Literature is biography in solution; for the human element is ever present in one form or another."

Sources of Biography.— Biography proper deals with historical personages, men and women of eminence who have lived and left traces of their lives. Hence, the biographer works with documents, for documents are the traces left by the thoughts and actions of men of former times; through documents the biographer learns all that can be learned of the illustrious persons of the past.

The Collection of Documents.— The first work of a biographer is to collect documents, all the accessible sources of information. This work was never easy, although much easier now than in ancient times. The increased facilities for consulting archives and libraries make the work much easier. The earliest scholars consulting, as they did, not all the documents, nor even the best documents, used whatever were at hand; and, hence, traces of their ignorance in the early biographical works. For example, Plutarch's " Lives " in which imagination so often goes into partnership with fact. At the present time the libraries and archives of the world are thrown open to the scholars; expeditions are sent out yearly by the various governments for the discovery and collection of documents. Besides the large public collections in museums and archives, there are equally valuable private collections. These are owned either by individuals or corporations. For example, the Monks of the East still hold in their monasteries invaluable documents. Several modern attempts have been made to centralize and create one large storehouse of documents; for example, the first Napoleon entertained the design of concentrating at Paris the archives of the whole of Europe, and for that purpose he actually conveyed to Paris the archives of Belgium, Castile, the Holy Roman Empire and others, all of which the French Government was compelled to restore. The British Museum at London represents another attempt to form a merger of international documents. But the most widely representative collection, and the most precious, is the Vatican Library, opened some years ago by Leo XIII to the scholars of Europe.

Various Methods of Making Documents Accessible to the Biographer.— Besides opening the large libraries of the world to those who wish to consult them, the study of original documents is now aided in various ways: First, by the publication of elaborate catalogues; each Government issues such catalogues of its own archives, museums, and libraries; and this policy, universal at the present time, enables the biographer to locate his material. Second, by the training of experts who pass upon the genuineness of documents; each government employs a number of these; they are assisted by various societies of research: for example, the Society of the Bollandists, the Imperial Academy of Vienna, the German Historical Society. Third, by transcription of original documents; they are transcribed or often photographed and spread broadcast, enabling the biographer to consult the documents in his home library. Fourth, by liberal appropriations from Governments, Universities, Societies, enabling research parties to visit distant countries and discover documents; for example, Palestine, Egypt and Greece at the present time have parties working in the interests of various governments. When Rénan began his Life of Christ, the French Government paid his expenses in Palestine and aided him in collecting material.

The Classification of Biographical Matter.— After finding the necessary sources, it remains to classify and arrange the material, so that no important section of it will be overlooked. Biographers adopt several methods of consulting documents and collecting material. First, they take notes from original documents and out of a mass of extracts, memoranda, etc., they construct their biographies. Another method is to read the original documents and quote from memory. This method is no longer in vogue on account of liability to error. In autobiography quotation from memory is sometimes employed when documents are not at hand. Now the documents are carefully grouped according to date, second, according to origin; third, according to contents; fourth, according to form. In this way, nothing essential is missed; all the facts necessary are present although in isolated form. It remains to organize these facts into a biographical synthesis.

The Various Kinds of Documents Consulted by the Biographer.— The biographer finds material wherever the individual has left a trace of his life-record. This record is large or small according to the prominence of the individual and his rank in society. Sometimes the life-record will involve almost all departments of contemporary literature; for example, the life of Napoleon, Bismarck, Leo XIII. Sometimes the record is confined to a small village or state and all the information obtainable would come from the consultation of a few documents. The immediate sources of information are six in number, and they are classified as follows: First, Church records giving information as to place and time of birth, baptism and church affiliation. Second, family records, dealing with parentage, ancestry, family connections, social standing, migrations, family possessions, etc. Third, City and State records showing the relation of the individual to civic society; the business, legal and political relations of the citizen to the State; for example, transfer of property, registrations for office, voting, marriage, death, offices held. Fourth, contemporary journals containing criticism of individual acts; the opinions of contemporaries regarding individual conduct. Fifth, private papers; among these the most important are diaries, memoirs and the letters of contemporaries. Sixth, the published works throwing light upon character, ability, attainments. Of the published works autograph letters are the most valuable, as a revelation of character. Very often, in the case of public or literary men the published works will contain autographical matter in the shape of memoirs, journals, reminiscences. These documents are the usual sources of information regarding individual life. But besides these there are other and more remote sources. For example, the private correspondence and the published works of contemporaries; opinions of associates handed down by tradition; records left in monuments, inscriptions, medals, in various arts, wherever traces of human life are preserved. The extent of such records will depend upon the prominence of the person.

The Grouping of Facts — Order of Time.— In biography it is the rule to follow the order of time, or what is known as the chronological order. This is done without difficulty in the case of individual life; whereas many difficulties present themselves when the story of collective life is written. The biographer uses each year as a central point for organizing and grouping his data; whereas the historian must constantly violate the order of time; he must go back constantly in order to bring up the details of his historical picture. This is very remarkable when history is written on a vast scale. For example, Gibbon's History of Rome. The biographer having the thread of only one individual life to follow, need never violate the order of time. There is a natural development from beginning to end.

Order of Place.— Besides the chronological order, there is the order of place. Human actions always involve the relation of place as well as time; and the facts of biography are arranged so as to correspond to the place where as well as the time when the individual lived. This order, sometimes called the geographical order, makes history so complex owing to the various centers for grouping facts; whereas, in biography it is subordinate to the chronological order, and makes no trouble whatever.

Minor Methods.— There are minor ways of grouping facts outside any direct consideration of space or time, though dependent on both. This grouping is based upon the four-fold activity of human life. First in the physical order: this grouping involves all questions regarding physical appearance and wellbeing; geographical or artificial environment and the physical development under such conditions. This grouping takes place at various times in the progress of the work. A second grouping of facts will involve mental activities, the conditions of mental life and growth, natural endowment and the various ways in which it was developed and expressed. A third grouping involves the moral life; various lines of conduct followed in relation to right and wrong or the claims of duty. This grouping is the most difficult as it involves all questions of character. The portrait of character must emerge from this group. In drawing this portrait, biographers and historians have committed untold crimes by suppressing facts, by ascribing false motives, by over-drawing positions, by interpreting acts, not according to the mind of the author, but according to the whim or prejudice of the biographer. Fourth, grouping of facts will center in the religious life of the individual, and will include all matters pertaining to religion. In biography, the last two groups, centering in morality and religion, furnish what is called the higher life of the individual; and the writer gives them the largest space, as the chief value of this kind of literature is to instruct by ethical and religious example.

CHAPTER XXIX

BIOGRAPHY (CONTINUED)

Various Kinds of Biography.— Authors of biography have selected various methods of describing individual life. First of all, they present the life-story either in an abbreviated or a complete form. The abbreviated form covering the larger part of this literature, includes many subdivisions.

The Obituary.— The first and most general of these divisions is the *obituary notice,* which contains only a few facts, such as the time of birth and death, the place where the life was spent, with a word perhaps about the occupation and character of the deceased. The majority of mankind must be satisfied with this meager account. The obituary notice is a feature of all modern periodicals from the lowest to the highest grade; for example, the most obscure newspaper; Harper's Monthly Magazine; both publish this kind of biography in every issue. In the best journals it is given the title of Necrology. This form also appears in dictionaries of biography where the editors, as a rule, are compelled to treat each life in the briefest possible manner. Each modern civilized nation publishes a dictionary of National Biography. Besides these National works, cities and towns prepare such dictionaries, limiting the scope to their own districts and defraying the expense from city funds. For example, the largest cities of the United States have all made provision of this kind. Various important societies in Church and State issue such publications — a recent work issued by the Masonic Fraternity gives brief lives of all the prominent Masons in our country, from George Washington to President Roosevelt. Religious Orders in the Church keep such records, which receive the name of annals or chronicles. This was the method of writing English history before the avowed historian appeared. For example, chronicles of Knight, Holinshed, the Anglo-Saxon chronicle, the chronicles of Monks. The Jesuits use the peculiar title " Relations; " their dictionary of biography has been frequently edited, and Parkman found it invaluable in writing of the Jesuit martyrs in America. These annals or chronicles sometimes extend to all prominent men of the country. For example, the early chronicles kept by the Religious Orders in England were national in scope and furnish the basis of English history for several centuries. The best of these is known as the Anglo-Saxon Chronicle — it covers the period from 853–1154, or from the reign of Alfred to that of Henry II. There are four divisions of it, corresponding to the four Monastic houses which were engaged in its compilation. It was kept in turn by the Monks of Winchester, Mercia, Abingdon and Northumbria. It supplies biographical data concerning the reigning kings, and prelates of the Church, with some meagre account of the various wars in which the Saxons were engaged. Supplementary to this is the chronicle kept by the Monks of Glastonbury, known as the Chronicle of St. Neot; and another, which belongs to the Monks of Peterborough. Besides the chronicles furnished by leading Monasteries, which are the composite works of monks, there are a number of valuable chronicles, the work of individual writers. For example, the Chronicle of Ingulphus, Abbot of Croyland in 1075. His chronicle extends from 650–1109, but it is chiefly occupied with the distinguished men of his order. Individual authors who have written biographical chronicles, are numerous in English literature. Besides Ingulphus, there are two well known examples: First,

Mathew Paris 1200–1259. He was a Benedictine Monk, and a graduate of the University of Paris. He received the patronage of Henry III, who requested him to write brief biographical accounts of all the celebrated men then living in the English realm. This account was afterward expanded by him into a dictionary of National Biography, and included the reigns of preceding kings. The second author, Raphael Holinshed (1577–1624) under orders from Queen Elizabeth compiled a biography similar to that of Matthew Paris. It is much larger and the separate biographies are more elaborate. At the present time Biographical Dictionaries are not confined to a particular class or nation. Two examples of this cosmopolitan character: the French Academy has recently published a Dictionary of Universal Biography; all the distinguished men of the world are given a place in it. In the English language our best Dictionary of Universal Biography is published by the Century Company, New York. It is much smaller than the French work, consisting only of one large volume, but more useful because more easily consulted.

The Eulogy.— A second form of abridged biography is known as the eulogy. It is more elaborate than the obituary notice, necrology or biographical chronicle. There are two classes of the eulogy: the essay which appears in periodicals; the panegyric prepared for delivery. Both kinds of eulogy appear at the death or on the anniversary of the individual. Both present the life-record in some detail, but both have this disadvantage: the eulogist selects only those facts which are worthy of praise and commendation; the justification being that only favorable things should be said concerning the dead. Hence, the abbreviated and one-sided view in the eulogy. This is particularly true of the national or religious hero. For example, in narrating the life of George Washington, our eulogists will never refer to the fact that he was rarely seen at public worship and that he was inclined to adopt a rather liberal moral standard. Or take the example of Pius IX: our eulogists remember all his saintly virtues, but omit any reference to the lack of statesmanship and his carelessness as a Temporal Ruler. The eulogist in the essay or panegyric is always a friend and special pleader; and hence this species of biography is very misleading and unreliable. But there is one advantage derived from a study of it, its method of condensation — it crowds the largest number of facts into the smallest compass, giving a rapid survey of a life with the omission of useless details.

Importance.—The eulogy, whether written or delivered, occupies a large place in English literature. Our leading essayists and orators almost without exception, have left examples of it. And its misleading character as to the individuals treated, does not impair its literary value. On the contrary, it is always considered a specimen of fine writing; the orator or essayist doing his very best for the person whom he sets out to praise. Three examples of the written eulogy: First, the essay on Saint John Chrysostom by Cardinal Newman. Second, the Eulogy on Shakespeare by James Russell Lowell. Third, the Eulogy on Napoleon by Channing. Three examples of the eulogy in the form of a panegyric: First, the the panegyric on O'Connell by Wendel Phillips. Second, the panegyric on Washington by Edward Everett. Third, the panegyric on Jefferson and Adams by Daniel Webster. The eulogy will always remain popular for two reasons: first, because it deals with persons and presents biography in a most pleasing form; secondly, because it gratifies a universal appetite for hero-worship.

The Diatribe and Philippic.— The eulogy presents the bright side of human life. There is a class of literature.

biographical in character, which presents the darker side. Various names are applied according to the degree of prejudice or hatred shown by the author. Thus, we have opposed to the eulogy, the diatribe, the libel, the satire. And opposed to the panegyric we have the philippic, or when the orator becomes violently partisan we have the tirade. These titles indicate the varying degrees of human hate or prejudice. Owing to intense party strife, freedom of the press, and freedom of speech, we have an abundance of this literature connected with the great names in English history. Most of this work is ephemeral, dying with the passions of the hour. But a percentage of it is permanent, owing to the literary skill of the author. For example: The satires of Swift or Junius; the philippics of Edmund Burke.

The Critique.— Between these extremes of the eulogy and the philippic there is a class of literature in which the authors avoid the extremes of love and hatred; they attempt to give a fair, impartial account of life and character. This literature appears in our best reviews and periodicals. It is commonly called a critique or essay in criticism. Like all abridged biography, it summarizes the main facts of the life, and bases a critical opinion upon this summary. The leading quarterly and monthly magazines publish this kind of biography in every issue. The essay in criticism is found not only in quarterly magazines, but also as prefaces to books. The prefatory sketch of the author's life is accompanied by a criticism of the work to which it forms an introduction. A more elaborate essay with an effort to be absolutely fair in criticism is found in encyclopedias where large numbers of these brief lives are published. For example, according to the announcement of the editors, the Encyclopedia Brittannica contains abridged biographies of 27,000 persons of all ages, races, and ranks in society. The American, National, and Chambers' Encyclopedias contain perhaps an equal number.

Biographical Critics.— The professional critic as represented in quarterly magazines, encyclopedias and elsewhere, combines biography with criticism. This example was set by John Dryden in the prefaces to his edition of the Shakespearean plays. Dryden introduced the essay, one-half of which was devoted to biography and the other half to criticism — a method faithfully followed ever since his day in what is termed the essay in criticism. Samuel Johnson employed the same method in his lives of the English poets. Francis Jeffrey, the Founder of the Edinburgh Review and its professional critic for twenty-six years, followed the same plan. Throughout the four large volumes of criticism left by Jeffrey, it is the uniform rule to give a biographical summary first, and criticism afterward. Lord Macaulay, who was a contributor to the Review, followed the example of the editor. The latest professional critic in English is Matthew Arnold, who left twelve volumes of prose, a large amount of which represents collected prefaces he wrote for the publishers of English classics. In the absence of any large or influential school of criticism, like the French Academy, we have depended upon individual authority. Hence, Dryden in his day made and unmade literary reputations; the same remark applies to such critics as Jeffrey, Macaulay, Johnson.

Private Papers.— Abridged biography sometimes takes the form of private journals, diaries, memoirs and letters. All these divisions come under the general head of private papers. These papers are autobiographical in character; they deal with particular periods or noteworthy incidents and reminiscences of the author's life. However numerous, these papers do not present a full biography; they are at best only detached fragments. But they give valuable information and help to interpret the life-record. In most cases the author of a complete biography relies upon the private papers for a confirmation of his statements regarding conduct and character; these papers are quoted continually; there is no other evidence so direct or convincing. One recent illustration: when Purcell charges Cardinal Manning with jealousy and spite toward Newman, he publishes fully a dozen letters written by Manning; and these letters leave no doubt in the reader's mind; for they prove that Manning used all his influence at Rome to keep Newman from the Cardinalate. These letters are a revelation of Manning's character A large number of private papers receive the title of memoirs. Sometimes they are called recollections or reminiscences. For example: The Recollections of an M. P., recently written. They are so named because as a rule they are written at the close of life when its labors and experiences may be calmly surveyed. Under these circumstances, we have the memoirs of Hume, Dryden, Gibbon, Carlyle. On the other hand, journals or diaries are kept during the period of active life; they bear the dates on which every fresh incident or reminiscence is chronicled. But like memoirs, they are only valuable fragments or partial views of the life-record.

The Private Journal.— The private journal was first kept by members of the various courts of Europe. It was the usual court practice during the Middle Ages. Each prince kept a private journal. On this point Lord Bacon remarks in the *Advancement of Learning:* "Princes hath, upon point of honor and policy, both, journals kept of what had passed day by day." These journals were filled with court gossip, the exchange of royal visits, the social events and functions. They had little literary merit, and were never published. From the court the custom spread to the nobility and to the officials of the Church. Then the private journal began to be of some use. It was elaborated by such writers as Madam De Stael, Montaigne, Fenelon. In England it was in general use during the age of Alexander Pope. He refers in the Dunciad to his age of "Journals, Medleys, Mercies, Magazines." And the implication is that it contained little literary merit. Private journals were kept by missionaries and travelers ever since the beginning of the era of discovery in the fifteenth century. For example, much of the biography of St. Francis Xavier is known from a private journal which he kept in India and China. The biography of Columbus depends upon a journal which he wrote during his voyages to America, as it was necessary to keep a private journal in order to give a true account of his travels to the home government. The private journal involving travel and exploration yields the most attractive material owing to incident and adventure. Some modern examples: The private journal kept by Livingstone while exploring South Africa; the recent visit of George Kennan to Siberia, of Nansen to the neighborhood of the Pole. These journals have been expanded into books of travel which are now general favorites. At the present time there is a tendency to publish these autobiographical fragments, journals and memoirs without weaving them into a formal life story. And there is no class of literature more popular than the journal of Amiel translated recently by Mrs. Humphrey Ward; the journal of Maria Baskertsief, the Russian artist; or the diary of the Opium Eater by Thomas De Quincey.

Memoirs and Letters.— Among private papers the memoir and the letter are highly valuable for purposes of biography. No biography is now compiled without including them, providing they may be obtained. The memoir is an essay dealing with some important event, incident or experience. As there are many such events in a lifetime, a number of these papers are written, and the plural form of the word is used. Memoirs may be as numerous as private letters. For example, the memoirs of Lord Nelson just published form two volumes. Memoirs, like private journals, are autobiographical; an exception to this rule occurs when an author writes of an intimate personal friend; but in such cases the author plays some part in the reminiscence. For example, in the memoirs of Napoleon written by Talleyrand the author is a factor in what he describes. Memoirs are now published in separate volumes; as views of life they are disconnected and fragmentary, and should be read in connection with a larger and more complete narrative. The reason for their present popularity is the fact that they treat of the more important and interesting events, leaving out all the minor details. Every rank of society now publishes memoirs. Some recent examples in the United States: in the army, the memoirs of Sheridan, Grant, Sherman; in the navy, the memoirs of Captain Mahan; in the Church, the memoirs of Edward E. Hale and Archbishop Spaulding. Among American men of letters, the memoirs of Poe, Bryant, Longfellow. Among American statesmen, the memoirs of Franklin, Marshall, and Lincoln. The publication of letters is now equally general. The very latest are those of Carlyle, Arnold, the correspondence of our colonial Governors; the letters written to Washington, now issued in five volumes.

Class Biography.— Abridged biography sometimes deals with certain classes of society, persons of the same calling or profession. The number of persons thus included, compels the biographer to be brief; and this kind of writing is called class biography. Class biography although abbreviated, is far more elaborate than necrology, biographical essays or private papers. It is the nearest approach that we have in abridged biography to the complete life-record of the individual. It aims at giving a connected account of the chief events, and these are unified by the particular calling or profession which is kept constantly in view.

Examples.— The example of writing class biography was set by Plutarch in the first century of the Christian era. He selected forty-six celebrated men from Greek and Roman history, and wrote their biographies by pairs according to their profession or calling. Thus he pairs off Cæsar and Alexander; Cicero and Demosthenes; Solon and Valerius; and so on down the list of celebrities and professions. Hence, his work is sometimes called Parallel Lives. These lives are works of great learning and research; and they are written at considerable length. They have been translated and frequently imitated, and the imitation of them has given us class biography.

English Imitators.— The earliest imitator of Plutarch among English authors was John Bale, a Protestant Bishop of the fifteenth century, who wrote a series of lives; taking for his subject the illustrious authors of England. The work was written in Latin, but has since been translated. A second example of the 17th century is Isaak Walton. Walton wrote the lives of Anglican divines. The series is incomplete, but the work is a good example of class-biography. A more representative work than either of these is the " Lives of the Poets," written by Samuel Johnson in the eighteenth century. This work written in ten small volumes appeared in 1781. These lives of the poets are, on the whole, the best of Johnson's works; the narratives are as entertaining as any novel; the remarks on life and on human nature are eminently shrewd and profound. The criticism contained in the work is the judgment of a mind vigorous and acute. A class-biography in imitation of Plutarch was written by Hartley Coleridge, son of Samuel Taylor Coleridge, in 1832. It is called "Lives of Northern Worthies," and deals with the celebrated men of Great Britain. These lives were written as essays for Black-

wood's Magazine; afterward, they were enlarged and published in volume form. The prose style of Coleridge, lively
and brilliant, is better adapted to biography than the lumbering
style of Johnson. In religion, we have a large number of class-
biographies. Three noted examples: First, the lives of English martyrs by John Foxe, who lived during the reign of
Queen Elizabeth. This work deals with the Protestant martyrs who died during the reign of Queen Mary. Second, Alban Butler, born at Northampton, England, 1711; died in St.
Omer's, France, in 1773. Published the Lives of the Saints,
a class-biography based upon the Acta Sanctorum. The work
is reliable as to facts; but the matter is poorly arranged and the
style is unattractive. This work has had a wide circulation because it has no competitors in English. Third, Walter Farquhar Hook — 1798–1875. He wrote two important works:
a dictionary of ecclesiastical biography and the "Lives of
the Archbishops of Canterbury "— the latter running through
14 volumes. Hook is a trustworthy biographer and he had access to all the materials.

Some Recent and Valuable Sets of Class-Biography.— The
Lives of the Saints, edited by S. Baring Gould, an English
clergyman of the Established Church. This series was begun
1872; is not yet completed. The Beacon Lights of History, a
series of the world's most distinguished men, written by John
Lord and published in fifteen volumes. Lives of the Popes,
a series in course of preparation; six volumes finished, written
by Ludwig Pastor, translated into English. Lives of Eminent Philosophers, a series of fifteen volumes, edited by William Knight, Professor of Moral Philosophy in the University
of St. Andrews. English Men of Letters, a series edited by
John Morley, forty-two volumes finished; others in course of
preparation. American Men of Letters, series edited by
Charles Dudley Warner. It has reached the fourteenth vol-

ume. Lives of American Statesmen, edited by John T. Morse, twenty-eight volumes completed; series unfinished. Lives of Eminent British Statesmen by John Morley, twelve volumes. Lives of Great Commanders, a series edited by General James Grant Wilson; eighteen volumes have appeared; series not yet completed. Lives of Great Artists, collected and edited by Frederick G. Stephens; thirty-nine volumes.

CHAPTER XXX

BIOGRAPHY (CONCLUDED)

Complete Biography.— Complete biography deals with individual life in the most satisfactory manner. It aims at furnishing a complete life-record; and to that end employs necrologies, eulogies, memoirs, letters, and whatever else may throw light upon the person's career. It supplies an amount of detail omitted in partial biographies. The author of such biography has access to Church, State and private papers; and quotes at considerable length the opinions of contemporaries. The publication is not hurried, as is often the case in class-biography; plenty of time is taken to collect and sift the material; so that a complete biography often takes several years in the preparation for the press. For example, John Morley has spent several years on his Life of Gladstone just published. Carlyle spent three years, and made several trips to Germany in his preparation of the Life of Frederick the Great.

Classification.— Complete biography is classified in various ways. On the part of authorship it is divided into three classes. It is written either by the author himself or by another, or by several others In the first case we have an *autobiography*. For example, the Apologia of Newman; in the second case, *individual biography*. For example: the Life of Christ by Geike; in the third case we have *composite biography:* for example, the Life of Lincoln by his secretaries, Nicolay and Hay. Of these three classes, autobiography is the most satisfactory. The author knows best where to get

materials relative to his own life.   He knows best the motives
which have governed his own life and conduct.   He should
be the best interpreter of his own acts.   Composite biography
is usually written by members of religious orders or by societies.   Biography is produced in this way: for example, the
lives and deeds of the Saints by the Bollandists.   Often a
composite biography is written by the family of the deceased.
A recent example: the life of Huxley by his wife and son.
The amount of this literature is comparatively small.   Biography, as a rule, is written by a single author.

Examples of Representative Biographers.— Some recent and
select examples of biographical writing: The Life of Thomas
Arnold by Dean Stanley.   Stanley was private chaplain of
Queen Victoria, dean of Westminster, and historian and theologian.   As an historian he wrote memorials of Canterbury
and a history of Westminster Abbey; essays on the Jewish
Church and the Apostolic Age.   As a theologian his chief
works are " The Relations of Church and State," a study of
Presbyterianism.   Dr. Arnold, the subject of his biography,
lived from 1795 to 1842.   He was a noted English educator,
head master of Rugby; the father of Matthew and Thomas
Arnold, both celebrated in English literature; professor of
Modern History in Oxford, 1841.   His historical works are
Lectures on Modern History, History of Rome.   A second
example: The Life of Samuel Johnson by James Boswell —
the most widely known and best written biography in English.
A word about the author: Boswell was born at Edinburgh
in 1740; died at London in 1795; a lawyer by profession; an
intimate friend and companion of Johnson for twenty years,
and, as he writes in the preface, thoroughly acquainted with
the story of Johnson's life.   A word about the work: The
author makes use of all the sources from which data could be
secured.   The private papers and correspondence of Johnson

were voluminous, as he was the leading litterateur of his age; besides the material which was turned over to him, Boswell makes use of his perosnal knowledge of the man, anecdotes, conversations and personal recollections. On the value of this supplementary knowledge Boswell writes as follows: "What I consider as the peculiar value of my work is the quantity it contains of Johnson's conversations." On this careful preparation of the materials, Boswell writes:

"The labor and anxious attention with which I have collected and arranged the materials of this biography will hardly be conceived by those who read it with careless facility. Were I to detail the books and papers which I have consulted, and the inquiries which I have found it necessary to make by various channels, I should probably be thought ridiculously ostentatious. But I will not suppress my satisfaction in the consciousness that by recording the life of the 'brightest ornament of the 18th century,' I have largely provided for the instruction and entertainment of mankind."

The following excerpts from the introduction to Johnson's Life written by Boswell, will throw light on the biographer's method:

"To write the life of him who excelled all mankind in writing the lives of others, and who, whether we consider his extraordinary endowments, or his various works, has been equalled by few in any age, is an arduous, and may be reckoned in me a presumptuous task. Had Dr. Johnson written his own life, in conformity with the opinion which he has given, that every man's life may be best written by himself; had he employed in the preservation of his own history, that clearness of narration and elegance of language in which he has embalmed so many eminent persons, the world would probably have had the most perfect example of biography that was ever exhibited. But although he at different times, in a desultory manner, committed to writing many particulars of the progress of his mind and fortunes, he never had persevering diligence enough to form them into a regular composition. Of these memorials a few have been preserved; but the greater part was consigned by him to the flames, a few days before his death. As I had the honor and happiness of enjoying his friendship for upwards of twenty years; as I had the scheme of writing his life constantly in view; as he was well apprised of this circumstance and from time to time obligingly satisfied my inquiries, by communicating to me the incidents of his early years; as I acquired a facility in recollecting, and was very assiduous in recording, his conversation, of which the extraordinary vigor and vivacity constituted one of the first features of his character; and as I have spared no pains in obtaining materials concerning him, from every quarter where I could discover that they were to be found, and have been favored with the most liberal communications by his friends; I flatter myself that few biographers have entered upon such a work as this with more advantages, independent of literary abilities, in which I am not vain enough to compare myself with some great names who have gone before me in this kind of writing. Instead of melting down my materials into one mass, and constantly speaking in my own person, by which I might have appeared to have more merit in the execution of the work, I have resolved to adopt and enlarge upon the excellent plan of Mr. Mason, in his Memoirs of Gray. Wherever narrative is necessary to explain, connect and supply, I furnish it to the best of my abilities; but in the chronological series of Johnson's life, which I trace as distinctly as I can year by year, I produce, wherever it is in my power, his own minutes, letters or conversation, being convinced that this mode is more lively, and will make my readers better acquainted with him, that even most of those were who actually knew him, but cou'd know him only partially; whereas there is here an accumulation of intelligence from various points, by which his character is more fully understood and illustrated. Indeed, I cannot conceive a more perfect mode of writing any man's life, than not only relating all the most important events of it in their order, but interweaving what he privately wrote, and said and thought; by which mankind are enabled as it were to see him live, and to 'live o'er each scene' with him, as he actually advanced through the different stages of his life. Had his other friends been as diligent and ardent as I was, he might have been almost entirely preserved. As it is, I will venture to say that he will be seen in this work more completely than any man who has ever yet lived. And he will be seen as he really was; for I profess to write, not his panegyric, which must be all praise, but his Life; which, great and good as he was, must not be supposed to be entirely perfect. To be as he was, is indeed subject of panegyric enough to any man in this state of being; but in every picture there should be shade as well as light, and when I delineate him without reserve, I do what he himself recommended, both by his precept and example. If the biographer writes from personal knowledge, and makes haste to gratify the public curiosity, there is danger lest his interest, his fear, his gratitude, or his tenderness, overpower his fidelity, and tempt him to conceal, if not invent. There are many who think it an act of piety to hide the faults or failings of their friends, even when they can no longer suffer by their detection; we therefore see whole ranks of characters adorned with uniform panegyric, and not to be known from one another but by extrinsic and casual circumstances. 'Let me remember,' says Hale, 'when I find myself inclined to pity a criminal, that there is likewise a pity due to the country.' If we owe regard to the memory of the dead, there is yet more respect to be paid to knowledge, to virtue and to truth. On this subject Plutarch writes: 'Nor is it always in the most distinguished achievements that men's virtues or vices may be best discerned; but very often an action of small note, a short saying or a jest, shall distinguish a person's real character more than the greatest sieges or the most important battles.'"

Boswell continues:

"To this may be added the sentiments of the very man whose life I am about to exhibit. The business of the biographer is often to pass slightly over those performances and incidents which produce vulgar greatness to lead the thoughts into domestic privacies, and display the minute details of daily life, where exterior appendages are cast aside, and men excel each other only by prudence and by virtue. The account of Thuanus is with great propriety said by its author to have been written that it might lay open to posterity the private and familiar character of that man, *cujus ingenium et candorem ex ipsius scriptis sunt olim semper miraturi,*— whose candor and genius will to the end of time be

by his writings preserved in admiration. There are many invisible circumstances, which, whether we read as inquirers after natural or moral knowledge, whether we intend to enlarge our science or increase our virtue, are more important than public occurrences. Thus Sallust, the great master of nature, has not forgot in his account of Catiline, to remark, that his walk was now quick, and again slow, as an indication of a mind revolving with violent commotion. Thus, the story of Melancthon affords a striking lecture on the value of time, by informing us that when he had made an appointment, he expected not only the hour but the minute to be fixed, that the day might not run out in the idleness of suspense; and all the plans and enterprises of De Witt are now of less importance to the world than that part of his personal character, which represents him as careful of his health, and negligent of his life. But biography has often been allotted to writers who seem very little acquainted with the nature of their task, or very negligent about the performance. They rarely afford any other account than might be collected from public papers, but imagine themselves writing a life, when they exhibit a chronological series of actions or preferments; and have so little regard to the manner or behaviour of their heroes, that more knowledge may be gained of a man's real character by a short conversation with one of his servants than from a formal and studied narrative, begun with his pedigree and ended with his funeral. There are, indeed, some natural reasons why these narratives are often written by such as were not likely to give much instruction or delight, and why most accounts of particular persons are barren and useless. If a life be delayed until interest and envy are at an end, we may hope for impartiality, but must expect little intelligence; for the incidents which give excellence to biography are of a volatile and evanescent kind, such as soon escape the memory, and are rarely transmitted by tradition. We know how few can portray a living acquaintance, except by its most prominent and observable particularities, and the grosser features of his mind; and it may be easily imagined how much of this little knowledge may be lost in imparting it, and how soon a succession of copies will lose all resemblance of the original."
(*Rambler,* No. 60.)

Boswell goes on to say:

" I am fully aware of the objections which may be made to
the minuteness on some occasions of my detail of Johnson's conversation, and how happily it is adapted for the petty exercise of
ridicule by men of superficial understanding and ludicrous fancy:
but I remain firm and confident in my opinion, that minute particulars are frequently characteristic, and always amusing, when
they relate to a distinguished man. I am, therefore, exceedingly
unwilling that anything, however slight, which my illustrious
friend thought it worth his while to express, with any degree of
point, should perish. For this almost superstitious reverence I
have found very old and venerable authority, quoted by our great
modern Prelate, Secker, in whose tenth sermon there is the following passage: 'Rabbi David Kimchi, a noted Jewish com-
mentator, who lived about five hundred years ago, explains that
passage in the first Psalm, ' His leaf also shall not wither,' from
Rabbis yet older than himself, thus: That ' even the idle talk,'
so he expresses it, ' of a good man ought to be regarded;' the
most superfluous things he saith are always of some value. And
other ancient authors have the same phrase, nearly in the same
sense.' Of one thing I am certain, that considering how highly
the small portion which we have of the table-talk and other anecdotes of our celebrated writers is valued, and how earnestly it is
regretted that we have not more, I am justified in preserving
rather too many of Johnson's sayings than too few; especially as
from the diversity of dispositions it cannot be known with certainty beforehand, whether what may seem trifling to some, and,
perhaps, to the collector himself, may not be most agreeable to
many; and the greater number that an author can please in any
degree, the more pleasure does there arise to a benevolent mind.
To those who are weak enough to think this is a degrading task,
and the time and labor which have been devoted to it misem-
ployed, I shall content myself with opposing the authority of the
greatest man of any age, *Julius Cæsar,* of whom Bacon observes,
that 'In his book of Apophthegms which he collected, we see that
he esteemed it more honor to make himself but a pair of tables,
to take the wise and pithy words of others than to have every
word of his own to be made an apophthegm or an oracle.' (Advancement of Learning, Book 1.) Having said thus much by

way of introduction, I commit the following pages to the candour
of the public."

John Morley.— He was born at Blackburn, Lancashire, Dec.
24, 1838. He received his education at Oxford where he
graduated in 1859; he entered the legal profession in 1860;
afterwards, he became the editor of the Fortnightly Review
and the Pall Mall Gazette. For a number of years he has
occupied a seat in Parliament and taken an active part in national politics. His literary work has been extensive, much
of it in the department of biography. The most recent contribution to this department is his Life of William Gladstone.

Criticism by The London Quarterly Review.—" There are
three aspects in which Mr. Morley's great work can, and in the
long run must, be appreciated — its aspect as a work of literary
art; its psychological aspect as a sympathetic appreciation of one
of the greatest personalities of his time; its historical aspect as
presenting a survey, which must needs be concise without being
inadequate, of the long series of political events associated with
Mr. Gladstone's career and subjected to his influence. These
several aspects are so organically connected in the biographical
synthesis that they cannot be wholly dissociated in the critical analysis. No biography which neglects any one of them can be held
to attain to the highest order of merit; but, if due allowance be
made for Mr. Morley's personal sympathies and political pre-
possessions, never suppressed, and yet never obtruded, we shall
hardly place Mr. Morley's biography in any class lower than the
first. It is a great portrait of a great man. The biography is
long, even as biographies go now; but its length cannot be said
to be excessive, in view of the unusual duration of Mr. Gladstone's public career, the unparalleled fullness of his life, and the
wide range of his interests. It has been said that only a syndi-
cate could write the life of such a man, and only an encyclopædia
could contain it. Mr. Morley has accomplished the work single-
handed; he has completed it in three years; and he has compressed the results into three volumes. Further than this com-
pression could not profitably go. His words are seldom wasted.

They are the distilled essence of documents innumerable, the condensed record of one of the most active and many-sided careers in British history, a brief epitome of more than half a century crowded with great political events, unexampled in social and economic change. Nevertheless, severely as Mr. Morley has condensed his materials, he retains at all times perfect mastery over them. His biography is no mere bald and jejune calendar of incidents, controversies, or events, but an articulated narrative, well proportioned in its parts, instinct with life and movement, in which the rare but necessary documents to be quoted fall naturally into their places as touches conducive to the completeness of the portrait. In style too, the book is admirably suited to its subject. The dominant note is a grave and lofty dignity, but lighter tones are not infrequent; and their introduction is well attuned to the spirit of the whole composition. It abounds in felicitous phrases and well chosen epithets; and there is no lack of those pungent apophthegms and pregnant reflections which bespeak the man of letters who has himself handled great affairs. As a single specimen of Mr. Morley's graver manner we may take his description of the scene on the introduction of the first Home Rule Bill. ' Of the chief comrades or rivals of the minister's own generation — the strong administrators, the eager and accomplished debaters, the sagacious leaders — the only survivor now comparable to him in eloquence or in influence was Mr. Bright. That illustrious man seldom came into the House in those distracted days; and on this memorable occasion his stern and noble head was to be seen in dim obscurity. Various as were the emotions in other regions of the House, in one quarter rejoicing was unmixed. There, at least, was no doubt and no misgiving. There, pallid and tranquil, sat the Irish leader, whose hard insight, whose patience, energy and spirit of command had achieved this astounding result, and done that which he had vowed to his countrymen that he would assuredly be able to do. On the benches round him, genial excitement rose almost to tumult. Well it might. For the first time since the Union, the Irish case was at last to be pressed in all its force and strength, in every aspect of policy and of conscience, by the most powerful Englishman then alive. More striking than the audience was the man; more striking than the multitude of eager onlookers from the shore was the rescuer with deliberate valour facing the

floods ready to wash him down; the veteran Ulysses who, after
more than half a century of combat, service, toil, thought it not
too late to try a further ' work of noble note.' In the hands of
such a master of the instrument, the theme might easily have
lent itself to one of those displays of exalted passion which the
House had marvelled at in more than one of Mr. Gladstone's
speeches on the Turkish question, or heard with religious reverence in his speech on the Affirmation Bill in 1883. What the
occasion now required was that passion should burn low, and
reasoned persuasion hold up the guiding lamp. An elaborate
scheme was to be unfolded, an unfamiliar policy to be explained
and vindicated. Of that best kind of eloquence which dispenses
with declamation, this was a fine and sustained example. There
was a deep, rapid, steady, onflowing volume of argument, exposition, exhortation. Every hard or bitter stroke was avoided.
Now and again a fervid note thrilled the ear and lifted all hearts.
But political oratory is action, not words-action, character, will,
conviction, purpose, personality. As this eager muster of men
underwent the enchantment of periods exquisite in their balance
and modulation, the compulsion of his flashing glances and animated gesture, what stirred and commanded them was the recol-
lection of natural service, the thought of the speaker's mastering
purpose, his unflagging resolution and strenuous will, his strength
of thew and sinew well tried in long years of resounding war,
his unquenched conviction that the just cause can never fail.
Few are the heroic moments in our parliamentary politics, but
this was one ' (iii, 311-2). ' Even the bitterest adversary of the
policy here referred to must acknowledge that this is literary
work of the highest order. We may follow it up with a few detached quotations illustrating Mr. Morley's felicities of expression and appreciation, premising at the same time that they lose
more than half their effect by being detached from their context.
Here, for a first example, is a shrewd attempt to explain the
baffling antinomies of Mr. Gladstone's personality. ' An illustrious opponent once described him, by way of hitting his singular quality of disposition, as an ardent Italian in the custody of
a Scotsman. It is easy to make too much of race, but when we
are puzzled by Mr. Gladstone's seeming contrarieties of temperament, his union of impulse with caution, of passion with circum-
spection, of pride and fire with self-control, of Ossianic flight with

a steady foothold on the solid earth, we may perhaps find a sort of explanation in thinking of him as a highlander in the custody of a lowlander' (i, 18). There are in Morley's portrait, at any rate, no dark or doubtful lineaments; and, did space permit, we could quote passage after passage to heighten the picture of his laborious, high-minded, and conscientious persistence in the profitable use of rare and high gifts, and in the scrupulous discharge of all the duties imposed on him by life and its circumstances. Nevertheless, it was a pre-established harmony between his best gifts and the proper field for their employment that made him a politician. He might have been anything, as Huxley said. But unless he had followed his early and rather *schwärmerisch* impulse to take orders, it is certain that in any civil walk of life he must have gravitated sooner or later to politics. He was essentially a man of action, although he was a great deal more, and had several qualities, gifts, and even failings which are seldom found so highly developed in men of action of the class to which he belonged. Mr. Morley puts all this very well in his opening pages. 'It is true that what interests the world in Mr. Gladstone is even more what he was than what he did; his brilliancy, charm, and power; the endless surprises; his dualism, or more than dualism; his vicissitudes of opinion; his subtleties of mental progress; his strange union of qualities never elsewhere found together; his striking unlikeness to other men in whom great and free nations have for long periods placed their trust. . . . Some may think in this connection that I have made the preponderance of politics excessive in the story of a genius of signal versatility, to whom politics were only one interest among many. . . . Yet, after all, it was to his thoughts, his purposes, his ideals, his performances as statesman, in all the widest significance of that lofty and honorable designation, that Mr. Gladstone owes the lasting substance of his fame. His life was ever '*greatly absorbed*,' he said, '*in working the institutions of his country.*' Here we mark a signal trait. Not for two centuries, since the historic strife of Anglican and Puritan, had our island produced a ruler in whom the religious motive was paramount in the like degree. He was not only a political force, but a moral force. He strove to use all the powers of his own genius and the powers of the state for moral purposes and religious. Nevertheless, his mission in all its forms was action. He had none of that detachment, often found among superior minds, which we honour for its disinterestedness, even while we lament its impotence in result. The track in which he moved, the instruments that he employed, were the track and the instruments, the sword and the trowel, of political action; and what is called the Gladstonian era was distinctively a political era." (The Quarterly Review, 1905, pp. 1, 2, 3.)

Minor Examples of Biography.— The Life of Audubon by Elliot Cowes and Maria Audubon — a composite biography. John J. Audubon, America's greatest ornithologist, born at New Orleans, 1780–1851; of French descent, and educated in France — celebrated for his drawings of birds. His chief works are, The Birds of America; Quadrupeds of America. The Life of John Ruskin, by W. G. Collingwood. Ruskin divides with Newman the honors of first place in English prose; celebrated as an art critic, and reformer of English taste in architecture and painting. Best known of his works are, The Seven Lamps of Architecture; the Stones of Venice; Modern Painters. Life of Louis Pasteur by Rene Vallery Radot. Pasteur, the leading scientist of France, in the past century, celebrated for his researches in bacteria, born at Jura, 1822–1895. Institutes bearing his name and founded for the treatment of hydrophobia and kindred germ diseases, exist in the large cities of America and Europe. Besides these lives we have as recent editions, the Life of Cromwell by President Roosevelt; the Life of Bismarck by Butler; the Life of Newman by Waller and Burrow.

CHAPTER XXXI

HISTORY

History is one of the most important of the standard prose-forms. It is the oldest prose-form of which we have an authentic account. It supplies material for every department of literature; and, in turn, borrows from all departments whether of verse or of prose. Hence, the interpretation and appreciation of literature depend in a large measure upon a knowledge of history.

Meaning of the Word.— It is derived from the Greek word, *istoria,* which signifies knowledge obtained by learned inquiry or investigation. According to the Greek, *istoor* signifies a wise man, a judge, or a critic. And the result of his investigation was known as history. This definition from the origin of the word does not differentiate history from the sciences, all of which are the result of learned investigation.

Definition According to Usage.— According to usage, history has both a general and a specific meaning. In general it means the prose narrative of past events, as probably true as human testimony will allow. In its widest sense it includes the record of all animate and inanimate orders of being. For example, the History of the Stars by Chambers; the History of the Earth by Seeley; the so-called Natural Histories dealing with animal and plant life. But in the strict sense history is confined to the human record. It is defined as the prose narrative of past events, having for its subject-matter collective human life.　In this way it is distinguished from biography, which deals with individual human life.　The collective life either of tribes or nations or the whole human race is the proper field and theme for the historical writer.

Factors in the Construction of History.— In the construction of history the two chief factors are science and art. Science collects the facts, ascertains their truth by an exhaustive examination of documents.　Thus science deals with the sources of history and supplies all the material.　An examination of these " sources " is precisely the same kind of work as an examination of the different strata of rock or the different flora and fauna of the earth.　Hence like geology and botany history is fundamentally scientific.　There is this difference, however, between the science of history and other sciences. Historical facts are only known indirectly by the help of their traces.　Historical knowledge is essentially indirect knowledge. The facts of other sciences are known by direct observation ; the facts of history depend upon documents and human testimony. One illustration :　By direct personal observation we can prove the existence of the law of gravitation.　We can prove the existence of an historical Alexander only on the testimony of contemporary witnesses and records.　Hence, history is called an indirect science in order to distinguish it from the direct sciences.　On that account it is none the less reliable.

Art as a Factor in History.— When the facts of history are authenticated and collected, the artist begins to group, coordinate and mass them in a literary structure.　Thus history may be compared to architecture, the brick and stone of which are historical facts.　The artist begins with a plan or outline, and he applies at once the fundamental principles of art — unity, harmony, balance, proportion.　The historian so arranges his facts as to give not merely a dead image, but a living representation of the past. On this point Symonds writes: "The magic wand of the historian touches the grave, and nations reappear clothed in their habit as they lived." Finally, the historian is a literary artist who gives to his subject-matter all the grace and charm of style found in other departments of literature.

History in Relation to Other Arts.— History is often compared with architecture on account of its massiveness, magnitude, the unity and complexity of its design. The Gothic cathedral in which a single unifying idea dominates a world of detail and complexity is not a greater work of art than the masterpieces of history. History bears a close resemblance to painting on account of the large amount of pictorial work involved. It is a succession of grand pictures of battlefield and forum and palace, a picture gallery of celebrities who figured in church, state, society. Hence history has many a foreground and back-ground — so many that the phrase, historical perspective, is a common one in criticism. It means that the artist must take the viewpoint of the age he is describing, and select those personages and events for the foreground of his pictures, which deserve prominence; at the same time outlining in the background all the others. But history is more nearly allied to dramatic art than to painting; for it attempts more than the mere picture of past heroes and events. It attempts to recreate the great characters of antiquity. Like the drama, it presents them as living and acting. Hence Balmez called history a grand drama. But while history contains most of the material out of which the drama has evolved, it is not concerned exclusively or even primarily with the individual hero. The nation, the state, the government; the acts of collective human life as revealed in the acts of a state or of a government hold first place and and are an historian's first concern. All individuals, whether heroes or not, should be subordinate to the main theme — a nation's origin, development, life.

The Art-Content of History.— It is a nation's life. Nation al life like individual life, obeys two laws: first, the law of continuity — this means that there are no breaks or leaps in the life of a people. Development may hasten or may slacken, but it is always continuous. The operation of this law of continuity makes history a unit; it is the basis for the organization of its facts into an artistic whole. The second law is that of differentiation. It means that the life of a people takes on new forms in the process of development; new ideas, new movements, new forms of government, new customs. These changes are not unlike the changes from childhood to maturity and old age in the life of the individual.

The Five-Fold Life of a Nation.*— "An examination of the life of any people will reveal certain permanent features common to the history of all civilized nations. These phases of national life are political, religious, educational, industrial and social. These are further emphasized by the fact that each has a great organization, called an institution, around which it clusters, and whose purpose, plan of work, and machinery are peculiar to itself. For political life the center is the institution called government; for religious life, the church; for intellectual life, the school; for industrial life, occupation; for social life, the family. Hence, the phrase, institutional life, which is often employed to designate this five-fold activity of the nation." The law of differentiation is now applied so thoroughly that we often think of the government without the church, the church without the school; and histories are written, which deal with only one of the five phases of national life, to the exclusion of all the others. For example, the history of the Church of

---

* For full development of this idea see Professor Mace: *Method in History,*page 11 seqq.

England; the political history of Great Britain; the history of British education; the history of the British industrial system.

The Origin of Institutional Life.— The primitive history of all peoples shows that, in the beginning, institutional life presented itself to man's consciousness as a simple and undivided whole. For example, in early Hebrew history Abraham did not separate in thought his political from his religious duties, nor did he think of his avocation and social interests as different and disconnected. In his time there were only the germs of a government, a church, a school, an industrial system; and these were so interwoven with other interests that they constituted one great life. But between that time and the present the principle of differentiation has done its work so perfectly that we often think of the government without the church coming into mind; and so with other institutions. These institutions have become great crystallized centers of life around which the thoughts and feelings of a people grow.

Value of Institutional Life.— Growth in the life of a nation becomes permanent by being embodied through law or custom, in its appropriate institution. For example, growth in political thought and feeling finds entrance into government, as the history of theocracy, monarchy and democracy clearly shows. Growth in religious life found entrance into the world, and paganism and Judaism yielded to Christianity, while Christianity itself has through the ages elaborated its appropriate institution. The same growth is permanent in our industrial, educational and social institutions.

Institutional Life the Basis of Civilization.— Because of this permanent institutional life, progress is possible, the advance of civilization is assured; for one generation profits by the achievements of all its predecessors.

The Organic Unity of Institutional Life.— While the life of a people flows in one mighty stream of five currents, it is nevertheless an organic whole. There is not one destiny for government, another for the church, another still for the school, and a different one for industrial and social interests; but all these constitute one life, one destiny. Hence, a great event cannot occur in one kind of institutional life without affecting all the others. One illustration: The liberation of the slaves in the Southern States. It affected religion by cleaving in twain all the religious denominations of the United States, save one. It affected politics by making the solid South forever democratic; it affected education by opening new problems in the intellectual test of voters; it affected industry by changing slave-labor to paid labor, thus bankrupting hundreds of Southern planters; finally, it affected society by raising the question whether a negro should be the social equal of his white companion and neighbor. A change in any kind of institutional life is bound to be felt in all the others. The degree to which it will be felt will depend upon the amount and character of the change. For example, the change from Paganism to Christianity was so radical as to be seriously felt in all phases of institutional life; whereas, the political change from monarchy to democracy in such countries as France and the United States did not materially alter other institutions.

Various Kinds of History.— Each kind of institutional life supplies material for history. The records of church, school, government and the social and industrial records comprise the material furnished to the historian. It remains to organize this material into an artistic unity. Various methods of organization are employed, giving us several distinct kinds of history.

Basis of Unity.— First of all, the basis of unity may be any one of the five national institutions, to the exclusion of all the others. Hence, the histories dealing separately with church, school, government, and so on. Secondly, the basis of unity may be any one of the five kinds of institutional life for a single period or in a single locality. For example, the history of the French Church in the Middle Ages; or the history of the Church in Brittany. Fourthly, the basis of unity may be all kinds of institutional life for a single period. For example, the colonial history of the United States; Hume's History of the Anglo-Saxons. Or it may concern only a locality, for example, the history of Rhode Island or Massachusetts. All these kinds of history are subject to national limitations and deal with the various phases of national life. Another class of history deals with institutional life independent of any national limitations. For example, a history of the Church universal; a history of government; a history of education. These histories are international or cosmopolitan in character.

Most Difficult Species.— Of these various kinds of history the most difficult to write is the complete life of a nation. This difficulty arises from two sources: the abundance of material supplied by the five phases of national life, an abundance which compels the historian to adopt a rigorous method of selection. The second difficulty is the exact disposition of selected facts in order rightly to portray the national life as contrasted with the political, social or religious life. The chief objection against national histories has been that they have given undue prominence to political life and neglected the industrial, social and intellectual life of the people. Such histories are not lacking in unity, but they violate the laws of symmetry and proportion.

Various Methods of Writing History.— In writing history the author deals with documents. Documents are the traces left in past time by the thoughts and actions of men. For the most part, these documents are found in archives, although monuments, coins, inscriptions or any traces of the human record are regarded and classified as documents. Each kind of institutional life possesses archives. There are archives of family, society, church and state. For the want of these archives the history of many periods in the past of humanity must remain forever unknown or only be guessed at from fragmentary traces in metal, brick, stone and mounds of earth. The cave-dwellers, mound-builders and Aztecs are examples in point — their history is almost unknown.

The Grouping of Facts.— The historical facts derived from documents are grouped in various ways. It is the second step in the construction of history. The primary method of grouping is to follow the order of occurrence. Each historical fact belongs to a definite time and place; so that the writer, no matter what be the place or scope of his history, will observe a chronological order which marks their succession of events *in time,* and a geographical order which marks their succession *in a given place.* Besides these two kinds of order, there is a larger grouping determined by the scope of the history itself, whether it be a partial or complete history of a nation. The method of grouping will then follow either the lines of institutional life taken separately, and covering a partial history of a people, or it will be fully national in scope.

Grouping of Facts (Continued).— The grouping of facts from which the customs and modes of life of a people are inferred is conducted along various lines; four of which are usual and common in history; these four lines are rustic, urban, provincial and national. Modes of country life differ from those of the city; while provincial traits are distinct from national traits. So that a separate grouping of facts will occur in each case. So marked are these lines of distinction that histories are written on the basis of each grouping. For example, the history of peasant life in Switzerland; the history of city life in London; the history of New England as contrasted with the history of the United States. The sixth and last order of grouping is based upon the biography of representative men. National life is expressed through individuals, whose personal career, at least for a time, is identified with that of the nation. So that history is filled with segments of biography which are used for the purpose of grouping national acts. In nations under monarchical rule, a complete biography is used, namely, that of the king or ruler; all national acts find expression through time and are grouped around the story of his life. Republics have a greater variety, but the same principle of grouping is employed. But history is more than the continuous narrative of events. It is the collective facts, plus the inferences which the historian draws regarding the habits of a people, their national traits, customs, character. While the process of grouping facts is going on, a second process occupies the mind of the writer. It is the process of interpretation. Without an attempt to interpret these facts, history would be a lifeless chronicle of past events. The true life of the nation, its manners, ethics, customs, character, would be wanting.

Various Methods of Interpreting Historical Facts.— After the grouping of historical facts takes place, the interpretation of these facts follows in order to determine the customs, habits, character, life of a nation. Historical interpretation means that the motives of national acts are set forth, together with the moral consequences. National life and conduct, like individual life, follows a code of morality and is governed by ethical principles. The historian must interpret national acts in the light of the principles. This is the most difficult task in relation to history. One illustration: The United States recent-

ly engaged in war and acquired foreign territory.　Three motives have been assigned.　First, a desire to extend the blessings
of free government to oppressed peoples.　Second, national
greed, selfishness, commercial advantages.　Third, a desire to
assert and extend national power, the policy of imperialism.
No matter how these national acts are interpreted, they affect
our national honor, our national character.　They have an ethical significance, because right and wrong, justice and honesty,
are involved.

CHAPTER XXXII

HISTORY (CONTINUED)

Various Methods of Historical Interpretation.— The interpretation of historical facts is the personal contribution of the author to history. It is his estimate of national morals, character and life from a review of national acts. It is the chief source of error in historical writing. So many false interpretations have been given that history is called a conspiracy against the truth. There are two ways in which to account for these false interpretations: an imperfect knowledge of the facts, the prejudice of the author. An imperfect knowledge of the facts may arise from a scarcity of material. Original documents are often scarce and fragmentary, especially in the case of nations of great antiquity. Inferences in such cases are in a large measure the guess of the historian. Imagination takes the place of fact. Hence, the fictitious narratives concerning the earliest inhabitants of America, Europe, or Asia. An imperfect knowledge of the facts may arise from lack of scholarship. The author is unable or unwilling to collect the facts available. Ancient historians were often unable to consult original documents owing to the poor condition of libraries and archives, their own poverty and the difficulties of travel. Much of this difficulty is now overcome by our modern facilities for editing and consulting manuscripts and by the large sums of money available for historical research.

Prejudice a Source of Error.— The most fruitful source of error is the prejudice of the historian. If history be a conspiracy against the truth it is so because all historians have suffered from some kind of prejudice. The historian belongs to some nation, some creed, some profession; is a member of some political party, is influenced by some social rank. Hence, his interpretation of historical facts is modified and colored by national, religious, political or social prejudice. In spite of many honest efforts at impartiality, these kinds of prejudice are traceable in every history written.

National Prejudice.— Of the various kinds of prejudice the most general and obvious is national prejudice. The tendency to exalt one's country at the expense of others is a universal weakness from which the historian has not escaped. The keen rivalry of neighboring nations often increases this prejudice. For example, the case of England and France. Centuries of rivalry between these nations have so vitiated historical writing that no one expects to learn the truth regarding France from English histories. In like manner the histories of other nations have been filled with falsehood. The tendency to defend one's country has led to all kinds of false interpretation, sometimes to the forging or suppression of documents. When it is a question of incriminating his own country the historian often prefers falsehood and the suppression of facts.

Religious Prejudice.— Religion has a firmer hold on the affections of men than love of country. It is a stronger kind of prejudice to overcome. It has left behind it a trail of falsehood wherever rival creeds have flourished. On account of this prejudice, most of the history composed since the Reformation must be rewritten. Catholic and Protestant historians are about equally guilty in the matter of prejudice. And the creed of the infidel has not saved him from similar error. For example, the history of Gibbon, so admirable and trustworthy in many ways, is poisoned by religious prejudice. The chapters dealing with Christianity, according to Dean Milman, are the most dishonest pages Gibbon has written. The prejudice of such writers as Froude, Macaulay, Freeman, is obvious, Even such an historian as Lingard, who made an heroic effort to be impartial, does not escape religious prejudice.

Party Prejudice.— The influence of party and social rank are minor kinds of prejudice but are equally effective in vitiating history. Party bitterness often reaches the same excess as religious or national prejudice. It is easy to discover from internal evidence to what party the historian belongs, and what may be his rank in society; that internal evidence will be a one-sided view of national events.

The Removal of Prejudice.— At the present time there are several agencies at work, tending to destroy prejudice and improve historical writing. Three of these are noteworthy: First of all, the modern facilities afforded for getting at historical truth. There never was a time when the honest historian had a better opportunity to do reliable work. The great archives of the world are all open to him. There never was a time when so many original sources of information were accessible. Today every government supports its own society of historical research, and spends thousands of dollars in equipping libraries and multiplying documents for critical investigation. In this matter, the example of governments is followed by two kinds of institutional life — the Church, and the school. The Church has opened her archives and placed a premium on historical investigation by inviting the leading scholars of the world to Rome. The leading universities of America and Europe send out bands of scholars annually for the purpose of collecting historical data. At the present time the University of Chicago has three bands at work, one in Mexico, another in South America, a third in Palestine. In like manner, other American universities and those of the old world, are engaged in historical investigation. As a result the historian is enabled to give a more accurate account, no matter what department he is working in. Along with increased facilities for knowing historical facts, there is a growing desire for accuracy, both on the part of writers and readers — the outcome of the modern scientific spirit. This spirit has opened a new era in the treatment of history.

Cosmopolitan Spirit.— A second agency at work is the cosmopolitan as opposed to the national spirit. National barriers are fast breaking down, enabling the historical writer to overcome the prejudice of race. Commerce and increased facilities of travel make it possible for one nation to become acquainted with another as never before. A truer concept of human brotherhood exists, and a better appreciation of what foreign peoples have accomplished. The narrow patriotism that would falsify the national record for the sake of national pride or glory, is fast disappearing.

Universal Toleration.— Religious prejudice, like national prejudice, is yielding to the spirit of universal toleration. Fanaticism which was mainly responsible for historical falsehood, is dying out. The historian who belongs to one creed can now write with tolerable fairness concerning another creed. An occasional writer still appears, like Charles Henry Lea, the historian of the Inquisition; but the class he represents no longer appeals to the general public. Perhaps the strongest corrective of prejudice is the modern diffusion of knowledge. A well-informed public will not permit repetition of the old lies concerning race or creed or party. A comparison of the recent work done by Jansen, Pastor, Bancroft and Freeman with previous historians will show a marked decline in all kinds of prejudice and an increasing respect for historical truth,

Literary Style in Historical Composition.— After grouping facts and interpreting them without prejudice, the historian considers the literary style in which his facts and inferences will be expressed. There is a general agreement regarding certain qualities of this style; that it be clear, animated, dignified, as befits a serious subject. Blair repeating the observations of Quintilian, has this to say concerning the style in which history ought to be written: "The purpose of history should determine its style, that purpose is to record truth for the instruction of mankind. The purpose of history is to enlarge our view of national and human character; it presents important facts which when seen in connection with their causes, and when studied in their effects, become our guides to right conduct, supplying our want of experience. History thus becomes our moral teacher, and on that account the style in which it is written ought to be grave and dignified, addressing itself to our judgment rather than to our imagination, and excluding flippancy, levity, sarcasm, invective, wit and humor, and all qualities which would detract from the seriousness of the subject." These characteristics, gravity and dignity, demand the periodic or long sentence, which is elaborated with all the wealth and force of language; these qualities do not exclude ornament, but the imagery must correspond with seriousness and dignity — no degrading similes or metaphors are permitted. These qualities demand the long paragraph as well as the long sentence, both of which add impressiveness and weight to the style.

Various Kinds of Style Employed.— Aside from the general characteristics of gravity and dignity, the historian varies his style in three ways. When presenting facts and telling the sequence of events he employs the *narrative style*. The main feature of this style is to set forth facts, incidents and events in the order of their occurrence and with as much economy of at-

tention as possible.　It is most frequently employed in historical composition because the author is dealing, for the most
part, with narrative.　Occasionally, however, he pauses in the
narrative to draw a picture or paint a scene; hence the *pictorial
style* in historical composition, which is a considerable variation from the narrative form.　Finally, after grouping a number of facts, incidents and events, the historian pauses to draw
a number of inferences, account for national acts by assigning
motives.　In doing so he employs the *philosophic style* which
varies considerably from either narrative or pictorial work.

The Narrative Style.— In the narrative style three qualities
are involved: the selection of facts, their combination in
the story, and the progress or movement of the story.　Hence,
the narrative style is the art of story-telling in historical
composition.　This art demands vividness, which makes the
story brisk and interesting; directness, which goes straight to
the conclusion toward which the sequence of incidents and
events is leading.　In using the narrative style the writer
must, first of all, select material; he must pick and choose, for
what can be said concerning a given story or train of events
is only a small portion of what might be said.　So that a good
story-teller is recognized by what he omits as well as by what
is said.　For example, in telling the story of a battle the
historian is confronted with a mass of details concerning the
movements of the troops and the incidents of the struggle.
He cannot narrate them all; he must leave out the larger number of them.　So many histories contain dull, wearisome
narrative because their authors have not mastered the art of
telling a story; they regard all incidents of equal importance;
they have not learned how to present those prominent events
which would suggest the others less prominent and of necessity suppressed.　No method of selecting details applies in
every case; but in every story we are concerned to know where

the scenes are laid, who are the leading characters; what are the motives and lines of their conduct; what is the aim or purpose of the story. As for the rest, it must be determined by circumstances and the skill of the artist.

Proportion.— A second quality of the narrative style is proportion. Proportion is a fundamental law of art. In this case it means some plan whereby a certain amount of space will be accorded to each group of facts or incidents — an arrangement based upon the relative importance of such groups to the whole work. Proportion, then, in the narrative, will depend upon the scope and extent of the work. If the plan allows of much detailed elaboration, we may expect the narrative to be crowded with incidents; we may expect the relations of cause and effect to be fully explained, and all the ideas associated with the main thread of the story to be given ample space in the composition. Such provision is always made in the plan of the best histories.

Movement.— A third and final quality of the narrative style is movement. Constant progression is demanded in the story. Something new and attractive is continually required in order to stimulate the curiosity of the reader and hold his attention. The motive of telling the story must often appear, in order to prevent it from being a mere bundle of disjointed facts. In the best histories the progress of the narrative is always rapid, a swiftly moving current which halts only when a scene is to be painted or when the end of each story requires the personal reflections and interpretation of the author. Among English historians, Hume, Gibbon and Prescott are regarded as our greatest masters of the narrative style.

Descriptive Style.— *Pictorial work* in history demands the descriptive style. Like the illustrations in a modern journal, pictorial work is necessary to impart vividness. It also supplies the theatre, stage and scenery for the action of the national drama. It presents the national heroes, the leading characters, giving a picture of each. Hence, the descriptive style is called word-painting. For example, in writing the history of any people it would be necessary to describe the country where they flourished; their principal cities, buildings, battlefields, and objects of a similar character. A variety of methods are employed in word-painting, two of which are in general use. The first is called the objective method, wherein an attempt is made to describe the object as truthfully as possible without any reference to the emotions it arouses. This attempted reproduction of the object is merely an enumeration of the principal features taken in the order in which they are presented to the eye. While reading these details, the imagination of the reader must construct the picture. The second is called the subjective method, when the author tells about the emotion excited by the details which he passes in review. The imagination and the fancy of the author play upon the object and transform it into something which reflects his own personality. This personal element is scarcely ever eliminated from descriptive work; although in historical composition it is less prominent than in any other kind of writing because the historian is acting in the official capacity of a critic or judge of national conduct, and accordingly, must suppress emotion and give an impersonal character to his work. On the other hand, the personal or subjective element has widest scope whenever history loses its judicial character and passes into the realm of fiction. For example, the personality of Walter Scott reflected in his historical novels. No historian can expect to succeed without a fair mastery of this style; for no matter how skilfully a narrative may be constructed, it will grow monotonous unless pictorial work be introduced from time to time; these pictures carefully executed and frequently introduced, enkindle the reader's imagination and appeal to his sense of beauty; they afford periods of relief and entertainment by allowing the eye to rest upon the leading personages and upon the scenes in which these personages are engaged. Thus, in a special manner, description is the artistic setting of historical composition, giving scope to the literary and æsthetic gifts of the writer.

The Philosophic Style.— Besides narrative and descriptive work, there is another kind of style employed in history. It is used whenever the historian offers an interpretation of historical facts, and, in consequence, it is named the philosophic or judicial style of writing. This style differs materially from narration or description. It is often called the judicial style, for the historian passes judgment upon historical acts in the same manner as a judge upon the bench. With the utmost degree of calmness and impartiality he is expected to deliver an opinion regarding national conduct, and the misfortune of history has been that, while preserving the judicial style and temper, his judgment has so often been contrary to the evidence. This style of writing is plain, severe, dignified, without ornament or much elaboration. The arts and decorations of rhetoric which characterize descriptive work are laid aside; the sole aim of the writer being to state his opinion in the clearest and most definite manner possible. This style is employed at the end of chapters, at the close of important national events, at the death of leading national characters or whenever the historian finds it necessary to pass judgment upon any group of events.

Some Representative Stylists in History.— Each nation possessing an extensive literature claims one or two historians distinguished for their style. Of ancient classic authors Thucydides among the Greeks and Livy among the Latins are celebrated for the exquisite literary finish given to their work.

The following comparison of the style of both writers is given by Blair: "Thucydides ranks as the greatest historian of antiquity; next to him we must place Livy; and both have attained that exalted position owing to the incomparable beauty of their style. Thucydides flourished in the golden age of Greek literature; he had enormous wealth, and leisure necessary to recast and polish his work. His history displays in full perfection that supreme and unapproachable beauty of form, of which the Greeks alone possessed the secret. Livy enjoyed similar advantages in wealth and leisure; but the language in which he wrote was not susceptible of the same polish and refinement." Thucydides' style is seen at its best in the orations which crowd the pages of his history; in his pen-pictures of the heroes who figured in the Peloponnesian war, and in his descriptions of the various battles by land and sea. His narrative work is not so successful; he tries often to compress facts within too narrow limits and shares with Tacitus the odium of being at times very vague and obscure; he did not possess the highest talent as a story-teller. Perhaps the strongest feature of his writing is his dramatic power, the vividness with which he paints the great scenes and events. Thucydides was the first who introduced orations; and the addresses with which his history abounds are among the most valuable remains which we have of ancient eloquence. On the other hand, Livy is excelled by no historian whatever in the art of narration. He manages to keep the attention of the reader even when recounting the driest details — the story never tarries, while the classic purity of his style, the eloquence of his speeches, the skill with which he depicts the play of emotion in his leading characters have deservedly entitled him to universal popularity. In style and language he represents the best period of Latin prose-writing. If he writes with less finish and less perfect rhythm than his model,

Cicero, he excels him in the varied structure of his periods and in the adaptation of the style to the subject-matter.

Method of the Ancients.— This criticism does not include questions of fact or fidelity to historical truth. For it was on the artistic rather than on the critical side of history that stress was almost universally laid in antiquity; and the thing that above all others was expected from the historian was not so much a scientific investigation and accurate exposition of the truth, as its skilful presentation in such a form as would charm and interest the reader. In this sense Cicero speaks of history as an oratorical work as if the oration were its predominant feature; and Quintilian speaks of it as a prose-poem. So that it was by their artistic merits that the ancient historians would stand or fall.

Modern Scientific Method.— The method of treating history as a species of literature was the method employed by Thucydides, and Livy, and the ancient classic writers generally. This method prevailed down through the Middle Ages to the close of the eighteenth century. The literary method was then superseded by the scientific method, the author of which was George Niebuhr. He was born in 1776 and died in 1831; of German parentage, although born in Copenhagen. He is known as the founder of the Modern Scientific School of History. He reversed the ancient classic conception regarding the purpose of history; declaring that history was science, not literature. In three particulars he represents a departure from the ancient canons of historical composition. First, he depreciates style, attaching no importance to literary form or finish. Concerning the proper style to be employed Niebuhr writes: "The style of history ought to be similar to the style of any scientific treatise, a plain statement of truth, nothing more. The attention given by the ancients to literary

finish was a mistake, a waste of time.   I expect that my readers will find sufficient attraction in the matter of my history
without pausing to consider the manner of writing." A
second departure from the ancient style was the stress laid
by Niebuhr upon institutions, tendencies, political and social
movements, not upon the lives of celebrated individuals.   Niebuhr continues: " The mistake of historians has been a love
of hero-worship which has made of history little more than
a tissue of inflated biography.   The great man has overshadowed every other consideration.   I prefer to transfer the
reader's attention to the acts of the nation, the manners, habits,
institutions, the vast and varied life of the people."   A third
departure was the elimination of the element of fiction.   The
beautiful orations which made ancient history so attractive
had to go, for history is a science, not literature.   Niebuhr is
responsible for eliminating the oration from modern history.
In the same manner the myths and legends which made excellent literature were excluded from history.   In his History
of Ancient Rome, he destroys many a beautiful legend about
the origin and early growth of the Roman race.   To Niebuhr
we may trace the beginning of that destructive criticism which
has dealt so unkindly with the records and legends of the
Hebrew people.

Influence of Niebuhr.— The appearance of Niebuhr marked
a new epoch in historical writing.   His example was followed
by all the German historians of any note.   They disregarded
style and literary finish, and worked upon history as they
would work upon any scientific treatise.   The immediate
effect of Niebuhr's example was the rise of the Tübingen
School, whose founder was Ferdinand Baur.   Baur was born
in 1792; died in 1860.   The same destructive criticism which
Niebuhr directed against Roman myths and legends, was
directed against the Bible by Baur and the Tübingen School.

This school is celebrated for its bitter attack upon the divinity of Christ and the supernatural element in the Bible. Baur's critical history of the Hebrews reduces miracle to the same status as a myth, or explains away the wonderful event by assigning natural causes. An unexpected application of Niebuhr's method was made to German history by Doctor Janssen. The traditional lies and calumnies concerning the old church were handled in the same manner as Roman myths. The publication of evidence placed many of the Reformers in an entirely new light before the public. The private life of Martin Luther was revealed by the publication of letters and official correspondence. Statements made by Janssen are in every case supported by documentary evidence. In his History of the Popes, now in course of preparation, Ludwig Pastor employs the same method, and certain Popes like Alexander VI suffer in the same manner as Martin Luther. Perhaps the most distinguished disciple of Niebuhr is Theodore Mommsen who continued Niebuhr's work in writing Roman history and employed Niebuhr's methods.

The following estimate of Niebuhr and the modern German historians is given by Mr. Garnett, an English critic:

Criticism by Garnett.—"From the point of view of industry and scholarship, modern German historians like Niebuhr and Mommsen are deserving of all praise; they have created a new era in historical writing when fact takes the place of fiction, and mere guesswork is supplanted by evidence. The best tribute to their painstaking zeal, and devotion to truth, is that the historians of other nations have imitated their example in trying to get at the truth of history. But the German historians, almost without exception, make the grave mistake of disregarding the artistic side of history; their style is almost uniformly dull and wearisome — it lacks life, color, movement. The narrative is painfully slow, owing to the mass of details crowded into the page. They gather all the facts with the greatest diligence, but seem to be unable to organize them to the best advantage."

CHAPTER XXXIII

HISTORY (CONTINUED)

Representative Stylists in French History.— In contrast with the unpolished style of German historians is the attention paid by the French to literary form and finish. French writers are conceded to be the unrivaled masters of modern prose; partly because of their language, and partly on account of the artistic instinct which is stronger in the French than in any other modern nation. It has often been remarked that if we could add the merit of German scholarship to their work, we would reach the ideal in the art of writing history. French historians are not so active as the Germans in collecting material, nor are they so careful in weighing evidence. Like the ancient classic writers, their chief concern seems to be the finished and attractive form rather than the matter.

Guizot.— Of the representative historians of France, William Francis Guizot deserves special mention, as being the best known and most widely appreciated historian outside his own country. Guizot was born in 1787; died in 1874; a prolific writer, Professor of Literature at the Sorbonne, and a member of the French Academy. His collected writings comprise sixty volumes, including translations of Shakespeare and Gibbon. His chief historical works are a History of Civilization in Europe, a History of Civilization in France.

The following estimate of Guizot is given by Richard Hutton, an English critic:

Criticism by Hutton.—" As an historian, Guizot reached the highest point of fame. His histories place him among the best writers of France and of Europe; his works must be regarded as classics of modern historical research, and an evidence of the great advance in the treatment of modern history, which has marked the last half century. Guizot approaches the German type in scholarship and accuracy. He is perhaps the most reliable of the French historians. Like the Germans, he employs a style which is not remarkable either for imagery or systematic narrative or beauty of description. In this respect he is unlike any of his countrymen. The strength of the style comes, above all things, from his thought; he has written grandly because he has thought profoundly. His phrase is never glowing or flowery, but always full of meaning. Without the aid of imagery his writings are powerful, with a flavor of sententiousness and at times a tendency to be dogmatic. It is the style of the logician, never yielding to levity or humor. Guizot treated history as a social science. He introduced among French historians a more critical spirit, and taught them the superior value of conclusions drawn from facts. He applied to history those laws which science applies to other phenomena. He was the first to present a complete analysis of the divers elements which compose the social body; he formulated the historic law of mutual dependences, pointing out the reciprocal influence of the individual upon society, and society upon the individual. He also applied the law of evolution to history, seeing therein successive and progressive transformations. To quote his own words: ' In the hands of an all-powerful Providence the history of a people is never interrupted or broken and never re-commences.' Guizot had many personal qualities which fitted him for historical writing: he was cool and cautious in temperament; without bias, either national or religious; a sincere believer, in an age of scoffing infidelity; and a consistent defender of liberty and order against the attacks of absolutism and anarchy."

Jules Michelet.— Besides Guizot, two other French writers should be mentioned in connection with French History. The first of these is Jules Michelet — born in 1798; died in 1874. He occupied the Chair of History in the College of

France. Like Guizot, he was a prolific writer, one who contributed to many departments of literature. His chief historical work is a History of France, upon which he spent forty years. Other works of considerable merit are his History of the Roman Republic; History of the Knights Templar and a History of the French Revolution.

Criticism by George Saintsbury.—" The literary characteristics of Michelet are among the most clearly marked, also among the most peculiar French literature. In the details of his style he is quite original and individual. His sentences and paragraphs are as different as possible from the orderly architecture of French classic prose. He often omits the verb, breaks or twists the phrase, and gives a grotesque finish to his work, in many points resembling Carlyle. His style is just the opposite of Guizot and the German school. To Michelet, history is always picturesque; it is a series of pictures. His imagination is constantly at work and excited — like Carlyle, images are continually dancing before his mind. Michelet called history ' the Resurrection '— the awakening of the dead; and while it is often difficult to adjust his work to ascertained facts, yet his pictures are always possible; his descriptions are instinct with genius, and always life-like. There are no dead bones in Michelet, no hint of the dissecting table as in Guizot; and whereas the style of Guizot is hard, cold and analytic, the style of Michelet is glowing with sentiment, full of fire, a synthesis true to life, and stimulating in the highest degree. In reading him one is constantly reminded of Victor Hugo or Carlyle."

Ernest Rénan.— A representative writer of modern French prose is Joseph Ernest Rénan who was born in 1823 and died in 1892. A member of the French Academy and recognized as one of the best prose writers France has produced. He wrote a History of the Origins of Christianity in six volumes, one of which is his celebrated Life of Christ. Besides the history, he left two valuable works in criticism; one on the origin of language, the other an estimate of the doctrines of Averroes.

Criticism by Mark Pattison.— The historical work of Rénan may be compared with that of Macaulay in style and in popularity; although Rénan deserves more credit for historical research, and he also had a greater regard for historical truth. In either case it was the style that won popular favor. As an illustration of the popularity of Rénan, twenty-four editions of his Life of Christ were sold in three years. ' In analyzing the style of Rénan we find,' says Mark Pattison, an English critic, ' the greatest care in the choice and collocation of words; each sentence is symmetrically formed with the nicest appreciation of rhythm and effect. His narrative never tires; on the contrary, it invites and allures the reader so that one is loath to lay down the volume. In his descriptive work there is a tendency to paint in glowing colors, and perhaps an undue prominence given to the flowers of fancy; so that, for example, in his descriptions of Palestine one feels like being introduced into fairyland. It would be difficult to name another modern French author who for grace and charm of diction can compare with Rénan."

English Historians.— If we compare the work of English historians with that of the French or Germans we find it somewhat inferior both in amount and in quality. We have not so large a number of specialists engaged in the department of history, nor is historical study so successfully prosecuted in English schools as in France or Germany. The greatest masters of English style like Newman, Ruskin, Kingsley, Stevenson, have given little attention to this species of composition; at best they have written only historical sketches or historical romances. For the most part they employed their talents in other departments of literature or science. Biography, oratory and fiction have made a much stronger appeal to them than history. As a consequence, the history of England is written in fragments; the British colonies and dependencies receive even scantier treatment. We have no history to place side by side with Michelet's History of France or Janssen's History of the German People. And although our literature is as rich and varied and as excellent as any in other departments, we have very few names to redeem our historical writing from an unenviable mediocrity.

Venerable Bede.— The first English writer of prominence who should be mentioned, although not a great stylist, is the Venerable Bede, justly called the Father of English History. His Ecclesiastical History, composed in the early part of the eighth century, is in reality a political history of England down to that date, for it comprises all that is known of early English history, whether ecclesiastical or poltical. A noteworthy feature of Bede's history is the amount of research which it represents. His method of quoting authorities and of weighing their evidence proves his unwillngness to imitate either classic authors or his own contemporaries in the matter of blending fact with fiction. As he states in the preface, "I have labored sincerely to commit to writing only such reliable things as I could gather from the works of scholars and from common tradition for the purpose of rightly instructing posterity. If I have written anything not delivered according to the truth, the reader must not impute the same to me, for in all that I have written I have labored honestly to render a faithful account." The Latin style of Bede is correct, plain and clear but not remarkable for any quality distinguishing it from ordinary Church Latinity. The charming personality of Bede, like that of Alfred, has won him even greater fame than his history.

Earl of Clarendon.— The first English historian who deserves to be ranked as a stylist is Edward Hyde, better known as the Earl of Clarendon. He was born in 1608; died in 1674. A university graduate and a member of the Long Parliament, Clarendon took part in the English Civil War, which he afterward made the subject of his history. As the materials were derived from the author's personal experience, the work is of high value, and places Clarendon among the leading historians of England; while the dignity, strength and polish of his style rank him as one of our classic prose-writers. Clarendon was a royalist, and his history in places is an excellent illustration of party prejudice. As the period covered is barely forty years, his work is also a fair illustration of how English history is written in fragments. There are two noteworthy features of his history — it is written rather in the form of Memoirs than of history, as if the Civil War were an episode in the author's own life rather than a part of the history of England. A second feature is the excellent manner in which the leading characters of the Civil War are delineated. The fine analysis of character and its dramatic presentation are not the least among the gifts of Clarendon. His prose is distinctively modern in tone and phrase as contrasted with the involved, lumbering style which Milton, Bacon and Raleigh employed in their historical writings.

David Hume.— The next stylist after Clarendon, in the order of time, is David Hume, the Scotch philosopher, essayist and historian. Some critics, like Henry Morley, regard Hume as our greatest stylist in the department of history, ranking him ahead of Macaulay, Gibbon or Prescott. The History of England, written by Hume, beginning with the invasion of Julius Cæsar, extends to the reign of James I. This was the first historical work in English planned on an extensive scale. The merits of the plan, says Morley, and the incomparable clearness and beauty of the narration soon overcame the indifference of the public, and the history gradually but successfully rose to the highest popularity and took its place among the prose classics of our language, a place it has ever since retained. There is a certain exquisite ease and vivacity about Hume's narrative which has never been surpassed. He

possessed all the qualities of a good story-teller; and, besides
this merit, his descriptive power was of the very highest order
— he pictures the great battles and scenes of important events
in such a way as to excite the interest of the dullest reader.
Perhaps the harshest criticism of Hume is of his indolence,
accepting so much of his material from second-hand sources
and not troubling himself too much about accuracy. Thus,
there are legendary and half-mythological stories told in the
first volume of his history which ordinary accuracy would
have excluded. In spite of his belief and attitude on religious
matters, Hume wrote a history which has at present a wider
circulation than any other on the same subject.

Lord Macaulay.— The best known stylist in English history
is Lord Macaulay, whose work, like that of Clarendon, is
fragmentary. Scarcely two hundred years of English history
are covered by it. Whatever be the correct estimate of his
work, Macaulay had a rather peculiar view of what a history
should be. In one of his critical essays he defines a perfect
history as a compound of poetry and philosophy, impressing
general rules on the mind by a vivid representation of particular characters and incidents. Elsewhere he defines the perfect
historian as one in whose work the character and spirit of an
age are exhibited in miniature. He relates no fact, attributes
no expression to his characters, which is not authenticated by
sufficient testimony; the true historian shows us the court, the
camp, the senate. He shows us also the nation. He considers
no anecdote, no peculiarity of manner, no familiar saying as too
insignificant for his notice, which is not too insignificant to
illustrate the operation of laws, of religion and of education,
and to mark the progress of the human mind

Criticism by Frederic Harrison.— Macaulay's theory of
what a history should be is far better than his performance.

His work is full of mistakes; although he had at hand all the material necessary for an accurate account. His love for striking antitheses led him to make statements which a sound judgment would have modified. The fact is, Macaulay was carried away by the glamor and glitter of a highly artificial style and sacrificed the truth of his narrative for the sake of striking effects; the sweeping generality, the grand climax, the splendid paradox — all needed the element of fiction in order that they might be sustained; but notwithstanding his lack of judgment and accuracy, the magnificence of his style won him instant popularity, and he remains the literary idol of those who mistake rhetorical tinsel for sound taste and genuine merit. We may not inappropriately call him the glorified journalist. While Macaulay had undoubted genius in the manipulation of words and the marshalling of sentences, he lacked the scholarship, patience, moderation and sound judgment necessary to the historian.

Edward Gibbon.— By far the greatest name in English historical literature is that of Edward Gibbon who was born in 1737; died in 1794. By turns a catholic, protestant and infidel, he finally settled down to a sort of philosophic deism. Educated at the English universities and in Switzerland, Gibbon displayed at all times an insatiable appetite for reading and study; he was known at home and in school as a diligent student.

Criticism by Thomas Shaw.— The History of the Decline and Fall of the Roman Empire is undoubtedly one of the greatest monuments of industry and genius. The task he undertook was to give a connected narrative of one of the most eventful periods in the annals of the world. It embraced a period of thirteen centuries, accounting for the greatest religious and social changes that have ever modified the destinies of our race; the rise and progress of Christianity and Mahomedanism. The institutions of Feudalism and Chivalry; the establishment of the modern European nations. The complexity of the subject was as remarkable as its extent. Not the least noteworthy feature is the full and varied references and quotations with which he supports his assertions. Very few statements made by Gibbon have been modified by more recent historical study. Guizot calls him the most accurate of our historians. The style of Gibbon is remarkably pompous, elaborate and dignified. Owing to the immense preponderance of the Latin over the Saxon element in his diction he is the least English of all our writers of the first class. The French idiom abounds. His chief sin against good taste is the too gorgeous and highly colored tone in his descriptions. His imagination was sensuous and he dwells with greater enthusiasm upon material than moral grandeur. There is in much of his work an offensive cynicism, as if he were recording the story of a race of fools. It is a trace of the influence of Voltaire upon his life and character.

Henry Hallam.— A modern English historian who illustrates the method of writing history on institutional rather than national lines, is Henry Hallam, who died in 1859. Hallam was a lawyer by profession, an excellent classical scholar, one who possessed an accurate and profound acquaintance with the language, literature, history and institutions of modern Europe. Hallam wrote a constitutional history of England, beginning with Henry VII. It covers a period of three hundred years

Criticism by Macaulay.—" On the whole, Mr. Hallam is far better qualified than any other writer of our time for the office which he has undertaken. He has great industry and great acuteness. His knowledge is extensive, various and profound. His mind is equally distinguished by the amplitude of its grasp and by the delicacy of its tact. His speculations have none of that vagueness which is the common fault of political philosophy. On the contrary they are strikingly practical, and teach us not only the general rule, but the mode of applying it to solve particular cases. In this respect they often remind us of the discourses of Machiavelli. The manner of the book is, on the whole, not unworthy of the matter. The language, even when most faulty, is weighty and massive, and indicates strong sense in every line. It often rises to an eloquence, not florid or im-

passioned, but high, grave and sober; such as would become a
state paper or a judgment delivered by a great magistrate. In
this respect the character of Mr. Hallam's mind corresponds
strikingly with that of his style. His work is eminently judicial.
The whole spirit is that of the Bench — he sums up with a calm,
steady impartiality, turning neither to the right nor to the left,
glossing over nothing, exaggerating nothing. On a general
survey, we do not scruple to pronounce the Constitutional History the most impartial book we have ever read."

Henry Buckle.— An English historian who imitated Guizot
in writing about civilization, is Henry Thomas Buckle, born
in 1821; died 1862. His History of Civilization in England,
complete in two volumes, appeared in 1860 and caused a sensation in Europe and America. The special doctrine he
sought to uphold was that climate, soil, food, and the aspects
of nature are the determining factors in intellectual progress.

Criticism by Robert Flint.—" Buckle had a high ideal of the
historian's duties, and he laboriously endeavored to realize it,
but he fancied himself far more successful in the attempt than
he really was, and greatly underrated what had been accomplished
by others. He brought a vast amount of information from the
most varied and distant sources to confirm his opinions, and the
abundance of his materials never perplexed or burdened him in
his argumentation; nevertheless, examples of well-conducted historical inductions are rare in his pages; he sometimes altered and
distorted the facts. He was very apt, when he had proved a
favorite opinion true, to infer it to be the whole truth. His intellect was comprehensive and vigorous, but neither classically
cultured nor scientifically disciplined; it was amazingly stored
with facts, but not rich in ideas; it was ambitious in aspiration,
confident to excess in its own powers, and exceptionally unconscious of where its knowledge ceased and its ignorance began.
Buckle was deficient in imagination, poetical feeling, and sympathy; hence he was narrow and harsh in his judgments on certain great periods of time and large classes of men, on antiquity
and the Middle Ages, on the clergy and statesmen, on heroes and
martyrs. But he was fearlessly honest according to his lights,

and gave expression to the most distasteful of his opinions with
a manly openness. He paid great attention to his style; it may
be pronounced equal to the subject, precise enough for the demands of science, full, flowing and flexible enough for every purpose of history. It is lucid when the business of the writer is to
state, explain, or illustrate; and whenever anger at the oppressor,
or sympathy with the oppressed calls upon it, it ascends to tones
worthy of Edmund Burke himself."

William Prescott.— Among authors of history, our greatest
stylist is William Hickling Prescott, born in 1796; died in
1859. A graduate of Harvard College, Prescott took up
the study of Spanish history, the result of his work being a
History of Ferdinand and Isabella; History of Phillip II;
The Conquest of Mexico; and The Conquest of Peru. He also
left a considerable volume of critical essays.

Criticism by Robert Wace.—" As an historian, Prescott
stands in the direct line of literary descent from Robertson, whose
influence is clearly discernible in his method and style. But
while Robertson was in some measure the initiator of a movement
dealing with Spanish history, Prescott came to the task when the
range of information was incomparably wider. He worked,
therefore, upon more assured ground; his sifting of authorities
was more thorough, and his method less restricted, both in the
selection of details and in their graphic presentation. At the
same time, Prescott cannot be classed as in the highest sense a
philosophic historian. His power lies chiefly in the clear grasp
of fact, in selection and synthesis, in the vivid narration of incident. For extended analysis he had small liking and faculty,
his critical insight is limited in range, and he confines himself
almost wholly to the concrete elements of history. When he does
venture upon more abstract criticism, his standards are often commonplace and superficial. And the world-scheme to which he
relates events is less profound than the thought of his time altogether warranted. If these things, however, indicate failure
from the point of view of ideal history, they at least make for
popularity. Few historians have had in a higher degree that

artistic feeling in the broad arrangement of materials which insures interest. The course of his narrative is unperplexed by doubtful or insoluble problems; no pretense at profundity or subtlety saps the vitality of his characters or interrupts the flow of incident with dissertation or digression. The painting is filled in with primary colors and with a free hand; and any sense of crudity which may be awakened by close inspection, is compensated by the vigor and massive effectiveness of the whole. Though Prescott did not bring to his work the highest scientific grasp, he brought to it scientific conscientiousness and thoroughness within his limitations, while his dominant pictorial faculty gave to his treatment a superscientific brilliancy. The romance of history has seldom had an abler exponent, and the large number of editions and translations of his works attests their undiminished fascination."

George Bancroft.— An American historian, whose name deserves mention with that of Prescott, is George Bancroft, who was born in 1800 and died in 1891; and who spent forty years of his life upon a history of the United States. The first volume was published in 1834, and the tenth or last, in 1874. Bancroft also wrote a history of the Constitution of the United States, which compares very favorably with Hallam's Constitutional History of England, both from the point of view of style and research.

Criticism by Henry Tuckerman.—" Mr. Bancroft carefully prepared himself for the task of writing a history of his country. After securing the best scholarship training that his own country afforded, he spent some years in the German universities of Gottingen and Heidelberg. To the task of writing a History of the United States he brought great and patient industry, an eloquent style, and a capacity to array the theme in the garb of philosophy. Throughout he is the earnest advocate of democratic institutions; and in the early volumes, where, by the nature of the subject there is little scope for attractive detail, by infusing a reflective tone he rescues the narrative from dryness and monotony. Instead of a series of facts arranged without any unity of sentiment, we have the idea and principle of civic advancement towards freedom, as a thread upon which the incidents are strung. He is remarkably diligent in unfolding the experiences of the first discoverers, and the political creeds of the early settlers; many curious and authentic details of aboriginal habits are also given; there are everywhere signs of research and genuine enthusiasm. Owing to the unequal interest of the subject, the same glow and finish are not uniformly perceptible in the style in which we occasionally discern an obvious strain after rhetorical effect. Sometimes, also, the author's political opinions are too often apparent. But these are incidental defects. The general spirit, execution, and effect of the work are elevated, genial, and highly instructive. Mr. Bancroft has vindicated his right to compose the annals of his country by giving to the record that vitality both of description and of thought which distinguishes true history from a mere collation of facts. He combines in his style the traits of a two-fold culture — the speculative tendency of the German, and the vivid delineation of the English historian; in a word, he gives us pictures, like the one, and arguments and suggestions, like the other, carefully stating the fact, and earnestly deducing from it the idea; he is more comprehensive as a philosopher than a limner, and yet no tyro in the latter's art, for here and there we encounter a character as tersely drawn, and a scene as vividly painted, as any of those which have rendered the best modern historians popular. But it is the under-current of thought rather than the brilliant surface of description which gives intellectual value to Bancroft's *History,* and has secured for it so high and extensive a reputation. In sentiment and principles, it is thoroughly American; but in its style and philosophy it has that broad and eclectic spirit appropriate both to the general interest of the subject and the enlightened sympathies of the age. Perhaps the best way to appreciate the literary merits of Bancroft's *History* is to compare it with the cold and formal annals familiar to our childhood. Unwearied and patient in research, discriminating in the choice of authorities, and judicious in estimating testimony, Bancroft has the art and the ardor, the intelligence and the tact, required to fuse into a vital unity the narrative thus carefully gleaned. He knows how to condense language, evolve thought from fact, and make incident and characterization illustrate the progress of events. This bold, active, concentrated manner is what is needed to give permanent and living interest to history. Portraits of individuals, scenes pregnant with momentous results and philosophic inferences alternate in his pages. The character of Pitt, the death of Montcalm, and the *rationale* of Puritanism, are very diverse subjects, yet they are each related to the development of the principle of freedom on this continent, and, accordingly, received both the artistic and analytical treatment of the American historian."

Francis Parkman.— Born at Boston, 1823; died, 1893. He studied at Harvard University, graduating with high honors in 1844; taught for one year in the University. His writings belong to the department of history and of fiction. His historical writings deal with early pioneer, missionary and Indian life in North America. Chief works: *Jesuits in North America; Montcalm and Wolfe; Pioneers of France in the New World.*

Criticism by Henry Tuckerman.—" Parkman hunted the buffalo, fraternized with the Indians, and thus gained that practical knowledge of aboriginal habits and character which enabled him to delineate the subject chosen with singular truth and effect. The result of his studies and experiences is not only a reliable and admirably planned narrative, but one of the most picturesque and romantic produced in America. Few subjects are more dramatic and rich in local associations; and the previous discipline and excellent style of the author have imparted to his historical work a permanent attraction."

John Fiske.— A native of New England, born at Hartford, Conn., 1842; studied the classics and law at Harvard University; held position of Librarian and Professor of Philosophy at Harvard for many years. His writings belong to the departments of history, philosophy, and criticism. His chief works are the " American Revolution " and the " Beginnings of New England." ¬

Criticism by the Editor of this Manual.—" The name of John Fiske is familiar to every American school boy. As a painstaking, conscientious historian he has few equals in the field of historical inquiry. Self-reliance, a freedom from prejudice, the very freshness of life, are characteristics which impress the reader at once; add to them the charm of a style flexible, vivid, picturesque, meeting all the requirements of historical narrative and description. Readers may differ from him in matters of evolution and theology, but all must be fascinated by his manner of treating historical subjects."

CHAPTER XXXIV.

THE ORATION

The oration is called a standard prose-form; it is recognized
as such in all ancient and modern literature. It has always
been a distinct division of prose; although oratory has found
occasional expression in history, in the drama and the epic.
The term, oration, is selected in preference to speech, discourse,
or address; although these words are often used as synonyms.
There are two reasons for this selection. First, the word,
oration, in its widest meaning, embraces all the work done in
this prose division — whatever is written or prepared for public delivery. For example, Lord Bacon writes in the Advancement of Learning: "Orations are pleadings, speeches,
invectives, apologies, laudations, polemics and the like."
Macaulay in his work on the Athenian orators, writes: "The
Greek oration from its humble beginnings in the Agora became the most powerful weapon against the encroachments
of tyranny." A second reason for its employment: the term,
oration, more strongly than any other, connotes the best literary work done by the orator. In the strictest sense it stands
for the most elaborate effort of the public speaker. Hence,
modern volumes of this species of prose are called orations
rather than addresses, discourses, or speeches; and the term,
oration, is selected to represent this prose-form in literature.

The Oration Defined.— The oration is a finished prose composition intended for public delivery. It is prepared for some
special occasion; hence, it is the best literary work of the ora-

tor. It involves the art of writing, and thus differs from oratory which is concerned with the art of interpreting to an audience what is written. Oratory is concerned with voice, gesture, manner — the personal appearance of the orator; the oration is his literary product.

The Oration Compared with the Essay.— The oration is similar to the essay in three particulars. First, in its briefness. Like the essay, it is a minor prose-form. However elaborate or finished an oration may be, it never reaches the proportion of a volume like history, biography or fiction. Hence it is classified with the letter and the essay as a minor prose-form. A second similarity: the oration, like the essay, possesses unity of theme and methodical development of thought. Hence both are fundamentally artistic. A final similarity: the oration, like the essay, demands the highest kind of literary talent. The orations holding a permanent place in literature are invariably the work of superior talent.

Some Differences.—The oration differs from the essay in five particulars. First, in purpose. The oration is intended to be spoken; the essay, to be read. The one appeals to the ear; the other, to the eye. Hence the oration must be so composed as to accomplish its purpose immediately; whereas, the essay admits of re-reading and careful survey. A second difference: the oration differs from the essay in power of appeal. Its success depends largely upon its power of arousing emotion in an audience. Hence, the art-content of an oration differs not in kind, but in degree, from that of the essay. Sublimity, humor, feeling, in fact all the elements of art-content are present in a larger degree, and their presence makes the oration a higher grade of literature than the essay. A third difference: the orator is permitted to repeat his thoughts until they are driven home and the required emotion is aroused.

The orator's success depends largely upon the skill with which these repetitions are made. Such repetitions would spoil the style of an essay. For example, the chief defect in Matthew Arnold's essays is the needless repetition of ideas. Aristotle speaks about the orator's gift of tautology; and all critics agree on this point, that in the oration the same ideas must be repeated in different words; the same thoughts must be restated until the orator is sure that he has made the necessary impression. Among orators Cicero excels for this talent of iteration — of repeating the same thought in diversified forms. This repetition, which is a merit in the oration, would be a serious defect in any other department of literature. A fourth difference between the oration and the essay: this difference is vividness of style. The oration makes a stronger appeal to the emotions than does the essay; hence the style of the former is characterized by frequent inversions, striking figures, by question marks and exclamations, by all the arts which make language impressive. This vividness of style is foreign to the essay, and out of place in any prose composition except the oration. The fifth difference between the oration and the essay lies in the plan or outline which the writer follows. The plan of the oration is more complex, more elaborate; the natural divisions of the theme are treated in a more formal way. If we compare the introduction of the essay with the introduction of the oration, this point of difference will appear. The orator usually recognizes his audience; the essayist as a rule proceeds directly to the development of the theme.

Characteristics of the Introduction.— An immediate recognition of the audience is required by the plan and purpose of an oration. " From the outset," says Aristotle, " the purpose is to gain admission, as it were, into the mind of the audience, and to establish a bond of sympathy between speaker and hearer. For, without some bond of sympathy and good feeling, an audience will not be open to enlightenment or persuasion." Quintilian writes: " In giving an introduction to his speech the orator must have as his object the preparation of his hearers to listen more readily and attentively." On the other hand, the essayist assumes that his work will be read; he makes no special effort either in the opening paragraph or in any other part to win recognition. His appeal is intellectual rather than emotional. He relies upon his literary reputation or upon the popularity of the magazine wherein his work appears. The purpose of an introduction in oratory is to win the audience as well as to introduce a subject for discussion. Hence, the introduction of the theme amounts to the introduction of a public speaker. And the speaker in his opening words must reveal certain qualities in order to gain admission into the mind and heart of his audience.

Qualities Required.—Among these qualities the first one favorably to impress an audience is calmness in manner and in language. Calmness implies strength, self-reliance, a mastery of the situation. Calmness at once disposes the audience favorably toward the speaker. Calmness in language is demanded in an introduction, because the audience at the beginning is passionless, unmoved. Emotion is to be aroused by gradual and growing appeals; hence, the vivid style which characterizes other parts of the oration is not a characteristic of the introduction. The style employed is plain, simple, without ornament; giving no expression to vehemence or passion.

An Exception.— When the emotion of the audience is already aroused before the speaker begins, then the calm, formal introduction is changed to an immediate, emotional appeal. For example, the orations of Mirabeau during the French Revolution; the orations of Cicero during the Catilinian rebellion; the orations of Wendell Phillips during the slavery agitation.

These, however, are exceptional cases; the orator as a rule must arouse the audience gradually; he begins calmly and proceeds with an ever-increasing warmth and vehemence.

Seriousness.— The second quality of an orator revealed by the introduction is seriousness. This quality is indispensable if the orator would exercise any considerable influence over his hearers. The subjects of the best orations do not offer any room for levity or pleasantry. They are subjects connected with temporal or spiritual salvation, or they represent great crises in life; and hence from the very outset the audience looks for seriousness in the speaker. Quintilian writes: " Only a serious, earnest, speaker can convince or persuade an audience when great interests are at stake." The pulpit orator above all others, says Fenelon, is required to be serious. On his word depends the salvation of souls. Hence, an amusing story, an anecdote or pleasantry of any kind must be kept out of the introduction in the highest type of the oration. There are certain classes of oratory in which pleasantry is suitable in the introduction and throughout the speech; but seriousness *in word* and *in manner* is demanded on all important occasions.

Politeness.— The third quality that an introduction should reveal is politeness. In the introduction of a speech an audience discovers at once whether the speaker is arrogant or proud or ill-mannered. An audience, like society, is won by a display of politeness. Hence, the opening words should be free from the slightest trace of vulgarity. Quintilian writes: " The first impression that a speaker makes upon an audience ought to be unmistakable evidence that he is a gentleman." Politeness implies two things: a respect for ourself and respect for the audience. And unless a speaker respects both himself and his hearers he cannot hope to exercise much influence or accomplish much in the matter of persuasion. The form of politeness most pleasing to an audience is modesty in the personal claims of the speaker. "Whatever be the talent or reputation of the orator," says Cicero, "he cannot afford to parade it; he must exercise a becoming reserve. Affectation of any kind ruins an orator as it does an actor." Cicero among the ancients, the French among modern orators, showed the greatest respect for the audience. Their exordiums are models of politeness.

The Plan.— The plan of the oration differs from that of the essay not only in the introduction, but also in the peroration. The closing paragraph in an essay does not differ from other parts. It completes the development of the theme; but there is no change in the style, and there is no purpose requiring special treatment of the subject. But there is a special purpose which the orator seeks to accomplish in the peroration. At the beginning, there is a direct effort to win the audience; at the close, there is an effort to leave a lasting impression. Hence, the closing part is written in a style extremely vivid. It is the best piece of writing in the composition. It is a summary of thought, a climax of feeling, and the literary form is the most highly finished of which the speaker is capable. Aristotle sums up the purpose of a peroration as follows: "In the peroration the orator endeavors for the last time to dispose the hearers favorably toward views or opinions already expressed; he summarizes the chief points in the oration and places his hearers under the influence of the passions; so that they feel most keenly pity, terror, hatred, emulation. He places that idea last upon which the strength of his case should rest."

Appeal to the Passions.— The plan of an oration, unlike the plan of an essay or of any other prose-form, makes the largest provision for the excitement of the passions; and the art displayed in this excitement is so subtle and complex as to place the oration among the highest grades of literature. The passions are the springs of human action. Men cannot be persuaded unless their passions are stirred. An orator cannot control his audience or persuade men to act unless he plays upon their feelings and emotions. This part, called the pathetic part in the oration, is the most difficult to handle. Hence, Cicero writes: "The highest power of an orator consists in exciting the minds of men to anger or to hatred or to grief, or in recalling them from these more violent emotions to gentleness and compassion." On the necessity of exciting the passions Aristotle writes: "When an audience has been brought to a state of excitement, then persuasion is effected, but not till then." Quintilian bears the same testimony to the pathetic part of an oration: "Throughout the whole of an oration there is room for addresses to the feelings; nor does the art of oratory present any subject that requires greater study; for the nature of the feelings is varied and should be treated with the greatest care." As to other parts of the oration, moderate and limited powers of mind will do. For example, the establishment of proofs — the appeal to reason and to the intellect — these things are of minor importance as compared with the power to make an audience weep or feel angry or respond to any other emotion. Yet it is this power that is supreme in oratory. The very life and soul of eloquence are shown in the effect produced on the feelings.

Ways of Exciting the Passions.— Various are the ways of exciting and controlling the feelings of an audience. The foundation of all successful literary work in the way of the pathetic is to place in concrete form, to paint in words, those objects which excite passion. This is called pictorial work in an oration. For example, the parables in the teaching of the Savior. Pictorial work ranks first in this connection, because it appeals to the multitude untrained in the development of abstract ideas. The multitude cannot follow a line of abstract reasoning without frequent and suitable illustration. A picture like the parable is necessary to stamp a truth on the mind of the people. Pictorial work in the oration embraces all the methods, whereby ideas are made concrete; hence, metaphor, simile, personification, all the figures of speech are pressed into service.

Scope.— Pictorial work in the oration will also include the illustrious events and characters of history. The orator depends as much upon the concrete examples of history as upon figures of speech. For instance, in sermon literature, the pictorial work dealing with the lives of the martyrs or with scenes of early conflict in Galilee, Greece or Rome. Pictures from history make a powerful appeal to the emotions, especially when they are drawn from the history of one's own country or when they concern objects made sacred by religion. Pictorial work in the oration owes a debt not only to history, but to the drama and the epic. The orator has always drawn heavily upon these sources. The department of literature represented by the oration, is perhaps the heaviest borrower in the matter of classic pictures. Milton and the tragedies of Shakespeare furnish the best pictorial work we have in English. English orators like Burke, Webster and Chatham show the greatest familiarity with the dramas of Greece, and the epics of Virgil and Homer.

Modern Use.— Pictorial work in the modern oration is characterized by briefness. The picture is drawn in a few lines, where the orators of a century ago would devote as many pages. Pictorial work in a large measure is required from the American orator. Our pulpit or platform oration when successful, contains a wealth of illustration. An English audience demands less pictorial work. For example, the parochial sermons of Newman and Liddon would be failures, if preached to American audiences. Plainness and freedom from illustration satisfy the unimaginative English mind.

Value.— Concerning pictorial work, Quintilian writes: " Whosoever shall best conceive images that will represent to the mind of the audience absent objects, will have the greatest power in moving the feelings. This power depends upon the fertility and the vividness of the orator's imagination. Hence the public speaker without imaginative power is of a certainty doomed to failure." Aristotle advises the greatest care in the training of the imagination for those who aim at becoming public speakers. He writes: " All audiences delight in surveying images, and they are moved far more by impressive imagery than by any mental work in an oration; because it is not by naked, bold, statements of fact, but by pictures that make them see the facts, that assemblies are moved." Accordingly, among figures of speech the metaphor is the orator's figure.

The Demand for Such Work.— Frequent and suitable illustrations are demanded in the oration addressed to the multitude. The orator meets this demand in two ways. He offers the work done by others, or his own work. The best speakers have adopted both methods. For example, in the Bunker Hill oration by Webster, there is the picture of Columbus on the deck of a vessel; the picture of the Battle of Bunker Hill; the picture of American prosperity — all drawn by himself — all original. There are also pictures from classic sources: Milton, Virgil, and Homer are quoted literally. A speaker is permitted to take a picture bodily from any source whatsoever, providing the borrowed work will illustrate his theme. And it is not necessary to give credit to the original author, as in other departments of literature.

Use of Poetry.— The employment of pictorial work done in poetry is an old custom with orators. Cicero recommends the study of poetry for the sake of imagery and illustration, because in this regard poetry bears the closest affinity to oratory. A favorite method with preachers is to paraphrase the psalms and other pictorial work of the Holy Scriptures, turning into prose and retaining the Biblical language of such pieces as suit the sermon. For example, in Newman these paraphrases not only of psalms, but of other Biblical passages, occur constantly. Another method followed by preachers is to take bodily the illustrations found in sermon-volumes — the work of other clergymen. A sermon written by a first-class author in any language is certain to contain some useful illustrations in the shape of texts or figures of speech. Sermons on the same subject by different clergymen will yield an abundance of pictorial work. Hence, the necessity of reading sermon literature, an extensive knowledge of which is the best equipment for the pulpit.

Original Work.— The orator must depend upon his own illustrations as well as upon those furnished from various literary sources. The work done by others may be extensive and abundant; nevertheless, he cannot always depend upon such sources; they are not always at hand. Illustrations demand a careful training in descriptive writing; because they are, for the most part, of a descriptive character. In this work the oration requires the greatest brevity and vividness. Hence, the orator should be a trained writer in all kinds of descriptive work. To draw a picture in words requires almost as much skill as to draw it in colors. It is the testimony of all speakers of eminence that years of practice in composition are necessary before one can effectively illustrate a sermon or an oration.

A Two-fold Need.— Without careful literary training, this material cannot be used to advantage, and hence among the qualifications of a successful speaker, two are worthy of special emphasis: extensive reading with a view to collect and employ the illustrations found in the various departments of literature; secondly, a careful training in composition enabling the speaker to prepare the raw material and supply his own illustration. Quintilian writes: "In order to gain a mastery over illustration, which means in turn a mastery over the audience, two kinds of work are required: the labor of critical reading and the greater labor of careful writing. Illustrations will never be forcible or energetic unless they acquire strength from great practice in both reading and writing. For the labor of writing, if left destitute of models from reading, passes away without effect, as having no director. Reading supplies the models for imitation; and writing enables us to make our own illustration as strong and effective as the model we imitate." Cicero observes: "What is so pleasant to be heard and understood as an oration adorned and polished, enriched with varied and beautiful illustrations; what, on the contrary, is so disappointing and barren as an oration without such ornament?"

CHAPTER XXXV

THE ORATION (CONTINUED)

ARGUMENT IN THE ORATION

Argument, like pictorial work, occupies a large place in the oration. It comes first in the order of development; and by some critics is ranked first in importance. Its importance is determined to some extent by the species of oration. For example, an oration in defense of some criminal at the bar of justice; an oration in praise of some hero. Argument in the oration is an appeal to reason; just as pictorial work is an appeal to the emotions. The selection and arrangement of arguments require as much care as the selection of suitable illustrations. Truths may be presented to an audience in two ways: first, in an abstract form, appealing directly to the intellect, and aiming at conviction; secondly, in a concrete form, appealing to the emotions and aiming at persuasion. The usual method in the oration is to state truths in the abstract form and then to apply illustrations, thus giving the same truth a concrete form. Two examples — Newman writes: "Theologians are apt to be lacking in the acquisition of science." The same truth follows in concrete form: "St. Augustine and St. Thomas knew less about science than a modern peasant." Lacordaire writes: "The Justice of God will prevail;" immediately afterward, in concrete form, "Consider the fiery furnace of Hell where fallen men and angels writhe in torment." When argument takes the abstract form it is occupied with principles, with genus and species, cause and effect. Inasmuch as it is applied logic, it employs the abstract vocabulary of logic; and, in every premise and inference, appeals directly to the intellect. Hence, argument exercises the reasoning power of an orator; just as illustration or pictorial work employs his imaginative power.

The Demands of Argument.— Argument involves both philosophy and rhetoric; philosophy, because its very existence depends upon that part of philosophy known as logic. And after arguments are constructed, rhetoric determines their order and arrangement in the oration. Rhetoric determines the place in the speech where they will be most effective, and the style and manner of expression. A debate among ancient critics took place over the relative value of philosophy and rhetoric in the making of an orator. Aristotle quarreled with the Rhetoricians of Greece. He declared that philosophy, inasmuch as it discovered the sources and aided in the construction of argument, was of more value to a speaker than rhetoric which merely arranged the argument and supplied suitable expression. The Rhetoricians contended that unless the arguments were properly arranged and most forcibly expressed, they might as well be omitted from a speech. The appeal would be lost upon the audience. Cicero, in summarizing the needs of an orator, places logic first. He writes: " The orator ought to have the subtlety of the dialectician, the grasp of a philosopher, the diction of a poet, the voice and gesture of the greatest actors." The amount of abstract reasoning in an oration will be determined by the character of the audience; a highly educated audience can follow it without much need of illustration. Hence, in orations before learned bodies, in all academic speaking, arguments are advanced in abstract form, demonstrating that which is true, but in a manner dry, bare and exact. The speaker proceeds in correct syllogistic form, and with mathematical precision. Very little else is given to the audience except the solid proofs of the proposition.

Logic and the Masses.— The abstract method of reasoning cannot be followed with success when a speaker addresses the uneducated masses. The common people do not understand abstractions. The terminology of the schools is a foreign language to them; they demand that the speaker lay aside those terms and employ a language known to all — words making a universal appeal; they demand that rhetoric be added to philosophy, not only in the construction and arrangement of arguments, but also, that each of these arguments be driven home by a number of forcible illustrations. For them the skeleton of thought requires flesh and blood. For example, the New Testament reveals the proper method and the proper language to use in speaking to the multitude. We cannot improve upon the method employed by the great Teacher of humanity.

Kinds of Argument Employed.— Among the various kinds of argument three are found most frequently in the oration. First, the abridged syllogism used in all kinds of deductive reasoning. The public speaker gives the syllogism a literary treatment. He argues *extra formam*. He cuts out either the major or the minor premise; and in doing so destroys the formalism of logic; yet the abridged syllogism is none the less effective. An example: "The human soul is a substance essentially spiritual; hence, it is immortal." Sometimes the whole syllogism is expressed in a single proposition. For example, "A just God punishes crime." The abridgment of the syllogism is usually accompanied by an extended paraphrase of the premise expressed. For example, Newman frequently devotes a paragraph to the amplification of a major or a minor premise. And in the paragraph immediately following, gives a similar expansion to his inference or conclusion. The public speaker may express both the major and minor of a syllogism, but he never does so in a formal way. He adds to each some amplification, either a proof or an exposition of the major or minor, and as in the case of an abridged syllogism, a paragraph or more may be devoted to each major or minor. Aristotle writes concerning the abridged syllogism: " It is the very body of proof in the oration. When one of the premises is not expressed, but understood, the style of the reasoner is rendered more natural and more in accordance with the demands of the popular assembly. The sword of the dialectician is hidden; only the velvet scabbard appears."

The Dilemma.— The dilemma is an argument frequently used by the orator. It consists of two or more alternatives presented to an adversary, and then follows a refutation of any he may select. Polemic oratory is filled with dilemmas. The great controversialists of the past used the dilemma as a favorite argument. A modern example: Mr. Bryan thus addresses the Republicans: " If you hold the Filipinos, you must hold them either as citizens or as subjects. But you cannot hold them as citizens without admitting them to a plane of equality with Americans; you cannot hold them as subjects without overthrowing the Constitution of the United States." The dilemma is not so popular now in the modern pulpit, because the pulpit has grown less controversial. The sermon literature of the Reformation period and down to the middle of the present century is full of the dilemma.

Arguments from Example.— The third kind of argument employed most frequently by the public speaker is the argument from example. It is a form of inductive reasoning that appeals to the multitude; because all men are constantly em-

ploying it. It is the source of many popular fallacies owing
to the hasty and incomplete generalization which characterizes the popular employment of this method. People often
draw a general conclusion from one or two examples; when a
hundred examples might be cited, proving the contrary. It
was a recognition of this popular weakness to leap at general
conclusions, that drew forth the awful condemnation of the one
by whom scandal cometh. In the moral order no argument
is more powerful for good or evil than the one drawn from
human example. Hence, the trite maxim of Cicero: *"Ex-
empla trahunt"*— Examples compel attention. Witness the
influence of example upon religious and political life; how the
multitude may be drawn into error and held in error by the
example of a few illustrious men. Hence, among the various
equipments of the orator ancient critics insist upon the study
of biography — a knowledge of those human examples which
may be employed with such telling effect. And Fenelon, in
his treatise on pulpit eloquence, places the study of religious
biography next to that of philosophy, so powerful is the example of the illustrious dead in the church to convince and
persuade the living.

Kinds of Argument.— The common means of argument
and persuasion are two — the example, and the abridged
syllogism. Of examples, there are two species; one species is
the quoting of real matters of fact, the events of time as they
have actually happened; the other species is the fabrification
of examples by the speaker. One species deals with fact; the
other, with fable or fiction.

Fictitious Example.— Both ancient and modern orators
made considerable use of the fable or fictitious example. Parables are fictitious examples which serve as well as those based
on fact. Pulpit orators have always employed fictitious ex-

amples. For example, experiences in their own lives or in the lives of others which are purely fanciful; yet illustrate or enforce some lesson. On the construction of fables Aristotle writes: " A speaker in bringing forward such fictitious work, should use for a model those examples that are actual fact. In the fable there should be all the force of probability, all the appearance of truth." For example, " The sower who went forth to sow, scattering grain on poor and stony soil "; legends concerning the martyrs, illustrating their courage and constancy. It is essential to all good fiction to resemble fact and truth; and fictitious examples in the oration are no exception to this rule.

Example as a Basis of Argument.— The example, whether real or fictitious, is the basis of several kinds of argument. The first kind is the general law or principle which is confirmed by the various examples adduced; they are either adduced as positive proof of a general proposition, or a general proposition is inferred from a number of them. In the first case they are used as a corroboration of the general law or principle; in the second case they are employed like the data of any science; they are the material for inductive reasoning. This is the ordinary way of employing examples. Another kind of argument based upon example is called *analogy*. Analogy is founded upon agreement, likeness, resemblance. A resemblance between two things may be so great as to warrant us in inferring that the resemblance extends beyond our actual knowledge. For example, the agreement that the planets around us are inhabited is an argument from analogy; because they resemble the earth in shape, movement, atmosphere, illumination, we infer that they also resemble the earth in the matter of inhabitants. One sentence in Patrick Henry's famous speech contains an argument from analogy: " Caesar had his Brutus; Charles the First, his Cromwell; and George the Third may profit by their example."

Abundance of Analogy.— The world is filled with analogies, with objects bearing some resemblance or likeness to one another; and hence the orator has a wide field and the choicest materials. Perhaps the most extensive works in English literature based upon analogy are Bishop Butler's Analogies between natural and revealed religion; and Henry Drummond's Natural Law and the Spiritual World. The pulpit orator uses the old but forcible arguments from analogy. The angels were all tempted once; and those that withstood the trial were confirmed in everlasting glory; so we stand in relation to the same goal. The martyrs fought the same spiritual fight under even more adverse circumstances. False analogies are as easily and as plausibly drawn as false inferences from a few examples. Hence, the sophistries and the mass of worthless argument in the orations of the special pleader.

Arrangement.— The arrangement of arguments in the oration is compared to that of men on a battlefield. It is the test of rhetorical power just as the construction of arguments is the test of rational power. John Quincy Adams in his Treatise on Oratory, writes: "You can find a hundred persons able to produce good ideas upon any subject for the one who can marshal them to the best advantage. Methodical argument is to the orator what tactics are to military art; and as victory has almost always fallen to the best tactician, so victory in eloquence belongs to him who can make the most methodical arrangement of his arguments and ideas. There is no part of the oration in which the consummate orator will be so decidedly manifest as in this arrangement."

Two Laws.— The various ways of making this arrangement will depend in a measure upon the kind of oration and upon the character of the audience. After allowing for various circumstances, critics insist upon the observance of two laws. The law of climax, an ascending scale of effects; an ever-increasing strength and force in the arguments which are advanced. An anti-climax in a speech is fatal unless the speech is a specimen of comedy. This law of climax is peculiar to the drama, the novel, the oration and the epic. The reader or hearer must be carried on by an ever-increasing emotional or intellectual appeal. The second law in the arrangement of arguments is called the law of exclusion. It is briefly the rejection of all kinds of argument either weak, or ineffective so far as the audience is concerned. An audience abhors weakness of any kind as Nature abhors a vacuum. Weakness in voice, physique, language or argument is always disappointing. Strength in these particulars challenges admiration and bespeaks an ideal orator. One of the most profitable literary studies is to dissect the great orations and compare the amount of argument with the amount of illustration, and note how rational and imaginative power are combined in the amplification of the theme.

CHAPTER XXXVI

THE ORATION (CONTINUED)

STYLE IN THE ORATION

Style.— There is a style or manner of writing which is peculiar to the oration; and this style contributes in a large measure to the success of the public speaker. The master-pieces of oratory in all languages are written in practically the same style. This style, sometimes called oratorical, is characterized by a subtle musical beauty or cadence running elusively through the prose. The cadences in the oration are not marked by the sameness of poetic lines; they are not governed like the regular measures in poetry, they are always wide-ranging and delicately shifting, so as never to compel direct recognition. Yet these prose rhythms are always symbolic of the mood of the passage. They are compared to tones which give to the human voice depth and tenderness and suggestiveness. " It is possible," says Aristotle, " to impose upon a series of simple words by delicately sensitive adjustment, a power over the feelings and imagination like that of an incantation." This power is exercised by the public speaker to the fullest extent; and results in fastening the attention of the audience upon what is said. The best grades of oratory will always include prose rhythm.

Variations of Style.— The manner of writing will vary according to the various parts of the oration and according to the various classes into which it is divided. Each distinct part of the oration, such as the exordium, the argumentative part, the peroration, will require a different style. The style of the exordium is plain, simple, passionless, except when passion is already aroused as in the case of Cicero against Catiline. The style in the peroration is almost the reverse of this; expression is taxed to the utmost in the final appeal — all the wealth and beauty of language are employed. Another contrast of style exists between the argumentative part and the appeal to the emotions. In the former, there is the utmost precision in thought and language; in the latter, there is the largest amount of freedom in the literary development — the manner of writing is free and easy because the pictorial quality which arouses emotion must have sufficient amplification. Thus there are sharp contrasts in the style of the oration, corresponding to the important divisions. A test of first-class workmanship is the power to vary the manner of writing so as to meet the requirements of each division. Good judgment demands these changes. " Style," says Aristotle, " will be in good taste, if it be not only expressive of feeling and character, but also if it be happily adjusted to the subject-matter." This adjustment is preserved, if the style be neither careless on questions of importance nor dignified on such questions or subjects as are mean and trifling. And a style which is thus made appropriate, invests the subject with persuasive efficacy; for the audience is thereby cheated into the persuasion that the orator is speaking with sincerity, even though he may not be; because under such circumstances men stand affected in that manner and employ exactly that kind of style which he employs. Moreover, every condition, habit and emotion of life must have style of language exactly suited to it; for example, the audience detects at once, knows instinctively, the natural language of passion; so also, the natural style of argument; hence, if there be no adjustment, if the orator keeps one manner of expression, regardless of the subject-matter, he is bound to be judged as artificial and unnatural; he loses his power to move the audience because the style makes it impossible for him to interpret his thoughts and emotions aright; his oratory becomes idle declamation.

All Orators Alike.— There is a family likeness among all great orators in this regard: by long practice in composition they can adapt their style of writing with perfect propriety to every shade of thought and emotion. This adaptation is termed the natural style — the style in which a writer speaks as he thinks and feels, and which depends on his temperament and the nature of his subject. Herbert Spencer, in his Philosophy of Style, calls this the perfect manner of writing. He says: "This style will sometimes be plain; sometimes ornate; sometimes the sentences will be balanced, and at other times unsymmetrical; for a time there will be sameness; then great variety; the mode of expression naturally responding to the state of feeling and the composition changing to the same degree that aspects of the subject change."

Variations of Style According to Species.— The style of writing varies, not only according to the various parts of an oration, but also according to the various species into which the oration is divided. In connection with the various species of the oration, Aristotle specifies three kinds of style. First, the demonstrative style. It is employed when the oration gives blame or praise to a particular person. Under this head is included all panegyrics, funeral orations, and orations on anniversaries, and at festivals. It is the manner of writing that belongs to the pulpit. The second is called the deliberative style. It is employed when the oration is delivered in parliament. It is the style of statesmen, and is sometimes called parliamentary oratory. The third is called the judicial style. It is employed in court trials. It is employed in accusation and defense; and it is sometimes called forensic.

The Demonstrative Style.— The demonstrative style, as Aristotle terms it, is employed in the forum and in the pulpit on great anniversaries and festivals. It is easily distinguished from other forms of oratory. The epithet, demonstrative, was used by Aristotle to denote the prevalence of emotion. The speaker has for his main purpose an emotional appeal. Hence, Quintilian calls it the impassioned style. It stands in sharp contrast with the calm, intellectual, appeal which characterizes the judicial style — the cold statement of the law and the evidence. Praise or blame is the object of demonstrative oratory. And the statement of either by a public speaker is always attended with emotion. Pulpit oratory is largely occupied with praise or blame. For example, the praise of God, angels, saints, the illustrious dead; or the condemnation of those whose lives are evil and vicious.

Emotion.— The chief characteristic, then, of demonstrative oratory is the element of emotion. It is the work of the heart, the affections; it is animated, magnetic, spirited; the passion of the speaker is communicated to the audience. It offers the widest scope to applause and enthusiasm. The prose development is akin to the external progress of the drama, each division becoming more vivid and vital than the preceding. Hence, in the forum, the praise of the national hero, amid increasing enthusiasm and excitement; or, in the pulpit, the mission and revival sermon with their dramatic intensity and fervor.

Examples.— For emotional effect compare the funeral orations of Bossuet with the Neglect of Divine Warnings by Newman; or the invective of Demosthenes against Philip of Macedon with the invective of Burke against Warren Hast-

ings or the invective of Cicero against Verres and Catiline.
Emotion in the demonstrative style follows two lines: the
tender and the pathetic; for example, the sufferings of the
hero praised; or, the bold and vehement, as the condemnation
of the criminal.   The subject-matter of pulpit oratory contains
the emotional element in perhaps the largest measure.   For
all theology centers in the saddest of all symbols — the cross
with its connotation of suffering, sacrifice, death.   There can
be no more powerful appeal than this to human emotion.
The subject-matter of pulpit oratory is filled with sublimity;
and this element of art-content always evokes emotion.   The
demonstrative style in the pulpit depends upon the sublime
themes of the supernatural world; and, outside the pulpit, on
the sublime actions of the human hero.   In either case, sublimity plays an important part as an emotional factor.

Element of Power.— A second characteristic of the demonstrative style is the element of power.   While all styles of
oratory have this element to a degree, the demonstrative style
possesses it in the largest measure.   The language of this style
is emphatically the language of power.   This element is a necessary consequence of the presence of feeling.   It follows from
the appeal to the emotions.   It is the literary result of passion.

Demands of the Multitude.— Accordingly,   those   methods
whereby a style is made vivid (for example, figures of speech;
short sentences with a repetition of noun and verb; the most
vigorous illustration; the question mark and interrogation
and other rhetorical devices,) are employed by the speaker.
There is a freedom from restraint in the demonstrative style,
as compared with judicial or parliamentary oratory.   The
speaker addresses the multitude, and hence is exempt from
the criticism of learned judges or select assemblies.   The
traditions, customs and criticism of court or parliament re-

strain an orator from exerting his power to the utmost. But the multitude impose no such checks or restraints; they demand the language of power, they look for the element of power which characterizes demonstrative oratory. This element often runs to excess both in style and in delivery, and the speaker is applauded and his purpose accomplished; whereas, such excess would excite only derision before a select audience — for example, a stump speaker before the Supreme Court.

The Deliberative Style.—The deliberative style is employed in oratory, when the oration is delivered before some representative assembly. For example, a congress or parliament. The individual members of such an audience are the select representatives of the people; and they act, as a rule, in some official capacity. Hence, the deliberative style of oratory flourishes wherever the people have full or partial representative government. For example, in a republic or limited monarchy. In modern times, with the growth of the national spirit and representative government, every parliament can boast of distinguished orators. Some examples: The Spanish Parliament, Emil Castelar; the Italian Parliament, Crispi; German Parliament, Windhorst; French Parliament, Mirabeau; English Parliament, Gladstone and O'Connell; American Parliament, Webster and Calhoun; Canadian Parliament, Sir John Macdonald and Wilfred Laurier. Every nation can boast of several masters of the deliberative style. In the parliaments of Greece and Rome, Socrates, Demosthenes, Cato, and Cicero.

Opinions of This Style.— This manner of writing an oration is partly explained by the term deliberative. To deliberate implies stress on the rational element; it indicates the prevalence of reason over emotion. Concerning the language employed in this style, Quintilian observes: " The language ought to be uniformly simple and grave, and more distinguished for studied thoughts than for studied phraseology. Canning writes as follows: " The House of Commons is a deliberative body of men, and the oration before the House should conform to its predominant character; the correct parliamentary speaker avoids mere ornament and declamation; or, if these be employed at all, they must seem to spring naturally out of the subject; the style should be that of an animated conversation on public business; there must be method also, but this should be felt in the effect rather than seen in the manner. No formal divisions, set exordiums, or perorations, as the old rhetoricians taught, will suit the deliberative style of oratory today. The deliberative oration owes much of its weight to the calm, rational, impressive manner in which it is written. But what adds most weight is the authority of the speaker who, as a member of parliament and often as premier, exercises the power entrusted to him by the people."

Changes in This Style.— Under what circumstances will this style of oratory change? In periods of great national excitement the ordinary calm manner yields to feeling and passion. Then the parliamentary speaker makes the most powerful appeal to the emotions; for indignation is then to be kindled or allayed, and the minds of the audience are to be moved to fear, hatred, pity, benevolence. During these periods or critical emergencies in national life, the very finest specimens of oratory have been produced; for example, the Athenian State in danger from Philip; the Roman State in danger from Catiline; the American Union in danger from secession.

Periods of Excitement.— It is noteworthy that in ancient as well as in modern times, the deliberative style has changed whenever parliament undertakes a great State trial. For example, the Trial of Warren Hastings, the Impeachment of President Johnson, or whenever parliament attempts some radical change in the laws of the realm. For example, the repeal of the May Laws in Germany, the Act of Union between Ireland and England; the imposition of taxes without representation in the American colonies. Because of such abnormal conditions, deliberative oratory undergoes a radical change; but calls forth as a consequence the best speakers both in ancient and in modern times — Demosthenes, Cicero, Burke, Webster, Sheridan, Gladstone, Chatham. All these men appeared during periods of abnormal national excitement.

Modern Influences.— In modern times deliberative oratory has come under the influence of two distinct forces — the commercial spirit, and the reduction of government to a science. These influences have taken away from the deliberative oration almost all traces of the demonstrative style. " A remarkable change," says Matthews, " has come over the House of Commons since the days of Edmund Burke, when English deliberative oratory was enlivened by explosions of passion which shook the House; when sallies of wit, graceful imagery and classic quotations adorned every deliberative effort. Today the deliberative speaker states his views plainly, tersely, with little preamble and less embellishment; and having delivered himself of what he has to say, he concludes as abruptly as he began. The brilliant speech has yielded to the cold business talk based upon a bundle of statistics. Rhetoric as such, and eloquence as such, seem to be no longer a part of the normal working of the British Parliament."

Our Parliamentary Style.— The American Parliament seems to be following the British example and employing the deliberative style in the strictest degree. The Congressional Record, which publishes the speeches of our parliamentary speakers, is little more than a mass of facts, analyzed testimony, cold reasoning, barren precedents and principles — the skeleton of oratory without flesh or soul. Hence, the unwarranted inference that the days of oratory are rapidly passing away. The deliberative style will always be affected by racial temperament; and, in the parliaments of the Latin races, we may expect it to give considerable scope to fancy, imagination, feeling. Yet, among all races, the style of parliamentary oratory should remain substantially as Quintilian defines it — a style, simple, grave, without much ornament or imagery — a style in which reason prevails over emotion. A deliberative assembly will always be engaged upon the discussion of what is honorable, useful or necessary to the State; and this three-fold subject-matter demands the largest exercise of reason and the smallest amount of fancy or imagination.

The Judicial Style.— This is the manner of writing or presenting arguments in a Court of Justice. It deals with evidence, with law, with a judge and jury. It is sometimes called forensic oratory; it belongs to the legal profession, just as demonstrative oratory belongs to the forum and pulpit, and deliberative oratory to parliament.

The Term.— The oration addressed to a judge, gives us the term judicial; it was in the days of Aristotle an elaborate appeal to reason, and a still more elaborate appeal to the passions. Hence, Aristotle in his treatment of the judicial style states the various ways of moving the judge, arousing his passions, so that he might sometimes decide according to his feelings and not according to the law and evidence. This method was universally employed by the pleaders in *ancient* Courts of Justice. It would be absurd to employ such a style in any high courts of justice today. For example, a case could never be won in the supreme courts of Great Britain or America by an emotional appeal. There is not the slightest chance for such success.

Trial by Jury.— Trial by jury has transferred this emotional appeal from the judge to the jurymen; and precisely with
the same purpose as the ancients had in view. The history of
jurisprudence shows frequent cases wherein a criminal, even a
murderer, has been acquitted because of the emotional appeal.
Two examples: Senator Voorhees of Indiana has secured the
acquittal of a number of murderers when the evidence was all
against them, and when their guilt was established beyond the
shadow of a doubt. The late Colonel Ingersoll has a similar
record as a lawyer. The lawyer of modern times is not more
successful with jurymen than the lawyer of ancient times
with judges who were often moved to grant a verdict against
the evidence.

Divisions.— The divisions of a forensic oration are five:
the exordium; statement of facts; the proof of what we advance; refutation of the opposing counsel; and the peroration.

Exordium.— The exordium in judicial oratory is far more
explicit and formal than in any other department of oratory.
The speaker at the outset states in clear, unmistakable terms
to judge and jury what he is going to prove concerning his
client; what he is going to infer from a statement of facts in
the case. This explicitness was accompanied in ancient times
by an attempt to conciliate the judges. Hence, we find in the
classic exordium a frequent digression in praise of the Judge
— his honesty, high-mindedness. These compliments are still
paid to juries; and they form a part of the exordium in modern
forensic oratory. The statement of facts is always made in a
peculiar style. Very much depends upon the coloring of these
statements. The best legal talent is often employed upon the
manipulation of facts, so as to blind or mislead a jury.

Some Characteristics of the Judicial Style.— The style of introduction in judicial oratory differs from that of the usual exordium : it is more explicit and formal. The speaker announces the points which will be the divisions of his oration; his style at the outset is characterized by the utmost clearness and brevity, in order that the jury may see the exact matter at issue. The history of the case in detail follows this explicit and formal introduction. And the judicial style is somewhat peculiar in the statement of details or the facts in the case. The success of an oration in a Court of Justice will often depend upon the manipulation of facts so as to give them an innocent, or guilty, coloring. As a lawyer is engaged for special pleading, all his legal talent will often be employed to make the worse appear the better reason; and he will manipulate the facts in the interests of his client — the story will be colored according to some pre-arranged plan. This manipulation of facts in judicial oratory is compared with the arrangement of objects in a picture. In the foreground of the picture the orator places all those facts that sustain and establish his side of the legal controversy. These facts are brought out in the clearest light, while the background is occupied with every detail that would invite an adverse decision. Purcell's Life of Cardinal Manning is an example in point; Purcell placed all the little defects and faults in the foreground of the picture, shrouding in the background all the grand redeeming traits in the character of the English Cardinal. A lawyer may destroy character in precisely the same way.

False Inferences.— The style of the judicial oration is peculiar not only in the arrangement of facts, but in the amount of false inferences drawn from facts. Hence, this kind of oration is filled with sophistry. False reasoning of every kind abounds. In attempting to prove his case, a lawyer is permitted to deceive the minds of the jury as well as to mislead their sympathies. He is permitted to do what would be ethically wrong outside a court-room.

The Peroration.— The peroration in the judicial style receives special attention. It is carefully written and memorized even when the body of the speech is extemporaneous or given from notes. The final impression made upon the jury is held to be of such importance as to warrant the elaborate perorations found in judicial oratory. The judicial oration does not offer the same scope that other kinds of oratory furnish. The speaker addresses only a small body of men; in the delivery there is not so much room for eloquence as before a parliament or popular assembly. In fact, a lawyer, accustomed for years to address juries, is unfit to make a success of popular or demonstrative oratory; his manner is that of the plain, quiet talker, not that of the orator.

Kinds of Pleading.— An interesting study in the judicial style is a comparison between the pleadings of the lower and higher courts; the former is a style akin to that of demonstrative oratory; the latter suggests the style of the deliberative assembly. In England eloquence has been comparatively rare in the court-room. One reason is the technicality which pervades every branch of English law. Special pleading seems to have the effect of cramping and confining the intellect. Owing to its enormous and unwieldly mass, the English law is unfavorable to the cultivation of oratory. The establishment of so many precedents, the growth of law reports, the statutes of parliament; the gradual extension of the province so as to cover every possible case — all combine to annihilate mere oratory as such. In ancient times, in the flourishing periods of Greek and Roman forensic oratory, the laws were few in number and very simple, and the judges were vested with large discretion; they were governed to a large extent by personal wishes and feelings. Hence, the frequent attempts to win their favor and to play upon their sympathies.

As years go on, we may expect the science of law to become more and more exact and comprehensive, leaving less room for the exercise of discretionary power on the part of judges, and, therefore, less room for aught else save precedent, fact, and evidence.

CHAPTER XXXVII

THE ORATION (CONTINUED)

HISTORY OF THE ORATION

Antiquity.— The oration, like the essay, is found in the oldest literature. It is as old as human society itself, because the most primitive society had a public speaker in its prophet or chief or high-priest. As soon as leaders of men appeared in any walk of life, the orator also appeared; for, aside from its literary value, the oration, like the sceptre, is a symbol of power exerted by one person over a multitude. The best proof of the antiquity of the oration is its presence in all the early histories of the world. The earliest historians quote the speeches of generals, statesmen and religious leaders. Sometimes these speeches form the bulk of a volume of ancient history. As example, Cæsar, Livy, Thucydides, and the historian of the Hebrews may be quoted. The oration occupies a prominent place in their narrative.

Among the Hebrews.— In Hebrew literature the oration is found, but rather in a fragmentary than in a complete form. Hebrew writers cared little for art-form; hence their oration is as crudely finished as their letter or their essay. The oration is represented partly by the elaborate speeches in the epic of Job. There are also numerous speeches scattered through the prophetical writings and New Testament; these cannot be well appreciated from a literary standpoint, because of the condensed and crude form in which they are

reported. The book of Deuteronomy is an exception to the
Biblical rule in the matter of speeches. This book might be
called the " Orations and Songs of Moses." There are four
orations in Deuteronomy; they were delivered by Moses to
the people of Israel, and they are reported with greater completeness than any other orations in the Bible. They resemble the orations found in the history of Livy, and Thucydides.
An intense interest is awakened in these orations from the
pathetic situation in which they are delivered: the leader of
the Hebrews, after wandering for years in the desert, at last
draws near to the Promised Land; and yet he realizes that he
can never enter it. For passionate appeal these orations are
unrivalled; they share the chief glory of Hebrew literature
in depth of feeling, sublimity, tenderness and an exalted style
in harmony with the sentiments expressed. In the orations
delivered by Moses, the subject-matter itself was calculated to
stir the strongest emotions — the captivity in Egypt where
Israel had suffered such long and cruel persecutions — the
years of sorrow in the wilderness — their struggles and tribu-
lations and the farewell of an old and faithful leader who
shared all their sufferings, but was not permitted to share
the happiness of the Promised Land. Nowhere is the tragic
note stronger in the mournful story of this exiled nation. The
only parallel in modern history is the Farewell of Napoleon to
the Old Guard of France.

Form of Hebrew Oratory.— Hebrew oratory frequently
takes the form of denunciation and complaint. This form is
conspicuous in the prophetical portion of Holy Scripture.
The prophets were, for the most part, men of great eloquence.
The invective of Demosthenes or Burke is often equalled by
these inspired reformers of Israel.

Among the Greeks.— The oration holds a prominent place
in Greek literature, because it played a prominent part in

Greek political life. The Greeks believed that eloquence was of celestial origin; they ascribed it to the invention of a god who, on account of this art, was the Messenger and Interpreter of Olympus. Oratory flourished in Greece because for a long time it was a free State; and, in the history of the world, free States alone have fostered oratory. One of the first acts of a tyrant, or of a despotic government, is to muzzle speech, destroy eloquence; it is their only safety. A despotic government wishes its subjects to be driven, not to be persuaded; hence there is no toleration for oratory.

Under Greek Democracy.— Oratory was a power in the flourishing periods of Greek democracy; it was the key to the highest dignities — the passport to the supreme dominion of the State. Hence, the eagerness to acquire this art; eloquence was taught as the occupation of a life. It was one of the chief objects of education in Greek schools. Literature, science, art, were to be mastered on the theory that an orator must be a man of universal knowledge. Moral duties were taught for the reason that none but a good man could be an orator. Learning, wisdom, even virtue itself, were valued only as they ministered to the purposes of eloquence. As a result of this passionate devotion and careful study, the Greeks brought this art to the highest perfection. The oration as a work of art, reached the term of its evolution in Greece; the orators of all nations since then have been mere imitators of Athenian models; just as all dramatic writers have imitated Sophocles or Æschylus, and all epic writers, Homer. It is the glory of Grecian literature to have supplied the best models in every department of verse and prose.

The Golden Age.— The golden age of Grecian eloquence extended from the time of Solon 600 B. C. to that of Alexander, 336 B. C. Within this space flourished the most re-

nowned orators of Greece; it was the brightest period in their
political history. Athens alone produced the great orators.
As an Ionian city, it possessed the rich intellectual qualities
of that brilliant race. The free form of government adopted
by Athens was also a factor. Cicero who studied at Athens,
as a member of the Greek Academy, writes: " The art of
eloquence is not the common property of all Greece, but seems
to belong to Athens alone. For I never heard of Argive,
Corinthian or Theban orators; and I never read of a single
orator among the Lacedæmonians."

The Athenian School.— The Athenians themselves were
conscious of their superiority in matters of eloquence. Isocrates, one of their brilliant speakers, wrote in his famous
panegyric, 380 B. C., as follows: " Athens has so distanced
the world in power of thought and speech, that her disciples
have become the teachers of all other men. She has brought
it to pass that the name of Greece should be thought no longer
a matter of race, but a matter of intelligence; and this name
should henceforth be given to the participators in our culture
rather than to the sharers in our racial origin." The school
of Athenian oratory claims seven distinguished names. The
first of these is Pericles. It is claimed for Pericles that he
was the first Athenian who composed and put into writing an
oration designed for the public. This speech, as reported to
us by Thucydides, is one of the noblest monuments of antiquity. It was delivered in the Westminster of Athens, *Cerami-
cus,* over the graves of those who fell in the Peloponnesian
war. Pericles was one of the most remarkable men of antiquity; he was the champion of Greek democracy, the ruler of
Athens for nearly forty years. He gained his marvelous influence over the Athenians by his moral character and his
eloquence. He spent vast sums in beautifying Athens and
making it an art-center. The names of the artists employed

by him would fill a small volume. He built the Parthenon and the Temple of Athens. In his long lifetime there flourished at Athens the poets, Æschylus, Sophocles and Euripides; the philosophers, Anaxagoras, Zeno, Socrates; the painter, Polygnotus; the sculptors, Myron and Phidias. The age of Pericles is compared, so far as literature and eloquence are concerned, with the age of Augustus in Rome; Louis XIV in France; Elizabeth in England.

Successors of Pericles.— Pericles was succeeded by six distinguished orators: Lysias, a lawyer by profession; Isocrates, a teacher of rhetoric, and known among the Greeks as the " Old Man Eloquent; " Isacus, the instructor of Demosthenes and the author of a treatise on Oratory; Æschines, a lawyer and rival of Demosthenes; finally, Demosthenes himself. These men are the best representatives of Greek eloquence; they compare favorably with Webster, Burke, Chatham and Sheridan in English; their work is, for the most part, preserved; they are known in Greek literature as the flower of the Athenian school.

Demosthenes.— Of these speakers, Demosthenes enjoys the widest reputation; he is more fortunate than the others in having a larger number of his speeches preserved, and thereby giving posterity a better chance to estimate his merits. Twenty-seven speeches known to be genuine are handed down; thirty-four of doubtful origin are ascribed to him, or sixty-one in all. He is also more fortunate in having appeared during a great national struggle when the occasion makes the orator. He enjoyed an advantage over all orators of other nations in having a more perfect medium for his art; inasmuch as the Greek language is admittedly a finer medium for expression than any other language either ancient or modern. In addition to this, Demosthenes owes the plan of his orations to Pericles, who left him perfect models of what the oration ought to be. With all these advantages, he is given first place; only three others, Cicero, Bossuet and Edmund Burke, approach him in excellence, although twenty-four centuries have passed since his birth, and a dozen nations flourishing in that time, have added hundreds of names to the list of orators.

The Oration Among the Romans.— The Romans derived their knowledge of the arts from the Greeks, including every department of literature. For several hundred years they were rude, illiterate, unskilled in anything except the art of war. After the conquest of Greece, they began to study the arts, and leading Roman scholars either studied at Athens, like Cicero, or had Greek teachers brought to Rome. The Greek masterpieces circulated widely in Italy. As a free state, Rome encouraged public speaking; and it was the opinion of Cicero that the art of eloquence, after that of arms, became the pride of the Roman commonwealth. The Romans had certain racial characteristics favorable to oratory. They were a grave people, serious almost to a fault. They were passionately devoted to their country; and patriotism is always an inspiration to eloquence. An additional inspiration came from their territorial expansion; they outgrew the narrowness and provincialism of Italy; a certain magnificence of thought and language followed their magnificent conquests; so that Newman could justly say of Cicero: " He spoke Roman, not Latin; and he was inspired, not by a petty State, but by the *orbis terrarum,* and the world-wide glance of the Roman eagle." Only one nation in modern history gives equal inspiration to the orator — the mistress of the seas, whose drum-beat is heard round the world.

Oratory and the Republic.— The Romans in the days of the Republic, added more names than the Greeks to the list of orators. In his dialogues on oratory, Cicero mentions fully one hundred names, including the famous generals, senators and statesmen of the Republic; such names as Brutus, Cato, Scipio, Antony, Cæsar, appearing among them. But if we make an exception of Cicero, the work of the others was much inferior to that of the Greeks. Oratory passed away with the Republic. A century after the death of Cicero, Tacitus bewails the decay of eloquence, in the following words: " Why is it that former ages were so distinguished for the genius and renown of orators and our own age so bereft of this glory as to scarcely retain the very name; for we style none such now except the ancients; the speakers of the present day are called pleaders, barristers, anything, in fact, rather than orators."

Studies of Quintilian.— Quintilian was the last Roman who distinguished himself by the study of oratory; but he sought fame as a teacher and critic, not as a public speaker. For twenty years he presided over the Roman School of Oratory. He resembles Aristotle in coming after the great orations of his country had been written, and in passing judgment upon them in a volume of criticism. Quintilian attempted a revival of the art, but a despot ruled in Rome, and the revival meant little more than the publication of some worthless panegyrics on a Roman tyrant. The world acknowledges a large debt to Quintilian; his work in criticism has been a text-book in the hands of students since his time.

Modern Oratory.— France and England are leading nations in modern eloquence; and they bear considerable resemblance to Greece and Rome. In relation to the arts, France seems to have inherited the genius of Greece, so that her capital city is justly styled the modern Athens; while London is the modern center of the *orbis terrarum;* and the imperial Eng-

lishman bears a striking resemblance to the imperial Roman.
France has produced two orators who are often compared
with Demosthenes: Mirabeau in the forum, and Bossuet in the
pulpit. The speeches of both contain those elements of passion and power which characterize the orations of the Athenian orator. Intense religious and political excitement gave
both the necessary opportunity. When Mirabeau appeared
in the French Assembly, he hurled defiance and scorn on the
nobility and King, as Demosthenes had done against Philip;
and he roused the people to the same passionate fury; he actually goaded them to madness by his eloquent recital of their
wrongs and his vehement denunciation of their rulers. It is
noteworthy that Mirabeau appeared with the Revolution and
the Republic; he would have been an impossibility under the
Monarchy.

Bossuet.— Besides Mirabeau, France produced another orator who compares favorably with Demosthenes. The orations
of Bossuet are often quoted as the highest standard of modern
pulpit eloquence. In comparison with the Greek masterpieces, these pulpit orations possess the same vehemence and
passion, the same power to influence the mind and captivate
the imagination. Bossuet had the advantage of a more sublime and inspiring theme, but the medium of his art was
less perfect. Many of the sermons of Bossuet exist only in
notes or rough sketches. His funeral orations are handed
down in complete form; as a funeral orator Bossuet is without
an equal. As a rule, Bossuet spoke from notes or outlines;
he did not memorize or write out a sermon except for some
great state occasion; he trusted to the inspiration of the moment; hence some of his best efforts, like those of Chatham,
are lost. Besides the classics, Bossuet relied upon three
sources of sacred eloquence: the homilies of St. Chrysostom
and St. Augustine and the Prophets of the Old Testament.

Fenelon writes that in Bossuet the Old Testament was transfigured into a man; next to these studies, his favorite author was Homer. A copy of Homer was his constant companion. In this particular, Bossuet resembles all the illustrious orators who made a life-long study of some epic — either Homer or Virgil or Milton. Bossuet flourished under a monarchy, but he enjoyed the immunity of the pulpit. Within the sanctuary he could thunder against regal vices and be amply protected by his sacred office. Paganism offered no such scope or safeguard to the eloquence of antiquity.

The Oration in England.— The characteristic difference between French and English eloquence is that which existed of old between Greece and Rome. The French, as greater artists, adopted higher ideals both of pleasing and persuading. The English took up eloquence on a lower key, adopting the utilitarian standard, caring little for polish or symmetry. The temperament of the people, their natural coldness, chilled the glow of emotion and destroyed that passionate fire which is the soul of eloquence; they demanded greater soberness than the French, and fewer flowers of the imagination. Hence, the custom, centuries old, in the English courts and parliament to argue from strict law, statute or precedent, which involves knowledge rather than oratory, reason rather than emotion. Hence, too, their ancient custom of reading sermons in the pulpit, as if oratory were a useless luxury. A strange national pride has materially assisted their phlegmatic temperament and compelled their statesmen, lawyers and clergymen to adopt the extreme of studied coolness and composure. Yet in spite of these drawbacks England has produced some of the finest orators known to history.

Reasons for Oratorical Growth.— Three reasons are assigned for the prominence of the oration in the literature of the English. The first is their freedom, and love of discussion; they have always enjoyed representative government, and the utmost freedom in debate is a marked characteristic of the British parliament which gives the same scope to oratory that it had in the republics of antiquity. A second reason is the vicissitudes, religious and political, through which England has passed from a small island kingdom to a world-wide empire. The revolutions that accompanied so many colonial settlements frequently roused the nation to intense passion and produced orators like Chatham and Sheridan and Burke. The religious revolutions were equally successful in making orators and in furnishing an opportunity for eloquence. Dissenters, Puritans, Calvinists; the long struggle for supremacy between Protestant and Catholic, were in turn an inspiration to the pulpit. "The clash of creeds," said Disraeli, "has kept the English pulpit at furnace heat from the days of Milton down to our own." The religious revolutions are represented by such orators as Latimer, Wiseman, Channing, Wesley. A final reason for the prominence of oratory in English literature is the clash of races, especially the struggle for independence as in the case of the American colonies and Ireland. These struggles are represented by Grattan, Curran, O'Connell, Patrick Henry, Gladstone, Disraeli. So long as there exists a clash of creeds and races in England, so long must oratory continue to flourish in spite of the temperament of the people.

The Future of Oratory.— The oration will remain an important factor in literature and in life, because the conditions which produced it in the past, will continue to exist. The growth of representative governments and the prevalence of Christianity over the world are conditions in its favor. Christianity opened a new avenue to the career of eloquence, and this more than compensates for any losses sustained in parliaments or in courts of justice. The modern scientific spirit has modified the appeal to the emotions and introduced more correctness in the development of thought. But the oration will remain substantially what it was — a composition appealing to reason, sentiment, passion, imagination. The masses will always demand it; and the leaders of men will always employ it.

CHAPTER XXXVIII

THE ORATION (CONTINUED)

REPRESENTATIVE ORATORS

Demosthenes.— He was born at Pæania, Attica, in 384 B. C., and died 322 B. C. He entered public life as a speaker in the Popular Assembly, in 355. His chief orations are the Philippics, the Olynthiacs, On the Peace, On the Embassy, and On the Crown. The best modern editions are those of Bekker (1823); Sauppe and Baiter (1850); Dindorf (1867); Whiston (1859). The orations of Demosthenes derived their inspiration from the struggle against the encroachments of Philip of Macedon.

Criticism by Blair.—" Despising the affected and florid manner which the rhetoricians of that age followed, Demosthenes returned to the forcible and manly eloquence of Pericles; and strength and vehemence form the principal characteristics of his style. Never had orator a finer field than Demosthenes in his Olynthiacs and Philippics, which are his capital orations, and, no doubt, to the nobleness of the subject, and to that integrity and public spirit which eminently breathe in them, they are indebted for much of their merit. The subject is to rouse the indignation of his countrymen against Philip of Macedon, the public enemy of the liberties of Greece; and to guard them against the insidious measures, by which that crafty prince endeavored to lay them asleep to danger. In the prosecution of this end, we see him taking every proper method to animate a people, renowned for justice, humanity, and valour, but in many instances become corrupt and degenerate. He boldly taxes them with their venality, their indolence, and indifference to the public cause;

while, at the same time, with all the art of an orator, he recalls the glory of their ancestors to their thoughts, shows them that they are still a flourishing and a powerful people, the natural protectors of the liberty of Greece, and who wanted only the inclination to exert themselves, in order to make Philip tremble. With his contemporary orators who were in Philip's interest, and who persuaded the people to peace, he keeps no measures, but plainly reproaches them as the betrayers of their country. He not only prompts to vigorous conduct, but he lays down the plan of that conduct; he enters into particulars; and points out, with great exactness, the measures of execution. This is the strain of these orations. They are strongly animated, and full of the impetuosity and fire of public spirit. They proceed in a continued train of inductions, consequences, and demonstrations, founded on sound reason. The figures which he uses are never sought after; but always rise from the subject. He employs them sparingly, indeed; for splendor and ornament are not the distinctions of this orator's composition. It is an energy of thought peculiar to himself, which forms his character, and sets him above all others. He appears to attend much more to things than to words. We forget the orator, and think of the business. He warms the mind, and impels to action. He has no parade and ostentation; no method of insinuation; no labored introductions; but is like a man full of his subject, who, after preparing his audience by a sentence or two for hearing plain truths, enters directly on business. Demosthenes appears to great advantage, when contrasted with Æschines in the celebrated oration ' *Pro Corona.'* Æschines was his rival in business, and personal enemy; and one of the most distinguished orators of that age. But when we read the two orations, Aeschines is feeble in comparison with Demosthenes, and makes much less impression on the mind. His reasonings concerning the law that was in question, are indeed very subtle; but his invective against Demosthenes is general and ill-supported. Whereas, Demosthenes is a torrent that nothing can resist. He bears down his antagonist with violence; he draws his character in the strongest colors; and the particular merit of that oration is, that all the descriptions in it are highly picturesque. There runs through it a strain of magnanimity and high honor: the orator speaks with that strength and conscious dignity which great actions and public spirit alone inspire. Both orators use great liberties with each other; and, in general, that unrestrained license which ancient manners permitted, even to the length of abusive names and downright scurrility, as appears both here and in Cicero's Philippics, hurts and offends a modern ear. What those ancient orators gained by such a manner in point of freedom and boldness, is more than compensated by want of dignity; which seems to give an advantage, in this respect, to the greater decency of modern speaking. The style of Demosthenes is strong and concise, though sometimes it must not be dissembled, harsh and abrupt. His words are very expressive; his arrangement is firm and manly, and though far from being unmusical, yet it seems difficult to find in him that studied, but concealed number, and rhythmus, which some of the ancient critics are fond of attributing to him. Negligent of these lesser graces, one would rather conceive him to have aimed at the sublime which lies in sentiment. His action and pronunciation are recorded to have been uncommonly vehement and ardent; which, from the manner of his composition, we are naturally led to believe. The character which one forms of him, from reading his works, is of the austere, rather than the gentle kind. He is on every occasion grave, serious, passionate; takes everything on a high tone; never lets himself down, nor attempts anything like pleasantry. If any fault can be found with his admirable eloquence, it is, that he sometimes borders on the hard and dry. He may be thought to want smoothness and grace; which Dionysius of Halicarnassus attributes to his imitating too closely the manner of Thucydides, who was his great model for style, and whose history he is said to have written eight times over with his own hand. But these defects are far more than compensated by that admirable and masterly force of masculine eloquence, which, as it overpowered all who heard it, cannot, at this day, be read without emotion."

Criticism by Henry Hardwicke.—" To his admirable delivery, Demosthenes, in his orations, joined the equal force of great and noble expressions, of lively descriptions, of pathetic passages, and of rhetorical images proper to affect and make strong impressions upon the mind. In short, nearly all of his orations are full of expressive figures, of frequent apostrophes, and reiterated interrogations, which gave life and vigor to, and animated all he said. Longinus, in his comparison between Demosthenes and Cicero, compares the eloquence of the former to lightning, and of the latter to a great fire. He says the eloquence of Demosthenes is a whirlwind and a clap of thunder that overturns all things, and that of Cicero like a great fire which devours all things. So that violence and impetuousness make up the character of Demosthenes' eloquence, and the progress of a great fire, which advances by degrees, together with the heat and insinuating virtue of fire, are the qualities of that of Cicero. The Grecian breaks out like thunder. The Roman warms and inflames like a great fire. Longinus therefore adds that Demosthenes never failed of success, when he was to strike terror into the minds of his audience, and to work upon them by strong representations and violent motions. But when it was necessary to go to the very heart, and to insinuate ones' self into the mind, by all those graces and pleasing charms which eloquence is mistress of; then it was that Cicero's art was triumphant, and that his diffused, enlarged discourse succeeded far better than the more close and concise style of Demosthenes; and the one has no more *eclat,* in the surprising strength of his reasons, than the other by the warming and affecting emotions he raises. It is said that before the time of Demosthenes, there existed three distinct styles of eloquence: that of Lysias, mild and persuasive, quietly engaged the attention, and won the assent of an audience; that of Thucydides, bold and animated, awakened the feelings and powerfully forced conviction on the mind; while that of Isocrates was, as it were, a combination of the former two. Demosthenes can scarcely be said to have proposed any individual as a model, although he bestowed so much untiring labor on the historian of the Peloponnesian war. He rather culled all that was valuable from the various styles of his great predecessors, working them up, and blending them into one harmonious whole: not, however, that there is such a uniformity or mannerism in his works as prevents him from applying himself with versatility to a variety of subjects; on the contrary, he seems to have had the power of carrying each individual style to perfection, and of adapting himself with equal excellence to each successive topic. In the general structure of many of his sentences, he resembles Thucydides; but he is more simple and perspicuous, and better calculated to be quickly comprehended by an audience. On the other hand, his clearness in narration, his elegance and purity of diction, and (to borrow a metaphor from a sister art) his correct keeping, remind the reader of Lysias. But the argumentative part of the speeches of Lysias are often deficient in vigor; whereas earnestness, power, zeal, rapidity, and passion, seated in his heart, and emanated from its profoundest depths. The mystery of his wonderful influence, then, lay in his honesty. It is this, joined to his action, that gave warmth and tone to his feelings, an energy to his language, and an impression to his manner, before which every imputation of insincerity must have vanished. The chief characteristics of Demosthenes' oratory were strength, energy, and sublimity, aided by an emphatic and vehement elocution. Liberty and eloquence, which are twin born, and which die together, expired in Greece, with their noble defender, Demosthenes, and eloquence relapsed again into the feeble manner introduced by the sophists."

Cicero.— A sketch of the life of Cicero has been given in this volume (see the Letter). It was at the age of thirty-nine that he began to distinguish himself as a deliberative orator. When he attained to the consulship he was forty-three. It was then that the moral qualities of his character were the highest, and his genius shone forth with the greatest splendor; for then he delivered his famous orations against Catiline.

Criticism by Rev. J. O'Conor.—" Cicero was always careful to lay out his oration, in accordance with the plan which he proposed in his rhetorical works. He pays greatest attention to the introductions containing the ethical proof; the body of the speech relating the facts and the arguments deducted from those facts; lastly the peroration, addressing itself to the moral sense of the judges. These were the parts to which he paid most attention. His skill as an orator is best shown in "the proof." He accounts for everything naturally, and converts objections into a confirmation of his own argument. Then he emphasizes all this by amplification and exaggeration. He has not the force of Demosthenes, but has what an ancient critic ascribes to him, 'the copiousness of Plato, and the sweetness of Isocrates.' Strength and simplicity cannot be claimed for him, but no one will deny that he has copiousness and soundness of treatment; we may add, wealth and harmony of diction, solid and sententious argument, a brilliant and poetic imagination. He carried his audience more by persuasion than by conviction. He captivates his hearers, flatters their vanity, rouses their selfishness, and stirs up their hopes and fears. Cicero had also a great fund of wit, in which respect he differed from Demosthenes, who, when he attempted to be facetious, made himself ridiculous. Cicero had also at his command, intense irony and sarcasm that never failed to be effective. Many faults have been attributed to the Roman orator; his copiousness sometimes runs to wordiness; the sound sometimes exceeds the sense; the style is too artificial; the speaker sometimes merely tries to display his verbal power, sacrificing everything to his vanity. However, his faults are more than outweighed by his excellences. Cicero said, ' the perfect orator is the perfect man; ' and there is no doubt that he tried to be a perfect man according to his own ideas. But his nature was decidedly weak. His constant aim was to do right, and his mistakes were those of the judgment rather than of the heart. His vanity and his desire to be popular with all men was his one great misfortune. But we can pardon many other faults in view of the eminence he attained in his art. Two magnificently planned orations are the one in 'Defence of Milo,' and the ' Manilian Law.' The *'Pro Archias'* is replete with the spirit of poetry, and the speeches against Catiline are models of invective."

Criticism by Blair.—" The object in this period most worthy to draw our attention, is Cicero himself; whose name alone suggests everything that is splendid in oratory. With the history of his life and with his character, as a man and a politician, we have not at present any direct concern. We consider him only as an eloquent speaker, and in this view, it is our business to remark both his virtues, and his defects, if he has any. His virtues are, beyond controversy, eminently great. In all his orations there is high art. He begins, generally, with a regular exordium; and with much preparation and insinuation prepossesses the hearers and studies to gain their affections. His method is clear, and his arguments are arranged with great propriety. His method is indeed more clear than that of Demosthenes; and this is one advantage which he has over him. We find everything in its proper place; he never attempts to move till he has endeavored to convince: and in moving, especially the softer passions, he is very successful. No man that ever wrote, knew the power and force of words better than Cicero. He rolls them along with the greatest beauty and pomp; and in the structure of his sentences is curious and exact to the highest degree. He is always full and flowing, never abrupt. He is a great amplifier of every subject; magnificent, and in his sentiments highly moral. His manner is on the whole diffuse, yet it is often happily varied, and suited to the subject. In his four orations, for instance, against Catiline, the tone and style of each of them, particularly the first and last, is very different, and accommodated with a great deal of judgment to the occasion and the situation in which they were spoken. When a great public object rouses his mind, and demands indignation and force, he departs considerably from that loose and declamatory manner to which he inclines at other times, and becomes exceedingly cogent and vehement. This is the case in his orations against Antony, and in those too against Verres and Catiline. Together with those high qualities which Cicero possessed, he is not exempt from certain defects, of which it is necessary to take notice. For the Ciceronian eloquence is a pattern so dazzling by its beauties, that, if not examined with accuracy and judgment, it is apt to betray the unwary into a faulty imitation; and I am of the opinion that it has sometimes produced this effect. In most of his orations, especially those composed in the early part of his life, there is too much art; even carried the length of ostentation. There is too visible a parade of eloquence. He seems often to aim at obtaining admiration, rather than at operating conviction, by what he says. Hence, on some occasions, he is showy, rather than solid; and diffuse, where he ought to have been pressing. His sentences are at all times round and sonorous; they cannot be accused of monotony, for they possess variety of cadence; but from too great a study of magnificence, he is sometimes deficient in strength. On all occasions, where there is the least room for it, he is full of himself. His great actions, and the real service which he had performed to his country, apologizes for this in part; ancient

manners, too, imposed fewer restraints from the side of decorum;
but, even after these allowances are made, Cicero's ostentation of
himself cannot be wholly palliated; and his orations, indeed, all
his works, leave on our minds the impression of a good man, but,
withal of a vain man."

The following comparison of Cicero and Demosthenes by
Blair is worthy of insertion here:

On the subject of comparing Cicero and Demosthenes, much
has been said by critical writers. The different manners of these
two princes of eloquence, and the distinguishing characters of
each, are so strongly marked in their writings, that the comparison is, in many respects, obvious and easy. The character
of Demosthenes is vigor and austerity: that of Cicero is gentleness and insinuation. In the one you find more manliness; in
the other, more ornament. The one is more harsh, but more
spirited and cogent; the other more agreeable, but, withal, looser
and weaker. To account for this difference, without any
prejudice to Cicero, it has been said that we must look to the
nature of their different auditories: that the refined Athenians
followed with ease the concise and convincing eloquence of
Demosthenes; but that a manner more popular, more flowery,
and declamatory was requisite in speaking to the Romans, a
people less acute, and less acquainted with the arts of speech.
But this is not satisfactory. For we must observe that the Greek
orator spoke much oftener before a mixed multitude than the
Roman. Almost all the public business of Athens was transacted
in popular assemblies. The common people were his hearers and
his judges; whereas, Cicero generally addressed himself to the
Patres Conscripti, or, in criminal trials, to the Praetor and the
Select Judges; and it cannot be imagined that the persons of
highest rank and best education in Rome required a more diffuse
manner of pleading than the common citizens of Athens, in order
to make them understand the cause, or relish the speaker. Perhaps we shall come nearer the truth by observing, that to unite
together all the qualities, without the least exception, that form a
perfect orator, and to excel equally in each of those qualities, is
not to be expected from the limited powers of human genius. The
highest degree of strength is, I suspect, never found united with

the highest degree of smoothness and ornament; equal attentions to both are incompatible; and the genius that carries ornament to its utmost length is not of such a kind as can excel as much in vigor. For there plainly lies the characteristical difference between these two celebrated orators. It is a disadvantage to Demosthenes that, besides his conciseness, which sometimes produces obscurity, the language in which he writes is less familiar to most of us than the Latin, and that we are less acquainted with the Greek antiquities than we are with the Roman. We read Cicero with more ease, and of course, with more pleasure. Independent of this circumstance, too, he is no doubt, in himself, a more agreeable writer than the other. But notwithstanding this advantage, I am of opinion that, were the state in danger, or some great public interest at stake, which drew the serious attention of men, an oration in the spirit and strain of Demosthenes would have more weight, and produce greater effects, than one in the Ciceronian manner. Were Demosthenes' Philippics spoken in a British assembly, in a similar conjuncture of affairs, they would convince and persuade at this day. The rapid style, the vehement reasoning, the disdain, anger, boldness, freedom which perpetually animate them, would render their success infallible over any modern assembly. I question whether the same can be said of Cicero's oration; whose eloquence, however beautiful, and however well suited to the Roman taste, yet borders oftener on declamation, and is more remote from the manner in which we now expect to hear real business and causes of importance treated.' Cicero's orations against Verres have been regarded by many writers as among the most splendid monuments of his genius. Of the six orations against Verres which have come down to us, Cicero delivered but one. Soon after the trial was begun, Verres, overwhelmed by the evidence of guilt which was produced against him, without awaiting the decision of the court, went into voluntary exile. If he had made a defence, the other five speeches would doubtless have been delivered."

Jacques Benigne Bossuet.— He was born at Dijon, France, September 27, 1627, and died at Paris, April 12, 1704. He ranks as the most celebrated orator France has produced. His chief works are an exposition of Catholic Doctrine, a

Treatise on Universal History, History of the Variations of the Protestant Church and the Funeral Orations upon which his fame as an orator rests.

Criticism by William Mathews.—" What schoolboy is not familiar with the religious terror with which, in his *oraisons funèbres,* the ' Demosthenes of the pulpit,' Bossuet, thrilled the breasts of *seigneurs* and princesses, and even the breast of that King before whom other kings trembled and knelt, when, taking for his text the words, ' Be wise, therefore, O ye kings ! be instructed, ye judges of the earth !' he unveiled to his auditors the awful reality of God the Lord of all empires, the chastiser of princes, reigning above the heavens, making and unmaking kingdoms, principalities and powers ; or, again, with the fire of a lyric poet and the zeal of a prophet, called on nations, princes, nobles and warriors, to come to the foot of the catafalque which strove to raise to heaven a magnificent testimony of the nothingness of man ? At the beginning of his discourses the action of ' the eagle of Meaux,' we are told, was dignified and reserved ; he confined himself to the notes before him. Gradually ' he warmed with his theme, the contagion of his enthusiasm seized his hearers ; he watched their rising emotion ; the rooted glances of a thousand eyes filled him with a sort of divine frenzy ; his notes became a burden and a hindrance ; with impetuous ardor he abandoned himself to the inspiration of the moment ; with the eyes of the soul he watched the swelling hearts of hearers ; their concentrated emotions became his own ; he felt within himself the collected might of the orators and martyrs whose collected essence, by long and repeated communion he had absorbed into himself ; from flight to flight he ascended, until, with unflagging energy, he towered straight upwards, and dragged the wrapt contemplation of his audience along with him in its ethereal flight.' At such times, says the Abbé Le Dieu, it seemed as though the heavens were open and celestial joys were about to descend upon these trembling souls, like tongues of fire on the day of Pentecost. At others times, heads bowed down with humiliation, or pale upturned faces with streaming eyes, lips parted with broken ejaculations of despair, silently testified that the spirit of repentance had breathed on many a hardened heart."

Criticism by F. O'Connor.—" The oratory of Bossuet knew three distinct phases, the first of which was marked by extreme detail in the treatment of the subject, the second by pathos in the narration and power of diction; the third by increased symmetry of construction, and propriety of arrangement. In point of merit the last is the least, and the first, the most praiseworthy. The speaker draws largely upon Holy Writ and sacred writings for means of rousing the emotions and depends principally upon the early classic writers for smoothness of style and grace of finish. The orator himself is no less deserving of admiration than his oratory is of praise. Living though he did, at a time when the king's will was supreme, he still recognized his conscience as his only guide, never stooped to flattery and never catered to the popular passions. He aimed especially at edification, consistency and truth, and seldom failed to reach his mark."

Edmund Burke.— He was born at Dublin, January 12, 1729, and died at Beaconsfield, England, in July, 1797. Burke was a celebrated writer as well as orator. His celebrated speeches were made at the trial of Warren Hastings, and in advocacy of the freedom of the press, fair treatment of America, Catholic emancipation and economical reform. His name is identified with whatever is great, elevated, and just, in statesmanship and legislation. He is also famous for his speeches and pamphlets on the French Revolution.

Criticism by John Morley.—" With all his hatred for the bookman in politics, Burke owed much of his own distinction to that generous richness and breadth of judgment which had been ripened in him by literature and his practice in it. Like some other men in our history, he showed that books are a better preparation for statesmanship than early training in the subordinate posts and among the permanent officials of a public department. There is no copiousness of literary reference in his work, such as over-abound in our civil and ecclesiastical publicists of the 17th century. Nor can we truly say that there is much, though there is certainly some, of that tact which literature is alleged to confer on those who approach it in a just spirit and with the true gift. The influence of literature on Burke lay partly in the direction of emancipation from the mechanical formulae of practical politics; partly in the association which it engendered, in a powerful understanding like his, between politics and the moral forces of the world, and between political maxims and the old and great sentences of morals; partly in drawing him, even when resting his case on prudence and expediency, to appeal to the widest and highest sympathies; partly, and more than all, in opening his thoughts to the many conditions, possibilities, and ' varieties of untried being,' in human character and situation, and so giving an incomparable flexibility to his methods of political approach. This flexibility is not to be found in his manner of composition. That derives its immense power from other sources; from passion, intensity, imagination, size, truth, cogency of logical reason. Those who insist on charm, on winningness in style, on subtle harmonies and fine exquisiteness of suggestion, are disappointed in Burke; they even find him stiff and over-colored. And there are blemishes of this kind. His banter is nearly always ungainly, his wit blunt, as Johnson said, and often unseasonable. As is usual with a man who has not true humor, Burke is also without true pathos. The thought of wrong or misery moved him less to pity for the victim than to anger against the cause. Again, there are some gratuitous and unredeemed vulgarities; some images that make us shudder. But only a literary fop can be detained by speeches like these. The varieties of Burke's literary or rhetorical method are very striking. It is almost incredible that the superb imaginative amplification of the description of Hyder Ali's descent upon the Carnatic should be from the same pen as the grave, simple, unadorned *Address to the King* (1777), where each sentence falls on the ear with the accent of some golden-tongued oracle of the wise gods. His stride is the stride of a giant, from the sentimental beauty of the pictures of Marie Antoinette at Versailles, or the red horror of the tale of Debi Sing in Rungpore, to the learning, positiveness and cool judicial mastery of the *Report on the Lords' Journals* (1794), which Philip Francis, no mean judge, declared on the whole to be the ' most eminent and extraordinary ' of all his productions. But even in the coolest and dryest of his pieces, there is the mark of greatness, of grasp, of comprehension. In all its varieties, Burke's style is noble, earnest, deep-flowing, because his sentiment was lofty and fervid, and went with sincerity and ardent disciplined travail of judgment. He had the style of his subjects; the amplitude, the weightiness, the laboriousness, the sense, the high flight, the grandeur, proper to a man dealing with imperial themes, with the fortunes of great societies, with the sacredness of law, the freedom of nations, the justice of rulers. Burke will always be read with delight and edification, because in the midst of discussions on the local and the accidental, he scatters apophthegms that take us into the regions of lasting wisdom. In the midst of the torrent of his most strenuous and passionate deliverances, he suddenly rises aloof from his immediate subject, and in all tranquillity reminds us of some permanent relation of things, some enduring truth of human life or human society. We do not hear the organ tones of Milton, for faith and freedom had other notes in the eighteenth century. There is none of the complacent and wise-borrowed sagacity of Bacon, for Burke's were days of personal strife and fire and civil division. We are not exhilarated by the cheerfulness, the polish, the fine manners of Bolingbroke, for Burke had an anxious conscience and was earnest and intent that the good should triumph. And yet Burke is among the greatest of those who have wrought marvels in the prose of our English tongue."

Criticism by Albert Smyth.—" Edmund Burke is sometimes ranked first among the writers of English prose of the eighteenth century. There is something imperial in his style. His sonorous sentences roll and toss in profuse and majestic eloquence. His thought streams from him, an impetuous and abundant torrent. His resplendent rhetoric surges forward with the pomp and state and endless barbaric variety of a Roman triumph. His eagerness and exuberance betrayed him at times into grave faults of manner. His early and successful imitation of Bolingbroke — by no means a flawless model — set a permanent mark upon him. The high virtues of simplicity and sobriety are not his. In imagination and expression he is magnificent, in the proudest sense of that much misapplied term; but his literary taste is not absolutely pure, nor his sense of proportion true, and his style is often overheated. Whatever the place to which he may be entitled among the masters of English prose, it is not likely that any writer will take precedence of him for subtle political wisdom and serious and fruitful reflection upon the principles of government and legislation. Mr. John Morley has said of Burke's three pieces on the American War: 'They are an example without fault of all the qualities which the critic, whether a theorist or an actor, of great political situations should strive by night and by day to possess. If their subject were as remote as the quarrel between the Corinthians and Corcyra, or the war between Rome and the allies, instead of a conflict to which the world owes the opportunity of the most important of political experiments, we should still have everything to learn from the author's treatment, — the vigorous grasp of masses of compressed detail, the wide illumination from great principles of human experience, the strong and masculine feeling for the two great political ends of Justice and Freedom, the large and generous interpretation of expediency, the morality, the vision, the noble temper.' However transient, commonplace, or personal the theme, Burke never left it without investing it with the splendor of history or introducing into it considerations drawn from the widest range of political institutions. Now that the violence of party strife has abated, and the figures and events of one hundred years ago may be impartially studied, it is unlikely that there should be any dissent from Mr. Lecky's opinion: 'No other politician or writer has thrown the light of so penetrating a genius on the nature and working of the British Constitution, has impressed his principles so deeply on both of the great parties in the State, and has left behind him a richer treasure of political wisdom applicable to all countries and to all times. . . . There is perhaps no English prose writer since Bacon whose works are so thickly starred with thought. The time may come when they will be no longer read. The time will never come in which men would not grow the wiser by reading them.' "

Daniel Webster.— He was born at Salisbury, New Hampshire, in 1782, and died at Marshfield, Massachusetts, in 1852. Like Edmund Burke, he was famous as a statesman, orator and lawyer. His chief public speeches, (aside from those delivered in Congress and at the bar) are orations delivered on the anniversary at Plymouth, on the laying of the corner stone of Bunker Hill Monument, on the deaths of Jefferson and Adams. By many critics he is regarded as the superior of Burke, and the greatest of English orators.

Criticism by Rufus Choate.—" Webster possessed in a wonderful degree an indefinable personal magnetism which impressed every one with a sense of greatness. His face, his eyes, his voice, were such that whoever looked upon him and heard him speak, felt intuitively that he was a man of most extraordinary powers. Sydney Smith, when he saw him, exclaimed, ' Good heavens he is a small cathedral by himself'; and Carlyle, writing of him, said, ' He is a magnificent specimen. As a logic fencer or parliamentary Hercules, one would incline to back him at first sight against all the extant world. The tanned complexion; the amorphous crag-like face; the dull black eyes under the precipice of brows, like dull anthracite furnaces needing only to be blown; the mastiff mouth accurately closed,— I have not traced so much of *silent Berserker rage* that I remember of in any man.' His multiform eloquence became at once so much accession to permanent literature, in the strictest sense, solid, attractive, and rich. Recall what pervaded all these forms of display, and every effort in every form: that union of naked intellect, in its largest measure, which penetrates to the exact truth of the matter in hand by intuition or by inference, and discerns everything which may make it intelligible, probable and credible to another, with an emotional and moral nature profound, passionate, and ready to kindle, and with imagination enough to supply a hundredfold more of illustration and aggrandizement than his taste suffered him to accept; that union of greatness of soul with depth of heart which made his speaking almost more an exhibition of character than of mere genius; the style not merely pure, clear Saxon, but so constructed, so luminous as far as becomes prose, so forcible, so abounding in unlabored felicities, the words so choice, the epithet so pictured, the matter absolute truth, or the most exact and spacious resemblance the human wit can devise; the treatment of the subject, if you have regard to the kind of truth he had to handle,— political, ethical, legal,— as deep as Paley's, or Locke's, or Butler's, yet that depth and that completeness of sense made transparent as crystal waters, raised on winged language, vivified, fused, and poured along in a tide of emotion fervid, and incapable to be withstood. The quality of Webster's imagination, which was of an historical, rather than poetical cast, had much to do with the power and peculiar charm of his oratory. But it was his simplicity of diction, and his perfect mastery of pure, idomatic English, which gave to his discourses their distinctive classic elegance, and made them worthy of a permanent place in our literature. As specimens, therefore, of a correct, clear, and vigorous style of composition, full of warmth and vitality, these orations are worthy of the most careful attention of every one who would perfect himself in the use of the English tongue; as notable examples of persuasive discourse, logical, forcible and convincing, they especially commend themselves to those who aspire to distinction as public speakers; as containing lessons of the purest and most disinterested patriotism, they appeal to Americans everywhere, and should be read and studied by every American youth."

Criticism by William Mathews.—" Webster was not a rhetorician like Everett and Wirt. Though nice in his choice of words, he was not, like Pinkney and Choate, constantly racking dictionaries to obtain an affluence of synonyms. Though possessing an ample command of expression, he rarely wastes a word. He once criticised Watts for saying in a hymn that an angel moved ' with most amazing speed.' The line, he said, conveyed no sense. ' It would amaze us,' he added, ' to see an oyster move a mile a day; it would not amaze us to see a greyhound run a mile a minute.' No one of our great orators had a greater horror of epithets and adjectives, or more heartily despised all grandiloquence or *sesquipedalia verba*. For all cant and rhetorical trickery,— for all ' bunkum ' talk and windy declamation about ' the shades of Hampden and Sidney ' and ' the eternal rights of man,'— for cheap enthusiasm and spread-eagles generally,— he had a supreme scorn. Few orators of equal imagination have so few figures of speech. There are more metaphors in ten pages of Burke than in all of Webster's works. In discussing a subject he loses no time in circumlocutions or digressions. He uses no scattering fowling-piece that sends its shot around the object to be hit, but plants his rifle-ball in the very center of the target. Commonly he prepared himself with conscientious care for his speeches,— not by writing them out, but by thinking over and over what he had to say, all the while mentally facing his audi-

ence. In many passages, no doubt, the very language was pre-
chosen,— selected with the nicest discrimination,— especially on
critical occasions, and in the closing paragraphs or the peroration. Some of Webster's indiscriminate eulogists are fond of
comparing him with Burke. The difference was, that one had
the very highest order of *talent,* the other had *genius.* Burke
was, like the poet, ' of imagination all compact,' and to this he
added profound culture, earnestness and moral sensibility; Webster's forte was in dialectics, in calm, masterly exposition, in massive strength of style, in all the qualities that give men leader-
ship in debate. As another has said, ' Where Webster reasoned,
Burke philosophized; where Webster was serene, equable, pon-
derous, dealing his blows like an ancient catapult, Burke was
clamorous, fiery, multitudinous, rushing forward like his own
' whirlwind of cavalry.' Webster was the Roman temple, stately,
solid, massive; Burke, the Gothic cathedral, fantastic, aspiring,
and many-colored. The sentences of Webster roll along like the
blasts of the trumpet on the night air; those of Burke are like the
echoes of an organ in some ancient minster. Webster advances,
in his heavy logical march, and his directness of purpose, like
a Caesarean legion, close, firm, serried, square; Burke, like an
oriental procession, with elephants and trophies, and the pomp
of banners. Webster never could have delivered any one of the
speeches of Burke on the trial of Hastings, blazing as they do
with the splendors of a gorgeous rhetoric; nor could Burke, on
the other hand, have made that overwhelming extempore reply to
Hayne, so full and running over with mingled logic, wit, irony,
satire, persuasion, and pathos."

**Various Estimates of the Oration, Oratory, and the Ora-
tor.**— In every age the oration has received extraordinary
praise and attention. Perhaps its most ardent admirers may
be found in the history of the English speaking race who from
time immemorial have defended and preserved the largest freedom of speech. So that in closing our study of this prose-
form it may be well to include some estimates of oratory furnished by modern men of genius.

Estimate by Henry Ward Beecher.—" I hold that oratory has this test and mark of divine providence, in that God, when He makes things perfect, signifies that He is done by throwing over them the robe of beauty; for beauty is the divine thought of excellence. All things growing in their earlier stages, are crude. All of them are in vigorous strength, it may be; but not until the blossom comes, and the fruit hangs pendant, has the vine evinced for what it was made. God is a God of beauty; and beauty is everywhere the final process. When things have come to that, they have touched their limit. Now, a living force that brings to itself all the resources of imagination, all the inspirations of feeling, all that is influential in body, in voice, in eye, in gesture, in posture, in the whole animated man, is in strict analogy with the divine thought and the divine arrangement; and there is no misconstruction more utterly untrue and fatal than this: that oratory is an artificial thing, which deals with baubles and trifles, for the sake of making bubbles of pleasure for transient effect on mercurial audiences. So far from that, it is the consecration of the whole man to the noblest purposes to which one can address himself — the education and inspiration of his fellow-men by all that there is in thought, by all that there is in feeling, by all that there is in all of them, sent home through the channels of taste and of beauty. And so regarded, oratory should take its place among the highest departments of education. It is said that books, and especially newspapers, are to take the place of the living voice. Never! never! The miracle of modern times, in one respect, is the press; to it is given a wide field and a wonderful work; and when it shall be clothed with all the moral inspirations, with all the ineffable graces, that come from simplicity and honesty and conviction, it will have a work second almost to none other in the land. Like the light, it carries knowledge every day round the globe. What is done at St. Paul's in the morning is known, or ever half the day has run round, in Wall Street, New York. What is done in New York at the rising of the sun, is, before the noontide hour known in California. By the power of the wire, and of the swift-following engine, the papers spread at large vast quantities of information before myriad readers throughout the country; but the office of the papers is simply to convey information. They cannot plant it. They cannot open the soil and put it into the furrow. They can-

not enforce it. It is given only to the living man, standing before men with the seed of knowledge in his hand, to open the
furrows in the living souls of men, and sow the seed, and cover
the furrows again. Not until human nature is other than it is,
will the function of the living voice — the greatest force on earth
among men — cease. Not until then will the orator be useless,
who brings to his aid all that is fervid in feeling; who incarnates
in himself the truth; who is for the hour the living reason, as
well as the reasoner; who is for the moment the moral sense;
who carries in himself the importunity and the urgency of zeal;
who brings his influence to bear upon men in various ways; who
adapts himself continually to the changing conditions of the men
that are before him; who plies them by softness and by hard-
ness, by light and by darkness, by hope and by fear; who stimu-
lates them or represses them at his will. Nor is there, let me
say, on God's footstool, anything so crowned and so regal as the
sensation of one who faces an audience in a worthy cause, and
with amplitude of means, and defies them, fights them, controls
them, *conquers* them. Great is the advance of civilization; mighty
are the engines of force, but man is greater than that which he
produces. Vast is that machine which stands in the dark unconsciously lifting, lifting — the only human slave — the iron slave
— the Corliss engine; but he that made the engine is greater than
the engine itself. Wonderful is the skill by which the most exquisite mechanism of modern life, the watch, is constructed; but
greater is the man that made the watch than the watch that is
made. Great is the press, great are the hundred instrumentali-
ties and institutions and customs of society; but above all is man.
The living force is greater than any of its creations — greater
than society, greater than its laws. 'The Sabbath was made
for man, and not man for the Sabbath,' saith the Lord. Man is
greater than his own institutions. And this living force is worthy
of all culture — of all culture in the power of beauty; of all culture in the direction of persuasion; of all culture in the art of
reasoning. To make men patriots, to make men Christians, to
make men the sons of God, let all the doors of heaven be opened,
and let God drop down charmed gifts — winged imagination, all-
perceiving reason, and all-judging reason. Whatever there is
that can make men wiser and better — let it descend upon the
head of him who has consecrated himself to the work of man-

kind, and who has made himself an orator for man's sake and for God's sake."*

Estimate by John Lancaster Spalding.—"Oratory is the greatest of the arts — greater than music, than poetry, than painting, than sculpture. The orator must gather into unity and harmony all that other artists achieve separately — must be at once musician, painter, poet, sculptor, architect; must be able to take the human mind and heart and imagination for his instrument and play upon it all the infinite divine cadences of rhythm and reason. He must stand forth before men as a man clothed with the resonance of the thunder-crash and with the searching power of the forked lightning; must sing to his audience and command them and subdue them to his every mood and thought; must have power to transport them into the midst of sublime scenes, of tumultuous oceans, of white and eternally serene mountain peaks; he must know all the melodies that soothe like the lullabies of mothers; must be able to plead as only love can plead — to rouse like a clarion's note; must be able to find his way through the labyrinthian windings of the heart of man, with all its passions and prejudices, and issue forth heralded as a conqueror. His words must be as full of music as a poet's, as clear-cut as a statue, as symmetrical as the noblest monument, as rightly ordered as an army in battle array; his thought must unfold itself like the budding leaves and the blossoming flowers; and from the center and heart of it all he must rise and reveal himself, not as an actor, but as a man and messenger sent by God to proclaim truth and vindicate the right. He must have knowledge of history, of literature, of religion, of science, of the world. He must be all alive with the subject he discusses. If his thoughts be not new, they must glow with a light not seen before; and they must be pure and high that they may appeal to what is best in man. He must utter, not what the arithmetical understanding would suggest, but what the soul would speak to souls. His language must be beautiful; his words simple, chaste and crystalline; his phrases must sparkle and glow like jewels on the brow of beauty. But he must ever bear in mind that mere vesture cannot hide the unreality and vacancy of what is false and

* *"Oratory"*— By permission of the Penn Publishing Co.

vulgar. Right words are born of true thoughts; and true thoughts of noble life. Those alone who take infinite pains can hope to become orators. There is no seeming trifle which may be neglected, for perfection is the result of attention to little things. He who would excel must inure himself to the labor of writing and rewriting what he would utter. The pen is to the mind what the plough is to the field. Ploughs do not sow the seed, but without the culture they give it will not thrive and yield rich harvest, however fertile the soil. When meditation and composition shall have made him familiar with every phase of his subject, lucid order, accurate expression, and copious language will come as the fountains burst and leap in spring. Having aroused and illumined his own spiritual being, he will have a message and the skill rightly to deliver it to his audience; and not to them only, but to the wider world to which the wings of the press shall bear his words. The public-speaking which has politics and business for its subject is useful and important, but Fame blows not her trumpet above the heads of those who do this work. They are talkers, not orators; fortunate if they talk logically, forcibly, to the point, while they keep themselves free from slang and other offense against the laws of speech. But he who would utter memorable things in perfect form must dwell in higher regions where gleams the light of ideal aims and ends; must think no labor too great, no self-denial too hard, if it help him to become a master. Like the mighty Grecian, he must love solitude, be willing, if need be, to dwell in caves by the resounding shores of the loud ocean; must take for his companions the immortal minds who have left record of themselves in books. He must abstain, train himself like an athlete, and accustom himself to all exercises that invigorate and sharpen the intellect or harden and supple the body. He must stand aloof from the crowds and despise the applause of the vulgar and the notoriety which is within the reach of criminals and prize-fighters. He must be wholly serious and sincere and keep his conscience pure, though he have not bread to eat. Great manhood alone can make great oratory possible. Above all, the orator must be a lover of truth and justice. His sympathies must go forth to the toilers who do the world's work and are God's children. Wherever there is oppression and wrong, he must be ready in the name of the Lord to defend and make good."

CHAPTER XXXIX

FICTION

Definition.— The term, fiction, is of Latin origin and has various meanings when employed in English. The widest meaning attached to the term makes it a synonym for fashioning, moulding, shaping, devising, or making. For example, Edmund Burke writes: "We never dreamt that parliaments had any right to force a currency of their own fiction in the place of that which is real." A second meaning attached to the word is that of fallacy or false deduction. Hence the phrase: "A fiction of the brain." Bacon writes: "They see thoroughly into the fallacies and fictions of this kind of reasoning." A third meaning connects fiction with literature; in a literary sense, fiction signifies that which is feigned, invented or imagined. Fiction is a term applied to any product of the imagination and has little to do with facts and realities. Like poetry, it gives to the imagination the largest possible range. Hence it may be applied to any literary product of the imagination, whether in prose or verse or in a narrative or dramatic form. For example, the parables of the Bible, or the Cyropædia of Xenophon or the Hind and Panther of Dryden may be considered as fiction. In fact, all departments of literature contain certain elements of fiction. Examples abound everywhere.

Restricted Meaning.— The term, fiction, is now employed in a restricted sense. It marks a sharply defined prose-form in literature, and it implies story-telling or narrative. In con-

nection with this prose-form three words are employed almost
as synonyms — the novel, romance, fiction. If we take
fiction in its strict modern meaning as a prose-form of literature, then romance and the novel may be accepted as names
for separate divisions of this prose literature; romance embracing the earlier work, and the novel, the later work done
in the field of fiction.

Origin of the Name Romance.— The term, romance, was
first applied to the fiction of the Middle Ages; originally, it
embraced not only stories of adventure and legend in prose
but also ballad forms and long narrative poems. The troubadours, who were the novelists and story-tellers of their time,
employed the Romance language; whence we have the term
romance which has become a synonym for fiction.

Subject-Matter.— The subject-matter of the romance embraces all kinds of heroic, marvellous and supernatural incidents derived either from history or from legend. For example, the Romance of Charlemagne; the Arthurian Romance.
Hallam writes: " The fiction of the Middle Ages rests upon
three columns — chivalry, gallantry, religion." This fiction
was designated as romance and written by natives of the north
of France. Knight-errantry, the crusades, feudalism, a general
spirit of adventure, furnished plenty of incident.

Scope.— But romance is not a peculiar creation of the Middle Ages. It is a characteristic of the youthful period in the
growth of every nation. The romantic period is sharply defined in every national literature. It embraces all that is
legendary, mythical and semi-historical in every age of the
world.

Three Kinds of Treatment.— The romance deals with its
subject-matter in three principal ways, thus producing three

varieties more or less distinct. In the first place, it may be frankly romantic in the exercise of the imagination, presenting events and characters that are beyond the range of any rational belief. The author has either a childish belief in what he relates or he tells the fanciful tale for the entertainment of his readers. For example, Oriental fiction belongs to this class: The Arabian nights, Arcadia, New Atlantis. In the second place, the author may relate impossible events, but in such a way as to give them a deceptive air of truth. For example, the adventures of Robinson Crusoe or the story of the Nautilus; Utopia. In the third place, the author may use these imaginary events and characters in a symbolic way; and then romance takes on the character of allegory. For example, Pilgrim's Progress, the Holy Grail, Gulliver's Travels.

The Structure of the Romance.— The romance resembles the epic in plan and purpose. It is divided into books and chapters; and like the epic introduces characters for the sake of the narrative or story. Like the epic, it employs the grand style, but it is hampered by the prose medium of expression. It resembles the epic in emphasizing the liberties rather than the limitations of the imagination. In spite of its prose-medium, it ranks with the epic as our most highly imaginative literature.

Plot in Romance.— The romance contains very little plot. The narrative is as simple and runs on with as little subtilty and entanglement as epic narrative. The grouping of events; the deeds and experiences of the various personages; their relations, thoughts, dispositions, all belong to a simple crude state of society. Hence, the plot is easily understood and unraveled. One reason why the plot is so simple: the romance follows the simple chronological order; and the skill of the writer is not expended in weaving subtilties, but in beautiful descriptions. The arts by which the narrative is made vivid and effective, are fully displayed. The plot may involve a single story, the adventures of a single hero like Robinson Crusoe; or it may deal with several distinct series of adventures or experiences. For example, King Arthur and the Round Table. There is always a common bond like the Round Table for these distinct narratives.

Characters.— The characters of the romance are seldom lifelike or human; they are giants, dwarfs, fairies, monsters, angels, demons; they are often animals or personified natural objects; but very rarely are they real men and women. The highly imaginative character of romance naturally implies its remoteness from the actual world; so that real men and women would be singularly out of place in it. Hence, the romance does not concern itself with the great problems of human life. It deals with human life in a superficial way; and if we except the great allegorical romances, God and the spiritual world receive superficial treatment in the romance. The modern romance comes nearer to earth and to reality than the romances of history, but the imagination still runs riot.

Sources of the English Romance.— The English romance drew its material from five chief sources: the native or Celtic source; the French source dating from the Norman conquest; the classic source reviving the story of Troy and the legends concerning Solomon, Alexander the Great and others; the Latin source divided equally between Spain and Italy. There are then in English literature five distinct cycles of romance.

Arthurian Cycle.— The first is called the Arthurian Cycle. It dates from the twelfth century when Geoffrey of Monmouth wrote a fanciful history of the old British kings. For 300 years myth and legend grew up around Arthur and the Knights of the Round Table. Sir Thomas Malory collected the various romances and published them in 1485 under one title, "The Death of Arthur." From this work of Malory comes the Arthurian Cycle; episodes from this cycle have been done into modern English by various writers; for example, the lyric treatment of "Tristram and Iseult" by Matthew Arnold. The fullest treatment of the Arthurian Cycle in modern English is found in epic form: the "Idylls of the King" by Tennyson. Tennyson drew all his material for this epic from Malory's collection. This cycle of Arthur contains all the elements of genuine romance, improbable adventures, marvellous struggles with giants and dragons — all that is widely imaginative. It also contains the chivalry and gallantry and the purity of life which mark the Middle Ages. Although Arthur was a British chieftain of the sixth century, the romanticists clothe him with all the glory of a contemporary knight.

Treatment of Passion.— The Arthurian Cycle is remarkable for its treatment of passion — religious passion is happily idealized in Sir Galahad's Quest of the Holy Grail; earthly passion in its highest and purest form in Arthur; guilty passion in Lancelot and Guinevere. In his epic narrative Tennyson gives prominence to the purifying and ennobling influence of religion. The second cycle of English romance comes from France and dates from the Norman conquest. During the Middle Ages, England had a French court, French schools, and for the most part French literature. French romance circulated in England. The marvelous stories concerning Charlemagne were the basis of a cycle similar to that of King Arthur. It assumed the form of extravagant history and biography. Charlemagne is represented as having twelve peers similar in character to the Knights of the Round Table. These romances first appeared in England in the thirteenth century. The most popular romance of the Charlemagne cycle was the song of Roland, one of the twelve peers. Several translations of it were made into English. But the cycle of Charlemagne had no permanent place or influence in English literature. An English version, called "Charles the Great," was published by Caxton in 1490. Besides the great cycle of Charlemagne, many separate romances from French sources came into England. For example, the Romance of the Rose, Flower and Leaf re-written by Chaucer. Another example: Valentine and Orson, translated into English and published by Copeland in 1560.

The Spanish Cycle.— Spanish romance centers in two heroes: Amadis De Gaul and the Cid. The former was a son of the French King; three books of romance concerning him appeared in the first years of the fourteenth century. They were in 1540 translated into French and brought to England. Many English translations of this cycle are extant. The best modern translation was made by Robert Southey, in four volumes, published in 1803. Spanish romance reached the height of its popularity during the age of Queen Elizabeth who was called the fair Oriana after one of the heroines in Amadis De Gaul. Besides Amadis De Gaul, there were romances concerning a native Spanish hero of the Middle Ages; they were called the "Chronicle of the Cid," as they first appeared in the form of history. French, English and Italian translations were made, that of Robert Southey being the best in English. Spanish fiction in the Middle Ages furnished a large amount of material for English authors. This influence continued until the religious and commercial rivalries of both countries developed an intense national hatred. The influence of Spanish romance upon English letters may be said to close with Cervantes. Spanish romance familiarized English readers with a larger variety of abnormal creatures than they found in native or French sources — giants, dwarfs, demons, and the wonders of fairyland.

The Outlaw.— The Spanish romance is also responsible for the literary treatment of the outlaw. English romanticists grew fond of this theme and a large portion of English romance is devoted to such heroes as Hereward The Saxon, Payn Peverel, and the Robin Hood cycle. Outlaw stories in Spain and England were first treated in ballad form, and were a part of the folk lore of both countries before their introduction into prose romance as episodes and cycles. The long struggle between the Moors and the Spaniards, and a similar struggle between the Saxons and the Normans supplied plenty of material for this kind of romance.

Italian Romance.— Italy shared the romantic life of the Middle Ages, and contributed a large number of stories to romantic literature. The stories of Boccaccio are an example. His " Amento " was improved by Sannazarro in the fifteenth century, and the title was changed to Arcadia. Sir Philip Sidney imitated the Italian model; he changed the setting of the story but retained the name. Thomas Greene, a contemporary of Shakespeare, wrote on the same subject; and Shirley finished the English series in 1640. The pastoral romance, although rather tame in comparison with stories of war and adventure, became very popular in the age of Elizabeth. Besides the pastoral romance, Boccaccio wrote in the genuine style of the romanticist. His Palamon and Arcite, a story of two Theban youths, gives the largest scope to the imagination. It was translated and considerably modified by John Dryden. Boccaccio wrote three romantic pieces which were closely imitated by Chaucer. The first was called Teseide — a story reproduced by Chaucer under the title of the "Knight's Tale;" a second called "Filostrato," the basis of Chaucer's "Troilus and Cressida." The Italian method of mixing prose and verse in the romance was not adopted by Chaucer, although later English writers employed it. For example, the romance of Lalla Rookh.

The Decameron.— The third and most important work of Boccaccio was the Decameron — a collection of one hundred stories with a common bond or thread of interest running through them. These stories mark a transition from the old romance; some of them are intensely realistic and even grossly licentious. They were written after the great plague of Florence in 1348. They represent a group of refugees from that city amusing themselves like Chaucer's Pilgrims by telling stories. On the influence of the Decameron, Dunlop the historian of English fiction, writes as follows: "There are few works which have had an equal influence on literature with the Decameron of Boccaccio. In England its effects were powerful. It inspired the Confessio Amantis of John Gower. From it Chaucer adopted the notion of the frame in which he has enclosed his Canterbury Tales. In some instances he has merely versified the stories and episodes of the Decameron. As early as 1566 an English translation of the Decameron was made by Painter under the title of the Palace of Pleasure; and the effect was speedily visible on the literature of the country. Henry Morley compares the Decameron with the Canterbury Tales, and finds the latter in accord with the high moral and religious ideals which characterize the romance of the Middle Ages. He writes: "The pilgrims to the Shrine of St. Thomas A'Becket are like the Knights of the Round Table, the very soul of honor and purity, while the men and women of the Decameron reflect the debased state of morals in the Italy of the fourteenth century."

As a Basis of English Romance.— Italian romance associates the names of Petrarch and Ariosto with that of Boccaccio. The romance of Petrarch, like that of the Middle
Ages, idealizes woman in the person of Laura. This work
cast in poetic form, involved the writing of several hundred
sonnets. The sonnets of Shakespeare are an English imitation of Petrarch; there is the same kind of connection or
thread of interest running through them, the same theme,
with a slightly different estimate of the felicities of married
life. Both writers agree upon the immortality which would
come from their literary effort to express a morbid and unnatural passion.

Ariosto.— Ariosto produced excellent types of medieval
chivalry. The story that influenced English writers, and became exceedingly popular in England was his Orlando Furioso; this story ranks ahead of the Decameron. It is placed
first in Italian romance. It involves all the old themes of
war, adventure, love, chivalry. Lord Byron, like Chaucer,
went to Italy for many of his subjects; he admired the Orlando
Furioso, and wrote an imitation of it, called Don Juan.
Byron contrived to infuse his own scepticism, melancholy, and
hatred of humanity into the English imitation; otherwise the
Italian romance is faithfuly reproduced. But Italy did more
than furnish models for English writers. Through Italy
came the revival of learning in Western Europe; and with it
came the classic cycles of romance. In Italy the Humanists
in the persons of Petrarch, Dante, Boccaccio, Leo X, revived the study of the ancient classics. The heroes of Pagan
mythology and early Greek and Roman history became themes
for romantic treatment. Long romances were written in
Italy, England and France concerning such persons as Alexander, Cyrus, Virgil, Cæsar, Priam; these were called the
classic cycles of romance.

Classic Cycles.— The classic cycles of romance come under four heads. First, those that were written by Greek or Latin authors and re-printed in Western Europe; for example, the Atlantis by Plato; Babylonica by Xenophon; Appolonius of Tyre by Dionysius; Æthiopica by Heliodorus. Secondly, those cycles that paraphrased the ancient classics: for example, the romance of Troy, of Annas, of Thebes. Thirdly, those cycles based upon classic history not yet versified; for example, the Cycle of Alexander. Fourthly, those cycles that merely reproduce the names of antiquity, the rest being the imaginative work of the medieval writer; for example the Romance of Thebes, and Carthage.

The Classic Cycle in England.— The oldest writer of classic romance in England was an Anglo-Norman trouvère named Benoit. He belonged to the Court of Henry II. In the year 1184 he brought out a story called " The Romance of Troy." It contained 30,000 lines, and covered the whole heroic period of Greek history. In this lengthy work he describes the arts, manners, life of the Middle Ages; although he does not state why such matters should be introduced in a romance of Greece. The romance of Benoit circulated in all the states of Western Europe. Another romance, called the " Trojan War," was published by Joseph of Exeter. It was written soon after Benoit's work, and had little merit compared with the former. The Troy-book of Lydgate, declared to be the first book printed in English, was a translation of it, brought out by Caxton, 1474. A popular romance of the classic cycle was the story of Thebes. Lydgate translated this story from the French, and Chaucer used part of it in his Canterbury Tales. It is noteworthy that the classic cycle in France and England was originally written in verse; as soon as the first prose composition appeared, in the second half of the fifteenth century, the reading public at once lost interest in the classic romance. The last classic romances published by Caxton were those of the Æneid and of Paris. Both were translated from the French. The most popular classic romance in England during the Middle Ages was the story of Alexander. It was published in seven languages. Caxton made an English translation at the close of the fifteenth century. Alexander appealed to the imagination of the Middle Ages, for it was a period of war with Asia. The crusaders, on their way to the Holy City, sang about the Asiatic expedition of Alexander. The ballad-writers and romanticists accumulated myth and legend until a whole library of romance centered in this hero.

Contributions from Northern Europe.— English romance was enriched with material from northern Europe, although the great cycles came from the south and the west. Romance in the north took the form of ballad or epic literature; the romance was called an Edda or a Saga by the Finns, Danes, and Scandinavian races. The best imitation of the northern Edda, as regards literary form, is the Indian romance, Hiawatha. Out of the northern material, two heroes were furnished to English romantic writers. The first and most important was Siegfried, who appeared in England as King Horn. Siegfried is the Arthur of Teutonic romance. He is the central figure of the Heldenbuch wherein is found a collection of German heroes. Siegfried is also the hero of the Nibelungenlied. This long narrative poem is written in the style of all medieval romance; and the work contains all the German legends concerning Siegfried. A comparison between the literary treatment of Siegfried and Arthur in English romance, reveals several points of similarity. War and love are the connecting links in each story. In each, the treatment of love, though often extravagant and fantastic, displays a genuine elevation of sentiment, and these northern romances reveal nowhere that shameless freedom taken by Boccaccio and other southern authors. In the treatment of war, there is some difference; Arthur of English romance is a knight who defies the power of men alone; whereas, Siegfried yields to no power whatsoever, whether of heaven, or earth, or hell. He has the old pagan temper of the hero who is invincible, making even the fates tremble. Hence, the Christian coloring of the German romance is not so marked as that of Arthur; the German hero is often compared to a Titan of Pagan mythology. In the English version of Siegfried, known as King Horn, the hero becomes a viking of the north; he is an adventurer on sea and land; he visits Iceland, where several Sagas record his deeds of bravery; he also fights the infidel in Holy Land. This German hero ranks with Alexander and Charlemagne as a fruitful source of romance.

Havelock.— The second hero from the north is Havelock, the Dane. The story is called an Anglo-Danish romance, because part of the scene is laid in England, part in Denmark. The basis of this romance is the frequent migration of Danes to England during the Middle Ages. Havelock, a Danish prince, weds an English princess and becomes king of both countries. The story belongs to the first half of the twelfth century. Havelock is a hero of much smaller proportions than Siegfried, although his struggles for both kingdoms were long and fierce. This romance first appeared in France; the oldest English version of it is ascribed to Geoffrey Gaimar, an Anglo-Norman trouvère. On account of its direct relation with England the story of Havelock became popular at once. Besides these romances of northern origin, a large amount of ballad literature and folk-lore came from the north. These ballads which may be styled miniature romances, dealt with the Vikings — adventurers from northern Europe, who went on perilous expeditions to England, Ireland, Iceland, and even

Greenland. The largest number of these Sagas are found in Iceland.

Reasons for Abundant Growth.— The romance of the Middle Ages owes its existence to four distinct causes which operated in England as well as on the continent. The first of these was the crusades, bringing western Europe into contact with Asia and opening a wide field for war and adventure. A second cause was the pilgrimage craze which spread over Europe, owing to the intense religious enthusiasm of the Middle Ages. Besides the international pilgrimages to the Holy Sepulchre in Palestine, and to the tombs of the martyrs in Rome, each nation had its special shrine. For example, the Shrine of St. Thomas A'Becket at Canterbury; Loch Deorg, in Ireland; Guadaloupe, in Spain; Mariazell, in Austria; Eberhardsclausen, in Germany. Hence, the basis for those numerous stories which circulated like the Canterbury Tales, the best modern copy of which is The Tales of a Wayside Inn. A third cause for the multiplication of romances in this period was the revival of learning and a quenchless zeal to outrank the ancient classics in the literary treatment of heroes. It is strange that the Middle Ages, revealing such good taste and genius in other fine arts (for example, sculpture, architecture, painting) did not reveal the same taste and judgment in literary matters. A final cause for the growth of romance was the national spirit; each nation of western Europe, as soon as it was carved out of the Roman Empire, began to cultivate its own national heroes, and these heroes were selected in preference to foreign themes.

CHAPTER XL

FICTION (CONTINUED)

Native English Romance.— English authors used materials from northern and southern Europe. In the beginning they merely translated or parodied the romances of the continent. In the fourteenth century they began to use English themes and English scenery, and gave to their work a native coloring. The age of Queen Elizabeth saw the best types produced of English romance. The first of these types is an allegorical romance, written in 1342. It was called the Vision of Piers Plowman. This allegory involves monks and knights, and the manners and customs of the Middle Ages. It also contains personified virtues and vices. All are introduced on a grand scale; and the romantic character of the piece is sustained by placing the characters in Dreamland. The author, while asleep, has nine visions, and his work is a faithful record of these. Throughout this allegorical romance there is a large amount of moralizing which is a distinct departure from the romance of the Middle Ages. The author aims at reforming the English Church and English society. Since the Vision of Piers Plowman was written, the allegorical romance has been a favorite in England. There are four noteworthy examples of this type, produced at later periods. Spenser's " Fairie Queen "; Dean Swift's " Tale of the Tub," Addison's " Vision of Mirza," Bunyan's " Pilgrim's Progress." The " Fairie Queen " ranks above the others in its rich blazonry of romantic ideals; the allegory involves an ethical system for the complete regulation of human conduct.

In this religious and ethical application of the romance, the practical side of English character is revealed. Mere romance as such, did not satisfy. Later on, the same practical trait of character gives us the novel with a purpose.

Romance of Travel.— The second type of native English romance is that of travel. English romance based upon travel began to develop when England became a great sea power and a rival of Spain and France in such remote regions as Asia and America. The wildest stories were circulated concerning the natives of those far-off lands. Imagination ran riot; mariners like Robinson Crusoe were wrecked on islands of which geography has taken no account. Travelers like Sir John Mandeville were finding cities of pearl and gold among the most barbarous peoples. Romantic marriages like that between Captain Rolfe and Pocahontas added the element of love to that of war and adventure. As adventure in the Holy Land inspired the romance of the Middle Ages, so adventure in the New World beyond the Atlantic inspired the romance of succeeding periods. English soldiers of fortune, like Frobisher and Drake, roamed the seas and brought home plenty of material for romantic treatment.

Euphues and Smith.— The first specimen of the romance of travel appears in the Age of Queen Elizabeth, written by John Lily. He describes the travels of an Athenian youth called Euphues. The Greek is represented as a wanderer in Italy and in England; and in both places he becomes a forsaken lover. Pictures of Italian and English landscape are drawn; the manners and customs of both peoples, portrayed. According to Euphues, the ideal woman of whom romanticists dreamed and wrote, was the Queen of England. Another example of this type is called the True Travels of Captain John Smith, reciting his adventures in America, his marvelous exploits with the Indians.

In Relation to the Drama.— Romance of travel by sea and land was reflected in the drama. For example, the Spanish Curate by Fletcher; The Tempest by Shakespeare. Both dramas are based upon adventures on land and sea. It was common for the hero of romance to meet with the fate of Prospero — to be wrecked on an island peopled by monsters of the Caliban type. Such were the stories told by sea-captains at English firesides when English vessels sailed every sea in search of new lands. Out of these stories came the finest type of the romance of travel — Robinson Crusoe.

Fictitious Travel.— Travel, both fictitious and real, has furnished romance. For example, " The Travels of Gulliver "; " The Ancient Mariner "; " The Citizen of the World "; " The Voyage of Wilkins"; "The Shipwreck of John Daniel." In modern times, travel forms an important feature in English fiction. For instance, the literary characters of Kipling move between England and India; Rider Haggard used Africa as a background and setting; Robert Louis Stevenson, America and the Islands of the Pacific. English authors of romance enjoy exceptional privileges, owing to the vast expansion of the British Empire.

The Historical Romance.— The third type of native English romance deals with history and is called the historical romance. It is more fruitful than all the others combined. The first historical romance was written by John Barclay in the closing years of the reign of Elizabeth. This first publication was called Argenis. The author describes it as a " stately fable in the manner of history." At once it was translated into five languages, and, since its publication, the historical romance has been popular in England. The story deals with England's struggle against Philip of Spain, and the destruction of the Spanish Armada. This type of romance flourished, owing to the long wars which England has kept up with races in remote quarters of the earth. The soldier of fortune, such as Thackeray describes at Waterloo, is the usual hero. In historical romances the history of some great war like the American Revolution, or the struggle against Napoleon, is involved. As an example, the stories of Waterloo by Maxwell; or the "Peninsular War," by the same author. The "Highlanders in Spain"; the "Spy" by Fenimore Cooper; the "Memoirs of a Cavalier," by De Foe, are illustrations of the same type.

In America.— Early American history is treated in the romances of Cooper and Irving; Carleton and Lever furnish that of Ireland; while the "Scottish Chiefs" fairly represents the historical romance of Scotland. A more adequate treatment of history is found in the historical novel such as that supplied by Bulwer Lytton. When the novel took the place of the romance in the development of fiction, two important changes were made; first, the events of history were narrated with greater regard for truth and accuracy; secondly, the characters of history were reproduced in their habit as they lived, not as impossible beings.

The Romantic Movement.— The romantic movement in English history began at the dawn of the nineteenth century. Five prominent authors are identified with its origin: Walter Scott, Wordsworth, Shelley, Burns, Coleridge. The movement is called a re-discovery and vindication of the concrete. It was a protest against eighteenth century methods; the moralizing, the abstractions, the perpetual search for *standards* and *canons,* the artificial classicism of such writers

as Alexander Pope. The romantic movement developed
along two lines: First, it aimed at giving the imagination
larger scope by discarding the abstract and the general, the
terminology and artifice of the schools; it substituted, instead, a treatment of concrete things, the individual realities
around us. Hence, the romantic movement was called a return to nature; and its most noteworthy representatives in the
beginning were Burns and Wordsworth. These writers were
constantly employed on scenes of nature; they described man
as he lives — a peasant on the Scottish highlands, or a shepherd in the Westmoreland Valley; whereas, the eighteenth
century writer would tell in rhyming couplets that man is a
rational animal. Compare the " Essay on Man " with the
" Cotter's Saturday Night " and the " Excursion," and the
meaning of the romantic movement becomes clear. It gave,
not general, but particular views of life — life concreted in
meadow, stream and cottage. Secondly, the romantic movement represented a return to the past, to that historical material which lends itself to imaginative treatment. Hence,
such writers as Walter Scott, who recalled the glory of the
Middle Ages. It is said of Walter Scott that he re-created
the Middle Ages. It is certain that his work revived a general interest in that period of English history.

Scott's Environment.— Walter Scott lived in what is known
as the Border District, between Scotland and England — the
home of romance where rival English and Scottish lords
struggled for mastery. A study of the legends connected
with his native place led Scott to write romance. After
writing in verse many of these legends, such as " Marmion "
and the " Lord of the Isles," he treated in prose and on a
larger scale the crusades and the romantic adventures of the
Middle Ages. He became the head of the romantic school
in England; his influence extended beyond England, and on

the continent his romances were translated and published. In England he had Coleridge, Shelley, Byron, for a following.

Growth of the Movement.— The romantic movement started by Burns and Walter Scott, soon spread throughout England; and the best writers either devoted their whole life to it, like Wordsworth, or contributed something to its advancement. Wordsworth spent fifty years on that part of his work which meant a " return to nature." Coleridge contributed the Lyrical Ballads in imitation of Walter Scott's early work; he also contributed the " Ancient Mariner." Byron's most extensive work, Don Juan, was a valuable addition in spite of its cynicism. Shelley made substantial contributions in the " Witch of Atlas," " Alastor," and the " Revolt of Islam." The " Witch of Atlas " is his best story — an allegorical romance wherein Fancy personified as a witch wanders over the face of the earth. The romantic movement, reviving the history of the Middle Ages, revived an interest in the religion of that period. The English Church of the nineteenth century was compared with the English Church of the Middle Ages. Hence, the reaction against protestantism and puritanism, and the return to Catholic ideals, doctrines and practices. Two classes of reformers arose: the ritualists who brought back the altars, lights, vestments, the sculpture and painting which characterized the English Church of the Middle Ages; the tractarians, who restored Catholic doctrine and dogma, as far as possible. Shortly after the romantic movement began, these two classes appeared. Cardinal Newman acknowledges his indebtedness to Walter Scott, whose writings first turned his attention toward Catholicism. Keble, another tractarian, tried to give the English Church a romantic character, and the result was a volume called the Christian Year. When Cardinal Newman wrote the " *Via*

Media " he believed that the English Church could be catholicized according to the ideals of the Middle Ages. Other tractarians were of the same opinion. These ideals are still cherished by Englishmen; and hence the romantic movement is silently but rapidly undoing the work of the Reformation.

The Revolt Against Realism.— The romantic movement, so popular at the present time, represents a revolt against realism, the school of which Dickens is the best type, and Zola the worst type. The reading public is weary of the realistic story with its dull commonplace and matter-of-fact, so that any fiction now aiming at popularity must be either wholly or in part romantic. Among the modern novelists who have made the largest contributions to this movement, Robert Louis Stevenson ranks first; Stevenson composed the wildest stories of adventure, in such books as " St. Ives," " Treasure Island," " The Master of Ballantrae " and " Tales of the Southern Sea." His stories are clean, wholesome; and he enjoys the distinction of being a great stylist as well as a successful author of romance. For the mastery of style, no better modern writer can be read or studied. Like Stevenson, William Morris has contributed largely to romance. His chief stories are " Ogier, the Dane " and " Sigurd, the Volsung." Morris opened a new field by treating the romances of Iceland. His translations of the Northern Sagas are a valuable addition to English literature. Since the death of Stevenson, the most striking figure in modern romance has been Rudyard Kipling. When his Anglo-Indian stories first found their way to the western world, they were immediately associated with the adventures of Rider Haggard in. Africa; and the adventures of Stevenson in the Southern Sea. Thackeray had prepared the way for Indian romance by writing about Colonel Newcome; but its fullest treatment is found in Kipling's stories. Kipling added what he called the true romance when he wrote his Jungle books. They are the romances of the animals. He interprets the conduct of wolves, bears, panthers, elephants, and translates their language into English. Kipling is not a romanticist in the sense that Stevenson was, for he employs always a realistic setting and says much about real things; whereas, Stevenson built his literary fabrics on dreams. Kipling is not a romanticist in the sense that Scott was, for while Scott was constantly looking backward to past ages, Kipling believes in the romance of the present; he believes there is as much romance in shot and shell as in the old tournaments or the older Round Table.

Romance and Science.— The romantic movement some thirty years ago began to develop along scientific lines; the discoveries of science, marvelous in themselves, became still more marvelous under this idealizing process. Examples of this kind of romance are " Elsie Venner," written in 1861 by Oliver Wendell Holmes; it was followed in 1871 by the "Coming Race," written by Bulwer Lytton. The "Coming Race" sets forth the Utopia of the age of electricity. Many of the sciences, notably Sociology, Political Economy and Astronomy, furnish a fruitful field to the romanticist; Bellamy's "Looking Backward," Ward's "Marcella" are examples in point. The romantic movement, at present so strong in the United States, deals with our early colonial history and with the types of character that flourished in such an environment. As yet American history has not sufficient perspective for romanticism. It is too recent; but the events connected with the discovery of America can be employed to advantage.

CHAPTER XLI

FICTION (CONTINUED)

THE NOVEL

Rank.— The novel holds a higher place in fiction than the romance. It presents a more careful study of life and character. Like the drama, it gives us character-creations; whereas the romance resembles the epic, because it gives the greatest prominence to incidents and adventures; and the hero in the romance is treated for the sake of the story. Hence, the ease with which a novel is dramatized in comparison with the romance whose characters like King Arthur are shadowy and uncertain even in outline; and whose situations are so often wildly impossible.

Meaning of the Word.— The word, novel, originally meant something new and striking, something strange and unusual; hence, at one time its use as a synonym for news or tidings. It had this meaning from the old French whence it is derived; and this meaning was retained during the age of Queen Elizabeth. For example, Ben Jonson writes, " Are there any novels this morning, sir? " Massinger writes, " You promise some novels that may delight us."

Restricted Meaning.— In fiction the novel is defined as a prose narrative involving as much plot and intricacy as a drama; it presents a picture of real life and possible men and women. It is like the drama in substance and purpose; plot and motive and character-revelation are similar in both, and the dialogue employed in both has the same purpose. Hence, the novel in its modern form, must be regarded as a part of dramatic literature. The many novels presented on the modern stage, are a proof of dramatic value. Marion Crawford, a leading modern novelist, has this to say on the dramatic value of the novel: "A novel is, after all, a play; and perhaps it is nothing but a substitute for the real play with live characters, scene-shifting and footlights. Accordingly, it is true that any really good novel can be dramatized." Again, he writes: "A novel is excellent according to the degree in which it produces the illusions of a good play."

Relation to Romance.— While the novel is thus allied with the drama, it retains many features of the romance from which it has evolved. First of all, it retains the prose-form; it also retains the method of direct prose narration. The dialogue is frequently supplemented by the narrative of the author. Hence, the action in the novel need not be so complete or so self-explanatory as in the drama; for the author can easily inform or explain where the dialogue fails to bring matters out clearly.

Stages of Evolution.— The novel has passed through three stages of evolution, and hence three distinct classes are found in literature.

The Romantic Novel.— The romantic novel comes first in the order of time. As the name indicates, it is closely allied to romance. As compared with other novels, it gives less prominence to the plot and less prominence to the characters. As it marks but the first step from romance toward reality the characters presented have greater definiteness — they are creations that approach more nearly to the real men and women of the world. But while these characters are less

vague and shadowy there is still, as in the romance, the largest
liberty of fiction. The plot is very slight. Hence, the romantic novel is rarely dramatized. For example, Richardson's " Pamela " published in 1740 and called the first novel
in English literature. The contents of this novel are quite
different from the romances that preceded it; there are no descriptions of gorgeous palaces; no warring knights or enchanted castles. Traces of the romance are found in the
allegory which forms a part of Pamela; also in the adventures of the heroine who is abducted and has several hair-
breadth escapes; finally, in the prose-form of the story there
is likewise the same slender plot. But the characters of
Pamela are all possible men and women; and because they
approach reality, Richardson has been called a realist. It is
significant that even in his early time, Richardson called one
of his novels a dramatic narrative. A more recent example
of the romantic novel is " The Last Days of Pompeii " by
Bulwer Lytton. Traces of the romance are found in such
characters as Arbaces, the Egyptian; and in such descriptions as the amphitheatre just before the eruption of Vesuvius. But the plot is not as subtle and elaborate as that of
a drama; yet the reader is brought face to face with certain
grim realities of life. According to the demands of the romantic novel the human element is for the most part natural
and life-like.

The Idealistic Novel.— A second class of novels was developed when the novel advanced completely beyond the limits of romanticism. The second class is called idealistic. It
differs from the romantic novel in that it never violates the
fundamental realities of life; although employing the liberties
of fiction; whereas, the romantic novel often presents a character or a scene that is wildly impossible. This truthfulness
to fundamental reality does not prevent the artist from treat-

ing his subject in a highly imaginative manner. In fact, the
term idealistic implies that the imagination is allowed sufficient range, and that it is continually at work redeeming from
their grossness and other defects the realities of life. Characters are idealized; the back-ground and stage-setting are
idealized views of nature. It is precisely this idealizing process which makes the novel a work of art; for, as De Quincey
wrote, art is such, not only because it imitates and reproduces
nature, but also because it *transforms, idealizes* and *beautifies*
the material offered by nature.

Indications of Idealism.— Idealism in the novel finds expression in three ways: first, in the scenery or stage-setting.
The picture work in the novel must supply the ever-changing
scenes which accompany the action of a drama. In this work
the author enjoys the privilege of a painter; and may choose
such background and scenery as will interpret and sustain
the dramatic action of the novel. These pictures reproduc-
ing landscape, forest, sea, are highly idealized views of nature; and in drawing them the author reveals his mastery
of words as an art-medium. And just as the modern stage
makes a special feature of its elaborate and beautiful scenery,
so the modern novel emphasizes this picturework of the
author in order to assist the dialogue. These idealized views
of nature are seen to best advantage when the author skilfully
chooses a region or district which easily lends itself to idealization. For example, " The Mill on the Floss," or, the Isle
of Man in " The Christian," or Trelingham Court by the sea,
in the " New Antigone." A still better effect is gained when
the author chooses a place with an historical background.
For example, Florence in " Romola "; or Rome in the novels
of Marion Crawford.

Idealization of Character.— This idealizing process involves
not only the scenery, but the characters as well. The novel,

like the drama, aims at character-creation; and the best novelists are those who create character as well as paint scenery. For example, such characters as Romola, Savonarola, Adam Bede, are as successfully drawn as Hamlet or Lear or Macbeth. The characters in the novel are expected to be perfect after their kind; and this perfection involves some departure from reality, though never to such an extent as to place any character beyond the pale of possibility. This idealizing process appears at its best in the chief hero or heroine of the novel. There is more room and a greater demand in such cases for idealization.

Idealization of Plot.— Idealism finds expression not only in characters and scenery; it also appears in the plot. The plot of a novel, like that of drama, attempts a portrayal of the entanglements of actual life. But this reproduction is accompanied by a considerable play of imagination. Situations are colored and improved so that the reality present in outline furnishes a basis for that work of beauty called art. It is quite enough if there be sufficient realism in the plot to produce an illusion on the mind of the reader. Next to the creation of character the development of the plot makes the heaviest demand upon the author who is an idealist. For the complex conditions of modern life must be portrayed with a large degree of truth; and these conditions do not favor idealism. Society in a crude and simple state yields much more readily to imaginative treatment.

Some Examples.— The writers of the idealistic novel are legion; the best representatives are Thackeray, Hawthorne, Meredith, George Eliot. Our best living representative in America is James Lane Allen. Some modern authors of idealistic fiction have written the romantic novel as well. For example, Lord Lytton; the bulk of his fiction is an example of modern idealism; but he has also written " Rienzi," the " Pilgrims of the Rhine," the " Last Days of Pompeii," in which the romantic element prevails.

The Realistic Novel.— Realism is the third and final step in the development of the novel. It is the outcome of two distinct influences exercised upon modern literature. The first influence is utilitarian; the novel for its own sake, or art for its own sake, becomes an untenable proposition; it should be employed for a higher purpose; hence, the use of the novel as a teacher to enforce some lesson in ethics, religion, politics. While the idealist aims at art for its own sake and is satisfied in gratifying our æsthetic nature by beautiful creations, the realist demands the novel with a purpose — the novel that goes beyond the realm of art and plays the role of instructor to mankind. In response to this utilitarian influence we have modern novels teaching all kinds of doctrines, from Bellamy's " Looking Backward " justifying socialism, to " Robert Elsmere," preaching agnosticism. The novel with a purpose teaches good and evil, according to the moral equipment of the author. It has worked several notable revolutions in modern history. For example, the novels of Dickens completely revolutionized the poor-law system and the educational system in England. A novel of Harriet Beecher Stowe was largely responsible for our late civil war, and the ultimate abolition of slavery. It is claimed that one million, four hundred thousand copies of Uncle Tom's Cabin were put into circulation before 1861.

Influence of Science.— The scientific spirit is a noteworthy influence exercised upon modern fiction. Like the utilitarian spirit, it demands the intensely realistic in the novel. Imagination or fancy must have no place in the story; things must be represented as they are — set forth in all their nakedness, deformity, ugliness. Those who, like Zola, have yielded fully to this influence, have ruined the novel as a work of art. The fundamental error of the realist rests in assuming that a higher grade of art is produced when every detail of nature is specified. Zola justifies his position in the following language: " The experimental novel which is sometimes called realistic, aims at presenting this whole truth of nature, not a beautiful fragment. The close observer finds relations which involve every possible aspect of the moral and physical world. And unless he be false to his profession the truly artistic writer will deal with every possible aspect and manifestation of nature."

The Position of Zola.— Zola defends his position by asserting that every manifestation of nature, no matter how repulsive, is a legitimate theme for art. The most satisfactory reply to Zola is furnished by Goethe; he writes: " It is the province of science to take note of all phenomena of nature; but the highest art must satisfy ethical and æsthetic demands, while remaining true to nature. It must pick and choose from the material offered. By its very nature art is selective and must discriminate; for it cannot find the beautiful or the ethically sound in every aspect of the material and moral world." Again, Goethe writes: " Art is, as Aristotle describes, an imitation of nature; but this does not mean to imitate blindly; it means that the artist must select and combine from nature those materials into which he breathes his own vivifying ideal." The best literary artists agree with Goethe; Matthew Arnold writes: " The province of art is to make a judicious selection of those views of life, which in themselves do not offend the moral or aesthetic sense. The drama or the novel, even when compelled to treat of the morally depraved, is never compelled to go beyond the bounds of decency." Ruskin writes: " The dissecting table has no place in the province of art. Under the plea of fidelity to nature and to the laws of art, novelists of the realistic school pander to the most vicious appetites, and thus lower the moral standard." The foremost living writers in modern literature belonging to the school of realism are Zola, Tolstoi, Ibsen, Henry James, William Dean Howells. The "Kreutzer Sonata," the "Resurrection" and "La Terre" are perhaps the vilest productions of this school. Modern English fiction is almost evenly divided between romanticism and realism in a modified form.

The Dramatic Element.— The dramatic element in fiction — plot, characters, dialogue, — are treated in full in the department of the drama. The technique of the drama, given elsewhere, should be studied in connection with the department of fiction.

CHAPTER XLII

FICTION (CONTINUED)

REPRESENTATIVE AUTHORS

The Story in Hebrew Literature.— Two charming stories — the Story of Ruth and the Story of Tobias — form interesting episodes in the history of Israel. They are the best examples of the short story obtainable from ancient sources. How much historic truth lies at the foundation of both is a question that does not concern us here; some critics refer to these stories as splendid examples of "poetic fiction." But the conservative view, as expressed by Dr. Francis Gigot seems to be more reasonable: "the books are both historical, were intended to be so by their authors; and, consequently, both stories rest upon a foundation of fact. Nevertheless, as stories they belong to the department of literature; in plot, character-sketching, dialogue and imaginative coloring, they approach more closely to the Greek ideal than any other species of Hebrew writing."

The Story of Ruth.— The authorship of the Story of Ruth is anonymous; some critics ascribe it to Samuel; others, to Ezechias. The precise date of its composition is likewise unknown, although from the mixture of styles it is regarded as a post-exile work based on a pre-exile narrative. The story which Goethe calls "the loveliest little idyl that has come down to us," tells about the marriage of Ruth and Boaz. In the time of the barley-harvest Ruth availed herself of the permission granted by the Mosaic Law and went to glean in the field of Boaz, a rich man of the place. Soon she makes known her claim of marriage to him, as next of kin. She marries him and becomes the mother of Obed, the grandfather of David. The story closes with a brief genealogy which constitutes its main historical value.

Criticism by Richard Moulton.— " If the chief distinction of the Idyl be its subject-matter of love and domestic life, then in all literature there is no more typical Idyl than the *Book of Ruth*. Following the *Book of Judges,* which has been filled with bloodshed and violence and the heroism of the sterner virtues, it comes upon us like a benediction of peace. It contains no trace of war or high politics; the disasters of its story are the troubles of family life — exile, bereavement, poverty; while its grand incidents are no more than the yearly festivities of country life, and the formal transfers of property that must go on although kingdoms rise and fall.

Now the interest of the idyl changes to the picturing of popular manners and customs. We have before us all the bustle and excitement of wheat and barley harvest in an agricultural community: the progress of the reapers, and the maidens gleaning behind them, the common meal in the heat of the day, the master coming down to look on and exchange greetings with his people. We see the stranger shyly joining the gleaners, the story of her faithfulness known to all, from the humblest reaper to Boaz himself. With a strange charm there come to us across the gulf of centuries the delicate attentions shown to Ruth by all, the little contrivances by which she is made to glean plentifully without knowing who has befriended her, the place of honor accorded her at the meal. No detail of social life is too petty for the idyl, not even the way in which Ruth eats her portion of food till she is sufficed, and what she leaves she brings to her lonely mother-in-law at home. The gloomy day of Naomi's life is to have light at eventide, and the first gleam of that light is the name of the master who has been so hospitable: Boaz is recognized as one near of kin, and Naomi rallies herself to the task of seeking a resting place for the loving Ruth. More manners and customs follow, and those of the quaintest. Ruth follows exactly the instructions of Naomi in going through the strange ritual by which she must claim the wealthy and powerful land-owner as next of kin. The story is not too short to prevent our catching the tenderness with which Boaz shields the stranger from the breath of gossip, nor the refined courtesy by which he treats the great service asked of him as a favor done to himself: ' Blessed be thou of the Lord, my daughter: thou hast showed more kindness in the latter end than at the beginning, inasmuch as thou followedst not young men, whether poor or rich.' The scene changes to give us the minutiæ of legal procedure in the gate of the city; and here again contrast of character appears, between the nameless kinsman who is ready to do everything that is just, and Boaz, who will go further and be generous. So, with all formalities, the land of Elimelech is redeemed, and Boaz takes Ruth to wife, in order that, according to the interesting Hebrew law, the child born to them may be considered to have revived the line of his grandfather. The long delayed happiness of Naomi becomes full as the women of the city move in procession to lay the new-born babe in her bosom, and sing to her how his name shall be famous in Israel: ' and he shall be unto thee a re-storer of life, and a nourisher of thine old age: for thy daughter-in-law, which loveth thee, which is better to thee than seven sons, hath borne him.' And the simple idyl in its last words joins itself on to the main stream of history by telling that the new-born Obed was the father of Jesse, and Jesse was the father of King David himself."

The Story of Tobias.— This story is the first of the deutero-canonical writings. It relates the virtues and trials of To-bias, a pious Israelite, who undergoes many afflictions, such as exile, captivity, blindness. Many critics regard the work as an historical romance inculcating moral lessons like the parables of our Lord.

Criticism by Gigot.—" It will be easily seen from these general contexts that the Book of Tobias inculcates important religious truths, such as the value of prayers and almsdeeds, the minis-terial function of the holy angels towards men, the power of evil spirits over wicked men, the chief duties of parents toward their children, gratitude to God for his various benefits. Hence, it is not surprising to find that scholars should have been divided concerning the actual purpose of the writer, and should have regarded as such the setting forth of these truths. The narrative was written to show that the truly righteous man who continues to trust in God, in good works and in prayer is amply rewarded at last. Piety may suffer for a while, it receives its recompense in the end. The story is not unlike our modern novel with a purpose."

Fiction in Greek Literature.— Much of Greek literature lies in the department of epic and drama where the imagination was given more scope. The Greeks had little inclination to clothe dramatic literature in the garb of prose. One recalls the Republic of Plato and the Cyropædia of Xenophon as examples of that imaginative treatment of a theme, akin to the best fiction. In point of fact, the Cyropædia is an historical romance. It belongs to the classic or golden age. In the silver age there are many examples of romance, such as the Babylonia of Jamblicus, the Habrocomes and Antheia of Xenophon of Ephesus, the Ethiopics of Heliodorus, the Clitopho and Leucippe of Tatius, the Daphnis and Chloe of Longus.

Criticism by Thomas Perry.—" In its own time, as we have said, this fantastic forged literature was of great service in furthering the development of a new form of composition which was destined to have much influence on modern writing, and the qualities of the Greek romance, the impossible adventures, the succession of catastrophes, the complicated intrigues, the intense love-making, had long formed the ingenious exercises of orators and speakers who lived by entertaining hearers and readers. The tendency of literature towards the discussion of love themes we have noticed even in Euripides, and we have seen how much more distinct it became when Greek letters found their new home at Alexandria. Obviously, the disconnected manner in which this favorite subject was treated in the later days by men who sought to concentrate all their acuteness upon a brief declamation or essay, stood in the way of a patient development of the study of the individual character. It furthered the production of rather a number of vivid scenes than of a carefully composed whole, and the Greek romances that have come down to us abound in incident; they lack psychological unity. Invention is exhausted in devising a succession of events; there is no growth, no careful study of character. The fragmentary nature of the previous studies for the romance were not the only cause of the absence of careful treatment of character; another explanation may be found in that law of intellectual economy which forbids the combination of exciting incidents with psychological analysis. If a succession of catastrophes will sustain the reader's interest, there is no necessity of strengthening this by describing the mental growth of the hero and heroine. It is only when readers have learned every possible combination of flood, flames, earthquakes, wild beasts, robbers, murderers, and poisons, and they no longer shudder at grewsome casualties because they know that there is salvation only a few pages ahead, that the more delicate and more difficult work of portraying a human being begins. The Greek romance did not attain this point, which was left for modern times, yet it is sufficiently creditable that before their final intellectual extinction this wonderful race should have completed their task of founding every form of literature on which posterity was to work.

Greek romances do not concern themselves, after the manner of contemporary English novels, with the instances of social life in the drawing-room but their whole tone is that of conventional society. The hero and heroine are always of gentle blood; the populace has its modern equivalent in the chorus of an Italian opera; they fill the humble position of rabble, citizens, soldiers, and the like. The action of the stories is distinctly busied only with the aristocratic victims of circumstances. This pastoral presents rustic life, devoid of its grimness, and only as it appears to people of position. Yet when this is granted it must also be acknowledged that although the picture drawn is a conventional one, it is yet well drawn. It is a fairyland, but a charming fairy-land that the author puts before us. The love of Daphnis and Chloe knows all the delays and hindrances that an ingenious invention can devise, but its setting is more attractive than the story itself. The pictures are the work of a time which lacked any real enthusiasm, which, indeed, was affected by some of the most worthless interests, but the idyllic touches here and there show that the old Greek spirit had not wholly died. It was, however, lamentably checked with rhetorical artifices; the language is a mass of wilful prettinesses, enough to place the story among the sophistical productions, although its exact date cannot be determined. It was translated by Amyot in 1559 A. D., but its ground was already taken, and although it enjoyed great popularity, the pastorals of Italy and Spain had firm hold of the popular taste, and the work of Longus remained a sort of literary curiosity, a wonderful example of grace mingled with the abundant literary artifice of a dying civilization."

Among the Latins.— The era of fiction among the Latins, like the same era among the Greeks, came after the golden age, so far at least, as prose is concerned. As Latin literature is, for the most part, an imitation of the Greek, Latin classic writers imitated the Greeks in employing poetic channels for all work of the imagination. After the Augustan age passed away, many prose romances appeared, representative authors of which are Petronius Arbiter and Apuleius.

Petronius Arbiter.— The date of his birth is unknown; he died about 66 A. D. He was a Roman author often identified with a certain Caius Petronius whom Tacitus mentions. Scarcely anything is known of his life. In their history of Roman Literature, Teuffel and Schwabe have this to say: "To Nero's time belongs the character novel of Petronius Arbiter, no doubt the same Petronius whom Nero compelled to kill himself. The novel was written in twenty books, only fragments of which remain. It was a satire on the society of Nero's time, and, doubtless, provoked the dissolute emperor to extreme measures. Though steeped in obscenity, this novel is not only highly important for the history of manners and language, but it is also a work of art, full of spirit, fine insight into human nature, wit of a high order and genial humor. The story contains a mixture of verse and prose.

Criticism by John Dunlop.—" The taste for the Sybarite and Milesian fables increased during the reign of the emperors. Many imitators of Aristides appeared, particularly Clodius Albinus, the competitor of the Emperor Severus, whose stories have not reached posterity, but are said to have obtained a celebrity to which their merit hardly entitled them. It is strange that Severus, in a letter to the Senate, in which he upbraids its members for the honors they had heaped on his rival, and the support they had given to his pretensions, should, amid accusations that concerned him more nearly, have expressed his chief mortification to arise from their having distinguished that person as learned, who had grown hoary in the study of old wives' tales, such as the Milesian-Punic fables.—" Major fuit dolor, quod illum pro literato laudandum plerique duxistis, cum ille neniis quibusdam anilibus occupatus, inter Milesias Punicas Apuleii fuit, et ludicra literaria consenesceret." But the most celebrated fable of ancient Rome is the work of Petronius Arbiter, perhaps the most remarkable fiction which has dishonored the literary history of any nation. It is the only fable of that period now extant, but is a strong proof of the monstrous corruption of the times in which such a production could be tolerated, though no doubt, writings of bad moral tendency might be circulated before the invention of printing, without arguing the depravity they would have evinced, if presented to the world subsequent to that period.

A story nearly the same with that in Petronius exists under the title of the Widow who was Comforted, in the book known in this country by the name of the Seven Wise Masters, which is one of the oldest collections of oriental stories. There, however, the levity of the widow is aggravated by the circumstance that the husband had died in consequence of alarm at a danger to which his wife had been exposed, and that she consented to mutilate his body in order to give it a perfect resemblance to that of the malefactor which had been taken down from the cross. This story of female levity has frequently been imitated, both in its classical and oriental circumstances. It is the *" Fabliau De le Femme qui se fist putain sur la fosse de son mari."* Père du Halde, in his History of China, informs us that it is a common story in that empire ; but the most singular place for the introduction of such a tale was the Rule and Exercise of Holy

Dying, by Jeremy Taylor, where it forms part of the 5th chapter, entitled, " Of the Contingencies of Death and Treating our Dead " (vol. 5). The Latin writers seem to have been uniformly more happy in their episodes than in the principal subject."

Lucius Apuleius.— He was born at Medaura, Numidia, about 125 A. D. He is known as a Roman Platonic philosopher and rhetorician. He is famous in literature for having written an " Apology " and the romance of the " Golden Ass."

Criticism by Henry Wilson.—" There is little of Apuleius' own invention in the work on which his fame principally rests. The *Metamorphoses* or *Golden Ass* (which latter title seems not to be the author's own, but to have been bestowed in compliment), was founded on a narrative in the Metamorphoses of Lucius of Patræ, a work extant in the time of Photius. From Photius' account (impugned, however, by Wieland and P. L. Courier) this book would seem to have consisted of a collection of marvelous stories related in an inartistic fashion, and in perfect good faith. The literary capabilities of this particular narrative attracted the attention of Apuleius' contemporary, Lucian, who proceeded to work it up in his own manner, adhering, as Photius seems to indicate, very closely to the original, but giving it a comic and satiric turn. Apuleius followed this *rifacimento,* making it, however, the ground-work of an elaborate romance, interspersed with numerous episodes, of which the beautiful story of Cupid and Psyche is the most celebrated, and altering the denouement to suit the religious revival of which he was an apostle. There is no reason to conclude with Warburton, that he wrote in direct antagonism to Christianity; or with Thomas Taylor, that ' his intention was to show that the man who gives himself to a voluptuous life becomes a beast.' The book is, nevertheless, a remarkable illustration of the contemporary reaction against a period of scepticism, of the general appetite for miracle and magic, and of the influx of Oriental and Egyptian ideas into the old theology. It is also composed with a well-marked literary aim, defined by Kretzschmann as the emulation of the Greek sophist, and the transplantation of their *tours de*

force into the Latin language. Nothing, indeed, is more characteristic of Apuleius than his versatility, unless that it be his
ostentation and self-confidence in the display of it. The dignified, the ludicrous, the voluptuous, the horrible, succeed each
other with bewildering rapidity; fancy and feeling are everywhere apparent, but not less so affectation, meretricious ornament,
and that effect to say everything finely which prevents anything being said well. The Latinity has a strong African colouring, and is crammed with obsolete words, agreeably to the taste
of the time. Few books accordingly suffer less by translation.
When these defects are mitigated or overlooked, the *Golden Ass*
will be pronounced a most successful work, original in treatment
though not in invention, invaluable as an illustration of ancient
manners, and full of entertainment from beginning to end. The
most famous and poetically beautiful portion is the episode of
Cupid and Psyche, adapted from a popular legend of which
traces are found in most fairy mythologies, which explains the
seeming incongruity of its being placed in the mouth of an old
hag. As observed by Friedländer, this discriminating recognition of the beauty of a wild flower of folk lore is as much to
the credit of Apuleius' taste and feeling as the invention of it
could have been to his imagination. The allegorical purport he
has infused into it is his own, and entirely in the spirit of the
Platonic philosophy. Don Quixote's adventure with the wine-
skins, and Gil Blas' captivity among the robbers, are palpably
borrowed from Apuleius; and several of his humorous episodes,
probably current as popular stories long before his time, reappear
in Boccaccio."

Cervantes.— He was born near Madrid in 1547; died in
Madrid, 1616. He became a soldier of fortune under Don
John of Austria, spent five years in slavery, in Algiers; and.
on the whole, led rather a romantic life. He wrote a large
number of novels, plays and romances. Outside of Spain
he is best known as the author of Don Quixote — a work
which entitles him to rank among the greatest authors of fiction.

Criticism by Henry Watts.—"There had appeared, up to 1605, no book since the invention of printing which had so many readers. To that artificial age, reared in the insipid extravagances of the successors of Amadis, *Don Quixote* was as the dawn of a new revelation. The humour, equally simple and deep, the easy, careless grace of the narrative, the fine wisdom and tenderness, the true charity, of this book which professed to be a burlesque of the romances of chivalry, were qualities as rare as they were delightful in Spanish literature. Even those who missed the allegory and were insensible to the satire could not but enjoy the story with its fresh and lively pictures of national life and character. That which has become, to use the phrase of Sainte-Beuve, 'The book of humanity,' was no less successful in its age as a book of popular recreation. The author himself was probably amazed at his own success. Like his great contemporary, Shakespeare, while careful of his lesser works he seemed to have abandoned his masterpiece to the printers with scarcely a thought of his literary reputation. All the first editions of *Don Quixote* swarm with blunders of the most extraordinary kind, proving that Cervantes could never have revised the printing, even if he had looked through his manuscript before committing it to the press. He is made to forget in one chapter what he had written in another. He confounds even the names of his characters, calling Sancho's wife Theresa in one place and Maria in another — the very blunders of which he afterwards accused his enemy, Avellaneda. He makes Sancho ride his ass immediately after it had been stolen by Gines de Passamonte, and bewail its loss when it had been recovered. He confounds time, place, and persons, and abounds in inaccuracies and anachronisms, to the distraction of his readers, the perturbation of his critics, and the serious grief of his admirers. The style of this first part of *Don Quixote,* in spite of occasional passages of beauty which are among the models of the Castilian tongue, is loose, slovenly and inartistic.

In one sense *Don Quixote* is indeed a satire; but the follies it ridicules are those common to all humanity and to every age, and the satire is of that rare kind which moves not to depreciation but to love and pity of the object — to sympathy rather than to contempt, and to tears as well as laughter. Don Quixote and Sancho Panza are permanent types individualized. They are as true for all times as for the sixteenth century — for all the world as for Spain. The antithesis of the pure imagination without understanding and the commonplace good sense without imagination which these two represent, is the eternal conflict which possesses the world. The secret of the marvelous success of *Don Quixote,* of the extraordinary popularity which makes it not only the great book of Spain but a book for all mankind, has been aptly described by Coleridge to lie in the rare combination of the permanent with the individual which the genius of the author has been enabled to achieve. Don Quixote is not only the perfect man of imagination, less the understanding, but he is a living picture of the Spanish *hidalgo* of the time of Philip II. Sancho is the ideal commonplace man of sense, less the imagination, and also the pure Manchegan peasant. In the carrying out of his happy conception, Cervantes was doubtless careless of his own main purpose, so that this burlesque of romance has become a real picture of life — this caricature of chivalry the truest chivalric model — this life of a fool the wisest of books."

Boccaccio.— He was born at Certaldo, near Florence, in 1313, and died in 1375. Like Cervantes in relation to Spanish literature, Boccaccio is the representative Italian novelist. He left works on history, geology, theology, and mythology, some of them written in Latin. His commentaries on Dante, together with many poems, are extant. His fame as a writer rests on the Decameron, a collection of one hundred stories.

Criticism by F. Hueffer.—" In the chronological enumeration of our author's writings we now come to his most important work, the *Decameron,* a collection of one hundred stories, published in their combined form in 1353, although mostly written at an earlier date. This work marks in a certain sense the rise of Italian prose. It is true that Dante's *Vita Nuova* was written before, but its involved sentences, founded essentially on Latin constructions, cannot be compared with the infinite suppleness and precision of Boccaccio's prose. The *Cento Novelle Antiche,* on the other hand, which also precedes the *Decameron* in date, can hardly be said to be written in artistic language according to definite rules of grammar and style. Boccaccio for the first time speaks a new idiom, flexible and tender, like the character of the nations, and capable of rendering all the shades of feeling, from the coarse laugh of cynicism to the sigh of hopeless love. It is by the name of 'Father of Italian Prose' that Boccaccio ought to be chiefly remembered. Like most progressive movements in art and literature, Boccaccio's remoulding of Italian prose may be described as a 'return to nature.' It is indeed the nature of the Italian people itself which has become articulate in the *Decameron;* here we find southern grace and elegance, together with that unveiled naïveté of impulse which is so striking and so amiable a quality of the Italian character. The undesirable complement of the last-mentioned feature, a coarseness and indecency of conception and expression hardly comprehensible to the northern mind, also appears in the *Decameron,* particularly where the life and conversation of the lower classes are the subject of the story. At the same time, these descriptions of low life are so admirable, and the character of popular parlance rendered with such humor as often to make the frown of moral disgust give way to a smile. It is not surprising that a style so concise and yet so pliable, so typical and yet so individual, as that of Boccaccio, was of enormous influence on the further progress of a prose in a manner created by it. This influence has indeed prevailed down to the present time, to an extent beneficial upon the whole, although frequently fatal to the development of individual writers. Novelists like Giovanni Fiorentino or Franco Sacchetti are completely under the sway of their great model; and Boccaccio's influence may be discerned equally in the plastic fulness of Machiavelli and in the pointed satire of Aretino. Without touching upon the individual merits of Lasca, Bandello, and other novelists of the *cinquecento,* it may be asserted that none of them created a style independent of their great predecessor. One cannot indeed but acquiesce in the authoritative utterance of the Academia della Crusca, which holds up the *Decameron* as the standard and model of Italian prose. Even the Della Cruscan writers themselves have been unable to deprive the language wholly of the fresh spontaneity of Boccaccio's manner, which in modern literature we again admire in Manzoni's *Promessi sposi.* A detailed analysis of a work so well known as the *Decameron* would be unnecessary. The description of the plague of Florence preceding the stories is universally acknowledged to be a masterpiece of epic grandeur and vividness. It ranks with the paintings of similar calamities by Thucydides, Defoe and Manzoni. Like Defoe, Boccaccio had to draw largely upon hearsay and his own imagination, it being almost certain that in 1348 he was at Naples, and therefore no eye-witness of the scenes he describes. The stories themselves, a hundred in number, range from the highest pathos to the coarsest licentiousness.

Victor Hugo.— He was born at Besancon in 1802, and died at Paris in 1885. He was celebrated both as a poet and as the leader of the French romantic school. He wrote a number of tragedies and several small volumes of lyrics. The number of his works in prose and verse would make a small library. Perhaps the best known outside of France are " The Toilers of the Sea," and " Les Miserables."

Criticism by Rene Doumic.—" What impresses the reader of Victor Hugo is the poetic quality of his style. This quality together with his love of romance, must impress the critic at once. It is not for originality or for vigor of thought that Victor Hugo is remarkable. He has very few ideas, and he relied rather on the initiative of others and the impulse that came from others. He defines his soul as a crystal reflecting the variegated colors of the world — a shell that echoed its thousand voices. In this way he vindicates his sincerity amid his various changes of opinion and the countless inspirations that govern his soul. His ideas were not grand, though he frequently employs the grand style. He never read profoundly in the book of nature; his psychology skimmed only the surface of truth. What was truly grand in him was the imagination which enlarged and distorted every object; throwing all things out of plumb and just proportion. Hence, his stories are filled with giants, titans, gods, heroes, monsters — he describes these with unwonted brilliance. But we do not find real men and women in his books. His emotion lacks the note of sincerity which we find in other great authors. It is in his literary form and finish that Victor Hugo must lay claim to all his superiority as a writer. In this respect he stands without a rival among his countrymen. The only modern

French authors who approach him are Balzac, Renan and Michelet. Although commonplace in his ideas and wholly incapable of analyzing the deeper emotions and dramatic play of the human heart, he excels in description, in word-painting, in evoking grand scenes where knight and hero may hold their most brilliant tournament. His ideas are images, he thinks in pictures. As an example of his style, read the Battle of Waterloo, or his descriptions of Notre Dame. He has a special talent for the grand narrative wherein the details are expressive and striking. Like Macaulay, he is famous for enumeration and striking antitheses. He also possessed the keenest sense of rhythm and mastered in a high degree the art of versification. Doubtless time will consign the greater part of his work to oblivion, but enough of it will remain to secure for him a permanent place among the great poets and romanticists of his age. Among authors of fiction his name will live with Balzac, Dumas, Zola and Flaubert."

Alexander Dumas.— He was born at Aisne, in France, 1803; died at Puys, 1870. He became noted as an author of plays and novels. Besides these he published a number of works dealing with history and personal reminiscence. Of his stories, the best known are the " Count of Monte Cristo "; " The Mohicans of Paris " and the " Three Musketeers." He shares with Hugo the glory of leading the romantic movement in France.

Criticism by James Farnsworth.—" Dumas is one of the most remarkable characters that the nineteenth century produced. His life was filled with romance, and his wildest work may be said to be only a reflection of his personal experience. His success in founding the ' Review of the World ' tempted him into trying his skill at historical romances. The influence of Walter Scott is plainly visible in the work that followed. The appearance of Monte Cristo excited universal interest; the effect was like the publication of Robinson Crusoe or Waverly. The extraordinary color, the never-flagging spirit, the endless surprises, and the air of nature which was cast over the most extravagant situations make this work worthy of the popularity it enjoyed in almost every country of the world. The vast quantity of his work interfered with its quality. He wrote too rapidly, some-thing after the fashion of Lord Byron, and paid too little atten-tion to recasting and revision. In this respect his son, ' Alex-andre Fils,' is far superior, although he does not exhibit the genius of his father. Owing to their undue expansion and in-terminable development many of his stories have grown decidedly unpopular. Of his numerous plays, two or three may be re-garded as a permanent contribution to French Comedy."

Walter Scott.— He was born at Edinburgh in 1771, and died at Abbotsford in 1832. He is one of the most cele-brated novelists in English literature, famed not only for the amount, but also for the quality of his work. Scott divided his labors between poetry and prose, and many of his ballads are familiar to every English household. The Waverly Novels are his literary masterpieces. Scott is the recognized leader of the romantic movement in England.

Criticism by William Henry Sheran.— Sir Walter Scott occu-pies a prominent place in English Fiction. He is the first, and perhaps the greatest, of our romantic writers. His early home was in the Border District, renowned for its traditions, folk-lore, and ballads, all harking back to the ages of chivalry and romance — Cumberland was near by, and the Eildon Hills and Edinburgh Castle. In his veins ran the blood of the Border chieftain. From youth his memory was stored with wild tales of what those Border chieftains had dared and done — their quarrels and raids, and feats of horsemanship. At his mother's knee, and in the library, he collected a mass of material, out of which came those beautiful pictures of the age of chivalry. Unlike Dickens, he gave no attention to contemporary manners or characters; he lived in the past with the knights and ladies, on the cloth of gold. He sought the romantic element in English and Scotch history; crusaders and pretenders to the English throne engaged his talent; for them he weaves the garment of medieval glory; he gives them spears and coats of mail, and richly caparisoned steeds, and bids them joust once more, or die in the Holy Land, fighting against the infidel. His historical romances are occupied with the crusades, whereas, those novels which are less romantic in character, have to do with queens and kings of Scotland and England. There are traces of the influence of Shakespeare in the work of Scott; for, just as Shakespeare based his historical plays on the actual record of the English kings, allowing his imagination free scope at the same time, so Walter Scott took a few facts from medieval history and used them as the basis of an imaginary wonderland. Like Shakespeare, he selected material which offered the finest opportunity for plot and imaginative treatment. But here the comparison closes, for while Shakespeare's imagination was in the highest sense *creative,* that of Walter Scott could only supply a fascinating story wherein characters with shadowy outlines are introduced for the sake of the narrative. These characters compared with Hamlet or Lear, are like splendid photographs or dissolving views compared with the living reality. Yet how many have been delighted with those dissolving views of an enchanting period which historical blasphemy has called the " Dark Ages."

Criticism by Alfred Welsh.—" The vast sums which Scott's prose and verse won, show how extensive was his popularity. He was the favorite of his age, read over the whole of Europe. He was the masterspirit that entered over the wide field of historical romance and gleaned its wealth for posterity. Without writing specifically for ethical aims, he wrote with ethical truth, and is full charged with the morality of the future. Apart from their historical value, which is great, the Waverly series created an improved taste — a taste for good sense and genuine feeling, as opposed to vapid sentimentalism and romantic extravagance. With all his delight in Highland chiefs and Border thieves, he has a true brotherhood with men, and continually hints some tie between the reader and the vast varieties of being, ever with an eye and a heart to — ' Make channels for the streams of love where they may broadly run.' Doubtless, without being professedly so, he wished to be useful. It filled his eyes with tears to be told that he was doing great good by his attractive and noble tales. His fundamental honesty and his wide humanity would form an *a priori* guarantee that his works, on the whole, should contribute to the amelioration of man and society. On his deathbed it consoled him that he had not com-

promised the interests of virtue. He said to his son-in-law:
'Lockhart, I may have but a minute to speak to you. My dear,
be a good man — be virtuous, be religious — be a good man.
Nothing else will give you comfort when you come to lie here.' "

Criticism by Richard Hutton.—" The most striking feature
of Scott's romances is that, for the most part, they are
pivoted on public rather than mere private interests and passions. With but few exceptions — (*The Antiquary, St. Ronan's
Well,* and *Guy Mannering* are the most important) — Scott's
novels give us an imaginative view, not of mere individuals, but
of individuals as they are affected by the public strifes and
social divisions of the age. And this it is which gives his books
so large an interest for old and young, soldiers and statesmen,
the world of society and the recluse, alike. You can hardly
read any novel of Scott's and not become better aware what
public life and political issues mean. And yet there is no artificiality, no elaborate attitudinizing before the antique mirrors
of the past, like Bulwer's, no dressing out of clothes-horses like
G. P. R. James. The boldness and the freshness of the present
are carried back into the past, and you see Papists and Puritans, Cavaliers and Roundheads, Jews, Jacobites, and Freeboot-
ers, preachers, schoolmasters, mercenary soldiers, gipsies and
beggars, all living the sort of life which the reader feels that in
their circumstances and under the same conditions of time and
place and parentage, he might have lived too. Indeed, no man
can read Scott without being more of a public man, whereas the
ordinary novel tends to make its readers rather less of one than
before. Next, though most of these stories are rightly called
romances, no one can avoid observing that they give that side
of life which is unromantic, quite as vigorously as the romantic
side. This was not true of Scott's poems, which only expressed
one-half of his nature, and were almost pure romances. But in
the novels the business of life is even better portrayed than its
sentiments. Mr. Bagehot, one of the ablest of Scott's critics,
has pointed out this admirably in his essay on *The Waverly
Novels.* ' Many historical novelists,' he says, ' especially those
who with care and pains have read up the detail, are often evidently in a strait how to pass from their history to their sentiment. The fancy of Sir Walter could not help connecting the

two. If he had given us the English side of the race to Derby, *he would have described the Bank of England paying in six-pences, and also the loves of the cashier.'* No one who knows the novels well, can question this. Fergus MacIvor's ways and means, his careful arrangements for receiving subsidies in black-mail, are as carefully recorded as his lavish highland hospitali-ties; and when he sends his silver cup to the Gaelic bard who chaunts his greatness, the faithful historian does not forget to let us know that the cup is his last, and that he is hard-pressed for the generosities of the future. So, too, the habitual thievish-ness of the highlanders is pressed upon us quite as vividly as their gallantry and superstitions. And so careful is Sir Walter to paint the petty pedantries of the Scotch traditional conser-vatism, that he will not spare even Charles Edward — of whom he draws so graceful a picture — the humiliation of submitting to old Bradwardine's 'solemn act of homage,' but makes him go through the absurd ceremony of placing his foot on a cushion to have its brogue unlatched by the dry old enthusiast of her-aldic lore. Indeed it was because Scott so much enjoyed the contrast between the high sentiment of life and its dry and often absurd detail, that his imagination found so much freer a vent in the historical romance, than it ever found in the romantic poem. Yet he clearly needed the romantic excitement of pictur-esque scenes and historical interests, too. I do not think he would ever have gained any brilliant success in the narrow region of the domestic novel. He said, himself, in expressing his ad-miration of Miss Austen, 'The big bow-wow strain I can do myself, like any now going, but the exquisite touch which ren-ders ordinary commonplace things and characters interesting, from the truth of the description and the sentiment, is denied to me.' Indeed, he tried it to some extent in *St. Ronan's Well,* and so far as he tried it, I think he failed. Scott needed a cer-tain largeness of type, a strongly-marked class-life, and, where it was possible, a free, out-of-doors life, for his delineations. No one could paint beggars and gipsies, and wandering fiddlers, and mercenary soldiers, and peasants and farmers and lawyers, and magistrates, and preachers, and courtiers, and statesmen, and best of all perhaps, queens and kings with anything like his ability. But when it came to describing the small differences of manner, differences not due to external habits, so much as

to internal sentiment or education, or mere domestic circumstance, he was beyond his proper field.

Charles Dickens.—He was born near Portsmouth, England,
in 1812; died at Rochester, in 1870. A portion of his
youth was spent in newspaper work; afterward, he became
a contributor to various magazines, quickly establishing his
unrivalled fame as a novelist. His name is a household word
wherever the English language is spoken. The most popular
of his novels are the "Pickwick Papers," "David Copperfield," and "Old Curiosity Shop."

Criticism by Adolphus Ward.—"Nature, when she gifted
Dickens with sensibility, observation, and imagination, had bestowed upon him yet another boon in the quality which seems
more prominent than any other in his whole being. The vigor
of Dickens — a mental and moral vigor supported by a splendid and physical organism — was the parent of some of his
foibles; amongst the rest, of his tendency to exaggeration. No
fault has been more frequently found with his workmanship
than this; nor can he be said to have defended himself very
successfully on this head when he declared that he did 'not
recollect ever to have heard or seen the charge of exaggeration
made against a feeble performance, though, in its feebleness, it
may have been most untrue.' But without this vigor he could
not have been creative as he was; and in him there were accordingly united with rare completeness a swift responsiveness
to the impulses of humor and pathos, an inexhaustible fertility in
discovering and inventing materials for their exercise, and the
constant, creative desire to give to these newly-created materials
a vivid, plastic form. And the mention of this last-named gift
in Dickens suggests the query whether, finally, there is anything
in his *manner* as a writer which may prevent the continuance of
his extraordinary popularity. No writer can be great without
a manner of his own; and that Dickens had such a manner his
most supercilious censurer will readily allow. His terse narrative power, often intensely humorous in its unblushing and un-
winking gravity, and often deeply pathetic in its simplicity, is as

characteristic of his manner as is the supreme felicity of his phrase, in which he has no equal. But no distaste for his mannerisms is likely to obscure the sense of his achievements in the branch of literature to which he devoted the full powers of his genius and the best energies of his nature. He introduced, indeed, no new species of prose fiction into our literature. In the historical novel he made two far from unsuccessful essays, in the earlier of which in particular — *Barnaby Rudge* — he showed a laudable desire to enter into the spirit of a past age; but he was without the reading or the patience of either the author of *Waverly* or the author of *The Virginians,* and without the fine historic enthusiasm which animates the broader workmanship of *Westward Ho.* For the purely imaginative romance, on the other hand, of which in some of his works Lord Lytton was the most prominent representative in contemporary English literature, Dickens' genius was not without certain affinities; but, to feel his full strength, he needed to touch the earth with his feet. Thus it is no mere phrase to say of him that he found the ideal in the real, and drew ˙his inspirations from the world around him."

Criticism by Beresford Chancellor.—"We are somewhat tenacious of applying the epithet of 'novelist' to the author of 'Pickwick,' however, for in the strict sense of the word he was not a novelist. 'He was a poor story-teller — he was not a great plotter,' says Mr. Lang; and this is only too apparent in most of the work he did, in 'Martin Chuzzlewit' no less than in 'Pickwick.' 'Our Mutual Friend' and 'Great Expectations' show, indeed, an effort not wholly unsuccessful to combine intricacy of plot with their author's peculiar genius for character sketching; but particularly in Dickens' earlier work, all such attempts are sadly to seek. It is for this reason that the small tale he wrote in collaboration with Wilkie Collins has more claim to be considered in the light of a novel, according to strict rules, than any of the larger works which emanated from his pen alone; for no greater English master of plot and sensation has lived than the author of 'The Moonstone.' But Dickens has been accused of other delinquencies besides that of being defective in the more important attributes of the novelist proper. He is called vulgar; he is said never to have succeeded in drawing a lady or a gentleman; he is attacked for want of true pathos, of being, in other words, a maudlin sentimentalist. Nowadays, it seems to have become an accepted proposition, that anything to do with the lowest classes is necessarily vulgar, for which reason 'Oliver Twist' is attacked on this head with more asperity than 'David Copperfield,' or 'Bleak House.' Nothing is so absurd. Vulgarity, using the word in its more extended significance, has its home almost entirely among the middle classes, more particularly the higher middle class, and often among those of a still more elevated standing. To pretend to be what one is not, to ape one's betters, to be ashamed of one's poorer relations, in short all the forms of snobbery which are nowadays so rampant, really form a vulgarity of the worst and most virulent type. Now there is no instance on record of a writer of fiction who set himself more sturdily to show up the falsity and baseness of such conduct, with the exception of Thackeray, than Dickens. It is, therefore, absurd to accuse him of harboring what he tried to destroy. Throughout the master's works, we see the same hatred of sham and cant, the same pity for poverty and oppression, the same noble endeavor to do his utmost to lighten the burdens of the poor by making them a bye-word and a scandal. 'Un honnête homme que la vue des iniquités humaines faisait bondir,' as a writer in the *Figaro* (of April, 1886), once described him. In the man himself what we find of kindly generosity, of large-heartedness, of tender sympathy, of joyous good-humor, of inexhaustible fun and unostentatious simplicity, is recorded by those who knew him best and loved him most. Sala and James Payne, Rimmer and Ward, Langton and Dolby, have all told us how the more intimate the association, the more lovable he became; and Thackeray has paid to him in the 'Four Georges' one of the noblest tributes which a writer can pay to a brother author who is being set in continual opposition to him. But, above all, it is in Forster's 'Life,' and in Dickens' own letters and speeches, that the true features of the man are best revealed. With less sterling qualities, few men could have come through the ordeal of applause and adulation which left Dickens unsullied. Like all pre-eminent men, he was self-made; but equally like every true leader, he was by birth and nature a gentleman. He was not a snob as Thackeray was, since he was not always imagining himself one.

He was florid in his tastes, and sometimes flashy in his dress, as he often was in his style; but it was the period in which much jewelry and obtrusive cravats were in vogue, in literature as well as in social life. But everything in his outward appearance became, we are told, subservient to the power of his eyes. 'Eyes,' says one who knew him, 'of the bluest blue; eyes which danced and sparkled with sunniest merriment and yet which quickly softened into serious sympathy; eyes which were brilliant and searching, and seemed always to be kindly, though keenly, reading the person to whom he was talking, yet which never hardened into sternness; eyes in which especially you could discern all the humanity and humour, the noble intellectual possibilities and the manly tenderness of their possessor.' "

George Eliot.— She was born in Warwickshire, England, in 1819, and died in London in 1880 — a woman of remarkable gifts and extraordinary achievements. As a scholar and writer she has few equals in our literature. Some critics regard her as our greatest novelist. Her literary work consists of poems, translations, essays, reviews and novels. For some time she was assistant editor of the Westminster Review. In fiction her best known books are 'The Mill on The Floss,' 'Romola,' and 'Adam Bede.'

Criticism by Richard Holt Hutton.—" What is remarkable in George Eliot is the striking combination in her of very deep speculative power with a very great and realistic imagination. It is rare to find an intellect so skilled in the analysis of the deepest psychological problems, so completely at home in the conception and delineation of real characters. George Eliot discusses the practical influences acting in men and women, I do not say with the *ease* of Fielding — for there is a touch of carefulness, often of over-carefulness in all she does,— but with much of his breadth and spaciousness,— the breadth and spaciousness, one must remember, of a man who had seen London life in the capacity of a London police magistrate. Nay, her imagination has, I do not say of course the fertility, but something of the range and the delight in rich historic colouring, of Sir Walter Scott's, while it combines with it something too of the pleasure in ordered

learning, and the laborious marshalling of the picturesque results of learning,— though her learning is usually in a very
different field,— which gives the flavor of scholastic pride to the
great genius of Milton. Not that I think George Eliot's fine
verse entitles her to be described as a poet, though the poetic
side of her mind has been deep enough and true enough to lend
richness, depth, and harmony to her romances. I am only
pointing out now how much she is besides a novelist,— how inevitable it was that in her novels she should range far beyond
the region of the most successful novelist of recent times,—far
beyond that little world of English society which has determined
for novelists of the most different type of genius,—for Miss
Austen, for Mrs. Gaskell, for Mr. Trollope, for Thackeray, and
for many less successful, but still very successful contemporaries,
— their peculiar field of work. It is, indeed, a great help towards
understanding her true genius to compare George Eliot with
the school of society-novelists of whom I have spoken. What
one remarks about the works of those who have studied any
particular society as a whole far more deeply than they have
studied the individual characters in it, is that their creations all
stand on one level, are delineated, with great accuracy, down
to the same not very considerable depth, and no further; that
all, in short, are bas-reliefs cut out on the same surface. The
novelists of this school are perfectly inexhaustible in resource on
the special social ground they choose, and quite incapable of
varying it. And all of them disappoint us in not giving more
insight into those deeper roots of character which lie beneath
the social surface. George Eliot as a novelist has points of
connection with both of these schools of art, besides some characteristics peculiarly her own. There is the same flowing ease
of manner, clearness of drawing, delicacy of finish, and absence
of excitement, which characterize the modern semi-satirical
school. But there is less of play in the surface-painting,— more
of depth in the deeper characters imagined,— a broader touch, a
stronger, direct fashion of delineation,— less of manner-paint-
ings, and more of the bare naturalism of human life. On the
other hand, there is nothing of the Rembrandt-like style of Miss
Brontë: the light flows more equally over George Eliot's pictures; one finds nothing of the irregular emphasis with which
Currer Bell's characters are drawn, or of the strong subjective

colouring which tinges all her scenes. George Eliot's imagination, like Miss Brontë's, loves to go to the roots of character,
and portrays best by broad, direct strokes; but there the likeness between them, so far as there is any, ends. The reasons
for the deeper method and for the directer style are hardly likely
to have been similar in the two cases. Miss Brontë can scarcely
be said to have had any large, instinctive knowledge of human
nature: — her own life and thoughts were exceptional, cast in
a strongly marked but not very wide mould; her imagination
was solitary; her experience was very limited; and her own personality tinged all she wrote. She ' made out ' the outward life
and manner of her *dramatis personae* by the sheer force of her
own imagination; and as she always imagined the will and the
affections as the substance and center of her characters, those of
her delineations which are successful at all are deep, and their
manner broad. George Eliot's genius is exceedingly different.
Her genial, broad delineations of human life have, as I said just
now, more perhaps of the breadth of Fielding than of any of
the manners-painters of the present day. For these imagine
life only as it appears in a certain dress and sphere, which are
a kind of artificial medium for their art,— life as affected by
drawing-rooms. George Eliot has little, if any, of their capacity
for catching the under-tones and allusive complexity of this sort
of society. She has, however, observed the phases of a more
natural and straightforward class of life, and she draws her
external world as much as possible from observation — though
some of her Florentine pictures must have been suggested more
by literary study than by personal experience — instead of *imagining* it, like Miss Brontë, out of the heart of the characters
she wishes to paint. The English manners she delights in, are
chiefly of the simplest and most homely kind,— of the rural
farmers and laborers,— of the half-educated portion of the country middle-class, who have learnt no educated reticence,— and
of the resident country gentry and clergy in their relations with
these rough-mannered neighbors. This is a world in which she
could not but learn a direct style of treatment. The habit of
concealing, or at most, of suggesting rather than downright expressing, what is closest to our hearts, is, as we know, a result
of education. It is quite foreign to the class of people whom
George Eliot knows most thoroughly, and has drawn with the

fullest power. All her deepest knowledge of human nature has probably been acquired among people who speak their thoughts with the directness, though not with the sharp metallic ring, of Miss Brontë's Yorkshire heroes. But instead of almost luxuriating, as Miss Brontë appears to do, in the startling emphasis of this mannerism, and making all her characters precipitate themselves in speech in the way best calculated to give a strongly-marked picture of the conception in her own brain,— George Eliot has evidently delighted to note all the varieties of form which varying circumstances give to these direct and simple manners, and takes as much pleasure in painting their different shades as Miss Austen does in guiding her more elaborate conversations to and fro so as to•elicit traits of personal character. Directness of delineation is, indeed, evidently natural to the author of ' Adam Bede,' but it has no tendency whatever to take, with her, that form of concentrated intensity which is assumed in Miss Brontë: her style has all the general composure and range of tone of the life she paints, and shows her as much in sympathy with the dumb and stolid phases of rural society as with its more active forms. There was something of the poet in both. But George Eliot's poetry is rooted in the more intellectual emotions, Miss Brontë's was in the most personal. George Eliot's poetic tendencies are rather of the kind to soften outlines and harmonize the effects of her pictures. Miss Brontë's, on the other hand, were adapted to express the passion of her own imagination; and while the effect was graphic and unique, it was monotonous, and not unfrequently, unreal. George Eliot, with a faith like that of her own ' Dinah,' would, to my mind, be one of the greatest intellectual personages the world had ever seen. Her imagination would gain that vivacity and spring the absence of which is its only artistic defect; her noble, ethical conceptions would win certainty and grandeur; her singularly just and impartial judgment would lose the tinge of gloom which now seems always to pervade it; and her poetic feelings would be no longer weighed down by the superincumbent mass of a body of sceptical thought with which they struggle for the mastery in vain. Few minds at once so speculative and so creative, have ever put their mark on literature. If she cannot paint the glow of human enterprise like Scott, or sketch with the easy rapidity of Fielding, she can do what neither of them could do — see and explain the relation of the broadest and commonest life to the deepest spring of philosophy and science. With a quicker pulse of life, with a richer, happier faith, I hardly see the limit to her power."

Thackeray.— He was born at Calcutta in 1811, and died at London in 1863. After finishing his education at Cambridge he devoted himself seriously to literature, and became one of England's greatest novelists. His best known works are *Vanity Fair, Pendennis* and *The Newcomes.*

Criticism by Thomas Shaw.—" Of his works as a whole it may be said that they are full of humor and irony, the moral purpose of the writer not so clearly evident, but yet present in them all. Social foibles, individual weaknesses, the lesser sins of society, are all shown up and treated with quiet satire. Most of his smaller writings are collected in the four volumes of *Miscellanies* published in 1857. Here appears the poetry of Thackeray. It has been well said, ' Thackeray was not *essentially* poetic; that is, he did not look at everything through the medium of the poetic faculty; his thoughts and imaginings were not always governed by a poetic law. He concealed what was poetic in his nature. He is half ashamed of the sentiment which must have expression. The characters he loves best are the characters where emotion and affection hold their sway, and he cannot keep telling you so, as he writes, but he does it with a sort of bashful reticence. He was thoroughly English in the structure of his mind. He could have wept as well as a native of Southern Europe, and sometimes the eye is moist, but the old Gothic spirit despises a man in tears; and so he stands proudly up in self-reliance and a generous manliness. The poetry of his nature was something he ever kept in the recess of his soul. It gave a tenderness to his rebuke, it shed a beauty on his conceptions; and as his countenance was lit with an expression of almost womanly tenderness, so his writing is pervaded with a gentle and loving pathos.

Hawthorne.— He was born in Massachusetts July 4, 1804; died at Plymouth, N. H., in 1864. After graduating at

Bowdoin College, he served some years as a State official, his
last public appointment being United States consul at Liver-
pool. He is the most celebrated among American novelists.
His best stories are *The Scarlet Letter, House of Seven
Gables,* and *The Marble Faun.*

   Criticism by Henry Tuckerman.—"Hawthorne is distinguished for the finish of his style, and the delicacy of his psychological insight. He combines the metaphysical talent of
Brown with the refined diction of Irving. For a period of more
than twenty years he contributed, at intervals, to annuals and
magazines, the most exquisite fancy sketches and historical narratives, the merit of which was scarcely recognized by the public
at large, although cordially praised by the discriminating few.
These papers have been recently collected under the title of
Twice-told Tales, and *Mosses from an Old Manse;* and, seen
by the light of the author's present reputation, their grace, wisdom, and originality are now generally acknowledged. But it is
through the two romances entitled *The Scarlet Letter,* and *The
House of the Seven Gables,* that Hawthorne's eminence has been
reached. They are remarkable at once for a highly finished and
beautiful style, the most charming artistic skill, and intense characterization. To these intrinsic and universal claims, they add
that of native scenes and subjects. Imagine such an anatomizer
of the human heart as Balzac, transported to a provincial town
of New England, and giving to its houses, streets, and history
the analytical power of his genius, and we realize the triumph
of Hawthorne. Bravely adopting familiar materials, he has
thrown over them the light and shadow of his thoughtful mind,
eliciting a deep significance and a prolific beauty; if we may
use the expression, he is ideally true to the real. His invention
is felicitous, his tone magnetic; his sphere borders on the supernatural, and yet a chaste expression and a refined sentiment
interlie his most earnest utterance; he is more suggestive than
dramatic. The early history of New England has found no
such genial and vivid illustration as his pages afford. At all
points his genius touches the interests of human life; now over-
flowing with a love of external nature as gentle as that of
Thomson, now intent upon the quaint or characteristic in life

with humor as zestful as that of Lamb, now developing the
horrible or pathetic with something of John Webster's dramatic
terror, and again buoyant with a fantasy as aerial as Shelley's
conceptions. And, in each instance, the staple of charming invention is adorned with the purest graces of style. Hawthorne
died with the pure and permanent fame of genius, having embalmed the experience he enjoyed in Italy and England in the
romances of *The Marble Faun* and *Our Old Home.* What we
admire in this writer's genius is his felicity in the use of common materials. It is very difficult to give an imaginative scope
to a scene or a topic which familiarity has robbed of illusion. It
is by the association of ideas, by the halo of remembrance and
the magic of love, that an object usually presents itself to the
mind under fanciful relations. From a foreign country our native spot becomes picturesque; and from the hill of manhood
the valley of youth appears romantic; but that is a peculiar and
rare mental alchemy which can transmute the dross of the common and the immediate into gold. Yet so does Hawthorne.
His *Old Apple Dealer* yet sits by the Old South Church, and the
Willey House is inscribed every summer-day by the penknives
of ambitious cits. He is able to illustrate, by his rich invention
places and themes that are before our very eyes and in our daily
speech. His fancy is as free of wing at the north end of Boston,
or on Salem turn-pike, as that of other poets in the Vale of Cash-
mere or amid the Isles of Greece. He does not seem to feel the
necessity of distance, either of time or space, to realize his
enchantments. He has succeeded in attaching an ethereal interest to home subjects, which is no small triumph. Somewhat of
that poetic charm which Wilson has thrown over Scottish life
in his *Lights and Shadows,* and Irving over English in his
Sketch-Book, and Lamb over Metropolitan in his *Elia,* has Hawthorne cast around New England, and his tales here and there
blend, as it were, with traits which endear these authors. His
best efforts are those in which the human predominates. Ingenuity and moral significancy are finely displayed, it is true, in
his allegories; but sometimes they are coldly fanciful, and do not
win the sympathies as in those instances where the play of the
heart relieves the dim workings of the abstract and supernatural.
Hawthorne, like all individualities, must be read in the appropriate mood. This secret of appreciation is now understood, as

regards Wordsworth. It is due to all genuine authors. To many, whose mental aliment has been exciting and coarse, the delicacy, meek beauties, and calm spirit of these writings will but gradually unfold themselves; but those capable of placing themselves in relation with Hawthorne, will discover a native genius for which to be grateful and proud, and a brother whom to know is to love. He certainly has done much to obviate the reproach which a philosophical writer, not without reason, has cast upon our authors, when he asserts their object to be to astonish rather than please."

Stevenson.— He was born at Edinburgh in 1850, and died in 1894. He received his education at the University of Edinburgh; was called to the bar, but never practiced law, devoting the whole of his life to literature. He is one of the great stylists in our language, ranking with Hume and Macaulay.

Criticism by William H. Sheran.— Mr. Stevenson enjoys the reputation of being the modern representative of the romantic school of fiction. There are others of high repute, for romanticism is now the vogue, but there is hardly any other whose name we would care to link with that of Walter Scott. In many respects Mr. Stevenson resembles Sir Walter; there is the same charm of personality, the same large-heartedness and nobility of soul, the same struggle with the unkind fate which in the one took the form of bankruptcy, and in the other, that of the great white plague. Like Scott, he loved adventure, romance, the 'call of the wild' in man and in nature. There was in him a combination of literary and story-telling charm, the former resulting from a long and severe apprenticeship. There can be no doubt but that Stevenson labored many years to acquire that charming style, which, so far as style goes, must rank him above Scott; for the latter wrote too much and too hurriedly to give minute attention to forms of expression and nicely adjusted word-combinations — such as we discover in Stevenson. It has been objected that the style of Stevenson is a little deficient in naturalness, a trifle over-wrought; critics detect here and there the artificial note. Yet it is the style which captivates the reader, and gives to his writings a claim to immortality. But the claim rests upon other ground as well, for Stevenson had the true genius for story-telling. The reader of 'Treasure Island' or 'The Suicide Club,' or 'John Silver' cannot escape the conviction that the author is a master in the art of weaving plot, and of holding the attention as if by spell or magic. The magic wand of Prospero seems to have been recovered by him, and, as he waves it over remote scenes and ages, all the burial places of romance give up their dead. His life was shortened by disease — the fate of many a literary genius, or he might have made a still stronger claim to universal recognition, but like Keats or Shelley, he has left ample proof of his genius.

Other Famous Writers.— The writers of fiction are legion, and all those who deserve special mention are so numerous that it is quite impossible to give them space in this manual. Writers like Mrs. Humphrey Ward, Sudermann, Tolstoi, William Dean Howells, Henry James, James Lane Allen and a host of others come to mind at once. But those mentioned and criticised may be taken as representatives of what fiction is at its best; they are names long identified with the highest and best that has been produced in this department of literary art. The following estimate of the value of fiction from the pen of one of our most accomplished critics and men of culture may fittingly close an extended analysis and study of the subject.

General Criticism by Hamilton Wright Mabie.—" Fiction, as a literary form, has steadily advanced in importance as the social idea has gained in clearness and control; has steadily deepened and broadened as the sense of social obligation and the feeling of social sympathy have deepened and broadened. 'Sir Charles Grandison' and 'Pamela' have a lessened interest for a generation who have known what life meant to 'Adam Bede' and 'Anna Karénina;' but the difference between the earlier and later novelists is not so great as the difference between our ancestors and ourselves. We no longer weep over the misfortunes of romantic gentlemen and the misery of lovelorn ladies of high degree; life has become so earnest, through our new consciousness of the community of suffering among all men, that we are no longer touched by the old conventional devices of the novelists. The great novels of today are so pervaded by life, so profoundly vitalized by genuine insight and sympathy, that they often seem more real to us than the experiences through which we actually pass. We accept nothing as art which does not first convince us of its reality as life. It would be easy and profitable to point out the individual contributions of the great novelists to the science which concerns itself with men in their social relations; but it must suffice to emphasize the significance of fiction as a form of literary art. Each master of this modern art has illustrated some aspect of social life, some form of social influence, some peculiar social condition. The novel of tendency has been only a little more emphatic, a little more consciously directed to a given end, than the great mass of novels of the first rank. 'Romola' and 'Anna Karénina' are as definite and decisive in their purpose as 'Uncle Tom's Cabin,' or 'Ramona.' Dickens, Thackeray, George Eliot, Björnson, Tourguéneff, Balzac, Spielhagen, Zola, Daudet, are never triflers; whatever their differences and their defects, they are always profoundly in earnest to represent the fact as they see it. The fact may be repulsive, even loathsome, but it is always a fact worth considering because of its human significance. Tourguéneff's 'Annals of a Sportsman,' Mrs. Stowe's 'Uncle Tom's Cabin,' Mrs. Jackson's 'Ramona,' Walter Besant's 'All Sorts and Conditions of Men,' have each produced results so definite and marked as to be unmistakable; but these stories have not been more earnest in tone than Daudet's 'Nabob' or 'Jack,' Thackeray's 'Vanity Fair,' Balzac's 'Eugènie Grandet,' George Eliot's 'Middlemarch.' Each of these admirable works, like all works of their rank, has touched life at first hand, and portrayed or interpreted it with masterly insight and power. In each the social instinct has been evident, and each in turn has disclosed some social fact in its large relations and results. To see life as it is and men as they are, is the common purpose of all great writers of fiction. So complete and searching has been the survey of social life by the novelists that the society of today, with all its gradations and differences, could be reproduced from the pages of fiction. From the days of Fielding to those of Charles Reade,

English life has never missed faithful record at the hands of those who have comprehended it, because they have pierced it with their sympathetic insight. Every great political movement like Chartism, every striking political incident like the Gordon riots, every form of discontent and agitation among the lower classes, has had fit and often lasting record. While George Eliot has set forth the tremendous force of inheritance and environment, the vigorous and often coarse brush of Dickens has painted, on a great canvas, the homely life of the common people; and the inimitable art of Thackeray, equally akin to irony and tears, has made us permanent possessors of the social habit and character of the last century. The virile genius of Björnson, in the latest work of his hand, ' Flags in the City and the Harbor,' deals with some of the most obscure problems of social and family life; Tourguéneff has made Russian character under the pressure of absolutism comprehensible to us; Tolstoi commands the attention of a new constituency of readers deeply moved by the marvelous fidelity with which he produces phases of experience, hidden processes of character, at once remote and familiar; while of Zola it must be confessed, whatever we think of his themes and his art, that he at least assumes to lay bare the very heart of certain social conditions in France. Fiction is unquestionably the most attractive and influential form through which men of literary genius express themselves today; and no fact of social significance, no human relationship, no class limitation, capacity or condition, will escape the instinctive search for life which possesses this generation. That which the student of social questions seeks as matter of science the novelist seeks as matter of art."

PART III

CHAPTER XLIII

POETRY

Before dealing with the main divisions of this department of literature, it is necessary to present some criticism on poetry in general, with the view to obtain a clear understanding of what poetry is, how it differs from prose, and what qualities of literary art are therein displayed to best advantage. The criticism that follows, taken from standard authors, is the best obtainable on the subject.

Criticism by William Wordsworth.—" What is meant by the word poet? What is a poet? To whom does he address himself? And what language is to be expected from him? He is a man speaking to men: a man, it is true, endowed with more lively sensibility, more enthusiasm and tenderness, who has a greater knowledge of human nature, and a more comprehensive soul, than are supposed to be common among mankind; a man pleased with his own passions and volitions, and who rejoices more than other men in the spirit of life that is in him; delighting to contemplate similar volitions and passions as manifested in the goings-on of the universe, and habitually impelled to create them where he does not find them. To these qualities he has added a disposition to be affected more than other men by absent things as if they were present; an ability of conjuring up in himself passions, which are indeed far from being the same as those produced by real events, yet (especially in those parts of the general sympathy which are pleasing and delightful) do more nearly resemble the passions produced by real events, than anything which from the motions of their own minds merely, other men are accustomed to feel in themselves: whence, and from practice, he has acquired a greater readiness and power in expressing what he thinks and feels, and especially those thoughts and feelings which, by his own choice, or from the structure of his own mind, arise in him without immediate external excitement. But whatever portion of this faculty we may suppose even the greatest Poet to possess, there cannot be a doubt that the language which it will suggest to him, must often, in liveliness and truth, fall short of that which is uttered by men in real life, under the actual pressure of those passions, certain shadows of which the Poet thus produces, or feels to be produced, in himself."

Principle of Selection.—" However exalted a notion we would wish to cherish of the character of a Poet, it is obvious that while he describes and imitates passions, his employment is in some degree mechanical, compared with the freedom and power of real and substantial action and suffering. So that it will be the wish of the Poet to bring his feelings near to those of the persons whose feelings he describes, nay, for short spaces of time, perhaps, to let himself slip into an entire delusion, and even confound and identify his own feelings with theirs; modifying only the language which is thus suggested to him by a consideration that he describes for a particular purpose, that of giving pleasure. Here, then, he will *apply the principle of selection* which has been already insisted upon. He will depend upon this for removing what otherwise would be painful or disgusting in the passion; he will feel that there is no necessity to trick out or to elevate nature; and, the more industriously he applies this principle, the deeper will be his faith that no words, which *his* fancy or imagination can suggest, will be comparable with those which are the emanations of reality and truth."

Language.—" But it may be said by those who do not object to the general spirit of these remarks, that, as it is impossible for the Poet to produce upon all occasions language as exquisitely fitted for the passion as that which the real passion itself suggests, it is proper that he should consider himself as in the situation of a translator, (who does not scruple to substitute excellencies of another kind for those which are unattainable by him; and endeavors occasionally to surpass his original, in order to make some amends for the general inferiority to which he feels that he

must submit. But this would be to encourage idleness and un-
manly despair. Further, it is the language of men who speak
of what they do not understand; who talk of poetry as of a matter
of amusement and idle pleasure; who will converse with us as
gravely about a *taste* for poetry, as they express it, as if it were a
thing as indifferent as a taste for rope-dancing, or Frontiniac or
Sherry. Aristotle, I have been told, has said, that poetry is the
most philosophic of all writing: it is so: its object is truth, not
individual and local, but general, and operative; not standing upon
external testimony, but carried alive into the heart by passion;
truth which is its own testimony, which gives competence and
confidence to the tribunal to which it appeals, and receives it
from the same tribunal. Poetry is the image of man and nature.
The obstacles which stand in the way of the fidelity of the Biographer and Historian, and of their consequent utility, are incalcu-
lably greater than those which are to be encountered by the Poet
who comprehends the dignity of his art. The Poet writes under
one restriction only, namely, the necessity of giving immediate
pleasure to a human being possessed of that information which
may be expected from him, not as a lawyer, a physician, a mariner,
an astronomer or a natural philosopher, but as a Man. Except
this one restriction, there is no object standing between the Poet
and the image of things; between this and the Biographer and Historian, there are a thousand."

Poet and Scientist.—" To this knowledge which all men carry
about with them, and to these sympathies in which, without any
other discipline than that of our daily life, we are fitted to take
delight, the Poet principally directs his attention. He considers
man and nature as essentially adapted to each other, and the mind
of man as naturally the mirror of the fairest and most interesting
properties of nature. And thus the Poet, prompted by this feeling of pleasure, which accompanies him through the whole course
of his studies, converses with general nature, with affections akin
to those, which, through the labor and length of time, the Man of
Science has raised up in himself, by conversing with those particular parts of nature which are the objects of his studies. *The
knowledge both of the Poet and the Man of Science is pleasure;
but the knowledge of the one cleaves to us as the necessary part
of our existence, our natural and inalienable inheritance; the other*

is a personal and individual acquisition, slow to come to us, and by no habitual and direct sympathy connecting us with our fellow-beings. The Man of Science seeks truth as a remote and unknown benefactor; he cherishes and loves it in his solitude: the Poet, winging a song in which all human beings join with him, rejoices in the presence of truth as our visible friend and hourly companion. *Poetry is the breath and finer spirit of all knowledge;* it is the impassioned expression which is in the countenance of all science. Emphatically may it be said of the Poet, as Shakespeare hath said of man, ' That he looks before and after.' He is the rock of defence for human nature; an upholder and preserver, carrying everywhere with him relationship and love. In spite of difference of soil and climate, of language and manners, of laws and customs: in spite of things silently gone out of mind, and things violently destroyed; the Poet binds together by passion and knowledge the vast empire of human society, as it is spread over the whole earth, and over all time. The objects of the Poet's thoughts are everywhere; though the eyes and senses of men are, it is true, his favorite guides, yet he will follow wheresoever he can find an atmosphere of sensation in which to move his wings. *Poetry is the first and last of all knowledge — it is as immortal as the heart of man.* If the labors of Men of Science should ever create any material revolution, direct or indirect, in our condition, and in the impressions which we habitually receive, the Poet will sleep then no more than at present; he will be ready to follow the steps of the Man of Science, not only in those general indirect effects, but he will be at his side, carrying sensation into the midst of the objects of the science itself. The remotest discoveries of the Chemist, the Botanist, or Mineralogist, will be as proper objects of the Poet's art as any upon which it can be employed, if the time should ever come when these things shall be familiar to us, and the relations under which they are contemplated by the followers of these respective sciences shall be manifestly and palpably material to us as enjoying and suffering beings. If the time should ever come when what is now called science, thus familiarized to men, shall be ready to put on, as it were, a form of flesh and blood, the Poet will lend his divine spirit to aid the transfiguration, and will welcome the Being thus produced, as a dear and genuine inmate of the household of man. It is not, then, to be supposed that any one, who holds that sublime notion of Poetry which I have attempted to convey, will break in upon the sanctity and truth of his pictures by transitory and accidental ornaments, and endeavor to excite admiration of itself by arts, the necessity of which must manifestly depend upon the assumed meanness of his subject."

Distinction of Language.—"What has been thus far said applies to Poetry in general; but especially to those parts of composition where the Poet speaks through the mouths of his characters; and upon this point it appears to authorize the conclusion that there are few persons of good sense, who would not allow that the dramatic parts of composition are defective, in proportion as they deviate from the real language of nature, and are colored by a diction of the Poet's own, either peculiar to him, as an individual poet, or belonging simply to Poets in general; to a body of men who, from the circumstance of their composition being in metre, it is expected will employ a particular language. It is not, then, in the dramatic parts of composition that we look for this distinction of language; but still it may be proper and necessary where the Poet speaks to us in his own person and character. To this I answer by referring the reader to the description before given of a Poet. Among the qualities there enumerated as principally conducing to form a poet, is implied nothing differing in kind from other men, but only in degree. The sum of what was said is, that the Poet is chiefly distinguished from other men by a greater promptness to think and feel without immediate external excitement, and a greater power in expressing such thoughts and feelings as are produced in him, in that manner.

Summary.—"I have said that poetry is the spontaneous overflow of powerful feelings: it takes its origin from emotion recollected in tranquillity: the emotion is contemplated till, by a species of reaction, the tranquillity gradually disappears, and an emotion, kindred to that which was before the subject of contemplation, is gradually produced, and does itself actually exist in the mind. In this mood successful composition generally begins, and in a mood similar to this, it is carried on; but the emotion, of whatever kind, and in whatever degree, from various causes, is qualified by various pleasures, so that in describing any passions whatsoever, which are voluntarily described, the mind will, upon the whole,

be in a state of enjoyment   If Nature be thus cautious to preserve
in a state of enjoyment a being so employed, the Poet ought to
profit by the lesson held forth to him, and ought especially to take
care, that, whatever passions he communicates to his reader, those
passions, if his reader's mind be sound and vigorous, should always be accompanied with an overbalance of pleasure. Now the
music of harmonious metrical language, the sense of difficulty
overcome, and the blind association of pleasure which has been
previously received from works of rhyme or metre of the same
or similar construction, an indistinct perception perpetually re-
newed of language closely resembling that of real life, and yet, in
the circumstance of metre, differing from it so widely — all these
imperceptibly make up a complex feeling of delight, which is of
the most important use in tempering the painful feeling always
found intermingled with powerful descriptions of the deeper passions. This effect is always produced in pathetic and impassioned
poetry; while, in lighter compositions, the ease and gracefulness
with which the poet manages his numbers are themselves con-
fessedly a principal source of the gratification of the reader. All
that is *necessary* to say, however, upon this subject, may be
effected by affirming, what few persons will deny, that of two
descriptions, either of passions, manners, or characters, each of
them equally well executed, the one in prose and the other in
verse, the verse will be read a hundred times where the prose is
read once."

CHAPTER XLIV

POETRY (CONTINUED)

Criticism by Shelley.—" Poetry, in a general sense, may be defined to be ' the expression of the imagination :' and poetry is connate with the origin of man. Man is an instrument over which a series of external and internal impressions are driven, like the alterations of an ever-changing wind over an Æolian lyre, which move it by their motion to ever-changing melody. But there is a principle within the human being, and perhaps within all sentient beings, which acts otherwise than in the lyre, and produces not melody alone, but harmony, by an internal adjustment of the sounds or motions thus excited to the impressions which excite them. It is as if the lyre could accommodate its chords to the motions of that which strikes them, in a determined proportion of sound ; even as the musician can accommodate his voice to the sound of the lyre. A child at play by itself will express its delight by its voice and motions ; and every inflexion of tone and every gesture will bear exact relation to a corresponding antitype in the pleasurable impressions which awakened it ; it will be the reflected image of that impression ; and as the lyre trembles and sounds after the wind has died away, so the child seeks, by prolonging in its voice and motions the duration of the effect, to prolong also a consciousness of the cause. In relation to the objects which delight a child, these expressions are what poetry is to higher objects. The savage (for the savage is to ages what the child is to years) expresses the emotions produced in him by surrounding objects in a similar manner ; and language and gesture, together with plastic or pictorial imitation, become the image of the combined effect of those objects, and of his apprehension of them. Man in society, with all his passions and his pleasures, next becomes the object of the passions and pleasures of man ; an additional class of emotions produces an augmented treasure of expressions ; and language, gesture, and the imitative arts become at once the representation and the medium, the pencil and the picture, the chisel and the statue, the chord and the harmony.

Origin of Poetry.—" In the youth of the world, men dance and sing and imitate natural objects, observing in these actions, as in all others, a certain rhythm or order. And, although all men observe a similar, they observe not the same, order, in the motions of the dance, in the melody of the song, in the combinations of language, in the series of their imitations of natural objects. For there is a certain order or rhythm belonging to each of these classes of mimetic representation, from which the hearer and the spectator receive an intenser and purer pleasure than from any other: the sense of an approximation to this order has been called taste by modern writers. Every man in the infancy of art observes an order which approximates more or less closely to that from which this highest delight results; but the diversity is not sufficiently marked, as that its gradations should be sensible, except in those instances where the predominance of this faculty of approximation to the beautiful (for so we may be permitted to name the relation between this highest pleasure and its cause) is very great. Those in whom it exists in excess are poets, in the most universal sense of the word; and the pleasure resulting from the manner in which they express the influence of society or nature upon their own minds, communicates itself to others, and gathers a sort of reduplication from that community. Their language is vitally metaphorical; that is, it marks the before unapprehended relation of things and perpetuates their apprehension, until the words which represent them, become, through time, signs for portions or classes of thoughts instead of pictures of integral thoughts; and then, if no new poets should arise to create afresh the associations which have been thus disorganized, language will be dead to all the nobler purposes of human intercourse. These similitudes of relations are finely said by Lord Bacon to be ' the same footsteps of nature impressed upon the various subjects of the world '— and he considers the faculty which perceives them as the storehouse of axioms common to all knowledge. In the infancy of society every author is necessarily a poet, because language itself is poetry; and to be a poet is to apprehend the true and the beautiful; in a word, the good which exists in the relation subsisting, first between existence and perception, and secondly between perception and expression. Every original language near to its source is in itself the chaos of a cyclic poem: the copiousness of lexicography and the distinctions of grammar are the works of a later age, and are merely the catalogue and the form of the creations of poetry."

Work of Poets.—"But poets, or those who imagine and express this indestructible order, are not only the authors of language and of music, of the dance, and architecture, and statuary and painting: *they are the institutors of laws, and the founders of civil society, and the inventors of the arts of life,* and the teachers who draw into a certain propinquity with the beautiful and the true, that partial apprehension of the agencies of the invisible world which is called religion. Hence, all original religions are allegorical or susceptible of allegory, and, like Janus, have a double face of false and true. Poets, according to the circumstances of the age and nation in which they appeared, were called, in the earlier epochs of the world, legislators, or prophets: a poet essentially comprises and unites both these characters. For he not only beholds intensely the present, as it is, and discovers those laws according to which present things ought to be ordered, but he beholds the future in the present, and his thoughts are the germs of the flower and the fruit of latest time.

Materials of Poetry.—"Language, color, form, and religious and civil habits of action are all the instruments and materials of poetry; they may be called poetry by that figure of speech which considers the effect as a synonym of the cause. But poetry in a more restricted sense expresses those arrangements of language, and, especially, metrical language, which are created by that imperial faculty, whose throne is curtained within the invisible nature of man. And this springs from the nature itself of language, which is a more direct representation of the actions and passions of our internal being, and is susceptible of more various and delicate combinations than colour, form, or motion, and is more plastic and obedient to the control of that faculty of which it is the creation. For language is arbitrarily produced by the imagination, and has relation to the thoughts alone; but all other materials, instruments and conditions of art have relations among each other, which limit and interpose between conception and expression. The former is as a mirror which reflects, the latter as a cloud which enfeebles, the light of which both are mediums of communication. Hence, the fame of sculptors, painters, and musicians, although the intrinsic powers of the great masters of these arts may yield in no degree to that of those who have employed language as the hieroglyphic of their thoughts, has never equalled that of poets in the restricted sense of the term; as two performers of equal skill will produce unequal effects from a guitar and a harp. The fame of legislators and founders of religions, so long as their instructions last, alone seems to exceed that of poets in the restricted sense; but it can scarcely be a question whether, if we deduct the celebrity which their flattery of the gross opinions of the vulgar usually conciliates, together with that which belonged to them in their higher character of poets, any excess will remain. We have thus circumscribed the word poetry within the limits of that art which is the most familiar and the most perfect expression of the faculty itself. It is necessary, however, to make the circle still narrower, and to determine the distinction between measured and unmeasured language; for the popular division into prose and verse is inadmissible in accurate philosophy. Sounds as well as thoughts have relation both between each other and towards that which they represent, and a perception of the order of those relations has always been found connected with a perception of the order of the relations of thoughts. Hence, the language of poets has ever affected a certain uniform and harmonious recurrence of sound, without which it were not poetry, and which is scarcely less indispensable to a communication of its influence than the words themselves, without reference to that peculiar order. Hence, the vanity of translation; it were as wise to cast a violet into a crucible that you might discover the formal principle of its color and odor, as to seek to transfuse from one language into another the creations of a poet. The plant must spring again from its seed, or it will bear no flower — and this is the burden of the curse of Babel."

Poets and Prose Writers.— "An observation of the regular mode of the recurrence of harmony in the language of poetical minds, together with its relation to music, produced metre, or a certain system of traditional forms of harmony and language. Yet it is by no means essential that a poet should accommodate his language to this traditional form, so that the harmony, which is its spirit, be observed. The practice is indeed convenient and popular, and to be preferred, especially in such composition as includes much action; but every great poet must inevitably innovate upon the example of his predecessors in the exact structure of his peculiar versification. The distinction between poets and prose writers is a vulgar error. The distinction between philosophers and poets has been anticipated. Plato was essentially a poet — the truth and splendor of his imagery, and the melody of his language, are the most intense that it is possible to conceive. He rejected the measure of the epic, dramatic, and lyrical forms, because he sought to kindle a harmony in thoughts divested in shape and action, and he forebore to invent any regular plan of rhythm which would include, under determinate forms, the varied pauses of his style. Cicero sought to imitate the cadence of his periods, but with little success. Lord Bacon was a poet. His language has a sweet and majestic rhythm, which satisfies the sense, no less than the almost superhuman wisdom of his philosophy satisfies the intellect; it is a strain which distends, and then bursts the circumference of the reader's mind, and pours itself forth together with it into the universal element with which it has perpetual sympathy. All the authors of revolutions in opinion are not only necessarily poets as they are inventors, nor even as their words unveil the permanent analogy of things by images which participate in the life of truth; but as their periods are harmonious and rhythmical, and contain in themselves the elements of verse; being the echo of the eternal music. Nor are those supreme poets, who have employed traditional forms of rhythm on account of the form and action of their subjects, less capable of perceiving and teaching the truth of things, than those who have omitted that form. Shakespeare, Dante and Milton (to confine ourselves to modern writers) are philosophers of the very loftiest power."

Functions of the Poetic Faculty.—" The functions of the poetic faculty are twofold; by one it creates new materials of knowledge, and power, and pleasure; by the other it engenders in the mind a desire to reproduce and arrange them according to a certain rhythm and order which may be called the beautiful and the good. The cultivation of poetry is never more to be desired than at periods when, from an excess of the selfish and calculating principle, the accumulation of the materials of external life exceeds the quantity of the power of assimilating them to the internal laws of human nature. The body has then become too unwieldy for that which animates it."

Poetry and Knowledge.— " Poetry is indeed something divine. It is at once the center and circumference of knowledge; it is that which comprehends all science, and that to which all science must be referred. It is at the same time the root and blossom of all other systems of thought; it is that from which all spring, and that which adorns all; and that which, if blighted, denies the fruit and the seed, and withholds from the barren world the nourishment and the succession of the scions of the tree of life. It is the perfect and the consummate surface and bloom of all things; it is as the odour and the colour of the rose to the texture of the elements which compose it, as the form and splendor of unfaded beauty to the secrets of anatomy and corruption. What were virtue, love, patriotism, friendship — what were the scenery of this beautiful universe which we inhabit; what were our consolations on this side of the grave — and what were our aspirations beyond it, if poetry did not ascend to bring light and fire from those eternal regions where the owl-winged faculty of calculation dare not ever soar? Poetry is not like reasoning, a power to be exerted according to the determination of the will. A man cannot say, ' I will compose poetry.' The greatest poet even cannot say it; for the mind in creation is as a fading coal, which some invisible influence, like an inconstant wind, awakens to transitory brightness; this power arises from within, like the colour of a flower which fades and changes as it is developed, and the conscious portions of our natures are unprophetic either of its approach or its departure. Could this influence be durable in its original purity and force, it is impossible to predict the greatness of the results; but when composition begins, inspiration is already on the decline, and the most glorious poetry that has ever been communicated to the world is probably a feeble shadow of the original conceptions of the poet.

A Record of the Best Minds.—" Poetry is the record of the best and happiest moments of the happiest and best minds. We are aware of evanescent visitations of thought and feelings sometimes associated with place or person, sometimes regarding our own mind alone, and always arising unforeseen and departing unbidden, but elevating and delightful beyond all expression: so that even in the desire and the regret they leave, there cannot be but pleasure, participating as it does in the nature of its object. It is, as it were, the interpenetration of a diviner nature through our own; but its footsteps are like those of a wind over the sea, which the coming calm erases, and whose traces remain only as on the wrinkled sand which paves it. These and corresponding conditions of being are experienced principally by those of the most delicate sensibility and the most enlarged imagination; and the state of mind produced by them is at war with every base desire. The enthusiasm of virtue, love, patriotism, and friendship is essentially linked with such emotions; and whilst they last, self appears as what it is, an atom to a universe. Poets are not only subject to these experiences as spirits of the most refined organizations, but they can colour all that they combine with the evanescent hues of this ethereal world; a word, a trait in the representation of a scene or a passion will touch the enchanted chord, and reanimate, in those who have ever experienced these emotions, the sleeping, the cold, the buried image of the past. Poetry thus makes immortal all that is best and most beautiful in the world; it arrests the vanishing apparitions which haunt the interlunations of life, and veiling them, or in language or in form, sends them forth among mankind, bearing sweet news of kindred joy to those with whom their sisters abide,— because there is no portal of expression from the caverns of the spirit which they inhabit into the universe of things. Poetry redeems from decay the visitations of the divinity in man. Poetry turns all things to loveliness; it exalts the beauty of that which is most beautiful, and it adds beauty to that which is most deformed; it marries exultation and horror, grief and pleasure, eternity and change; it subdues to union under its light yoke all irreconcilable things. It transmutes all that it touches, and every form moving within the radiance of its presence is changed by wondrous sympathy to an incarnation of the spirit which it breathes: its secret alchemy turns to potable gold the poisonous waters which flow from death through life; it strips the veil of familiarity from the world, and lays bare the naked and sleeping beauty, which is the spirit of its forms. All things exist as they are perceived: at least in relation to the percipient. 'The mind is its own place, and of itself can make a heaven of hell, a hell of heaven.' But poetry defeats the curse which binds us to be subjected to the accident of surrounding impressions. And whether it spreads its own figured curtain, or withdraws life's dark veil from before the scene of things, it equally creates for us a being within our being. It makes us the inhabitants of a world to which the familiar world is a chaos. It reproduces the common universe of which we are portions and percipients, and it purges from our inward sight the film of familiarity which obscures from us the wonder of our being. It compels us to feel that which we perceive, and to imagine that which we know. It creates anew the universe, after it has been annihilated in our minds by the recurrence of impressions blunted by reiteration. It justifies the bold and true words of Tasso: *'Non merita nome di creatore, se non Iddio ed il Poeta.'"*

Qualities of a Poet.—" A poet, as he is the author to others of the highest wisdom, pleasure, virtue and glory, so he ought personally to be the happiest, the best, the wisest, and the most illustrious of men. As to his glory, let time be challenged to declare whether the fame of any other institutor of human life be comparable to that of a poet. That he is the wisest, the happiest, and the best, inasmuch as he is a poet, is equally incontrovertible: the greatest poets have been men of the most spotless virtue, of the most consummate prudence, and, if we would look into the interior of their lives, the most fortunate of men: and the exceptions, as they regard those who possessed the poetic faculty in a high, yet inferior degree, will be found on consideration to confine rather than destroy the rule. Let us for a moment stoop to the arbitration of popular breath, and usurping and uniting in our own persons the incompatible characters of accuser, witness, judge, and executioner, let us decide, without trial, testimony, or form, that certain motives of those who are 'there sitting where we may not soar,' are reprehensible. Let us assume that Homer was a drunkard, that Virgil was a flatterer, that Horace was a coward, that Tasso was a madman, that Lord Bacon was a peculator, that Raphael was a libertine, that Spenser was a poet-laureate. It is inconsistent with the division of our subject to cite living poets, but posterity has done ample justice to the great names now referred to. Their errors have been weighed and found to have been dust in the balance; if their sins ' were as scarlet, they are now white as snow;' they have been washed in the blood of the mediator and redeemer, Time. Observe in what a ludicrous chaos the imputations of real or fictitious crime have been confused in the contemporary calumnies against poetry and poets; consider how little is as it appears — or appears as it is; look to your own motives, and judge not, lest ye be judged."

Poetry and Logic.—" Poetry, as has been said, differs in this respect from logic, that it is not subject to the control of the active powers of the mind, and that its birth and recurrence have no necessary connection with the consciousness or will. It is presumptuous to determine that these are the necessary conditions of all mental causation, when mental effects are experienced unsusceptible of being referred to them. The frequent recurrence of the poetical power, it is obvious to suppose, may produce in the mind a habit of order and harmony correlative with its own nature and with its effects upon other minds. But in the intervals of inspiration, and they may be frequent without being durable, a poet becomes a man, and is abandoned to the sudden reflux of the influences under which others habitually live. But as he is more delicately organized than other men, and sensible to pain and pleasure, both his own and that of others, in a degree unknown to them, he will avoid the one and pursue the other with an ardour proportioned to this difference. And he renders himself obnoxious to calumny when he neglects to observe the circumstances under which these objects of universal pursuit and flight have disguised themselves in one another's garments."

Sources of Criticism.— Besides the critics quoted in the foregoing pages, the criticism of Aristotle, Horace, Vida, Boileau, not to mention such critics as Johnson, Puttenham, Sidney, Gosse, Stedman, Lacy, Arnold. in our own tongue, ought to be familiar to the student. Authorities ancient and modern form a small library. But throughout this mass of criticism there is a large amount of repetition; and the passages quoted here, while avoiding such repetition, exhibit the matter fairly well out of English stores, giving the student a fair estimate of what poetry is, and the place it holds in literature. There remains to consider the chief divisions of poetry: the *drama,* the *epic* and the *lyric.*

CHAPTER XLV

THE DRAMA

Definition.— The word, drama, is derived from the Greek (*drawo*) and signifies action. Aristotle defines the drama as an action complete, organic, with unity of theme and purpose. Lessing defines it as the mirror of human life; he calls it the highest form of literary art inasmuch as the dramatic artist holds the mirror up to life in its most complex and subtle relations. The drama is a work of art because it is an imitation; it imitates action; it presents personages as real and as acting. Hence, Schlegel calls dramatic art an imitation in the way of action. The drama originated in man's love of imitation. "To imitate," says Aristotle, "is instinctive in man from his infancy; and from imitation all men naturally receive pleasure — imitation in voice and gesture, in dress and decoration, in character and action." But of these various imitations, character and action are vitally related to the drama.

Meaning of an "Action."— The action in dramatic art has a specific meaning. It implies an operation of the will; a fulfillment or carrying out of a personal resolution. The action must, therefore, present itself to the human mind as having its source in a human or superhuman will; in other words, persons, and not brutes or the inferior creation, must be represented as acting. Hence, the standard phrase, *Dramatis personae*. The action of a drama connotes an actor; hence, dramas are written to be acted — to be interpreted by an actor. Therefore, properly speaking, the literary drama is a misnomer. The title, literary drama, is sometimes used of works kept apart from the stage; but the true drama is inseparable from the actor and the stage. The action of the drama has for its necessary correlative the actor. He is the interpreter of the action; and he is always kept in mind by the dramatic artist. Hence, there is a vital connection between the dramatic art and the histrionic art.

The First Requirement for the Action.— The drama appeals, in the first place, to our intelligence. Therefore, the action of the play should have a logical sequence — a beginning, a middle, and an end. The beginning states the cause of the action; the middle, the development of the action; the end, the result of the action; hence, in the drama there is a premise, an argument, and a conclusion.

The Second Requirement for the Action.— The action should contain a unifying idea — an idea that gives organic unity and completeness to the drama. Aristotle calls it the dramatic idea; he calls it dramatic, because it involves such a theme as love, jealousy, ambition — a theme which impels men to act; the dramatic idea involves, besides the general theme of love or ambition, a particular theme such as the love of Romeo; the ambition of Caesar. In other words, the dramatic idea is concreted in some personal example. For example, the personification of ambition leading to moral ruin in Macbeth.

A Third Requirement for the Action.— The drama is based on the truth of life; hence, probability is essential to the action. An improbable theme, or the improbable treatment of a theme, is but a travesty of dramatic art. The action must appeal to the audience as natural and likely to occur.

A Fourth Requirement for the Action.— The action involves incidents, a series of happenings; these incidents lie about every dramatic idea in greater or less proportion. The dramatic idea cannot stand unless supported by these incidents. For example, the assassination of a man or the beheading of a woman would give no other sensation than that of horror; but when we know with all the attendant circumstances, that one is Robespierre and the other Marie Antoinette, we feel at once the force of the dramatic idea. In other words, the conditions and the cause, as well as the result of the action, are essential. The incidents and happenings that support the action are organized into acts. Custom has divided dramas of serious import into five acts; but this is largely a convenience; there is no arbitrary number. Aristotle makes no mention of acts; though the Greek plays had irregular pauses sustained by the chorus. Shakespeare's plays were not originally so divided. The acts as parts of a drama, are separated by an interval. The spectator supposes certain things to pass in the intervening time — things of no material interest, though occurring in the natural development of the dramatic idea. For example, the twenty years' sleep of Rip Van Winkle. Moreover, there are particular reasons why there should be periods of rest. There are many plays of great intensity where the chief actor could not bear the strain, physical, mental, and emotional. For example, Julius Caesar, Richelieu; among modern dramas, Cyrano de Bergerac. The intervals between the acts allow rest and a husbandry of resources. Again, the several acts present distinct pictures, and so assist in the final and full understanding of the drama. Modern custom divides a drama into acts; the acts, into scenes; and all contribute to intelligent work and to the general understanding of the play in the performance. Each scene accomplishes something, and the sum of these scenes makes the act, as the sum of the acts makes the play.

The length of acts and scenes cannot be determined with mathematical precision. The length of an act is determined by what that act has to accomplish. Acts are long and short, and vary like paragraphs in an essay, according to the importance of their subordinate themes.

The Fifth Requirement for the Action.— The action of the drama must possess importance and magnitude. The object of the struggle such as the drama implies, ought to have sufficient dignity to command general attention. Hence, the chief characters of the drama are, as a rule, people from the higher walks of life — statesmen, kings, cardinals, commanders; also supernatural beings — angels, devils, gods. These characters naturally excite interest. The importance and magnitude of the action depend not only upon the natural dignity of the chief characters, but also upon the importance of their acts. For example, a king playing chess; a king playing for a neighboring crown. In other words, both character and action should be important. Judged by this standard the Crucifixion furnishes the best material for a drama.

The Sixth Requirement for the Action.— The action of the drama should represent all that is important to the understanding of the play, in the strong excitement of the characters and in a continuously progressive increase of effects. The action must be capable of the strongest dramatic excitement; that is to say, it must contain many thrilling moments, climax succeeding climax, till the final catastrophe; personages must be represented in their most intimate emotional relations with each other, in order to excite a corresponding emotion in the audience. Moreover, the struggle of the hero should be such as the audience may easily understand and sympathize with. Hence, the elemental and universal passions — love, hatred, cruelty, revenge, ambition, are the best themes for the drama. They make the widest appeal, and are capable of the strongest dramatic excitement.

Divisions of the Action.— The smallest division of the action is the scene. Scenes are of two kinds: first, the painted picture, commonly known as the scenery of the stage; secondly, what actually takes place, what is said and done by the players. It is, therefore, a segment of the action. Each act has its special function — a distinctness and a relative completeness of its own. An act is made up of scenes, just as a play is made up of acts. Each act, to the smallest particle, must have a definite purpose; so with each scene. All scenes are incidents leading up to a main incident called the climax. Threads run through the drama, binding the smallest parts together, like nerves in the human body.

First Requirement for the Scene.— A scene must accomplish something toward the general result. The impression made by a scene may be very strong of itself, very beautiful or very pathetic; but if it does not belong in every fibre to the action, dramatic law has no pardon for it.

Second Requirement for the Scene.— Each scene must be in sequence. It must occupy its proper place in the development of the action; it must sustain a gradual scale leading up to the climax and down to the catastrophe. The skill of the dramatic artist is shown by so arranging the scenes as to secure an orderly, yet ever-increasing momentum in the action of the drama.

The Dialogue in the Scene.— The dialogue is, as a rule, required to make a scene. The greater part of the action is carried on in dialogue. The dialogue implies two persons either in harmony with each other, or at variance. Their agreement or opposition furthers the action. Most scenes are, of necessity, dialogues. Human life is thus best presented to an audience. Like every particle in the dramatic structure, the dialogue must follow certain laws. First, it must be organic, with definiteness of purpose. Secondly, it must always advance the action. Thirdly, it should be suitable to character *in thought* and *dialect;* so as to express the finer relations between the people of the play.

Some Characteristics of the Dialogue.— As variety in speech is the rule of life, so great variety marks the dialogue. It is as varied as character and social standing. The second characteristic of the dialogue is contrast of thought. This contrast is its great stimulus. It is carried on, not by words alone, but by look and gesture. In fact, the manner and bearing of the actors should figure quite as prominently as the words exchanged. The action of the drama would be quite tame without such aids. Finally, the dialogue gets over ground rapidly; hence, its common use in dramatic scenes. The greater the number of persons in the scene, the slower the action; and slowness of action is fatal; the audience grows weary. With the dialogue usually go "asides," or remarks aside, and the monologue. "Asides" are natural and common enough in life. They appear artificial only when actors are clumsy. They are a part of the dramatic machinery. They keep the audience in touch with the development of the action. They are sometimes a material part of the action. For example, Macbeth: "Stars, hide your fires."

The Monologue.— The monologue is also very useful. In supreme moments it is entirely natural. The drama is life, and men make their most serious resolves in solitude — alone. Hence, the naturalness of the monologue. The monologue gives the hero of the modern stage opportunity to reveal to the audience his most secret feeling and volition. Its use, however, is limited; because the influence of the struggle of each man on every purpose of the drama is so great that every isolation of the individual must be specially justified. Only where a rich inner life has been concealed for a long time in the general play, does the audience tolerate its private revelation. The audience cares little for the quiet expression of an individual so long as the connection and contrasts may be gleaned from a dialogue.

Pauses.— Monologues represent a pause for rest in the action. They place the speaker in a significant manner before the audience. Hence, they need in advance of themselves an excited tension of feeling in the audience. They may open a scene, or be placed between two scenes of an exciting character. But they must always be constructed *dramatically;* that is, by weighing both sides of the struggle they must win something significant for the action itself. For example, Hamlet's two soliloquies; Macbeth's air drawn dagger. Aside from dramatic uses, the monologue, which is as a rule a literary gem, becomes a favorite passage with the public. In the construction of scenes the monologue, dialogue, and "asides" represent the lyric or emotional element; the epic element is represented by the messenger. Hence, the announcements by messenger are an important part in our drama. They relieve the tension, give the audience a pause for breath. These announcements are called the epic element because they recite in the third person the deeds of the hero or chief character. These narratives represent portions of the action which cannot be conveniently staged. For example, a great battle or popular commotion, the results of which are reported by messengers to the audience. In this connection, announcements by messenger are essential to the integrity of the action. In the Greek drama, notably those of Æschylus, whole scenes were given up to narratives from messengers; in the modern drama there are no messenger-scenes as such; but messengers are still an important part, a necessary adjunct.

Groups in the Scene.— The grouping of characters was unknown to the Greeks. It necessarily belongs to the modern drama wherein there is a large scope of life. Groups consist of three or more persons on the stage; hence, they introduce the picturesque element and heighten the effect. It becomes the dramatist's care to give employment to all these people; for the picturesque element has its share in dramatic composition. Groups impress the audience partly by their picture, as in pantomime or tableaux; and partly by their energy or movement which prepares or closes a situation, thus binding together the common action of the drama. In plays that concern an uprising of the people, or in historical dramas, frequent grouping of characters is essential. In modern plays it is customary to have all the prominent characters on the stage in the closing scene, just before the last fall of the curtain. The final result of the action is thus more clearly understood, and the picturesque effect upon the audience is vivid and lasting. It is a vivid summary of the action, having the same office in the drama that a peroration has in a speech.

The Episode in the Scene.— An episode is an interruption of the action, or, as the Greeks term it, a " standing still." The episode concerns some element in the piece, or it may be a mere interruption without any reference to the drama. For example, the boy playing the harp for Brutus in his tent on the calm night before the battle of Pharsalia. In Denman Thompson's " Old Homestead," the Salvation Army marching and playing before Grace Church, New York; in the " Sign of the Cross," the Pagan girl's song before Mercia.

Shakespeare's clowns and fools are introduced mainly for episode to give the audience pleasing moments of rest from the intensity of the action. The episode should permit the action to be resumed without a jar to the memory or the attention. Hence, the episode should be brief. But of all these elements in a scene, the dialogue is most important, inasmuch as it carries on the action. The purpose of every dialogue is to bring into prominence from the assertions and counter-assertions a result which impels the action further. The dialogue stands for strife and struggle; in it perception is matched against perception; emotion against emotion; volition against volition, and out of this storm and stress the action grows. Hence, as Schlegel observes, "Dialogue is the creator of Dramatic action; for man thus appears under powerful restraint, excitement, or transformation. In the dialogue appear those peculiarities which bring men effectively into conflict with other men, namely, force of sentiment, violence of will, achievement hindered through passionate desire; in a word, all the issues of moral conflict appear in the dialogue; and dramatic action is nothing more than a condensed history of these moral issues."

The Painted Picture in Relation to the Scene.— A scene consists not only of what takes place in dialogue, monologue, episode, but it also consists of a painted picture, commonly known as stage scenery. Scenery plays a large part in the economy of the modern drama. The first principle to be observed in its use, is laid down by Aristotle: "The scenery should be organic with the play and should never by imperfection destroy the illusion." Imperfections in scenery arise in various ways: 1st, by over-elaboration; 2d, by undue proportion in mechanical effects; by too much color and impressiveness.

A Second Principle.— Scenery should be subordinate to the acting; scenery, after all, is only the background. Hence, it should give the largest showing to the human element. Poor dramas require elaborate scenery for support. The classic drama needs but a minimum of such assistance. As a matter of fact, too much scenic display mars the action, divides and distracts the attention of the audience. Moreover, the inanimate can only have an accidental contact with man in the matter of action; the pictorial scene is valuable for impressions; and it may go a step beyond that and " garnish a moment of influence in the progress of the story "; but it is necessarily subordinate. Change of scenery is demanded by the changing environment of the action; time and place must be considered in the pictorial scene. Considerable skill and taste may be shown in this regard, so much so that the " pictorial staging of a play " is now considered a fine art.

The Act in the Drama.— Horace is the main authority for dividing a drama into five acts. In the *Ars Poetica* he writes: *" Neve, minor, neve sit quinto productior actu fabula."*— " Let your play consist of five acts, nor more, nor less." The authority of Horace is enforced by modern custom and practice. But the five-act division is purely arbitrary. " There is nothing," writes Dr. Blair, " in the nature of dramatic composition which fixes this number rather than any other; and it had been much better if no such number had been ascertained, but every play had been allowed to divide itself into as many parts or intervals as the subject naturally pointed out." In the Greek tragedies at certain intervals the actor retired and the chorus continued with songs; but these intervals were extremely unequal and irregular, sometimes dividing the play into three parts; sometimes into seven or eight parts. As custom has now divided every play into five acts, it remains to consider the especial office assigned to each act.

The Special Office or Function of the First Act.— The first act ought to contain a clear exposition of the subject. This exposition Aristotle calls the prologue of the drama. The first act ought to be so managed as to awaken the curiosity of the spectators; it ought to furnish them with materials for understanding the sequel. The first act should make the audience acquainted with the personages who are to appear, with their several views and interests, and with the situation of affairs at the time when the play commences. In early times, a single actor appeared and recited the situation in a few lines: for example, the plays of Æschylus and Euripides began in this way; hence, the strict meaning of the word, prologue, corresponding exactly to the preface of a book. Now, the situation appears and the subject is made to open itself by conversation among the first actors who are brought upon the stage. In other words, the prologue, formerly distinct, becomes a function of the first act. Thus, for example, the first act of Macbeth: it presents the chief characters — Macbeth, Lady Macbeth, Duncan, Banquo, The Weird Sisters. It presents the exact situation. Macbeth tempted in three ways: by an ungovernable ambition; by the powers of evil; by a heartless wife. The relations between the chief actors are at least indicated; also the lines along which the play will develop. In other words, the situation of affairs is clearly set forth. Facts of time, place, circumstances, color, tone, character — all furnish the basis of the action.

The Special Office of the Second Act.— As the first act is occupied with the basis of the action, so the second act is devoted to the development of the action. The action of a drama proceeds from the very outset toward a point called the climax; and from the very outset should speed like an arrow from the string. This rapidity is gained in the second act by a change from general impressions to particular and specific ones. The first act presents all the needful general impressions; the second act is devoted to a specific treatment of the hero. For example, the murder of Duncan occupies the whole of the second act in Macbeth. In other words, the hero does something which keeps the attention and promises a climax. The object of the first act is to get the attention of the audience; the object of the second act is to hold the attention, and the drama must do this at all hazards. Hence, the second act will present the hero as doing something which keeps the audience in suspense. Suspense as to the issue should remain in the mind when the second act closes. For example, the murder of Duncan and the flight of his sons: will Macbeth succeed to the throne? will the sons of Duncan return and be revenged? Suspense as to the outcome always heightens the interest. Hence, the second act presents what is called a *situation*. A situation is the state of persons in a scene with regard to others. In a sense, all scenes are situations, but the technical meaning is confined to points of special interest where expectation is peculiarly alert as to what the characters will say and do. The second act is called by critics the act of ascent owing to the rising movement of the action. And while it advances the hero toward the climax, it has another function to perform: it introduces the counter-play. By counter-play is meant the action of those characters opposed to the hero. Such action begins at the close of the second act. For example, in Macbeth the flight of Duncan's sons into England and Ireland, which is the basis of the counter-movement against the hero. The complications resulting from the counter-play prolong the suspense and give a necessary delay to the action, which otherwise too direct, would bring the drama too quickly to an end.

The Third Act in the Drama.— The function of the third act is to present the climax. By climax in a drama is meant the highest point in the ascending scale of dramatic action. Dramatic action is compared to a pyramid in its rise and fall. On the one side it mounts to the apex which is called the climax of the action; thence it falls on the other side to the base which is called the catastrophe.   The third act is held to be most important inasmuch as it presents the hero at the height of his success and at the same time on the threshold of his reverses.   It is not necessarily the act that excites greatest sympathy; for the catastrophe as a rule stirs deeper emotion. It simply indicates that the hero or figure of chief interest has reached a decisive moment in his career.   For example, in Macbeth, when Banquo is slain and his son escapes. Here Macbeth has reached the culminating point in his successes and is on the threshold of reverses.   Hence, the climax in the third act is called the turning point of dramatic action. Suspense continues, for the solution is not yet in sight, though dimly indicated; but expectation is quickened; for the chief character or hero is in the supreme crisis of the drama; he is placed in a position of peril.   As the climax presents the results of the rising movement; as all that preceded finds therein a crowning point, the poet needs to use all the splendor of poetry and all the skill of dramatic art, in order to make vividly conspicuous this middle or turning point of his artistic creation.   For example, the banquet scene in Macbeth — the murderer's struggle with the ghost, the fearful struggles with his own conscience, the social festivity and royal splendor — all are pictured with the finest art of Shakespeare.

The Fourth Act in the Drama.— The special office of the fourth act is to present the return of the action; hence, it lies between the climax and the catastrophe, between the apex and the base of the dramatic pyramid.   As the second act represents the ascent of the action; so the fourth act represents the descent.   The second and third acts are filled with obstacles and entanglements; the fourth opens a solution. Up to the climax of the drama, the hero, as a rule, appears in a desire working from within outward, changing by his own force the life-relations in which he came upon the stage. From the climax on, what the hero has done reacts upon himself and gains power over him. The external world which he fought in the ascent of the action, now stands in the strife above him. And this adverse influence becomes continually more powerful and victorious until at last in the final catastrophe it compels the hero to yield to its irresistible force. The gradual fall of the hero, called technically, the return of the action, is exemplified in Macbeth, fourth act. What the royal murderer has done reacts upon himself. First, the witches show a long line of future kings — Banquo's descendants; thereby foreshadowing Macbeth's defeated purpose in slaying Banquo. Secondly, Macduff escapes to England, forms an alliance with Malcolm for the overthrow of Macbeth; thereby completing the counter-play against the hero. In this alliance the murder of Duncan reacts upon the hero, threatening to overwhelm him. Thus the fourth act in every drama is occupied with the fatal consequences of the hero's deeds.

The Special Office of the Fifth Act.—The fifth act completes the drama. It presents the last stage of the falling action. The conditions of the plot are about to be fulfilled. There are suggestions of finality in the words and deeds of the characters. Vigor, intensity, interest, surprise, still continue, but the horizon closes down. For example, when Lady Macbeth walks in her sleep and reveals her madness we know that the springs of action in the play, at least from this side, are available no more. One by one, the hopes of Macbeth, based on prophecy, are destroyed. In the fifth act, movement is more rapid than in any part of the play; details, as far as possible, are omitted. There is no broad elaboration of scenes. The fifth act presents the catastrophe or what the ancients called the exodus. It is, briefly, an important deed overcoming the hero and closing the action. Through this deed the chief characters of the drama are relieved from trouble. For example, the battle between Macbeth and Macduff in the fifth act. The external world which the hero conquered, deals a death-blow in the catastrophe; whence comes the term tragedy. The catastrophe is, as regards literary form, brief, simple, free from ornament. The dramatic artist aims solely at being impressive. Hence, the brief scenes pulsate with life. For rapid and skilful handling of the catastrophe there is no better example than the closing scenes of Macbeth. But however sudden, and even in manner of accomplishment, surprising, may be the catastrophe, it should not be unprepared, but like every other part of the action, should preserve its organic connection with the whole. Sudden suicides which terminate so many tragedies, and the paternal blessings which close an equal number of comedies, should be something more than a signal for the fall of the curtain; they should be a logical outgrowth and natural close of the drama. The end of the play must be organic; that is, it must be in proportion with cause and effect; it should afford a commanding point where the whole action may be recalled; the interest and curiosity of the audience must be fully satisfied.

CHAPTER XLVI

CHARACTERS OF THE DRAMA

The Characters.— The action of a drama, divided into scenes and acts, is carried on by means of characters; these characters are called *dramatis personae*. The dramatic artist must create these characters; and in so doing must justify the claim of the drama that it holds the mirror up to nature. As an artist, he will give to his characters those general traits and dispositions which make them natural and human. Secondly, he will clothe them with specific traits which individualize each one. His art is tested chiefly in this regard; to individualize his creations, distinguishing by happy strokes the one from the other. The inventive power of the poet is taxed in producing the artistic appearance of a rich individual life; because he puts together a few vital expressions in such a manner that the person, understood and felt by him, is intelligible to the audience as a characteristic being. The artist can present only single strokes; out of these the audience or the reader must picture the fullness of characteristic life. This is made possible by the suggestive power of the artist; just as a few lines drawn on a canvas by a skilful hand bring out the form of a human countenance; so a few words skilfully used on the literary canvas may sharply define any character in a drama. This suggestive power, in order to accomplish its purpose, implies the active co-operation of the audience. The imagination of the audience must be at work upon the suggestions given.

Three Underlying Principles.— However the method and scope of characterization may vary under the influence of

different historical epochs and different tendencies and tastes
of races or nations, there are three principles underlying this
branch of dramatic art. The first principle: the character
in a drama must have distinctiveness. Whatever its part in
the action, it must be sufficiently marked in its distinctive features to interest the audience. This is particularly true of the
leading characters; and even the lesser characters should have
distinctive and distinguishing traits. As in real life so in
dramatic art, individual and personal traits ought to be sufficiently pronounced to awaken interest, and furnish a distinct
type. The second principle: besides impressing the imagination with distinctness, each character must be consistent
with itself; this consistency must appear between its conduct in the action and the features it has established as its
own. In order to secure this result, the dramatic artist will
first have distinctly conceived the character; and his conception expressed in the growth and progress of the play, will
determine the totality of the character he creates. If it be a
historical personage, the character in the drama should harmonize, as far as possible, with the character established by
the facts of history. But while the creative artist is permitted
to modify the historic character, he is obliged to present his
own character creation as consistent from the first act to the
last. For example, Shakespeare could not introduce Macbeth
as a courageous man; and in the last act show him to be a
coward. A character may be complex and at the same time
consistent with itself; that is, it may exhibit good and evil
traits, as men in real life exhibit them; but consistency demands that these traits, once emphasized, be carried through
the drama. The third principle: a character should be directly *effective* with regard to the dramatic action in which
it takes part; that is to say, the influence it exerts upon the
progress of the action, should correspond to its distinctive
features — in other words, the conduct of the play should al-

ways spring from the nature of the characters. Hence, even the minor characters should not idly intervene; their conduct should be significant, vitally related to the action. The only exception to this rule is the episode which may be detached from the action, placed as it were, in parenthesis as a breathing space for actors and audience. On the other hand, the chief characters should determine the course of the action which should harmonize with their distinctive traits and features. Chance is thereby excluded from dramatic action, inasmuch as it flows naturally from the characters. Whatever is said or done in the drama springs as naturally from the characters as the herb from the earth or light from the sun. For example, given the character of Macbeth or his wife, and we may naturally expect murders. However the method and scope of characterization may vary among different races or in different historical epochs, these principles:—distinctiveness, self-consistency, effectiveness,— always and everywhere apply to character-drawing.

Characters Most Suitable and Proper for the Drama.— Aristotle furnishes two rules respecting the selection of characters. First, as to external dignity; the chief characters of a drama, like those of the epic, should be illustrious, of high rank, thereby dignifying the action of the drama, and giving it magnitude; but as the drama is a mirror of life, all ranks and conditions ought to be represented, omitting, of course, the most degrading and mean circumstances. The second rule, as to morals; the persons represented should be mixed characters, in which good and evil traits are found, such in fact as we meet in the world; they afford the most proper field for displaying without any bad effect on morals, the vicissitudes of life. They interest us most deeply, as they display emotions and passions which we have all been conscious of. Human nature in its strength and weakness is thus presented as found in actual life. On the other hand, perfectly unmixed characters either of good or ill men are not the fittest; for the distress of the one, being wholly unmerited, hurts and shocks us; and the sufferings of the other excite no pity. The dramatic artist should so introduce his personages, and the incidents relating to them, as to leave upon the audience impressions favorable to virtue and to the administration of Providence. The drama should excite pity for the virtuous in distress. Under no conditions is the dramatic artist permitted to exhibit human life so as to render virtue an object of aversion. If innocent persons suffer, their sufferings ought to be attended with such circumstances as will make virtue appear amiable and admirable.

The Chief Character of the Drama.— The drama should have only one chief character or hero, about whom all the the persons, however great their manner, arrange themselves. Hence, the drama is thoroughly monarchical in arrangement; the unity of its action depends essentially upon this fact, that the action is controlled by one dominant character. The interest of the audience must be directed for the most part toward one person. The highest dramatic processes of but few persons can be elaborated in a single drama; and of these few the audience should not be left in doubt as to the most important person. One exception to this rule is permitted when the relations of two lovers form the material and plot of the drama, these persons are looked upon as enjoying equal privileges; and are treated as a unit in leading and controlling the action. Hence, we have dramas called " Romeo and Juliet "; " Troilus and Cressida "; " Anthony and Cleopatra." With this exception, dramatic unity demands a single hero, as the leading character. The scenes at the beginning of the drama, giving color to the whole piece, should also give the moral fibre of the hero. Shakespeare manages his heroes with wonderful skill. Before his heroes are entangled in the difficulties of a tragic action, he allows them to express the trend of their character, so that the audience may know distinctly what is to follow. For example, Hamlet, Othello, Macbeth, Brutus, Richard III, Cæsar.

Subordinate Characters.— Besides being distinct, self-consistent and effective, the subordinate characters should present a variety and contrast to the audience; because dramatic action relies chiefly upon contrast for its development; the weak will must clash with the strong one; virtue must battle with vice; one social rank must cross swords with another, as happens in actual life. The intermingling of races and creeds in modern life gives the widest scope to the dramatic artist, adding the clash of nationalities and religions. Lessing calls this contrast of character the soul of the modern drama; and his remark is equally applicable to the drama of the ancients.

Revelation of Character.— Every person in the drama, whether chief or subordinate, should show the fundamental traits of his or her character, as distinctly, as quickly and as attractively as possible. The dramatic artist has no place for a hidden character howsoever subordinate. His skill lies exclusively in the revelation of those traits and features which make character what it is — a moral engraving, the imprint and impress of a life-struggle upon an inherited moral individuality. Beyond these rules which have an universal application, no general law can be laid down respecting the manners, speech, costume, of persons in the drama; inasmuch as these accidents are regulated by place and time, the particular customs of different countries.

Forms of the Drama.— The drama is divided into two forms, according as it is employed upon the light and gay or upon the grave and affecting incidents of human life. The one is called *comedy;* the other, *tragedy.* Tragedy embraces the high passions, the virtues, crimes and sufferings of men; comedy tells of their humors, follies and pleasures. Tragedy is the highest form of literary art, inasmuch as it exhibits human life under the strongest emotion and under the most trying and critical situations; thereby demanding all the wealth of expression and the profoundest knowledge of the human heart. It ranks higher than the epic, because the epic exhibits human character by narrations and descriptions of the poet; whereas tragedy sets the personages themselves before us, as living and speaking.

The Aim of Tragedy.— Aristotle defines the aim of tragedy as the purging and purifying of our passions by means of pity and terror. Dr. Blair interprets this to mean that tragedy is intended to improve our virtuous sensibilities; to make men more sensible to virtue. The purpose of tragedy is accomplished when we are interested in behalf of virtue; when we are moved to compassion for the distressed; when we are led to guard against errors in our own conduct, by seeing their consequences in the lives of other men. Tragedy is thus a great moral force — a literary power making for righteousness.

Origin of Tragedy.— The word tragedy comes from the Greek *tragos,* signifying a goat, and *ode,* a song. The origin of tragedy was none other than the song sung at the festival of Bacchus when a goat was offered in sacrifice. After the sacrifice the priests sang hymns or lyric poems; these hymns were sung sometimes by the whole company, sometimes by separate bands answering alternately to each other; making what we call a chorus with its strophe and antistrophe. In order to throw some variety into this entertainment and to relieve the singers, a person was introduced who, between the songs, should give a recitation. Thespis, who lived about 536 years before the Christian era, made this innovation; and, as it met with approval, Æschylus, who came 50 years after him, and who is properly the father of tragedy, went a step farther, introduced a dialogue between two persons or actors, in which he contrived to interweave some interesting story and brought his actors on a stage adorned with proper scenery and decorations. All that these actors recited was called episodes or additional song. The songs of the chorus were made to relate no longer to Bacchus, their original subject, but to the story in which the actors were concerned. This began to give the drama a regular form, which was soon after brought to perfection by Sophocles and Euripides. It is remarkable in how short a space of time tragedy grew up among the Greeks, from its rudest beginnings to its most perfect state. For Sophocles, the greatest and most correct of all the tragic poets flourished only seventy years after Thespis. The chorus was the foundation of the ancient tragedy. It was not an ornament added to it, or a contrivance designed to render it more perfect. It was the original entertainment to which the dramatic dialogue was an addition. In process of time the chorus, from being the principal, became a mere accident of the tragedy, until at last in the modern tragedy the chorus has disappeared altogether. All there is to remind one of the chorus in a modern theatre, is the orchestra before the footlights.

Recitations.— The recitations introduced were of an epic character, parts of the Iliad, or epic poems relating to the gods and the Greek heroes. The Greeks employed bands of wandering minstrels at their feasts of Bacchus, to recite their epic pieces, just as Shakespeare and his strolling players were employed at the court of Elizabeth or James. These declaimers were called rhapsodes. They exercised their art in mutual emulation; by long recitation they strove to tire each other down. Out of this emulation came the dialogue. Thus we have the epic element presented by the rhapsodes and the lyric element by the chanting priests of Bacchus, who were called the chorus. The chorus and the rhapsodes alternated in the divisions of the work, called strophe and antistrophe. Thespis (535 B. C.) made a change; he introduced an actor chosen from the rhapsodes. This actor, instead of merely alternating his recitations with the song of the chorus, carried on a dialogue with its leader. The chorus stood round its leader, upon the steps of the Bacchic altar. The actor himself stood on a table near by and wearing a mask, personated some deity or hero. Thus, the epic element changed to the tragic. Æschylus introduced a second actor, and cut down the functions of the chorus. Sophocles added a third actor, and the preponderance of the dialogue was made complete. The actor introduced by Thespis played in turn the part of all the prominent figures in the legend, from gods and kings down to heralds and messengers. He counterfeited their appearance, spoke their sentiments, exhibited their passions. Afterwards, when two or three actors were introduced, the vital elements of all tragic performance were present — namely, impersonation and dialogue — and tragedy became distinguished as a new art. Thespis separated tragedy from the function of religious worship; he exhibited tragedies in Athens dealing with Greek history and mythology. The actors gradually changed places with the chorus; the steps of the Bacchic altar were transformed into a stage. The chorus and its leader were relegated to the footlights where now, in the form of a rudimentary organ, they furnish music while the curtain is down. Here a question arises, Has the drama gained or lost by the abolition of the chorus? Dr. Blair observes in reply: " It must be admitted that the chorus tended to render

tragedy more magnificent, more instructive and more moral."
Carried on by singing and accompanied by music, the chorus
no doubt diversified the entertainment greatly, and added to
its splendor. But these advantages were outweighed by such
difficulties as render the exclusion of the chorus from modern
plays almost imperative. Private transactions, plots and
schemes of confederates, must go on at times; hence, the
scenery demanded excludes the old-time chorus which always
occupied the stage. Again, the tragic drama is a natural and
probable imitation of human life; hence, no persons should appear, save those necessary to the action; any others are unnatural and improbable. Moreover, the mixture of music and song
with the dialogue of the actors is an unnatural circumstance,
destroying resemblance to actual life. It was warranted somewhat by the ritual of Bacchus and the pastoral life of Greece,
but it has no resemblance to the real life of today. "One use,"
says Dr. Blair, "might still be made of the ancient chorus,
and it would be a considerable improvement to the modern
theatre. While the curtain is down between the acts, the
chorus might be introduced, whose music and songs should
have a relation to the incidents of the preceding act, and to the
disposition which those incidents are presumed to have awakened in the audience. By this means the tone of passion
would be kept up, and all the good effects of the ancient chorus
preserved, whereas our modern orchestra strikes a foreign
and discordant note; and as a rule the musical selections have
no relation whatever to the play in progress."

Growth of the Dialogue.— With the decline of the chorus
the dialogue came more and more into prominence. In the
Thespian drama it had a prominent part; but consisted of long
narratives and had little resemblance to conversation in real
life. Æschylus corrected this artistic error; he made the
dialogue vivid and lively; to give more life he introduced a

second actor; thus drawing the attention of the audience from the songs of the chorus to the spoken and acted parts of the play. The variety and vividness of the dialogue was still further increased by Sophocles who introduced a third actor. The unnatural conversations between actor and chorus were set aside; and the choral odes were treated as so many resting-places in the dialogue. With the addition of a third actor, Sophocles made the dialogue embrace a greater complexity of incidents and exhibit a more varied play of character. He brought the three actors simultaneously upon the stage in a manner suggestive of the group-scenes in the modern drama, thereby increasing the effect. The dialogue of Greek tragedy differs from that of the modern drama in two important points.. First, and especially, in the greater prominence which it as-signs to narrative, a prominence due partly to the epic element in its origin; partly to the refinement of Greek feeling which preferred the narrative to the actual exhibition of deeds of blood and violence; and partly to the infrequency of soliloquies and asides which were impossible owing to the presence of the chorus. The dialogue of the Greek tragedy varied in length from the modern drama, sometimes embracing forty lines, sometimes four or five hundred lines. As a rule its parts were longer and exhibited less passion than the modern dialogue.

Characters of Greek Tragedy.— In the development of Greek tragedy Æschylus, Sophocles and Euripides represented characters after an ideal fashion. In delineating the charac-ters of heroes, their aim was not like Shakespeare to hold the mirror up to nature, but to people their stage with heroes of ideal strength and grandeur; and the force of their genius is no where more apparent than in the success with which they accomplished their task. They elevated the minds of the audience by a majestic picture of the heroic world. The gods and heroes of their tragedies are the offspring of a heroic age. Superhuman strength, courage, iron will and iron endurance are their characteristic qualities. They have none of the frailties and weaknesses of human beings. No force can bend them nor tender motive allure them from their course. For example, Prometheus, Clytemnestra. In contrast with the heroes, the lesser characters exhibit the weaknesses and frailties of humankind. For example, the nymphs in Prometheus; the maidens in the Septem. Female characters played an unimportant part, especially in the earlier tragedies, for the tender passions were touched but slightly. Arms and the hero were the favorite themes; the heroism sung in the epic was impersonated in the tragedy.

General Characteristics of Greek Tragedy.— With the rise of tragedy, the poetry of Greece completed the natural process of its evolution. From the epic, tragedy derived its legendary subjects and its graceful and majestic measure. From lyric poetry it inherited a wealth of metrical forms and a splendor of diction which were capable of expressing every shade of feeling and passion. The new art in turn transformed the material of the epic, giving it a more brilliant and impressive shape. The serene and leisurely narrative of the epic was intensified into an action rapid, concise, transacted before the very eyes of the audience. The narrow and personal interests of the old lyric were exchanged for meditations of deeper moment, the great principles and eternal problems of the universe. The result was a new art surpassing all previous work in vividness of effect and in profound earnestness of moral feeling. The general characteristics of the Greek tragedy as thus evolved are four in number. First, ethical elevation of tone and purpose. The tone of the Greek tragedy is essentially meditative and religious. A vein of earnest thoughtfulness runs through it. The chief actors meditate upon the dark mystery of existence, the ways of

Providence, the destiny of mankind, much after the fashion of Hamlet. The modern tragedy seldom rises to the same level of impressiveness. The second characteristic of Greek tragedy is a graceful harmony of form and structure which has never been surpassed. Beauty, no less than truth and impressiveness, was the constant aim of the ancient tragic writers. The influence of a keenly developed æsthetic sense appeared in every part of their work, in choice of subjects as well as in mode of treatment. Scenes are laid before stately palaces and temples of the gods. Plots are invested with the charm of romance and legend, graceful movement, gorgeous dress, princely language and bearing — the commonplace raised into a region of ideal splendor; over all is the air of a lofty and exalted idealism. A third characteristic: the simplicity and lucid clearness of the plot. Everything tending to confuse or divert the mind, is carefully excluded. The action is brief, straightforward, concentrated, as it should be, on a single point. Characters are few in number, only three at most appearing at the same time. This severe and lucid form of the Greek tragedy makes a sharp contrast with the modern play, which is more involved and obscure, requiring at times considerable effort on the part of the audience to unravel and understand it. A fourth characteristic: the delicate treatment of those deeds of physical horror and atrocity which form the catastrophe of most tragedies. Such deeds must either be exhibited before the eyes of the spectators or enacted behind the scenes and revealed by narrative. The Greeks preferred the latter method. Scenes of active violence and brutal murder such as the Elizabethan dramatists delighted to exhibit, were rarely shown upon the Greek stage. Only two examples can be found in the extant Greek plays: that of Ajax in Sophocles, and Evadne in Euripides. The reason for their exclusion was a refinement and delicacy which regarded the actual commission of such atrocities as a sight too terrible for the feelings of the audience. The Greek tragedy exhibiting these four general characteristics, ethical grandeur of tone, graceful harmony of form, clearness of plot, and delicacy of treatment, assumed, as was natural, a somewhat different aspect in the hands of the three greatest artists. In Æschylus the grandeur and religious depth of the conception were more conspicuous than artistic form. In Euripides the moral impressiveness and ideal beauty of the older drama give place to a more secular tone and a more realistic manner of treatment. Plots became more complex; music, as in the modern opera, began to encroach upon the sense and the poetry. It was only in Sophocles that the various elements of classical tragedy — moral inspiration, simplicity, ideal beauty — were blended together. Hence, Sophocles, though excelled in some respects by Æschylus and Euripides, has justly been regarded as the typical representative of Greek tragedy in its highest perfection. Tragedy completed its evolution in Sophocles; it has not been improved or vitally modified since his day. Roman, French and English tragedy are simply imitation with some accidental modifications peculiar to these races.

CHAPTER XLVII

ETHICS OF THE DRAMA

The Ethical Side.— The drama may be viewed from an ethical as well as an æsthetic standpoint. As a work of art, it appeals to the æsthetic sense, and forms a separate department of literature. As a work involving the operations of the human will, it belongs to the department of Ethics. It is a mirror of human conduct, and therefore has an ethical significance. The ethical purpose of the drama is stated by Aristotle to be the purification of our passions by means of pity and terror. That is to say, we should be terrified by the misdeeds, the crimes of men as presented in the drama; we should be moved to pity on account of the misfortunes which follow these misdeeds, the awful suffering resulting both to the innocent and the guilty. And the benefit arising from this two-fold effect should be a purification of the passions so as to conform them to right conduct. The ethical proposition underlying the drama is this: vice must be punished; virtue must be rewarded. Not only this, but virtue must be represented as more attractive than vice, and more worthy of imitation. For example, in " King Lear," the vice of Goneril and Regan is punished by murder and suicide; the victims of Edgar and Kent are rewarded by their joint succession to the throne of Britain.

Opinion of Blair.— On the ethical purpose of the drama, Dr. Blair writes as follows:

" The purpose of the drama is accomplished when we are interested in behalf of virtue; when we are moved to compassion for the distressed, when we are led to guard against errors in our own conduct, by seeing their consequences in the lives of other men. The drama is thus a great moral force making for right-eousness."

The Extent of This Ethical Purpose.— An ethical purpose is commonly confined to all serious drama of which tragedy is the chief representative. In the lighter forms of the drama there is no ethical purpose, the aim being simply to furnish amusement. Yet there are forms of comedy so vile and suggestive that the modern stage in this particular is universally condemned as immoral. So popular have become these light plays thus mixed with suggestions of vice, that outside the domain of tragedy, by far the greater number of dramas are unclean and ethically unsound. The drama has furnished evidences of the most shocking immorality. For example, the living pictures on the ancient Roman stage; the drama of the Restoration, to which Dryden was a contributor; the modern Extravaganza or Vaudeville; modern plays like " Iris," " Sappho " and the " Resurrection."

The Basis of Morality in the Drama.— The drama is the mirror of contemporary life; hence, its ethical standard is determined by the morality of the age in which it is produced. Every age sets up its own principles of right and wrong. In general, there is a marked difference between the drama of Christian and pagan times. The pagans were more licentious, lax; their moral standard was lower than that of Christian times. Hence, the ancient classic drama cannot compare with the modern drama in the matter of purity. Scenes which the Greek and Roman applauded, would be hissed from the modern stage. An immoral incident in a modern play is often tolerated, but an immoral object as a sustained purpose, would be fatal. Hence, the withdrawal of so many plays like Sappho, or the re-casting of them, so as to eliminate the immoral purpose.

Reasons for the Low Pagan Standard.— First, the idea of Fate, or Destiny, which was resistless and inexorable. This religious belief contributed directly to lower the moral standard of the ancient classic drama; because it annihilated free will; it taught the hero that it was vain for him to struggle against vicious inclination. The hero was doomed by Destiny to follow a certain course, whether right or wrong. Some examples: In Æschylus, Clytemnestra murders Agamemnon, and afterwards pleads that it is not she, but Destiny that has done the deed. In Euripides, Orestes is pursued by the furies, and he cries out in justification of the murder that Fate was guilty of the crime. He could not avert what the gods had in store for him. In other words, he was not responsible for his own acts. In Sophocles, Antigone breaks the existing laws of the realm: "Destiny wills it." Besides the influence of Fate or Destiny the Pagan gods in many cases set a poor example of moral conduct. Like Venus, many of them were the deification of vice. They were reproduced on the Greek and Roman stage in all their moral deformity. Hence, religion among the pagans was the great enemy of virtue and morality. Another reason for the depravity of the ancient classic stage was the pagan treatment of woman. In real life and on the stage, she was treated as the toy and plaything of passion. The pagan concept of marriage permitted concubinage and polygamy. Hence, the hero of the pagan drama was often represented with as many wives as the divinity he adored. An instance of this freedom is furnished by Shakespeare in King Lear; the pagan Gloster and his illegitimate son, Edmund. A new sense of decency seems to have been created by the Christian exaltation of woman; just as a new ethical standard arose from the vindication of free-will and individual accountability.

Religion and the Ethics of the Drama.— The Church used her influence to redeem the drama, just as she was instrumental in improving and elevating all the arts. She made the drama the teacher of religion and morality; hence, the existence of the old mystery and morality plays. The oldest reference to the mystery plays in our literature is the play of St. Catherine, presented in the Convent of Dunstable in 1119. The play deals with the miracles and martyrdom of the Saint. Mysteries, or miracle plays abound in the early literature of all the Catholic countries of Europe: Spain, Germany, France, Italy, possess an abundance of this literature. Every large cathedral, monastery and convent school had its stage. The Divine Comedy of Dante is only a long narrative form of mystery plays enacted at Florence — plays that dealt with heaven, hell and purgatory. These plays were composed and acted by Monks; the cathedral was often transformed into a theatre; the costumes were furnished by the rich vestry of the church; they personified angels, devils, saints and martyrs. The comic element was supplied by the Devil who took the part of a clown or jester.

Materials.— The material for the mystery plays was drawn from the Bible and from early church history. For example, we have such titles as the Creation of the World, the Fall of Man, the Massacre of the Innocents, the Crucifixion of our Lord. In this manner the church utilized the drama as a teacher of religion. The church employed the drama as a teacher of morality, and the morality plays are the result. These plays were contemporary with the old mystery or miracle plays; they were a product of the Middle Ages, and the first to employ them were the Norman trouveres.

They can be traced back through short Latin texts to the eleventh century. From France these plays were brought into England where they at once became popular. They also spread to Germany, Italy and Spain; so that we may say the church employed the drama for five centuries as the teacher of morality. The morality plays satisfied the love for moral allegory which manifests itself in so many periods of English literature.

Earliest English Example.— The earliest English morality play extant dates back to 1343. It was called the Pride of Life. This drama supplies a good definition of the morality play. Man is represented as the King of life; the various virtues and vices — pride, anger, envy, avarice, patience, humility, abstinence, come in turn and make their appeals to him; the ethical lesson being that he repels all the vices and welcomes all the virtues. Thus the earlier English morality plays from the reign of Henry VI, to Henry VIII, throw into allegorical form the conflict between good and evil in the mind and life of man. Every virtue is personified and held up for admiration. Every vice takes also some hideous, repellent form. Such titles as the Punishment of Gluttony, the Fall of Pride, the Rebuke of Envy, indicate the ethical lesson and purpose of the morality plays.

Absence of Art.— Neither the mystery nor morality plays exhibit any high degree of art. These plays are little more than loose bundles of dialogues thrown together without plot, coherence or unity. In English literature not one of these has survived as an artistic model. This is all the more strange since they were written at a time when painting, sculpture, architecture, and all the other fine arts flourished. The fact is explained in two ways: first, the imperfect condition of the medium made a high grade of art impossible.

The languages of Western Europe were in a very crude, imperfect condition. If we except the Italian, the medium through which Dante and Petrarch worked, no living language at the time was sufficiently flexible or polished for the best grades of literary art. For example, in English, the plays of Shakespeare could not have been written before his time, even if the genius to produce them had previously existed. A second reason is the lack of training on the part of the monks. They had not the best models before them, or at least did not use them to advantage. In their dramatic works there is little trace of classic training. It is also urged that in the case of the miracle plays the monks did not wish to depart from the simplicity of the Biblical narrative; whereas the morality or allegorical plays could be only lengthy dialogues at best; no room existing for character creation or subtlety of plot. But however it may be explained, whether on the ground of lack of medium or genius or training or unsuitableness of material, it cannot be urged that Christianity antagonized the drama. The very existence of the miracle and morality plays is proof of the very opposite attitude. Although not a high grade of art, miracle and morality plays accomplished the purpose for which they were written; they taught religious truth, and the very highest standard of morality. And these religious and ethical lessons were of supreme value to the multitude, even though they were not enforced by all the subtlety and charm of dramatic art.

The Ethics of the Modern Drama.— It is generally admitted that the modern drama represents neither a high grade of art nor a high standard of morality. Zangwill, the English critic, says of the modern play that it consists of drivel and devil. The criticism is just, for all our representative authors of dramatic literature seem to be afflicted with moral degeneracy. Some examples: Henry Ibsen, representing Scandinavian literature; he has written some thirty dramas, most of which are unfit for reading or presentation on the stage; the vilest are Love's Comedy, the Doll House, and the Lady from the Sea. A few of his expurgated plays have been well received in England and America, on account of their literary merit. In his dramas, Ibsen aims at destroying the marriage bond, and giving unrestrained liberty to all the natural passions. Like Ibsen, Tolstoi has corrupted Russian literature. His novels as soon as written, are dramatized, not only in Russia, but throughout the English speaking world, where he enjoys a large and unsavory reputation. As an example of his ethical standard, the Kreutzer Sonata was forbidden to pass through the United States mails, but the English translators and publishers managed to dispose of half a million copies. His latest work, The Resurrection, was hissed from the London stage, recast, and played in New York City. Tolstoi, like Ibsen, is a pure pagan in morals, believes in no restraint. His recent excommunication from the Greek Church happened more on account of his ethical than his religious teaching. Herman Sudermann, the leading living German dramatist, belongs to the same category as Ibsen and Tolstoi. His chief plays, the End of Sodom, Home, and a Question of Honor, were prohibited by the German Government on account of their immorality. These plays were welcomed in Paris, and Sudermann is acting as playwright for Sara Bernhardt, supplying a new drama every year. He is a prolific writer, a dramatic genius, but he has used his pen to degrade the modern stage.

The Outlook.— From an ethical standpoint, we may hope for better things, at least in the English-speaking world where there has always been a healthy reaction from stage disease and corruption. Already our playwrights show signs of returning moral sanity. The public is beginning to demand a higher standard, and the playwrights respond, as a matter of course.

CHAPTER XLVIII

THE DRAMA (CONTINUED)

REPRESENTATIVE AUTHORS

The Drama of Job.— The authorship of this drama is still an unsettled question in Old Testament criticism. Jewish tradition, as expressed in the Talmud, assigns it to Moses — a view in which some modern critics concur. Modern scholarship can fix neither the date nor the authorship, although from internal evidence it is clear that the drama was written some time between the seventh and fourth centuries before Christ. In matter, if not in form, Job may be regarded as one of the oldest specimens of dramatic literature.

Criticism by William Davidson.—" The Poem of ' Job' so remarkable for imaginative power and literary skill, was unquestionably intended to set forth theological doctrine — God, man, evil, good, suffering, hope, destiny. The thesis of the book is that suffering in the present life is not precisely proportioned to ill desert. On the contrary, the righteous suffer; yet the drama teaches that God is, and God is good. Job's attitude throughout is that of the man who is trying to understand God, not denying His existence or mocking at His rule. Job teaches us, first of all, that the drama of our earthly life has a significance which earth does not exhaust. Secondly, the government of the Most High contemplates issues which are beyond us. Thirdly, it may be necessary to prove disinterested goodness to men, angels and devils. This drama of human suffering teaches that pain may be a privilege rather than a punishment; that the loftiest spirits may have to pass through it as a trial of their loyalty rather than a chastisement for their transgressions; and that in such cases it behooves them to bear, as the Lord's chosen ones, the burden and the mystery of life, as pregnant with a deeper significance hereafter to be made known."

Literary Form.— A majority of writers agree in calling Job a drama, although Milton refers to it as an epic with a dramatic setting. On this point Driver writes as follows: " It is of the nature of a drama not yet emancipated from the lyric element. It may be termed a dramatic poem, for its principal parts are constructed in the form of a dialogue, and the action which it represents passes through the successive stages of entanglement, development and solution. The action is, however, largely internal and mental, the successive scenes exhibiting the varying moods of a great soul struggling with the mystery of fate, rather than trying external situations. The constructive imagination of the writer is conspicuous throughout; it reveals itself in the bold conceptions, the free, flowing outlines of the whole poem; also in the wealth, variety and finish of its detailed imagery. Only a close study of the book can give an idea of the richness and multitude of its metaphors, the concentrated vigor of its phraseology, its depth of human feeling, its portraiture of life and the expressiveness of the descriptions of external nature."

Criticism by Professor Moulton.—" The dominant impression is that of a magnificent drama. No element of dramatic effect is wanting — the great ash-mound is the stage — the crowd of spectators resemble the Greek chorus — the changes of the sky are a fitting dramatic background. Interest in character abounds — Eliphoz, Jophar and Bildad are distinct creations. But the essence of the drama lies in the action. The whole world of literature hardly contains a more remarkable piece of dramatic movement than the changes of position taken by Job in the course of the dialogue with the Friends. To dramatic effect, however, must be added epic; the description of the Heavenly Court is epical; also in the mode in which Heaven deals with Job — the seeming conspiracy of earth and heaven, which robs Job of all his possessions. The lyric element is also present, as for example in the Curse — the elegy of a Broken Heart. As to the central idea of the dialogue, it is a philosophical discussion dramatized. The subject discussed is the mystery of human suffering and its bearing upon the righteous government of the world. Each section of the drama is the representation of a different philosophical attitude to this question."

Æschylus.— He was a native of Attica, born in the year 525 B. C., and died in Sicily, 456 B. C. He took part in the great battles of the Persian War, having been wounded at Marathon. Afterward he gave his attention to the drama. He is called the " Father of Greek Tragedy." More than sixty dramas were written by him; seven are extant; of these, the best are the Persæ, Seven Against Thebes, Prometheus Vinctus, and the Orestean Trilogy.

Criticism by William Ward.—" The classic period of the Greek drama includes Æschylus, Sophocles and Euripides. These are the names of its three great masters; in the progress of their art there is an unbroken continuity. Æschylus had fought against those Persians whose rout he celebrated with patriotic pride in the " Persæ." He was trained in the Eleusinian mysteries, and was a passionate upholder of the institution most intimately associated with the primitive political traditions of the past — the Areopagus. He had been born in the generation after Solon, to whose maxims he fondly clung; he must have belonged to that anti-democratical party which favored the Spartan alliance, and it was the Warian development of Hellenic life and the philosophical system based upon it with which his religious and moral convictions were imbued. Thus, even upon the generation which succeeded him, the chivalrous spirit and diction of his poetry, and the unapproached sublimity of his dramatic imagination, fell, as it falls upon later posterity, like the note of a mightier age."

Criticism by A. E. Haigh.—" Æschylus, if we consider the variety and significance of the work which he accomplished, appears to have been one of the greatest poetic geniuses that the world has ever seen. The influence which he exercised upon the growth of Greek tragedy was so powerful and decisive, that he may be regarded as its founder. In the hands of Thespis and his successors, the drama had scarcely advanced beyond the embryonic stage, and its future was still uncertain. Æschylus, in the course of a single generation, expanded and developed its latent capacities with such masterly power and such completeness of result, that its general character was henceforth finally settled, and the task of subsequent poets became comparatively easy. His activity was not confined to any one branch of theatrical representation, but covered the entire field, and effected an equal transformation in the structure, the spirit and the external appearance of tragedy. The most obvious characteristics of Æschylus, are grandeur, loftiness and massive strength. His dramas are colossal creations, planned and executed with a largeness of design and a depth of purpose to which it would be difficult to find any parallel. Every part of the composition, from the plots and characters to the language and versification, is fashioned on the same imposing scale, and the effect of the whole is to impress the mind with a sense of unapproachable power and majesty. The material for his tragedies is drawn from very various quarters, and covers nearly the whole ground of Greek mythology. Some of them seem to be based on mere oral tradition and not on previous literature. As regards plot, there is very little of it in his dramas, at least, in the modern sense; there are no sudden obstacles, unexpected developments or rapid vicissitudes of situation. The construction is so simple that the ultimate issue is known to the audience from the very first. The choral odes are long; between these come the brief but impassioned dialogues in which the characters work out their doom, and the inevitable justice of the gods advances slowly but surely to its appointed end."

Sophocles.— He was born at Colonus, near Athens, 495 B. C.; died at Athens, 406 B. C. He was one of the Athenian generals in the Samian War. He contended for the tragic prize in 468, defeating Æschylus; in turn, he was defeated by Euripides. Of his extant plays the best known are Œdipus Tyrannus, Antigone, Electra, and Ajax.

Criticism by Professor Mahaffy.— " Sophocles devoted all his energy to the production of those famous works of art, which gave him such a hold over the Athenian public that he came to be considered the very ideal of a tragic poet, and was worshipped after his death as a hero, under the title of Dexion. He is said to have won twenty tragic victories. The author of the " Poetic " and the Alexandrian critics follow the judgment of the Attic public, and most modern critics have agreed with them that the tragedies of Sophocles are the most perfect that the world has seen."

Criticism by Thomas Sergeant Perry.—" The general custom of critics is to refer to Sophocles as the great poet of the age of Pericles, as is Shakespeare of the Elizabethan age, Racine of that of Louis XIV. The inevitable comparison between his work and that of Æschylus makes clear the difference between the man who works with unfamiliar tools in rapidly changing conditions, and his successor who finds the paths cut and laid out, so that it falls to him to devote himself to perfecting the task in hand. Sophocles found the drama established, and he developed its capacities ; he deepened its human interest by modifying sublimities and heroics in the direction of real human life, changing the mythological monster into a man with perfectly natural sorrows, joys, ambitions, sufferings, etc. Again, Æschylus made full use of his opportunities to terrify the spectators with ghastly scenes. Sophocles, on the other hand, lets solemn pathos and religious awe take the place of complete terror. In reviewing the total impression of what has come down to us from the hands of Sophocles, what strikes us is the calmness and self-possession of his art, a quality that is more readily perceived than described, for the nearer an object comes to perfect beauty, the more difficult it is to define it, except with that one word. When it has marked qualities that give one side more prominence than another, we are no longer dumb. In English literature, for example, Milton has been described with exactness, whereas countless volumes have struggled with Shakespeare, and his work, at its best, yet defies the most industrious commentators to say just wherein its merit lies. In the same way the rounded perfection of Sophocles baffles anyone who tries his hand at conveying a full impression of his many attractive qualities.

Criticism by Blair.—"Sophocles is the most masterly of the three Greek tragedians, the most correct in the conduct of his subjects, the most just in his sentiments. He is likewise eminent for his descriptive talent; for example, the description of the death of Œdipus or of Haemon is a perfect pattern of what description should be in a tragedy. While Æschylus is the Father of Greek Tragedy, he exhibits the defects as well as the beauties of an early original writer; he is bold, nervous, animated, yet very obscure and difficult to be understood; his style is crowded too much with metaphors; it is often harsh and abrupt. He has much fire, elevation, force, but less of tenderness than Sophocles. He delights in the marvellous, the uncanny, the blood-curdling; for example, the Ghost of Darius, or the furies in Eumenides. On the contrary, Sophocles is content with the human, the natural — the mirror held up, not to mythology, but to nature."

Euripides.— The third and last of the famous Greek tragedians was born 480 B. C., and died 406 B. C He was a native of Salamis, lived during the invasion of Xerxes, studied rhetoric under Prodicus, and at the age of twenty-five began to write dramas. He wrote seventy-five plays in all; eighteen of which are extant. The most famous are " Hecuba," " Iphigenia," " Electra," " Ion " and " Bacchæ."

Criticism by Professor R. C. Jebb.—" Euripides is the mediator between ancient and modern drama No great poet is more difficult to estimate justly, and none has been judged more unfairly. Euripides was only fifteen years younger than Sophocles. But when Euripides began to write, it must have been clear to any man of his genius and culture that, though an established prestige might be maintained, a new poet who sought to construct tragedy on the old basis would be building on sand. For, first, the popular religion itself — the very foundation of tragedy — had been undermined. Secondly, scepticism had begun to be busy with the legends which that religion consecrated. Neither gods nor heroes commanded all the old unquestioning faith. Lastly, an increasing number of the audience in the theatre began to be destitute of the training, musical and poetical, which had prepared an earlier generation to enjoy the chaste and placid grandeur of ideal Tragedy. Euripides made a splendid effort to maintain the place of tragedy in the spiritual life of Athens by modifying its interests in the sense which his own generation required. Could not the heroic persons still excite interest if they were made more real — if, in them, the passions and sorrows of everyday life were portrayed with greater vividness and directness? And might not the less cultivated part of the audience at least enjoy a thrilling plot, especially if taken from the home-legends of Attica? Euripides became the virtual founder of the Romantic Drama. In so far as his work fails, the failure is one which probably no artistic tact could then have wholly avoided. The frame within which he had to work was one which could not be stretched to his plan. The chorus, the masks, the narrow stage, the conventional costumes, the slender opportunities for change of scenery, were so many fixed obstacles to the free development of tragedy in the new direction. But no man of his time could have broken free from these traditions; in attempting to do so, he must have wrecked either his fame or his art. It is not the fault of Euripides if in so much of his work we feel the want of harmony between matter and form. Art abhors compromise; and it was the misforune of Attic tragedy in his generation that nothing but a compromise could save it.

Aristophanes.— Among authors of Greek comedy, Aristophanes is fairly representative. He was born 446 B. C. and died not later than 380 B. C. He is sometimes called the Pagan Voltaire, because his plays tend to bring the gods into contempt. His best known plays are the " Frogs," the " Clouds," the " Wasps " and the " Birds."

Criticism by Professor R. C. Jebb.—" Comedy, as we have it in Aristophanes, is a public commentary on the every-day life of Athens, in great things and small. Politics and society, statesmen and private persons, are criticised with unsparing freedom. The satire is unscrupulously personal. Old Athens knew no respect for private life when it seemed to be for the good of the city that the vices of a citizen should be lashed. Aristophanes was not only a great satirist, but a great poet. His comedies unite elements which meet nowhere in literature. There is a play of fancy, as extravagant as in a modern Burlesque. The whole world is turned topsy-turvy. Gods and mortals alike are whirled through the motley riot of one great carnival. There is a humor as delicate, a literary satire as keen, as the most exquisite wit could offer to the most subtle appreciation. And there are lyric strains of a wild woodland sweetness hardly to be matched, save in Shakespeare. He claims for himself, and justly, that he is outspoken on the side of virtue and against vice."

Criticism by Thomas Sergeant Perry.—" Aristophanes represents, not only wit and satire, but half of the divided spirit of Athens, and to speak of him merely as a great writer is to do him but scant justice. Aristophanes is great because he personifies an important part of the Athenian people; his hatred of the destructive war; his detestation of the new intellectual ferment, his abhorrence of the democracy, are beyond and outside of his personal feelings — they count as the expression of a large part of an eager people. As regards the laws of the drama, Aristophanes adhered strictly to them, and his dramas are some of the finest specimens we have in the department of Comedy."

Among the Latins.— The regular Roman drama was of foreign origin — a mere imitation of the Greek. Unfortunately there is very little of the Roman drama extant, especially those creations that belong to the classic age. We know only the titles of the tragedies written by Lucius, Andronicus and Ennius. The tragedies of Seneca are the only ones which we possess, plays in which not only the Greek themes are employed, but likewise the Greek method. However, two writers of Roman comedy are famous; their extant dramas rescue Latin literature from absolute sterility in this department.

Plautus.— M. Accius Plautus was a celebrated comic poet; he was the son of a freedman, born in Umbria about 525 A. U. C. He was called Plautus from his splay-feet, a defect common to the Umbrians. Twenty plays of this writer have come down to us; although, in his age, about one hundred and thirty plays bore his name. His best known plays are the " Captive," " Rudens," " Mostellaria," and " Menæchmi."

Criticism by Charles Anthon.—" In each plot of Plautus there is sufficient action, movement and spirit. The incidents never flag, but rapidly accelerate the catastrophe. But if we regard his plays in the mass, there is a considerable, and perhaps too great uniformity in his fables; they hinge for the most part on the love of some dissolute youth for a courtesan, his employment of a slave to defraud a father of a sum sufficient for his expensive pleasures, and the final discovery that his mistress is a free-born citizen. The Latin style of Plautus excels in briskness of dialogue as well as purity of expression, and has been extolled by the learned Roman grammarians who declared that if the Muses were to speak Latin, they would employ his diction. There can be no doubt but that Plautus wonderfully improved and refined the Latin language. The chief excellence of Plautus is generally reputed to consist in the wit and comic force of his dialogue. At times he degenerates into buffoonery and scurrility, but like other dramatists he was obliged to appeal to baser elements of society."

Publius Terentius.— He was a celebrated Latin comic poet, born about the 560th year of Rome. In his earliest youth he was a slave. He composed, or rather adapted from the Greek, a large number of plays, six of which are extant. Of these the " Adelphi," " Hecyra " and " Eunuchus " are best known.

Criticism by Professor Smith.—" The plots of Terence, as a rule, are taken from Greek sources. In the additions and alterations which he made, he has given proof of good taste and judgment. He was a more careful observer of the unities of time and place than Plautus or any of his predecessors. Terence instead of resorting to buffoonery in order to hold his audience, had recourse to the double plot, thus increasing the public interest in the play without pandering to the viler tastes of the rabble. Ancient critics are agreed that the special talent of this author is revealed in the delineation of characters and manners, and in the inimitable art with which he wove incidents into the dramatic story. All the inferior passions which form the scope of comedy are nicely observed and adequately expressed. Like Plautus, he did much to polish the rugged Latin: Cicero refers to him as "*omnia dulcia dicens*." His comedies are remarkable for their elegance of dialogue, presenting a constant flow of easy, genteel, polite conversation. The difference between Terence and Plautus lies in the fact that the former wrote for the refined and educated few, whereas the latter strove to satisfy the ignorant multitude."

Goethe.— Among the Germans, Goethe ranks first as a poet and dramatist. He was born at Frankfort in 1749 and died at Weimar in 1832. His father, a man of means, bore the title of Imperial Councillor. Goethe graduated in Law from the University of Strasburg, but gave up the legal profession for literary pursuits. He held many positions of honor under the government; his travels were confined to Italy. He was on familiar terms with Carlyle and knew English literature thoroughly. Schiller, his contemporary, was a life-long friend. The best known dramas of Goethe are " The Accomplices," " Stella " and " Faust," the last play winning him international fame.

Criticism by William Lindemann.—" Goethe passed through a number of stages as a poet and dramatist. As he grew in years and in knowledge he responded to the influence of the Romantic Movement. He laid aside classic canons and joined the procession led by Walter Scott and Wordsworth in the ' return to nature.' As years went by, he gave himself up more and more to the contemplation and study of nature. Like Wordsworth he began to assent to a higher pantheism. Nature became all to him, as the last traces of Christian teaching faded from his mind. In 1776 he wrote as follows: " All things are to be found in nature. Nature is wholly and at all times complete. Her crown is love. All debt and merit alike belong to her. No original being corresponds wholly to the root-idea; behind each the higher idea lies hidden — *that* is my God.' Again, he writes to Herder concerning Christ: ' The legend of Christ is a proof that the world can continue ten million years and no one reach a correct judgment regarding these matters.' Goethe developed an extraordinary love of nature, a love which led him to pursue so ardently the study of the physical sciences. Evidence of such study appears in all his later poetry. As an author of lyrics, Goethe deserves the highest commendation. Many of his ballads are household treasures throughout the Fatherland. It is customary to regard Goethe as a poet of the head rather than the heart; and the bulk of his writings may be quoted in support of this contention. Nevertheless, Goethe possessed the passionate heart of the poet; his lyrics thrill with emotion. And if we had not these, the many love affairs in which he was personally involved, would be ample proof of the existence of extraordinary passion. In the language of England's bard, Goethe ' loved not wisely, but too well.' If one would doubt that he possessed a heart or affection in the highest degree, let him read the poem to Faust. In his treatment of the drama, Goethe, while employing classic themes, departed somewhat from classic canons of taste, and from classic methods. In place of belief in the gods, which inspired fear in man, Goethe substituted a religion of humanity, a humanitarianism which was intended to ennoble human nature. While preserving the skeleton of the ancient fables, Goethe dressed them out in modern motive, breathing modern life into the dead past. Goethe observes strictly the three dramatic unities. The number of acts is limited to five. He preserves the form and the admirable simplicity of the Greek drama.

Criticism by Thomas Carlyle.—" Shakespeare and Goethe, unlike innumerable others, are *vital;* their construction begins at the *heart,* and flows outward as the life-streams do, fashioning the *surface,* as it were, spontaneously. Those Macbeths and Falstaffs, accordingly, those Fausts and Philinas, have a verisimilitude and life that separates them from all other fictions of late ages. All others, in comparison, have more or less the nature of hollow wizards, constructed from without inwards, painted *like* and deceptively put in motion. Many years ago on finishing our perusal of *Wilhelm Meister,* with a very mixed sentiment in other respects, we could not but feel that here lay more insight into the elements of human nature, and a more poetically perfect combining of these, than in all the other fictitious literature of our generation. In Goethe's works, chronologically arranged, we see this above all things: a mind working itself into clearer and clearer freedom, gaining a more and more perfect dominion of its world. "*Werther*" we call the voice of the world's despair; passionate, uncontrollable is this voice; not yet melodious and supreme — as nevertheless we at length hear it in the wild apocalyptic "*Faust,*" like a death-song of departing worlds; no voice of joyful 'morning stars singing together' over a Creation, but of red, nigh-extinguished, midnight stars, in spheral swan-melody, proclaiming, 'It is ended.' In the next period we have what might be styled Pagan or Ethenic in character; meaning thereby an anthropomorphic character akin to that of old Greece and Rome. '*Wilhelm Meister*' is of that stamp: warm, hearty, sunny, human endeavor, a free recognition of Life in its depth, variety, and majesty; as yet no divinity recognized there. Also, the '*Venetian Epigrams*' are of the like Old Ethenic tone — musical, joyfully strong; true, yet not the whole truth. The Old World is now in ashes; doubt has been reduced to denial. But after the smoke and flame are blown away, the sun shines clear again over the ruin. In the third and final period, melodious reverence becomes triumphant. "Faust" is saved, redeemed. What all must admire in Goethe is his utmost clearness, all-piercing faculty of vision. A nobler power of insight than this of Goethe you in vain look for, since Shakespeare passed away. For Goethe, as for Shakespeare, the world lies all translucent. Again, we must admire in both, but especially in Goethe, an extraordinary "*Figurativeness,*" for this grand light-giving intellect, as all such are, is an imaginative one. Because of the spell of such a powerful imagination, perennial, as a possession forever, Goethe's history and writings abide: a thousand-voiced 'melody of wisdom,' which he that has ears may hear. He who was of compass to know and feel more than any other man, this is the record of his knowledge and feeling."

Criticism by Bishop Spalding.—"Goethe, whom the consent of the enlightened has placed in the narrow circle of the few really great minds of the world, was not an ideal man. He had even grave faults. In his relations with women he was not always either wise or moral. He never wholly outgrew the influence of Spinoza, Voltaire, and Rousseau. He was not a Christian. In the presence of his country's awful humiliations he remained passive and seemingly indifferent, consented even to receive the decoration of the Legion of Honor from Napoleon, in the hour of his triumph over Germany. In fact, he dearly loved a king or a duke, however uninteresting or vulgar the man might be. They who would make him a demi-god, do not see him as he is; and he is great enough as he is, not to need the doubtful help of false praise. Even as a writer he is not without serious defects. It is only in his best lyrics that he is altogether admirable. In his prose he is not unfrequently diffuse, commonplace, tiresome even. As he grew older he became the victim of allegory, symbolism, and didacticism. Few find " Wilhelm Meister " an interesting novel, and still fewer can read the second part of " Faust " at all. Yet, find fault with him as one may, he is, both as a man and as an author, worthy of the most serious study, for the world has had few men who teach so well the things we all most need to learn. His industry was unwearying, his sympathies were all-embracing, and whatever concerned man interested him. His aim, which he never lost sight of even for a moment, was to up-build his own being, to raise, as he said, as high as possible the apex of the pyramid whose base and foundation had been given him. His ideal is life in its completeness, life brought into harmony with all that is true, good and fair. Think of living, is his motto — Live in the whole, in God and in all that He has made. Whatever he does, and his occupations are of the most varied kind, he always holds in view his own self-culture. He was Counselor of a Grand Duke, Minister of ·Public Instruction, superintendent of the theatre, and of public works, a scientist, an antiquarian, a critic of literature and of art, as well as a poet, a dramatist, and a novelist. He practiced drawing, painting and engraving. He strove to make himself a sculptor. He studied everything, and sought to find in everything he did or learned, the means of his own improvement. In power of imagination he is inferior to Shakespeare, but he is his superior in culture, in seriousness of purpose, and in the painstaking care with which he followed his vocation, throughout a long life, even to the very end. He was not only acquainted with the best which was known, but he had studied human life in all its phases, had meditated profoundly on all the great problems, had traveled and beheld the masterpieces of art, had observed everything, investigated everything. His thoughts are elevated and profound; his attitude toward the world is uniformly tolerant and kindly; his style is classic. He is full of patience, courage, and cheerfulness.

His appreciativeness and interest are active and enlightened. His faith in reason is absolute; his poetic insight and inspiration are deep and genuine; his moral teaching is wholesome and invigorating. If not a Christian, he is still less a denier and scoffer. On the contrary, the spirit in which he thinks and strives is that of modesty, reverence, and self-renunciation, of mildness, sympathy, and helpfulness. He is a builder, not a destroyer; a diffuser of light and sweetness, not a sower of discord and hatred. His coldness is apparent only; his selfishness is that of the man of genius, whose work is imperative, whose task is imposed by a master who must be obeyed. Of the poets, he is the greatest moralist and the most suggestive thinker. He may be called the creator of the literature of Germany; he is the author of the best educational novel, and of one of the few world-dramas. He gave the impulse which led Scott to write the Waverly novels, and he was the inspirer of Carlyle, who, however, never, attained the clearness of vision, the repose, the breadth, the amenity, the kindliness, and sanity of the master. He is less intense than Dante, who was too preoccupied with the hatreds and strifes of his age; he is more conscious of a high purpose than Shakespeare, who hardly seems to have personal views at all, who comes so near saying everything that it is difficult to divine his real thoughts. Goethe knows what he wants, and he perceives clearly the means by which his aims are realized."

Henrik Ibsen.— He was born at Skien, Norway, in 1828. He studied medicine, but, later on, applied himself to literature. Few literary men have shown greater zeal and devotion to their life-work. Already he has earned the title of " Shakespeare of the North." His dramas (outside the drama there is very little from his pen) are translated into every modern language. The best known plays are " Love's Comedy," " Brand," " Ghosts," the " Master-Builder " and " An Enemy of the People."

Criticism by William H. Sheran.— It is customary to refer to Ibsen as the modern Shakespeare. Certainly, it may be said of him that no foreign playwright has had such welcome, both in

England and America, as has Ibsen. His plays have been translated several times into English, and our best critics are of the
opinion that even in translation they outrank anything produced
by our native genius during the past two hundred years, if they
have not actually won a place beside the immortal productions
of the Bard of Avon. Ibsen served a brief apprenticeship in
" Catilina " and the " Feast at Solhaug," when the skill of the
master workman began to assert itself; for the " Vikings " and
" Ghosts," which followed soon after, are the perfect flowering
of his genius. In selecting materials, Ibsen, like Shakespeare,
made use of the early history of his country ; thus, the " Vikings "
resembles " King Lear " and " Cymbeline." In this connection
it may be said that no playwright illustrates better than Ibsen
the dramatic possibilities of northern mythology. But Ibsen,
unlike Shakespeare, traveled in foreign lands, and studied human
life and the masterpieces of art in France, Italy, and other
countries. Yet, true to his Norwegian or Teutonic temperament,
he admires moral beauty rather than sensuous beauty, and disappointed in his quest after moral beauty, he distrusted his fellow man and became a pessimist of the most pronounced type.
He is a pessimist who distrusts his fellow man, and who permits
his pessimism to assume an iconoclastic attitude toward the existing conventionalities of society. In his greater tragedies there is
an echo of Shelley's hatred for the existing order of things. But,
although a pessimist, he does not proceed to the lengths of
Schopenhauer — he does not teach that life itself is an evil, or that
happiness is unattainable. He believes, on the contrary, that
man would be happy under other conditions. He believes that
if man is robbed of happiness, it is because of society, the conventional rules and ideas of duty, which starve and slay man's
moral nature. This is exactly the plea of Shelley. And one
reason for the popularity of Ibsen is, that such doctrine has struck
a responsive chord in the English speaking world. Not that the
English race would do away with the accepted canons of right
conduct, but there is a feeling that the accepted conventionalities
of modern society exact too much — impose too much restraint.
Ibsen, therefore, quarrels with man for retaining these traditional conventionalities — his pessimism is the pessimism of indignation; he is indignant because man allows himself to be
swayed by a social tyrant. Another characteristic is Ibsen's lack

of sympathy with any kind of suffering. He believes that man's road to greatness lies through pain and sorrow; the discipline of suffering is needed for the development of a healthy moral nature. Therein we find an echo of Shakespeare — sweet are the uses of adversity. In pain, adversity and oppression the highest virtues of our race grow and blossom.

Finally, the critic of Ibsen notices how much he has accomplished with commonplace material; his characters are not the great personages of the earth, kings, queens, statesmen, heroes, etc., they are taken from the lower walks of life; yet his dramas hold an audience spellbound by economy of attention, the skilful management of plot, the subtle analysis of motive, and a wierd, grim atmosphere like that which hangs over a volcano ready to belch forth at any time " redounding smoke and ruddy flame." Perhaps there is not sufficient relief afforded to the audience from this morbid intensity, and, therefore, Shakespeare, if not so strictly artistic, is far more natural by introducing clowns and episodes as a needed relief. But Ibsen writes the *drama with a purpose,* whereas, Shakespeare holds up the mirror to nature, smiling amid her tears. In either case tragedy has gained the highest peaks in the mountain range of human passion.

Hermann Südermann.— He was born at Matzicken, East Prussia, in 1857. By common consent he is regarded as one of the world's greatest dramatists, promising to excel even his own gifted countryman, the creator of Faust. He is a disciple of Ibsen. His best known plays are the " Joy of Living," " The End of Sodom," " Home," and " Honor."

Criticism by William Lindemann.—" The fame of Hermann Südermann began with the drama called ' Honor,' which was published in 1889. The technique of this drama followed traditional lines, although throughout the work we see evidences of the Romantic movement or ' return to nature,' which characterizes the modern drama in Germany and elsewhere. The thesis of the play is revolutionary in the extreme, an echo of the pessimism of Ibsen. It amounts to this, as stated in Südermann's own words: there is no such thing as honor. What we call honor is merely the shadow which we cast when the bright sun of popular applause shines full upon us. The saddest feature about 'honor' is that there are as many kinds as there are classes of society. But in passing this judgment the dramatist has forgotten to note that there is such a thing as 'guilty honor,' the shadow cast by evil deeds when the light of conscience falls on them. There is throughout the play a shameful realism which paints the lower classes in all their viciousness and naked deformity. The author seems to take a special delight in creating harrowing scenes such as excite one's indignation rather than one's pity. Similarly, in the 'End of Sodom,' although the avowed purpose of the author is to cause a wholesome terror of evil in the minds of those disposed thereto. The author would thus work a moral reformation by painting the immoral in the most hideous and revolting light. But this position cannot be maintained either from the standpoint of good art or good morals. For, first of all, according to the laws of art, a character must be possible; and the hero of the 'End of Sodom' is an impossible character; he is absolutely unthinkable. Again, the highest art while yielding to us the largest amount of æsthetic pleasure, should never wound our moral sentiments and feelings. Yet, from the beginning to the end of this drama, the author makes such a mistake — he leads us into a world from whose stifling atmosphere we would as gladly escape as from a charnel house. By placing the morals of the upper and lower classes in opposition, Südermann secures his most powerful dramatic effects. It cannot be denied that the artist has presented to us the most powerful scenes that passion can display; although we must confess that many of them are at the same time inartistic and gruesome. The contrast and conflict of classes are splendid material for the modern dramatist, and Südermann has taken advantage of it."

"In the tragedy called 'John,' Südermann attempted the historical drama with some success. Three distinct motives are disclosed in it: the first is the love of Salome, the daughter of Herodias, for John the Baptist; the second is the desire of the Baptist for the Holy One; the third is the story of Josephus that John was murdered because they feared the effect of his socialistic speeches. Only the first motive is dominant throughout the play. The others fail, or rather are brought to no definite issue. This drama, like the preceding, reveals Südermann's mastery over the springs of passion; also, a decided improvement in character-creation. The technique or finish indicates that Südermann has attained the zenith of his glory as an artist.'

" The proper sphere or province of Südermann is the romance. 'Frau Sorge' is, on the whole, his finest work; he does not dabble in modern problems, socialistic or ethical, nor does he go back to the infant ideals of Romanticism. In this romantic novel he teaches the supreme lesson of life — the performance of duty. In the struggle between duty and inclination, his ideal character is always on the side of the former, and attains symmetry of growth and perfection of moral nature in the divinely appointed way — the way of trial and toil and suffering. Südermann, in spite of his many and obvious defects, will doubtless end his career by winning the very highest place in German dramatic literature."

Moliére.— He was born at Paris in 1622, and died there in 1673. He was a graduate of the Jesuit College in Paris. At the early age of twenty-three he began to devote his entire time to acting and play-writing. He placed himself at the head of a troop of actors, performing both in the provinces and in Paris where he settled down. He is by far the most celebrated of the French dramatists, occupying the same place in French comedy that Shakespeare does in English tragedy.

Criticism by Réné Doumic.—" Molière is a genius purely French or Gallic. His literary ancestors were not Greeks, as in the case of Racine, nor Romans and Spaniards, as in the case of Corneille, but our own story-tellers, the ancient authors of French legend and song, that hallowed group of which Rabelais and Reguier are worthy representatives. The inspiration drawn from those old fables and stories pervades Molière's work, traceable alike in his minor pieces and in his most important dramas. It is a grave mistake, sometimes made, to distinguish between the Molière of high and low grade comedy. The most we can affirm is that while the method differs somewhat, the spirit and mannerisms remain the same; so that we may recognize in " the Misanthrope " and " The Fourbiers De Scapin " the hand of the same author. Molière's relationship to the older Gallic authors of comedy is also revealed in his freedom of treatment; he has the greatest contempt for traditional rules and conventionalities. He writes: 'You are a gay lot with your rules and conventionalities whereby you only embarrass the ignorant and stultify us more and more every day. For my part, I adopt only one rule — is it not the greatest of all? — *to please?*' This freedom of treatment is manifested not only in the construction of the drama but in the author's manner of viewing life, a view so comprehensive as to include all that is dark, unlovely and frivolous. One looks in vain throughout Molière for those splendid poetic impulses which are manifest in Aristophanes and Shakespeare — outbreaks of passion which often occur in the midst of the grossest buffoonery. Apart from so many characters capable of exciting laughter or ridicule, there are none illumined by the rays of the ideal. Among his numerous coquettes and prudes, only Henriette represents true feminine virtue, and she is lacking in the ideal grace and charm of a woman. How much different in this respect are the women of Shakespeare! Molière considers that the ridiculous is essential to man's nature. According to him, it is indissolubly wedded even to virtue. Hence, he is never afflicted at the sight of it; the sentiment he reveals in the presence of vice is not anger but only curiosity. He takes little care to preach virtue or to attach any moral lessons to the conclusion of his drama. In fact, Molière gives no precepts, he simply chronicles facts. He knows that in reality evil men who are the most clever, are also the strongest, at least in most cases. He demonstrates this; and the only lesson we may learn from his plays is to mistrust them. But we recognize Molière's Gallic ancestry in his gaiety of spirit and the tone of his raillery. With him, however, raillery is often cruel. Certain misfortunes which are tragic and which should excite sentiments of pity, have only a comic side for Molière. He treats as comic some materials which rightly belong to tragedy."

"Notwithstanding the fact that Molière is the greatest French comedian, the impression we get from his work is one of sadness and bitterness. This is not a proof that the author was morose, or that his laugh was not genuine. It is only a proof that he was a profound student of human nature, penetrating more deeply, perhaps, than any other author into the secrets of the human heart. For sadness is the last word of all profound investigation of life. If we study the art of Molière from the viewpoint of external qualities the merit that strikes us most is deftness of touch and a certain magnificence of execution. His characters are exhibited on a grand scale, in a somewhat princely fashion; grand traits are pictured at the expense of minor tones and tints, and these almost overshadow the finer points of character. Each scene is made up of one idea, and one only — this with a view to produce but one effect. Richness and magnificence of language accompany the elaborate scenes, and add much to a style that is strong, firm, and natural. Molière adopts a free and easy style of versification, such as becomes the comic dialogue. In this particular he broke with tradition. There are some violations of idiom, forced turns of phrase and wild, uncouth metaphor — errors due in a measure to the astonishing rapidity with which he wrote. Then, too, it must be remembered that he wrote not for reading but for recitation, and the stage has its own rules and liberties peculiarly its own. Properly speaking, Molière has no style, for style with him varies with every character and shapes itself according to such demands. In this respect Molière proves his kinship with the great masters of dramatic art. The humor of Molière while sometimes of a common-place order, never degenerates into punning; he indulges in all kinds of pleasantry, and his jokes are sometimes perpetrated with thrilling effect."

"Molière is without question the greatest of comic writers in a nation devoted to comedy. His plays reflecting the national love of art, are perfect models of artistic skill: more than this, they are a perfect mirror of the society of his own age, and of humanity in all ages."

William Shakespeare.— He was born at Stratford-on-Avon 1564, and died there in 1616. Very few facts concerning his life are known. Where or when Shakespeare was educated is unknown. About 1587 Shakespeare went to London and sought his fortune in connection with the stage. His relationship with the Globe and Blackfriars is well known. He gained considerable wealth, the result of his labors both as an actor and author. Of the numerous plays left by him the best known tragedies are "Othello," "King Lear," "Hamlet," "Macbeth" and "Julius Cæsar"; the best known comedies are,

" Taming of the Shrew," " Merchant of Venice," " Measure for Measure," " Comedy of Errors " and the " Tempest."

Criticism of Shakespeare.— The amount of criticism dealing with Shakespeare, if collected, would easily fill a small library. Critics of every nation and age have vied with each other in sounding the note of praise. By universal consent he is styled the greatest of dramatists, unapproached by any ancient or modern writer. Among English critics, Dryden, Johnson, Pope, Carlyle, Hazlitt, White, Lowell, Moulton, Mabie, Dowden, have given special attention to Shakespeare. And foreign critics, like Goethe, Schlegel, Ulrici, not to mention a host of others, have gleaned in the same fruitful field. A volume is needed to deal adequately with such a theme.

Criticism by James Russell Lowell.—" It may be reckoned one of the rarest pieces of good luck that ever fell to the share of a race, that (as was true of Shakespeare) its most rhythmic genius, its acutest intellect, its profoundest imagination, and its healthiest understanding should have been combined in one man, and that he should have arrived at the full development of his powers at the moment when the material in which he was to work — that wonderful composite called English, the best result of the confusion of tongues — was in its freshest perfection. The English speaking nations should build a monument to the misguided enthusiasts of the Plain of Shinar; for, as the mixture of many bloods seems to have made them the most vigorous of modern races, so has the mingling of divers speeches given them a language which is perhaps the noblest vehicle of poetic thought that ever existed. Had Shakespeare been born fifty years earlier, he would have been cramped by a book-language not yet flexible enough for the demands of rhythmic emotion, not yet sufficiently popularized for the natural and familiar expression of supreme thought, not yet so rich in metaphysical phrase as to render possible that ideal representation of the great passions, which is the aim and end of Art, not yet subdued by practice and general consent to a definiteness of accentuation essential to ease and congruity of metrical arrangement. Had he been born fifty years

later, his ripened manhood would have found itself in an England absorbed and angry with the solution of political and religious problems, from which his whole nature was averse, instead of that Elizabethan social system, ordered and planetary in
functions and degrees as the angelic hierarchy of the Areopagite,
where his contemplative eye could crowd itself with various and
brilliant pictures and whence his impartial brain — one lobe of
which seems to have been Normanly refined and the other Saxon-
ly sagacious — could draw its morals of courtly and worldly
wisdom, its lessons of prudence and magnanimity. In estimating
Shakespeare, it should never be forgotten, that, like Goethe, he
was essentially observer and artist, and incapable of partisanship.
The passions, actions, sentiments, whose character and results he
delighted to watch and to reproduce, are those of man in society
as it existed ; and it no more occurred to him to question the right
of that society to exist than to criticise the divine ordination of
the seasons. His business was with men as they were, not with
man as he ought to be — with the human soul as it is shaped or
twisted into character by the complex experience of life, not in its
abstract essence, as something to be saved or lost. The scope
of the higher drama is to represent life, not every-day life, it is
true, but life lifted above the plane of bread-and-butter associations, by nobler reaches of language, by the influence at once inspiring and modulating of verse, by an intenser play of passion
condensing that misty mixture of feeling and reflection which
makes the ordinary atmosphere of existence into flashes of
thought and phrase whose brief, but terrible, illumination prints
the outworn landscape of every-day upon our brains, with its
little motives and mean results, in lines of tell-tale fire. The
moral office of tragedy is to show us our own weaknesses idealized in grander figures and more awful results — to teach us that
what we pardon in ourselves as venial faults, if they seem to have
but slight influence on our immediate fortunes, have arms as
long as those of kings, and reach forward to the catastrophe of
our lives, that they are dry-rotting the very fibre of will and conscience, so that, if we should be brought to the test of a great
temptation or a stringent emergency, we must be involved in a
ruin as sudden and complete as that we shudder at in the unreal
scene of the theatre. But the primary *object* of a tragedy is not
to inculcate a formal moral. Representing life, it teaches, like

life, by indirection, by those nods and winks that are thrown away on us blind horses in such profusion. We may learn, to be sure, plenty of lessons from Shakespeare. We are not likely to have kingdoms to divide, crowns foretold us by weird sisters, a father's death to avenge, or to kill our wives from jealousy; but Lear may teach us to draw the line more clearly between a wise generosity and a loose-handed weakness of giving; Macbeth, how one sin involves another, and forever another, by a fatal parthenogenesis, and that the key which unlocks forbidden doors to our will or passion leaves a stain on the hand, that may not be so dark as blood, but that will not out; Hamlet, that all the noblest gifts of person, temperament, and mind slip like sand through the grasp of an infirm purpose; Othello, that the perpetual silt of some one weakness, the eddies of a suspicious temper depositing their one impalpable layer after another, may build up a shoal on which an heroic life and an otherwise magnanimous nature may bilge and go to pieces. All this we may learn, and much more, and Shakespeare was no doubt well aware of all this, and more; but I do not believe that he wrote his plays with any such didactic purpose. He knew human nature too well not to know that one thorn of experience is worth a whole wilderness of warning — that, where one man shapes his life by precept and example, there are a thousand who have it shaped for them by impulse and by circumstances. He did not mean his great tragedies for scarecrows, as if the nailing of one hawk to the barn-door would prevent the next from coming down souse into the hen-yard. No, it is not the poor bleaching victim hung up to moult its draggled feathers in the rain that he wishes to show us. He loves the hawk-nature as well as the hen-nature; and if he is unequalled in anything, it is in that sunny breadth of view, that impregnability of reason, that looks down all ranks and conditions of men, all fortunes and misfortunes, with the equal eye of the pure artist."

Criticism by Thomas Shaw.—" A general conception of the dramatic genius of Shakespeare must be founded upon an examination of *all* his pieces; and while the historical dramas show how he could free his mind from the trammels imposed by the necessity of adhering to real facts and persons, the romantic portion of his pieces, or those founded upon fiction, will equally prove that the freedom of an ideal subject did not deprive him of the strictest fidelity to general nature. The characters that move through the action of these latter dramas exhibit the same consummate appreciation of the general and the individual in humanity; and though he has occasionally stepped over the boundary of ordinary human nature, and has created a multitude of supernatural beings, fairies, spirits, witches and other creatures of the imagination, even in these, the severest consistency and the strictest verisimilitude never for a moment abandoned him. They are always *constantes sibi;* we know that such beings do not and cannot exist; but we irresistibly feel, in reading the scenes in which they appear, that if they did exist, they could not exist other than as he has painted them. The data being established, the consequences, to the most remote and trivial details, flow from them in a manner that no analysis can gainsay. In the *mode* of delineating passion and feeling Shakespeare proceeds differently from all other dramatic authors. They, even the greatest among them, create a personage by accumulating in it all such traits as their reading and observation show to usually accompany the fundamental elements which go to form its constitution: and thus they all, more or less, fall into the error of making their personages embodiments of such a moral peculiarity. They give us admirable and complete *monographies* of ambition, of avarice, of hypocracy, and the like. Moreover, in the expression of their feelings, whether tragic or comic, such characters almost universally *describe* the sensations they experience. But men and women of Shakespeare exactly resemble the men and women of strong emotion or other powerful moral impression; we indicate to others what we feel, rather, and far more powerfully, by what we suppress than what we utter. In this respect the men and women of Shakespeare exactly resemble the men and women of real life, and not the men and women of the stage. Nor has he ever fallen into the common error of forgetting the infinite complexity of human character. If we analyze any one of the prominent personages of Shakespeare, though we may often at first sight perceive in it the predominance of some one quality or passion, on a nearer view we shall find that the complexity of its moral being goes on widening and deepening with every new attempt on our part to grasp or sound the whole extent of its individuality.

" In the expression of strong emotion, as well as in the delineation of character, Shakespeare is superior to all other dramatists, superior to all other poets. He never finds it necessary, in order to produce the effect he desires, to have recourse in the one case to violent or declamatory rhetoric, or in the other to unusual or abnormal combinations of qualities. In him we meet with no sentimental assassins, no moral monsters,—

'Blessed with one virtue and a thousand crimes.'

Without overstepping the ordinary limits of human experience, he is always able to interest or instruct us with the exhibition of general passions and feelings, manifesting themselves in the way we generally see them in the world. He is like the great painter of antiquity, who produced his ever-varying effects by the aid of four simple colors. In the expression, too, he uniformly draws, at least in the finest passages, his illustrations from the most simple and familiar objects, from the most ordinary scenes of life. When a great occasion presents itself, he ever shows himself equal to that occasion. There are, indeed, in his works many passages where he has allowed his taste for intellectual subtleties to get the better of his judgment, and where his passion for playing upon words — a passion which was the literary vice of the day, and the effects of which are traceable in the writings of Bacon as well as in his — is permitted to cool the enthusiasm excited by the situation or the feelings of the speaker. But the indulgence in conceits generally disappears in the great culminating moments of intense passion: and while we are speaking of this defect with due critical severity, we must not forget that there are occasions when the intense moral agitation is not incompatible with a morbid and feverish activity of the intellect, and that the most violent emotion sometimes finds a vent in the intellectual contortions of a conceit. Nevertheless, it cannot be denied that Shakespeare very often runs riot in the indulgence of this tendency, to the injury of the effect designed and in defiance of the most evident principles of good taste. His style is unquestionably a very difficult one in some respects; and this obscurity is not to be attributed, except of course, in some particular instances, to the corrupt state in which his writings have descended to us, and still less to the archaism or obsoleteness of his diction. Many of the great dramatists his contemporaries, for example Massinger and Ford, are in this respect as different from Shakespeare as if they had been separated from him by two centuries of time — their writings being as remarkable for the limpidity and clearness of expression as his are occasionally for its complexity. It is, therefore, not to the remoteness of the period that we must ascribe this peculiarity. Indeed in this respect Shakespeare's language will present nearly as much difficulty to an English as to a foreign student. We must look for the cause of this in the enormously developed intellectual and imaginative faculty in the poet; leading him to make metaphor of the boldest kind the ordinary tissue of his style. The thoughts rise so fast under his pen, and successively generate others with such a portentous rapidity, that the reader requires almost as great an intellectual vivacity as the poet, in order to trace the leading idea through the labyrinth of subordinate illustration. In all figurative writing the metaphor, the image, is an ornament, something extraneous to the thought it is intended to illustrate, and may be detached from it, leaving the fundamental idea intact: in Shakespeare the metaphor is the very fabric of the thought itself and entirely inseparable from it. His diction may be compared to some elaborate monument of the finest Gothic architecture in which the superficial glance losses itself in an inextricable maze of sculptural detail and fantastically fretted ornamentation, but where a close examination shows that every pinnacle, every buttress, every moulding is an essential member of the construction. This imitation union of the reason and the imagination is a peculiarity common to Shakespeare and Bacon, in whose writings the severest logic is expressed in the boldest metaphor, and the very titles of whose books and the very definitions of whose philosophical terms are frequently images of the most figurative character. There is assuredly no poet, ancient or modern, from whose writings may be extracted such a number of profound and yet practical observations applicable to the common affairs and interests of life; observations expressed with the simplicity of a casual remark, yet pregnant with the condensed wisdom of philosophy; exhibiting more than the acuteness of De Rochefoucauld, without his cynical contempt for humanity, and more than practical good sense of Molière, with a far wider and more universal applicability. In the picturing of abnormal and supernatural states of existence, as in the delineation of every phase of mental derangement, or the sentiments and actions of fantastic and supernatural beings, Shakespeare exhibits the same coherency and consistency in the midst of what at first sight appears altogether to transcend ordinary experience. Every grade of folly, from the verge of idiocy to the most fantastic eccentricity, every shade of moral perturbation, from the jealousy fury of Othello to the frenzy of Lear or the not less touching madness of Ophelia, is represented in his plays with a fidelity so complete that the most experienced physiologists have affirmed that such intellectual disturbances may be studied in his pages with as much profit as in the actual patients of a madhouse."

Other Dramatists.— Perhaps there is no department of literature so rich and varied as the drama. Every nation, ancient as well as modern, lays claim to excellence in gifted playwrights and stage productions. The student of English literature is familiar with the contemporaries of Shakespeare — Marlowe, Fletcher, Greene, Chettle, Ford, Massinger, Beaumont, Webster, Dekker, and many others. Continental literature can boast a Schiller in Germany, a Corneille, Racine and Hugo in France, a Camœns in Portugal, a Cervantes in Spain; for every nation has had its golden age when the dramatist flourished. At all times the stage has appealed to the people; they have seen thereon, as in a mirror, a reflection of their own human life, its faults and foibles, its glory and shame; they have seen the smiles of comedy and the blinding tears of tragedy. The drama shows us the soul in action, and its greatest works reveal the individual soul in collision with a higher will, a stronger force, as represented by the decrees of fate, the family or the State. There is no literary work more complex, instructive or fascinating — none which repays the student so much for his time and application. We may close the criticism of the drama with two observations made by master minds — the life of humanity is a grand drama — the whole world is a stage, and we are the players.

CHAPTER XLIX

THE EPIC

Origin of the Epic.— At the root of the epic was the popular worship of heroes. This worship filled heaven with the gods of mythology; and around their earthly career legends and myths grew up and flourished in the traditions of the people. In these legends the epic writer found material for his long narrative poem. The mythology furnishing the basis for epics, deals with the forces and elements of nature which were deified, as well as with the human hero. In this connection Professor Jebb writes of Homer: "The early religion of the Greeks was chiefly a sense of divinity in the forces of outward nature; so that among the gods of Olympus are those representing the elements, the seasons, the divisions of earth and water, etc.; these gods were fully as heroic in character as those who had inherited heaven or those who, as human heroes, earned deification." The epic treatment of this material corresponds with the traditional treatment of it; hence, it is almost wholly fictitious. But certain elements of truth remain in the composition of the epic. For example, Jebb finds three elements of truth in Homer. First, his epics are true in employing historical material for setting and outline; they are true in selecting some characters or heroes who actually have a place in human history, although the events in their lives as given in the epics are for the most part fictitious. Finally, they are true in giving a faithful picture of the social manners and institutions which existed at the time. These elements of truth found in Homer, extend throughout the whole realm of epic literature.

The Epic Compared with the Lyric— The epic deals with the real or fictitious events of history; hence, it is objective in character; whereas, the lyric deals with the writer's own thoughts and emotions. In other words, the lyric is purely subjective. It is self-expression in the matter of love, hatred, grief, hope, or in any other of the various passions. As distinguished from the lyric, epic poetry was recited, not set to music; the author was kept in the background; the events of the story, not the personal feelings of the author, held the attention of reader or hearer. As a natural result of the material treated, the lyric is a brief poem. The expression of intense emotion, like the duration of any passion, is incapable of long continuance. For example, the climax of grief, joy, hatred, or any passion is brief in nature; and must be so in art; and the lyric which is its form of expression cannot be drawn out to any length without violating the law of nature. This is true, even when a large number of lyrics cluster around a single theme as in the *In Memoriam* of Tennyson; for each lyric is brief, having a separate topic. Tennyson defines these lyrics as " short swallow-flights of song that dip their wings in tears and skim away." The epic, on the contrary, is a long narrative poem, dealing with the story of some hero, and involving a large number of events and episodes. The material is such that the epic must run through many chapters or cantos; it often reaches the proportions of a good-sized volume.

Epic and Lyric Combined.— The epic often contains lyric elements, because it frequently gives expression to intense emotion. For example, the hymns of the angels or the prayers of our first parents quoted in Milton; the frequent and passionate invocation of the gods in Virgil and Homer. These are purely lyrical in character. While they do not change the form and matter of the epic line, they are separated by quotation marks, and are understood by the author and reader to be distinct from the epic story.

The Epic Compared with the Drama.— As compared with the drama, the epic is narrated; the drama is acted. The drama is concerned primarily with character creation. The events in a drama are stated in order to unfold character; they are seen in the light of character-development; whereas, the events in the epic, like the events of history, are made interesting on their own account.

Leading Characters Compared.— If we compare leading characters of the epic, for example, Achilles or Ulysses, with leading characters of the drama, for example, Hamlet or Othello, the difference between epic and dramatic treatment appears at once. The main point of difference is magnitude and uncertainty of outline. The epic hero as represented in Achilles or Ulysses, is unreal, a human shadow, distorted and magnified beyond the range of probability; as a rule, this hero is an impossible idealization of human qualities and human deeds. Thus, epic characters are aptly described as sprites, goblins, ghosts, flitting with magnified forms in the twilight of history. Hence, too, the frequent introduction of the supernatural in order to sustain epic grandeur and magnificence. The epic writer constantly destroys human limitations and his imagination takes refuge in the supernatural. For example, Homer forgets Achilles and the plain of Troy, and spends much of his time and talent around Olympus. In *Paradise Lost*, Adam is made a mere pigmy among supernatural heroes. In the broad light of day the traditional epic hero is an absurd creation; hence, Milton felt that he was born an age too late, because he could not clothe Adam with that unnatural, super-human magnificence, as older epic writers had done with primitive heroes. But he found a remedy in the heroes of an other world and another race. Angels take the place of pagan gods; and heaven and hell, like Olympus, claim the splendid imagery of the epic. The drama, on the other hand, is a mirror of nature; Hamlet and Othello are real human beings. The characters of the drama are all possible human types; they are perfectly natural in their qualities and deeds; the success of the drama depends upon faithfulness to reality; whereas in the epic there is a constant tending toward an impossible idealism. Hence, in the drama we have character-creation in the true sense of the word; while the creations of the epic are extravagant and imaginary.

Dramatic Use of Epic Material.— Drama often makes use of epic material, just as the epic often embraces lyric material. But the long narrative undergoes almost a complete transformation. The supernatural machinery is either cut out or relegated to the back-ground; the long speeches are cut down to those of ordinary conversation; the extravagant imagery and language are so modified as to suit an ordinary human being; the dramatic situations are multiplied; so that while one trait of character was displayed in the epic, half a dozen appear in the clash of wills and motives peculiar to the drama. The heroes live and act and interpret themselves to us by all the complexity of movement known to actual living. The Homeric narrative was thus treated by the Greek dramatists; the epic of *Faust* by Goethe is a striking modern example of such treatment. *Paradise Lost,* on the contrary, has never been dramatized because the supernatural machinery could not be staged or eliminated with success. It is made a vital part of the story. Adam's life, as written by Milton, presents too small a number of dramatic situations; the whole story would have to be re-written, in order to constitute a drama.

Types of the Epic.— The two most notable and most typical forms of epic poetry are the primitive epic and the so-called modern epic. The former is a growth rather than a creation; at least the people who handed down the myth or tradition are responsible for its enlargement, quite as much as the poet whose name it bears. The poem is written on a grand scale and relies upon the supernatural as well as the human element in the story.

The modern epic is likewise on a grand scale and uses the supernatural. But there is this main point of difference. The modern epic writer is self-conscious and introduces the personal element frequently. Milton devotes a page to his own blindness, he speaks of having fallen on evil days; of having started the epic late in life, and other matters quite foreign to the narrative. This self-consciousness is stronger still in Dante, who uses the epic in order to place many of his personal enemies in hell. This self-consciousness or personal equation is quite unknown in the older epics. And the epic writer, like the historian or the dramatist, ought to keep himself in the background.

Rank of the Epic.— The epic poem is universally allowed to be, of all poetical works, the most dignified, and at the same time, the most difficult of execution. To contrive a story which shall please and interest all readers, by being at once entertaining, important and instructive; to fill it with suitable incidents; to enliven it with a variety of characters, and of descriptions; and throughout a long work, to maintain that propriety of sentiment, and that elevation of style, which the epic character requires, is unquestionably a very high effort of poetical genius. Hence, so very few have succeeded in the attempt, that strict critics will hardly allow any other poems to bear the name of epic, except the Iliad and the Æneid.

Dispute as to Definition.—There is no subject, it must be confessed, on which critics have displayed more pedantry, than on this. By tedious disquisitions, founded on a servile submission to authority, they have given such an air of mystery to a plain subject, as to render it difficult for an ordinary reader to conceive what an epic poem is. By Bossu's definition, it is a discourse invented by art purely to form the manners of men by means of instruction disguised under the allegory of some important action, which is related in verse. This definition would suit several of Æsop's Fables, if they were somewhat extended, and put into verse; and accordingly, to illustrate his definition, the critic draws a parallel, in form, between the construction of one of Æsop's Fables and the plan of Homer's Iliad. The first thing, says he, which either a writer of fables, or of heroic poems does, is to choose some maxim or point of morality, to inculcate which, is to be the design of his work. Next, he invents a general story, or a series of facts, without any names, such as he judges will be most proper for illustrating his intended moral. Lastly, he particularizes his story; that is, if he be a fabulist he introduces his dog, his sheep and his wolf; or, if he be an epic poet, he looks into ancient history for some proper names of heroes to give to his actors; and then his plan is completed.

Correct Definition.— The plain account of the nature of an epic poem is the recital of some illustrious enterprise in a poetical form. This is as exact a definition as there is any occasion for, on this subject. It comprehends several other poems besides the Iliad of Homer, the Æneid of Virgil and the Jerusalem of Tasso, which are, perhaps, the three most regular and complete epic works that ever were composed. But to exclude all poems from the epic class, which are not formed exactly upon the same model as these, is the pedantry of criticism. We can give exact definitions and descriptions of minerals, plants, and animals; and can arrange them with precision, under the different classes to which they belong,

because nature affords a visible unvarying standard, to which
we refer them. But with regard to works of taste and imagination, where nature has fixed no standard, but leaves
scope for beauties of many different kinds, it is absurd to attempt defining, and limiting them with the same precision.
Criticism, when employed in such attempts, degenerates into
trifling questions about words and names only. One, therefore,
can have no scruple to class such poems, as Milton's Paradise
Lost, Lucan's Pharsalia, Statius' Thebiad, Ossian's Fingal
and Temora, Camœn's Lusiad, Voltaire's Henriade, Cam-
bray's Telemachus, Glover's Leonidas, Wilkie's Epigoniad,
under the same species of composition with the Iliad and the
Æneid; though some of them approach much nearer than
others to the perfection of these celebrated works. They are,
undoubtedly, all epic; that is, poetical recitals of great adventures; which is all that is meant by this denomination of poetry.

Moral Value.— Though one cannot by any means allow
that it is the essence of an epic poem to be wholly an allegory,
or a fable contrived to illustrate some moral truth, yet it is
certain that no poetry is of a more moral nature than this.
Its effect in promoting virtue is not to be measured by any
one maxim, or instruction which results from the whole history, like the moral of one of Æsop's fables. This is a poor
and trivial view of the advantage to be derived from perusing
a long epic work, that at the end we shall be able to gather
from it some common-place morality. Its effect arises from
the impression which the parts of the poem separately, as well
as the whole taken together, make upon the mind of the reader;
from the great examples which it sets before us, and the high
sentiments with which it warms our hearts. The end which
it proposes is to extend our ideas of human perfection, or,
in other words, to excite admiration. Now this can be accomplished only by proper representation of heroic deeds and

virtuous characters. For high virtue is the object which all mankind are formed to admire; and, therefore, epic poems are, and must be, favorable to the cause of virtue. Valor, truth, justice, fidelity, friendship, piety, magnanimity, are the objects which, in the course of such compositions, are presented to our minds, under the most splendid and honorable colors. In behalf of virtuous personages, our affections are engaged; in their designs, and their distresses, we are interested; the generous and public affections are awakened; the mind is purified from sensual and mean pursuits, and accustomed to take part in great heroic enterprises. It is indeed no small testimony in honor of virtue, that several of the most refined and elegant entertainments of mankind, such as that species of poetical composition which we now consider, must be grounded on moral sentiments and impressions. This is a testimony of such weight that, were it in the power of skeptical philosophers to weaken the force of those reasonings which establish the essential distinctions between vice and virtue, the writings of epic poets alone were sufficient to refute their false philosophy; showing by that appeal which they constantly make to the feelings of mankind in favor of virtue, that the foundations of it are laid deep and strong in human nature.

Characteristics of the Epic.— The general strain and spirit of the epic composition sufficiently mark its distinction from the other kinds of poetry. In pastoral writing the reigning idea is innocence and tranquillity. Compassion is the great object of tragedy; ridicule, the province of comedy. The predominant character of the epic is, admiration excited by heroic actions. It is sufficiently distinguished from history, both by its political form and the liberty of fiction which it assumes. It is a more calm composition than tragedy. It admits, nay, requires, the pathetic and the violent, on particular occasions; but the pathetic is not expected to be its general character.

It requires, more than other species of poetry, a grave, equal, and supported dignity. It takes in a greater compass of time and action than dramatic writing admits, and thereby allows full display of characters. Dramatic writings display characters chiefly by means of sentiments and passions; epic poetry, chiefly by means of actions. The emotions, therefore, which it raises are not so violent, but they are more prolonged. These are the general characteristics of this species of composition. But, in order to give a more particular and critical view of it, let us consider the epic poem under three heads; first, with respect to the subject or action; secondly, with respect to the actors or characters; and lastly, with respect to the narration of the poet.

The Action of the Epic.— The action, or subject of the epic poem, must have three properties; it must be one; it must be great; it must be interesting: First, it must be *one action* or enterprise which the poet chooses for his subject. I have frequently had occasion to remark the importance of unity in many kinds of composition in order to make a full and strong impression upon the mind. With the highest reason, Aristotle insists upon this, as essential to epic poetry; and it is, indeed, the most material of all his rules respecting it. For it is certain that, in the recital of heroic adventures, several scattered and independent facts can never affect a reader so deeply, nor engage his attention so strongly, as a tale that is one and connected, where the several incidents hang upon one another, and are all made to conspire for the accomplishment of one end. In a regular epic, the more this unity is rendered sensible to the imagination, the better will be the effect; and, for this reason, as Aristotle has observed, it is not sufficient for the poet to confine himself to the actions of one man, or to those things which happened during a certain period of time; but the unity must lie in the subject itself; and arise from all the parts combining into one whole. In all the great epic poems, unity of action is sufficiently apparent. Virgil, for instance, has chosen for his subject, the establishment of Æneas in Italy. From the beginning to the end of the poem, this object is ever in our view, and links all the parts of it together with full connection. The unity of the Odyssey is of the same nature; the return and re-establishment of Ulysses in his own country. The subject of Tasso, is the recovery of Jerusalem from the infidels; that of Milton, the expulsion of our first parents from Paradise; and both of them are unexceptionable in the unity of the story. The professed subject of the Iliad is the anger of Achilles, with the consequences which it produced. The Greeks carry on many unsuccessful engagements against the Trojans, as long as they are deprived of the assistance of Achilles. Upon his being appeased and reconciled to Agamemnon, victory follows, and the poem closes. It must be owned, however, that the unity, or connecting principle, is not quite so sensible to the imagination here, as in the Æneid. For, throughout many books of the Iliad, Achilles is out of sight; he is lost in inaction, and the fancy terminates on no other object than the success of the two armies which we see contending in war.

Interpretation of Epic Action.— The unity of the epic action is not to be strictly interpreted, as if it excluded all episodes, or subordinate actions. It is necessary to observe here, that the term episode is employed by Aristotle, in a different sense from what we now give to it. It was a term originally applied to dramatic poetry, and hence, transferred to epic; and by episodes in an epic poem, it should seem that Aristotle understood the extension of the general fable, or plan of the poem, into all its circumstances. What his meaning was, is indeed not very clear; and this obscurity has occasioned much altercation among critical writers. Bossu, in particular, is so perplexed upon this subject, as to be almost unintelligible. But dismissing so fruitless a controversy, what we now understand by episodes, are certain actions or incidents, introduced into the narration, connected with the principal action, yet not so essential to it, as to destroy, if they had been omitted, the main subject of the poem. Of this nature are the interview of Hector with Andromache, in the Iliad; the story of Cacus, and that of Nisus and Euryalus, in the Æneid; the adventures of Tancred with Erminia and Clorinda, in the Jerusalem; and the prospect of his descendants exhibited to Adam in the last books of Paradise Lost.

Episodes.— Such episodes as these are not only permitted to an epic poet, but provided they are properly executed, are great ornaments to his work. The rules regarding them are the following: First, they must be naturally introduced; they must have a sufficient connection with the poem; they must seem inferior parts that belong to it; not mere appendages stuck to it. The episode of Olinda and Sophronia in the second book of Tasso's Jerusalem is faulty, by transgressing this rule. It is too detached from the rest of the work, and, being introduced so near the opening of the poem, misleads the reader to an expectation that it is to be of some future consequence, whereas it proves to be connected with nothing that follows. In proportion as any episode is slightly related to the main subject, it should always be the shorter. The passion of Dido in the Æneid, and the snares of Armida in the Jerusalem, which are expanded so fully in these poems, cannot with propriety be called episodes. They are constituent parts of the work, and form a considerable share of the intrigue of the poem. In the next place, episodes ought to present to us objects of a different kind from those which go before, and those which follow in the course of the poem. Because it is principally for the sake of variety that episodes are introduced into an epic composition. In so long a work they tend to diversify the subject and to relieve the reader by shifting the scene. In the midst of combats, therefore, an episode of the martial kind would be out of place; whereas Hector's visit to Andromache in the Iliad, and Erminia's adventure with the shepherd in the seventh book of the Jerusalem, afford us a well-judged and pleasing retreat from camps and battles. Lastly, as an episode is a professed embellishment, it ought to be particularly elegant and well finished; and accordingly, it is, for the most part, in pieces of this kind that poets put forth their strength. The episodes of Teribazus and Ariana, in Leonidas, and of the death of Hercules, in the Epigoniad, are the two greatest beauties in these poems.

The Unity of the Epic Action.— This necessarily supposes that the action be entire and complete: that is, as Aristotle well expresses it, that it have a beginning, a middle, and an end. Either by relating the whole, in his own person, or by introducing some of his actors to relate what had passed before the opening of the poem, the author must always contrive to give us full information of everything that belongs to his subject; he must not leave our curiosity, in any article, ungratified: he must bring us precisely to the accomplishment of his plan, and then conclude. The second property of the epic action is that it be great; that it have sufficient splendor and importance both to fix our attention and to justify the magnificent apparatus which the poet bestows upon it. This is so evidently requisite as not to require illustration; and, indeed, hardly any who have attempted epic poetry, have failed in choosing some subject sufficiently important, either by the nature of the action or by the fame of the personages concerned in it.

Advantage of Antiquity.— It contributes to the grandeur of the epic subject, that it be not of a modern date, nor fall

within any period of history with which we are intimately
acquainted.   Both Lucan and Voltaire have, in the choice of
their subjects, transgressed this rule, and they have, upon that
account, succeeded worse.   Antiquity is favorable to those
high and august ideas which epic poetry is designed to raise.
It tends to aggrandize, in our imagination, both persons and
events: and what is still more material, it allows the poet the
liberty of adorning his subject by means of fiction.   Whereas,
as soon as he comes within the verge of real and authenticated
history, this liberty is abridged.   He must either confine himself wholly, as Lucan has done, to strict historical truth, at
the expense of rendering his story jejune; or if he goes beyond
it, like Voltaire in his Henriade, this disadvantage follows,
that, in well-known events, the true and the fictitious parts of
the plan do not naturally mingle and incorporate with each
other.   These observations cannot be applied to dramatic writing, where the personages are exhibited to us, not so much
that we may admire, as that we may love or pity them.   Such
passions are much more consistent with the familiar historical
knowledge of the persons who are to be the objects of them;
and even require them to be displayed in the light and with
the failings of ordinary men.   Modern and well-known history, therefore, may furnish very proper materials for tragedy.
But for epic poetry, where heroism is the ground-work and
where the object in view is to excite admiration, ancient or
traditionary history is assuredly the safest region.   There the
author may lay hold on names, and characters, and events not
wholly unknown, on which to build his story, while, at the
same time, by reason of the distance of the period, or of the
remoteness of the scene, sufficient scope is left him for fiction
and invention.

The Third Property.— The third property required in the
epic poem is, that it be interesting.   It is not sufficient for

this purpose that it be great. For deeds of mere valor, how heroic soever, may prove cold and tiresome. Much will depend on the happy choice of some subject, which shall by its nature, interest the public; as when the poet selects for his hero one who is the founder, or the deliverer, or the favorite, of his nation; or when he writes of achievements that have been highly celebrated, or have been connected with important consequences to any public cause. Most of the great epic poems are abundantly fortunate in this respect, and must have been very interesting to those ages and countries in which they were composed.

Management of Plan.—But the chief circumstance which renders an epic poem interesting, and which tends to interest not one age or country alone, but all readers, is the skilful conduct of the author in the management of his subject. He must so contrive his plan as that it shall comprehend many affecting incidents. He must not dazzle us perpetually with valiant achievements, for all readers tire of constant fighting and battles; but he must study to touch our hearts. He may sometimes be awful and august, he must often be tender and pathetic, he must give us gentle and pleasing scenes of love, friendship, and affection. The more an epic poem abounds with situations which awaken the feelings of humanity, the more interesting it is; and these form always the favorite passages of the work. No poets are so happy in this respect as Virgil and Tasso.

Characters of Heroes.— Much, too, depends upon the characters of the heroes for rendering the poem interesting, that they be such as shall strongly attach the readers, and make them take part in the dangers which the heroes encounter. These dangers, or obstacles, form what is called the nodus or the intrigue of the epic poem, in the judicious conduct of which, consists much of the poet's art. He must rouse our attention, by a prospect of the difficulties which seem to threaten disappointment to the enterprise of his favorite personages; he must make these difficulties grow and thicken upon us by degrees; till, after having kept us for some time in a state of agitation and suspense, he paves the way, by a proper preparation of incidents, for the winding up of the plot in a natural and probable manner. It is plain that every tale which is designed to engage attention, must be conducted on a plan of this sort.

The Close.— A question has been moved, whether the nature of the epic poem does require that it should always end successfully? Most critics are inclined to think that a successful issue is the most proper; and they appear to have reason on their side. An unhappy conclusion depresses the mind, and is opposite to the elevating emotions which belong to this species of poetry. Terror and compassion are the proper subjects of tragedy; but as the epic poem is of larger compass and extent, it were too much, if after the difficulties and troubles which commonly abound in the progress of the poem, the author should bring them all at last to an unfortunate issue. Accordingly, the general practice of the epic poet is on the side of a prosperous conclusion; not, however, without some exceptions. For two authors of great name, Lucan and Milton, have held a contrary course; the one concluding with the subversion of the Roman liberty; the other, with the expulsion of man from Paradise.

Time.— With regard to the time or duration of the epic action, no precise boundaries can be ascertained. A considerable extent is always allowed to it, as it does not necessarily depend on those violent passions which can be supposed to have only a short continuance. The Iliad, which is formed upon the anger of Achilles, has, with propriety, the shortest duration of any of the great epic poems. According to Bossu, the action lasts no longer than forty-seven days. The action of the Odyssey, computed from the taking of Troy to the peace of Ithaca, extends to eight years and a half; and the action of the Æneid, computed in the same way from the taking of Troy to the death of Turnus, includes about six years. But if we measure the period only of the poet's own narration, or compute from the time in which the hero makes his first appearance till the conclusion, the duration of both these last poems is brought within a much smaller compass. The Odyssey, beginning with Ulysses in the island of Calypso, comprehends fifty-eight days only; and the Æneid beginning with the storm which throws Æneas upon the cost of Africa, is reckoned to include, at the most, a year and some months.

Personages.— As it is the business of an epic poet to copy after nature and to form a probably interesting tale, he must study to give all his *personages* proper and well-supported characters, such as display the features of human nature. This is what Aristotle calls giving manners to the poem. It is by no means necessary that all his actors be morally good; imperfect, nay, vicious characters may find a proper place; though the nature of epic poetry seems to require that the principal figures exhibited should be such as tend to arouse admiration and love, rather than hatred or contempt. But whatever the character be which a poet gives to any of his actors, he must take care to preserve it uniform and consistent with itself. Everything which that person says or does must be suited to it, and must serve to distinguish him from any other. Poetic characters may be divided into two kinds, general and particular. General characters are wise, brave, virtuous, without any further distinction. Particular characters express the species of bravery, of wisdom, of virtue, for which any one is

eminent. They exhibit the peculiar features which distinguish
one individual from another, which mark the difference of
the same moral quality in different men, according as it is
combined with other dispositions in their temper.   In drawing
such particular characters, genius is chiefly exerted.   How far
each of the three great epic poets have distinguished themselves
in this part of composition, shall afterwards be shown in remarking upon their works.   It is sufficient now to mention,
that it is in this part that Homer has principally excelled;
Tasso has come the nearest to Homer; and Virgil has been the
most deficient.   It has been the practice of all epic poets to
select some one personage whom they distinguish above all
the rest, and make the hero of the tale.   This is considered
essential to epic composition, and is attended with several advantages.   It renders the unity of the subject more sensible,
when there is one principal figure, to which, as to a center,
all the rest refer.   It tends to interest us more in the enterprise
which is carried on, and it gives the poet an opportunity of
exerting his talents for adorning and displaying one character with peculiar splendor.   It has been asked, Who, then,
is the hero of Paradise Lost?   The devil, it has been answered
by some critics; and, in consequence of this idea, much ridicule
and censure have been thrown upon Milton.   But they have
mistaken that author's intention by proceeding upon a sup-
position that in the conclusion of his poem the hero must needs
be triumphant.   Whereas, Milton followed a different plan
and has given a tragic conclusion to a poem otherwise epic
in form.   For Adam is undoubtedly his hero; that is, the capital and most interesting figure in his poem.

Supernatural Personages.— Besides human actors, there are
personages of another kind that usually occupy no small place
in epic poetry, that is, the gods, or supernatural beings.   This
brings us to the consideration of what is called the machinery

of the epic poem; the nicest and most difficult part of the subject. Critics appear to have gone to the extreme on both sides. Almost all the French critics decide in favor of the machinery as essential to the constitution of an epic poem. They quote that sentence of Petronius Arbiter, as if it were an oracle, *" per ambages, Deorumque ministeria, procipitandus est liber spiritus,"* and hold that, though a poem had every other requisite that could be demanded, yet it could not be ranked in the epic class, unless the main action was carried on by the intervention of the gods. This decision seems to be founded on no principle or reason whatever, unless a superstitious reverence for the practice of Homer and Virgil. These poets very properly embellished their story by the traditional tales and popular legends of their own country; according to which all the great transactions of the heroic times were intermixed with the fables of their deities. But does it thence follow that in other countries and in other ages, where there is not the like advantage of current superstition and popular credulity, epic poetry must be wholly confined to antiquated fictions and fairy tales? Lucan has composed a very spirited poem, certainly of the epic kind, where neither gods nor supernatural beings are at all employed. The author of Leonidas has made an attempt of the same kind, not without success; and beyond doubt, wherever a poet gives us a regular heroic story, well connected in its parts, adorned with characters, and supported with proper dignity and elevation, though his agents be, every one of them, human, he has fulfilled the chief requisites of this sort of composition and has a just title to be classed with epic writers. But though one cannot admit that machinery is essential or necessary to the epic plan, neither can one agree with some late critics of considerable name, who are for excluding it totally, as inconsistent with that probability and impression of reality which they think should reign in this kind of writing. Mankind do not consider poetical writings with so philosophical an eye. They seek entertainment from them; and for the bulk of readers, indeed for almost all men, the marvelous has a great charm. It gratifies and fills the imagination; and gives room for many a striking and sublime description. In epic poetry in particular, where admiration and lofty ideas are supposed to reign, the marvelous and supernatural find, if any where, their proper place. They both enable the poet to aggrandize his subject by means of those august and solemn objects which religion introduces into it; and they allow him to enlarge and diversify his plan, by comprehending with it heaven, and earth, and hell, men, and invisible beings, and the whole circle of the universe. At the same time, in the use of this supernatural machinery, it becomes a poet to be temperate and prudent. He is not at liberty to invent what system of the marvelous he pleases. It must always have some foundation in popular belief. He must avail himself in a decent manner either of the religious faith or the superstitious credulity of the country wherein he lives or of which he writes, so as to give an air of probability to events which are most contrary to the common course of nature. Whatever machinery he employs, he must take care not to overload us with it; not to withdraw human actions and manners too much from view, not to obscure them under a cloud of incredible fictions. He must always remember, that his chief business is to relate to men the actions and the exploits of men; that it is by these principally he is to interest us and to touch our hearts; and that if probability be altogether banished from his work, it can never make a deep or a lasting impression. Indeed, there would seem nothing more difficult in epic poetry than to adjust properly the mixture of the marvelous with the probable, so as to gratify and amuse us with the one without sacrificing the other. It seems needless to observe that these observations affect not the conduct of Milton's work: whose plan being altogether theological, his supernatural beings form not the machinery but are the principal actors in the poem. With regard to allegorical personages, fame, discord, love, and the like, it may be safely pronounced that they form the worst machinery of any. In description they are sometimes allowable, and may serve for embellishment; but they should never be permitted to bear any share in the action of the poem. For being plain and admitted fictions, mere names of general ideas to which even fancy cannot attribute any existence as persons, if they be introduced as mingling with human actors, an intolerable confusion of shadows and realities arises and all consistency of action is utterly destroyed.

Narration.— In the narration, which is the last head that remains to be considered, it is not material whether the poet recounts the whole story in his own character, or introduces some personages to relate any part of the action that had passed before the poem opens. Homer follows the one method in his Iliad, and the other in his Odyssey. Virgil has, in this respect, imitated the conduct of the Odyssey; Tasso, that of the Iliad. The chief advantage which arises from any of the actors being employed to relate part of the story is that it allows the poet, if he choose, to open with some interesting situation of affairs, informing us afterward of what had passed before that period; and gives him the greater liberty of spreading out such parts of the subject as he is inclined to dwell upon in person, and of comprehending the rest with a short recital. Where the subject is of great extent, and comprehends the transactions of several years, as in the Odyssey and the Æneid, this method therefore seems preferable. When the subject is of smaller compass, and of shorter duration, as in the Iliad, and the Jerusalem, the poet may without disadvantage relate the whole in his own person, as is done in both these poems. In the presentation of the subject, the invocation of the muse, and other ceremonies of the introduction, poets may vary at their pleasure. It is perfectly trifling to make these little formalities the object of precise rule, any farther than that the subject of the work should always be clearly proposed, and without affected or unsuitable pomp. For, according to Horace's noted rule, no introduction should ever set out too high, or promise too much, lest the author should not fulfil the expectations he has raised. What is of most importance in the tenor of the narration is that it be perspicuous, animated, and enriched with all the beauties of poetry. No sort of composition requires more strength, dignity, and fire, than the epic poem. It is the region within which we look for everything that is sublime in description, tender in sentiment, and bold and lively in expression; and, therefore, though an author's plan be faultless, and his story never so well conducted, yet if he be feeble, or flat in style, destitute of affecting scenes, and deficient in poetic coloring, he can have no success. The ornaments which epic poetry admits, must all be of the grave and chaste kind. Nothing that is loose, ludicrous, or affected, finds any place. All objects which it presents, ought to be either great, or tender, or pleasing. Descriptions of disgusting or shocking objects, should as much as possible be avoided; and therefore the fable of the Harpies in the third book of the Æneid, and the allegory of Sin and Death in the second book of Paradise Lost, had been better omitted.

CHAPTER L

THE EPIC (CONTINUED)

REPRESENTATIVE AUTHORS

Homer.— He is the poet who, according to very ancient tradition, is credited with the authorship of the Iliad and the Odyssey, besides a number of hymns written in honor of the gods. Nothing is known of his life or his personality; indeed, modern destructive criticism has led us to doubt whether such a person as Homer ever existed at all. Seven Grecian cities claim to be his birthplace. According to Professor Mahaffy, the home of the original Homer seems to have been about Smyrna; and although his date is quite uncertain, it need not be placed before 800 B. C., and not after 700 B. C.

Criticism by William E. Gladstone.—" The poems of Homer do not constitute merely a great item of the splendid literature of Greece; but they have a separate position, to which none other can approach. They, and the manners they describe, constitute a world of their own; and are served by a sea of time, whose breadth has not been certainly measured, from the firmly set continent of recorded tradition and continuous fact. In this sea, they lie as a great island. And in this island we find not merely details of events, but a scheme of human life and character, complete in all its parts. We are introduced to man in every relation of which he is capable; in every one of his arts, devices, institutions; in the entire circle of his experience. There is no other author whose case is analogous to this, or of whom it can be said that the study of him is not a mere matter of literary criticism, but is a full study of life in every one of its departments."

Homer His Own Witness.—" When we use the word Homer, we do not mean a person historically known to us, like Pope or

487

Milton. We mean in the main the author, whoever, or whatever he was, of the wonderful poems called respectively, not by the author, but by the world, the *Iliad* and the *Odyssey*. His name is conventional, and its sense in etymology is not very different from that which would be conveyed by our phrase, ' the author.' Great artists may be knowable from their works; and there is a singular transparency in the mind, as there is also in the limpid language of Homer. Old as he is, the comprehensive and systematic study of him is still young. It had hardly begun before the 19th century. With the primary source of information found in his text, we have to combine two others: (1) the scattered notices supplied by ancient tradition; and, (2) the valuable and still growing illustrations furnished by the study of language, and by the discoveries and learned study of ancient remains."

Our Earliest View of Him.—" At the first dawn of the historic period, we find the poems established in popular renown; and so prominent that a school of minstrels takes the name of *Homeridae* from making it their business to preserve and to recite them. Still, the question as to whether the poems, as we have them, can be trusted, whether they present substantially the character of what may be termed original documents, is one of great, but gradually diminishing difficulty. It is also of importance, because of the nature of their contents. In the first place, they give a far greater amount of information, than is to be found in any other literary production of the same compass. In the second place, that information, speaking of it generally, is to be had nowhere else. In the third place, it is information of the utmost interest, and even of great moment. It introduces to us, in the very beginnings of their experience, the most gifted people of the world, and enables us to judge how they became such as in later times we know them; how they began to be fitted to discharge the splendid part, allotted to them in shaping the destinies of the world. And this picture is exhibited with such a fulness both of particulars and of vital force, that perhaps never in any country has an age been so completely placed upon record. Finally, amidst the increase of archaic knowledge on all sides, we begin to find a multitude of points of contrast between the Homeric poems and the primitive history of the world, as it is gradually revealed by records, monuments, and language; so that they are coming more and more to constitute an important factor in the formation of that history."

" The place and office of the Greeks in regard to letters, and to the culture of the human mind throughout all time, have been admirably described in the opening section of Mr. Jebb's *Primer of Greek Literature*. It is quite idle for modern theorists to suppose that we can dispense with their aid, or shake off what some would call a thraldom. This could only be done by going back to a state which, whatever its equipments in certain respects, would be, in essential points, one nearer to barbarism than that which we now hold. The work of the Greeks has been done once for all, and for all mankind.

Homer's Relation to It.—" The qualities that mark Greek letters in general are pre-eminently found in Homer; such as force, purpose, measure, fitness, directness, clearness, and completeness. To these he adds a richness and variety, a comprehensive universality, which is given only to the highest genius. The force, which marks a full and healthy development in mind and body, is in the Greeks generally, not thrown idly about, but addressed to an aim. The thought is in strict proportion to the subject, and the language is fitted exactly to the thought. It goes to its end by the straightest road. The clearness of Homer is unrivalled in literature. The passages in which his meaning is open to the smallest shade of doubt, either as to thought or language, might perhaps be counted on the fingers. Such a clearness could hardly survive the advent of philosophy. It was the privilege of the childhood of the race, a true, though an Herculean childhood. Lastly; the assertion may create greater surprise in some, but it is true, that Homer's forms of expression are in a very high degree complete, as a statue shaped and polished to the fingernail was in the Roman proverb complete; not merely in their main outlines, but in refined and subtle detail. The whole of these eminently Greek qualities may be summed up in one phrase — poetic truth."

His Characteristic Style.—" Besides his general prerogative as an universal genius, and besides the properties in which Homer is followed, and as it were, reproduced, in his countrymen, he has other particular gifts of his own. For example, he is probably the most characteristic of all poets. Traits personal to him-

self, inhere in his whole work, and perpetually reappear upon the
surface. Sir Walter Scott has admirably described the fine style
of Swift as the style which puts the right words in the right
places. No more just sentence could have been written on the
style of Homer. But the merit thus described is essentially general. Homer has also the special quality, that all he produces
carries the maker's mark. But the maker's mark, when too
prominent, constitutes what is called mannerism. With Homer,
the maker's mark never obtrudes the maker, or places him between the reader and the theme. It never interferes with the
aim and matter of the poem. Only it is there, ready when
wanted. If we look for it, we find it. We then discover that in
him what we call style, while he has the simplest of all styles, is
also, setting aside the class of mannerists, perhaps the most peculiar to the individual. It would be hardly possible to quote five
lines from him, which must not at once by internal evidence be
recognized as his. Even in the smallest shred of the painting, the
painter's touch is seen. So that though imitated often, in form
and in material, the imitations of him are known by their trick and
effort, not by their likeness."

Homer's Relation to Greek Poetry in Its Several Branches.—
"Passing from these fragmentary remarks, a few words may
be added on Homer's more direct contributions to the literature
of his country, and indeed of the world. From him has been
drawn the epic, which I suppose contests with the drama the
title to supremacy among the kinds of poetry. It seems to me,
however, that Homer stands in a nearer relation, than has commonly been perceived, to the theatre of his country. And this,
not only on account of the remarkable degree in which he con-
ducts the action of his poems through the medium of the speeches.
In its earliest acknowledged stage the Greek drama shows us but
a single actor or reciter, together with a chorus chanting odes
in honor of Dionusos : upon which chorus there certainly devolved
the office of passing judgments, according to right and truth,
upon the action of the piece. Now Homer, reciting his own
poems, was himself an actor, using a musical accompaniment :
and he introduces from time to time, under the name of Tis (tis),
a personage extrinsic to the action, who performs the part of
a judicious observer, and is the organ, like the chorus, of a

sound public opinion. The poetry of Homer appears to have supplied the basis of the hymns which are untruly associated with his name as their composer; and it is easy to perceive how the elegy might find food from his laments (*threnos*) over the dead, and the war-song of Turtaios derive its inspiration from the whole strain of the *Iliad*. In the view of Aristophanes, he seems to have been properly the poet of war. The triumphal hymn of praise, or *paian,* is commemorated in the *Iliad,* as already established in use."

To Oratory.—" There is one noble branch of Greek Literature, which we cannot but refer markedly to Homer, namely, its political oratory. For the oratory of argument and sarcasm, we turn to the embassy of the Ninth *Ilaid* in the barrack of Achilles: for the oratory of passion and withering invective, to the debate in the assembly of the First Book, or to the wonderful speech of Odysseus in reply to the insolence of the Scherian Prince, given in the Eighth *Odyssey*. I know not where to find grander models; and I cannot think Achilles in any way inferior to Demosthenes. Nor was this a bye-blow of the poet's genius. We have seen that the subject of public speech had a large and well-defined place in his mind; and one of the very few passages in his poems, that can be called properly descriptive (introduced however in a speech), will be found in the eight splendid lines of the Third *Iliad* (216-223), which celebrate the eloquence of Odysseus."

To History.—" Less direct than the relation of Homer to the oratory of Greece, but still sufficiently perceptible, is the manner in which his poems supply the first suggestion of the great work of the historians. Apart from the mere incidents of the war of Troy, or from whatever nucleus of truth there may be in the adventures of Odysseus. Homer is the historian of their age in the picture he has given us of its mind, its institutions and its manners. Nor does it seem possible to account for the large number of important pre-Troic Legends that he has introduced, especially into the *Iliad,* upon any other ground than this, that the bard of the heroic age, making use of the only vehicle it afforded, worked with positive historic aims."

Philosophy a Marked Exception.—" But if Homer can thus be exhibited as the father of Greek letters in most of their branches, there is one great exception, which belongs to a later development. That exception was the philosophy of Greece, which seems to have owed its first inception to the Asiatic contact established after the great eastern migration. The absence of all abstract or metaphysical ideas from Homer is truly remarkable. Of all poets, he is the most objective and the least speculative. Of the impersonated Unseen, no poet has made such effective employment; of the Unseen, except as connected with impersonation, he never I think makes use, unless on two occasions; one (vol. vii. 36) where the ships of the Phaiakes are as swift as a wing, or as a thought; and the other, when he compares the agitated mind of Hera with the quickened intelligence of a man stimulated and informed with much travel (*Il.* xv. 30). The nearest approach to these cases is perhaps to be found in such passages as the reflection of Achilles on the mixed dispensation of life, and its preponderating sadness. But this is incorporated thought. Two caskets are on the floor of heaven: the contents are respectively good and evil. From them Zeus dispenses the mixed fortunes of some, and the unmixed misery of others. Homer was not an optimist. But neither did he multiply gratuitous perplexities. The controversies of materialism were unknown to him. All the world, all life, all experience, filled his magazine; for him mind and matter had suffered no breach of harmony. Human life had an aspect mostly sad: but the universe, as to its general constitution, was still in tune."

Criticism by Professor R. C. Jebb.—"Achilles and Odysseus are two characters which always had a strong hold upon the Greek imagination. The Greek idea of human perfection was a wise mind in a beautiful body, good counsel joined to a noble action. Noble action is pre-eminently represented by Achilles, good counsel by Odysseus. Odysseus is brave, but he is especially the man of subtle intellect and ready resource. It was a grave fault of the Greeks that they cared too little whether that quickness of wit which they so much admired, was or was not honest. It is strange that the noble Homeric conception of Odysseus should have been lowered by later Greek poets who, dwelling chiefly on his subtlety, sometimes made him an unscrupulous knave, reckless of everything except personal gain. No such shadow ever fell on the Homeric Achilles. His irresistible might and splendor in war, his stormy human passions, his fine sense, fitting in the son of a goddess, for what is soothing or strengthening in the messages of the gods, his love passing the love of women, his foresight of an early death, even when life was most dazzling, made him glow before the Greek imagination with an immortal youth, as the very type of chivalry in their race. The early ambitions of Alexander the Great were fired by this Homeric vision of Achilles. Nothing can show better how vividly the Homeric Poems wrought in Greek life and history than to see how real the young Greek hero at Troy was to the young Greek conqueror of the East."

Homeric Theology.—" The *Odyssey* bears the marks of a later time than the *Iliad*. Still, there is a general agreement between the two poems in the broad features of the age which they describe. Each poem is a picture of an heroic age on which the poet looks back as far-off in the past, but for his idea of which, he draws in some measure on his own days. The deities of the *Iliad* are colossal men and women, stronger and fairer than mortals, able to work wonders and to take any form they please, but not all-powerful or all-wise, and often immoral. They dwell on the high-crowned mountain Olympus, and are called the Olympian gods. Zeus, a sensual, passionate, but genial person (Jupiter, the sky), is their chief, having overthrown the dynasty of his father Cronus (Saturn), which preceded the Olympian dynasty. Next to Zeus are four great deities — Here, his queen, with whom he quarrels much; Apollo; Athene (who represents especially intelligence); and Poseidon, god of the sea. Other gods sometimes dispute the supremacy of Zeus, and he quells them by threats or by force. The gods act on man chiefly by hurting or comforting his body in some way, and expect some offerings of savoury food and wine. In the *Odyssey* we find a more spiritual conception. Olympus has become a shadowy, far-off place, where the gods dwell apart. Zeus is now indisputably supreme. The gods now act not only on man's body, but also, and chiefly, on his mind and heart. They also wander over the earth in disguise, spying out who are just among men. The Homeric poems did much towards establishing a fixed standard type for each deity, and reconciling the inconsistencies of different local worships.   But they did not *create* this theology, which was far older."

Homeric Morality.—" The Homeric gods punish a man for disobeying or affronting them in any way; but they do not always punish him for immoral actions.   Fear of the gods, then, though powerful as far as it goes, would not go very far towards making the Homeric man moral.   For that he needs a moral law, independent of his religion.   Among the warriors of the *Iliad,* such a law is represented chiefly by what the Greeks call *Aidôs,* and which is often nearly what we call the sense of honor.   Along with this, there is another principle which comes out more clearly in the *Odyssey* than in the *Iliad,* this is *nemesis,* literally ' distribution, then, that feeling which is roused in the mind by an unjust distribution — moral indignation.   A man feels *aidôs* for the opinion of his neighbors.   He feels *nemesis* when his own sense of right is shocked.   In the *Odyssey* we find a riper moral sense than in the *Iliad,* and a much larger number of words to express moral distinctions.   The age of reflection has begun, as the bits of proverbial philosophy in the *Odyssey* show.   Homeric morality is high relatively to Homeric relation; but, as a rule, the Homeric man recognizes duties, not towards his fellow-creatures as such, but only towards certain classes of them, who stand in a special relation to himself, as masters, or dependents, or guests, or suppliants."

Criticism by Frederick Schlegel.—" The relish with which the ancient Greeks appreciated the Homeric poems was materially enhanced by patriotic associations, whilst we are interested in them chiefly as vivid and beautiful representations of heroic life.   They are free from the charge of narrow views, or adulatory panegyrics exclusively bestowed on a particular lineage — a charge such as may be justly preferred against the old songs of Arabia, or those of Ossian.   Breathing the spirit of purest freedom, their representations of the phenomena of nature and of the varieties of human character, evince a sensibility pure and universal.   A whole world opens out before us as we read them, a world of living and moving imagery.   The two prominent figures, Achilles and Ulysses, seem to start from the canvas into warm life; yet they are but characters and ideas so general as to be found repeated in nearly all Greek Hero legends; though never again sketched with so masterly a hand, or so exquisitely finished. Achilles, a hero destined to exhaust all the delights of mortality, whilst still in the bloom and pride of youthful vigor, doomed moreover to be cut off by tragic fate in the prime of his days, is the loftier conception of the two: an echo of this chord may be found in the character of many a hero in the legends of various lands; next in beauty to the Grecian, perhaps, those of our own northern clime. The legendary traditions of heroic times, among the sprightliest nations, are overshadowed by elegiac sensibilities, plaints full of tenderness, and sometimes shrouded in sombre grief. As if the transition from an age of glorious freedom and heroism had impressed succeeding generations with a feeling of dreary confinement, or the bard would transfer to the fictions of those times exclusively, reminiscences of some pristine state of bliss, deep-seated in the bosom of the whole human family. A less magnificent, but still richly-attractive form of poetic heroism is presented in the person of Ulysses, the roving, travelled hero, discreet, and experienced as brave, fitted to undergo danger and encounter adventures of every sort. Ample scope is thus afforded for portraying, in easy flowing style, the rare sights and products of foreign lands. In energy and pathos, the epics of the north, in brilliant coloring, those of the east, as far as our acquaintance extends, may compare with, if they do not surpass, the Homeric poems. But the peculiar distinction of the latter is the amount of living truth and clearness blended in harmonious unison with an almost infantile simplicity and affluent fancy. The narrative, whilst entering into minute detail with all the garrulousness of age, never grows tiresome, owing to the extreme freshness and grace of imagery ever and anon dextrously shifted. Character, passion, and dialogue are unfolded with dramatic skill, and individual circumstances described with almost historical fidelity. From this last quality, which completely distinguishes Homer from all other — even Grecian — bards, he possibly derives his name. Homeros signifies a surety or witness: and on account of his truthful accuracy as a minstrel of the heroic time, he richly deserves this appellation. To us he is, indeed, *Homeros,* a surety as well as a witness of the epic ages in their genuine state. As for the other meaning, relative to his blindness, also involved in the word, it is clearly conjectural, forming part of a tissue of inventions respecting the life of one wholly unknown to us in his person, and it is undeserving of a moment's consideration. Without the direct testimony of Milton it would be sufficiently apparent from internal evidence in his poems, that he saw only with the eye of the spirit, and tasted not the exhilarating joyousness of sunlight. A melancholy haze broods over the page of Ossian, and it may reasonably be inferred that the gloom of night shaded the minstrel's brow. But whoever would ascribe the composition of the *Iliad* and *Odyssey,* the most lucid and transparent of all the poems of antiquity, to a blind bard must, before pronouncing such a verdict, determine to shut his own eyes to every kind of proof and argument. In whatever century the Homeric poems originated, they transport us into times when the heroic element was fast approaching dissolution, or had just expired. Two worlds appear to meet in them: the wondrous past which seemed to be never very far removed from the poet's gaze, whilst occasionally it stood vividly before him; and the present breathing world, in the midst of which he lived and moved.

Virgil.— Publius Virgilius Maro was born near Mantua in 70 B. C.; died at Brundisium in 19 B. C. Next to Homer, he is the most famous of classic epic writers. He was an intimate friend of Horace and enjoyed the patronage of Mæcenas. The last years of his life were spent in Campania. Besides the Æneid, he wrote a number of Eclogues and Georgics.

Criticism by Professor W. Sellar.— "The work which remained for Virgil to accomplish was the addition of a great Roman epic to literature.

It was desirable to select a single heroic action which should belong to the cycle of legendary events celebrated in the Homeric poems, and which should be associated with the whole fortunes of Rome and with the supreme interests of the hour. The only subject which in any way satisfied these apparently irreconcilable conditions was that of the wanderings of Æneas and of his final settlement in Latium. The story, though not of Roman origin, but of a composite growth, had been familiar to the Romans from the beginning of their literature; and had been recognized by official acts of senate and people as associated with the national fortunes. The subject enabled Virgil to tell over again and to give novelty to the tale of the fall of Troy, and to tell a tale of sea-adventure similar to that of the wanderings of Odysseus. But the special applicability of his subject to his purposes was determined by the claim which the Julii, a .patrician family of Alban origin, made to descent from Iulus, the supposed son of Æneas and founder of Alba Longa. The personal, as distinct from the national and artistic, motives of the poem could be satisfied by this subject alone. The *Æneid* is thus at once the epic of the national life under its new conditions and an imitative epic of human actions, manners, and character. The true keynote of the poem is struck in the line with which the poem closes: —

'Tantæ molis erat Romanam condere gentem.'

The idea which underlies the whole action of the poem is that of the great part played by Rome in the history of the world, that part being from of old determined by divine decree, and carried out through the virtue of her sons. The idea of universal empire is thus the dominant idea of the poem. With this idea, that of the unbroken continuity of the national life is intimately associated. The reverence for antiquity, for old customs and the traditions of the past, was a large element in the national sentiment, and has a prominent place in the *Æneid*. So, too, has the feeling of local attachment and of the power of local association over the imagination. It might be said of the manner of life represented in the *Æneid* that it is no more true to any actual condition of human society than that represented in the *Eclogues*. But may not the same be said of all idealizing restoration of a remote past in an age of advanced civilization? The life represented in the *Œdipus Tyrannus* or in *King Lear* is not the life of the Periclan nor of the Elizabethan age, nor is it conceivable as the real life of a prehistoric age. The truth of such a representation is to be judged, not by its relation to any actual state of things ever realized in the world, but by its relation to an ideal of the imagination — the ideal conception of how man, endowed with the gifts and graces of a civilized time, but who had not yet lost the youthful buoyancy of a more primitive age, might play his part under circumstances which would afford scope for the passions and activities of a vigorous personality, and for the refined emotions and subtle reflections of an era of high intellectual and moral cultivation. The verdict of most readers of the *Æneid* will be that Virgil does not satisfy this condition, as it is satisfied by Sophocles and Shakespeare. Yet there is a considerable attraction in the compromise which Virgil has produced, between the life which he knew by experience and that which he saw in the past of his imagination. There is a courtesy, dignity, and consideration for the feelings of others in the manners of his chief personages, such as might be exhibited by the noblest and most commanding natures in an age of chivalry and in an age of culture. The charm of primitive simplicity is present in some passages of the *Æneid,* the spell of luxurious pomp in others. The actual delight of voyaging past beautiful islands, familiar to travelers in the Augustan age, is enhanced by the suggestion of the adventurous spirit which sent the first explorers abroad in search of unknown settlements. Where Virgil is least real, and least successfully ideal, and where consequently he is most purely imitative, is in the battle-scenes of the later books. They afford scope, however, to his patriotic desire to do justice to the martial energy of the Italian races; and some of them have a peculiar beauty from the pathos with which the death of some of the more interesting personages of his story is described."

Even those who have been insensible to the representative and to the human interest of the *Æneid,* have generally recognized the artistic excellence of the poem. This is conspicuous both in the conception of the action and the arrangement of its successive stages and in the workmanship of details. In variety of interest and finish of execution the first eight books are superior to the last four. Each of the former has a large and distinct sphere of interest, and they each contribute to the impression of the work as a whole. In the first book, we have the spectacle of the storm, of the prophecy of Jove, and of the building of Carthage; in the second, the spectacle of the destruction of Troy; in the third, the voyage among the islands and coasts of the Mediterranean; in the fourth, the tragedy of Dido; in the fifth, the rest in the Sicilian bay, at the foot of Mount Eryx; in the sixth, the revelation of the spiritual world of Virgil's imagination, and of the souls of those who built up the greatness of Rome in their pre-existent state, in their shadowy dwelling-place; in the seventh, the arrival of the Trojans at the mouth of the Tiber and the gathering of the Italian clans; in the eighth, the first sight of the hills of Rome, and the prophetic representation of the great crises in Roman history leading up to the greatest of them all, the crowning victory of Actium. Among these books we may infer that Virgil assigned the palm to the second, the fourth, and the sixth, as he selected them to read to Augustus and the members of the imperial family. The interest flags in the last four; nor is it possible to feel the culminating sympathy with the final combat between Hector and Achilles. Yet a personal interest is awakened in the adventures and fate of Pallas, Lausus, and Camilla. Virgil may himself have become weary of the succession of battle-scenes — 'eadem horrida bella,'— which the requirements of epic poetry rather than the impulses of his own genius or the taste of his readers called upon him to portray; and this may partly account for the sense of discouragement which he is supposed to have felt at the end of his labors. There is not only a less varied interest, there is greater inequality of workmanship of the later books, owing to the fact that they had not received their author's final revisal. Yet in them there are many lines and passages of great power, pathos, and beauty. Virgil brought the two great instruments of varied and continuous harmony and of a rich, chastened, and noble style to the highest perfection of which the Latin tongue was capable. The rhythm and style of the *Æneid* is more unequal than the rhythm and style of the *Georgics,* but is a larger and more varied instrument. The note of his supremacy among all the poetic artists of his country is that subtle fusion of the music and the meaning of language which touches the deepest and most secret springs of emotion. He touches especially the emotions of reverence and of a yearning for a higher spiritual life, and the sense of nobleness in human affairs, in great institutions, and great natures; the sense of the sanctity of human affections, of the imaginative spell exercised by the past, of the mystery of the unseen world. This is the secret of the power which his words have had over some of the deepest and greatest natures both in ages of faith and in more positive times. No words more subtly and truly express the magic of his style than those in which Dr. Newman characterizes 'his single words and phrases, his pathetic half-lines, giving utterance as the voice of nature herself to that pain and weariness, yet hope of better things, which is the experience of her children in every age.' "

Criticism by Charles Anthon, LL.D.—"The *Æneid* has for its subject the settlement of the Trojans in Italy. This production belongs to a nobler class of poetry than the *Georgics,* and is, perhaps, equally perfect in its kind. It ranks, indeed, in the very highest order, and it was in this exalted species that Virgil was most fitted to excel. Undisturbed by excess of passion, and never hurried away by the current of ideas, he calmly consigned to immortal verse the scenes which his fancy had first painted as lovely, and which his understanding had afterward approved. The extent, too, and depth of the design proposed in the *Æneid,* rendered this subjection to the judgment indispensable. It would be absurd to suppose, with some critics, that Virgil intended to give instruction to princes in the art of settling colonies (Catrou, *Œuvres de Virgile,* vol. 3, p. 486), or to supply Augustus with political rules for the government and legislation of a great empire; but he evidently designed, not merely to deduce the descent of Augustus and the Romans from Æneas and his companions, but, by creating a perfect character in his hero, to shadow out the eminent qualities of his imperial patron; to recommend his virtues to his countrymen, who would readily apply to him the amiable portrait; and perhaps to suggest that he was the ruler of the world announced of old by the prophecies and oracles of the Saturnian land. (Æn. 6, 789, seqq.) No one who has read the *Æneid,* and studied the historical character of Augustus, or the early events of his reign, can doubt that Æneas is an allegorical representation of that emperor. The chief objection which critics in all ages have urged against the *Æneid,* or at least, against the poetical character of its author, is the defect in what forms the most essential quality of a poet, originality and the power of invention. It has never, indeed, been denied that he possessed a species of invention, if it may be so called, which consists in placing ideas that have been preoccupied in a new light, or presenting assemblages, which have been already exhibited, in a new point of view. Nor has it been disputed that he often succeeds in bestowing on them the charm of novelty, by the power of more perfect diction, and by that poetic touch which transmutes whatever it lights on, into gold. But it is alleged that he has contrived few incidents, and opened up no new veins of thought. It is well known that the Roman dramatic writers, instead of contriving plots of their own, translated the masterpieces of Sophocles, Euripides, and Menander. The same imitative spirit naturally enough prevailed in the first attempts at epic poetry. When any beautiful model exists in an art, it so engrosses and intimidates the mind, that we are apt to think that, in order to execute successfully any work of a similar description, the approved prototype must be imitated. It is supposed that what had pleased once, must please always; and circumstances, in themselves unimportant, or perhaps accidental, are converted into general and immutable rules. It was natural, then, for the Romans, struck with admiration at the sublime and beautiful productions of the epic muse of Greece, to follow her lesson with servility. The mind of Virgil also led him to imitation. His excellence lay in the propriety, beauty, and majesty of his poetical character, in his judicious contrivance of composition, his correctness of drawing, his purity of taste, his artful adaptation of the conception of others to his own purposes, and his skill in the combination of materials. Accordingly, when Virgil first applied himself to frame a poem, which might celebrate his imperial master, and emulate the productions of Greece, in a department of poetry wherein she was as yet unrivalled, he first naturally bent a reverent eye on Homer; and, though he differed widely from his Grecian master in the qualities of his mind and genius, he became his most strict and devoted disciple. The Latin dramatists, in preparing their pieces for the stage, had frequently compounded them of the plots of two Greek plays, melted, as it were, into one; and thus compensated for the want of invention and severe simplicity of composition by greater richness and variety of incident. From their example, Virgil comprehended in his plan the arguments both of the *Iliad* and *Odyssey;* the one serving him as a guide for the wanderings and adventures of his hero previous to the landing in Latium, and the other as a model for the wars which he sustained in Italy, to gain his destined bride, Lavinia. He had thus before him all the beauties and defects of Homer, as lights to gaze at and as rocks to be shunned with the judgment of ages on both, as a chart which might conduct him to yet greater perfection."

Dante.—Dante Alighieri was born in Florence in 1265, and died at Ravenna in 1321. He was, like his father, a member of the Guelph party. Later on, he strove to unite the Guelph and Ghibellines, and thus became known as the "First Italian." His immortal poem was written while the author suffered exile for his political views. He wandered from one country to another, according to one account, visiting Oxford. He shares with Homer, Virgil and Milton the honor of being one of the four great epic writers of the world. His English translators, Cary, Norton and Longfellow, are widely known.

Criticism by Thomas Carlyle.—"I give Dante my highest praise when I say of his *Divine Comedy* that it is, in all senses, genuinely a Song. In the very sound of it there is a *canto fermo;* it proceeds as by a chant. The language, his simple *Terza rima,* doubtless helped him in this. The essence and material of the work are themselves rhythmic. Its depth and rapt passion and sincerity make it musical; go deep enough, there is music everywhere. A true inward symmetry, what one calls an architectural harmony, reigns in it, proportionates it all: architectural; which also partakes of the character of music. The three kingdoms, Inferno, Purgatorio, Paradiso, look out on one another like compartments of a great edifice, a great supernatural world-cathedral, piled up there, stern, solemn, awful. It is at bottom the *sincerest* of all poems, and sincerity is also the measure of its worth. It came deep out of the author's heart of hearts; and it goes deep, and through long generations, into ours. Perhaps one ought to say that *intensity* is the prevailing character of Dante's genius; his greatness has concentred itself into fiery emphasis and depth; he pierces down into the very heart of Being—I know nothing so intense as Dante. There is a brevity, an abrupt precision in him: Tacitus is not briefer, more condensed. It is strange with what a sharp, decisive grace he snatches the true likeness of a matter; cuts into the matter as with a pen of fire. Dante's painting is not graphic only, brief, true, and of a vividness as of fire in dark night; taken on the wider scale it is every way noble, and the outcome of a great soul. Dante is the spokesman of the Middle Ages; the thought they lived by stands here, in everlasting music. These sublime ideas of his, terrible and beautiful, are the fruit of the Christian Meditation of all good men who had gone before him. As to his influence and permanence, Dante speaks. to the noble, the pure and great, in all times and places. Neither does he grow obsolete; he burns as a pure star, fixed there in the firmament, at which the great and high of all ages kindle themselves: he is the possession of all the chosen of the world for uncounted time."

Criticism by Brother Azarias.—"A study of the 'Divina Commedia,' in any of its aspects, must needs be a study of the age in which it was produced, of the man out of the fulness of whose soul it issued in notes strong and clear, and of the various influences that made their impress upon both the man and the poem. Of all the supreme efforts of creative genius, the 'Divina Commedia' is that that can least be taken out of the times and circumstances that gave it birth. Its contemporary history and its contemporary spirit constitute its clearest and best commentary."

"The age of Dante was preeminently a Catholic age. It was an age when men lived in one faith, had one ritual, recited one creed, were taught one and the same doctrine and practice, and breathed a common religious atmosphere. In this respect there is a marked contrast between the Time-spirit of that day and the Time-spirit of the present. The great chorus of modern thought is a loud proclaiming of pessimism and the despair that would destroy a hereafter, annihilate the soul, and ignore a Personal Divinity. It acts in open defiance of the whole Christian codes of the spiritual truth and the spiritual law that are essential elements in all modern conduct and modern thinking. 'Its crowning dogma,' says a recent writer, 'is written even now between the lines in many a dainty volume, that evil has a secret holiness, and sin a consecrating magnificence.' Now of this agnostic spirit must we divest ourselves in entering upon a study of Dante's masterpiece. There we will find no doubt. All is intense earnestness. The light of faith guides the poet's steps through the hopeless chambers of Hell with a firmness of con-

viction that knows no wavering; it bears him through the
sufferings of purgatory, believing strongly in its reality; it raises
him on the wings of love and contemplation into heaven's empyrean, where he really hopes to enjoy bliss far beyond aught
whereof he sings. If we would understand the animating
principle of the poem, it behooves us to cast aside all idea
that these divisions of it were a mere barbarous and cumber-
some machinery. Not in this fashion are epoch-making works
constructed. Dante believed in the existence of these places
and in the reality of their woes and their joys as firmly as he
believed in himself. The simple faith pervading this poem
contrasts strikingly with the spirit animating 'Faust.' The latter is designed to represent the innate conflict of the savage
in man against established law and order in the moral, social, and
physical world. Mephistopheles is the evil genius of the hero.
He impersonates the negation of truth and goodness. But much
as the spirit-world figures in Goethe's masterpiece, it does so
not as a living reality, but as a mere scaffolding whereby Goethe
builds up the artistic structure of the experiences gathered from
study and observation, or found in the recesses of his own large
worldly heart. And what is the uppermost lesson that one may
read on every page of that wonderful panorama of modern life?
As we understand it, we read simply the dark lesson, that only
through the experiences that come of all manner of self-indul-
gence and self-gratification may one reach the broader view of
life and attain perfection. This is attempting to make one's
own way out of the wood of error and wrong-doing at the risk
of being devoured by the beasts of predominant sin and passion.
The hero is guilty of crime the most atrocious; he brings ruin
in his wake; up to his last hour, he is sensual and covetous; he
deserts not his sins; rather his sins desert him. There are
regrets; in one instance there is remorse; but there is no con-
version. And yet, as though in mockery of the Christian ideal
of personal purity and holiness, this sinful soul is triumphantly
borne to heaven amid the songs of angels. The poet represents
him as saved by the only saving principle on, or above, or under
the earth — the principle of Love: 'Whoever striving exerts
himself, him can we redeem, *and if he also participates in the
love from on high, the Blessed Host shall meet him with heartiest
welcome.*' Faust, like Dante in his poem, is the special object

of womanly love. She whose heart he broke pleads in his behalf before the Mater Gloriosa, and her prayer is heard. Faust is saved. Through wreck and ruin of soul and body he reaches the solution of life's riddle. 'Faust' is a poem of selfishness. How does Dante treat the same theme of struggle and salvation? How does he introduce the same element of womanly love? Beatrice, after upbraiding Dante for his sins, says: 'God's high destiny would be broken if Lethe were passed and such food were tasted without the repentance that breaks forth in tears.' Such is womanly love in Dante's conception: spiritual, elevating, ennobling, strengthening, ideal. These characteristics we fail to see in Goethe's conception. To his mind, womanly love is merely a blind love, all-enduring and all-forgiving. But 'Faust' is the world-poem of this century, even as the 'Divina Commedia' is of the thirteenth. Goethe is the mouthpiece of the modern world; the Middle Ages sing through Dante. And as each was a child of his age, the personality of each is a determining element written into the fibre of both great poems."

"The music of the 'Paradiso' is the music of spiritual life; and the music of spiritual life can be interpreted only by those into whose existence spiritual life enters as a living, breathing reality. It is a music articulate and familiar to each religious man. It throbs in his every aspiration. His ear has been attuned to its exquisite cadences; its harmony vibrates through the pages of the spiritual book he reads; it is re-echoed in the sermons and exhortations he hears and in the hymns he chants; his whole life is the clearest commentary upon this poem — rather his life is itself the living poem from which Dante has made a marvelous though still imperfect transcript. In the noblest themes of that transcript, he recognizes echoes of the thoughts, sentiments, and aspirations that in his own breast are continuously humming unspeakable music. The fervor and love and high thought that are all so grandly intensified in the terse rhythm of the 'Divina Commedia" are the ferver and love and high thought that are daily moving tens of thousands of men and women to lead the spiritual life therein portrayed in obedience to the Love Divine that rules hearts and sways the heavens in perpetual harmony. The religious man in sauntering through the vast aisles and chapels of this noble cathedral of song, here admiring a tender and touching picture, there gazing upon a

scene of terror penciled in vivid colors, again drinking in the
sweet and inspiring strains of its clear organ-tones, feels that
beneath its solemn arches his soul may rest, for he is at home
in his Father's House."

Milton.— John Milton was born in 1608 and died in 1674.
He was the son of a London Scrivener. He studied at St.
Paul's School and at Christ's College, Cambridge. Milton
was made Latin Secretary to the new Commonwealth which
was inaugurated by Cronwell. The writings of Milton are
voluminous, divided between verse and prose. Much of his
prose work is polemic; his verse is lyric and dramatic as well
as epic; the *Ode on the Nativity,* the *Sonnet to Shakespeare,*
the *Samson Agonistes* share with *Paradise Lost* the glory of
being supremely great literature. Milton is the fourth great
epic writer in the order of time.

Criticism by Mark Pattison.—" Poetry has been defined as
' the suggestion of noble grounds for the noble emotions,' and,
in this respect, none of the world-epics — there are at most five
such in existence — can compete with *Paradise Lost.* The
melancholy pathos of Lucretius, indeed, pierces the heart with a
two-edged sword more keen than Milton's, but the compass of
Lucretius' horizon is much less, being limited to this earth and
its inhabitants. The horizon of *Paradise Lost* is not narrower
than all space, its chronology not shorter than eternity; the globe
of our earth a mere spot in the physical universe, and that universe itself, a drop suspended in the infinite empyrean. His aspirations had thus reached ' one of the highest arcs that human
contemplation circling upwards can make from the glassy sea
whereon she stands.' (Doctr. and Disc.). Like his contemporary, Pascal, his mind had beaten her wings against the prison
walls of human thought.

" Milton's diction is the elaborated outcome of all the best
words of all antecedent poetry, not by a process of recollected
reading and storage, but by the same mental habit by which we
learn to speak our mother-tongue. Only, in the case of the poet,
the vocabulary acquired has a new meaning superadded to the

words, from the occasion on which they have been previously
employed by others. Words, over and above their dictionary
significance, connote all the feeling which has gathered round
them by reason of their employment through a hundred generations of song. In the words of Mr. Myers, ' without ceasing
to be a logical step in the argument, a phrase becomes a centre
of emotional force. The complex associations which it evokes
modify the associations evoked by other words in the same passage, in a ·way distinct from logical or grammatical conception.'
The poet suggests much more than he says, or, as. Milton himself has phrased it, ' more is meant than meets the ear.' For
the purpose of poetry, a thought is the representative of many
feelings, and a word is the representative of many thoughts.
A single word may thus set in motion in us the vibration of a
feeling first consigned to letters 3,000 years ago. For oratory
words should be winged, that they may do their work of persuasion. For poetry, words should be freighted with association
of feeling, that they may awaken sympathy. It is the suggestive
power of words that the poet cares for, rather than their current
denotation. How laughable are the attempts of the commentators to interpret a line in Virgil as they would a sentence in
Aristotle's *Physics!* Milton's secret lies in his mastery over the
rich treasures of this inherited vocabulary. He wielded it as
his own, as a second mother-tongue, the native and habitual
idiom of his thought and feeling, backed by a massive frame of
character, and ' a power which is got within me to a passion.'
(*Areopagitica.*)

  " When Wordsworth came forward at the end of the eighteenth century with his famous reform of the language of
English poetry, the Miltonic diction was the current coin paid
out by every versifier. Wordsworth revolted against this dialect
as unmeaning, hollow, gaudy, and, in phraseology altogether
abandoned it, reverting to the common language of ordinary life.
It was necessary to do this in order to recount poetry with the
sympathies of men, and make it again a true utterance, instead of
the ingenious exercise in putting together words which it had
become. In projecting this abandonment of the received tradition, it may be thought that Wordsworth was condemning the
Miltonic system of expression in itself. But this was not so.
Milton's language had become, in the hands of the imitators of

the eighteenth century, sound without sense, a husk without the kernel, a body of words without the soul of poetry. Milton had created and wielded as instrument which was beyond the control of any less than himself. He wrote it as a living language; the poetasters of the eighteenth century wrote it as a dead language, as boys make Latin verses. Their poetry is to *Paradise Lost,* as a modern Gothic restoration is to a genuine Middle-Age church. It was against the feeble race of imitators, and not against the master himself, that the protest of the Lake poet was raised. He proposed to do away with the Miltonic vocabulary altogether, not because it was in itself vicious, but because it could now only be employed at second-hand. One draw-back there was attendant upon the style chosen by Milton, viz., that it narrowly limited the circle of his readers. All words are addressed to those who understand them. The Welsh triads are not for those who have not learnt Welsh; an English poem is only for those who understand English. But of understanding English there are many degrees; it requires some education to understand literary style at all. A large majority of the natives of any country possess, and use, only a small fraction of their mother-tongue. These people may be left out of the discussion. Confining ourselves only to that small part of our millions which we speak of as the educated classes — that is, those whose schooling is carried on beyond fourteen years of age — it will be found that only a small fraction of the men, and a still smaller fraction of the women, fully apprehend the meaning of words. This is the case with what is written in the ordinary language of books. When we pass from a style in which words have only their simple significance, to a style of which the effect depends on the suggestion of collateral association, we leave behind the majority even of these few. This is what is meant by the standing charge against Milton that he is too learned.

"The style of *Paradise Lost* is then only the natural expression of a soul thus exquisitely nourished upon the best thoughts and finest words of all ages. It is the language of one who lives in the companionship of the great and the wise of past time. It is inevitable that when such a one speaks, his tones, his accent, the melodies of his rhythm, the inner harmonies of his linked thoughts, the grace of his illusive touch, should escape the common ear. To follow Milton one should have at least tasted the same training through which he put himself. ' *Te quoque dignum finge deo.'* The many cannot see it, and they complain that the poet is too learned. They would have Milton talk like Bunyan or William Cobbett, whom they understand. Milton did attempt the demagogue in his pamphlets, only with the result of blemishing his fame and degrading his genius. The best poetry is that which calls upon us to rise to it, not that which writes down to us.

" There is an element of decay and death in poems which we vainly style immortal. Some of the sources of Milton's power are already in process of drying up. I do not speak of the ordinary caducity of language, in virtue of which every effusion of the human spirit is lodged in a body of death. Milton suffers little as yet from this cause. There are few lines in his poems which are less intelligible now than they were at the time they were written. This is partly to be ascribed to his limited vocabulary, Milton, in his verse, using not more than eight thousand words, or about half the number used by Shakespeare. Nay, the position of our earlier writers has been improved by the mere spread of the English language over a wider area. Addison apologized for *Paradise Lost* falling short of the *Æneid,* because of the inferiority of the language in which it was written. " So divine a poem in English is like a stately palace built of brick." The defects of English for purposes of rhythm and harmony are as great now as they ever were, but the space that our speech fills in the world is vastly increased, and this increase of consideration is reflected back upon our older writers. But if, as a treasury of poetic speech, *Paradise Lost* has gained by time, it has lost far more as a storehouse of divine truth. We at this day are better able than ever to appreciate its force of expression, its grace of phrase, its harmony of rhythmical movement, but it is losing its hold over our imagination. Strange to say, this failure of vital power in the constitution of the poem is due to the very selection of subject by which Milton sought to secure perpetuity. Not content with being the poet of men, and with describing human passions and ordinary events, he aspired to present the destiny of the whole race of mankind, to tell the story of creation, and to reveal the councils of heaven and hell. And he would raise this structure upon no unstable base, but upon the sure foundation of the written Word. It would have been a thing incredible to Milton that the hold of the Jewish Scriptures over the imagination of English men and women could ever be weakened. This process, however, has already commenced. The demonology of the poem has already, with educated readers, passed from the region of fact into that of fiction. Not so, universally, but with a large number of readers, the angelology can be no more than what the critics call machinery. And it requires a violent effort from any of our day to accommodate our conceptions to the anthropomorphic theology of *Paradise Lost*. Were the sapping process to continue at the same rate for two more centuries, the possibility of epic illusion would be lost to the whole scheme and economy of the poem. Milton has taken a scheme of life for life itself. Had he, in the choice of subject, remembered the principle of the Aristotelean Poetic (which he otherwise highly prized), that men in action are the poet's proper theme, he would have raised his imaginative fabric on a more permanent foundation; upon the appetites, passions, and emotions of men, their vices and virtues, their aims and ambitions, which are a far more constant quantity than any theological system. This, perhaps, was what Goethe meant when he pronounced the subject of *Paradise Lost* to be abominable, with a fair outside, but rotten inwardly.' "

Criticism by Lord Macaulay.—" The only poem of modern times which can be compared with the *Paradise Lost* is the *Divine Comedy*. The subject of Milton, in some points, resembled that of Dante; but he has treated it in a widely different manner. We cannot, we think, better illustrate our opinion respecting our own great poet, than by contrasting him with the father of Tuscan literature. The poetry of Milton differs from that of Dante as the hieroglyphics of Egypt differed from the picture writing of Mexico. The images which Dante employs speak for themselves; they stand simply for what they are. Those of Milton have a signification which is often discernible only to the initiated. Their value depends less on what they directly represent than on what they remotely suggest. However strange, however grotesque, may be the appearance which Dante undertakes to describe, he never shrinks from describing it. He gives us the shape, the color, the sound, the smell, the taste; he counts the numbers; he measures the size. His similes are the illustrations of a traveler. Unlike those of other poets, and especially of Milton, they are introduced in a plain, businesslike, manner; not for the sake of any beauty in the objects from which they are drawn; not for the sake of any ornament which they may impart to the poem; but simply in order to make the meaning of the writer as clear to the reader as it is to himself. The ruins of the precipice which led from the sixth to the seventh circle of hell, were like those of the rock which fell into the Adige on the south of Trent. The cataract of Phlegethon was like that of Aqua Cheta at the monastery of St. Benedict. The place where the heretics were confined in burning tombs resembled the vast cemetery of Arles.

" Poetry which relates to the beings of another world, ought to be at once mysterious and picturesque, indeed, beyond any that ever was written. Its effect approaches to that produced by the pencil or the chisel. But it is picturesque to the exclusion of all mystery. This is a fault on the right side, a fault inseparable from the plan of Dante's poem, which, as we have already observed, rendered the utmost accuracy of description necessary. Still, it is a fault. The supernatural agents excite an interest; but it is not the interest which is proper to supernatural agents. We feel that we could talk to the ghosts and demons, without any emotion of unearthly awe. We could, like Don Juan, ask them to supper, and eat heartily in their company. Dante's angels are good men with wings. His devils are spiteful, ugly, executioners. His dead men are merely living men in strange situations. The scene which passes between the poet and Farinata is justly celebrated. Still, Farinata in the burning tomb is exactly what Farinata would have been at an *auto da fé.* Nothing can be more touching than the first interview of Dante and Beatrice. Yet, what is it but a lovely woman chiding, with sweet, austere composure, the lover for whose affection she is grateful, but whose vices she reprobates? The feelings which give the passage its charm would suit the streets of Florence as well as the summit of the Mount of Purgatory.

" To return for a moment to the parallel which we have been attempting to draw between Milton and Dante, we would add that the poetry of these great men has in a considerable degree taken its character from their moral qualities. They are not egotists. They rarely obtrude their idiosyncrasies on their readers. They have nothing in common with those modern beggars for fame, who extort a pittance from the compassion of the inexperienced, by exposing the nakedness and sores of their minds. Yet it would be difficult to name two writers whose works have been more completely, though undesignedly, colored by their personal feelings. The character of Milton was peculiarly distinguished by loftiness of spirit; that of Dante, by intensity of feeling. In every line of the *Divine Comedy* we discern the asperity which is produced by pride struggling with misery. There is perhaps no work in the world so deeply and uniformly sorrowful. The melancholy of Dante was no fantastic caprice. It was not, as far as at this distance of time can be judged, the effect of external circumstances. It was from within. Neither love nor glory, neither the conflicts of earth nor the hope of heaven, could dispel it. It turned every consolation and every pleasure into its own nature. It resembled that noxious Sardinian soil of which the intense bitterness is said to have been perceptible even in its honey. His mind was, in the noble language of the Hebrew poet, ' a land of darkness, as darkness itself, and where the light was as darkness.' The gloom of his character discolors all the passions of men, and all the face of nature, and tinges with its own livid hue the flowers of Paradise and the glories of the eternal throne. All the portraits of him are singularly characteristic. No person can look on the features, noble even to ruggedness, the dark furrows of the cheek, the haggard and woeful stare of the eye, the sullen and contemptuous curve of the lip, and doubt that they belong to a man too proud and too sensitive to be happy. Milton was, like Dante, a statesman and a lover; and, like Dante, he had been unfortunate in ambition and in love. He had survived his health and his sight, the comforts of his home and the prosperity of his party. Of the great men by whom he had been distinguished at his entrance into life, some had been taken away from the evil to come; some had carried into foreign climates their unconquerable hatred of oppression; some were pining in dungeons; and some had poured forth their blood on scaffolds. Venal and licentious scribblers, with just sufficient talent to clothe the thoughts of a pander in the style of a bellman, were now the favorite writers of the sovereign and of the public. It was a loathsome herd, which could be compared to nothing so filthy as to the rabble of 'Comus,' grotesque monsters, half bestial, half human, dropping with wine, bloated with gluttony, and reeling in obscene dances. Amidst these, that fair Muse was placed, like the chaste lady of the lofty, spotless, and serene, to be chattered at, and pointed at, and grinned at, by the whole rout of satyrs and goblins. If ever despondency and asperity could be excused in any man, they might have been excused in Milton. But the strength of his mind overcame every calamity. Neither blindness, nor gout, nor age, nor penury, nor domestic afflictions, nor political disappointments, nor abuse, nor proscription, nor neglect, had power to disturb his sedate and majestic patience. His spirits do not seem to have been high, but they were singularly equable. His temper was serious, perhaps stern; but it was a temper which no sufferings could render sullen or fretful. Such as it was when, on the eve of great events, he returned from his travels, in the prime of health and manly beauty, loaded with literary distinctions, and glowing with patriotic hopes; such it continued to be when, after having experienced every calamity which is incident to our nature, old, poor, sightless, and disgraced, he retired to his hovel to die."

Minor Epics.—The minor epics of the world are the Ramayana, Maha-bharata, Kalevala, Beowulf, Nibelungen Lied, Song of Roland, Shah-namah, Poem of the Cid, Orlando Furioso, Lusiad, Jerusalem Delivered, Messiad. The conditions for the production of the primitive epic exist but once in a nation's growth; and most nations have been fortunate enough to take advantage of the opportunity. Constructed upon the noblest principles of art and pervaded by the eternal calm of the immortals, the above-mentioned epics are of undying interest to the nations whose gifted sons produce them. But it was given to their more exalted brethren — Homer, Virgil, Dante, and Milton — to break down national barriers and appeal with almost equal interest to every nation and to every age; and for this reason the latter were selected here as the best representatives of the epic.

CHAPTER LI

THE LYRIC

Its Place.— The lyric occupies the third, or lowest place, among standard verse-forms. It is preceded by the drama and the epic, and like the letter in prose, is lowest on the scale, so far as value and importance are concerned.

Origin of the Term.— The term, lyric, derived from the word, *lyra,* was first applied to a musical instrument of the harp family. At a later date it was applied to the songs adapted to the harp or lyre, and in this connection involved both music and poetry. For the lines thus written were composed for the sole purpose of being set to music. Hence, lyric poetry among the ancients was known as songs or psalms.

Present Scope.—At the present time the lyric has a wider significance, meaning not only poetry set to music, but all miscellaneous work outside the domain of the epic and the drama.

Exceptions.—An exception is made of what is called didactic poetry. This class lies outside the domain of epic and drama, yet it cannot be classified as lyric. Its length and sustained thought, together with an almost complete absence of emotion, give it anything but a lyric character. The fact is that didactic poetry represents an abnormal creation; it is an attempt to combine philosophy or science with the imaginative process of poetry. The result is neither good philosophy nor genuine poetry. The didactic poem, as Blair remarks, differs only in form, not in scope or substance, from a philosophical, a moral or a critical treatise in prose. Thus, so far as it can be classified at all, it belongs to the department of philosophy rather than poetry. A second exception is sometimes made of the satire, and pastoral poetry. But these often take a lyric form. Otherwise, they are heroic in character, and belong to epic literature.

Marks of the Lyric.— *Briefness.*— The lyric is recognized in four ways. First, by its briefness. It is invariably a brief production. This is due to the fact that the author uses the lyric as a vehicle for intense passion or a passing mood. Intense passion is by nature of short duration, and in art must have the briefest expression. It is, therefore, as Tennyson describes it, " a short swallow-flight of song."

Emotional Value.— The lyric is also recognized on account of its emotional value. It is always intended to arouse the feelings of the reader or hearer. Its success depends upon the amount of passion thus aroused. And because of this appeal to the emotions, the lyric is made the most musical of all literary work. Among primitive or savage races, it acted as a spell or incantation, so strong was its influence over the emotions. Among the most highly civilized nations, the lyric known as the national anthem has an almost equal influence.

Subjectivity.—The lyric is recognized on account of its subjectivity. It expresses the feeling of the writer; it represents his own mood or passion, not the mood or passion of another. Hence, it is quite different from the drama wherein the author describes the thoughts and feelings of characters which he has created; also, from the epic wherein external events and circumstances are described. Both the drama and the epic are objective, whereas the lyric is a self-revelation on the part of the author.

Flexibility of Form.— The lyric is known by its flexibility of form. The least art is required in the plan of a lyric. It is adjusted so as to express every feeling, mood and fancy. Like the letter, it may be made highly artificial; but in such cases the charm is lessened or destroyed. Its normal condition is one of largest freedom. Thus, the psalm in Hebrew literature and the ballad in the folk-lore of all nations are unrivalled representatives of the lyric.

Meter and Style in the Lyric.— Lyric poetry is nowhere more varied than in its metre, and it offers an interesting field for the study of this element of poetic form. It uses feet of all kinds and lines of every length. No particular foot is especially characteristic, the kind of foot being determined by the spirit of the poem. The most common lines are the tetrameter and pentameter. The use of end rhyme is almost universal in modern lyrics. There is also an abundance of alliteration and assonance; and likewise a studied effort to give vowel sounds the preference. These elements determine in large measure the quality and effect of the music. The very diversity of lyric meter makes specific directions impossible.

Style.— In style the lyric is subject to the same laws as other literature; but the various qualities are nowhere manifested more fully and vividly. Intellectual qualities of style are less strongly marked, for the lyric is not predominantly intellectual in substance. As a rule, however, it is more subtle and abstruse than the epic; because subjective moods or states often so highly complex are less easy to express than simple epic narrative. Emotional qualities of style are expected to be present in the fullest measure. Wit, humor, pathos, sublimity, beauty, melody, are all present. The lyric covers the whole range of feeling. The emotion that is universal and thoroughly human prevails. Hence, grief, devotion, love, patriotism, hope, are the constant theme and determine the style of the lyric.

Suggestiveness.— One characteristic of the lyric style is its suggestiveness. The lyric is the most highly suggestive form of literature, owing to the narrow limits within which the artist must work. This suggestiveness applies both to thought development and to illustration or picture work. The artist has not room to give every thought or every picture in detail. Often the slightest hint must serve where a paragraph of amplification would be given in prose, and would be required to express the thought in full. Hence, the condensed or concise style of the lyric. The intellect and imagination of the reader are thus kept active. This is particularly true of the lyric produced in a highly civilized state of society. For example, Pindar, Horace, Tennyson.

In Relation to Epic and Drama.— As a work of art, the lyric is inferior to the epic or the drama. It requires neither an elaborate plan nor character creation. Like the letter in prose, the lyric is ubiquitous; it enters into the composition of both drama and epic. These higher verse forms originated in the lyric, and both retain lyric elements. The drama grew out of the hymn; the epic came from the hymn and the ballad. At the present time the lyric retains a three-fold relation to the drama — first, in the songs sung by the various characters in the progress of dramatic action; second, in the orchestral music or interludes between the acts; third, in the prelude and epilogue of the drama. For example, the lyrics scattered through the plays of Shakespeare would form a small volume. And they are still more numerous in the Greek drama, owing to the important part taken by the chorus.

In the Epic.— The lyric is frequently employed in the construction of the epic. Both ancient and modern epics employ material drawn from the supernatural world. Epic heroes are invariably associated with angels or deities. Hence, hymns, prayers, invocations, are woven into the story. For example, the prayers of Æneas on his voyage to Italy; the prayers of our first parents in *Paradise Lost;* the invocations of Dante in passing through purgatory, hell, heaven.

In Relation to Prose.— The lyric finds its way into almost every department of prose, especially the letter, essay, oratory, and fiction. It is there in the form of quotation, and is often demanded by the highly emotional character of the work.

Classification.— Lyrics are classified, first of all, on the basis of form; so that we have, for example, the song, the sonnet, the ode, and the quatrain. Secondly, they are classified according to the emotion which they excite. These emotions may be religious, patriotic, amorous, humorous; hence, the hymn or dirge, the national anthem, the love-song, the ballad, lampoon. As the prevailing mood is identified with the subject-matter, this last division is really based upon the themes treated, such as God, country, man, art, nature.

The Sacred Lyric.— As the title indicates, it deals with God and the supernatural world. It is inspired by religion. It is the oldest lyric in literature; for besides such ancient productions as the Indian and Vedic Hymns, this lyric was sung by Moses and Miriam after the passage of the Red Sea. The Book of Psalms is the best known collection of sacred lyrics in the Hebrew literature; although throughout the books of the Old Testament a number of fine lyrics are scattered, as, for example, the odes of David and Hannah in the books of Samuel, celebrating the mercy and goodness of the Lord.

Causes of Lyric Growth.— On account of their national isolation the Hebrews developed a subjective quality in their character; they brooded, meditated upon themselves and their

Creator, and their many sacred lyrics are the literary result of such meditation. To this cause we may add the rich and varied natural scenery of Palestine. All the charm and variety of Oriental tropic scenery are present; so that no country furnishes better material for imaginative work. As a consequence, we have the grand imagery of the Hebrew Psalms.

The Sacred Lyric in the Christian Era.— The hymns of Christians in all countries and ages are classified as sacred lyrics which have about the same significance as the psalms under the old dispensation. There are several references to hymns in the New Testament, as for example, after the institution of the Lord's Supper, our Lord and His Apostles sung a hymn; the words of St. Matthew are, " And when they had sung a hymn they went out into the Mount of Olives." So also when St. Paul and Silas were thrown into prison, they had a song-service in the jail at which their fellow prisoners attended. It is clear from St. Paul's letters that hymns and singing were a part of the divine service in the oldest Christian churches, notably in the Church of Corinth. Pliny wrote to Trajan that on appointed days the Christians assembled and sang hymns to Christ. Tertullian writes that after the Love-feast (*Agapæ*) each worshipper was invited to come forward and sing a hymn in God's praise.

Greek and Roman Missals.—The mass-book, or missal, employed in all branches of the Catholic Church is, for the most part, a collection of sacred lyrics. From a literary view-point, the missal is an attempt to regulate the song-service accompanying the Eucharistic sacrifice; hence, from the *Introibo* or opening hymn, to the last *oration* or prayer, we find such lyric pieces as the *Gloria, Kyrie, Offertory, Preface, Agnus Dei, prayers and sequences.* The meter and form of the lyric are preserved in many of the sequences. For example, the

Dies Iræ and *Lauda Sion*. Besides the sacred lyrics incorporated into the missal, there were special hymns for important feasts, processional hymns in which the Greek and Latin Churches were equally productive. The *Te Deum* may be taken as a fair illustration.

Breviaries.— The breviary, like the missal, is lyric in character. The majority of the hymns are taken from the Book of Psalms. In connection with these there are a number from Christian sources. The addition of hymns from Christian writers can be traced as far back as the ninth century. The breviary is an outgrowth of monastic life, as the compilation of the hymns clearly indicates. Before the Council of Trent, each monastery, diocese and large city had its own lyric collection; now only three kinds of breviaries are permitted — the Mozarabic, Ambrosian, and Roman; the latter being the official breviary of the Catholic clergy. An admirable translation of the Roman breviary was made into English by the late Marquis of Bute.

Christian Hymn Books.— The third and most important source of the sacred ode is the Christian hymn-book. The Therapeutæ or Essene Jews were the first to use hymn-books; and Eusebius, the historian, declares that the early Christians borrowed the hymn-book from them. The hymn-book was first used in the Church of Antioch, 107 A. D. Ignatius counsels congregational singing in his letter to the Christians of Antioch: "Let the brethren form themselves into a choir and sing praise to the Father in Christ Jesus." From Antioch, congregational singing spread throughout the eastern churches. In the Greek Church hymn-books were called *tropologia;* a few of these date back as far as the fifth century, and they are preserved in manuscript form in the libraries of Moscow and Rome. Famous compilers of the tropologia were Anatolius, Patriarch of Constantinople; St. John Chrysostom; Saints Cosmas and Saba. The tropologia contain hymns from almost every saint on the Greek calendar down to the seventh century. The writing of hymns seemed to be one of the requisites of canonization. In the Latin Church the use of hymn-books began with Saint Hilary and Saint Ambrose. The earliest reference that we have to a hymn-book in the Latin Church is found in Saint Jerome's Commentary on Galatians; in the preface Jerome refers to a book of hymns written by Saint Hilary and in use in the Diocese of Poitiers in 356. Saint Ambrose introduced congregational singing into the church at Milan. Saint Augustine refers to this as follows: "Then it was first appointed that, after the manner of the Eastern Church, hymns and songs be sung, lest the people grow weary." Ambrosian music and the Ambrosian hymn-book were in vogue down to the time of Gregory the Great, when the Gregorian service came into use. After the downfall of the Roman Empire all the nations of Western Europe had hymn-books, each in its own language. The chief writers in the Western Church were Venerable Bede, (who wrote eleven hymns) and Alfred the Great, for the Saxon Church; Charlemagne and St. Bernard in France; *Jesu Dulcis Memoria* is a celebrated hymn by St. Bernard. In Italy, Thomas De Celano, who wrote the *Dies Iræ;* he was the companion and biographer of Saint Francis of Assissi. Jacobus De Benedictis, a Franciscan, who wrote the *Stabat Mater*. In Germany, Peter the Venerable, Abbot of Cluny, who wrote the celebrated hymn, "Jerusalem the Golden." And Hartmann, who compiled the German hymn-book in the fourteenth century. Martin Luther deserves special mention; he re-established congregational singing, which had fallen into disuse; he composed a German hymn-book, still in use in the Lutheran Church. His most famous hymn is a para-

phrase of the 46th psalm: Our Lord, a tower of strength —
" *Ein feste berg ist unser Gott.*"

English Hymns.— The first English hymn-book in the native tongue was published by order of Henry the Eighth, 6th
of May, 1545. It was called the "King's Primer," and by
royal mandate was used throughout the kingdom. It was
modeled on the Breviary and it contained English translations
of the best known Ambrosian and other early hymns. The
English hymn-book changed with each succeeding reign.
Under Queen Elizabeth, the King's Primer was thrown out
as ungodly, and a Geneva hymn-book, tinctured with Calvin-
ism, was substituted. It was a strange combination of Lutheran, Catholic and Biblical hymns, with considerable additions
from the original work of William Keith, an exiled Scotchman
at Geneva.

Books of Common Prayer.— From the middle of the sixteenth century to the present time, the English Church has employed Books of Common Prayer. These Books were author-
ized by law; they were modified from time to time by the
reigning sovereigns, notably by Edward the Sixth and Queen
Elizabeth. The Book of Common Prayer is one of the finest
products in English literature, and like King James' version
of the Bible, should be read for its literary value. This Book
contains all the lyric pieces in the Mass, besides a choice selection from the Book of Psalms and early Christian hymns.

Notable Compilations.— Besides the Book of Common
Prayer, five hymn-books have been compiled, and used from
time to time in English church service. First, the Puritan
Hymn-book compiled by George Wither, still used in some
of the non-conformist churches. Second, the hymn-book written by John Wesley who imitated Luther in providing original

hymns for the Methodist Church. Third, Bishop Heber's. The hymns of Heber are found in every Protestant hymn-book. The Church of England employed his collections at the beginning of the seventeenth century. His hymns are still popular with all classes of Protestants. Fourth, John Keble's. His collection provides a hymn for every Sunday and feast day; it is known as the "Christian Year." It is all original work. Cardinal Newman wrote as follows concerning the Christian Year: "The Christian Year made its appearance in 1827. It is not necessary for me to praise a book which has already become one of the classics of the language. When the general tone of religious literature was nerveless and impotent, Keble struck an original note and woke up in the hearts of thousands a new music, the effect of his lyrics was so deep, so pure, so beautiful." Fifth, Frederick William Faber's. Faber is best known to Catholic England. In 1836 Faber took the Newdigate prize at Oxford for a poem on the Knights of St. John. Wordsworth and Coleridge were his intimate friends. Wordsworth said that Faber might easily become the first poet of his time, if he gave his whole attention to poetry. His hymns forming a considerable volume, are used by Catholics and Protestants alike. The present Catholic hymn-book owes a large debt to Faber. He was the most fervent and zealous convert of the Oxford movement.

Other Contributions to the English Sacred Lyric.— The chief classic writers have contributed hymns to sacred literature. Among these John Milton ranks first. There are three famous hymns written by Milton: the Nativity, the Passion, Circumcision. The ode on the Nativity, constructed on the model of the Pindaric odes, is very elaborate, and by all critics regarded as one of our very best lyrics. Milton translated into verse many fine selections from the Hebrew psalms; among them the psalm, "The Lord is My Shepherd," is regarded as the best. John Dryden gave some attention to hymnology. The English translation of the *Veni Creator* now in use, is from his pen. Dryden's ode on Sacred Music (in honor of Saint Cecelia) is accorded the first place in our literature. Alexander Pope gave less attention than Dryden to hymn-writing; his lyric work is devoted to epitaph and elegy. His ode on Saint Cecilia has been admired for its correctness of diction, but it is cold and labored. His best hymn is called the " Universal Prayer," opening with the line, " Father of all, in every age." It was written to correct the impression that the author of the " Essay on Man " was a pantheist. Addison began a translation of the psalms in 1698, but never completed it; and, although the fragment left us is highly polished, it has never been popular. He also wrote thirteen original hymns, the most remarkable of which is " The Soul's Sabbath." Robert Burns left one lyric among his poems; its title is, " To Mary in Heaven." Wordsworth wrote on a similar subject. One line of Wordsworth has immortalized his hymn, his description of the Blessed Virgin as " our tainted Nature's solitary boast." Lord Byron published a small volume of lyrics in 1815, dealing with religious subjects. The volume was called Hebrew Melodies; many of the themes were furnished by the Old Testament, such as the Song of Saul, Jeptha's Daughter, All is Vanity. Modern hymn-books have two selections from Byron, one called the Destruction of Sennacherib —" The Assyrian came down like the wolf on the fold." The other lyric is a paraphrase of the 137th psalm —" By the waters of Babylon we sat down and we wept." A section of the lyrics left by Thomas Moore is devoted to hymns. There are thirty-three pieces in all, some of them quite as musical as anything he has written. The most popular one is the hymn beginning with the line, " Sound the loud timbrel o'er Egypt's dark sea."

Miscellaneous Contributions.— The great English prose writers of the nineteenth century, Newman, Ruskin, Arnold, Lowell, have each contributed to the department of the lyric. A volume by Newman, styled " Occasional Verses," is devoted almost exclusively to religious subjects; this volume contains the hymn so universally admired, " Lead, Kindly Light." Hymns approaching it in popularity are the " Holy City " and the " Recessional." Among American authors, John Greenleaf Whittier holds first place as a lyric writer, dealing with religious themes. Like John Wesley, Whittier belongs to the evangelical school; his lyrics are hymns of prayer and praise, and he rarely descends to polemics. The " Invocation " and the " Centennial Hymn " may be taken as fair examples of his work. Many of his hymns are prayers for the abolition of slavery; and he became a strong factor in the Abolition movement. The modern non-Catholic hymn-books contain selections from the lyrics of Longfellow, Tennyson, Whittier, and Kipling. The " Recessional " and the " Holy City," " The Psalm of Life " and the " Salutation to the New Year," are four hymns of exceptional merit; and with " Lead, Kindly Light," form the richest contribution which the 19th century has made to hymnology.

The National Lyric.— This species is known under the title of the national song or anthem. As the name idicates, it is inspired by patriotic feeling. No nation is so poor or so insignificant as not to have a favorite national song or anthem. Englishmen are familiar with " God Save the King "; Americans, Frenchmen and Germans respond to the " Star Spangled Banner," the " Marseillaise " and the " Watch on the Rhine." Similarly, all peoples have consecrated some lyrics as the highest expression of patriotic feeling. In watching the effect of such anthems upon the multitude, one may easily understand how poetry, even in its primitive crudeness, acted upon the savage like a spell or incantation. The effect of this lyric is best seen when the nations are marching to battle and keeping time to the wild, grand music of war.

The Heroic Lyric.— The sacred lyric deals with the supernatural hero and the supernatural world. The heroic lyric is confined to the human hero and the present world which has been a theatre for the display of his exalted character and shining virtues. This species of lyric, like the epic, is inspired by hero-worship. The oldest lyric of this class referred to in Hebrew literature, begins with the line: " Saul slew his thousands; David, his tens of thousands." It is the keynote of all the ancient literature under this head. In modern times, the heroes of peace are added to those of war, and this lyric has gradually widened in scope so as to include all orders of brilliant individual achievement. Each nation has supplied a number of lyric poets who were devoted to such lyric work. Each nation of any note has produced poets like David, Pindar, Horace, Tennyson, who have sung about national heroes — laureate poets who have immortalized the noble living and the noble dead.

The Plaintive Lyric.— The plaintive lyric is called the elegy. It is expressive of sorrow — the sorrow caused by death and separation. Sometimes, it expresses the gentler emotions unconnected with death; but its usual theme is the bier, the pall, the grave, and the dark cypress that guards God's acre. As it is a poem of a temperate character, it admits no boldness of meter, thought or language, nor any sudden or violent transitions of emotion. It has the muffled, subdued movement of the dirge, thus sanctifying but not concealing the grief that must have way. Perhaps the most perfect illustration of this lyric is Gray's *Elegy in a Country Churchyard*. Among ancient classic poems, the " Tristia " of Ovid are the most celebrated elegies. Shelley's lament over Keats, Milton's " Lycidas " and Tennyson's " In Memoriam " are well known examples in English literature. Some of the psalms are splendid examples of lamentation. The Lamentations of Jeremias and of the captives by the " Waters of Babylon " are the very soul of sadness clothed in lyric form.

The Ballad.— The word is derived from the old French, *baller,* to dance, and originally meant a song sung to the rhythmic movement of a dancing chorus. Later, the word was applied to a particular form of old French lyrics. In England, the ballad was the common name given to simple tales told in a simple verse. It signified the poetry of the common people; so that Folk-song and Ballad were synonymous, as they are so considered in Germany. The ballad is noted for its directness, freshness and freedom from those artificial restraints which the learning of the schools inflicts upon poetry. On this point Stedman observes : " Primitive ballads have a straightforward felicity; many of them a conjuring melody, as befits verse and music born together. Their gold is virgin, from the rock-strata, and none the better for refining and burnishing. No language is richer in them than the English." Gummere, quoting Stevenson, describes the ballad as verse dealing with the eternal life of man spent under sun and rain, and in rude physical effort. Further, he calls the ballad, " the poetry of the people, poetry which once came from the people as a whole, from the compact body as yet undivided by lettered or unlettered taste, representing the sentiment neither of individuals nor of a class. It inclines to the narrative, the concrete and exterior, and it has no mark of the artist or his sentiment; it must be the outcome and expression of a whole community, and this community must be homogeneous — must belong to a time when, in a common atmosphere of ignorance, so far as book-lore is concerned, one habit of thought and one standard of action animate every member from prince to ploughboy. When learning came among the folk, it drove the ballad first into byways, and then altogether out of living literature."

Content of the Ballad.— Simplicity of thought and speech and a naturalness peculiar to the primitive man are ear-marks of the ballad. It gives us a sense of tradition and a flavor of spontaneity, riches of the emotions and of direct vision, poverty of intellect and reflection. Its poetic diction is unschooled, close to life.

Meter and Imagery.— The meter is not labored, irregular, and hardly melodious when judged by the strictest canons; however, it shows a clear and certain sense of general harmony. Assonance often does the work of rhyme. Figures are few and recurrent, always unforced, and for the most part unconscious. The language of primitive or simple passion is iteration, not figure; so that ballads poor in imagery are full of iteration.

Purpose.— The ballad, like other species of the lyric, was made for singing, and to some extent was made in singing. The melody was by no means the device of a minstrel to entertain the throng, but the concerted work of a throng to entertain itself. There can be no doubt that from the dance came the fact and the terms of meter — the steps and windings of both are inseparable. The dance was the center and in one way the origin of all the songs of the people. "No singing, no dance; and conversely, no dance, no singing"— this, as Gummere puts it, is the history of the ballad in a nutshell.

Communal Origin.— The question has often been discussed whether the community or the individual should be credited with the authorship of the ballad. Writers like Müllenhoff and Schlegel declare that the making of ballads could never have been a communal process; because all poetry rests upon a union of nature and art; it has a purpose and plan, and therefore belongs to an artist. On the other hand, such authorities as Grimm assert that it is the " folk," not the individual, which pours its own flood of poetry over far-off events, thus giving to us the folk-lyric or ballad. It is probably the most reasonable solution of the difficulty to say that both the individual and the community were factors; the individual originating the poem, the " folk " changing and amplifying it, adding stanzas and changing lines to suit the communal fancy. As it is difficult to see how a ballad could begin to be without some individual conceiving and originating it; so, in like manner, it is unreasonable to suppose that the " folk " adopted and sung it without many alterations and variations; perhaps, after some generations, recasting the whole piece.

Amount and Use of Such Literature.— The ballad literature of every nation is voluminous. Much of it is not collected, notably the ballads of the Celt, the Spaniard and the Italian. Child has collected the ballads of Scotland and England, basing his work on the previous labors of Motherwell and Scott. Bugeaud and Champfleury have collected the ballads of France, and those of Northern Europe have been edited and criticised by Taloy, Kretschmar and Grimm. The Gælic League promises to do as much for the rich folklore of Ireland. The use of the ballad is admitted by all critics in the construction of primitive epics. It is easy to show survivals of the ballad in the poetry of Homer and in all the older epics. Moreover, it may be added that the Greek drama sprang from the sacred choruses of village vintagers. Ballads are the joy of the peasant class. " Let me make the people's songs, and I care not who makes their laws "— thus spoke O'Connell.

Ballads reach the heart of the people. The country seems to have aided in their making; the bird's note rings in them, the tree has lent her whispers, the stream its murmur, the village bell its tinkling tune. Ballads are a voice from secret places, from silent peoples, and old times long dead; and as such they stir us in a strangely intimate fashion to which artistic verse can never attain.

The Sonnet.— The sonnet forms an important division of the lyric. The word, sonnet, is a diminutive for song, and signifies a short poem. As used in literature, the sonnet is a lyric of fixed form, limited to fourteen lines, with a prescribed disposition of rhymes. The form is of Italian origin. A sonnet, according to the Italian model, is written in five-foot measure; though the lines may be eight feet in length.

Divisions.— The sonnet consists of two divisions or groupings. The first is called the major group and contains eight lines — hence the term, octave, which is applied to it. The second or minor group, contains six lines, and is called a sextette. According to Petrarch, this divison corresponds to question and answer; the octave presenting some problem or question; the sextette furnishing some solution or reply. But the modern sonnet often fails to meet this requirement. In the construction of the sonnet the Italian writers observed certain rules which still prevail. *First,* the sonnet must confine itself to one leading idea, thought or feeling. *Second,* it must be so developed as to leave in the reader's mind a sense of completeness; it must be a complete composition in miniature. *Third,* the rhyme, however varied, must have not more than three variations in the sextette; and two in the octave. Finally, the style of the sonnet must be free from any vagueness or obscurity, and from all harsh-sounding words or word combinations. In the last particular, the musical speech of

Italy has a decided superiority over the English tongue. Owing to the application of these rules, the sonnet is the most perfect work of art in the department of the lyric.

Origin of the Sonnet.— The sonnet made its first appearance at the beginning of the twelfth century, and in Italy. Like many forms of Italian poetry it originated in Provence. At once it came into popular favor. And the Italian writers famous for their connection with the revival of learning, all wrote sonnets. Dante, Petrarch and Michael Angelo are representative authors of the sonnet. During his youth, and before his exile from Florence, Dante wrote lyric poetry in the ballad and sonnet form. Seventy-eight genuine sonnets were collected and published in a work called the "Lyrics of Dante." These lyrics were translated into English by Frederick Pollock in 1843.

Petrarch an Author.— But the most famous Italian author of sonnets is Petrarch. His volume written on the life and death of Laura has no equal in sonnet literature. Shelley describing these lyrics says, "They are as spells which unseal the inmost enchanted fountains of delight." Besides the cycle of sonnets dedicated to Laura, there are a number dealing with such miscellaneous subjects as virtue, fame, Divinity. There are various English translators of Petrarch; the best translation of the sonnets was made by Reeve in 1868.

The Sonnet in England.— The sonnet was brought from Italy to England where it appeared in the form of translation. The first English author of the sonnet was Sir Thomas Wyatt, who lived during the reign of Henry the Eighth. Wyatt was likewise the first English author of satires in classical form. His work in the sonnet began by translations from Petrarch. His lyrics are preserved, not on account of their merit, but as a literary landmark — the beginning of Italian influence upon English literature.

English Classic Writers of the Sonnet.— The first of these is Shakespeare. The sonnets of Shakespeare were completed in 1598. The whole collection, 156 in all, was published in 1609, or 13 years before the first folio edition of the plays. These sonnets are divided into two groups — one group dealing with Shakespeare's friendship for a man whose name is withheld. This group contains 126 sonnets which are connected like the lyrics of the *In Memoriam.* The second group of forty sonnets are written in imitation of Petrarch's Laura; they idealize some unknown woman whose name is also kept secret. The sonnets of Shakespeare are often obscure and irregular in form. In some measure they follow the Italian model, but like the dramas, often violate the rules of art. The sonnets of Milton come next in the order of time; they are not so numerous as those of Shakespeare, but in technique they are a higher grade of work. Milton wrote in both the English and Italian languages, and he had a better appreciation of musical values. Three of his sonnets are famous: the *Massacre of Piedmont;* the *Assault on the City;* his *Dead Wife.* With Milton, the sonnet disappeared from English poetry for 100 years. It was despised by Pope and Dryden. It reappeared in England with the Romantic movement. Coleridge, Wordsworth and Shelley employed it. Two large collections were left by Wordsworth — the Ecclesiastical sonnets which run through several hundred, and give the history of Christianity in miniature. The bigot and the artist are equally evident in this collection. The second collection is dedicated to the River Duddon, and a more charming collection outside Keats and Shakespeare cannot be found in our literature. The sonnets of Keats are compared to a tropic flower garden. They are unrivaled examples of sensuousness. Other authors who deserve mention are Tennyson, Longfellow, Rossetti, Richard Watson Gilder, Maurice Francis Egan, Aubrey De Vere. Modern magazines and periodicals take kindly to the sonnet; and perhaps it represents a sufficient tax upon the modern Muse accustomed to only short swallow-flights of song.

CHAPTER LII

THE LYRIC (CONTINUED)

REPRESENTATIVE AUTHORS

Pindar.— The celebrated lyric poet of Bœotia was born in 522 B. C., and died at the age of eighty years. He was in the prime of life when Xerxes invaded Greece and when the battles of Thermopylæ and Salamis were fought. He had among his patrons Hiero of Syracuse, Theron of Agrigentum; Amyntas, king of Macedonia; also, many of the free cities of Greece. He was honored and loved by the Ionian states for himself as well as for his art. The Athenians made him their public guest. The only class of poems which enable us to judge of Pindar's general style are his Triumphal Odes, although he wrote hymns and dirges and almost every variety of lyric. He is regarded as the father of lyric poetry.

Criticism by Charles Anthon.—" Pindar begins an ode full of the lofty conception which he has formed of the glorious destiny of the victor; and he seems, as it were, carried away by the flood of images which his conception pours forth. He does not attempt to express directly the general idea, but follows the train of thought which it suggests into details, though without losing sight of their reference to the main subject. There is in the Pindaric odes an extraordinary variety of style and expression. In respect of metre, every ode of Pindar has an individual character, no two odes being of the same metrical structure. A severe dignity pervades the odes; the mythical narrations are developed with great fullness; the ideas are limited to the subject; there is throughout a general character of calmness and elevation. The language has a slight Doric tinge

534

which adds to its brilliancy and dignity. The scholar comes to the study of Pindar, as to that of one whom fable and history, poetry and criticism have alike delighted to honor. The writers of Greece speak of him as the man whose birth was celebrated by the songs and dances of the deities themselves, in joyous anticipation of those immortal hymns which he was to frame in their praise. Pindar is not merely a devout, but he is also an eminently moral poet. Plato observes of him, in the Menon, that he maintained the immortality of the soul; and he lays down with remarkable distinctness, the doctrine of future happiness or misery. Hence, his poems abound with maxims of the highest morality. Of his extensive literary labors, we have remaining at the present day forty-five triumphal odes, together with some few fragments of his other productions."

Criticism by Doctor Blair.—" Pindar is the great father of lyric poetry; his genius was sublime; his expressions are beautiful and happy; his descriptions picturesque. The ancients admired him greatly. Our pleasure in reading him is somewhat diminished by his rapid and abrupt style and by his obscure allusions to particular families and cities unknown to us. He was imitated by Euripides and Sophocles in the choral lyrics and by the Latin School."

Sappho.— She was a native of Lesbos, and probably spent most of her life at Mytilene. Her date cannot be fixed with certainty, but she must have lived about the beginning of the 6th century B. C., as she was a contemporary of Alcæus and Pittacus. Her life, like that of Homer, is unknown, although legend and fable have been busy, sometimes at the expense of her morals and character. Her poetry is preserved only in fragments, but from these fragments it is clear that she was incomparably the greatest lyric poetess the world has ever seen.

Criticism by James A. Plowden.—" In antiquity the fame of Sappho rivalled that of Homer. She was called ' the poetess ' as he was called ' the poet.' Different writers style her ' the tenth

Muse,' ' the flower of the Graces,' a ' Miracle,' ' the beautiful ';
the last epitaph referring to her writings. Her poems were arranged in nine books. The few remains which have come down
to us amply testify to the justice of the praises lavished upon
Sappho by the ancients. The perfection and finish of every
line, the correspondence of sense and sound, the incomparable
command over all the most delicate resources of verse, and the
exquisite symmetry of the complete odes raise her into the very
first rank of technical poetry at once, while her direct and fervent
painting of passion has never been since surpassed. Her fragments bear witness to a profound feeling for the beauty of
nature; we know from other sources that she had a peculiar
delight in flowers, and especially in the rose. The ancients also
attributed to her a considerable power in satire."

Horace.— Quintus Horatius Flaccus was born at Venusium,
65 B. C., and lived to the age of fifty-eight years. Like Pindar and Sappho among the Greeks, Horace is known as the
best lyric writer among the Romans. Horace took part in the
civil war, joining the army of Brutus and flying from the
field of Philippi. After the accession of Augustus, he lived
under the patronage of Mæcenas, who provided the poet with
an ample stipend. His works are divided into odes, epodes,
satires and epistles; his fame and merit as a lyric writer have
been admitted by the critics of every nation and age.

Criticism by Alexander Smith.—" The lyrics of Horace are
imitations of the Greek poets. One cannot escape the conviction
that, like the poetry of Alexander Pope, these lyrics are constructed in a highly artificial manner; the stronger and more
powerful feelings of human nature are seldom displayed in them,
owing to the presence of this artificial note. His best lyrics are
those descriptive of country life; for the beauties of nature he had
as keen an appreciation and relish as Sappho. Besides this, he
had clear judgment, strong good sense and purity of taste."

Criticism by Blair.—" The name of Horace cannot be mentioned without particular praise; that ' Curiosa Felicitas ' which

has been remarked in his expression; the sweetness, elegance and spirit of many of his lyrics; the thorough knowledge of the world, the excellent sentiments and natural easy manner, which distinguish his satires and epistles — all contribute to render him one of those very few authors whom one never tires of reading, and from whom, were every other monument destroyed, we should be led to form a very high idea of the taste and genius of the Augustan age. Of all the writers of lyrics, ancient or modern, there is none that, in point of correctness, harmony, and happy expression, can vie with Horace. He has descended from the Pindaric rapture to a more moderate degree of elevation, and joins connected thought and good sense with the highest beauties of poetry. The peculiar character in which he excels, is grace and elegance; and in this style of composition no poet has ever attained to a greater perfection than Horace. No poet supports a moral sentiment with more dignity, touches a gay one more happily, or possesses the art of trifling more agreeably when he choses to trifle. His language is so fortunate that with a single word or epithet he often conveys a whole description to the fancy. Hence, he ever has been, and ever will continue to be, a favorite author with all persons of taste."

Petrarch.—Francesco Petrarch was born at Arezzo, Italy, in 1304, and died near Padua in 1374. He studied at Montpelier, where he remained until he was eighteen. He was crowned poet laureate in Rome, 1341. His chief works belong to the department of the lyric; they are sonnets and odes in honor of Laura. His letters and orations are numerous, and he wrote a number of controversial and polemical treatises. All critics admit his title to first place among Italian lyric poets.

Criticism by Frederick Schlegel.—"The lyric poetry of Petrarch must be classified as love-song, and should be compared with the love-song of Spain and Germany to be duly comprehended. On instituting a comparative examination, Petrarch's especial characteristic will be found to consist in a more artistic spiritual platonism than is evinced by any other love-

poet of the Middle Ages. Some of his commentators have gone
so far as to contend that his Laura was no historic personage
at all, but a mere personification of his ideal fancy. This, in
turn, has been stoutly denied; proofs have been adduced from
the church registers not only of her actual existence, but also
of her marriage and her numerous family. A still stronger proof
is a lovely portrait of her in the Petrarch collection at Florence.
The verse of Petrarch is not deficient in that allegorical spirit
which is so generally characteristic of mediæval minstrelsy. In
metrical skill, as also in the cultivation of his native idiom, he
is undoubtedly entitled to be ranked among the foremost bards
who composed in any of the Romanic tongues."

Criticism by J. A. Symonds.—" As an author, Petrarch must
be considered from two points of view — first, as a writer of
Latin verse and prose; secondly, as an Italian lyrist. In the
former capacity he was speedily outstripped by more fortunate
scholars and contemporaries. His epistles, and ' Epic of Africa '
on which he set such store, exhibited a comparatively limited
command of Latin metre; his treatises and orations are not
remarkable for purity of diction. But as a lyrist, Petrarch occupies a very different position. We can say with Shelley that
his lyrics are spells which unseal the inmost enchanted fountains
of the delight which is the grief of love. Petrarch, in his mon-
umental series of odes and sonnets, depicted all the moods of a
real passion, and presented them in a style of such lucidity, with
so exquisite a command of rhythmical resources, and with humanity of emotion so simple and so true, as to render his portrait of a lover's soul applicable to all who have loved and will
love for ages. Regarding Laura, we derive no clear conception
either of her person or her character. She is not so much a
woman as woman in the abstract; and perhaps on this very account the poems written for her by her lover have been taken
to the heart by countless lovers who came after him. The
method of his art is so generalizing, while his feeling is so
natural, that every man can see himself reflected in the singer,
and his mistress shadowed forth in Laura. The same criticism
might be passed on Petrarch's description of nature. That he
felt the beauties of nature keenly, is certain, and he frequently
touches them with obvious appreciation. Yet he has written

nothing so characteristic of Vancluse as to be inapplicable to any solitude where there are woods and water. His lyrics are, therefore, one long melodious monody poured from the poet's soul, with the indefinite form of a beautiful woman seated in a lovely landscape, a perpetual object of delightful contemplation. English readers may be referred to a little book on Petrarch by Henry Reeve, and to Symond's 'Renaissance in Italy.'"

Schiller.— He was born in Wurtemberg in 1759 and died at Weimar in 1805. He became a famous German lyric poet, dramatist and historian, publishing in all seventeen volumes. He divides honors with Goethe in the department of the drama, but is superior to every other German poet in the sweetness and tenderness of his lyrics.

Criticism by Professor Sievers.—" Schiller began his literary career at the age of twenty-two. He wrote dramas of which the best known are ' The Robbers,' ' Maria Stewart ' and ' William Tell.' These dramas alone would place an author high on the ladder of literary fame. But Schiller wrote ballads and lyrics as well — lyrics which place him first among German writers in this species of composition. His great lyric rival was Goethe who admitted that Schiller outstripped him in the race. Schiller's masterpiece is the world-famous lyric the ' Song of the Bell.' This lyric within a small compass presents an impressive picture of the course of human life, varying its melody with subtle art to suit the changing aspects of the theme. ' The Genius,' ' The Ideal,' and ' The Walk ' are lyrics which compare favorably with the ' Song of the Bell.' These lyrics of Schiller express in clear and noble language some of the highest feelings excited in a poetic mind by the contemplation of human life and destiny."

Criticism by Frederick Schlegel.—" In the impassioned productions of his early prime, we see Schiller incessantly moved by the conflict of inner emotions; he is urged onwards by the enthusiastic hopes to improve the existing state of all things. A sort of violent optimisim has taken possession of him and this optimism finds the sweetest of lyric expression. In the serious lyrics of every nation, feeling must preponderate over thought, and have as it were a commanding aim if it is to be suitably expressed in melody. Now seriousness is a characteristic of all the lyrics written by Schiller; they are poems with a purpose; the feeling pervading them is genuine, and no lyric poet ever lived who knew better how to touch the springs of feeling. The same observation holds good of his dramas, as anyone who has read Maria Stewart or William Tell can bear witness."

Heine.— Heinrich Heine was born in 1799 and died in 1856. He was of Jewish descent. At one time he studied with the view of entering the legal profession, but he attended no lectures at the University except those on literature, by Schlegel. He began to write lyric poems in 1822 and continued to do so until his death. Heine devoted himself to journalism and satire as well as to lyric poetry. His prose is sullied by irreverence and blasphemy, his satire, like that of Swift, touches at times the lowest depths of vulgarity, and the prose style itself is not calculated to contribute to his literary fame. Heine will be remembered as a lyric writer who in this species of composition ranks next to Schiller.

Criticism by Matthew Arnold.—" I wish to mark Heine's place in modern European literature, the scope of his activity, and his value. I cannot attempt to give here a detailed account of his life, or a description of his separate works. In May, 1831, he went over his Jordan, the Rhine, and fixed himself in his new Jerusalem, Paris. There, henceforward, he lived, going in general to some French watering-place in the summer, but making only one or two short visits to Germany during the rest of his life. His works, in verse and prose, succeed each other without stopping; a collected edition of them, filling seven closely-printed octavo volumes, has been published in America; in the collected editions of few people's works is there so little to skip. Those who wish for a single good specimen of him should read his first important work, the work which made his reputation, the *Reisebilder,* or ' Travelling Sketches ': prose and verse, wit and seriousness, are mingled in it, and the mingling of these is characteristic of Heine, and is nowhere to be seen practiced more naturally and happily than in his *Reisebilder*.

"The magic of Heine's poetical form is incomparable; he chiefly uses a form of old German popular poetry, a ballad-form which has more rapidity and grace than any ballad-form of ours; he employs this form with the most exquisite lightness and ease, and yet it has at the same time the inborn fulness, pathos, and old-world charm of all true forms of popular poetry. Thus in Heine's poetry, too, one perpetually blends the impression of French modernism and clearness with that of German sentiment and fulness; and to give this blended impression is, as I have said, Heine's great characteristic."

Alfred De Musset.—He was born in 1810 and died in 1857. He studied and lived in Paris. In his twentieth year he published his first volume of poetry. He wrote several plays and a number of short stories, all well received; but his chief work lay in the department of the lyric. If not the greatest French lyric author, he is among her foremost lyric representatives; all critics admit the supreme excellence of his work.

Criticism by Réné Doumic.—"The three qualities which Alfred de Musset possessed were elegance, insight and inspiration; with these he achieved the grandest flights of epic poetry. One more quality should be added, sadness. No French poet is more uniformly sorrowful. He seems to be master of all the ideas associated with grief, and he has clothed them all with exquisite imagery. His definition, or rather law of poetry is that the more sorrowful and hopeless the poet is, the more beautiful he will sing. This law certainly applies to De Musset and his class of lyrists. His poems, for the most part, are gloomy meditations on death and oblivion and the insufficiency of human love to satisfy man's heart, the disappointment and final regret which attends pleasure. The deepest emotions are aroused by his meditations on such themes — meditations which stamp this lyric genius as the worst kind of a pessimist. For, out of this vale of tears and lamentation and despair, Faith points to no exit or deliverance — De Musset has neither Faith nor Hope. As to literary form, De Musset is unrivalled, his technique is perfect, yet not the result of overmuch study or artifice. In moments of passion his style reaches a precision and exactness which form the basis of lasting merit. One may observe throughout his work traces of a strong and rich and varied imagination; his genius not wide in scope gained thereby in profundity. We may conclude by remarking that he has fathomed and depicted the intensity, the depth of the agony of the human soul for all time. Higher praise than this cannot be accorded to a lyric poet. We may also observe in conclusion that his poetry is a reflection of his own life — its gloom and pessimism, its vices and excesses — it was a life of sin with the inevitable sorrow, the primrose path that closed in dejection and despair."

Tennyson.— He was born at Somersby, in Lincolnshire, 1810, and succeeded Wordsworth as Laureate in 1850. He was educated at Cambridge, where in 1829 he gained the Chancellor's medal for a prize poem. In 1830 he published his first volume under the title of " Poems, Chiefly Lyrical." It had a very cold reception, some reviewers calling it " Dismal Drivel." Ten years of study and retirement, and Tennyson again ventured to publish his lyrics, this time with marked success. His popularity has grown ever since. It is safe to claim for him first place among the lyric writers in English literature. His chief poems are Locksley Hall, the Princess, the Idylls of the King, Maud, The Lotus Eaters, In Memoriam. Short pieces of exquisite beauty are " Break, Break, Break"; " Crossing the Bar "; " The Poet "; " Spring "; " Vastness."

Criticism by William H. Sheran.— If we compare Tennyson with his predecessors, we find that he differs from them, or rather is superior to them, in several respects. First of all, we note his greater power of condensation in accordance with the genius and method of lyric poetry; he is able to compress his thought within narrower limits; he is able to say in a few lines what his predecessors would spread over as many pages. Terseness is, then, a characteristic of Tennyson. As an example, one may cite the ' Splendor Falls on Castle Walls,' or, ' Break, Break,

Break,' or, 'Flow Down Cold Rivulet.' Within equal limits it seems quite impossible to make language more expressive. A second characteristic in which he excels his predecessors, is the happy union of word-picture and music. The 'Splendor Falls on Castle Walls' may be taken as an illustration in point. Here we have a complete medieval picture in four short lines, and framed in the most exquisite music. The 'Palace of Art' is another illustration, any stanza of which would offer a theme for a canvas — any stanza of which would convince the reader that Tennyson is a very great master of English harmonics, perhaps the greatest of all our musical writers, at least on a plane with Shelley, Keats, Spenser and Milton. Besides the exquisite character of Tennyson's painting and music, the critic must note his perfect technique, the happy choice of themes, the high moral tone, and the sustained quality of his work. In the matter of literary form, he has fewer imperfect lines and meters than any other great English writer; the subjects which he selected gave the largest scope to lyric genius — subjects like the 'In Memoriam,' or 'Enoch Arden,' exciting the deepest emotion. It is not necessary to publish an abridged edition of his works, either to exclude unsavory passages, or to secure a just estimate of his poetic talent. Every line of Tennyson may be read for beauty of form and fancy, for painting and music, as well as for moral and spiritual profit.

Shelley.— He was born in Sussex, England, August 5th, 1792; died in Italy, July 8th, 1822. He was educated at Eton and Oxford. Like many men of Literary genius, Shelley suffered from moral lapses; a wild, uncontrollable passion which set at defiance all laws and restraints imposed by State, Church, or society. Generosity, charity, a passionate love of liberty, were the better traits of his character. As an artist in the department of lyric poetry, he has no superior, and few equals among Englishmen. Representative lyrics are his odes to the Skylark and to the West Wind.

Criticism by Professor Dowden.—"Although Shelley wrote narrative poems and one great tragedy, his genius was primarily lyrical, and his poetry tells more to a reader who is acquainted with his character and events of his life than to one who knows the poems only as if they had fallen out of the air from some invisible singer. No poet ever sang more directly out of his own feelings — his joys, his sorrows, his desires, his regrets; and what he has written acquires a fuller meaning when we understand its source and its occasion. Shelley's poetry belongs also to a particular epoch in the world's history — the revolutionary epoch — and what may fairly be described as the body of doctrine which forms the intellectual background of his imaginative visions can be comprehended only when we consider his work in relation to the period of which it is the outcome. ' A beautiful and ineffectual angel, beating in the void his luminous wings in vain '— so Matthew Arnold, with a variation of Joubert's sentence on Plato, defined his conception of Shelley. The charm of the phrase must not render us insensible of its remoteness from the fact. Shelley was no angel, whether of celestial or diabolic race, but most human in his passions, his errors, his failure, his achievement. Nor was it in the void that he lived and moved; he belonged in an eminent degree to the revolutionary movement of his own day."

Longfellow.— He was born in Maine, February 27, 1807; died at Cambridge, 1882. He studied at Bowdoin College, became a distinguished linguist, traveled much in foreign countries, taught Belles-Lettres in Harvard College. Longfellow wrote a considerable amount of prose and verse; his chief literary distinction is that of a lyric writer. As a lyrist, he divides with Poe the first honors in American literature. His best work associates his name with Keats and Tennyson.

Criticism by Martin Williston.—" It is not a gracious office to analyze the qualities of the true poet or to attempt to classify his work after scientific canons. Longfellow did not belong to that class of singers who are rapt away with violent and uncontrollable inspirations; his creations are never spasmodically born. He was no ' God intoxicated ' man, across whose unconscious spirit the madness of a mighty mood sweeps and carries him into what heavens and deeps he knows not. Rather he was a listening soul, bringing an intelligent ear to the oracle, and interpreting through his own calm and generous wisdom the message learned. He communed with nature; he kept her fellowship, but was never made beside himself by even her greatest communications. He was an intent observer of the universe, never losing his own judgment or surrendering his thoughtfulness. Whether he would have been more Pythian in his muse and less calmly wise had he not at the outset of his course been immersed in the Romanticism of modern Europe, and felt the subduing power of mediæval reminiscence amid the stately temples of the Old World, is questionable. He was fully in sympathy with whatever is valuable or nobly characteristic in the civilization of this America of ours which is at once the youngest and the oldest on earth. It was his nature to see things as he did, meditatively, deliberatively, with an instinctive reference to the things that had been. He delighted in the twilight view of men who had passed by, and he loved to spend dreamy hours amid the withdrawn centuries, musing on the life that had filled this world, a life so like and so unlike that which was even then going past under the high noon of the glaring present. As he went further down the descent of years he imbibed somewhat more fully than at first the spirit of a primitive age, and looked at the universe with deeply questioning eyes, less and less disposed to think most things explicable. He was nearly seventy when he wrote the ' Mask of Pandora,' and in this impressive poem he reveals his altered mood toward the mysteries of being. Nature has grown more oracular, her explanations less distinct than he had believed them to be. At all times he held his soul devoutly ready to be awakened by the voices of God to the world; his was the reverent and worshipful muse, and his singing, therefore, was eagerly heard by the multitude. He wished to utter that which the usual man could take into his heart and find food for his diviner self. It was this lofty humanity that gave him the unwearying love of so many millions. He loved to find the field of celestial enterprise among homely and familiar experiences. He chose for his themes brave deeds of simple men, the patient suffering of quiet and inconspicuous people, heroism where no pageantry surrounded it. He culled the flowers of history for their sweetness of self-sacrifice, and searched the past to illumine by its most radiant examples the nobler possi-

bilities of the sober present. He never thought himself a solar
genius, to be set at last among the fixed stars of the heaven of
fame, but he valued the fame of his genius for the light it
could shed upon the path that is daily trod by the working
throng of our crowded world. He was completely subjective to
his method. What is the best way to employ this interior man?
How can we make our lives sublime? What is beautiful and
suitable in this middle world between the final good and ill?
These are the questions that may be heard beneath the harmonies
of his perfect verse. Longfellow is not the most original of
poets. He does not attempt the profundities of psychology, nor
venture new explanations of the frame of things. On the other
hand, he was never a slavish adherent of dogmatic opinions,
whether in the realm of faith or science, though most of his life
satisfied with the ordinary Christian account of the higher revelation of man to his God. He did not care for an agitating investigation into the undeclared secrets of moral and material existence.
His genius did not lead him to search for his first principles. He
rested in a large faith in the Invisible. He was willing to be
quiet in a noble agnosticism that assumed what knowledge could
not assert, but was luminous with a rational trust in the all-
enfolding goodness of God. He believed that so long as man
continued on earth, he could not learn all things, quite ready
to concede

> 'I do not know, nor will I vainly question
> Those pages of the mystic book which hold
> The story still untold.
> But without rash conjecture or suggestion
> Turn its last leaves in reverence and good heed
> Until 'the End' I read.'

He had no fondness for that morbid analysis of human nature
so characteristic of the modern school of fiction, whose most
distinguished and principal representative is found in George
Eliot. Art he held to be constructive and creative, not inquis-
itorial nor surgical. It was no vivisection of the human soul he
was aiming at, but the vivifying of human nature with divine impulses. He penetrated his descriptions and reports of the world
with his own pure spirit, and so conveyed a virtue with every
reception of his blessed communication. We become better as
we confer with this unordained priest of moral beauty, this

singing servitor of all truth, who has the gifts of God to bestow, and the highest promises of existence to declare to us. He pictures the exquisite things, honor, magnanimity, love and all events, using the outer life as studio and canvas for this scenic art of the soul."

CHAPTER LIII.

CONCLUSION

Thoughts from Matthew Arnold's Essay in Criticism.—
" The critical power is of lower rank than the creative. True;
but in assenting to this proposition, one or two things are to be
kept in mind. It is undeniable that the exercise of a creative
power, that a free creative activity, is the highest funtion of
man; it is proved to be so by man's finding in it his true happiness. But it is undeniable, also, that men may have the sense
of exercising this free creative activity in other ways than in
producing great works of literature or art; if it were not so, all
but a very few men would be shut out from the true happiness of
all men. They may have it in well-doing, they may have it in
learning, they may have it even in criticising. This is one thing
to be kept in mind. Another is, that the exercise of the creative
power in the production of great works of literature or art,
however high this exercise of it may rank, is not at all epochs
and under all conditions possible; and that, therefore, labor may
be vainly spent in attempting it, which might with more fruit be
used in preparing for it, in rendering it possible. This creative
power works with elements, with materials; what if it has not
those materials, those elements, ready for its use? In that case
it must surely wait till they are ready. Now, in literature — I
will limit myself to literature, for it is about literature that the
question arises — the elements with which the creative power
works are ideas; the best ideas on every matter which literature
touches, current at the time. At any rate we may lay it down
as certain that in modern literature no manifestation of the
creative power not working with these can be very important
or fruitful. And I say *current* at the time, not merely accessible
at the time; for creative literary genius does not principally show
itself in discovering new ideas, that is rather the business of the
philosopher. The grand work of literary genius is a work of
synthesis and exposition, not of analysis and discovery; its gift

548

lies in the faculty of being happily inspired by a certain intellectual and spiritual atmosphere, by a certain order of ideas,
when it finds itself in them; of dealing divinely with these ideas,
presenting them in the most effective and attractive combinations — making beautiful works with them, in short. But it
must have the atmosphere, it must find itself amidst the order
of ideas, in order to work freely; and these it is not so easy to
command. This is why great creative epochs in literature are
so rare, this is why there is so much that is unsatisfactory in
the productions of many men of real genius; because for the
creation of a master-work of literature two powers must concur,
the power of the man·and the power of the moment, and the
man is not enough without the moment; the creative power has,
for its happy exercise, appointed elements, and those elements are
not in its own control. Nay, they are more within the control
of the critical power. It is the business of the critical power,
as I said in the words already quoted, ' in all branches of knowledge, theology, philosophy, history, art, science, to see the object
as in itself it really is.' Thus, it tends, at last, to make an intellectual situation of which the creative power can profitably avail
itself. It tends to establish an order of ideas, if not absolutely
true, yet true by comparison with that which it displaces; to
make the best ideas prevail. Presently, these new ideas reach
society, the touch of truth is the touch of life, and there is a
stir and growth everywhere; out of this stir and growth come the
creative epochs of literature.

" The critic should have a disinterested endeavor to learn and
propagate the best that is known and thought in the world and
thus to establish a current of fresh and true ideas. By the very
nature of things, as England is not all the world, much of the best
that is known and thought in the world cannot be of English
growth, must be foreign; by the nature of things, again, it is
just this that we are least likely to know, while English thought
is streaming in upon us from all sides, and takes excellent care
that we shall not be ignorant of its existence. The English critic
of literature, therefore, must dwell much on foreign thought, and
with particular heed on any part of it, which, while significant and
fruitful in itself, is for any reason specially likely to escape him.
Again, judging is often spoken of as the critic's own business, and
so in some sense it is; but the judgment which almost insensibly

forms itself in a fair and clear mind, along with fresh knowledge, is the valuable one; and thus knowledge, and ever fresh knowledge, must be the critic's great concern for himself. And it is by communicating fresh knowledge, and letting his own judgment pass along with it•— but insensibly, and in the second place, not the first, as a sort of companion and clue, not as an abstract law-giver — that the critic will generally do most good to his readers. Sometimes, no doubt, for the sake of establishing an author's place in literature, and his relation to a central standard (and if this is not done, how are we to get at our *best in the world?*) criticism may have to deal with a subject-matter so familiar that fresh knowledge is out of the question, and then it must be all judgment; an enunciation and detailed application of principles. Here the great safeguard is never to let oneself become abstract, always to retain an intimate and lively consciousness of the truth of what one is saying, and, the moment this fails us, to be sure that something is wrong. Still, under all circumstances, this mere judgment and application of principles is, in itself, not the most satisfactory work to the critic; like mathematics, it is tautological, and cannot well give us, like fresh learning the sense of creative activity. I am bound by my own definition of criticism: *a disinterested endeavor to learn and propagate the best that is known and thought in the world.* How much of current English literature comes into this "best that is known and thought in the world?' Not very much, I fear; certainly less at this moment than of the current literature of France or Germany. Well, then, am I to alter my definition of criticism, in order to meet the requirements of a number of practicing English critics, who, after all, are free in their choice of a business? That would be making criticism lend itself just to one of those alien practical considerations, which, I have said, are so fatal to it. One may say, indeed, to those who have to deal with the mass — so much better disregarded — of current English literature, that they may at all events endeavor, in dealing with this, to try it, so far as they can, by the standard of the best that is known and thought in the world; one may say, that to get anywhere near this standard, every critic should try and possess one great literature, at least, besides his own; and the more unlike his own, the better. But after all, the criticism I am really concerned with — the criticism which alone can much help us for the future, the criticism which, throughout Europe, is at the present day meant, when so much stress is laid on the importance of criticism and the critical spirit — is a criticism which regards Europe as being, for intellectual and spiritual purposes, one great confederation, bound to a joint action and working to a common result; and whose members have, for their proper outfit, a knowledge of Greek, Roman, and Eastern antiquity, and of one another. Special, local, and temporary advantages being put out of account, that modern nation will in the intellectual and spiritual sphere make most progress, which most thoroughly carries out this program. And what is that but saying that we too, all of us, as individuals, the more thoroughly we carry it out, shall make the more progress? There is so much inviting us! — what are we to take, what will nourish us in growth towards perfection? That is the question which, with the immense field of life and of literature lying before him, the critic has to answer; for himself first, and afterwards for others. I conclude with what I said at the beginning: to have the sense of creative activity is the great happiness and the great proof of being alive, and it is not denied to criticism to have it; but then, criticism must be sincere, simple, flexible, ardent, ever widening its knowledge. Then it may have, in no contemptible measure, a joyful sense of creative activity; a sense which a man of insight and conscience will prefer to what he might derive from a poor, starved, fragmentary, inadequate creation. And, at some epochs, no other creation is possible. Still, in full measure, the sense of creative activity belongs only to genuine creation; in literature we must never forget that. But what true man of letters ever can forget it? It is no such common matter for a gifted nature to come into possession of a current of true and living ideas, and to produce amidst the inspiration of them, that we are likely to underrate it. The epochs of Æschylus and Shakespeare make us feel their pre-eminence. In an epoch like those is, no doubt, the true life of literature; there is the promised land, towards which criticism can only beckon. That promised land it will not be ours to enter, and we shall die in the wilderness: but to have desired to enter it, to have saluted it from afar, is already, perhaps, the best distinction among contemporaries; it will certainly be the best title to esteem with posterity."

APPENDIX I.

WORKS USED IN THE COMPILATION OF THIS HANDBOOK

SELECT CRITICISM

Aristotle ....Rhetoric and Poetics.
Azarias, Brother...................Philosophy of Literature.
Arnold, Matthew...................Essays in Criticism.
Bagehot, Walter....................Literary Studies.
Boyesen, Hjalmar Hjorth..........Literary Criticism.
Bates, Arlo........................Talks on Literature.
Bosanquet, Bernard.................History of Æsthetics.
Brink, Bernard Egidius Ten........Literary Elements.
Brooke, Stopford...................English Literature.
Blair, Hugh........................Rhetoric.
Brunetière, Ferdinand..............History and Literature.
Burke, Edmund.....................The Sublime and Beautiful.
Coleridge, Samuel Taylor...........Biographia Literaria.
Cook, Albert Samuel...............Art of Poetry.
Corson, Hiram.....................Aims of Literary Study.
Crashaw, William Henry...........Interpretation of Literature.
Courthope, William John...........Life in Poetry.
De Quincey, Thomas...............Essays on Style and Language.
Dryden, John......................Essays on Dramatic Poetry.
Dowden, Edward...................Studies in Literature.
Emerson, Ralph Waldo ....Thoughts on Modern Literature.
Gibbon, Edward ....Essay on Study of Literature.
Goethe, Johann Wolfgang von......Art and Nature.
Horace ....Art and Poetry.
Hartmann, Ernest von.............Theory of Aesthetics.
Higginson, Thomas Wentworth......Literature as an Art.
Hunt, Theodore William...........Studies in Literature and Style.
Hazlitt, William ....Dramatic Literature.
Jordan, Alfred ....Literature and Science.
Kingsley, Charles ....Literary Lectures.
Kames, Lord ....Elements of Criticism.
Lewes, George Henry ....Success in Literature.
Longinus ....The Sublime.
Lowell, James Russell ....Literary Criticism.
Mabie, Hamilton Wright ....Short Studies in Literature.
Macaulay, Thomas Babington......Critical Essays.
Minto, William ....Manual of English Prose.
Moulton, Richard Green ....Shakespeare as a Dramatic Artist.
Morley, Henry ....Manual of English Literature.
Müller, Max ....Science of Language.

Newman, John Henry ....Lecture on Literature.
Pallen, Condé Benoist ....Philosophy of Literature.
Pater, Walter ....Appreciations.
Pope, Alexander ....Essay in Criticism.
Quintilian ....Institutes.
Renton, William ....Logic of Style.
Sainte-Beuve, Charles Augustin.....Theory of Literature.
Sears, Lorenzo ....Principles of Literary Criticism.
Schopenhauer, Arthur ....Art of Literature.
Sherman, L. A....................Analytics of Literature.
Spencer, Herbert ....Philosophy of Style.
Staël, Madame de ....Literature and Society.
Stevenson, Robert Louis ....Essay on Style.
Stedman, Edmund Clarence ....Nature and Elements of Poetry.
Symonds, John Addington ....Essay on Literature.
Taine, Hippolyte Adolphe ....English Literature.
Warner, Charles Dudley ....Literature and Life.
Whitney, William Dwight..........Language Study.
Whitman, Walt ....Poetry of the Future.
Winckelmann, John ....History of Ancient Art.
Wolff, Eugene ....Studies of Poetry.
Wylie, Laura Johnson ....Evolution of English Criticism.
Winchester, Caleb Thomas ....Some Principles of Literary Criti-
                                  cism.

APPENDIX II

BIBLIOGRAPHY — SELECT READING

THE LETTER

Arnold, Matthew ....Letters, 1 Vol.
Browning, Elizabeth Barrett ......Letters, 2 Vols.
Browning, Robert ....Letters, 2 Vols.
Burke, Edmund ....Letters on a Regicide Peace.
Bismarck, Prince Otto von ....Letters to a Noble Lord.
Bismarck, Prince Otto von ....Love Letters, 1 Vol.
Carlyle, Thomas ....Letters, 2 Vols.
Cicero ....Letters, 1 Vol.
Chesterfield, Lord ....Letters to His Son.
Clifford, Mrs. William ....Love Letters, 1 Vol.
Fraser, Mrs. Henry ....Letters from Japan.
Gallienne. Richard Le............Love Letters of the King.
Guérin, Eugénie de...............Letters.
Goldsmith, Oliver ....Letters of a Nobleman.
Hugo, Victor ....Letters, 1 Vol.
"Junius" ....Letters.
Kingsley, Charles ....Letters and Memoirs.
Lang, Andrew ....Letters to Dead Authors.
Montagu, Lady Mary Wortley......Letters, 1 Vol.
Newman, John Henry ....Letters, 2 Vols.

Nicoll, William Robertson ....Letters on Life.
Paul, Saint ....Letters.
Pliny ....Letters.
Swift, Dean ....Letters.
Stevenson, Robert Louis ....Letters, 2 Vols.
Stowe, Harriet Beecher ....Letters and Life.
Schiller, Johann Friedrich von......Correspondence.
Sévigné, Madame De.............Letters.
Thaxter, Celia ....Letters.
Walpole, Horace ....Letters, 4 Vols.
Webster, Daniel ....Letter on the Impressment of American Seamen.
Wallace, Henry ....Letters to a Tom Boy.

APPENDIX III

BIBLIOGRAPHY — SELECT READING

THE ESSAY

Arnold, Matthew ....Essays in Criticism.
Addison, Joseph ....The Spectator.
Barry, William ....Essays.
Bacon, Francis ....Essays, 1 Vol.
Browne, Sir Thomas ....Essays and Reviews.
Brownson, Orestes ....Essays and Reviews.
Carlyle, Thomas ....Essays, 6 Vols.
Coleridge, Samuel Taylor ....Essays.
De Quincey, Thomas ....Essays.
Emerson, Ralph Waldo ....Essays.
Fairbairn, Andrew Martin ....Essays and Reviews.
Goldsmith, Oliver ....Citizen of the World, and Miscellaneous Essays.
Hume, David ....Essays, Literary, Moral and Political.
Huxley, Thomas ....Essays, 4 Vols.
Harrison, Frederic ....Essays.
Hunt, Leigh ....The "Indicator."
Hazlitt, William ....The Round Table and Political Essays.
Jeffrey, Francis ....Critical Essays and Reviews.
Johnson, Samuel ....Lives of the Poets.
Lamb, Charles ....Essays of Elia.
Lilly, William Samuel ....Essays Political and Moral.
Locke, John ....Essays on Human Understanding.
Lowell, James Russell ....Among My Books, etc., and Reviews.
Macaulay, Thomas Babington......Essays.
Montaigne, Michel Eyquem de.....Florios Edition.
Mivart, St. George ....Essays Critical and Scientific.
Mabie, Hamilton Wright ....Essays and Appreciations.

Newman, John Henry.............Essays Critical and Historical; Essays on Miracles.
Pater, Walter ....Appreciations.
Repplier, Agnes ....Essays.
Ruskin, John ....Modern Painters.
Spencer, Herbert ....Philosophy of Style.
Saintsbury, George ....French Novelists.
Stephen, Leslie ....Hours in a Library.
Spalding, John Lancaster..........Opportunity, and Other Essays.
Smith, Sydney ....Essays and Reviews.
Swift, Jonathan ,..................Battle of the Books.

APPENDIX IV

BIBLIOGRAPHY — SELECT READING

BIOGRAPHY

Austin, George Lancaster..........Life of Wendell Phillips.
Barrows, John Henry.............Life of Beecher.
Boswell, James ....Life of Johnson.
Butler, Arthur John..............Life of Dante.
Carlyle, Thomas ....Biographical Essays.
Cavendish, George ....Life of Wolsey.
Century Company ....Dictionary, Proper Names.
Chateaubriand, François René,
   Vicomte de . ...Memoirs.
Cross, John Walter...............Life of George Eliot.
Cooper, Thomas ....Biographical Dictionary.
Farrar, Frederick William.........Life of St. Paul.
Fields, James Thomas.............Biographical Sketches.
Froude, James Anthony........ Life of Carlyle.
Geike, Cunningham ....Life of Christ.
Gibbon, Edward ....Memoirs.
Hale, Edward Everett.............Life of Lowell.
Hewlett, Maurice ....Life of Richard Yea and Nay.
Hudson, Henry .... Life of Shakespeare.
Huxley, Leonard ....Life of Thomas Henry Huxley.
Jesse, John Heneage..............Memoirs of the English Court.
Lang, Andrew ....Life of Mary Queen of Scots.
Morley, John ....Life of William Ewart Cladstone.
Newman, John Henry.............Apologia Pro Vita Sua.
Purcell, Edmund Sheridan.........Life of Cardinal Manning. .
Plutarch ....Biographical Essays.
Renan, Ernest ....Recollections of Childhood.
Raleigh, Walter Sir...............Life of Milton.
Roche, James Jeffrey.............Life of Boyle O'Reilly.
Sanborn, Francis Benson..........Life of Emerson.
Talleyrand, Charles Maurice de.....Memoirs of Napoleon.
Tennyson, Hallam ....Memoir of Tennyson.
Tyler, Moses Coit.................Life of Patrick Henry.
Warner, Charles Dudley...........Life of Cromwell.

Watson, John .... Life of The Master.
Ward, Adolphus William .... Life of Charles Dickens.
American Men of Letters........... Series.
English Men of Letters............ Series.
Famous Women of the French Court Series.
Foreign Statesmen .... Series.
Franklin Series of Biography......
Great Commander .... Series.
Public Men of To-day............ Series.
Saintly Lives .... Series.
Women of Colonial Times.......... Series.
World's Epoch Makers............ Series.

APPENDIX V

BIBLIOGRAPHY — SELECT READING

HISTORY

Acton, Lord .... Historical Lectures.
Bancroft, George .... History of the United States.
Buckle, Henry Thomas............ History of Civilization.
Beers, Henry Augustin .... English Romanticism.
Courthope, William John.......... History of English Poetry.
Cheney, Mrs. Emma .... The Civil War.
Donaldson, James .... History of Education.
Farrar, Frederick William .... History of Interpretation.
Freeman, Edward Augustus .... The Norman Conquest.
Fischer, George .... History of the Reformation.
Froude, James Anthony .... History of England.
Fay, Theodore .... History of Germany.
Gardiner, Samuel Rawson .... History of England.
Gibbon, Edward .... Roman Empire.
Guizot, Francois .... History of Civilization.
Grote, George .... History of Greece.
Hartmann, Sadakichi .... American Art.
Harnack, Adolf .... History of Dogma.
Hume, David .... History of England.
Janssen, John .... German People.
Irving, Washington .... The Conquest of Granada.
Lodge, Henry Cabot .... American Colonies.
Livy .... History of Rome.
Lecky, Wm. E. H. .... European Morals.
Lea, Charles Henry .... Spanish Inquisition.
Lingard, John .... History of England.
Mahaffy, John P. .... Greek Literature.
Maitland, Samuel Roffey .... Dark Ages.
Macaulay, Lord .... History of England.
Merivale, Charles .... History of the Romans.
Motley, John Lothrop .... The Dutch Republic.

Milman, Henry Hart ....Latin Christianity.
MacMaster, John Bach ....United States, History of
McCarthy, Justin ....Our Own Times, History of
Mommsen, Theodor ....Roman History.
Newman, John Henry ....Historical Sketches.
Napier, Sir William ....The Peninsular War.
Niebuhr, Barthold Georg ....Roman History.
Painter, Franklin Verzelius Newton.History of Education.
Parkman, Francis ....Pioneers of North America.
Prescott, William Hickling.........The Conquest of Mexico.
Prior, Edward ....Gothic Art.
Roosevelt, Theodore ....Naval War of 1812.
Schlegel, Frederick ....Modern Europe.
Schwill, Ferdinand ....Philosophy of History.
Saintsbury, George ....History of Criticism.
Tarbell, Frank Bigelow ....History of Greek Art.
Taine, Hippolyte Adolphe..........The French Revolution.
Van Dyke, John ....History of Painting.
Watson, Thomas ....History of France.
Wilson, Woodrow ....History of American People.

APPENDIX VI

BIBLIOGRAPHY — SELECT READING

THE ORATION

Adams, John ....Speeches.
Beecher, Henry Ward ....Speeches and Lectures.
Bossuet, Jacques ....Funeral Orations.
Bourdaloue, Louis ....Sermons.
Brougham, Lord ....Orations.
Burke, Edmund ....Speeches.
Chatham, Lord ....Speeches.
Choate, Rufus ....Addresses.
Chrysostom, St. John.............Homilies.
Cicero ....Against Catiline.
Clay, Henry ....Speeches.
Curran, John Philpott ....Addresses.
Demosthenes ....Against Philip.
Edwards, Jonathan ....Sermons.
Erskine, Lord ....Defense of Gordon and Paine.
Everett, Edward ....Plymouth Addresses.
Fénelon, Archbishop ....Sermons.
Fox, Charles ....Addresses.
Farrar, Frederick William ....Sermons.
Gladstone, William Ewart ....Speeches.
Gough, John Bartholomew.........Temperance Addresses.
Grattan, Henry ....Speeches.
Henry, Patrick ....Speeches.

Jefferson, Thomas .... Orations.
Lincoln, Abraham .... Gettysburg Speech.
Little, Canon Knox................ Sermons.
Liddon, Henry Parry.............. Sermons.
Mirabeau, Gabriel Comte de......... Orations.
Montalambert, Comte de............ Orations.
Newman, John Henry.............. Sermons and Lectures.
O'Connell, Daniel .... Speeches.
Pitt, William (The Younger)...... Orations.
Sheil, Richard Lalor............... Speeches.
Sheridan, Richard Brinsley......... Speeches.
Stanley, Lord .... Lectures and Addresses.
Wesley, John .... Addresses.
Walpole, Horace .... Speeches.
Webster, Daniel .... Orations.

CONTEMPORARY ORATORS

Bryan, William Jennings........... Dolliver, Senator.
Castelar, Emilio .... Finerty, John.
Cockran, William Bourke........... Augustino, Fra.
Hillis, Newell Dwight.............. Morley, John.
Hirsch, Rabbi .... Didon, Père.
Ireland, John .... Redmond, John.
Little, Canon Knox................ Roosevelt, Theodore.
Choate, Joseph H.................. Spalding, John Lancaster.
Bülow, Count von................. Harper, William Rainey.

APPENDIX VII

BIBLIOGRAPHY — SELECT READING

FICTION

Allen, Grant .... Tents of Shem.
Alcott, Louisa May .... Little Women.
Austen, Jane .... Pride and Prejudice.
Barry, William .... New Antigone.
Barrie, James Matthew .... The Little Minister.
Balzac, Honore de................ A Lily of the Valley.
Beaconsfield, Lord .... Vivian Grey.
Black, William .... In Silk Attire.
Björnson, Björnstjerne .... The Fisher Maiden.
Blackmore, Richard Doddridge..... Lorna Doone.
Boccaccio .... Decameron.
Brontë, Charlotte .... Jane Eyre.
Cable, George Washington .... Old Creole Days.
Caine, Hall .... The Christian.
Cervantes .... Don Quixote.
Cooper, James Fennimore .... Leather Stocking Tales.

Corelli, Marie ....Wormwood.
Crawford, Marion ....Saracinesca.
Croly, George ....Tarry Thou Till I Come.
Defoe, Daniel ....Robinson Crusoe.
Daudet, Alphonse ....Little Masterpieces.
Dickens, Charles ....Pickwick Papers.
Doyle, Conan ....Hound of the Baskervilles.
Dumas, Alexandre ....Monte Cristo, The Count of.
Edgeworth, Maria ....Castle Rack Rent.
Eggleston, Edward ....The Graysons.
Eliot, George ....Romola.
Fielding, Henry ....Tom Jones.
Frederic, Harold ....The Damnation of Theron Ware.
Goldsmith, Oliver ....Vicar of Wakefield.
Hawthorne, Nathaniel ....The Scarlet Letter.
Haggard, Rider ....Montezuma's Daughter.
Hugo, Victor ....Les Miserables.
Ingelow, Jean ....John Jerome.
Hart, Francis Bret ....Ward of the Golden Gate.
Howells, William Dean ....World of Chance.
James, Henry ....The Ambassadors.
Jerome, Jerome Klapka ....John Ingerfield.
Kingsley, Charles ....Hypatia.
Kipling, Rudyard ....The Light That Failed.
Landor, Walter Savage. ....Pericles and Aspasia.
Lang, Andrew ....Gold of Fairnilee.
Lever, Charles ....Charles O'Malley.
Lytton, Lord ....Last Days of Pompeii.
McCarthy, Justin Huntley ....If I Were King.
MacLaren, Ian ....Beside The Bonnie Brier Bush.
Malet, Lucas ....Sir Richard Calmady.
Mallock, William Hurrell ....The Old Order Changeth.
Meredith, George ....Diana of the Crossways.
Moore, George ....A Mummer's Wife.
Oliphant, Mrs Margaret ....A Beleagured City.
Parker, Gilbert ....Seats of the Mighty.
Phelps, Elizabeth Stuart..........Gates Ajar.
Rabelais, Francois ....Pantagruel.
Richardson, Samuel ....Pamela.
Rives, Amelie ....The Quick or the Dead.
Schreiner, Olive ....Story of an African Farm.
Scott, Walter ....Waverly Novels.
Sienkiewicz, Henryk ....Quo Vadis.
Stevenson, Robert Louis ....Dr. Jeykel and Mr. Hyde.
Smollett, Tobias ....Humphrey Clinker.
Sterne, Laurence ....Tristram Shandy.
Stowe, Harriet Beecher ....Uncle Tom's Cabin.
Thackerey, William Makepeace.....Vanity Fair.
Trollope, Anthony ....Orley Farm.
Tolstoi, Count Leo...............War and Peace.
Turgenev, Ivan ....Rudin.
Twain, Mark ....Prince and Pauper.
Ward, Mrs Humphrey ....Robert Elsmere.
Wallace, General Lew ....Ben Hur.
Wharton, Edith ....Valley of Decision.

Weyman, Stanley ....Castle Inn.
Wiggin, Kate Douglas ....Timothy's Quest.
Wister, Owen ....The Virginian.
Westcott, Edward Noyes ....David Harum.
Zangwill, Israel ....Children of the Ghetto.
Zola, Emile ....Rome and Paris.

APPENDIX VIII

BIBLIOGRAPHY — SELECT READING

THE DRAMA

Beaumont & Fletcher ....Philaster.
Byron, Lord ....Manfred.
Browning, Robert ....Pippa Passes.
Congreve, William ....Love for Love.
Dryden, John ....Spanish Friar.
Euripides ....Tragedies.
Æschylus ....Tragedies.
Ford, John ....The Broken Heart.
Goethe, Johann Wolfgang von......Faust.
Goldsmith, Oliver ....She Stoops to Conquer.
Howells, William Dean ....Out of the Question.
Ibsen, Henrik ....Ghosts.
Jonson, Ben ....Masques.
Longfellow, Henry Wadsworth......Christus.
Molière, Jean Baptiste ....Comedies.
Marlowe, Christopher ....Tamburlaine.
Massinger, Philip ....The New Way to Pay Old Debts.
Milton, John ....Samson Agonistes.
Phillips, Stephen ....Herod.
Racine, Jean Baptiste.............Tragedies.
Shakespeare, William ....Greater Tragedies.
Sophocles ....Tragedies.
Schiller, Johann Friedrich von.....William Tell.
Sheridan, Richard Brinsley.........The Rivals.
Shelley, Percy Bysshe ....Prometheus Unbound.
Swinburne, Charles Algernon.......Atalanta in Calydon.
Symonds, John Addington..........Francesca Da Rimini(a translation).
Shaw, Bernard ....Plays for Puritans.
Stevenson, Robert Louis ....Deacon Brodie.
Strong, L. C. (editor) ....Stage Lovers' Series.
Südermann, Hermann ....The Joy of Living.
Terence ....Comedies.
Tennyson, Alfred, Lord...........Becket.
Tolstoi, Count Leo ....The Resurrection.
Udall, Nicholas ....Ralph Roister Doister.
Upton, George ....Standard Operas.
Webster, John ....The Duchess of Malfi,
Wagner, Wilhelm Richard,........,Valkyrie, and Parsifal,

APPENDIX IX

BIBLIOGRAPHY — SELECT READING

THE EPIC

Arnold, Edwin ....The Light of Asia.
Arnold, Edwin ....Light of the World.
Arnold, Matthew ....Sohrab and Rustum.
Ariosto, Ludovico ....Orlando Furioso.
Barham, Alfred ....Nibelungen Lied (Translation).
Browning, Elizabeth Barrett ....Aurora Leigh.
Browning, Robert ....The Ring and the Book.
Byron, Lord ....Childe Harold.
Camöens, Luis de..................The Lusiad.
Campbell, Thomas ....Gertrude of Wyoming.
Chapman, George ....Homer (Translation).
Crawford, John ....The Kalevala (Translation).
Dante ....The Divine Comedy.
Dryden, John ....Hind and Panther.
Eliot, George ....Legend of Jubal.
Fairfax, Sir Edward ....Jerusalem Delivered.
Griffith, Robert ....Ramayana (Translation).
Goldsmith, Oliver ....The Deserted Village.
Hall, John Leslie ....Beowulf (Translation).
Homer ....The Iliad, and the Odyssey.
Klopstock, Friedrich Gottlieb .....The Messiad.
Longfellow, Henry Wadsworth.....Evangeline, and Hiawatha.
Lowell, James Russell ....The Vision of Sir Launfal.
Milton, John ....Paradise Lost, and Paradise Re-
                                  gained.
Moore, Thomas ....Lalla Rookh.
Montgomery, Robert ....Omnipresence of Deity.
O'Hagan, John ....Song of Roland (Translation).
Ormsby, John ....The Cid (Translation).
Pope, Alexander ....Homer (Translation).
Roy, Chandra ....Maha-bharata (Translation).
Scott, Sir Walter ....The Lady of the Lake.
Spenser, Edmund ....Fairie Queen.
Tasso, Torquato ....Jerusalem Delivered.
Tennyson, Alfred, Lord ....Idylls of the King, and The Princess.
Virgil ....Aeneid.
Wilkinson, Richard Cleaver........Saul.
Wordsworth, William ....The Excursion.

APPENDIX X

BIBLIOGRAPHY — SELECT READING

THE LYRIC

Arnold, Matthew ....Lyrics.
Austin, Alfred ....Lyrics.
Aldrich, Thomas Bailey ....Later Lyrics.
Burns, Robert ....Lyrics.
Browning, Robert ....Lyrics.
Bryant, William Cullen ....Thanatopsis, Waterfowl, and other Lyrics.
Browning, Elizabeth Barrett.......Sonnets.
Byron, Lord ....Lyrics.
Campbell, Thomas ....Lyrics.
Dryden, John ....St. Cecilia's Day.
Emerson, Ralph Waldo.............Threnody.
Egan, Maurice Francis............Sonnets.
Field, Eugene ....Songs, and Other Verse.
Goldsmith, Oliver ....The Traveler.
Golden Treasury ....American Songs and Lyrics.
Guiney, Louise Imogen ....Lyrics.
Gray, Thomas ....Elegies and Odes.
Gilder, Richard Watson ....Sonnets.
Goethe, Johann Wolfgang von......Lyrics.
Holmes, Oliver Wendell ....The Last Leaf.
Henley, William Ernest ....Hawthorn and Lavender.
Herbert, George ....Religious Hymns.
Horace ....Odes, and Lyrics.
Heine, Heinrich ....Lyrics.
Keats, John ....Odes, and Sonnets.
Keble, John ....The Christian Year.
Kipling, Rudyard ....The Recessional.
Longfellow, Henry Wadsworth.....Lyrics.
Lowell, James Russell.............Commemorative Odes.
Lanier, Sidney ....Songs, and Lyrics.
Moore, Thomas ....Irish Melodies.
Milton, John ....Lycidas, and Sonnets.
Mackay, Eric ....Lyric Love Letters.
Meynell, Alice ....Lyrics.
Newman, John Henry ....Lead Kindly Light.
O'Reilly, John Boyle.............Landing of the Pilgrims.
Poe, Edgar Allen ....The Bells, Raven, etc.
Pindar ....Lyrics.
Riley, James Whitcomb ....Pipes O' Pan.
Rossetti, Dante Gabriel ....Sonnets and Lyrics.
Sappho ....Lyrics.
Swinburne, Algernon Charles.......Songs of North Sea.
Stedman, Edmund Clarence ....Mater Coronata.

Shelley, Percy Bysshe..............Skylark, Cloud, etc.
Shakespeare, William ....Lyrics.
Spenser, Edmund ....Epithalamium.
Spalding, John Lancaster...........Poet's Praise.
Schiller, Johann Friedrich von.....Lyrics.
Tennyson, Alfred ....Lyrics.
Tabb, John Batholomew...........Sonnets.
Wilcox, Ella Wheeler..............Poems of Passion.
Wordsworth, William ....Sonnets, and Odes.
Whittier, John Greenleaf...........Lyrics.

INDEX

Abbot of Croyland, 202.
A'Becket, St. Thomas, 334.
Abelard, 72.
Act in the Drama, 413; the 1st function of, 414; the 2nd, 414; the 3rd, 415; the 4th, 416; the 5th, 417.
Action, Divisions of, 408; meaning of, 404; requirements for, 405, 406, 407.
Adam, origin of words, 9.
Adam Bede, author of, 380.
Adams, John Quincy, on oratory, 280.
Addison, Joseph, 155, 524; elegant style, 98; essayist, 175, 185; essays of, 100.
Adjectives, 13.
Æneid, 498.
Æschines, orator, 307.
Æschylus, 158, 297, 425, 441; characters of, 428; dramas of, 5, 410; epochs of, 551.
Æsop, memoirs, 166.
Æsthetic Sense, improvement of the, 4; its practical value, 6; its primary appeal to literary art, 3; lines of development, 5; ultimate judge of merit, 5; a universal endowment, 4.
Affinity of Literature to other Fine Arts, 1.
Ajax, in Sophocles, 430.
Alciphron, letters of, 126.
Alexander, example of moral sublime, 57.
Allen, James Lane, idealistic novelist, 352.
Allibone, criticism on Addison, 186.
America, romance in, 343.
Analogy, in argument, 279.
Ancients, method of, 245.
Anglo-Saxon, chronicle, 202.
"Anna Karénina," 385.
Anthon, Charles, criticism on Pindar, 534; on Plautus, 447; on Virgil, 500.

Antiquity, advantage of, 477.
Apologia of Newman, memoir, 165.
Apology of Socrates, memoir, 165.
Arabic, use in literature, 23.
Aratus, poet, 124.
Arbaces, 350.
Arbiter, Petronius, Roman author, 361.
Argument, arrangement of, 280; definition of, 50; demands of, 275; in composition, 47; in oration, 274; kinds of, 276.
Ariosto, 73; romance, 335.
Aristophanes, 445; errors in wit, 76.
Aristotle, 406; dialogues of, 158; on drama, 404; on force, 43; on oration, 265; on oratory, 290; remarks, 1.
Arius, letter of, 121.
Arnold, Matthew, 32, 99, 209; critic, 206; criticism on Heine, 540; essay in criticism, 548; essayist, 191; letters of, 112; model on paragraph, 39; on Lowell's allusions, 43; on the letter, 108; on the novel, 354; outlines work, 41.
Arnold, Thomas, 214.
Arrangement of words, purpose of, 24.
Art, absence of in morality plays, 436; content, 61, 69.
Art-Form, elements of, 7.
Arthur, King, 331.
Arthurian Cycle, 330.
Artist, Divine, 68; human, 68.
Artists, Great, lives of, 12.
Ashburton, Lord, letter to, 116.
Athenian School of Oratory, 298.
Attachment to Country, 71.
Atterbury, pamphlet, 172.
Atticus, 134.
Audubon, life of, 224; memoirs, 166.
Aurelius, Emperor Marcus, 135.

Autobiography of Cicero, 131.
Azarias, Brother, criticism on Dante, 503.

Bacchic altar, 426.
Bacchus, 425.
Bacon, Lord, 207, 253, 395; essayist, 182; on oration, 263.
Bain, on balanced sentence, 28; rhetoric, 34, 74; says, 59.
Balance, 68.
Baldwin, rhetoric, 44.
Bale, John, imitator, 210.
Ballad, The, 527; content of, 528.
Balmez, 227.
Bancroft, George, historian, 238, 259, 260.
Barren Style, 93.
Bascom, on sublimity, 52.
Basil, letters of, 126.
Basis, of feeling, 69; of humor, 77; of melody, 80; of melody-words, 81.
Baskertsief, Maria, 208.
Bates, Arlo, on application of argument, 51; says of clearness, 42.
Battle of Waterloo, 369.
Beauty, definition of, 61; in literary art, 66; of form, 67.
Bede, Venerable, writer, 252.
Beecher, Henry Ward, on oratory, 323.
Bennett, James Gordon, journalism, 177.
Benoit, writer of romance, 336.
Beowulf, alliteration carried to excess, 82; epic, 513.
Berkeley, Bishop, dialogue-essay, 158.
Bernhardt, Sara, 438.
Bible, sublime passages in, 60.
Biblical Essay, definition, 153.
Biographer, 166, 197, 198.
Biographers, examples of, 214.
Biographical Matter, classification of, 197.
Biography, 108, 194; class, 209; class, sets of, 211; complete classification, 213; definition of, 193; kinds of, 201; minor examples, 224; sources of, 195.
Biology, 193.
Bjornson, 387.
Black Forest, example of silence and solitude, 56.

Blair, Dr., comparison of style, 244; criticism on Addison, 185; criticism on Cicero, 311; criticism on Demosthenes, 306; criticism on Horace, 536; criticism on Pindar, 535; criticism of Pliny letters, 142; criticism on Sophocles, 444; on beauty, 62; on drama, 426, 427; on ethical purpose, 432; on figures of speech, 45; on sublimity, 52; on the importance of verbs, 12, 13; style in history, 239.
Boaz, field of, 357.
Boccaccio, Italian writer, 73, 366.
Bolingbroke, 171, 172.
Bollandists, Society of, 197.
Book of Psalms, 71.
Book of Wisdom, epistle, 122.
Books of Common Prayer, 522.
Bossuet, Jacques Benigne, orator, 302, 314; sincerity of, 46; writings of, 66.
Boswell, James, 214, 215; example of narration, 50; Life of Johnson, 110.
Bowdoin College, 382.
Breviaries, Lyric, 520.
Briefness of Lyric, 515.
Brontë, Miss, 379; poetry of, 380.
Browning, defines love, 72; errors of, 43; obscurity of, 43; use of foreign words, 23.
Bryan, William Jennings, example, forcible style, 95.
Bryant, preference of Saxon, 17.
Buckle, Henry, historian, 257.
Buffon, saying of, 103.
Bunyan's Pilgrim's Progress, 340.
Burke, Edmund, explains effect of the sublime, 56; model of argument, 51; on beauty, 64; on power of sublime, 53; orator, 316; pamphlet, 171; philippics of, 205; sincerity of, 46; use of periodic sentences, 26.
Burroughs, John, memoirs, 166.
Burrow, biography, 224.
Butler, biography, 222.
Butler, Alban, 211.
Butler's, Bishop, analogies, 280.
Byron, Lord, 172, 370; Lyrics, 524.
Cæsar, Julius, 219; example of moral sublime, 58; oration, 295.
Caine, Hall, use of love letters, 120.

Campbell, on force, 43.
Carlyle, Thomas, 209; criticism on Dante, 502; criticism on Goethe, 449; errors of, 43; essay, 175; essayist, 188; force of, 45; "French Revolution," 101; letters of, 112; sublime writer, 66.
Catholic Historians, 236.
Cato, tragedy of, 151.
Celt, ballads of the, 529; excels in wit, 77.
Celtic, Anglicising of, 23; affected by the Latin, 15; use in literature, 23.
Century Company, biography, 203.
Century Dictionary, reference, 16.
Century, Nineteenth (British), symposium, 162.
Cervantes, model in wit and humor, 76; Spanish writer, 364.
Chamber's Encyclopedia, 206.
Chambers, History of Stars, 225.
Chancellor, Beresford, criticism on Dickens, 375.
Channing, sublime passages, 60.
Character, idealization of, 351; revelation of, 423.
Characters of the Drama, 419, 468; compared, 468; the chief, 422; subordinate, 423.
Charlemagne, of romance, 338.
Chartism, 387.
Chaucer, erotic poet, 73; force of, 44; preference of Saxon, 17.
Chesterfield, Lord, 180; biographical data, 137; charm of manner of, 138; letters of, 137, 138.
Chesterfield, literary work of, 138.
Chesterfield, on good manners, 140.
Chesterfield urges energy and application, 140.
Chesterfield's Letters, literary merit of, 141.
Choate, Rufus, criticism on Webster, 320.
Christ, biography of, 193; life of, 250.
Christian Hymn Books, 520.
Christian Year, by Keble, 345.
Christianity, origin of, 250.
Chrysostom, Saint John, eulogy on, 204; letters of, 126.
Cicero, 32, 313, 398; as a writer, 129; career of, 128; character of, 131; classic representative of ancient letter writers, 128; criticism of, 133; De Amicitia, 71; epistolary style, characteristics of, 132; essayist, 179; expressions, 1; friendship for Atticus, 131; general estimate of, 128; letters of, 111, 129, 130, 131; melody, 83; model of argument, 51; on history, 245; on oration, 273; on style, 94; orator, 265, 310; use of periodic sentences, 26.
Cicero's Letters, literary value, 132.
Civil War, English, 252.
Civil War, our late, 109.
Clarke, Richard, on letters of Leo XIII., 117.
Classic Cycles, in England, 336.
Classification, of letters, 123; of lyric, 518.
Clearness, errors regarding, 42; of composition, 41; of style, 86.
Cleopatra, 72.
Climax, law of, 281.
Clytemnestra, 429.
Cobbett, William, 509.
Cochran, Bourke, forcible style, 95.
Coherence, of paragraph, 34.
Coleridge, essay, 175; on Don Quixote, 366; romance, 343.
Coleridge, Hartley, imitator, 210.
Color, applied to words, 67; source of beauty, 62.
Columbus, 208; example of moral sublime, 58.
Comedy, 424; relation to wit, 79.
Composition, complete, 40; kinds of, 47; qualities of complete, 41.
Concise Style, 90.
Conclusion, 548.
Conjunction, cumulative, 37.
Construction, rules of, of paragraph, 33.
Corneille, 465.
Correctness, of style, 85.
Cosmopolitan Spirit, history, 238.
"Count of Monte Cristo," 369.
Cowley, 151.
Crawford, Marion, novels of, 351; use of love letters, 120.
Criticism, 550; sources of, 402.
Critics, Biographical, 206.
Critique, The, 205.
Crusoe, Robinson, 171.
Cyropædia. 155; of Xenophon, 327, 359.

Dana, Charles A., journalism, 177.
Dante, 73, 502, 504, 511; force of, 44.
David, platonic love, 70.
David's sling, 77.
Davidson, William, criticism on " Job," 439.
Davis, Richard Harding, news-letters, 114.
Decameron, The, romance, 334, 367.
Definition of epic, dispute as to, 470; of essay, 151.
Deistic School, 173.
Demosthenes, 313; orator, 299, 306; prose of, 66; sincerity of, 46.
De Musset, Alfred, lyric poet, 541.
De Quincey, Thomas, 27, 102, 208; diffuse style, 91; on defects of long sentence, 126; on essay, 152.
Description, Literary, 48; meaning of, 48; scientific, 48.
Descriptive composition, 47; style, 241.
De Sevigné, Madame, letter writer, 148.
Design in Art, 65; in literary art, 66; source of beauty, 65.
Deuteronomy, orations in, 296.
De Vere, Aubrey, sonnets of, 533.
Dialogue, 155; characteristics of, 409; definition of, 156; essay, in English literature, 158; growth of, 427; kinds of, 157.
Diatribe, 204.
Dickens, Charles, novelist, 374, 376.
Diderot, 173.
Dido, in Virgil, 73.
Diffuse Style, 89.
Dignified Style, 96.
Dilemma, The, argument, 277.
Disraeli, on pamphlet, 167.
Divisions of beauty, 61; of literary art, 108; of sonnet, 530.
Documents, collection of, 196.
Doll House, The, drama, 438.
Don Quixote, 365, 366; adventure, 364; comic character, 79.
Doumic, Réné, criticism on De Musset, 541; criticism on Hugo, 368; criticism on Molière, 456.
Dowden, Professor, criticism on Shelley, 543.
Drama, The, definition, 404; ethics of modern, 437; forms of, 423;

of Job, 439; religion and ethics of, 435.
Dramatic element, in fiction, 355.
Dramatis Personæ, of Miss Brontë, 379.
Dramatists, 465.
Dryden, John, 151; critic, 206; memoir, 166; sacred music, 524; symposium, 161.
Duke of Norfolk, letter to, 146.
Dumas, Alexander, French writer, 369.
Dunlop, John, criticism by, 362.

Earl of Clarendon, historian, 252.
Edinburgh Review, 175.
Edmund, son of Gloster, 434.
Egan, Maurice Francis, sonnets of, 533.
Elegance, etymological meaning, 46; scope of, 46.
Elegant Style, 97.
Elements of Art-Form, 7.
Eliot, George, genius of, 379; ideal-istic novelist, 352; model on para-graph, 39; novelist, 377; poetry of, 380; symposium, 161.
Elizabeth, Queen, 203.
" Elsie Venner," romance, 347.
Emerson, 97; errors of, 43; on eulo-gy, 164; words illustrated by, 7.
Emotion, in oratory, 285.
Emotional Value, of lyric, 515; of melody, 80.
Emphasis, places of, 24.
Empire, Holy Roman, 196.
Encyclopedia Brittannica, 205.
England, 383; Church of, 170; son-nets in, 531.
English Historians, 251.
English Hymns, 522.
English Literature, eulogy in, 163.
English, morality play, 436.
English Romance, 335, 340; sources of, 330.
English Sacred Lyric, 523.
English Words, French and Latin elements, 18; native, 16; sources of, 15; their universal indebted-ness, 15; value of Latin element, 19.
Epic, characteristics of, 473; close of, 480; compared with drama, 468; heroes of, 479; in the, 517; management of plan, 479; moral

value, 472; origin of, 466; personages of, 481; rank of, 470; supernatural personages, 482; third property of, 478; types of, 469.
Epic Action, 474; interpretation of, 475; time of, 480; unity of, 477.
Epic Material, dramatic use of, 469.
Episodes, 476.
Essay, 165; among the Greeks, 154; meaning in literature, 150; meaning of, 150; modern use of word, 151.
Essayists, English, 185; representative, number of, 178.
Ethical Purpose, extent of, 433.
Ethical Side, of drama, 432.
Eulogistic Literature, 59.
Eulogium, 162; modern use of, 163.
Eulogy, 155, 203, 204.
Euphues, romance, 341.
Euripides, 444; characters, 428; dramatist, 179.
Europe, Northern, romance from, 337.
Evadne, in Euripides, 430.
Evolution of the novel, 349.
Example, argument from, 277; fictitious, 278.
Exposition, in composition, 47; meaning of, 47.

Faber, hymn books, 523; platonic love, 70.
Facts, grouping of, 199; minor ways of grouping, 200; order of place, 199.
Farnsworth, James, criticism on Dumas, 369.
Falstaff, comic character, 79.
Family Relationship, 69.
Feeling, element of art-content, 69.
Ferdinand, history of, 258.
Fiction, 108, 340; meaning of, 327.
Fielding, 386.
Figure, source of beauty, 62.
Figures of Speech, 44.
Fiske, John, criticism of, 262; historian, 261.
Flaubert, author, 369.
Flexibility of Form, of lyric, 515.
Flint, Robert, criticism on Buckle, 257.
Florence, mystery plays at, 435.
Force, Basis of. 44; in composition, 43

Forcible Style, 95.
Forensic Oratory, 293.
Form, source of beauty, 62; source of literary beauty, 67.
Foxe, John, 211.
Franklin, memoirs, 209.
Freeman's, essay, 151; history, 237.
French Academy, 206.
French Church, middle ages, 231.
French Element, 21; on English words, 18.
French History, stylists in, 248.
French Sources, b.
French Words, Domestication of, 21.
Froude, history, 237; letters of, 110.
Funeral Oration of Bossuet, 315.

Gaelic League, The, of Ireland, 529.
Garnett, criticism on Niebuhr, 247.
Gaskell, Mrs., 378.
Genung, Professor, says on paragraph, 35.
German Historical Society, 197.
German Sources, b.
Germans, not remarkable for wit, 77.
Germany, 550; morality plays, 436.
Gibbon, Edward, example of narration, 50; historian, 241, 255; history, 236; History of Rome, 199; use of long words, 20.
Gigot, criticism on Book of Tobias, 358.
Gilder, Richard Watson, sonnets of, 533.
Gladstone, William E., 220, 223; criticism on Homer, 487; his personality, 222.
Goethe, 448, 504; on ideals, 354; platonic love, 70.
Golden Ass, The, 364.
Gospel, employs figures of speech, 44.
Gothic Cathedral Illustrates, 2.
Goths, invasion of, 58.
Gould, S. Baring, 211.
Grattan, sublime passages, 60.
Greek Democracy, oratory, 297.
Greek, drama, 70, 410.
Greek Element, names used in science, 19; use in literature, 23.
Greek Essay, 158.

Greek Literature, fiction in, 359.
Greek Missals, 519.
Greek Tragedy, 429; characters of, 428.
Greeks, principles expressed, 1.
Greeley, Horace, journalism, 177.
Greenough, on loose sentences, 27.
Guizot, 249; historian, 248.

Habrocomes, of Xenophon, 359.
Haggard, Rider, adventures of, 346.
Haigh, A. E., criticism on Æschylus, 441.
Halifax, Lord, tracts, 170.
Hallam, Arthur, 71.
Hallam, Henry, historian, 256.
Hamlet, example of feeling, 70; sublimity, 60.
Hamlet's Ghost, example of obscurity, 55.
Handbook treats literature, a.
Hardwicke, Henry, criticism on Demosthenes, 308.
Harmony, 68; of paragraph, 34; of principles, 1.
Harper's Weekly, letters in, 114.
Harris, Russell, letters of, 114.
Harrison, Frederic, criticism on Macaulay, 254.
Harvard College, 258.
Havelock, romance, 338.
Hawthorne, 381.
Hay, 213.
Heber's, Bishop, hymn book, 523.
Hebrew Literature, story in, 356.
Hebrew People, 60.
Hebrews, oration, 295.
Heine, lyric poet, 540.
Helen, in Homer, 73.
Heloise, 72.
Henry, Patrick, example, forcible style, 95; sincerity of, 46; speech, 102, 279.
Hereward, the Saxon romance, 333.
Herodotus, historian, 126.
Hesiod, eulogium, 162.
Hill, on abuse of particles, 38.
Historical Composition, literary style in, 239.
Historical Facts, methods of interpreting, 233.
Historical Interpretation, methods of, 235.
Historical Value of Letters, 109.

History, 108; art as a factor in, 226; art-content of, 228; difficult species, 231; factors in construction of, 226; grouping of facts, 232; kinds of, 230; meaning of word, 225; method of writing, 231; of the letter, 121; relation to other arts, 227.
Hogarth, definition, 63; on beauty, 63.
Holinshed, chronicles of, 202.
Holy City, 337.
Holy Writ, 70.
Homer, epic poet, 487; epics of, 5; eulogium, 162; his own witness, 487; poetry of, 66; relation to Greek poetry, 490; relation to history, 491; relation to oratory, 491; relation to philosophy, 491; style, 489; sublime passages of, 56; view of, 488.
Homeric Morality, 494.
Homeric Theology, 493.
Hook, Walter Farquhar, 211.
Horace, lyric writer, 536; platonic love, 70; theme, love, 73.
Howells, William Dean, realistic writer, 355; use of love letters, 120.
Hueffer, F., criticism on Boccaccio 366.
Hugo, Victor, French writer, 368; sublime writer, 66.
Hume, David, 254; historian, 241; History of Anglo-Saxons, 231; stylist, 253.
Humor, in art-content, 75; in fiction, 78.
Hutton, Richard Holt, 141; criticism on Arnold, 192; criticism on George Eliot, 377; criticism of Guizot, 249; criticism on Scott, 372.
Huxley, Life of, 214; monograph, 156.
Hymn Books, notable compilations, 522.

Ibsen, Henrik, 438, 452; realistic writer, 355.
Idealism, indications of, 351.
Idealistic Novel, 350.
Idiomatic Style, 91.
Ignatius, letters of, 126.
Imitators, English, 210.

Impassioned Style, 101.
Imperial Academy of Vienna, 197.
Importance of the Letter, 109.
Infinity, as source of the sublime, 54.
Influences, on oratory, 289.
Ingersoll, Colonel, oration, 291.
Institutional Life, basis of civilization, 229; unity of, 230; value of, 229.
Intellectual Style, 98.
Intellectual Sublime, 58.
Irving, 383; elegant style, 98.
Isabella, history of, 258.
Italian, ballads of the, 529; romance, 333; use in literature, 23.
Italy, 383; morality plays, 436.

James, Henry, realistic writer, 355; use of love letters, 120.
Janssen's History of the German People, 109, 238, 247.
Jebb, Prof. R. C., criticism on Aristophanes, 445; criticism on Euripides, 444; criticism on Homer, 492; on Homer, 466.
Jeffrey, 175.
Jerusalem Delivered, epic, 513.
Jesuits, in North America, 261.
Job's Vision, example of obscurity, 55.
Johnson, Dr. Samuel, 98; eulogy, 163; example of narration, 50; imitator, 210; use of balanced sentence, 28.
Jonathan, platonic love, 70.
Judicial Style, characteristics of, 292; in oration, 290.
Junius, 105; letters of, 144; satires of, 205.

Kalevala, epic, 513.
Keats, 385.
Keble, letters of, 110, 112.
Keble's Christian Year, 71.
Kinds of letters, 110; of style, 88.
King Alfred, 59.
King Lear, 434; example of feeling, 70; example of sublimity in sound, 57.
Kipling, Rudyard, 347, 525; novelist, 346.
Knight, chronicles of, 202.
Knowledge, 399.

Labored Style, 93.
Lacordaire, on oration, 274.
"Lalla Rookh," romance of, 334.
Lamb, 383; essays of, 100.
Language, described by Renan, 9; distinction of, 392; in poetry, 389.
Lanier, Sidney, remarked, a.
"Last Days of Pompeii," 353.
Latin Element, on English words, 18; value of, 19.
Latin language, an element in construction, 15; names used in science, 19; vehicle of civilization, 15.
Latins, among the, 361; among the drama, 446.
Lea, Charles Henry, historian, 238.
Lead Kindly Light, example of feeling, 74.
Leader, The, literary merit of, 175; popularity of, 177; publication of, 175; subjects treated in, 176.
Lear, sublimity, 60.
Lessing, describes æsthetic sense, 3; on drama, 404.
Letter in Hebrew literature, 121.
Letter of friendship, 111.
Letters of the Church Fathers, 126.
Lilly, dialogue-essay, 158.
Lincoln, memoirs, 209.
Lincoln, President, secretaries of, 109.
Lindemann, William, criticism on Goethe, 448; criticism on Sudermann, 454.
Lines of beauty, 63.
Lingard, history, 237.
Literary Art and the æsthetic sense, 3; its widest appeal, 17; Latin element in, 20; relationship to science, 2, 3; words in relation to, 7.
Literary examples, 74.
Literary Form of Job, 440.
Literary Style, 100.
Literary use of love letters, 120.
Literary value of news-letters, 116.
Literature as a fine art, 1; of the sublime, 60.
Livy, historian, 126; oration, 295; style, 244.
Locke, definition of wit, 75; essay, 151.
Logic, 276.

London Quarterly Review, criticism on Morley, 220.
London Times, editorials in, 176; letters in, 114.
Longfellow, 545; lyric poet, 544; preference of Saxon, 17; sonnets of, 533.
Longinus, on sublimity, 52.
"Looking Backward," romance, 347.
Lord, Angel of the, 67.
Lord, John, 211.
Love, source of literature, 72.
Love Letters, 119.
Lowell, James Russell, 97; criticism on Carlyle, 190; criticism on Shakespeare, 459; obscure literary allusions, 43.
Lucian, dialogue-essay, 159.
Luther, Martin, 247, 521; letters of, 110.
Luxuriant Style, 94.
Lydgate, translator, 336.
Lyric, in Christian Era, 519; marks of, 515; meaning and scope of, 514; meter and style, 516; relation to prose, 518; suggestiveness, 517; the heroic, 526.
Lyric Growth, causes of, 518.
Lyric Poets, miscellaneous, 525.
Lyric and Epic, comparison of, 467.
Lytton, Bulwer, 350, 352; historical romance, 343.

Mabie, Hamilton Wright, general criticism, 385.
Macaulay, Lord, 32, 97, 255; criticism on Hallam, 256; criticism on Milton, 510; essay, 175; essayist, 186; eulogy, 163; example of narration, 50; history, 237; melody, 83; model on paragraph, 39; stylist, 254; use of balanced sentence, 28; use of long words, 20.
Macbeth, 416, 418; "Knocking at the Gate," example of sublimity in sound, 57; sublimity, 60.
Maha-bharata, epic, 513.
Mahaffy, Professor, criticism on Sophocles, 443,
Mallock, dialogue-essay, 158.
Malory, Sir Thomas, romance, 331.
Man, in relation to society, 70.
Manning, Cardinal, Life of, 292.
"Mar-Prelate Tracts," 169.

Marsh, explanation of use of French words, 21; observations on oldest Latin, 19; words described by, 7.
Marshall, memoirs, 209.
Material, for mystery plays, 435.
Mathews, William, criticism on Bossuet, 315; criticism on Webster, 321; on oratory, 289.
Mead, Professor, 25; on adjectives, 13.
Melody, in art-content, 80; in paragraph, 82; in thought, 82.
Memoir, 155; as an essay, 165; basis of, 166; definition of, 165.
Memoirs, 253; literary value, 167; of Gibbon, 165.
Memorabilia, of Xenophon, 165.
Messiad, epic, 513.
Meter and Imagery, of ballad, 528.
Method, of paragraph arrangement, 35.
Michelet, Jules, historian, 249.
Middle Ages, 257, 337.
Müller, Prof. Max, b.
Mill, John Stuart, observations on apt words and phrases, 10.
Milman, Dean, criticism on Macaulay, 188.
Milton, John, 253, 511, 506; epics of, 5; essays of, 170; Paradise Regained, 72; preference of Saxon, 17; sublime passages, 56, 60.
Minto, on length of sentence, 25.
Mirabeau, orations, 266.
"Mr. Dooley," wit and humor, 79.
Mivart, dialogue-essay, 158; monograph, 156.
Molière, 456.
Monograph, 155; modern use of, 156.
Monologues, 409, 410.
Montagu, Lady Mary, letter writer, 148.
Montague, letters of, 112.
Montaigne, essayist, 180.
Montcalm, history, 261.
Moore, Thomas, lyrics of, 524.
Moralia, opera, 179.
Morality in Drama, basis of, 433.
More, Sir Thomas, pamphlets, 168.
Morley, John, 211, 212, 213, 220; criticism on Burke, 316; says, 117; Life of Gladstone, 110; on Montaigne, 181.

Morris, William, novelist, 346.

Morse, John T., 212.

Moses, orations by, 296.

Moulton, Professor Richard, criticism by, 440; criticism on Book of Ruth, 357; on essay, 153; on the letter, 121.

Movement, narrative style, 241; source of beauty, 63, 68.

Napoleon, documents, 196.

Narration, 485; definition of, 49.

Narrative composition, 47; style, 240.

Nation, five-fold life of a, 228.

National Biography, 201.

National Lyric, 525.

Native English Words, 16.

Naturalness, of style, 88.

Nature, animated source of sublime, 57.

Nelson, Lord, memoirs, 209.

Nepos, essayist, 179, 180.

" New Antigone," 351.

Newman, Cardinal, 32, 145, 345; criticism by, 105, 126; dialogue-essay, 159; essay, 151; letters of, 110; model on paragraph, 39; on oration, 274; outlines work, 41; platonic love, 70; says of Cicero, 129; sublimity, 60; tracts of, 168.

Niagara, 68.

Nibelungenlied, epic, 513; romance, 337.

Nicolay, 213.

Niebuhr, history, 245; influence of, 246.

Nightingale, Florence, 59.

Norman Conquest, 22.

Norman trouveres, 435.

Notre Dame, 369.

Nouns, selection of, 11.

Novel, meaning of the, 348; realistic, 353; relation to romance, 349.

Nye, William, wit and humor, 79.

O'Connell, Daniel, wit, 76.

O'Connor, F., criticism on Bossuet, 316.

O'Conor, Rev. J., criticism on Cicero, 310.

Obituary, 201.

Obscurity, as source of the sublime, 55.

Occasion for open letter, 118.

Onias, letter to, 121.

Open letter, 118.

Oration, 263; estimates of, 322; history of, 295; in England, 303; plan of, 268; style in, 282.

Orator, qualities required for, 266.

Oratorical Growth, 303.

Orators, representative, 306.

Oratory, compared with essay, 264; future of, 304; modern, 301.

Origin, of ballad, 528.

Othello, sublimity, 60.

Outlaw, The, romance, 333.

Outline, method of, 41.

Outlook, The, in drama, 438.

Ovid, theme, love, 73.

Oxford Movement, 173; letters on, 110.

Pagan Standard, low, 434.

Paine, Tom, 173.

Painted Picture, relation to scene, 412.

" Pamela," 385.

Pamphlet, a special pleader, 167.

Pamphlets, of 18th century, 171.

Paradise Lost, 508.

Paragraph, 33; connection of sentences in, 33; divisions of, 35; linking of, 36; prevised, 35.

Parkman, Francis, historian, 202, 261.

Parliamentary Style, in oration, 289.

Parthenon, 299.

Particles, 14.

Pascal, letters of, 143.

Passion, treatment of, 331.

Passions, appeal to, 268; exciting of, 269.

Pasteur's Monograph, 156.

Pastor, historian, 238.

Pater, describes humor, 75; essays on style, 104; on biography, 195; on individuality, 103; on method of study, 39.

Pattison, Mark, criticism on Macaulay, 187; criticism on Milton, 506; criticism on Rénan, 251.

Pauses, in drama, 410.

" Payn Peverel," romance, 333.

Penry, tracts, 170.

Percentages at present of foreign words, 22.

Pericles, 108; orator, 299.

Period of Criticism, 154.

Perry, Thomas, criticism by, 359; criticism on Aristophanes, 446; criticism on Sophocles, 443.

Personality in Literary Art, 84, 103.

Petrarch, 73; an author, 531; lyric poet, 537.

Phædo, 158.

Pharisees, 45.

Philippic, 204.

Phillips, Wendell, orations, 266; sublime passages, 60.

Philosophic Style, 243.

Pickwick, comic character, 79.

Pindar, lyric poet, 534.

Pioneer Press, The, editorials in, 176.

Plaintive Lyric, 526.

Plan, evolution of, 40; for composition, 40.

Plato, dialogues of, 158; says, 3; symposium, 160; words described by, 7.

Platonic love, 70.

Plautus, 446.

Pliny, 142; author, 125.

Plot, idealization of, 352; in romance, 329.

Plowden, James A., criticism on Sappho, 535.

Plutarch, essayist, 178; historian, 126.

Poe's " The Bells," example of sublimity in sound, 57.

Poet, 390; qualities of, 401.

Poetic Faculty, functions of, 398.

Poetry, 399; in pictorial work, 272; materials of, 396; origin of, 395.

Poetry and Logic, 402.

Poets and Prose Writers, 397.

Politeness, quality of orator, 267.

Pompous Style, 97.

Pope, Alexander, 344; errors in wit, 76; letters of, 146.

Popes, Lives of the, 211.

Popular Style, 102.

Power, as source of the sublime, 55; maleficent source of sublime, 58; national and religious, 236.

Prejudice, of historian, 235; removal of party, 237.

Preliminary Study, a.

Prescott, William, historian, 241, 258.

Principle, A Second, in drama, 413; of selection, 389.

Principles Applied, in paragraph, 34; underlying of drama, 419.

Private Journal, 207.

Private Papers, 206.

Prometheus, 429.

Propertius, theme, love, 73.

Proportion, 68; law of art, 241.

Prose-forms, a.

Protestant Historians, 236.

Providence, 422.

Publication of love letters, 120.

Publicity of open letters, 118.

Punic Faith, illustrated by, 10.

Purcell, 207.

Puritanism, history, 261.

Purpose, of ballad, 528.

Pusey, tracts of, 168, 174.

Quackenbos, on loose sentence, 27; on sublimity, 53.

Qualities of Style, 85.

Quintilian, eulogy, 162; history, 239; on conclusion of sentence, 31; on history, 245; on oration, 266, 269, 273; studies of, 301.

Rabelais, errors in wit, 76.

Radot, Rene Vallery, 224.

Raleigh, 253.

Rank of letters among prose forms, 109.

Reade, Charles, 386.

Realism, revolt against, 346.

Recitations, 425.

Record of the Best Minds, 400.

Redeemer, example of moral sublime, 58.

Relation of Lyric to Epic and Drama, 517.

Religious Feeling, 71.

Rénan, Ernest, 197; description of language, 9; historian, 250.

Republic of Letters, The, 108.

" Resurrection, The," by Tolstoi, 438.

Review, North American, symposium, 162.

Revolution, French, 172.

Richelieu, 406.

" Robin Hood," romance, 333.

" Robinson Crusoe," romance, 369, 341.

Roman, oration, 300.

Roman Catholic Church, precepts conveyed by native language, 15.

Roman Missals, 519.

Roman Republic, The, oratory during, 300.

Romance, characters of, 330; growth of, 339; historical, 342; of travel, 341; origin of name, 328; relation to drama, 342; structure of, 329.

Romantic Movement, 343; growth of the, 345.

Romantic Novel, 349.

Rome, history, 237.

Roosevelt, President, biography, 224.

"Root and Branch Pamphlets," 169.

Rossetti, sonnets of, 533.

Round Table, Knights of, 334.

Rule, general, for choosing sentence, 29.

Ruskin, John, 32; life of, 224; model on paragraph, 39; outlines work, 41; sublimity, 60; use of cumulative conjunction, 38.

Russell, news-letters of, 114.

Russians, not remarkable for wit, 77.

Ruth, story of, 73.

Saint Paul, letters of, 124, 130; representative Hebrew author of letters, 122.

Saint Peter, epistle of, 122.

Sacred Lyric, 518.

Saintsbury, George, criticism on Montaigne, 181; criticism on Michelet, 250; criticism on Pascal, 143.

Sappho, lyric poetess, 535.

Satanic School, 172.

Savonarola, 352.

Saxon-English, lack of expressive words in, 22.

Saxon Words, brevity of, 16; concreteness of, 17; sound and sense, 17; special value to literary artist, 16; syntactic structure, 18; tendency to compound, 18; the significance of, 17; their appeal. 17.

Scene, dialogue in, 408; episode in, 411; groups in, 411; requirements for, 408.

Scenery, 412.

Schaefer, Prof. F. J., b.

Schiller, lyric poet, 539; platonic love, 70.

Schlegel, Frederick, criticism on Homer, 494; criticism on Petrarch, 537; criticism on Schiller, 539; on dialogue, 412; on drama, 404; words likened by, 7.

Schoolmen, 169.

Schwabe, 180.

Science, 226; influence of, 353; relationship to literary art, 2, 3.

Scientific Method, modern history, 245.

Scientist, 390.

Scope, in oration, 270; of romance, 328.

Scott, Walter, 242; environment of, 344; "Heart of Midlothian," 101; novelist, 370; romance, 343; treatment of mediæval history, 116.

Scribes, 45.

Scripture, Holy, figures of speech, 45.

Seeley, History of Earth, 225.

Sellar, Professor W., criticism on Virgil, 496.

Sentence, balanced, 28; coherence of, 29; harmony of, 30; linking, in paragraph, 37; use of long, 25; loose, 27; use of short, 24.

Sentences in connection with melody, 81; number of, in paragraph, 35; periodic, 26.

Seriousness, quality of orator, 267.

Shakespeare, William, 420, 458; dramas of, 5; epochs of, 551; model in wit and humor, 76; no letters of, 112; preference of Saxon, 17; sonnets, 120; wit of, 77.

Shaw, Thomas B., criticism of letters, 148; criticism on Bacon, 183; criticism on Gibbon, 255; criticism on Shakespeare, 461; criticism on Thackeray, 381.

Shelley, criticism on poetry, 394; lament over Keats, 527; lyric poet, 542.

Sheran, William Henry, criticism on Arnold, 191; criticism on Carlyle, 189; criticism on Ibsen, 452; criticism on Scott, 370; criticism on Stevenson, 384; criticism on Tennyson, 543.

Siegfried, Teutonic romance, 337.

Sievers, Professor, criticism on Schiller, 539.

" Sigurd, the Volsung," romance, 346.

Silence, as source of the sublime, 55.

Smith, Professor Alexander, criticism on Horace, 536; criticism on Terentius, 447.

Smith, Captain John, travels of, 341.

Smith, Professor, criticism on Terentius, 447.

Smith, Sydney, on humor, 77.

Smyth, Albert, criticism on Burke, 318.

Solitude, as source of the sublime, 55.

Solon, 59, 297.

Some features of style, 100.

Sonnet, The, 530; classic writers of the, 532; origin of the, 531.

Sophocles, 158, 297, 425, 442; characters, 428; dramas of, 5.

Sound, as source of the sublime, 57.

Source, subjective of force, 45.

Sources of principles, 1.

Southey, Robert, translations by, 332.

Spain, 435; morality plays, 436.

Spaniard, ballads of the, 529.

Spanish Cycle, romance, 332.

Spalding, Bishop John Lancaster, criticism on Goethe, 450; on oratory, 325.

Special literary merit, of letters, 123.

Spectator, 171.

Spencer, Herbert, describes perfect artist, 29; model on paragraph, 39; on brevity of words, 16; on oration, 284; on the perfect artist, 105; philosophy of style, 20, 90; translation of his definition of evolution, 19; use of cumulative conjunction, 38.

Spenser, Edmund, epithalamium, 120.

Stanley, Dean, biographer, 214.

Stedman, elements of poetry, 83; on the ballad, 527.

Steele, 155.

Stevenson, Robert Louis, novelist, 346, 384.

Stewart, Dugald, criticism on Bacon, 183.

Story of Ruth, Hebrew literature, 356.

Story of Tobias, Hebrew literature, 356, 358.

Style, deliberate, 287; demonstrative, 285; in literature, 84; in history, kinds of, 239; is made vivid, 286; of love-letters, 120; of news-letters, 113, 117; of open letter, 119; variations of, 284.

Stylists in History, 243.

Subject-matter of letters of friendship, 111; of news-letter, 114; of romance, 328.

Subjectivity, of lyric, 515.

Sublimity, depends upon, 56; meaning of, 52; sources of, 53.

Südermann, Hermann, 454, 455.

" Suicide Club, The," 385.

Swift, Dean, 108, 170, 172; errors in wit, 76; letters of, 146; pamphlet, 171; satires of, 205; tale of the tub, 340; wit of, 76.

Swinburne, prose and verse, 82.

Switzerland, history, 233.

Syle, in oration, 282.

Syllogism, in argument, 276.

Symonds, J. A., criticism on Petrarch, 538; on history, 227.

Symposium, 155; Greek, 161; modern, 161.

Tallyrand, 117; correspondence of, 116.

Tartars, invasion of, 58.

Tasso, 401.

Tennyson, 525; lyric poet, 542; platonic love, 70; preference of Saxon, 17; sonnets of, 533; use of foreign words, 23.

Terence, language employed by literary art, 3.

Terentius, Publius, 447.

Teutonic Language, an element in construction, 15.

Thackeray, 381; author, 376.

" The Ancient Mariner," romance, 342.

The Essay, 108; a standard prose form, 150; a work of art, 152.

The Holy City, example of feeling, 74.
"The House of the Seven Gables," 382.
The Letter, 108; among the Greeks and Latins, 125; in relation to other literary forms, 110.
"The Mill on the Floss," 351.
The News-Letter, definition of, 113; in relation to literary criticism, 115.
The Official Letter, 115.
The Oration, 108.
"The Scarlet Letter," 382.
The Sermon, 108.
"The Shipwreck of John Daniel,' romance, 342.
"The Tales of a Wayside Inn," 339.
"The Travels of Gulliver," romance, 342.
"The Voyage of Wilkins," romance, 342.
Theories regarding words, 9.
Thespis, 426.
Thompson's, Denman, "Old Homestead," 411.
Thucydides, oration, 295; style, 244.
Throgmartin, tracts, 170.
Tasso, 73.
Tolstoi, 387, 438; realistic writer, 355.
Tracts, 167; history of, 168; of 19th century, 173; Puritan, 169.
Tragedy, aim of, 424.
Trajan, Emperor, letters to, 142.
Travel, Fictitious, in romance, 342.
'Treasure Island," 385.
Treatment of Love, ancient and modern, 73.
Treatment of Romance, 328.
Trelingham Court, in "New Antigone," 351.
Trench, observation on words, 10; theories on the origin of words (two), 8; words described by, 8.
Trollope, Mr., 378.
Troubadours, in France, 73.
Trial by Jury, oration, 291.
Tuckerman, Henry, criticism on Bancroft, 259; criticism on Hawthorne, 382; criticism on Parkman, 261.
Thucydides, historian, 126.
Turks, invasion of, 58.
Twain, Mark, wit and humor, 79.

Tyndall's monograph, 156.

Udal, tracts, 170.
United States, colonial history, 231.
Unity, 68; basis of, 230; in paragraph, 34; of principles, 1.
Universal Toleration, history, 238.
Universality of Appeal, 119.
University of Chicago, history, 237.
Utility of letters, 112.

Value of humor, 78; of Junius letters, 144; of pictorial work, 271; of wit, 77.
Variation, how secured, 24.
Vatican Library, 196.
Verbs, 12.
Verse-forms, a.
Vesuvius, eruption of, 350.
Virgil, 496; epics of, 5; poetry of, 66; platonic love, 70.
Virchow's monograph, 156.
"Vision of Piers Plowman," romance, 340.
Vividness, of style, 86.
Vocabulary of Sublime, 59.
Voorhees, Senator, oration, 291.

Wace, Robert, criticism on Prescott, 258.
Wagner, music of, 5.
Waller, biography, 224.
Walpole, letters of, 112; memoirs of, 147.
Walton, Isaac, imitator, 210.
Ward, dialogue-essay, 158.
Ward, Adolphus, criticism on Dickens, 374.
Ward, Mrs. Humphrey, 208.
Ward's "Marcella," romance, 347.
Ward, Wilfred, dialogue-essay, 158.
Ward, William, criticism on Æschylus, 441.
Warner, Charles Dudley, 211.
Washington, George, 203.
Watts, Henry, criticism on Cervantes, 365.
Webster, Daniel, melody, 83; model of argument, 51; oration by, 271; orator, 319; result of theory, 8; sincerity of, 46.
Welsh, Alfred, criticism on Macaulay, 187; criticism on Scott, 371.
Wendel, Barrett, says of paragraphs, 35.

Wesley, John, 525.

Whately, on force. 43.

Whittier, 525.

Williston, Martin, criticism on Longfellow, 544.

Wilson, General James Grant, 212.

Wit, in art-content, 75; of different peoples, 77.

Wolfe, history, 261.

Word-painting, 242.

Words, combinations, 24; in relation to literary art, 7; law of selection, 23; multiplied, 9; new, 9; origin of, 8; partial agreement of theories, 9; particles, 14; selection of adjectives, 13; selection of nouns, 11; selection of verbs, 12; two-fold function, 11; various definitions of, 7.

Wordsworth, William, criticism on poetry, 388.

Work of Poets, 396.

Works on letter criticism, 149.

Xavier, Francis, 59, 208.

Xenophon, 155; essayist, 154, 179; eulogy, 162.

Xenophon, symposium, 160.

Zola, realistic novelist, 354; realistic writer, 355.

How to Study Literature

By B. A. HEYDRICK, A. B.

DEPARTMENT OF ENGLISH, HIGH SCHOOL OF COMMERCE
NEW YORK CITY

There are many text-books on rhetoric, many histories of literature, some annotated editions containing directions for the study of particular books. But so far no other work has appeared which provides systematic instruction in the study of literature itself, applicable to every classic, let us say, or to any classic.

Such a book is *How to Study Literature.* It is a guide to the study of literary productions. Taking up Narrative Poetry first, an outline is given, in the form of questions, which will lead the student to comprehend the subject matter, to analyze the structure, to study the characters, the descriptions, the style, and the metre —of such a work for example as Tennyson's "Princess" or Coleridge's "Ancient Mariner." Next follows Lyric Poetry, with questions for the study of the thought, the mood, the style, the metre; and suggestions for comparative study and collateral reading. In a similar way the drama, the essay, the oration and the novel are taken up and questions given which will lead to a full comprehension of the work studied.

This book was recently adopted by the Kansas State Agricultural College (Manhattan, Kansas) as a handbook in one of their required courses in English Literature, and the Professor in charge writes us as follows:

"It seems to give in concise and definite form certain *fundamentals* in *literary criticism* and *appreciation* which the college freshman or sophomore usually lacks and to *give them* in a *more effective way* than does any other text which we have examined."

NOBLE AND NOBLE - - *Publishers*
76 Fifth Avenue - - - - New York

Writing the Short-Story

By J. BERG ESENWEIN, A. M., Ph. D.

EDITOR OF "THE WRITER'S MONTHLY," SOMETIME EDITOR OF
LIPPINCOTT'S MAGAZINE

A Practical Handbook on the Rise, Structure, Writing and Sale of the Modern Short-Story

This volume embodies the practical principles of short-story structure as recognized by American and British magazine editors, and as practiced by authors whose products are judged to be of the first order. At the same time, the body of sound scholarship has not been lost sight of in considering the popular and marketable short-story, so that the treatise is peculiarly adapted to the needs of college and senior secondary-school classes, as well as suited to inspire and guide the individual writer, amateur or professional, who wishes to improve his art.

CHAPTER HEADS

I. History of the Short-Story
II. What is a Short-Story
III. Kinds of Short-Story
IV. Choosing a Theme
V. Gathering the Materials
VI. Fact in Fiction
VII. The Plot
VIII. What Constitutes a Good Plot?
IX. Plot Development
X. How Stories Are Told
XI. The Opening of the Story
XII. The Setting of the Story
XIII. The Elements of the Setting
XIV. The Body of the Story
XV. Characters and Characterizations
XVI. Dialogue
XVII. Style
XVIII. Some Special Characteristics of the Short-Story
XIX. What is Originality
XX. Talent and Training
XXI. Acquiring a Vocabulary
XXII. Studying the Short-Story
XXIII. The Laboratory Method
XXIV. Writing the Short-Story
XXV. Selling the Short-Story
XXVI. Why Stories are Rejected

APPENDICES

APPENDIX A—Collections of Short-Stories, Sketches and Tales
APPENDIX B—One Hundred Representative Short-Stories
APPENDIX C—The Plots of Twenty Short-Stories
APPENDIX D—Digest of Rhetorical Rules Applicable to Short-Story Writing
APPENDIX E—Books for a Fiction-Writer's Library
APPENDIX F—Bibliography

NOBLE AND NOBLE   -   - *Publishers*
76 Fifth Avenue - - - - New York